INVESTING ON
YOUR OWN

INVESTING ON YOUR OWN:

HOW TO FIND WINNING STOCKS IN YOUR OWN BACKYARD

RICHARD L. THORSELL

McGRAW-HILL BOOK COMPANY
New York St. Louis San Francisco Auckland Bogotá
Düsseldorf Johannesburg London Madrid Mexico
Montreal New Delhi Panama Paris São Paulo
Singapore Sydney Tokyo Toronto

Library of Congress Cataloging in Publication Data

Thorsell, Richard L.
  Investing on your own: how to find
winning stocks in your own backyard.

  Includes index.
  1. Investments.   2. Stocks.   I. Title.
HG4521.T475   332.6'3223   78-23333
ISBN 0-07-064540-X

1234567890   BPBP   7865432109

The editor for this book was Kiril Sokoloff,
the designer was William Frost, and the production supervisor
was Sally Fliess. It was set in Palatino
by Monotype Composition Company, Inc.

Printed and bound by The Book Press.

TO CAROLYN

CONTENTS

ACKNOWLEDGMENTS

Kiril Sokoloff, Senior Editor at McGraw-Hill, contributed much valuable advice and criticism. The manuscript was prepared with great patience and care by Sheilagh Stevick Ross, Rebecca Madrigal, Donald Lee Cooper, and Valda Aviks. I am very grateful to Pamela Haskins for copy editing, to Rose Jacobowitz for her careful supervision of the manuscript, and to Rachel In for the index.

During the years in which this project was in gestation, many former clients and colleagues gave generously of their time and ideas. While the synthesis is my own responsibility, the components grew from long dialogues with dozens of bright and helpful Wall Street people.

In moving from the world of money to the exploration of the mind, I especially appreciate the insights and profound integrity of Elizabeth Thorne, J.D., Ph.D.

RICHARD L. THORSELL

INTRODUCTION

The stock market today is badly distorted by too much interest in a few big companies and too little interest in the vast majority of medium-sized and smaller firms.

This distortion is not justified by real differences in earning power between the favorite few and the many exceptional smaller companies buried in with the rest of the market. As a result, an extraordinary opportunity has been created for individual investors in these "uncommon stocks."

This mother lode of value in the heart of the market will yield its profits to anyone with good common sense and a willingness to work at stock selection. You can't succeed if you sit and read other people's buy and sell tips, but you can if you will take a few hours to discover the path to wealth described in this book.

While making money in stocks isn't easy, it isn't as difficult as the losers would like you to believe. The ideas and methods you need are spelled out in these 22 chapters. Read the Table of Contents carefully before jumping into the text. It will give you a good framework and perspective.

The overall plan of the book is shown in Figure 1.

Chapter 22 is devoted to some of the common questions people ask about uncommon stocks. The Appendix contains a unique Prospect List of 7,200 companies, including the name and address of the president of each one. Since the best place to look for uncommon stocks is in

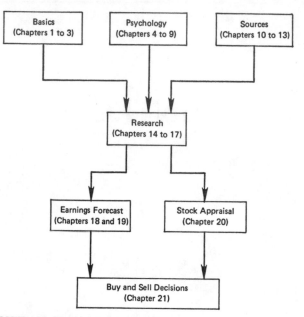

FIGURE 1.   OVERALL PLAN OF THE BOOK.

your own backyard, the Prospect List is organized geographically right down to your local ZIP code. However, you should screen this Prospect List very carefully in accordance with the analytical tools provided in the book. The author does not intend to pass judgment on the investment merits of the companies in the list. These companies are mentioned here not as recommendations, but only to suggest to you where to begin your search.

There is a lot of material here. Select the ideas and stocks which are of interest to you now. Then keep the book on your desk. It will be a continuing source of advice and direction. It can shorten by several years the time it will take you to be an investor who is independent not only in spirit but financially as well.

One last comment: While investing is a serious venture, it is also the ultimate do-it-yourself hobby. So try to relax and enjoy the pleasures it offers. You will meet lots of interesting people, and you will see some fascinating places and things in your own area that you didn't know existed. There's no law against making friends and having some fun while you travel down the path to wealth.

INVESTING ON YOUR OWN

BASICS

Many individual investors have been badly burned by the stock market over the last decade. Since the end of 1968, only a few have made much money. The market has been through, and is now only partially recovered from, the most massive erosion of stock prices since the 1930s, especially in medium-sized and smaller companies. Meanwhile, the trend has continued toward concentration of assets in institutions such as banks, insurance companies, and mutual funds.

Many people are asking: What's left for the individual investor? In our judgment: Everything!

The greatest opportunity in 30 years has been created by the twin forces of a still depressed market in the uncommon stocks and the professionalization of most investable assets. A huge area of potential value has opened up in the heart of the market. The great majority of stocks have become oversold, while the favorite few are heavily overused. You can beat the pros and the market and find these uncommon stocks.

Follow this path to wealth, and you have a solid shot at eventually making more money from your part-time investing than from your full-time job. There is real opportunity, and those who cannot see it have just been looking in the wrong places.

1

THE CASE FOR UNCOMMON STOCKS

WHAT IS AN UNCOMMON STOCK?

An uncommon stock is a stock which is not yet followed by the crowd. Often it is a local company, located practically in your own backyard. The company's stock has the potential to go up severalfold in price over the next few years. Most important of all, you can easily get to know this company personally, in your spare time, ahead of everyone else. You can learn how to spot this uncommon stock, determine what it is worth, and decide when to buy and when to sell.

Uncommon stocks are the blue chips of the future. They are not yet recognized by professional investors and the general investing public. Someday those in the investment world will catch on and include your uncommon stock on their list of the top few hundred companies. By that time, when everyone else is buying and the stock has gone up to a price many times above what you paid, you will be selling to take your well-earned profits.

You really can get in and out of the right stocks at the right time on your own. You can do it in a few hours a week with no expensive help from the professionals. You will no longer rely on secondhand information from advisory services or on self-serving advice from stockbrokers.

You can do a better job of making stock decisions than the people you may now be paying to make them for you.

By following this simple revolution in stock market methods, you can gain personal control of your own financial destiny and feel a new sense of accomplishment and independence. At the same time you will broaden your contacts in your community, which could lead in all kinds of interesting new directions. You might eventually make more money from uncommon stocks than you do now from your full-time job. How else could you spend a few spare hours per week and get so much out of it?

WHAT ABOUT REAL ESTATE, COMMODITIES, ANTIQUES, AND OTHER ALTERNATIVES?

Growth money could have been put in several places which have done better than the average stock over the last decade. The surest place was real estate, but big gains have also been made in commodities, in collectibles such as antiques and coins, and in quality gemstones.

So why do we think you should now buy certain kinds of stocks? There are three main reasons:

1. We are looking for uncommon stocks, not average stocks. The difference between the two is the difference between a thoroughbred racehorse and a tired old plow horse.

2. Inflation has driven up enormously the prices of so-called non-paper investments (land, houses, commodities, antiques, etc.). We think that the big surge is now over and that future gains will at best match the inflation rate rather than exceed it, as in the past 10 years. In short, prices in this area of investment have risen to reflect our current higher inflation rate.

3. Meanwhile, inflation has driven down the value of paper assets (such as stocks), while earnings of many companies have grown much faster than inflation. As a result, certain stocks are once again the most undervalued investment vehicle.

There is no permanently superior type of investment, but certain basic trends do stay intact for many years before changing. In 1946 stocks were cheap and out of favor. In 1968 it was the opposite: Smart money sold stock and bought land and gold. Once again the trends are changing, and certain kinds of stocks are very underpriced.

The investment services will always find some numbers to show how well their particular investment program or idea has worked. You have seen all the ads for gold, growth funds, income funds, commodity letters, etc. Remember, though, that the fact that an investment medium has done well for one period does not mean that it will continue in the future to outperform all the alternatives. Just the opposite may be true: By the time ads and stories are all over the financial pages, you have to wonder who is not already in the game—who is left still waiting to buy. This is just what causes cycles of undervaluation and overvaluation in every kind of investment.

In our opinion, uncommon stocks are the outstanding opportunity of the 1980s. We will give you more information and ideas to back this up throughout the book. Keep in mind, though, that the only way we can prove our opinion beyond any doubt is to wait for prices of uncommon stocks to go way up. By then, of course, the big recovery cycle will be over, and this tremendous opportunity will have been missed.

You are bound to be skeptical and uncertain. The prevailing investment opinion at the moment is still on your side: Stocks in general are sickly, and lesser-known stocks are dead. What else would people be saying at the bottom of an investment cycle?

In the mid-1960s all the bright young millionaires laughed at the idea of buying gold. It had been $35 per ounce since before they were born! Yet 10 years later it was up 500 percent in price, and most of these young millionaires went down the drain in stocks in the crashes of 1970 and 1974. If they had sold stocks and bought gold, they would have been 10 times better off or more. That's the power of an idea whose time has come. And the time has come again—for that special area of the market we call "uncommon stocks."

THE CHANCES OF GETTING RICH

After a few bad months in the market, a discouraged friend once grumbled: "The chance to get rich went out with the robber barons." We have all heard variations on that theme. The Sherman Anti-Trust Act of 1898 and Teddy Roosevelt's trust-busting activities were supposed to spell the end for freewheeling capitalism. They didn't. Fortunes were made in the second two decades of this century. Then, after the crash of 1929, Franklin Delano Roosevelt was supposed to have ruined the country with his "socialist schemes" and "reckless fiscal policies." But those who bought while others panicked made a fortune before World War II. Then the enormous dislocation and growth of government bureaucracy during the war were supposed to have created an impossible burden for the nation's economy to carry. In 1947, there were very good reasons to expect another major depression to be lurking around the next corner. Yet smart buyers found bargains which were not matched again for over a quarter of a century!

During the 20 years before the crash of 1974 the rise of powerful institutional investors was often said to have taken away much of the opportunity from private individuals. Great teams of analysts, advisers, and administrators were thought to be required to produce investment performance. However, since 1974 just the opposite has happened! In more recent years the big banks, trust departments, mutual funds, and other large institutions have come under tremendous fire for their poor performance records. Meanwhile, the individual private investor now actually leads the market more often than the institutions do.

It is our conviction that individual opportunity to get rich in the stock market will continue to exist into the indefinite future. This is more than a statement of faith based on history. It is also a statement of a belief in the continuing process by which new enterprises sprout and take hold of a firm place in our economy. Some people will always save a portion of their income and put this money and their minds and souls into ideas for new small businesses. New service concepts, better technology, and more efficient or appealing products continue to come along every month. Some of these ventures will get off the ground floor and become large enough to sell stock in the public markets. Then you can buy when these companies are proved but still young and growing. There will always be an ample supply of small to medium-sized companies which are capable of growing to become many times greater in value within our investment time horizon. With common sense and hard work you can find these uncommon stock market opportunities.

BIG BUSINESS AND BIG GOVERNMENT CANNOT STOP UNCOMMON COMPANIES

There are other reasons why many people mistakenly believe that opportunity is dead. For example, an enormous proportion of capital formation, or "saving," occurs in large corporations, since they pay out less than half of their earnings in dividends. The rest of their net profit after taxes is available for investment, usually back into the business itself. This "closed loop" is important to big, mature firms, but they are attractive mostly to institutional investors. The smaller, growing firms cannot generate enough savings on their own and cannot depend on the institutions, and so these firms must come to us to join them in the rewards and risks of their expansion. Genius in people, like excellence in a company, shows itself early. You can learn to spot such opportunities and take advantage of them as they flower into maturity.

Another argument put forth by the pessimists is that the federal government, and the state and local governments to a lesser degree, is going to be increasingly active in setting up rules of the game for business people to follow. Thirty years from now, they claim, we may come to view the 1950s and 1960s in the same light that we now view the 1870s and 1880s: the last period of opportunity for economic growth and the achievement of personal fortune. Socialism of some sort, they feel, will have strangled the private sector and destroyed most business and stock market opportunities.

However, contrary to what many seem to believe, this country does not appear to be headed toward socialism per se. What does seem to be going on is much more akin to mercantilism, which is a detailed involvement of the government in the regulation of business enterprise, rather than its direct ownership. The difference is enormous. Under a socialist doctrine, individual opportunity is heavily constrained, and small enterprises are far less apt to be permitted to struggle to life against the entrenched state monopolies. On the other hand, under the "new mercantilism," while business decisions may be more complex and difficult to make, the payoffs to those who are successful will be undiminished in comparison with payoffs in the past. The new mercantilism is not the end of the stock market as a source of personal fortune for individual private investors.

Thus it is our very firm belief that real opportunity still exists, and while the game has become more difficult, the players such as yourself have become more capable. For example, technological change continues at a rapid pace, but product cycles as short as five years are now being routinely dealt with by business managers and investors alike. The whole process of opportunity creation is occurring on a scale at least equal to that of the last 100 years in this country, and that is opportunity enough by any standard.

HOW MUCH CAN YOU MAKE?

The answer is that you can make a great deal of money if you are able to stay in over the long term. Unfortunately, much of the general public was driven from the market in the late 1960s by excessive and irresponsible claims based on only short-term performance. People are only now beginning to come back. Let's take a look at past claims for investment results.

A mutual fund or other high-growth-oriented investor who is successfully taking reasonable risks can and should have occasional spectacular years of 50 percent or more gain. Such investors must have unusually profitable years, in fact, to offset the bad years and average out at a high enough return to justify the risk being taken. However, that does not mean that these short-term performances can be peddled to the public as a long-term prospect.

During the last period of really good times for the broad, overall market (1967–1968), portfolio managers could not resist the temptation to trumpet claims of great financial wizardry and genius. They raised their clients' hopes to new heights—and, of course, attracted thousands of new and eager investors in the process. And, as you know, the result was a humiliating disaster for one and all.

Let us apply a little bit of common sense to test the sanity of claims you may hear this time around as the broad bull market gets rolling. Ask yourself: What would happen if very high rates of return were continued for many years? As you will see shortly, this simple question makes casual claims of 25 to 50 percent annual appreciation completely absurd. Table 1 shows what would happen if you started with a pool of $10,000 and performed consistently for 20 years at various rates of return.

TABLE 1.   Earnings on $10,000 after 20 Years at Various Rates of Return

Performance or Rate of Return	Approximate ending value
5% (typical interest rate on savings)	$26,000
9% (long-term stock market return)	$56,000
12% (good results)	$96,000
15% (a figure unreached by any mutual fund)	$160,000
25% (A target often claimed)	$860,000
50% (a very good single year at optimum risk)	$3,400,000
100% (a double every year)	$10+ billion!

As you can see from the table, if you compounded performance on a modest pool of $10,000 at 100 percent a year for 20 years, your capital would amount to over $10 billion! You would have made five times more money in two decades than any individual in history has made in an entire lifetime. Compounded at "only" 25 percent a year for 31 years, the results would still come out the same.

Howard Hughes started with $10 million; 40 years later, when he died, he was worth $2 billion. That sounds like an astounding performance, but it works out to about 12 percent a year compounded on his original $10-million inheritance! And keep in mind that he is considered to have been one of the world's most successful people. Well, financially anyway.

So an average 12 percent a year obtained over the long term, through depressions and wars and other great dislocations, is nothing to sneeze at. It is for this reason we believe that one of the most important advantages of our methods is that you can reduce the risk of not achieving decent long-term performance.

Don't shoot for doubles every year or two, even though you probably will get such surges in performance for short periods. From peak to peak in the market, though, if you can average just over 12 percent, you can make 10 times on your capital in 20 years even with no new savings. In general, targets of 10 to 15 percent per year will give you a double in about six years, or 5 to 15 times on your money over the next 20 years.

This level is high enough to lift you above inflation problems and is enough above savings rates to be worth the added risk. Yet you are not shooting for the very difficult targets, such as 25 to 50 percent per year on average, which are more likely to lead you to bitter disappointment than down the path to wealth.

Your targets are your decision alone, of course. You may want to take more risk and roll the dice for a few big hits and then get back to the middle level of risks. Or you may want to take almost no risk and accept more conservative targets. Whatever your choice, we just want you to know the risk-versus-return trade-off you will be making. Watch the risks first, and the long-term return will come. If you don't take reckless risks or let others take them for you, you can get where you are trying to go.

HOW YOU CAN BEAT THE MARKET

DON'T BE SNOWED BY THE PROFESSIONALS

In Chapter 1 we asserted that money can still be made in the stock market. But why do we think that you, the individual investor, can be successful? You may believe that the stock market is just too competitive and that you just can't expect to do a better job than the professionals. That lack of self-confidence is wrong. You can beat the pros, the public, and the entire market.

There is one basic reason why you may not yet believe you can make money on a part-time basis. You know from your own experience that someone who spends full time on something should logically be able to do a better job than a part-timer or an amateur. Experience in business, sports, entertainment, the professions, and elsewhere confirms this belief. In the world of investments, also, the professionals want you to carry this belief into their offices and to give yourself into their hands. Most investment advisers, stockbrokers, mutual fund managers, and bank trustees honestly believe that they can do a better job for you than you could ever hope to do for yourself. They are absolutely wrong.

Investing is not really a full-blown profession like law or business management. There are some useful skills involved, to be sure, but they can be learned in far less time than the two to four years it takes to become a professional in other fields. You can become as skilled as the professionals in a few months, and this book can show you how.

The professionals have an advantage over you mainly because they have more experience with a few hundred major companies. They have spent 90 percent of their time not on acquiring special skills which you don't have but on learning specific information about giant "institutional-quality" stocks.

However, there are thousands of companies to choose from, and most are ignored by the pros. They spend thousands of hours pouring over General Motors and several dozen other favorites, but they are totally ignorant about 95 percent of all publicly traded companies. Learn some basic professional techniques and then apply your skills to these lesser-known companies. Then you can know more about your stock relative to what everyone else knows than the pro does about GM! That knowledge is your key to successful investing.

YOU HAVE THE ABILITY

Certainly it is necessary for you to be well prepared. Fortunately, though, the overall educational level has increased, and the requirements for what might be termed an "adequate" background are far less difficult to meet today than they were 20, 40, or 60 years ago. It is no more difficult for a person to get a college degree today than it was for his or her grandfather to get a high school education—not when measured in relation to the conventions and standards of today, the family and other sacrifices required, and the personal capabilities which might be demanded.

You are better informed and more sophisticated about the practical world around you than all but the shrewdest professional operators of only two generations ago. You have the general education and background to be a successful private investor, and you can probably find a few hours per week to spend on this if you really want to grow wealthy.

There are tens of thousands more people who are in this position now than there were a generation ago. Meanwhile, the investment business has become so specialized and concentrated that most companies are simply ignored. No one with any real ability to judge these stocks' prices is even looking at them. When the new legions of private investors such as yourself finally come out to explore this gold mine within the stock market, the combination will produce a massive shift in stock prices. As they sort through the many thousands of lesser-known companies and find the truly uncommon stocks among them, the prices of these shares will move up dramatically in just a few years. This is a major new force behind the expected emergence of uncommon stocks in the 1980s.

HOW DO BARGAINS ARISE?

How do bargains arise in the supposedly efficient modern stock market? Let's look briefly at the real economics of future stock prices.

The economist defines capital as any facilities which may be used to produce future goods and services. It is a nonhuman factor of future production. It is the "something else" beyond human time and effort which is needed to produce goods and services. There are many varieties of definitions, all of which would lead us into a dull and unnecessary review of economic theory. The central theme of all definitions for our purposes, however, is that capital is measurable only in terms of its future ability to help produce income—not income only in the sense of interest or dividends, but rather in the sense of a total future flow of goods and services.

Implicit in the concept of capital are the ability and willingness of people to save, that is, to postpone consumption today to create rights to the facilities for future consumption. This definition focuses our attention on the one fundamental property of capital in general and common stocks in particular: The current or present value of a stock is wholly determined by estimates of the future. The past is relevant only as it helps us estimate that future.

Why recite this very simple and basic idea? Because most people, including most professionals, do not really grasp the basic law of stock valuation: Changes in stock prices arise out of changes in the market's expectations for the future. Therefore, we are essentially in the business of forecasting changes in expectations for the future.

Stock bargains are being created continuously in the market. The price of any stock always reflects a consensus judgment of value. All the interpretations of all the known facts come to balance in the current market quotation. Prices continuously change to reflect either (1) public awareness of something previously unknown or (2) a change in the public's interpretation of already known facts.

This is another way of saying that when expectations change, prices change, and so we had better be ready to forecast such shifts. Therefore, we are interested in the discontinuities of information, not the consensus forecast of obvious and accepted trends which are already reflected in the current prices. We want to know when the market consensus (or market price) is wrong, not when it is right. And we cannot find that out by chasing after the professional opinion makers, since all they.can tell you is why the stock is selling where it is now!

THE VALUE OF RESEARCH

As a result of this economic logic—and, more importantly, on the basis of years of practical experience—we have become very strong believers in business research. What is research? Just what is it that is being researched?

We are trying to put together a body of information which is not already discounted or reflected in the stock's price—and information which is legal to trade on. In other words, the problem boils down to finding out whether there is something between common knowledge and illegal inside information. You are going to learn to sort out those stocks in which the market's consensus view of the company is significantly different from yours—where a disparity exists between what is thought to be the case and what you have learned will really happen.

That may sound difficult, and for the giant stocks of wide interest it is almost impossible. These are the "favorite 50" or the "institutional favorites," on which the pros focus all their effort and therefore cancel out one another's effectiveness. For most stocks, though, you can get a perfectly legal edge with the right information.

What type of research information is of value to you? Suppose for the purposes of this discussion that you somehow have total access to all information available on a company. That is, assume that you are in the position of top management, that you have a good sense of what is relevant, and that you have the time to search around inside the company. Clearly under such circumstances even the worst pessimists about the value of research (the so-called random-walk proponents) would agree that such fundamental information would be of great value in predicting the future course of the company's earnings and the future price of its stock. Unfortunately, it is quite illegal for any investor to trade on such information if it has not been fully disclosed to the public either through the media or by means of documents filed with the regulatory agencies.

Now let us take a look at the other extreme. The pure "chartists," or "technicians," by choice do not get involved in such fundamental information at all! It is their opinion that by simply looking at past stock price patterns, they can make a useful forecast about future price patterns and make buy and sell decisions accordingly. While there is no long-term evidence whatever to support this view, it does represent a convenient bench mark for our purposes in defining the "zero information" position.

The debate rages over whether there is anything in between, that is, whether by any legal method, including those developed in this book, a private individual investor can produce information which will make real money. We believe it is possible because we have done it, and so can you. It is our conviction that, by concentrating your research on a limited number of less-than-giant companies, you can get as close to the position of an insider as necessary and still be able to buy and sell stocks profitably and ethically.

Such concentration of research effort means that once you find a good company you should normally stay with it and continue to follow its progress. By steady accumulation of data and through experience with a small number of specific companies you can know a lot more than the market. (This does not mean that if you once buy one of your closely followed stocks, you should never sell it. You should, and we will show you how to make such decisions. A stock frequently gets overpriced as well as underpriced, and you can sell in the hope of buying it back at a lower price, or even at the same price but a lot further in the future.) This research effort requires a personal involvement on your part. You cannot rely solely upon outside opinions, however helpful they may be. You must get involved in the nuts and bolts of fundamental business research on companies you invest in. If you do, it is our conviction, based on personal experience, that you will be successful.

It is really quite surprising how much you can gradually come to learn about a company and how easy it is to do so. In fact, from an investment standpoint it is actually possible to develop a better-informed and more reliable view of a company than that of its own top management! You will not have more facts, of course, but you will have the most important facts, and you will have them sorted out better. Therefore, you can sometimes understand their investment significance better than so-called insiders can. Management people must spend 99 percent of their time on operations and specific planning; they cannot and do not work on the topics addressed by you as a sophisticated private investor. Even if they did, their position would make it more difficult for them to do the kind of field research required; they just would not get the same straight answers which you will get from competitors, suppliers, and rank-and-file employees. Finally, their personal involvement and commitment prevent them from making an objective analysis. The only advantage maintained by insiders in top management is, of course, completely open access to company records. However, since they usually cannot and do not trade on such information, their special position has no market impact. The penalties for insider trading on privileged information have become very high, and the level of ethics really has improved markedly in recent years.

So, you really can know a stock better than its management. If this opinion seems a bit presumptuous, consider an analogous situation. How much more does your doctor know about your future health than you do? Normally, a great deal more. Yet you live in your body and have much more specific information. You're literally an insider. However, the doctor is better trained and better organized in this field than you are. Although you have a more intimate knowledge of yourself, for the narrow purpose of predicting your future health the doctor will on average outperform your estimates. Similarly, your special skills as an objective part-time observer of company activities can make you a better stock price forecaster than the insider.

However, you don't need to worry about getting quite that good. You can learn enough to get the edge on the market, and that's what the game is all about. It is not as hard as you might have thought, although naturally not every person on the street can do it. But the job is very manageable with a few hours of work per week.

We'll come back to this central idea in subsequent chapters and also give you a lot of specific advice. First, let's go inside the professionals' world so that you can see for yourself the reality of what they do and don't do.

INSIDE THE PROFESSIONALS' WORLD

During the generations before World War II, before tremendous funds were amassed in institutional hands, pros were essentially generalists rather than specialists. Pros were just like other people, except that they spent full time in the stock market. They prided themselves on knowing what was going on in the world, and quite frequently they spent full time in the investment area because it gave them a perch from which to view the passing scene.

The amount of specific knowledge about the big companies they needed to absorb was not great. They did not have to read 100-page reports about General Motors from each of 10 specialized security analysts. They knew what business the company was in, and they knew generally what phase the economy was in and when it was appropriate to be in or out of GM stock. They tried to keep up with the gossip about the "pools" (now very illegal) and whether there was one running in GM. In short, they were ordinary people applying themselves to the investment world.

With the post-world War II burgeoning of assets under professional management and in institutional hands, there was a tremendous flood of money to spend on the investment decision process. The professionals suddenly had millions of dollars in fees coming in. They spent money on bigger staffs and bureaucratic procedures. One person no longer did the whole job. The last quarter of a century has seen a tremendous proliferation of stock market information and intensive debate about methods and technique.

Most investors, especially professionals, hold the view that all this expansion in methodology and specialization came about because of the increased complexity of the world. We don't think so. The world is not any more complex now than it was two generations ago. In the framework of the people and the problems they were facing, the world was just as difficult at that time as it is today. They had to figure out what was going to happen to resolve the Great Depression; surely this was no less complex than our central problem of today, which is that of trying to figure out how to resolve the worldwide inflation.

The main reason for all this volume of new ideas was that the money was available and the huge size of institutional funds forced professional managers into a highly specialized world. They could not run $1 billion the way they ran a few million. They had to concentrate on only big companies in which they could buy $10 million worth of a single stock at a time. They had to wring out every nickel with esoteric trading techniques which are useless to individual investors. Some cynics even think that part of the huge increase in fees had to be spent to justify the once fat profits being made—in some cases millions of dollars in personal compensation for one manager in one year.

All this specialization resulted in less and less interest in smaller and medium-sized companies. (The exception was a brief period in the late 1960s.) Yet the number of such companies on the public market has increased dramatically. The situation today is that the supply of lesser-known stocks exceeds the demand, and prices have been unusually depressed.

Very little of value to you in judging these companies is known today which wasn't known 40 years ago. Again this may seem pretty unbelievable, since there have been such great advances in so many other fields. But most of the new investing ideas are of value only for multimillion-dollar funds. Today's stock market is wide open to you, and there are plenty of good bargains around for the simple reason that no one is looking for them.

TWO PROFESSIONAL FLOPS:
THE GENIUS AND THE COMPUTER

Professional managers learned their current way of doing things from bitter experience. In the last 15 years there have been two extremes. First, people thought that the human being was going to be eliminated and that investments would be run entirely by computer. Then came those who thought that the "Renaissance man" of the prewar world had come back on the scene and that a 19-year-old genius with a $100-million portfolio and a telephone and a secretary could outperform anybody or anything else.

As many of you know, neither of these approaches has worked in the real world. Their failure was not due simply to the fact that the stock market fell apart between 1968 and 1974. In our judgment, neither of these methods could have worked in the first place even if they had been blessed with good markets.

Let's take a look first at the computer approach. The thesis of the computer people was that you can build a decision-making model that will replace human decision making to a large degree. The human being was to become essentially a data gatherer for the machine. Wells Fargo Bank in San Francisco was a pioneer in this method, and in the early 1960s it was spending a quarter of a million dollars a year on computer applications. That budget level went on for a decade until Wells Fargo finally gave up trying to beat the market and just bought the averages.

The first difficulty with the computer approach was independent of whether it might or might not have worked; instead, it was the age-old problem of office politics. How could you have taken a group of three or four dozen old-time investment professionals who had in the aggregate a couple of hundred years of investment experience and explained to them that they were obsolete? Even if it had been true, they wouldn't have accepted it. It would have taken decades for the internal bureaucratic changes to take place.

The principal problem with the computer approach was that all the decision-making models were just extraordinarily complex. They had to be complex, of course, to get even a very crude approximation of the real world. To solve this problem, various theoreticians came up with some very elegant approaches to simplifying the models. Unfortunately, the simplifying assumptions destroyed what little predicting value the models might have had.

The computer models were also extraordinarily sensitive. Very small changes in the underlying assumptions (the input) caused port-folios to shift around wildly. As a result, to run money on a computer, you must accept a very, very elaborate model of the world, give it a tremendous amount of input from a data-gathering group, and turn over the portfolio about 100 percent a month. At this point any sane chairman of the board would fire the entire investment department! Nobody is going to accept that nonsense. Even if top-management people felt that such an approach would provide good performance (which is absurd), they couldn't go out and sell the idea to trust clients and pension trustees.

Most of the computer models were focusing on the wrong information anyway. They were attempting to take readily available published information and incorporate it into various programs to come up with new information that wasn't already discounted in the stock market. That's awfully difficult to do. If you've been an investor for a while, you know that most of the information circulating in the investment community is of little value. The valuable information is not printed in annual reports or brokers' blurbs. You have to go out in the business world and dig for it. You get it from other people. Sitting behind a desk (or under the desk, as we prefer to characterize it), the computer technicians were simply not dealing with the information which was of primary value: the new information. They weren't even in touch with the people who possessed it! They were not doing the necessary fieldwork to uncover information which would have produced exceptional investment performance.

One of the ironic and humorous by-products of most of the computer work done over the last 20 years is that the computer technicians have satisfactorily demonstrated (to themselves, at least) that all stock price fluctuations are random and unpredictable. Thus, in their opinion, we are all obsolete, pros and independent amateurs alike. Even if the computer people were able to produce a practical investment decision-making model, the best it would be able to do would be to track the market averages. That means that you could then simplify your model enormously (just own the Dow-Jones average, for example) and reduce your staff to one person! The whole thing has gone around full circle.

Our personal opinion is that there are valuable ideas ("undiscounted information") available about stocks and that they are not all that difficult to get hold of—but some careful ferreting about is required. (We will go into that in much more detail later in the book.) Unfortunately, most professionals destroy valuable information by the way in which they organize it. They take it back to their office and spend three or four months digesting it, writing reports (which nobody reads), and running it through all kinds of complex committees and decision-making processes. By using some of the better professional research techniques and our decision-making methods, you can skip all the bureaucratic nonsense and act on your own good ideas.

What about the genius approach? At roughly the same time the computer approach was peaking out, human professional investors looking for real growth of capital had evolved into two types of people. First there were the "go-go" operators, whom we don't need to beat to death again. Then there were the more serious and highly competent generalists. They felt that if they just sorted out the very best companies and then bought and held them forever, they would do better than if they traded in and out. Their thesis was that you find a growth company with outstanding management, buy it at any price, and hold onto it come hell or high water. This approach worked for several years—up until about the same time the go-go operators began to come unglued. When the market fell apart in 1969–1974, however, they and their counterparts rode their beautiful treasured stocks all the way back down again. If you were on that trip, you know what a heartbreaking experience it was.

Professional investors have now concluded that the problem with all the old approaches is that the "supergeneralist" is an impossible job specification. The latest professional line is that, while it was possible 50 years ago to make money as a lone operator, today it is not possible because of the tremendous proliferation of information. Professional investors think that because we now have full disclosure of information as a matter of law (and there are some pretty heavy teeth in those laws), it is much more difficult today to dig out unknown information because so much is already freely available. The supergeneralist would have to be able to follow dozens of areas, read voraciously, and keep up on all kinds of trends. That is an impossible job for a single individual, or so the argument goes. In accepting this false conclusion, institutions and brokers have developed a whole cadre of specialists who go around analyzing the same few companies in unnecessary detail and depth, while ignoring thousands of attractive but smaller companies.

WHO ARE YOUR REAL COMPETITORS?

With whom do you, as an individual investor, compete for uncommon stock ideas? Most of the nation's millions of other investors are too busy with jobs or other pursuits to perform business research, and/or they lack the training this book provides. Only a fraction of 1 percent of these people are making decisions on a basis other than random reaction to gossip, prejudices, and self-serving advice from brokers and useless advisory services.

There are 100,000 professional stockbrokers who regularly advise clients, but only a small number of them actually spend any amount of their time on research. They are in the business of selling, not researching, and so they are not much competition for a serious private investor.

There are roughly 10,000 security analysts who do spend full time on business research. However, fewer than one in ten does anything other than rehash and report already known facts about the same few hundred companies. This is not a criticism of the abilities of analysts, many of whom are brilliant people, but simply a recognition of the limits under which most of them work. There are several thousand portfolio managers, and the same observations apply to them. They spend almost all their time trying to second-guess one another about the big companies. In reality, there are only a few thousand real competitors in the field.

This sounds incredible, but keep in mind that we are discussing the gathering of significant information and its use in systematic pricing decisions. While all these ideas will be developed in detail as the book unfolds, the short version of the path to wealth is this: (1) Learn the few really basic and ageless professional research and price forecasting techniques; (2) trust your common sense and ignore most professional advice; (3) spend a few hours learning the new decision-making methods we have spent 20 years developing for you; and (4) start looking into some local medium-sized and smaller companies which are ignored by everyone else so that you can become the expert.

By using a few of the best professional methods and by concentrating your efforts on a small number of local stocks, you can run your own portfolio in just a few hours per week, do a better job at less cost, and beat the market!

WHERE TO FIND UNCOMMON STOCKS

LOOK CLOSE TO HOME

The best place to look for interesting companies is in your own back-yard. Personal research is one feature which separates you, the success-ful private investor, from the tip-chasing gamblers who believe what-ever two-bit expert they last heard. Therefore, it makes sense that the closer you live to a company, the easier and cheaper it will be for you to call and visit and the more likely you are to meet people who know what is really going on.

Chapters 14 to 17 are devoted to research and related subjects, and so we will not discuss that now. The purpose of this chapter is simple: to show you where to find uncommon stocks, starting with our unique Prospect List. If you haven't already done so, please turn to this list (pages 181 to 438) and flip through it quickly.

Your Prospect List includes 7,200 companies. Every one is traded publicly, either on the major exchanges or over the counter. The name and address of the president of each are listed also. The list is organized geographically by ZIP code.

Even if you didn't have a single idea before for a stock to research, you will have all you can handle in just a few more minutes. Here is how to get started:

1. Get out your local telephone book and look up the ZIP-code map for your area. In addition to your own ZIP code, list the codes of several more areas that are within easy reach of your home or office.

2. Open the Prospect List to your own ZIP code and then find your other selected codes.

3. On any basis at all, pick out about five or ten companies in your area and adjacent areas. It's great if you already know something about them, but it's not essential. You are just fishing for ideas.

4. Write a personal letter, not a form letter, to the president of each prospect company you select. Keep it short and simple. Say that you are a private investor and ask for information and for the president's referral to a contact inside the company. You will want to compose your letter in your own style, but as an example, the letter shown in Figure 2 seldom fails to get a response.

Mr. Malcolm Jones, President
XYZ Company, Inc.

Dear Mr. Jones:

I am a private investor considering buying stock in your company. To help me do my homework, would you please send me a copy of your latest two years' annual reports, any interim reports issued since, and, if possible, a copy of your SEC Form 10-K annual report. I would also appreciate marketing literature, the house newspaper, press clippings, or any other material you think could round out my understanding of your company.

When I have finished studying what you send, I may have a few questions left unanswered. Could you refer me to the right person in your company to contact for a personal meeting?

Perhaps sometime in the future, when I have become much more knowledgeable about XYZ Company, you will find a few minutes to let me come in to meet you personally. Meanwhile, thank you for your consideration of this request.

Sincerely

John Wilson

FIGURE 2. SAMPLE LETTER TO THE PRESIDENT OF A PROSPECT COMPANY.

Within one week you will begin getting all kinds of material from your prospects. Forget about companies that fail to respond. You don't need communication problems right from the start. You will find that the better-quality companies and the promotional companies (need we say that these are two completely separate types?) will both respond fully. The secretive company or the marginal company will send you only the bare bones or nothing at all. That is just what you want for this first sorting out. The rule at this stage is that if a company doesn't impress you right up front as being open and interesting, stop spending your valuable time on it.

THE PROSPECT LIST OF 7,200 STOCKS

What are the chances that a stock on our Prospect List will turn out to be an uncommon stock? There are almost 10,000 publicly owned companies in which one might invest. We eliminated about one-third of them in developing the Prospect List.

First, of course, we dropped those very large companies which get regular attention from investors, since you really can't learn much new about them. For example, you could easily waste weeks studying IBM only to finally understand why it sells where it does. There are three very smart and ambitious analysts who do nothing but study IBM for institutional investors, and there are hundreds more who put in over five hours per week on the stock. The chances are very slim indeed that you will ever learn anything that is not already reflected in the price of this kind of stock.

Next we cut out a large number of local utilities, railroads, telephone companies, and other regulated businesses. While sometimes such stocks are cheap, we would stay away from them because their profits are heavily controlled by political pressures and no one seems to want them to make more than a bare minimum return.

Further cuts were made on the basis of direct experience that indicated you might have trouble dealing with the company for all kinds of reasons we don't have space to discuss. Since we have owned over 700 companies at one time or another, it seemed only fair to spare you some blind alleys where possible. We also probably missed some stocks out of error or oversight, and a few will have moved or appointed new presidents since this book was published.

The presence or absence of any stock on this list is not a recommendation of any sort. The sole purpose of the Prospect List is to provide you with the most convenient way possible to start looking for uncommon stocks.

WHAT ARE THE CHANCES OF FINDING AN UNCOMMON STOCK?

There is no solid formula concerning your yield of good ideas from prospecting. While you may find a real potential gem in the first batch, don't be discouraged if you have to wade through dozens of information packages from your friendly local company presidents. You are looking for just a few (maybe two to five) which are worth your effort to research in depth.

We have done work on dozens of good, interesting companies that no qualified investment person, professional or amateur, has so much as visited for over a year—and some of these firms have had market value capitalizations of hundreds of millions of dollars! One of our favorite uncommon companies, Rogers Corporation, had no one but a few wire-house reporters even telephone it for several years. The pros are just out of the market for the vast majority of stocks, and some of these are incredible bargains. Because of this experience in the real world of today, it is impossible to accept the view that all publicly available information is accurately and properly discounted in the current market price. There is real opportunity, and those who cannot see it have just spent their time looking in the wrong places.

A SCREENING CHECKLIST

How can you tell at this stage whether you should begin really digging in to learn about a company? While there is no perfect screening technique, here are some of the tests a company should pass on the basis of your first hour-long survey of its information package:

1. The material sent to you should be sufficient to give you a good, clear picture of what the company does and how well it is doing financially. If you have received a lot of abstract nonsense and glossy but irrelevant photos, quit, don't fight. If you have made a reasonable effort to understand and still can't, it's the company's fault, not yours.

2. You should feel capable of getting deeper into what you first see. If you will get snowed under by technology, avoid the company; if you're an engineer and don't relate to ladies' dresses, so be it. You don't really have to know a thing about the business to start with, but until you've done a few research projects, you might as well stay in comfortable territory.

3. The stock should still trade at least a few hundred shares per day. The Prospect List was 100 percent accurate when we last revised it, but markets do dry up. So check the newspapers or ask your broker just to be sure your prospect is still breathing regularly.

4. There should be no time bombs or major problems which won't be resolved in the next few months. Time bombs are issues which easily could move the stock up or down 75 percent once settled but whose outcome is so unpredictable that no one can even guess at it. Two examples are basic lawsuits and exploration programs. The reason to avoid such stocks is that your research efforts will leave you no better able to make a price forecast than anyone else. And without a research edge, you're back in the flock with all the other sheep again.

When you have selected your first real candidate, then begin your research work, picking ideas and directions from the later chapters of the book. You still may drop the stock at any point in your research, so don't be overly critical at this early stage. Don't be afraid of companies with erratic records or normal problems. Very few firms have perfect records anymore. Remember, you are trying to find stocks whose future price you can have a better idea about than you can about the overall market. Such undervaluation (or overvaluation) can arise in almost any kind of company.

THE PSYCHOLOGY OF INVESTING

Our human foibles and hidden capacities are as important to stock market success as all the more technical skills combined. In Chapters 4 to 9 we will look at how behavior gets intertwined with issues of economics. These ideas are distilled from the most frequent or severe problems investors have which are related not to investing but to their own ways of thinking and feeling.

WHAT MAKES STOCKS MOVE?

THE MARKET ISN'T MOMMY

The stock market does not care about you or about your hopes, ambitions, or needs. Many investors act as if what they want somehow magically influences what they will get. You must keep your head clear and not slip into the more subtle versions of this narcissistic position. Agonizing over the stock pages won't bring comforting price gains. Cheering on your favorite stock is like clapping at the end of a movie. Gerry Goodman ("Adam Smith") said it best in *The Money Game*: "The stock doesn't know you own it."

For example, most sensible investors try to think about their investment objectives before buying stocks. We agree, and strongly encourage this idea. (See Chapters 6 and 9.) However, you cannot simply decide that you want to make 15 percent per year and then push the 15 percent button on the market machine. The best rate of return attainable at a given level of risk is determined only by current market opportunities. Therefore, the mere fact that you take more risk does not mean that you will get a higher return.

The basic idea of risk versus return can be displayed in a graph as shown in Figure 3.

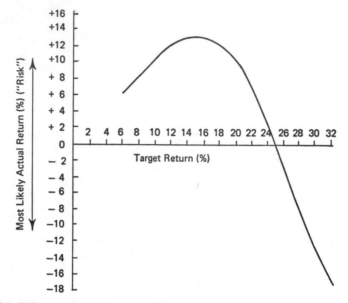

FIGURE 3. RISK-VERSUS-RETURN CURVE.

The curve in the figure illustrates that as you increase your target return (investment objective) and therefore the risks you are willing to take, you can increase the actual long-term return you achieve—up to a certain point. After this point, you begin to get too speculative, and your most likely actual long-term rate of return begins to drop. When you get completely speculative and take real long shots, you are in the absurd position of taking very large risks and producing a zero or a negative rate of return.

Obviously, this relationship does not hold true in the short term, within a year or two, but it does hold true over the longer term. The shape of this curve at any point in time is subject to great debate, of course, but the general principle is well accepted.

THE BUSINESSMAN'S RISK

The highest average return point on the curve (a target return of 12 to 18 percent in our illustration) is often called a "businessman's risk" on the assumption that a rational, experienced risk taker with adequate earning power would aim for the best return. Let's look at this businessman's-risk area. You can reasonably expect to produce average long-term annual compound rates of return in the area of 12 percent or a bit more. At this level of risk, over a period of several years you have the best chance to achieve multifold increases in your capital.

In the process of reaching for fairly high rates of long-term gain, however, it is not unusual to suffer temporary reversals for a year or two amounting to 20 percent or more. Unfortunately, there is no way to achieve real wealth over the long term without accepting short-term fluctuations of this magnitude.

This can be very upsetting for even the sophisticated investor in the short run. However, it is a fact of investment life, and if you truly feel uncomfortable with high risk, then reduce your risk and your expectations.

Don't be misled by the occasional spectacular successes of others. Some investors have achieved extraordinary rates of return for short periods, but only by taking large risks, either with or without an awareness of what they were doing. For example, we made over $1 million in one single year (1968), but risked every dime we had and all we could borrow. That speculation was not smart, even though it worked and even though every step of the way we knew how dangerous our position was. We could have dug a financial hole that would have taken 10 years to climb out of—but we were lucky instead.

Many investors have specific future obligations to meet and really cannot take the businessman's risk. In fact, they are at the other extreme from the speculator and just want to increase their probability of achieving at least a respectable basic return. This is the left side of the curve, where one can aim for 6 to 8 percent average gains with a very good chance of achieving them. (The bulk of professional money management activity is also in this area of the risk-versus-return curve.) If your risk tolerance is low (or should be!), your portfolio will be quite different from that of the businessman's-risk investor who is in the 12 to 18 percent area.

THE CHANCE-OF-SUCCESS CURVE

The specification of risk, therefore, is your first priority. Yet most investors are operating completely blind with respect to risk. Very few investors (or even professional managers) can tell you what the chances are of their stocks' falling by 10 or 30 or 90 percent if their judgment turns out to be wrong. More importantly, most investors have no idea what the chances are of their not achieving their targeted rate of return over the long term.

To make this important point a different way, we have provided another kind of illustration: the "chance-of-success" curve, shown in Figure 4. The bottom scale shows the targeted return, and the scale at the left shows the chances of achieving it. This curve, like the risk-versus-return curve, is just one man's opinion at a particular time, and you may feel the lines should be drawn differently. The important thing is that it is another expression of the commonsense idea that the higher the goal, the harder it is to reach. So set your risk levels realistically and don't let your reach exceed your grasp!

HOW CURRENT TRENDS AFFECT STOCKS

Fairly early in your work on a company you should get acquainted with its short-term or current trends. While you are usually intending to have a long-term interest in the company, you may decide to shift the priority of your work on the basis of what is happening right now.

The biggest single determinant of short-term stock price moves is relative earnings performance. (That is simply the next few quarters' percentage changes in earnings per share relative to changes in overall corporate profits for all public companies.) As you begin to assemble your research on the longer-term trends (one to five years), you will find that you can sharpen your foresight by trying to identify a few of the most significant of the short-term indicators of profits.

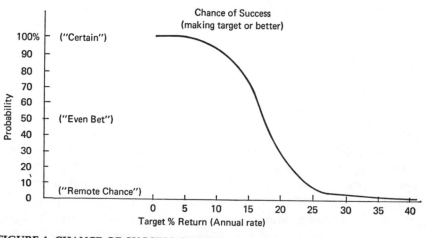

FIGURE 4. CHANCE-OF-SUCCESS CURVE.

For example, sales figures are often publicly available on a monthly or even shorter interval, even though profits are released only quarterly. Are sales stagnant or declining? Maybe this was planned for, and expenses were cut in advance to protect profits. Or maybe the sales slowdown does mean lower profits ahead. Are sales rising? If so, are they above expectations? Does the sales trend really mean anything? Maybe weekly or monthly sales normally jump around a lot (as in machinery manufacturing) instead of being normally stable (as in an electric utility).

Here are some more preliminary ideas for possibly significant short-term profit indicators:

1. New or incoming orders

2. Physical measures of shipments (i.e., units or barrels or tons, as opposed to the dollar value of sales)

3. Employment-level changes caused by hirings and layoffs or even strikes and other disputes

4. Advertising-program changes, where expenditures often move up or down quickly in sensitive response to changing expectations of company profits

Look past the indicator itself. It can mean the obvious, or it can mean the opposite of what you might expect. Try to get clearly focused on the significance of the data. Generalizations are meaningless. You must find a specific perspective on each company individually. Get it from the historical record if it is available. Otherwise, look to people inside the company who have lived with the short-term ups and downs long enough to set you straight.

Ask your company contact for help in understanding the general relationship between current sales trends (and other indicators) and current profits. Your contact may not want to talk about profits themselves in advance of public release, but he or she can ethically give you a short course on the possible meanings of indicators such as sales. You might also ask what are the most important specific topics currently being discussed by top management. An honest answer to that one can save you a lot of time.

Getting to the heart of this issue of short-term profit trends is your most important starting point in understanding what makes stocks move.

KEEPING STRAIGHT WITH YOURSELF

THE SINGLE BIGGEST MISTAKE IN INVESTING

Telling yourself lies can hurt your stock market performance more than any other mistake. That seems strange, doesn't it? You don't lie to yourself, you think. But you do, and so does everyone else. It is quite natural. Even if we operate on a minimum of fantasy and wishful thinking, inevitably our memory will play tricks on us. It will warp our recollections of past decisions, amplify our smart moves, and subdue the painful knowledge of our mistakes. Even the most experienced investor with few personal hang-ups is subject to the expensive human trait of selective perception or selective memory. Inadvertent self-deception is the biggest factor in success or failure in the stock market, and yet almost nothing is ever written about it.

You can avoid the risks associated with self-deception by keeping straight with yourself. To keep straight, you must be as explicit or as specific as possible on important issues. It requires plainness and distinctness. It requires precision in selection of words and clarity of definitions. In short, it requires that you define your expectations.

Those last three words sum up a subject about which we have the strongest feelings. Investing is not a science, and quite frankly it is not even a particularly well-developed business practice. There is nothing very predictable about the future. We just don't know what profit might be earned next year by the persistent efforts of the Avon ladies or what Avon stock itself may sell for. We can only make an educated guess or rough estimate. All this notwithstanding, it is still relatively easy to introduce some useful discipline into the practice of buying and selling stocks. The heart of this discipline is to strive at all times to make absolutely explicit your assumptions regarding the future events which will create changes in stock prices. *Write it down.* Put down on a piece of paper the underlying assumptions on which you are operating so that you can keep things clear in your mind.

Successful investing is often a lonely job. True productive cooperation among investors is very rare, despite the hundreds of investment committees and dozens of research teams which are rampant on Wall Street. In practice, the identification of truly outstanding long-term values is essentially a one-person job. Creative investors usually are solitary searchers rather than organization people. It is precisely because of this that you must be completely honest with yourself about your beliefs and prejudices. You usually cannot depend on someone else to question your judgment at every turn. For this you need a brief written record of your own ideas and thoughts.

WINSTON CHURCHILL'S RULE

Winston Churchill used to demand from his World War II staff that they cover an entire complex subject on one side of an ordinary sheet of paper! The discipline was enormous. Similarly, we have never seen an investment situation which could not be summarized in its essentials on one sheet of paper. You might find this exercise in willpower and self-direction to be very valuable.

There is an analogy in speech making. It has been our experience that the amount of preparation necessary is inversely proportional to the length of the speech. That is, if you have an entire hour to talk about a topic, you really don't have to do very much preparation (assuming you know something about the subject to begin with). However, if you have been given just a few minutes to cover a subject, you will find that it can take several hours to condense your thoughts carefully enough.

The Churchill rule applies directly in summarizing for yourself the key determinants of the future price of a stock. If you have 10 or 20 pages on which to scribble, you can simply pick up a pencil and start writing. Condensing your thoughts on one page can be of far more help to you.

The Churchill rule is nowhere more important than in making your price estimates. There is more nonsense written on the question of when to buy and when to sell than on any other subject in the investment field. Such discussions usually fall into one of two categories. The first is simply a listing of types of situations in which one should buy or sell; these rules of thumb are supposed to provide some guideline. For example: "Cut your losses and let your profits run." When such rules are examined simply and explicitly, in an attempt to understand just exactly what they mean, frequently it is found that they mean almost nothing at all.

The other major school of theories attempts to build systems for buying and selling. These systems are usually simplistic and mechanistic, and they have performance records lasting from a few months to a couple of years. One example: "Buy a stock when it first appears on the daily 'new high' list and sell it when it first falters." Unfortunately, we have never seen a system which would survive a long-term statistical test. When the realities of gathering investment information and the cost of brokerage commissions are taken into account, these theories just fall apart in practice. Future price estimates and buy and sell decision making are among the most glaring weaknesses in the entire investment field. Because of this, Chapters 18 to 21 are devoted to a careful development of more useful methods for making buy and sell decisions.

THE DECISION NOTEBOOK

One of the greatest sources of education for anyone is objective reflection upon his or her own experiences. This is particularly true in analyzing past mistakes and successes in the stock market. Therefore, we suggest the habit of keeping a "decision notebook." This is a diary in which you enter your reasons for doing what you are doing, your expectations, and any other key information on a stock. As events unfold in the months and years which follow, it is painfully impossible to get away from those original expectations! Naturally you will be forced by events to alter your expectations, sometimes in minor ways and sometimes drastically. But you can never escape from them. You cannot hide in a faulty memory or in the well-meaning flattery or the unthinking criticisms of friends.

By acting in harmony with your explicit expectations, you will perform consistently better than if you follow the short-term trading urges of the moment. This process is called "trading with your expectations." It means, for example, that while you can fall in love with a company, you should never fall in love with its stock. You can and should continue to follow a company's progress without owning its shares at all times. The reason for this is that opportunities to sell will arise from time to time because of big fluctuations and distortions in the price of your stock in comparison with your long-term price estimates.

One of the best examples of this is Raychem Corporation in California. Astute investors could have made about 10 times on their original investment over the period of a decade in this company. This is excellent performance by any reasonable standard. Notwithstanding this, however, if one had simply followed the expedient of buying the company when its price/earning (P/E) ratio was below 30 times and selling it when its P/E ratio was above 70 times (certainly not unreasonable outside limits), a great deal more money would have been made.

It might reasonably be argued that making such judgments is virtually impossible ahead of time and misleadingly easy in hindsight. There are those in the profession who feel that identification as a great company is cause enough to hold the stock virtually indefinitely. However, by setting up your explicit price expectations for a period of one to three years in advance, you will often discover that a stock has already moved up so much that even after allowing for a healthy margin of error the risks clearly outweigh the remaining potential rewards. You can know this only if you have written down your expectations in advance.

Returning to the example of Raychem, in the early 1960s, when that stock was selling in the mid-30s, we recommended it to our institutional clients as an intelligent long-term speculation. At that point the stock had already gone up some, and Raychem was known to a few other investors on the West Coast as a small but high-quality growth company. It was not long before Raychem gained national popularity; eventually it went up to almost $300 per share at the peak of the market in the late 1960s.

However, before that we recommended sale of Raychem at a price of around 150. While we were briefly embarrassed by its subsequent double even from that price, we saw that it was just as likely to have fallen back to 75 as to have doubled. That kind of bet you can get in Las Vegas or Atlantic City! Certainly, it was a great company, and it may very well still be. But there must come a time to sell any company, even Raychem—and a time to buy it back. Incidentally, the stock finally did tumble by 75 percent from 300 back to about 75, and then it went almost all the way back up to 300 again a few years later. By having careful price targets thought out in advance, you can avoid some of the roller-coaster rides and get more out of your work in the stock market.

WHAT ABOUT INTUITION?

"Intuitive" investors who do not stay straight with themselves are only temporarily lucky freewheelers. Stock market performance is a business and a serious hobby, not a game. The concept of an intuitive "performance game" was very popular in the 1960s. While stock price performance is certainly the ultimate goal, at that time methods of picking stocks became more and more superficial and detached from reality. Many professionals who should have known better began to act like tourists on their first trip to the gambling casinos. They began to play hunches and operate on very little information, and they seldom took the time to write down explicitly just what their expectations were for a stock. They had no really clear idea why they owned a stock.

At the height of the nonsense in the late 1960s, hundreds of portfolio managers were acting on no better information and with no more discipline than the proverbial shoeshine boy of the 1920s. Since then, needless to say, most have been burned badly and have either left the business or gotten a lot more careful.

Investing is a serious business, and sometimes the job can seem a bit tedious. Intuition alone and snap judgments are tempting. It is not always great fun to sit down and carefully summarize your expectations, nor is it the most exciting thing in the world to build up good files on your companies. However, keep in mind that you do not need to know every detail of a company's existence, nor do you need to agree with other people's opinions as to what is really important. The critical thing is that you know that you don't know something, in the sense that you have deliberately reviewed a situation and have concluded that those particular details would not have much influence on the price of the stock.

Your results in stock selection do not depend on the detailed knowledge you carry around and display or on the wealth of anecdotes you are able to relate about a given company. Instead, your results will come from your ability to concisely summarize the key determinants of the future price of a company's stock and from your ability to act on your own judgment.

Being a solid winner is a lot more satisfying than experiencing the quick thrills or defeats of mindless gambling. When you really want to make big money, you don't treat it like a game! There can be a lot of very real fun in disciplining yourself in the methods outlined in this book and in watching your net worth cross your "financial security zone" for the first time! Keeping straight with yourself may not be flashy, but it is a much surer and more self-reliant path to wealth.

A GOOD STRATEGY IS WORTH A THOUSAND CLEVER TACTICS

TIME HORIZONS

One difficult question, even for very sophisticated investors, concerns the right time horizon to use in seeking and judging investment performance. Our opinion is that to maximize your long-term rate of return, you need the patience to hold for at least two to three years. Sometimes you will get lucky and be out in a year, but other times your stock may take four or five years to develop and be recognized. Your time horizon must avoid the extremes. Try to operate somewhere in between the self-destructive frantic trading behavior of the compulsive plunger and the equally mindless "put-'em-away-forever" school.

Very few investment people have successfully operated at one extreme or the other of the time-horizon question. Most short-term-oriented investors are not successful with their tactics when they keep going over several years. Their long-term records are fair to poor. They can sound clever and can perform well for short periods of time, especially in a bull market, but a time horizon measured in days or weeks or months is doomed to produce only random results over the long term.

THE PITFALLS OF THE CHARTISTS

The usual exponents of short-term tactics are the chartists, or technicians. It is their theory that future price action over the near term (a few days to a few months) can be predicted just on the basis of a careful examination of past price patterns. They study detailed charts showing data on past stock prices and trading volume, and they use only these data to make fast moves in and out of the market. Stockbrokers love them because they usually generate lots of commissions.

When technicians act as investment advisers, their opinions are usually so hedged that the investor can't tell what they are recommending. However, the most successful technician-advisers have been quite careful to be very clear about what they want their clients to do. Then, when they happen to hit a period when they have been right for a few times in a row, they promote their record and develop enormous followings. Almost invariably, these records blow up when the market makes a major shift in direction, and their followers are left to wander off in search of a new guru.

We have spent a lot of time talking to technicians over the years and trying to work through their methods. If there was anything there which could be of use, it would save a lot of work! We have always had access to computers and have offered to help technicians test the statistical validity of their ideas. Unfortunately, however, these and other studies indicate that there is very little of economic value going on in the technical approach. Chartists generate a lot of action, but when the dust settles, the results have been no better than would have been obtained by throwing darts at the stock page.

In the few cases in which technical methods seem to work, it has turned out that the technician, without being fully aware of it, was using a great deal of nontechnical experience. Even chart watchers are exposed over the years to much fundamental and background material in addition to their cherished price and volume charts. Just reading the papers and talking to friends in the market would give them a mountain of useful facts. Consequently, while the rare successful technicians may be giving full credit and emphasis to their chart work, it is their entire mental process which is producing the results. They are seeing chart patterns in relation to their store of other and more significant knowledge. They are not giving enough credit to the other things that are going on in their own minds.

There is some merit to doing technical work in conjunction with business research, but do not try to use it exclusively or even primarily. In addition to practical limitations, there is another reason for this attitude. You must maintain your composure in the midst of the continuous (and almost always insignificant) jiggling and changing of stock prices. It takes a sense of perspective to buy and sell stocks successfully, and there is no point in tearing your hair out over minute-by-minute price fluctuations on the tape.

Even if you have easy access to a full set of electronic equipment at the present time, give some thought to ignoring it all in the interest of saving time for more important work. It is too tempting to spend half an hour punching out stock prices and watching short-term swings, making totally frustrating attempts to read meaning into them. That time could be much better spent in calling up a company's competitor for a little gossip, making a short check with a financial VP on the current outlook for the company, or doing some other bit of basic research. Once you have set your buy and sell points (which we will discuss in detail in Chapter 21), normally you need not be concerned with price fluctuations within that range. For most individual private investors, short-term trading activity is really of no concern.

WHY A BUY-AND-HOLD STRATEGY WON'T WORK

Now let's take a look at the other extreme of the time-horizon question. There are two schools of thought which maintain that the best thing to do is find a good stock and hold on to it indefinitely. The first is the traditional version of the "put-'em-away-forever" school. It is based primarily on an outdated bank trust department practice geared to extremely low costs for research and administration. It is usually just a capital preservation or holding action based on producing the lowest common denominator of performance. You should avoid any involvement with this type of investment practice.

The other buy-and-hold school is one which seems to put too much faith in the wisdom of business research. In this case, decisions to buy and hold are based on a conviction that if the research work is done properly and a good company is discovered, no extreme of overvaluation in the marketplace should cause you to sell that stock. Similarly, no depression in its price should cause you to lose faith in it.

While we have the highest respect for the business analysis done by some proponents of this theory, we completely disagree with their view on stock price decisions. No stock, no matter how it stacks up on a checklist of ideal characteristics, is inherently and permanently suitable for anyone. The investment character of a company changes not only with the slowly changing circumstances of the company itself but also with the more rapid changes in the price of its stock. When these factors are moving in opposite directions, the suitability can shift very rapidly, sometimes in just a few months. An investor should be willing to sell any stock when the risks outweigh the rewards over the next year or two.

You will often want to continue to do research on an overvalued company whose stock you have sold. You may have a very high opinion of its prospects and fully expect that if the market becomes bearish or if the company itself temporarily stumbles, you will be able to buy it back cheaper. And, even if neither of these things occurs, you may be able to buy that stock back two or three years from now at its current price, having had the use of that money for other projects in the meantime.

Consequently, while you should be very reluctant to sell a good stock, assuming you were thoughtful when you bought it, often it is necessary. We must not get too enamored with the notion of the "inherent superiority" of any product or company or industry. In the very long term—say, fifteen years or more—there does not seem to be any such thing as an inherently superior investment vehicle. Some great investment research has been brought to virtual ruin by a failure to recognize this basic concept.

This outlines the extremes of time horizon. Do not attempt to invest for very short fluctuations, say, 5 or 10 percent over a few months. On the other hand, it is not realistic to have an investment policy which looks beyond five years or so, and certainly not beyond 10 years.

As a matter of practice, a realistic time horizon tends to run about two to three years. Sometimes you will get lucky and realize your target price in a year or less. Sometimes you may have to endure work-out situations well beyond three years. But every stock you own should be for sale at a price.

THREE MAJOR INVESTMENT MYTHS

"I'VE GOT TO GET EVEN BEFORE I GET OUT"

How often have you heard people say this? "If only General Widget would get back to the 40 bucks a share I paid, I'd be even and could sell the damn stock." That is a very expensive myth you're hearing. In reality, for the purposes of making decisions now, you should ignore what you once paid for a stock.

A sounder principle is what is known as the "doctrine of sunk cost." It is enormously difficult for most investors to accept that cost is irrelevant—that it is "sunk" and gone and that no future action should be guided by it. The original price or cost lives on in our minds and gets in the way of new decisions which need to be made. Therefore, we need to forget what we paid for a stock.

Unfortunately, if you bought XYZ stock at 25 and it's now at 15, even after the most serious-minded and careful discussion you are still going to harbor the notion somewhere deep in your heart that you haven't yet really lost the money. You will feel that you really haven't given up that $25 per share until you sell the stock. When you get in that mythical frame of mind, try reminding yourself that a stock is worth only what you can get for it today. A decision to buy or sell should be based on what you think the stock will be worth in the future rather than on what it was worth in the past. It isn't easy to ignore the sunk cost of your stocks, but it must be done.

Of course it is still true that, on average, when you sell stocks their cost had better be less than what you get for them, or something is wrong somewhere! It is this basic truth of profit or loss that most investors are reaching for when they focus on past cost. Unfortunately, however, in an attempt to get a handle on the profit and loss controls, they frequently make decisions on the basis of past cost, and these may not make sense in today's conditions.

Even otherwise sophisticated institutional brokers have often asked us, "What did you pay for your XYZ stock?" Our standard answer was in the form of a question: "What did the stock close at today?" That is the real cost in the sense that the only decision left to make is whether to hold or sell. If the stock is held, its "cost" is the price someone would have paid for it today. That's the cost or price of continuing to own the stock, not what was paid for it in the past.

The most common error caused by ignorance of the doctrine of sunk cost is the decision to "sell when I get even." This is a sad statement because it reveals the muddled thinking that probably pervades the speaker's whole portfolio. Such investors are just a few more bad players in the market, helping create opportunities for others. They are like bad poker players or $2 bettors at the track, and maybe we should be thankful they're sitting in on the game. But how can they imagine that the future price of a stock has any connection with their cost? They should instead be making their best estimate of where the stock is going and then hold or sell on the basis of that.

To make the case clearer, suppose such an investor had gotten the stock for nothing. Would that affect where it is going or when it should be sold? Suppose the investor paid $1,000 a share and it is now at 10. Isn't the real question whether the stock is going to 5 or 15 or wherever from 10? Sure, there are tax considerations and also some powerful feelings involved, and real decisions can be tough. But they aren't going to be made less complex by being confused with painful, hard-to-face irrelevancies.

"I HAVE TO CHOOSE BETWEEN INCOME AND GROWTH"

It has been drummed into investors' heads for years that the basic trade-off they must make is income now versus potential growth or capital gains in the future. In the narrow sense of current dividend yield on current market price, perhaps there is some truth in this. Basically, however, you should instead think in terms of the total rate of return, that is, the income and change in price taken together. The combined rate of return can be measured in relation to the risk of loss involved and can be compared with market averages to measure your performance.

The modern measure of true economic income from stocks or bonds combines the ordinary income (dividends or interest) with the change in market value (realized and unrealized capital gain or loss). This combined, or total, rate of return may then be reduced to reflect taxes (whether paid or reserved) and inflation.

For the sake of clarity, let's go through an example. If you buy 1,000 shares of XYZ at $15 per share, receive a $1-per-share annual dividend, and could sell for $30 per share three years later, the aftertax total rate of return* works out as follows:

STEP 1: Ordinary income portion

- $1 per share times 1,000 shares equals $1,000 per year (pretax return).

- $1,000 taxable at 50 percent equals $500 per year (aftertax return).

- $500 per year (aftertax return) times three years totals $1,500.

STEP 2: Capital gains portion

- $30 current price per share less $15 cost equals $15 per-share gain (pretax return).

- $15 per-share gain times 1,000 shares equals $15,000 (pretax return).

- $15,000 gain taxable at 35 percent totals $9,750 (aftertax return).

STEP 3: Total return

- Income of $1,500 plus gain of $9,750 equals total return of $11,250.

- Percentage return on $15,000 cost equals 11,250/15,000, or 75 percent.

---

* To the statisticians: You are right that this calculation is a simplified version, but for practical purposes it is the same as the complex computer-oriented formula.

- 75 percent over three years is equal to a compound annual return of 20.5 percent.

- Inflation can be deducted at a compound annual rate of 6.5 percent.

- 20.5 percent aftertax return less 6.5 percent inflation is 14.0 percent.

That 14 percent figure is the true economic return, adjusted for taxes and inflation. It is a far better indicator of investment performance than yield, growth rates, or other more familiar measures.

Whether a stock pays a high or a low dividend, the only reason to own it is to achieve an appropriate total return in relation to the risks assumed. It is the lower-risk investors who are often mixed up by this subject, since most of their total return comes in the form of dividend and interest income. Businessman's-risk investors (see Chapter 4) are interested in substantial capital gains and will usually be less concerned about the level of current income in the form of dividends or interest payments. Most of their return must come from price changes over a period of several years.

These capital gains (taxable at lower rates, with taxes payable many years from now) can provide far more dramatic additions to a portfolio's value than quarterly dividends which are taxable as received at higher ordinary income rates. At the businessman's-risk level of performance, the primary objective is to own shares in a business which will prosper and be many times more profitable in the future. Sometimes you can get a high dividend in the process, but not usually.

This brings us to the issue of how to generate spendable cash from your portfolio if its dividend and interest income is too low. What should you do if you need to earn spendable income from your investment portfolio? Does this mean you must invest only in "income" stocks or in bonds? The answer is definitely "no."

A much better approach to the production of spendable cash from a portfolio is to have a well-disciplined withdrawal program. Under such a system, you draw out a fixed amount of money on a regular basis, probably quarterly. The amount of this cash withdrawal must be geared to your needs, and only you can make that decision.

However, we caution against an annual withdrawal rate above 6 percent of the total portfolio. The reason is that an otherwise sound long-term program could be permanently sidetracked by a couple of bad market years coming on top of overly heavy withdrawals, forcing you to sell near the bottom to keep your withdrawals flowing.

In the "proper Bostonian" sense, the withdrawal-program idea was thought to be an ill-advised "invasion of principal," an old notion that still has some truth in it. Experience in managing larger estates gave rise in the nineteenth century to the idea of "spending only the dividends," and even this old-fashioned guideline is better than no discipline at all.

However, for the intelligent individual investor, having a fixed withdrawal program not geared to specific dividend or interest income is a much more sensible and more profitable approach to the generation of spendable cash than focusing investment policy solely on current income. Selling shares every few months to supplement low ordinary income is preferable to owning high-dividend dogs which seldom move up or which may eventually have to cut their dividend anyway.

"I CAN'T PUT ALL MY EGGS IN ONE BASKET"

How many individual stocks should you own? It depends primarily on the risk tolerance and return targets you have selected, and to some degree on how big your account is. In an extremely large and very low risk account (one worth $100 million and up) the number of securities can be over 50, while in a very small businessman's-risk account you should be willing to use as few as three.

There is only one main reason for diversification: spreading the risk of errors by reducing your exposure to any one company. The effect of diversification versus concentration can be demonstrated with elaborate statistical techniques, showing the separate influence of the general market, the volatility of the individual stock, and many other factors.

A far simpler illustration tells the basic story. Table 2 shows percentage changes in the value of a portfolio that result from a double in the price of any one stock (while the prices of the others remain constant).

From this table it can be seen that a highly concentrated portfolio— say, one with four stocks—still gets a very nice boost from the price action of just one stock. A 50-stock portfolio, on the other hand, gains only about 2 percent from the strong appreciation of just one security. The other side of the coin, of course, is that if one stock turns sour, the impact is lessened or intensified in the same ratios.

TABLE 2.   PERCENTAGE CHANGES IN THE VALUE OF A PORTFOLIO
DUE TO A DOUBLE IN THE PRICE OF ONE STOCK

Number of Stocks Owned	Appreciation in Portfolio Value Due to a Double in Just One Stock
1	100%
2	50%
3	33%
4	25%
5	20%
10	10%
20	5%
50	2%

When this simple observation is combined with an understanding of the limited number of hours most people want to devote to investing, it becomes apparent that most portfolios should be concentrated in a limited number of stocks rather than being widely diversified in a scattering of poorly understood stocks. We suggest that you own between three and ten carefully picked situations, and preferably five to seven. Beyond that number, the benefit of the additional diversification is offset by a dilution of your research work over too many stocks.

The ownership of a much larger list is called for only when a very low-risk target is selected. In that case the influence of the general market becomes most important rather than the impact of any one carefully picked stock. In such larger and/or lower-risk accounts, you may own several dozen fairly mature and better-known companies and do very little original research. However, your long-term results will more closely reflect the general market. Your cost in time spent on analysis of each company is far lower, and you can use your commission dollars to buy reasonably reliable research on these bigger issues. However, the closer you get to that position of low risk, high diversification, and reliance on the research of others, the more your portfolio will resemble a giant pooled fund. If that is the case, it is better to own a no-load mutual fund because its cost will be lower. For some, of course, this is the best answer, but in today's opportunity-strewn market it seems a shame to settle for such mediocre performance.

Most individual investors can and should use somewhat smaller companies and do most of the work themselves, since brokers cannot afford to spend time on small companies. As we discussed in earlier chapters, brokers view these lesser-known stocks, which are golden opportunities for us, as "low-turnover merchandise" and leave them unresearched.

An important issue within the subject of diversification concerns your principles and prejudices and what stocks you might need to exclude from consideration, regardless of their potential return. For example, conflict-of-interest interpretations by the counts and insider rules have broadened in recent years. This has caused many private individual investors simply to exclude from their portfolios certain companies which might expose them to nuisance suits, to misleading press articles, or just to possible misunderstanding on the part of clients, patients, or friends.

For individuals with a wide range of business connections and interests, stocks on the "excluded list" could number in the dozens, having been rejected on the basis of officerships and directorships, family affiliations, regulatory or other conflict situations, or former associations, for example. There is so much other opportunity available that it is best to be very strict with yourself in drawing up your list of real conflict companies.

Other stocks may appear on the excluded list for more personal reasons, commonly involving religious or moral convictions. Examples are stocks of tobacco companies, brewers or distillers, drug companies, and military contractors. However, if the list begins to broaden into whole segments of the economy, these restrictions may begin to impair performance. This should not distract us, of course, for we all have the responsibility to put our basic convictions ahead of our narrower commercial pursuits.

Some investors have strong convictions about the inherent and permanent investment worth of certain companies or industries and therefore may want to create even more restrictions. At this point you will begin to run into the so-called rules for investment success, most of which are unsound or even dangerous. (See Chapter 2.) To anyone who proposes such restrictions we repeat that no company or industry or type of stock is permanently and inherently superior or inferior from an investment standpoint. Spectacular gains have been made by those who recognized ahead of time new economic patterns emerging in such once "inherently inferior" areas as furniture retailing (Levitz), truck rentals (Ryder Systems), measurement devices (Hewlett Packard), gas transmission (Coastal States), insurance (Equity Funding), and hamburger stands (MacDonald's). And, in the very cases just cited, three out of the six subsequently reversed their position (Levitz, Ryder, and Coastal

States), and one (Equity Funding) almost went under entirely! Hewlett Packard and MacDonald's have become so entrenched in the "favorite 50" that your chances of knowing more than the market are now pretty slim.

The same process continues today, with changes occurring in materials technology, fast foods, air and water purification, aviation, and many other fields. We readily admit to a certain prejudice against "commodity" companies (cement, lumber, copper, aluminum, gold, etc.) "luck" companies (e.g., oil exploration and new product plays) and regulated industries (especially utilities).

However, these prejudices have caused us to overlook major changes. For example, while we picked Hewlett Packard very early, we turned down stock on the initial offering of MacDonald's without really looking at it because it was "just a hamburger stand"!

So it is best to keep an open mind and a short excluded list. Some exclusions are legal necessities, and some are legitimate matters of personal moral convictions. Beyond this, however, try not to make further permanent exclusions from your portfolio.

THE BIG PICTURE: ECONOMISTS AND OTHER EGGHEADS

ECONOMISTS ARE SELDOM RIGHT
BUT ALWAYS USEFUL

Wall Streeters spend great amounts of time and money on an attempt to predict the future course of the economy and its effect on the stock market. Some banks have an entire staff of Ph.D.'s in economics, and no self-respecting brokerage house would be without at least a consulting economist who can crank out an occasional memo on the economy.

In spite of this, most professional observers of the scene grumble that all this produces little of value to investors. That is to say, if one consistently followed the advice given by economists, the investment results would be approximately the same as those achieved by throwing a dart at the stock page and buying whatever it struck.

Yet economists can still be enormously helpful. The apparent problem with their forecasting record lies not in their human fallibility but in the way we are handling the data they are giving us. We are asking them to tell us about a rate of inflation, a rate of economic growth, or a level of interest rates. That is one role they can play, but only poorly, and it detracts from their greater value to us.

A good economist is a provider of perspective. As private investors, we should be interested in the views of economists as well as those of historians, political scientists, psychologists, sociologists, and other intellectuals. Sometimes these sources can be extremely productive for an investor. They can weave together some disconnected threads of evidence into a tantalizing tapestry of perspective.

EXTRAORDINARY POPULAR DELUSIONS
AND THE MADNESS OF CROWDS

Most of the major discontinuities in the apparent trends of our times may have to come as surprises. It just may not be practical to pick stocks which will do well during an unexpected major turn in history. But even if we won't often know in advance, we must gear ourselves to survive occasional major storms. Many situations of this type are illustrated in the beautiful and classic book entitled *Extraordinary Popular Delusions and the Madness of Crowds*. It was written by Charles Mackay in 1841 and describes recurring surges of fads throughout history. The book offers us perspective. Like the work of contemporary intellectuals, its value is impossible to document.

We can sometimes know the truth of our times, though, and it is a wisdom worth seeking. Fortunes have been made by being in fine tune with popular madness. The trick is to keep hold of such fortunes through the inevitable ensuing period of correction. In the process of becoming tuned to a fad you are very likely to be swept along with it and thus be unable to recognize that it is coming to an end. That is why many fortunes are quickly made, but few are kept. The perspective of intellectuals is thus a useful tool to have in your investment kit, even though you cannot depend upon it for the main thrust of your investment policy.

It is terribly easy to get carried away in the tides of emotion which can sweep the market and the general population. But as one old hand pointed out, "Crises usually ain't crises." An assassination or a natural disaster or a sudden welling up of a regional war has a tremendous psychological effect on us even if we are so fortunate as to be spared any direct involvement. Great changes in currency exchange rates, involving strange-sounding institutions and unfamiliar terms, can throw a profound sense of unease into investors generally.

Sometimes the market can simply feed on its own pessimism and for several months at a time continue to go down for no other apparent reason than that it has already gone down. This happened in April and May of 1970 and again in late 1974. There were abuses and distortions and excessive valuations rampant in the preceding markets of 1967–1969 and 1972–1973. But to survive as an investor means to at least not sell out at those bottoms!

To avoid this fate, one has only to conclude that the world is not coming to an end, as many people come to think every few years. For example, it was entirely appropriate to invest in the midst of the two recent madnesses (1970 and 1974), with confidence that the economy would straighten itself out and that when it did the abject fear which gripped the stock market would lift, propelling stocks up by huge percentages. That is the value of the egghead's perspective, when it works: "to keep your head when all about you are losing theirs."

SOME SPECIFIC WAYS TO KEEP
YOUR PERSPECTIVE

It's all very nice that Mackay wrote a great book in 1841, but how do you keep your head in today's nitty-gritty world of stock picking? Let's switch gears from philosophy to some practical advice on how to put together the "big picture" on a company.

At the very first try to define or describe to yourself the business your company is in. Instead of using vague words, such as "financial services," use the clearest, simplest, and most specific terms: "a commercial bank operating in an area of 60,000 people, writing mainly house mortgages and auto and appliance loans."

Once many years ago a small company proclaimed that it was in the "leisure products industry." The concept of leisure as a growth industry was popular at that time (although it is much less so today), and the company naturally wanted to be thought of as a growth situation. After reading the package of material the company sent and making a one-hour visit to the main plant, the analyst drove home and wrote this description of the business: "The firm buys dry seasoned wood and employs nonunion semiskilled labor to make baseball bats, which it sells directly to four chain stores and through about 25 distributors." That tells you something real and useful, whereas "leisure products" doesn't tell you a thing. Feel the difference?

Be prepared to change your description as you learn more about the company. Keep it current. Refer to it for guidance later on when you are thinking about the parts of the business and how they fit together.

Many researches never get around to the apparently simple task of writing a description. Maybe that's because the answer seems obvious. It's not! Right now, stop reading this book and try writing down a description of your full-time business or profession in concrete terms. (Yes, right now!)

See how much this exercise forces you to think about what really happens? We all live in a world of symbolic shorthand and easy abstractions. That's fine for chatter at cocktail parties, but keeping your perspective means being more direct and specific.

Here is another way to get the big picture. Take a look at the history of the company. Did it open shop in 1968 as a promotion and linger on to ensnare you? Or is it an old local institution, hog-tied and bound by a web of self-serving managers and owned by their predecessors' widows? A little time spent on history at this stage in your thinking can save you a lot of time and aggravation in the future, either by better focusing your efforts or by causing you to drop the study.

Don't let superficial prejudices stop you, though. Rogers Corporation, one of the finest companies we've ever seen, started over 100 years ago as a small paper mill in northeastern Connecticut. However, the annual report gave a totally different impression of the company's current business, as contrasted to its past history. The report included a detailed listing of key managers by age and tenure, some excellent product descriptions, and a simple, honest letter from the president summing up the year. You had to wonder why an "old paper company" would do that. It caused us to drive over and ask.

Rogers Corporation turned out to be made up of a group of very bright people who are now formulating and making fiber-reinforced plastic materials and devices for such tough customers as General Motors (gas tank floats), IBM (computer connectors), and Xerox and Polaroid (flexible distribution circuits). The company doesn't even make paper anymore. Its sales have been doubling every five years, and with new products for which it has a special talent, rather than in commodity lines like the old paper business. Rogers's unpromising history had disguised a very uncommon company.

A SHORT ECONOMICS CHECKLIST

Finally, here is a short economics checklist to use in thinking about a company. In general, ask yourself: What are the most significant determinants of the firm's future earnings? If necessary, take at face value the facts as given about the firm's operations for the time being. Think about its economics, in terms of leverages, correlations, price structure, cost of entry and exit, regulations, and protection.

You don't need to be trained in economics to do this type of analysis. The issues are largely commonsense ones. Just as you did when you wrote your description of the business, keep pushing toward simple and basic relationships which are really important:

1. Leverages. How are the firm's profits likely to move as sales increase or decrease? Are there high fixed costs? How is the firm leveraged financially?

2. Correlations. Here we are speaking of correlations of company sales with readily available economic indicators such as consumer disposable income. What outside indicators (even including the weather) can be helpful?

3. Price Structure. Who controls the product price decision: the company, the middleman, or the consumer? Does the consumer really care about the product's price (drugs, no; cars, yes)? What would happen to profits if the firm raised or lowered its prices by 10 percent? By 50 percent?

4. Cost of Entry and Exit. Could a lot of new competition spring up quickly? If it did, what form would it take? If this firm wanted to get out of a losing part of the business, could it? What would it cost?

5. Regulations. What special costs and restrictions exist because of rules and government regulations? Are those worse than those faced by most businesses?

6. Protection. Does some unusual condition exist which gives the company special rights or power, such as patents, a geographic monopoly (as in the case of a grocery store or cement plant), a well-established brand, unique individual talents, or unique relative size?

CHAPTER 9

YOUR PERSONAL INVESTMENT CONSTITUTION

Your "investment constitution" is an honest self-appraisal of your real ability to take risk. It is analogous to the United States Constitution; that is, it's a permanent written statement of your most basic investment tenets.

Your investment constitution is your set of standing instructions to yourself, written in terms which are meaningful to your specific practical decisions in the stock market. It is analogous to a written constitution because it sets forth some practical general tenets which give continuity and discipline to everyday decision making. It expresses your long-term basic guideposts even when you may have temporarily lost sight of them yourself.

Your investment constitution should include:

I. Risk Tolerance: your decision as to the maximum level of risk you are willing to assume.

II. Return Targets: your personal standard of performance and, if necessary, a plan for taking spendable cash out of your portfolio regularly.

III. Diversification: how many stocks you have decided to own and your permanent areas of investment interest or lack of interest.

It is not difficult to put together your own investment constitution. The discussions in Chapters 4 to 8 might be reviewed if necessary. Figure 5 is a typical investment constitution. Naturally it will not be entirely suitable for you. But it helps to illustrate how simple it can be to draw up such a document once you have thought through the issues involved.

Your investment constitution should be reviewed or revised at least every two years. As your wealth increases, you will need to update the

THE INVESTMENT CONSTITUTION OF JOHN WILSON.

PREAMBLE

I have thought carefully about the following simple guidelines. I remind myself not to violate them without the most thorough and searching reappraisal. They should not be abandoned in haste in the midst of crisis. This policy is set down after long and calm reflection to protect my progress toward financial freedom.

I. RISK TOLERANCE

The maximum amount of money I can afford to lose under the most reasonable conditions is $10,000. My total money available for investment is $25,000. Therefore, my average risk tolerance is $10,000 divided by $25,000, or 40%. Thus I should own stocks which on average are unlikely to drop more than 40% under the worst reasonable conditions that I foresee.

II. RETURN TARGETS

a. At this level of risk tolerance, even a 40% short-term drop will not force me to sell out at the bottom. Therefore, I should be able to hold on through these unpredictable short-term moves to achieve a long-term compound annual return of 10 to 15% with a single-figure target of 12%. If I am successful, this will double my net worth in six years and raise it 1,000% in 20 years.

b. My spendable cash needs are not dependent on this investment portfolio, and so my current cash withdrawal rate is zero.

III. DIVERSIFICATION

a. I will own no one stock worth over 50% of my total money available for investment, which is $25,000. Therefore, the maximum I will keep invested in one stock (at current market value) is $12,500, regardless of cost. This means I will need at least three stocks if fully invested to allow for flexibility.

b. The maximum number of stocks I feel I can know well enough to risk my money is five.

c. Thus the number of stocks I will own at any one time will vary from zero to five.

d. I am excluding the following industries or types of companies: utilities and banks (because I do not feel I can adequately understand them) and tobacco stocks (because of my moral objection to their products).

John Wilson

FIGURE 5.   TYPICAL INVESTMENT CONSTITUTION.

key figures regarding how much you can afford to lose and your total available for investment. A change in either of these will of course alter your risk tolerance. As demands on your time change or as you get better at stock selection, you may change your diversification rules. If you retire or if your obligations change, you may add or delete a cash withdrawal program.

All this may seem unnecessary to you, and maybe a little foolish. It really is not. This short formal exercise is based on experience with tens of thousands of individual investors and hundreds of institutions through some of the wildest market gyrations. The majority of these investors, including many otherwise fine professionals, could have saved themselves a lot of grief or made a lot more money by this one act of self-determination.

The value of a written investment constitution is that it is explicit. It brings your thinking out of the shadows. It forces you to operate according to a self-disciplined plan rather than by intuition alone. While this may seem unnecessary to you right now, it will save you from some terrible and costly blunders later on. It is a vital step on your path to wealth.

SOURCES

The creative use of sources is involved in every aspect of the investment process. Chapters 10 to 13 are concerned with some specific things you should know to get firsthand information from original sources. We will tell you about your legal rights to information and about the three main sources: the company, the Securities and Exchange Commission (SEC) reports, and the newspapers. Then we move from public to private sources and learn about the "who" and "how" of interviewing. There is a chapter containing very candid advice about stockbrokers. Just for the fun of it, we have included a chapter entitled "Spying: The Fine Art of Industrial Espionage."

CHAPTER 10

WHERE TO GET FIRSTHAND INFORMATION AT ALMOST NO COST

YOUR LEGAL RIGHTS TO INFORMATION

Information must be made publicly available by companies so that everyone can have equal access to the facts. Popular impressions aside, professional investment managers cannot by law have significant information made available to them that is not also made available to the general public. This principle of equal but limited public access to company information is usually stated in glossier terms: "full, timely, and accurate public disclosure of all material information." This principle is the legal foundation of the stock market.

In contrast to people outside the company, the board of directors and the officers of a company are entitled to all information. They then decide what is "material" and therefore must be made public. Needless to say, great debates arise as to what is material and how to choose from among equally "accurate" methods of presentation. The courts become the final arbiter, of course, of whether the insiders have complied with the disclosure laws.

Publicly owned companies are permitted to maintain this selective secrecy from their own shareholders for very good reasons. The conduct of the affairs of the firm often requires specialized or proprietary skills, technology, and information. Complete public disclosure could hurt the company's competitive position and impair its earnings power. Members of the public, especially stockholders and professional investment managers, may think that all their questions deserve an answer. However, company officers quite obviously often tell us a good deal less than we would like to know.

There is strong justification for a company management to operate with some secrets, and it is proper that the law recognize and protect this right. If a company is not disclosing material facts as it goes along, the shareholders' legal remedy lies in their right to sue the officers and directors for damages after the facts do come out. Such suits are rare, however, because they are very expensive. Consequently, this countervailing force is seldom used. The important question for us is whether such withholding of answers is in the company's best interests or, instead, is a symptom of hidden troubles.

The whole problem of access to information is a legal jungle, but for the individual private investor it is not really hard to handle properly. As a matter of practice most people will sell stock in an overly secretive company rather than get into a big fight with its management over what is or is not material. You should adopt the same attitude and not get mired down in a big hassle defending your rights. Spend your time more productively researching companies which welcome your interest rather than fear it.

THE COMPANY IS YOUR FIRST STOP

The first and last source of information is the company itself. While your other sources are also an important part of your research effort, it doesn't pay to get too sophisticated too early.

Almost any company will send to anyone who asks for it a set of basic financial materials, such as annual and quarterly reports, news releases, and reprints of articles and speeches. The company will also send product literature if you ask and a subscription to its in-house newspaper. A trip to the local library may produce recent articles on the firm and its people, technology, industry, and markets. The Securities and Exchange Commission (SEC) will give you access to all recent filings, and this is another useful "first stop." Getting this information is very simple and inexpensive, and you can do it in just a few hours.

Contacting the company was covered in Chapter 3, and the library trip needs no elaboration. In case you are not familiar with what company-originated material is available from the SEC, here is a run-down on that source.

THE SEC REPORTS

Every publicly traded company must file several documents each year with the SEC in Washington, D.C. These filings are required by the United States government to promote "full and fair disclosure." The system works fairly well and is always being improved—usually to increase the quantity of data disclosed and also to make the information easier to read and understand. The SEC is one corner of the federal bureaucracy in which you can have confidence.

There are three types of documents filed with the SEC which you should have available if you get really serious about a stock. If the company itself cannot supply them, you can get copies directly from the SEC. These reports are the Annual Report (Form 10-K), the Quarterly Report (Form 10-Q), and the "Current Events" Report (Form 8-K). To get these reports, write to:

The Securities and Exchange Commission
Public Reference Section
500 North Capital Street
Washington, D.C. 20549

There is a copying charge of 10 cents per page, and delivery takes about two weeks. Be sure to specify exactly the name of the company, the type of report you want, and the year. In your note, say that you agree to be responsible for billing, and prepayment will not be required. If you live in or near Washington, you may want to go in person to the Public Reference Section, which is actually located at 1100 L Street N.W., Room 6101. Much of the same information is available in regional offices in New York, Chicago, and Los Angeles. Smaller collections are also available in the six other regional offices: Boston, Atlanta, Fort Worth, Denver, Seattle, and Arlington.

These reports are important, and so we will describe them in detail. Don't be overwhelmed by all the material. This is your basic reference source, and, as with a dictionary, you don't need to know every word in it.

THE ANNUAL REPORT (Form 10-K).

This filing must disclose a good deal more information than the annual reports printed up for mailing to stockholders. It is the cornerstone of the SEC's full and fair disclosure principle and is the greatest single printed source of information on a company's affairs. The SEC Annual Report (the 10-K) is available on every one of the companies in your Prospect List. With the steady pressure on corporations to provide more data, many are beginning to print up the longer 10-K and make it their annual report to shareholders as well. The added cost is well worth it to any public company.

The contents of the 10-K are prescribed by SEC regulations. The report consists of two parts. Part I includes 10 items:

1. Business. An identification of the company's principal products or services, its principal markets and methods of distribution, and, if material, competitive factors; backlog and expectation of fulfillment; availability of raw materials; importance of patents, licenses, and franchises; estimated cost of research; number of employees; and effects of compliance with ecological laws. If there is more than one line of business, for each of the last five fiscal years there is a statement of total sales and net income for each line which, during either of the last two fiscal years, accounted for 10 percent or more of total sales or pretax income.

2. Summary of Operations. A summary of operations for each of the last five fiscal years and any additional years required to keep the summary from being misleading (per-share earnings and dividends are included). Any change in accounting principles or practices is noted with date and reasons along with a letter from the registrant's independent accountants.

3. Properties. A listing of the location and character of principal plants, mines, and other important properties also indicating whether owned or leased.

4. Parents and Subsidiaries. A list or diagram of all parents and subsidiaries and, for each one named, the percentage of voting securities owned or other basis of control.

5. Legal Proceedings. A brief description of material legal proceedings, including where pending; when civil rights statutes are involved, proceedings may be disclosed.

6. Increases and Decreases in Outstanding Securities. Information for each security, including reacquired securities; new issues; securities issued in exchange for property, services, or other securities; and new securities resulting from modification of outstanding securities.

7. Approximate Number of Equity Security Holders. A list of the holders of record for each class of equity securities as of the fiscal year.

8. Executive Officers of the Company. A list of all executive officers, the nature of family relationships between them, and positions and offices held.

9. Indemnification of Directors and Officers. A statement of any arrangement under which any director or officer is insured or indemnified against any liability which he or she may incur in his or her capacities as a director or officer.

10. Financial Statements and Exhibits Filed. A list of all financial statements and exhibits filed as part of the 10-K.

Five additional items are required in Part II of the 10-K. Firms often meet this requirement by filing the proxy statement for the annual meeting, since, as you will note, these five items are usually subjects for this meeting.

11. Principal Security Holders and Security Holdings of Management. An identification of the owners of 10 percent or more of any class of securities and a listing of securities held by directors and officers according to amount and percent of each class.

12. Directors and Officers. A listing of the names, offices, and terms of office of the directors and officers, including specific background data on each.

13. Remuneration of Directors and Officers. A listing of the directors and the three highest-paid officers with aggregate annual remuneration exceeding $40,000—and total paid all officers and directors.

14. Options Granted to Management to Purchase Securities. A listing of options granted to, or exercised by, directors and officers since the beginning of the fiscal year.

15. Interest of Management and Others in Certain Transactions. A statement of material changes in significant transactions involving such things as assets; pension, retirement, savings, or other, similar plans; and unusual loans.

THE QUARTERLY REPORT (FORM 10-Q)

This report is filed within 45 days of the end of each of the first three quarters. It is a quarterly update of the 10-K, except that the requirements are slightly relaxed. The important difference is that quarterly financial data do not have to be audited. However, the regulations do require that management still provide a "fair statement" of results and alert the reader to any significant special factors (such as seasonality or strikes) which affected the quarter.

THE CURRENT EVENTS REPORT (FORM 8-K)

This form is filed not on a calendar basis, as the 10-K and the 10-Q are, but whenever a key event occurs. It therefore often discloses things not found anywhere else, and it is sometimes the first place where significant new events are uncovered. This is especially true in medium-sized and smaller companies, since even when they issue a press release, the papers often ignore them. However, you can't count on just the 8-K because information that has been disclosed in other filings (in the 10-K or the 10-Q usually) need not be repeated in the 8-K. Here are some specific items required to be disclosed:

1. A change in control of the company

2. The acquisition or disposition of a significant amount of assets other than in the normal course of business

3. Legal proceedings other than routine proceedings normal to the business.

4. Changes in securities involving a material change in the rights of the holders of any class of registered securities for any reason

5. A material withdrawal or substitution of assets securing any class of registered securities

6. Defaults upon senior securities not covered within 30 days and affecting more than 5 percent of the total assets

7. An increase in amount of securities outstanding if it exceeds 5 percent

8. A decrease in amount of securities outstanding if it exceeds 5 percent of the previously outstanding amount

9. Options to purchase securities if the total unreported exceeds 5 percent of the securities of the class

10. Extraordinary item charges and credits, other material charges and credits to income of any unusual nature, material provisions for loss, and restatements of capital share account

11. The submission of matters to a vote of security holders

12. A change in certifying accountant

13. Other important events that the company believes are material

14. Financial statements and exhibits as supporting documentation

We have gone into detail about these three SEC reports to make the point that with a few direct sources such as these, plus a few good company contacts, you will have plenty of information to work with. You really don't need a lot of secondary sources such as investment service reports. They are often derived from these same original documents and are written by junior people on a production-line basis. Get used to working with the basic materials. In no time you will be able to skip over dozens of pages of trivia and focus on the really significant disclosures.

SOME ADVICE ON HOW TO
READ THE NEWSPAPER

There is no shortage of other places to look for information, but only one is "must" reading on a regular basis: *The Wall Street Journal*. You probably already know it casually, but now you should really get into it regularly. We hope you won't be insulted by our telling you how to read the paper, but there are a few points which might save you some time and money.

Decide in advance what features you want to cover for sure. A good list includes the overall market statistics (inside back page); however, ignore the nonsense in the daily market column itself. The quarterly earnings reports are good to scan regularly also, just to develop a feel for the current corporate profit picture as it unfolds. The front-page news can be skipped over lightly. Most of it is topical among the boardroom hangers-on for just a few days and doesn't affect your invesments.

At least once a week, though, the *Journal* does a feature on a broader subject, and these are an excellent way to get a gradual education on the full range of investment topics. The human-interest stories ("Troubles at Rolls Royce," for example) are often well written and entertaining, but they won't make you a dime, so try to skip them if you can.

Finally, you can develop and post your own charts or tables on any of the hundreds of statistical series which appear regularly. For example, suppose that current interest rates are critical to one or more of your stocks. You don't need to pay $50 per year and up for interest rate reports. Just pick out a few rates each day (try commercial paper, Treasury bills, and long-term government bonds) and post them on a chart. Then read the stories about interest rates. In a few weeks you will begin to get a real feeling for rates, and that direct experience will be far more useful to you than a canned report which arrives a week or two later.

Similarly, there are regular features (including charts if you're too busy to do your own) on such things as prices (of everything!), chain-store sales, hourly and weekly earnings, factory orders, construction expenditures, shipments, inventories, economic indicators, the money supply, productivity, the balance of trade, corporate profits by industry (in addition to reports from individual companies), national income series, unemployment and layoff rates, housing starts, overall industrial output, purchasing agent surveys, consumer credit—and on and on!

If you read the paper selectively, you can meet most of your general investment information needs, and you will require few additional services. If you don't read the paper this way, you can pay thousands of dollars a year for services which will be less valuable than the *Journal* itself. Once again, our advice is to use the primary sources—they really are easy to get used to, and you eliminate the information middleman.

Your local paper probably has a terrible financial section, but it can be a gold mine and takes practically no time to cover. Your investment risk tolerance may lead you to smaller companies with mostly regional followings, and your local paper will often run stories on your stocks which escape national attention. A friend of ours once made $400,000 in a few minutes because he noticed an apparently routine story which appeared one morning only in *The Los Angeles Times*. The financial vice president of a local company in which this friend had a 100,000-share position had resigned. Our friend knew this man only casually, but well enough to be so surprised at his resignation that he strongly suspected something terrible was happening. Therefore, he sold his 100,000 shares of stock in a block at $20 per share before the close of trading the same day.

Within a week the news broke that earnings were terrible. Only when national attention focused on the surprising profit problems did *The Wall Street Journal* pick up the whole story. The stock sank like a rock to 16 and never went above that price again.

Whatever big institution bought those 100,000 shares for $2 million had just taken a $400,000 loss—a quick and expensive lesson on simple, basic sources of public information. Yet this institution probably pays at least $400,000 per year for a lot of highly sophisticated services and electronic equipment which this time just got in the way and diverted it from the key issues.

You would have sold the stock too under the same circumstances— as long as you had done your homework and then trusted your instincts. The seller had spent only about an average of half an hour per week on the company, and every one of his sources was open to you: SEC filings, company literature, a visit by car to the company, chats on the phone with a few customers—and a copy of *The Los Angeles Times*! Total out-of-pocket cost of the analysis: $35.76!

11

INTERVIEWING MADE EASY

WHAT TO EXPECT

Interviewing, whether conducted in person or over the phone, makes most people nervous. Let's discuss what to expect and try to dispel some of your resistance to the idea.

Even if you have no experience at interviewing, you can become effective at it very quickly. A good approach to interviewing is really not much different from a commonsense approach to any personal relationship. Do not attempt to use a special interviewing technique and don't try to be tricky or devious in your approach to potential sources of information.

Some professional researchers disagree with this natural style. For example, one rather manipulative technique is called the "stress interview." Under the rules of this game, interviewers try to make the people they are interviewing feel under mild attack concerning their facts and opinions. The theory is that they will protect themselves by offering more information to defend their positions. However, very little of any use comes out of that type of meeting, and what does emerge is not worth the aggravation involved. Even if you were willing to be that way with people, it really isn't necessary anyway. There are so many potential contacts and sources on a company that there is no need for you to get overly anxious and become pushy or tactless with anyone.

Before you approach a contact, take the trouble to do at least some preparation. During the interview, simply show an honest interest in the subject at hand. It is surprising how helpful many people are willing to be. This seems to be just as true of people on the inside of a company as it is of those on the outside. (Exceptions are top-management people in larger companies, who are trained into extreme caution, and some special groups, such as attorneys, who are discussed later on.)

You should try to suspend your disbelief during an interview. Your own anxiety can make you a bit uptight, and you may behave in some unnatural way to overcome those feelings. Try instead to remain open to what your source tells you. Do not, for example, cast yourself in a trial lawyer role by exhibiting signs of distrust and challenging everything your source says. You can ask questions that will elicit elaboration of certain points, or you can invite your source to give both sides of an issue, but you want to avoid making this person feel ill at ease or on the defensive. Whatever your legal rights may be, at that moment your source usually feels that he or she is freely doing you a favor talking to you. Don't interfere with this natural capacity and desire to communicate to you.

Above all, you must convey to your source that you will keep whatever you are told strictly confidential. And, since the business world can be a very small place sometimes, it is essential that you not repeat what your source tells you. You must keep your promise of confidence. In addition, do not overly impose on a source at any one time. If you want to use that source again in the future, it will be a tremendous saving of introductory time to have that person receptive again when you do call.

Relax, be yourself, and behave naturally. With that attitude you will come to enjoy your interviewing and will do more of it, which will show up in improved stock market profits as well as fewer ulcers!

THE REAL PURPOSE OF AN INTERVIEW

Before we discuss specific sources, let's be clear about what we are looking for. We are not on a search for inside information; this can cause legal problems. Fortunately, a good part of our looking and listening is done outside the company, and what we learn there is in the public domain already. Our purpose is to improve our understanding of the real world in which the company operates. We thereby improve our ability to predict the company's performance under varying conditions, and we may avoid many of the mistakes made by lazy, desk-bound investors.

It is at this level of research that profitable insights begin to emerge. Such work is especially valuable on less well known companies which are no longer of interest to professionals. They aren't looking at much of anything except the largest few hundred companies, and most private investors are too timid to realize that they can go out and get their information firsthand. It is precisely because of this situation that interviewing can be so profitable to those who take the few hours necessary to really do it.

Getting and using your own personal sources is not as subtle or complicated as the pros would lead you to believe. You will usually form some very clear impressions during your first interview which are quite different from the conclusions you might have drawn from your reading alone. After just a few meetings with a small variety of sources, many investors have said that "things fall into place." Their whole level of confidence is higher, and rightfully so.

THE SEVEN SOURCES

Here is a checklist of potential sources:

1. The company

2. Former employees

3. Competitors

4. Customers

5. Suppliers

6. Trade associations

7. Professionals

Let's look at each of these seven sources:

1. THE COMPANY. Anyone at any level can give you a start. Eventually meet someone in the financial department and a

second contact in the key nonfinancial part of the company. This will give you a much better bearing on most issues, since you will meet people who usually see things from quite different perspectives. If you do not have two contacts, be sure you really can get along with just one. You will see the value of this method very quickly for yourself when you get back home after your first research interview. (Chapter 17 is devoted to appraising management.)

2. FORMER EMPLOYEES. These are a fountain of information and misinformation. They are almost always overlooked, and yet they will often talk more openly than current employees. The only problem is finding them. There are two simple ways of doing this:

    a. Ask someone in the company straightforwardly to introduce you to the most senior person he or she knows who left in the last year or so.

    b. Look in the prior years' annual reports (you did ask for the last two years' reports, right?) and just pick out an officer who is not listed this year. Ask your company contact where this person is now employed or where he or she lives.

    Both these prospecting methods work well and will get you on the phone with an ex-employee. Getting at least some cooperation is also far easier than you may think. Just be honest about your interest as a prospective individual investor; make it clear that you have no connection with the company or anyone else and that everything is off the record.

    A much rarer find is someone who was offered a senior job at the company but who turned down the offer. You may find "job rejectors" by asking your inside contacts, of course, but don't depend on finding this type of source. If you happen on one, though, who is willing to speak openly, you can really learn a lot because he or she has probably just finished asking some of the same questions you have. Even if this person's reasons for not joining the firm are irrelevant to its merits as a stock, you are bound to have a rewarding conversation.

    One note of obvious caution: Former employees (and even job rejectors) are bound to be a bit defensive, and often downright bitter. Treat what they tell you with special care. It's a bit like learning about someone through the opinions of a mother-in-law!

3. COMPETITORS. To find a company's competitors, look them up in industry directories (see the discussion of trade associations below). Sometimes they are even in the Yellow Pages of the phone book. Competitors can be a mother-in-law type of source too, but they are one of our favorites anyway. They are often headquartered in a distant city, but don't be afraid to call them. Even a brief phone call will be of some help. Also, a local branch or sales outlet can give you some idea of where your company stands. With competitors, however, you may have to find a tactful way to get them to stop the sales pitch and give you a straight story.

4. CUSTOMERS. These are usually the most objective source, and sometimes they give you a strikingly clear picture in a hurry. If these sources are consistently negative, drop the stock like a hot rock. You will never make money on companies whose customers are all mad at them! Conversely, if the customers are unusually pleased, you may be on to a big winner. Most of the time you will get a middle-ground response—"a problem now and then, but they're pretty good"—but you will pick up a sense of the company's reputation in the process.

   How do you find customers? Sometimes it's obvious (who buys farm equipment?), but if it isn't, ask your company contact. Sometimes contacts balk at this, but don't blame them. They are just fearful of your messing up a valuable business relationship and getting them into hot water. If your contact is reluctant at first, wait until he or she begins to trust you more; then you'll usually get the information you want.

5. SUPPLIERS. Suppliers, or "vendors," as they are often called, are people who sell to your company. They are especially knowledgeable, and they are not as closemouthed as you might think, even though they seem to have little to gain by telling you a straight story and risking a backlash from a customer. Like anyone else, they like to tell about their business, and that will involve their relations with the company you are researching. By being patient and keeping information strictly to yourself, you can establish a nice pipeline to this very valuable type of source.

6. TRADE ASSOCIATIONS. Trade associations will never say anything revealing about a member company. So why bother to contact them? Because these groups have unique data on the

whole industry, often all packaged and free for the asking. They exist to provide a legal way for competing firms to communicate with one another, and you should be on the grapevine too.

Ignore the propaganda and concentrate on the specific facts they have to offer, such as total industry sales, lists of industry participants, market share of each company, trade manuals or directories (with all kinds of leads and perspectives), press releases, and comparative data on products. Your company's trade association is probably located too far away to visit easily, so write a nice letter and be prepared for several tries before the communications get rolling. An introduction from the company would help open the door; this will not inhibit the response, as it might with other sources, since the association wouldn't have said anything negative anyway. PROFESSIONALS. This group includes attorneys, accountants, bankers, consultants, and even architects. These people deal with the company only occasionally, and often they have privileged access to inside information. Your purpose in approaching them is not to tap them for illegal tips, of course, but your talks with them will be inhibited by their fears of just that. Also, of course, they will be careful to avoid any appearance of violating the company's confidence. Despite these natural inhibitions, professionals can be good sources. They are capable of making perceptive judgments about the company because of their special skills and because they see a lot of other companies with which to compare the one you are interested in.

Always get an introduction to professional sources from the company and never try to approach them in an offhand way. For example, if you run into the company's lawyer at a party, the most you should do is tell him you are doing some research and ask him whether he would be willing to talk to you at his office, after you have the company's approval. Keep your initial approaches clean, proper, and formal. Later on, if your relationships with professionals become more intimate, that's just fine. But don't make the mistake of raising their defenses and turning them off prematurely.

WHAT YOU NEED TO KNOW ABOUT STOCKBROKERS

SAVING 50 PERCENT PLUS ON COMMISSIONS

No matter how self-reliant you become as an individual investor, you still have to buy and sell through a stockbrokerage firm. However, you have a wide choice of services and costs from full-service firms to those which do only order execution.

For your purposes as an independent private investor, there has been an important change in the brokerage industry. Since May 1, 1975, the rates or commissions charged by brokers have become negotiable and competitive. Before "May Day" (as the people on the Street call that day) rates were fixed, and everybody charged the same thing, at least for the smaller trades originated by individuals. Firms competed for business on a nonprice basis, just as airlines did, stressing service, safety, reputation, and convenience. Now, however, you can easily and safely get your trades done at about 50 percent lower rates through so-called discounters. These firms advertise regularly in *The Wall Street Journal* or the financial pages, and their ads invariably headline big commission rate savings. You will not have any trouble finding one.

There are some pros and cons to consider in a decision to use a discount broker instead of a full-service firm. First, you will be doing most of your own research, if you don't already, and therefore you will not be seeking buy and sell advice from your broker. You also may not need your broker to act as custodian of your certificates since you should not be jumping in and out of stocks so frequently as to be inconvenienced by trips to your own safe-deposit box. You may not need to borrow from your broker, either, because you may get lower interest rates directly from your bank or because you just don't want to invest with borrowed money. In any case, you can save money by going to a broker who offers only order execution and not all these other services. The discounters have expanded very rapidly since commission rates became unfixed. You should seriously consider running your trades through one of them if you don't use advice, custodial service, or credit.

The one major disadvantage of discounters (in addition to their bare-bones service) is that you will not have a live broker or account executive who will pamper you and watch over you and call you up with news and gossip. For some experienced investors that is a blessed relief. However, maybe you would like someone down at the boardroom to talk with, and that's perfectly all right. Just be advised that now you are paying for personal service you may not need and that you can get lower commission rates elsewhere.

THE INHERENT CONFLICT

One problem with the brokerage industry is that the commission system creates an inherent short-term conflict of interest between brokers and their clients. Almost all brokers are paid directly or indirectly in proportion to the volume of trading in which they get you to engage. On the other hand, your profits from investing are inversely proportional to turnover. That is, you will usually do better buying and selling over a period of one to three years than you would trading in and out every few weeks or months.

Commissions based on turnover or sales volume work well in motivating used-car salesmen and door-to-door peddlers, but they seem to be inconsistent with the provision of a professional service such as investment advice. Unfortunately, brokers' emphasis must be on selling, not advising, whatever their personal convictions. Young brokers become rich senior partners; young advisers become old advisers. Most of the brokerage industry's leaders have strong selling experience and instincts. Marketing is a fine background for senior management in any field, of course, and most of the top people we've known are genuinely honest. However, the ordinary boardroom brokers you will meet must conform to the system somewhat in order to make a living, which means "write that ticket."

While you do need to be well aware of the inherent conflict, you should also know that the standards of integrity and efficiency among brokers are higher now than ever and are as good as those among any other professionals. The fact that most brokers do operate ethically is a credit to their personal backbone and basic decency; the system tends to put you and your broker into a hidden conflict of interest.

What is the industry's alternative? Unbundle. That is, charge a low rate for pure transactions. Then add optional fees or retainers which entitle the client to other services such as research, buy and sell advice, custody of certificates, and a credit line.

With the advent of commission rate competition, these changes have begun. The brokerage industry is now going through a difficult period of experimentation with the addition of new services and the repackaging of the traditional ones. You and all other private investors are going to benefit, but not only because you will be able to buy just what you need. A longer-term consequence of these changes is that the brokerage industry can stop "selling the sizzle" (as brokers are so fond of saying) and start selling the steak. In those who are doing the selling they can encourage and reward the concept of fiduciary obligation to clients, making it a principle that handling a family's savings is something more socially serious than selling them an encyclopedia.

QUALITIES OF A GOOD BROKER

Suppose you have decided that you do not want to do all your own work and instead want a broker to help you with decisions. In that case, here is a short profile of a "good broker."

First and foremost, you must be able to trust his* motives. Maybe you have a nose for honest people, and so you will be all right. If not, by all means get a referral from someone you have already learned to

---

* The use of masculine pronouns is for convenience only. It is increasingly likely that your broker could be a woman, particularly given the large recruiting effort to attract women to the brokerage industry.

trust. Ask about the issue of the broker's honesty and separate it from how well he did. A good recent track record makes a broker popular, but it doesn't make him honest.

Next look at what you have to offer a broker. He wants to make money, which means he expects you to buy or sell something often enough to justify the time he spends with you. A good broker expects to make $50,000 per year and up, and he has only about 2,000 hours per year to allocate. Therefore, he must net at least $25 per hour, which means he has to generate gross commissions of about $50 to $100 per hour. Think about that in your relations with your broker, and you will get along with him much better.

The other thing you can offer a broker is ideas. While the advice is supposed to go all the other way, toward you, there are exceptions. When you find an uncommon stock and he appreciates that you really know what you're talking about, he can use that idea with his other clients. As long as you buy and sell first, you can't get hurt by a little extra interest in your pet stock. You must still expect to generate enough commissions to keep him happy, of course, but a real interchange of ideas can make him value your account more highly. This can pay off in better service, occasional preference in new issues, and more careful and thoughtful attention to your needs.

A good broker for your purposes must be familiar with the tools of research. Only about one in ten brokers really takes research seriously and knows how to use it. Your broker's firm should have a first-rate institutional research department, and their facts and opinions should be available to you in at least condensed form. Your broker should have direct access by telephone to a liaison person who sits right in the research department itself and who knows what the professional analysts are thinking and doing. Three national retail firms which also have excellent research departments are Paine Webber,* Merrill Lynch, and E. F. Hutton. There are a few others, as well as a dozen smaller regional firms with good research departments. Every firm says it does research, but only a handful sponsor multimillion-dollar programs. If you are going to pay high commissions, you should have the benefit of such a major research department.

Good brokers are hard to define, beyond saying that they should

---

* The author was Chairman of the Investment Committee of Paine Webber until early 1977, but has no current affiliation with this or any other brokerage firm.

be honest and have a solid research orientation. You may have to look around in a few places to find someone with these two key qualities. Most brokers are good at instilling in you a certain confidence and at inspiring an irresistible urge to buy something. If you make it clear that you want specific help in research and a consultative kind of guidance rather than a push toward decisions, you should be able to get what you need.

CHAPTER 13

SPYING: THE FINE ART
OF INDUSTRIAL
ESPIONAGE

WASTEBASKET RESEARCH

As part of your liberal education in the stock market you should learn something about the fascinating topic of "industrial espionage." The top management of any company which operates with sensitive information is well aware of the threats and opportunities of the James Bond approach to information gathering. More commonly, such practices involve trade secrets, confidential market data, product formulations, unique circuit or mechanical designs, and similar operating information. When industrial espionage is turned to the field of investment research, however, it might be called "wastebasket research."

It is totally illegal, of course, and must be rejected on those grounds alone. However, even though no responsible private investor would get involved, it would be naïve to assume that spying does not occur at all. Therefore, you should know something about such activities.

One of the most blatant incidents in the field of wastebasket research actually did involve a wastebasket! Like all good espionage schemes, it was simple and direct. It seems that Herman, an enterprising young security analyst from New York, found a certain janitor who every evening cleaned the executive offices of a big blue-chip company.

Herman bribed the janitor to deliver to him each evening around midnight the contents of the wastebaskets from the private offices of the chairman of the board and the president of this company.

Within a month his efforts paid off. The scene now shifts to Boston and the oak-paneled office of a Mr. Lawrence, who was one of Herman's best institutional clients. Herman telephoned to report his progress—and to set up a time and place to deliver his findings. In one of the 16 bags of trash Herman had uncovered a coffee-stained and crumpled copy of a special memorandum from the chairman of the board to the president. The memo contained the chairman's detailed comments about the company's budget for the following year, including the earnings-per-share forecast. The chairman was known to be quite active and candid, and Herman assured Mr. Lawrence that the document was very juicy indeed.

They agreed to meet that evening at a quiet bar by the waterfront, where Mr. Lawrence took delivery of the memo from his spy. Whatever he did with the information, there is no doubt that it was genuine. Herman returned to New York the next day and found a very large order waiting for him from Mr. Lawrence.

THE BUGGING OF FAST FRED

Another brush with wastebasket research, or industrial espionage, happened to put a well-known fund manager, whom we will call Fast Fred, on the receiving end of the spying. Because of some flattering publicity, Fast Fred's decisions had become a matter of widespread curiosity. Everyone wanted to know what he was buying. One day he began to notice that when he placed buy orders, the stocks moved quickly up, even before his brokers could get to the floor of the New York Stock Exchange. The first two times he thought that it was just bad luck, but by the fourth time his suspicions had grown rapidly. Someone was making Fast Fred look very bad indeed.

Fast Fred called in a special private "communications consultant" without telling anyone else except his secretary, whose integrity was above question. The consultant suggested checking for a wiretap by electronically sweeping, or testing, the lines from the phones on his desk back to the main cable.

Within an hour three men showed up carrying a huge black box. Fast Fred remembered thinking that this bunch looked more like plumbers than counterespionage agents, and all this happened five years before Watergate! The "plumbers" set to work efficiently and had the phones swept in an hour or two. They found the tap they were looking for and, without touching it, reported back to the fund manager.

Fast Fred had two options. He could just pull the tap, and the problem would be stopped. Or he could leave the tap connected a while longer and set a trap to catch the SOBs who were listening in on his buy orders. However, setting a trap involved a serious risk of loss to the fund because the buy orders would have to be real and a publicity leak could mess up the market in the stocks he was trying to buy. There was no way to carry the investigation any further by tracing the culprits' transactions, since the buyers were heavily disguised through blinds. He couldn't risk losing a fortune to catch the eavesdroppers, and he couldn't call the police since he certainly didn't want his stockholders to know what had happened. That would tarnish his reputation as a clever stock market operator. Therefore, despite great frustration, that had to be the end of it. Fast Fred would never learn who was behind the tap.

Any company which has sensitive information is faced with the same security problem. Telephone taps and other eavesdropping and espionage devices are readily available through your local private detective or electronics store. Their use is clearly illegal, of course, and it would be complete foolishness for an investor to get involved.

Perhaps in the public's mind the use of such techniques as these might seem to be an enormous temptation. It really is not, for a number of reasons. First, there is simply the old-fashioned risk of getting caught, a deterrent which should not be minimized. Also, the information itself likely would prove of very little value and might be completely misleading. However, the most important practical reason why such activities are not more widespread is that they are simply not necessary. The researching and interviewing process can be carried out quite comfortably in the open and can provide better information at lower cost—and obviously it is perfectly legal. Chapters 14 to 17 are a practical guide to these more traditional research methods.

RESEARCH

Business research is the process of understanding a company well enough to make reliable estimates of its future earning power. It does not involve an estimate of the future price of that company's stock. That is a separate process which follows research. (See Chapters 18 to 21.)

Even though you will develop competence in both disciplines, the separation of investment analysis into business research and decision making is essential to retaining objectivity about a stock. Try to imagine that the stock is not even publicly traded—that it is a private company and you are temporarily concerned only with its "fundamentals."

How do we get at these fundamentals on a specific company? The purpose of Chapters 14 to 17 is to guide you through this task. In these chapters we will get into a lot of specifics and illustrations. Don't be concerned by the apparent difficulty or detail involved in business research. You will never need to cover all this material on any one company. To do so would take far too much time and is really unnecessary anyway. Instead, select those issues which seem most relevant to the particular company you are investigating. Before doing any piece of work, always ask yourself: How will what I learn help me to forecast profits? In other words: What good will it do me to know what it is I am about to explore?

THE RESEARCH CHECKLIST

The Research Checklist is a highly condensed outline which you can add to and change on the basis of your own experience. It is a shopping list of potential questions and topics to consider. Some of the material in Chapters 4 and 8 is based on it, as well as all of Chapters 15 to 17 and part of Chapter 18.

The Research Checklist is not a standard form to fill out, however, since each company investigation will be different. Also, the sequence of your work will be far more informal than this structured outline, which is a composite of the key subjects from hundreds of company research projects.

As you read through the Research Checklist and the chapters based on it, keep in mind that you will never actually do all this work on any one company. In your work on any particular company you will safely be able to ignore many of the issues raised. The benefit of this discipline is largely that you will have at least considered a subject, even if you quickly decide it is not a key issue for the company that holds your immediate attention. Apply your own creative common sense when you use the checklist. As long as you keep that kind of balance, business research can be enjoyable in itself as well as profitable without taking an unreasonable amount of your time.

The best business researchers often ask the simplest questions:

1. Who?	3. Where?	5. When?
2. What?	4. How?	6. Why?

The following topics and questions are an extension of these six basic words.

1. Background of the company. (See Chapter 8.)
   a. Description: a clear, simple, specific description of the firm's business or businesses.
   b. History: a summary of the past 10 years and of the last year or two in more detail. What are the implications?
2. Basic economics of the company. (See Chapter 8.) What are the most significant determinants of the firm's future earnings?
   a. Leverages.
   b. Correlations.
   c. Price structure.
   d. Cost of entry and exit.
   e. Regulations.
   f. Protection.
3. Connections and communications with the world outside the company. (See Chapter 16.)
   a. Who are the company's main outside connections?
   b. What are the key dates for both regular and upcoming events?
   c. When new material information develops, how is it communicated to each of the firm's "publics"?
4. The current trends. (See Chapter 4.)
5. Analysis of the main business functions. (See Chapter 15.)
   a. Marketing.
   b. Production.
   c. Finance.
   d. Compliance.
   e. Research.
6. Statistical analysis. (See Chapters 18 and 19.)
7. Fifteen ways to judge top management. (See Chapter 17.)
   1. Who are the top managers?
   2. How are the key activities organized?
   3. What are the key decisions? How are they made?

4. What is the philosophy of business management, both as your source expresses it and as you observe it?
5. How does the planning and control system work?
6. What does it take to be good in this business, beyond what it takes to be successful in any business?
7. What changes in management have occurred in the last 12 months? In the last three to five years?
8. What incentives are there for management? How are they tied to our interests as stockholders?
9. How do the top people define themselves? What is their self-perception?
10. How could management people steal? What makes you think they don't?
11. How would you characterize the relations between the key executives? Is this pattern of interaction meaningful, or is it just an idiosyncrasy?
12. Does management seem to have clear ideas or plans?
13. Does management have a command of the facts? Does each member of management tell the same story about the facts? How does management's story compare with what outsiders are telling you?
14. How does the company develop new people?
15. What are your intuitive feelings and reactions?

THE FIVE MAIN BUSINESS FUNCTIONS

Any business can be viewed as a working association of a few major functions. Most companies of any size are organized along these functional lines, although there is a great variety of specific detail and terminology. A company employee (other than one of the top few people) whom you meet will identify as much with his or her functional department as with the company itself.

Here is one typical listing of the main business functions:

1. Marketing

2. Production

3. Finance

4. Compliance

5. Research

In this chapter we will discuss each of these subjects. This should give you some ideas and questions for interviews with people in each of these areas. (For more on interviewing, see Chapter 11.) Naturally you will never get around to covering all these topics, nor will you usually even meet someone from each of the five parts of the company.

As in all your research, try to focus on what seems to be most important to future profitability and stock market appeal.

MARKETING

Marketing encompasses every aspect of creating a sale or gathering revenues. It is far more than selling, advertising, and packaging. Marketing is the art of pulling all the following elements together into a coherent and effective program:

1. What does the company sell, and why? ("Product or service policy" is the usual jargon.)
2. Who is the immediate customer or buyer?
3. Who is the ultimate consumer of the product, if this is not the immediate buyer?
4. Why does each customer buy? What need is being filled?
5. What are the statistical dimensions of the market?
   a. Market size.
   b. Market share.
   c. Rate of growth or decline.
   d. Recent changes.
6. Competitors.
   a. Who are they?
   b. How do they compete? (On price? On quality? On convenience?)
7. Does the company really know the answers to questions 1 to 6? How?
   a. Review the market research and analysis program.
   b. Who does the research and analysis?
   c. To whom do the market research people report?
8. What is the company's marketing strategy, and how is it related to your observations from questions 1 to 7?
   a. Specifically how is the strategy implemented?
   b. Does the company have a direct sales force, or does it sell mostly through middlemen?
   c. How and where does the company advertise or promote its products or services?
   d. What provisions has the company made for a follow-up program to provide service and maintain quality control?
9. What are the current industry conditions, and what is this company's position?

PRODUCTION

Production involves the whole process of delivering what marketing has sold. It includes making a product or organizing a service, distribution, inventory, labor policy and relations, and many other related activities. The word "production" as used here does not necessarily mean just the manufacturing of a physical item, like a wristwatch or a tractor. It means the creation of economic value of any sort. For example, production also includes such diverse activities as services (building maintenance or computer programming), contracts (insurance policies or savings accounts), and even entertainment (racetracks or movies).

The real issues are the same no matter what is being produced:

1. What facilities are required?

2. What is their cost structure, and how does it compare with that of the competition's facilities?

3. Where is the current production rate in relation to economies of scale or volume? Could costs per unit change significantly over the next year or two?

4. Who are the people (professional and labor) needed in production? How many such people are there? What skills are they required to have? What is their turnover, both absolutely and relative to competition? Does the firm have a waiting list of potential employees? What labor contracts are outstanding, and when do they expire? What is the climate of relationships (you should be especially concerned with how grievances are aired and settled)?

5. What are the other key inputs, particularly in the areas of prices of materials and potential shortages?

6. How does the firm decide to make or buy what it sells? What degree of integration is considered best, from simple assembly operation up to total self-sufficiency, and what are the reasons for the policy?

7. How is the product (or service) quality-controlled and quality-assured?

FINANCE

Finance is the function which is responsible for raising the funds needed by the marketing and production operations, and in most firms it also houses the accounting department. The company's general planning and control work also is often done by a small staff of people within the finance department, but top management will share direct supervision of this special group. (See Chapter 17 for more details on top-management appraisal.)

The following are a few important examples of issues involving accounting, financial planning, and money management:

1. What is the effect of inventory valuation methods on the cost of goods sold? How is obsolete inventory kept off the books?

2. Are any unusual revenues (such as a profit or loss on a sale of assets) mixed in with ordinary revenues from sales?

3. Has any change been made in accounting for the company's subsidiaries? What would the figures look like if the change had not occurred?

4. Are there any significant items in the footnotes of the annual report which you don't understand? Ask for a simple explanation.

5. The AICPA (American Institute of Certified Public Accountants) for several years has been making major changes in accounting methods. Are any of these changes coming in areas which affect the company? Is the financial staff well enough aware of these changes to guide top management away from potential problems?

6. What is the effect on profits of changes in "product mix" (i.e., the percentage of overall sales coming from each product line)?

7. Are there any nonrecurring charges? If there were to be any in the future, from what would they most likely arise?

8. If foreign earnings are involved, how predictable are they?

9. How is the computer useful? Just in routine accounting (payroll and inventory), or in overall planning and management?

10. What does the company regard as realistic and desirable figures for such key indicators as pretax profit margin, tax rate, current ratio, debt as a percentage of equity, return on equity, and dividend payout? (See Chapter 19 for a discussion of key indicators.)

11.   If any of the key indicators are not now where they should be, what does the company plan to do about it? For example, if debt is regarded as too high (as a percentage of equity), then the company must either slow down growth or sell stock to raise equity.

12.   When does the company plan its next addition of long-term capital, and will it be debt or equity or a combination?

13.   Does the company's planning and control system indicate clearly enough how all the parts of the business relate? For example, unexpected sales could result in a big increase in accounts receivable and inventories. Unless its planning system gives an early warning about this, the company might have a tough scramble to find the money to finance its success.

14.   If the company has excess assets, does it keep them in riskless short-term deposits, or does it make long-term investments? Who decides, and how? Is the company taking risks as intelligently as you are with your investment assets?

15.   Acquisitions can be a great way to grow rapidly, or they can lead to disaster. Have any acquisitions been made in recent years? What was their contribution to sales and earnings? If the company is interested in acquisitions, what is it looking for in a prospect? What impact is the company willing to let an acquisition have on the whole firm? Are there any preconceived terms or conditions?

16.   In general, does management seem to know enough about long-term investing and/or acquisitions to justify your confidence? Do these activities make sense in relation to the company's main business, or are they a diversion or even a dangerous adventure?

COMPLIANCE

The term "compliance" refers to the effort required to keep the company in harmony with present governmental laws and rules and to enable it to anticipate and possibly influence future regulations. Not all companies recognize this legal area as a full-fledged function with the same status as marketing, production, and finance. However, the massive involvement of the federal government is being further complicated by the more activist attitudes of state and local governments, and a far greater number of issues are now considered to be in the public interest. Therefore, more and more companies now have a compliance department, which then usually also handles day-to-day contact with outside law firms.

Here are some of the considerations regarding compliance:

1. What is the general attitude of management toward this topic?

2. What special regulations and laws apply to this company, in addition to those which affect any corporation?

3. What is the company's degree of understanding about its legal environment?

4. When were the most recent conversations or correspondence with the SEC, other regulatory agencies, the IRS, or any other government body? To the extent that these matters can be discussed, how does the company characterize the current situation?

5. What are the most significant matters that the company's compliance people are currently concerned with?

RESEARCH

Research is any current spending (other than capital investments) which is not associated with the generation of current income. As in the case of compliance, not all companies have elevated research to parity with the three traditional line departments. Be prepared to accept the fact that in some cases research is truly not relevant even in the broad sense in which we have defined it.

The best test of whether research is important is the average age of existing products. That is, what percentage of current sales are coming from products or services developed in the last five or ten years? If over 25 percent of current sales are in this category, then research and related issues may be worth investigating carefully. Even if research is a new activity, if it accounts for 1 percent or more of expenses, you still had better look into it.

1.   What are the goals of research? Has the company defined its new-product criteria?

2.   How would you describe the research staff (in terms of degrees, specialties, tenure, and motivation)?

3.   Is the research program concerned mostly with product engineering and design, with fairly predictable results, or is there a major "breakthrough potential" and an accompanying risk of major failure?

4.   Who owns the results?

5.   How is research managed? Who is in charge, and to whom does this person report? How is each project supervised? How does research coordinate with marketing to determine salability? How does research coordinate with production to confirm that a new product can be produced in adequate quantities and at acceptable quality and cost levels?

6.   What are the research expectations? What seems to be coming from research over the next year or two, and what can it mean in terms of sales and profits?

7.   What does the company plan to spend on research in the next few years, and what factors could significantly alter these plans?

"WHO KNOWS WHO": CONNECTIONS AND COMMUNICATIONS

THE COMPANY YOUR COMPANY KEEPS

The people and institutions a company associates with are a meaningful indication of its quality. That sounds like nineteenth-century snobishness, doesn't it? Well it is! A company should pick its outside associates with the question "What can they do for the business?" uppermost in mind. You are looking for a management and a company in which to invest and risk your capital. You should expect them to operate in a somewhat narrow commercial way and to find their social outlets and drinking buddies someplace else. A strong management looks for strong outsiders, and vice versa.

To make an appraisal of the "company your company keeps," look at these five key outside connections: (1) outside (nonmanagement) members of the board of directors; (2) directorships held by members of this management in other companies, foundations, government boards, etc.; (3) the company's commercial banker; (4) the company's investment banker; and (5) the social pattern.

1. OUTSIDE (NONMANAGEMENT) MEMBERS OF THE BOARD OF DIRECTORS

Do they exist at all? Are they old cronies who will vote as they're told, or are they accomplished and independent people who could be true representatives of your interest? What is the real reason why each is on the board?

2. DIRECTORSHIPS HELD BY MEMBERS OF THIS MANAGEMENT IN OTHER COMPANIES, FOUNDATIONS, GOVERNMENT BOARDS, ETC.

Directorships are financially dangerous to the person serving because of the personal liability now attached to being a director. For a variety of good reasons, though, a company's top few people still may serve on other boards.

You will sometimes find some surprising indications of power and competence and connections in your management. We know of one executive of a medium-sized company who has been on close terms with every United States President since Kennedy. The regulatory agencies are careful to treat him very fairly at worst. Another small company has a financial vice president who has family members on the boards of the biggest corporations in his region. As a result, he is seldom surprised by shifts in the business scene. However, you may also find that your company's president is too busy raising money for the Red Cross to take care of mundane things like corporate profits. You won't really know for sure, but directorship patterns can be a very useful piece of the overall pattern of connections.

3. THE COMPANY'S COMMERCIAL BANKER

Does the company have a solid and long relationship with a bank that is big enough to handle its loan needs? You will seldom find the bank disclosed in the printed reports, but your contact will tell you without any difficulty. Banking relationships are less close and more flexible now than in earlier generations, but good access to short-term loans is still critical for most smaller companies.

4. THE COMPANY'S INVESTMENT BANKER

In case you are not familiar with this term, an investment banker is the company's securities underwriter or broker. This is the person responsible for raising long-term or investment capital, as contrasted with short-term loans obtained from the commercial banker. In addition, a good investment banker will help introduce the company to the financial community, make a trading market in the stock (if it is not listed on an exchange), act as an intermediary in mergers and acquisitions, and often extend advice concerning the nonfinancial affairs of the company as well.

The investment banker can be a powerful friend or a complete parasite. There are many examples of both extremes. The firm the banker is with makes some difference, since the best-known investment banking houses seldom tolerate a real charlatan. However, a lot of the very best investment people are partners in smaller firms, and the major houses are something of a training ground for bright but very young people on the way up.

How do you tell whether such outside connections are live wires? There are two ways. First, check their background. Are they on any impressive boards? What are their positions within their own firms? How many years of experience do they have? Second, ask top-management people what their investment bankers have done for them in the last couple of years. This will give you a pretty clear reading on whether a company has a strong investment banking connection or a weak one.

5. THE SOCIAL PATTERN

Companies, like people, usually form and maintain a distinctive social pattern. For example, is there a single family which dominates? If so, it will create a pattern of corporate life which revolves around the "old family ties." While that is not always bad, it usually stifles new ideas and discourages bright but "unconnected" people from joining the firm. If there is a family power system operating, you had better make sure the old family tree is populated with enough relatives who are capable of pursuing business careers and interested in doing so.

Another social pattern is the "old school tie." The most pervasive such system in the United States involves graduates of the Harvard Business School. Some firms are so dominated by H.B.S. graduates that in recruiting new people they very actively favor those with the same school tie. This also occurs with graduates of other top private schools with large enrollments, such as Stanford, Yale, and M.I.T. The public universities seem to be less of a focus for this phenomenon.

Should you regard the old school tie as a negative? In itself, yes. Any non-job-related discrimination is unhealthy to some degree, and maybe even illegal. However, against this social preference system you must weigh the other management skills evidenced. It is a fact of life that the best schools have themselves screened out and attracted individuals with higher-than-average qualifications and then given them some useful training along with the emotional bonds which are encouraged to develop. As long as you decide the company's managers are on the ball in other respects, count this as only a mild negative.

Similarly, many companies show clear signs of being dominated by self-perpetuating social patterns focused on religion, ethnic background, or political beliefs. If the pattern is maintained by recruiting practices, it is illegal. However, you and everyone else know that even among public firms there exist so-called Jewish companies, Italian companies, Chinese companies, conservative Republican companies, and so forth. These patterns almost invariably grew up with a company and relate more to its early history than to any present advantage in the pattern.

What should you think of this? Your moral reactions are your own business and must be considered first. Don't go out of your way to look for problems in this sensitive area, but if you do object to a social pattern, then avoid the company. You can't really objectively dig into a company which tramples on your principles.

From a strict investment standpoint, you must ask whether there are any practical business benefits. For example, in the diamond trade it helps to be Jewish. In the oil business it helps not to be if you want to do business with the Arabs. Most of the time, though, the only business benefit is that people from similar backgrounds may work better together and relate more easily to others in their industry.

CONCERN FOR COMMUNICATIONS

In smaller and medium-sized companies there is often little careful thought given to communications, at least compared with the sophisticated way the giant corporations go about it. For your purposes as a private investor, the important issue really is whether a company you are researching is well tuned to the benefits of good communications or, at the other extreme, is hurting itself by a crude or thoughtless approach. You don't need to get involved in all the subtleties as long as you can form an overall judgment on this issue, and that is not hard to do.

The first step is, of course, to know when things are likely to happen. A handy system is to keep a calendar of events for each of your closely followed companies. This will enable you to see all the material as it comes out. Occasionally you will be alerted to problems by unusual delays in reports or other scheduled happenings, but the main purpose is to keep on top of facts as they unfold. Here is a short list of events to mark on your calendar:

1. The release to the public of preliminary reports of quarterly and annual earnings.

2. The mailing of printed quarterly and annual reports to shareholders.

3. Annual meeting.

4. Major contract closings due, especially renewals.

5. Union agreements expiring.

6. Filings with the SEC. (See Chapter 10 for details.)

7. Filings with any other regulatory agencies.

8. Industry trade shows, exhibits, and symposia, at which new products are likely to be unveiled.

THE FIVE PUBLICS

There are five "publics" which a company that is well tuned to communications should be able to discuss with you:

1. Stockholders

2. The financial community

3. Customers

4. Special groups

5. The general public

STOCKHOLDERS

Stockholders are always on the minds of any company management. Sometimes this is reflected in an open and honest attitude, but occasionally the reaction is an almost paranoid mistrust and secretiveness. Your key concern here is whether the communications to stockholders indicate that management people feel there is a healthy identity of interest between themselves and the owners of the company.

The best preliminary evidence is your own reaction when you finish reading the stockholder reports and letters for the first time. For the moment, don't think about whether you like the facts presented. Do you understand the message? Is it conveyed with candor and directness or with vagueness and indirection? If you have an uneasy feeling that you're not getting a straight story, the chances are that your reaction is right. Also, whatever you feel, you can bet that many stockholders will share your response.

Another easy test of the way material is communicated to stockholders is to look at reports in a bad period. (If you don't see an obvious one, try 1970 or 1974.) Any manager can be honest in good times, but how well did your management square up to bad news? The ability to keep a level flow of honest news coming, no matter what, is a clear sign of outstanding leadership. This is a very difficult attribute to fake; as you have seen in other areas of life, people often show their true character most clearly in times of adversity.

THE FINANCIAL COMMUNITY

The financial community may be said to include all those who influence stockholders. More concretely, the financial community is made up of stockbrokers, security analysts, investment counselors, bankers, insurance executives, mutual fund managers, and financial journalists. When we speak of "Wall Street," we usually mean this group.

While these people will be given all the same material you get, a company should be making a modest additional effort to attract their steady and growing interest. This is done not by favoring them with more information but by spoon-feeding them. For example, the company's president may allocate one or two days a year to appear before a meeting of the Security Analysts Society, then drop in to visit a few major institutional stockholders, and finally be interviewed by a financial columnist. Rarely anymore does a company president tell these people anything new. Rather, the president is just making their job easier by giving an organized presentation of the company's story and by showing a willingness to meet on their own turf to answer questions.

There was a time when you, as an independent private investor, were at a disadvantage in not being included in the inside doings of the financial community, or Wall Street. For several reasons, this is no longer true. First, the law has gotten tough in requiring fair and full disclosure to everyone. (See Chapter 10.) Your company's top officers would be rare fossils indeed if they hadn't tightened up their compliance with the disclosure laws since the 1960s. Second, the financial community has lost interest in all but the largest few hundred companies and simply doesn't invite officers of smaller companies to come and visit. This is changing back slowly, though, and so eventually the Street will be chasing companies of our size once again. By the time that happens, you will already be in first if you have done your homework.

The third reason you aren't missing out by not being in on these private meetings is that they are usually useless anyway! The largest corporations have honed their presentations to the point where the most controversial statement of the day is "Good morning, ladies and gentlemen." Representatives of smaller companies, when they are invited at all, are often so nervous and inexperienced that they bore everyone stiff with details and then are too frightened to answer the really important questions.

While most financial community meetings would be a waste of time for you, they do help the working members of the Street. The security analysts will come back and write memos to the public clients (and to one another). The brokers will talk to clients about "their" lunch with the president. The columnist will more easily grind out a story for the morning edition. These meetings may not show up right away in increased stockholder interest, but they are all part of getting a company's name in circulation. Be sure your company is at least extending an open hand.

CUSTOMERS

Even though this is mainly the daily concern of marketing people, the company should be aware of the interplay of regular advertising with its other business communications. For example, all too often a company projects an image in its advertising which contradicts the theme of its annual reports. Naturally the messages must be quite different since one has the prime purpose of selling, while the other has the prime purpose of a maximum long-term stock price. However, to continue our example, the company should show some awareness of the selling value of its annual report and the stock price effect of its routine advertising.

How do you know whether this connection is being made? One simple way to find out is to ask your company contact to tell you about the preparation of both the latest advertising campaign and the annual report. Were some of the same people (other than the chief executive) contributing to both projects? Or did the marketing department work on the ads in isolation from the financial people, who in turn cranked out the annual report all by themselves? By requesting a specific recent illustration rather than posing a direct question, you will get the overall impression you're looking for. That is a good method in general, since it doesn't force your contact to draw a possibly uncomfortable conclusion. Instead, your contact can just tell you a story, and you can make your own judgments.

SPECIAL GROUPS

There are other special groups which are particularly important to your company or its industry. Does management have a clear idea of who these people are, what their needs and interests may be, and how to get the story to them?

For example, airline managers should be intimately familiar with the Civil Aeronautics Board and should have a good, businesslike connection at several levels. They should not rely on their industry lobbyists in Washington or on routine filings of reports. They will get personally involved with this regulatory process.

As another example, a proprietary (nonprescription) drug company should be acutely aware of the antipill subculture. People who are strongly opposed to all except vital medications are poor customers, but they can still raise havoc with a product if they get the wrong (or maybe the right) information.

THE GENERAL PUBLIC

The general public includes all the four subgroups discussed above as well as people in general. The field of public relations is much maligned and misunderstood. The term "PR man" has come to be an insult. Yet a good PR man can be a valuable counselor in an area where everyone else may stumble.

You should expect to find a balanced awareness of this fact in a company you are researching. Evidence of this awareness is unmistakable: If a good PR man has been around for long, everyone will know the jargon. "What message are we communicating?" "Through which media?" "To which public?" A little of that goes a long way, to be sure, but ignorance of PR is a bad sign also. As is true in several other areas of our research, only the discovery of extremes should concern you.

FIFTEEN WAYS TO JUDGE TOP MANAGEMENT

The top few management people have a tremendous influence on the success or failure of your investment. A complete evaluation could require several meetings over a long period of time. However, as we always point out, you can pick a few of the most relevant ideas for whatever company you are now researching and fairly quickly form a good, reliable impression of management quality.

The payoff from this kind of research is your sense of real conviction about the quality of management. A truly uncommon company is run by uncommon people. You must come away from your work feeling strong confidence in management before you can justify owning a company's stock.

In Chapters 18 to 21 we will get down to the quantitative specifics about forecasting stock prices and coming to a final buy or sell decision. The purpose of this chapter is more qualitative—to give you the broad, subjective underpinnings for forecasting. Moreover, your conversations with management and others (see Chapter 11 for interviewing methods) will give you the contacts you need to refine your forecast and come up with the best possible price estimate for the stock.

Thus your work on management appraisal has two purposes: It will enable you to judge the people and to build your lines of communication with them.

Judging people is not new to you, of course. You have always sorted out the winners from the losers, whether in school or on the job. You know that some people seem to have what it takes to succeed, while others just stumble through life. Don't lose track of that experience as you read this chapter. Instead, try to connect these time-tested ways of judging company managers with your intuitions over the years about people in general. The 15 ways of judging top management described in this chapter are effective only when embedded in, or added to, your own good common sense.

Here is an outline of what we will discuss in detail:

1. Who are the top managers?

2. How are the key activities organized?

3. What are the key decisions? How are they made?

4. What is the philosophy of business management, both as your source expresses it and as you observe it?

5. How does the planning and control system work?

6. What does it take to be good in this business, beyond what it takes to be successful in any business?

7. What changes in management have occurred in the last 12 months? In the last three to five years?

8. What incentives are there for management? How are they tied to our interests as stockholders?

9. How do the top people define themselves? What is their self-perception?

10. How could management people steal? What makes you think they don't?

11. How would you characterize the relations between the key executives? Is this pattern of interaction meaningful, or is it just an idiosyncrasy?

12. Does management seem to have clear ideas or plans?

13. Does management have a command of the facts? Does each member of management tell the same story about the facts? How does management's story compare with what outsiders are telling you?

14.   How does the company develop new people?

15.   What are your intuitive feelings and reactions?

1. WHO ARE THE TOP MANAGERS?

Whoever actually makes the key decisions is a top manager. Usually, of course, the highest titles are given to the same people who really carry out the top functions. If so, you need pick out only the chairman of the board and/or the chief executive officer, the president and/or the chief operating officer, and the vice presidents in charge of marketing, finance, production, compliance, and research. (See Chapter 15 if you need to review these five main business functions.)

Occasionally, however, titles are misplaced. For example, there is a company in Boston in which the treasurer is in reality the top person. However, this is pretty unusual, and you won't have any trouble discovering where the power is located. Just ask your sources inside the company who had the last word on a few recent major decisions.

The company can usually give you résumés of the key people. Put these in your files and add to them as you pick up more information. Focus on the meaning of the events in each manager's life. Don't spend a great deal of time on verifying facts such as salary at a previous job. You are really looking for broad patterns of personal behavior. Some examples are excessive job hopping, inadequate qualifications or excessive qualifications, and particularly strong or weak functional experience such as a heavy marketing background or a lack of experience in financial matters. Résumé work will provide you with additional leads for new sources (Chapter 10), and it should also help you appraise the pattern of outside activities and connections (Chapter 16).

2. HOW ARE THE KEY ACTIVITIES ORGANIZED?

As an aid to your general understanding of the business, it is usually worth taking some care to go through the so-called organization chart. Look at it both as it appears on paper and as it actually seems to function.

3. WHAT ARE THE KEY DECISIONS? HOW ARE THEY MADE?

In any business there are certain decisions which are obviously pivotal. For example, if the company is a restaurant chain, the selection of sites for future restaurants is a key decision. Such decisions need to be made many times during the course of the year's operations. They contrast with those which either are routine administrative matters or are made very infrequently, such as decisions on major financing or acquisitions. In trying to identify the key decisions, your preliminary work in analyzing the economics of the firm (Chapter 8) should lead you to the answers.

Direct questions to management will probably produce nothing but an organization chart and some vague job descriptions. Instead, try the case method. Picking up on our example of a restaurant chain, you might identify one or two of the newest restaurant sites and then ask which people were involved in the decision to select those particular locations. Was an unnecessarily large amount of staff work done? Or, at the other extreme, was one person running the whole show?

In this particular case, the best method seems to be to have one highly experienced, well-seasoned field person, supported by perhaps one or two assistants, who gets involved with the whole process—from the time research is done on traffic flows and zoning and soil conditions right up until the time the entire real estate package is put together. This field person in turn then needs to be working directly with the chief operating officer of the company, with as little red tape in between them as possible.

Another illustration of key decisions is provided by an airline. Here the job of flight scheduling has a major impact on a company's costs and competitive position on a week-to-week basis. Key operating decisions need to be made by a full-time, highly experienced person, well supported but not bureaucratized into a committee, and with a direct line-reporting relationship to the president of the airline. As another example, a manufacturer of automobile parts has extremely important decisions to make in two areas: pricing bids and production order scheduling. You can learn a lot about the efficiency and competitive position of a company by going through one of these decisions step by step.

One disconcerting but useful insight will sometimes come out of an investigation of the key decisions. It may turn out that the company really does not have very much control over its own destiny and that even its most important decisions cannot have any major effect on year-to-year profitability.

This is particularly true in commodity-oriented companies. Examples of such situations are lumber companies, cement plants, basic chemical producers, oil refineries, and mining companies. For such companies, price decisions are completely in the hands of the market-place rather than being at the firm's discretion. As a result, incremental profit calculations force the company to work at 100 percent of capacity, if at all possible, because the costs of production are of the high fixed and low variable type. In such situations, it does not matter whether the coal mine or whatever is run by Albert Einstein or Mortimer Snerd! External factors of price and sunk costs will pretty well control the company's destiny.

We are not normally intrigued by investments of this character. However, if for some reason you have developed a high degree of confidence in the direction of the external factors which control the company and you are simply looking for a vehicle to play this situation, under those unusual circumstances you should be willing to invest with Mortimer Snerd and his coal-mining company. Such situations are rare, of course, primarily because the external factors are often so difficult to predict: commodity prices, political events, short-term interest rate fluctuations, and other such unanalyzable situations.

4. WHAT IS THE PHILOSOPHY OF BUSINESS MANAGEMENT, BOTH AS YOUR SOURCE EXPRESSES IT AND AS YOU OBSERVE IT?

This has a lot in common with the question of top management's self-perception (item 9 below). In this case, we are looking for management's theories or prejudices or judgments regarding the appropriate method of conducting a business. Does management believe in gathering facts from the troops, retiring to reach a decision, and then barking orders back down the line? This is the so-called Theory X organization. Or does management believe in collaboration in the business decision-making process and an open flow of information in both directions? This is the Theory Y organization. The extreme cases would be the United States Marine Corps as a Theory X organization and a psycho-analytic institute as a Theory Y organization.

It is quite unlikely that what the top people tell you about their philosophy of business management will be the way they actually run the company. There are some terrible martinets who honestly think they are collaborative decision makers and open-handed communicators! On the other hand, a rough and tough and gruff-sounding old bull of the woods can still do a beautiful job of involving his people in the decision-making process.

To make matters even more complicated, it is hard to argue that either method of management is inherently superior. You will just have to make a judgment as to whether the company's philosophy and methods are appropriate to the specific business involved. For example, if the Marine Corps were a business and you were to find out that it was going to revolutionize its methods of operations and set up committees of privates to second-guess the commands of generals, I suspect you would want to be out of that stock in a hurry! At the other extreme, if a highly productive and imaginative research group was for some reason faced with a new manager who was a retired Marine Corps general, you would certainly want to have some second thoughts about continuing your involvement with that situation as well.

5. HOW DOES THE PLANNING AND CONTROL SYSTEM WORK?

This is the heart of any investigation of top management's ability to run a business. A planning and control system is the entire process by which information is gathered and processed, the way in which future plans and expectations are formulated and interrelated, and the way in which the daily flow of physical events is compared with the expectations which have come out of the planning process. (See also Chapter 15.)

To start an investigation in this area, request samples of reports which circulate at the middle-management and top-management levels. It doesn't matter if these reports contain figures which are out of date. In fact, it is better if they do because this makes it much easier to obtain them without raising the problem of inside information, which is usually the reason for management's reluctance to show the forms for the planning and control process. Asking for out-of-date reports is a good way to avoid this problem. While the current information may be proprietary, just the format of basic planning and control documents need not be kept secret.

Most of the time you will have no trouble getting a look at the system. In fact, you may have to politely extract yourself from a several-hour dissertation by a very proud financial vice president on the subject of his or her planning and control work. Apparently not very many people outside the company take more than a cursory interest in this subject. However, such controls are just as basic to a company as a steering wheel is to an automobile, and the consequences of their absence or sudden failure can be devastating.

The mere existence of planning documents and elaborate computer printouts does not by itself ensure you that they are used effectively and properly. Spend some time going into the way in which controls were developed. Who did the basic system design? Was it someone in the firm, or was an outside consultant brought in? Was the project initiated by the top management, or is it something that came up gradually through the staff? How does management know the information is being assimilated by the people to whom it is sent? Has management ever tried cutting off all reports and reinstituting only those which are missed and then asked for?

The essential purpose of any planning and control system is to monitor what is actually happening versus what was supposed to happen. If the budget called for monthly sales of 3.7 million units and the actual sales were 3.1 million, what were the causes of the variation from budget? Was it something ordinary and of little concern, such as vacation schedules, a large shipment during the previous month, or a seasonal variation not specifically anticipated in the budget? On the other hand, was it something serious, like an indication of declining product acceptance, price erosion, a new product from a competitor, or a sales falloff after an advertising promotion which didn't catch fire?

Finally, what are the consequences of deviation from the plans? It is well and good to have realistic plans and adequate data gathering and comparison, but if action does not take place as a result of variances, then the whole process becomes academic. What recent actions have been taken as a consequence of data which have turned up from the planning and control process? How far from budget can a manager get before running into trouble? Is the manager's compensation directly related to the variances, as it should be, or is it still pegged outside the system?

6. WHAT DOES IT TAKE TO BE GOOD IN THIS BUSINESS, BEYOND WHAT IT TAKES TO BE SUCCESSFUL IN ANY BUSINESS?

Most company people will tell you that to be good at their business you must possess a list of qualities which reads like the Boy Scout oath. In almost all cases, they drastically overstate the requirements for reasonable success in their particular field. Usually it is not general traits but a specific set of experiences or background which gives them the real edge over their competitors. We all like to make great virtues out of our own skills, and, of course, it would be quite tactless to challenge this harmless conceit. The real issue is whether such skills or backgrounds are in particularly scarce supply and whether they seem to be possessed by the competitors as well.

For example, consider the case of Carlos Perez, a nice old man who is in the business of scavenging clothing for resale through deep discount merchandisers in Harlem. Carlos has a sort of "pack-rat" character. He seems to really love getting into flooded or burned-out stores and warehouses to pull out the salable merchandise from among the completely ruined goods. He says that if he had an opportunity to make an extra $200 a week working instead in a clean, modern textile factory, he would still rather stay with his life as a scavenger. Carlos has only ordinary mental and physical capacities. His small list of merchandising connections and his other practical business experience could fairly easily be duplicated by most people. What is special, and what it takes to be really good at his business, is that old pack-rat instinct. That observation is not very scientific, but if we had an opportunity to bet somehow on Carlos Perez's special skills, we would do it without hesitation.

7. WHAT CHANGES IN MANAGEMENT HAVE OCCURRED IN THE LAST 12 MONTHS? IN THE LAST THREE TO FIVE YEARS?

You should certainly be quite curious about the reasons behind any recent changes in top management. Make a real effort to speak to any top managers who have left the company in the last several years.

One of the favorite reasons given by analysts for buying a particular stock is that the management has changed. This is usually the best reason in the world for not buying the stock. If there are problems in a company serious enough to require a major management change, it would be very unusual if they could be solved by new people over a period of a few fiscal quarters. It is more likely to take several years. In addition, it is very common for incoming managers to write off everything but the kitchen sink at the next possible opportunity, making it absolutely certain that all potential future problems will also be charged to the past management.

One of the most startling reversals of opinion during the process of looking at management changes occurred while a private investor was researching a fairly small company in the pollution control business in Los Angeles. The investor had done all his desk work and was beginning the field interviewing. After spending an hour with the president, he was unusually impressed by this executive's awareness of all the major issues of business management. The two of them then walked over to the office of the treasurer, who went through the financial controls. In the course of that conversation the investor formed a strong impression that the president had an excellent personal rapport with the people around him. At that time the investor was still digging around the company itself and had done only one outside check. This had been with a customer, and the response had been extremely favorable.

Everything was beginning to point to the possibility that this was a fine little company—an uncommon stock which could produce outstanding multiples of price over a long period of time. The investor was tempted at this point to begin buying stock. It was fairly thinly traded, and he was afraid that he would not be able to get a position because the price would run up and away before he could get in. He had already spent what is considered a normal amount of research time, and his gut feeling at this point was positive. Instead of buying, he decided to get one more personal contact. He found the former general manager of one of the company's largest operating units and called him for an appointment.

Charley Z. had left the company about six months before on what seemed amicable terms. The president and treasurer had in the earlier meeting said nice things about Charley, and there seemed to be nothing "between the lines" in their comments. When the investor met alone with Charley, however, the former manager began to talk about the day-to-day work he used to do. It was soon obvious that Charley was reliving a terribly frustrating experience. The financial controls, which looked good on paper in the treasurer's office, turned out to be quite inappropriate for the practical realities of running the business out in the real world. In addition, the cooperative spirit the investor had noted at the head office was viewed instead as a "fraternity house" by Charley and the operating people. In Charley's words, "We were running all over southern California getting the goddamned work done while all those people played patty-cake with each other in their fancy offices."

When the investor got over his initial keen disappointment, he became fascinated by the facade of competence and camaraderie which he had initially mistaken for "quality of management." He then began looking around for what had led him astray. The answer came fairly quickly once the question was properly framed. A professional research analyst had become very close to management. This analyst knew so much about the company that he was, in effect, an informal member of the board. After the investor had talked to this analyst for 30 minutes, the picture became complete. In that time, the analyst used a half dozen phrases which were identical, right down to the words and inflection, with those used by the president and treasurer of the company. The investor had found the source of that superficial layer of competence. The professional analyst had been coaching management on all the right things to say!

The analyst was doing his "stage managing" with the best of intentions and was not himself fully aware of the resentment which had built up among the people who were doing the work. He was a brilliant but not a very experienced or ethical young man, and he hoped that the company's operational troubles would not get too serious. He thought that if everything held together long enough, the stock could be promoted to the public on the basis of the company's good recent record and fairly direct involvement in pollution control activities. All these observations or impressions could have been wrong, of course, but they were sufficient for the investor's purposes. He dropped any further work on the company.

During the next 12 months, the company's earnings inched up a bit, and the stock went up 40 percent in price! The investor thought maybe he had been too critical but decided not to go back to complete his work. Then a real squabble developed inside the company, and all hell broke loose. Several middle managers resigned. In spite of a generally improving market for the firm's products, earnings dropped off very sharply. The stock began to falter; then it fell slowly and finally collapsed entirely. Within another six months, it was selling at a fraction of its price when the investor had looked at it originally.

One brief contact with a former member of management had saved this investor from a disastrous mistake. If you had made that same call to Charley and spent a half hour with him, you would have had the same uneasy feelings about the stock. As in this case, quite often there is really nothing mysterious or subtle about researching management. On the contrary, most of the time you too will turn up any serious problems if you just make a few phone calls. That's the beauty of smaller companies: Charley was not an inaccessible big executive at a giant corporation, but rather an ordinary local man who didn't mind sharing some gossip about his former job.

8. WHAT INCENTIVES ARE THERE FOR MANAGEMENT? HOW ARE THEY TIED TO OUR INTEREST AS STOCKHOLDERS?

There should be strong incentives for the top-management people, and this compensation should be tied to the earnings progress of the company and perhaps also to the price of the stock. This produces the least conflict of interest between the operating management of a company and the outside stockholders. Rising earnings and, one hopes, a rising stock price have got to be good for both under this arrangement.

However, this line of reasoning is sometimes abused by well-entrenched managements so that they can provide themselves with very large payments for very little real performance. Consequently, in some companies you may want to look more carefully at this subject and be less willing to accept the good intentions of management at face value.

This issue is not important on its own, but it gives clues to attitudes which can have an important influence on the earning power of a firm. As an illustration, how many top managements take really significant cuts in pay during times of earnings reversal? Not very many do, of course. Among those which do, you will find a much higher proportion of truly investor-oriented managements.

Changes have occurred in the tax laws which badly hurt the value of stock options, and so this traditional incentive has considerably less power than it used to. The proceeds of the exercise of a stock option are taxable at ordinary rates unless the stock is held up to eight years from the date of issue. The paper gains (unrealized profits) may be subject to a preference tax in the meantime, and the profits can be taken away by the market while the manager is locked in.

This change in the aftertax value of an option and its excessively long time horizon have made stock options much less useful as a source of management incentive compensation. At the same time, the maximum tax on ordinary income has come down, making the plain old-fashioned cash bonus a much more attractive incentive than it used to be. These facts are widely recognized by incentive compensation consultants and are rapidly being reflected in revised programs now going into effect.

Information concerning compensation arrangements is usually very scanty. Only the largest deals are adequately disclosed in the SEC filings. You should pursue these things quite carefully if you are looking for more insight into management's general attitude and character. It is a big red warning flag when you see a lot a special deals being made at the top level without the knowledge and participation of middle-management people. Rather than giving them a stronger urge to work hard to join the "clubhouse at the top," it almost invariably breeds a deep resentment which affects their daily work. It often causes them to begin to look outside the company for their own personal opportunities.

This and other sources of irritation between middle management and the top-management group are seldom recognized by outside investors.

The whole issue of compensation is a highly charged one, particularly at the top level. Most people really don't want to talk about it unless they are pressed a bit, but it should be researched. People may work for love or prestige or group involvement, but our perhaps old-fashioned opinion is that they work first and foremost for money. You simply have to find out how much they get and under what conditions they get it before you have an adequate view of the firm.

9. HOW DO THE TOP PEOPLE DEFINE THEMSELVES? WHAT IS THEIR SELF-PERCEPTION?

This subject is worth pursuing because people tend to act in a way which will reinforce their own self-image. They may not do it right away, but eventually they will take action which they hope will make reality conform to their fantasies.

At the early stages of your investigation and cross-checking work, it is very difficult to get much in this area. Most company managements have become quite sophisticated in recent years about expressing the so-called right buzz words to any and all casual acquaintances, and they are particularly cautious about this with potential investors. In time, however, if you use a tactful and thoroughly honest approach with your contacts, they will open up on the subject with a bit more candor. We are looking for "stability of self-image." This means that managers are not excessively searching or questioning their role in the world or their current situation, but instead seem genuinely to be at ease and in harmony with their work. Such people seem to be happy at what they are doing to have a sense of rootedness, at least insofar as that is possible in the mobile and fast-moving corporate world.

This stability of self-image is sometimes manifested by a somewhat provincial manner, and it is very easy to mistake this characteristic for narrowness and timidity. However, it does not follow that people with a well-developed and stable sense of who they are and where they are going are not curious and imaginative. Quite the contrary; it is frequently from this base of personal security that managers are able to venture forth and test out and accept changes which can be important to their firms over the long term. On the other hand, the insecure, ego-ridden, hard-driving, compulsive manager, which is the more popular conception of the corporate president, is not usually the type of character you should want running your firm. Such a person is apt to make decisions for change for its own sake and can be even more dangerous than the bureaucrat who makes decisions against change regardless of merit.

The consequences of self-image are illustrated in the case of a small Midwestern company which makes automobile radiators. This is a simple nuts-and-bolts sort of business. "Time-in-grade" type of experience is probably more important than any other special skills or traits. In interviewing the president of this company, it was learned that he had a very clear image of himself as the head of a dynamic business enterprise. Moreover, he was much preoccupied with a confused version of the Harvard Business School way of running a company, possibly because his son was off at that institution in their M.B.A. program. Whatever the reasons, he had surrounded himself with a staff and used methods far more appropriate to a complex multidivisional company several times the size of his prosaic radiator business. Therefore, his overhead costs were too high, as you might expect. The most important consequence was the development of an extremely premature bureaucratization and a general hardening of the arteries for no good reason whatever. The president simply viewed himself in this capacity, and he moved to create that world around him whether realities justified it or not.

10. HOW COULD MANAGEMENT PEOPLE STEAL? WHAT MAKES YOU THINK THEY DON'T?

Obviously, no one would want anything to do with a company whose management is dishonest. What we are aiming at here is not quite that black and white. In most cases, if there is any really flagrant dishonesty afoot, your chances of knowing about it ahead of time are very slim.

You should be far more concerned about the question of so-called corporate opportunity than about the much rarer forms of common criminality which are inherently unpredictable.

Despite the popular view of the overworked executive, all well-organized managers will have a certain amount of free time on their hands. Also, by the time top people have reached their present positions, they should have some money saved. Consequently, company managers will quite commonly be on the lookout for opportunities to invest for themselves in small businesses where their special expertise and their small capital might be parlayed into a big killing. Such opportunities circulate quite commonly at this level, and it is perfectly appropriate and ethical for managers to take advantage of them, providing, of course, that they are not taking time away from their essential activities in the management of their own company. Also, the investments should not be anything that the company itself should more appropriately be involved with. This is what is meant by the term "corporate opportunity."

How does the company decide that a venture is a corporate opportunity, as opposed to something that the key people are free to devote their own extra money and time to? There are no hard-and-fast rules, and the board of directors of the firm can define their business strategy narrowly or broadly as they feel appropriate to the talents and resources of the company. In addition, most managements are on reasonably good terms with their boards and have little difficulty getting letters of authorization for outside activities. Our role in this situation is not that of a watchdog, but again we are looking for insights into the character of the top people.

This is a very fertile field to plow. The essential information is uncovered by an investigation of the outside investments, affiliations, and directorships of the top-management personnel. If you work from these preliminary facts, a few short talks with the outside parties will tell you just how extensive a drain is created by these activities.

Usually by this stage of the work, you will be familiar enough with the company's business to have a personal opinion about the degree of conflict which might be involved. While you should keep such opinions to yourself by and large, it is the moral equivalent of embezzlement for a top management to take an opportunity which rightfully belongs to the public corporation. Outside activities are legitimate, and they help keep people mentally alive and provide them with some very valuable moneymaking opportunities. It is a matter of your own judgment when the bounds have been overstepped and you get the feeling that the company is just providing a vehicle for the outside activities and interests of its top people. If the company's prospects do not capture the imagination and take most of the time of the key people, then maybe the stock should be of even less interest to you.

11. *HOW WOULD YOU CHARACTERIZE THE RELATIONS BETWEEN THE KEY EXECUTIVES? IS THIS PATTERN OF INTERACTION MEANINGFUL, OR IS IT JUST AN IDIOSYNCRASY?*

This topic is related to item 14 below, which concerns the development of new people, but it focuses particularly on the ongoing relationships of the existing decision makers rather than on the question of continuity of management. We are concerned specifically with the flow of communications in the firm, since much valuable information flows outside the normal planning and control system on fragile lines of personal interaction.

The single most visible evidence is the question of "access." Do the key people interact with one another frequently? Can the middle managers be heard satisfactorily and in turn instructed through direct contact and in human terms? The textbooks are full of advice and rules regarding communications and interactions in top management. However, you do not need to be a communications consultant to sense pretty quickly whether the lines are basically open or heavily clogged.

The comfortable old-shoe familiarity among the more experienced managers in smaller companies can sometimes throw you off the trail. There can be evidence of great cordiality and good humor when you see these people together. Frequently, of course, the appearance is the reality, and that is about all there is to it. Occasionally, however, you can stumble into a really sick situation in which the values of internal cooperation have subverted those of profits. Such managers will still be smiling happily at one another as the water laps up over the deck and the ship goes down.

One good way of getting at this issue is to look at a few events in the recent history of the company, whether they seem to have any great investment significance or not—for example, a stock split, a new officer, or a settlement of a long-standing lawsuit. Then, in the process of your work, try to find out how the decisions on this event were made and how the information was communicated through the ranks. A few short examples of this sort, brought out during your conversations on other subjects, will tell you a great deal more than management's direct assertions on the subject.

12. DOES MANAGEMENT SEEM TO HAVE CLEAR IDEAS OR PLANS?

Almost all management people in this day and age will give you a rosy story about their future expectations for growth and prosperity. In order to judge the clarity of any underlying plans, we have to probe and push a bit more than we would normally like to do. When a glossy plan for future growth is sketched out in easy strokes, at some appropriate time you will have to ask your contact to have enough confidence in you to be a bit more specific. If the plan is any good and if your contact does in fact have a reasonable degree of confidence in your ability to keep your mouth shut, then he or she may be willing to give you some of the specifics you will need to evaluate management's judgments.

Here again you are not trying to second-guess the plan as a whole, or at least that is not your primary objective. Instead, you will find out whether future plans are just documents of wishful thinking ("letters to Santa Claus") or reasonable, practical blueprints for real action. For example, if the company plans to sell 50 percent more baseball bats or computers or doorknobs in the next two or three years, where is it going to build the plant necessary to produce them? How is the company going to finance the plant, its equipment, and the inventory? Which competitors are going to have to give up market shares? What additional channels of distribution are to be opened up? What strains will that put on the existing channels? What price actions may be necessary to achieve this objective? Who is leading the project internally at the present time? How much of the total time of top management does it seem to be taking? It won't take much of this kind of probing before your impressions are clearly formed.

13. *DOES MANAGEMENTS HAVE A COMMAND OF THE FACTS? DOES EACH MEMBER OF MANAGEMENT TELL THE SAME STORY ABOUT THE FACTS? HOW DOES MANAGEMENT'S STORY COMPARE WITH WHAT OUTSIDERS ARE TELLING YOU?*

There is no great virtue in possessing a clutter of unnecessary and unrelated facts. However, we always feel much more comfortable with a manager who either has the important facts at hand or at least can reach over to the bookcase or into a briefcase and produce them in short order.

Facts are the raw materials of decisions, and good managers frequently have a librarian's sense of data storage and retrieval. They will have their information layered according to its relative importance and will have their offices or their secretaries' offices well stocked with those things they may need to know on fairly short notice. They will probably insist that their subordinates be equally well armed and prepared, and they will be pretty intolerant if there is a confused scramble through the file cabinets every time a question is asked.

Good managers are comfortable with their facts and do not consider that acquiring and working with them is beneath their dignity. Even the President of the United States is a fact gatherer to some extent in addition to being a decision maker. A comfortable professional competence with the world of statistics and a grasp of mundane events are signs of strength rather than indications of a lack of breadth.

You will often get conflicting facts in field research, and they can be fascinating to explore. It is not very often that people deliberately lie to you, in the sense of telling you one thing while believing another to be true. But there are perceptual differences which are bound to occur, and when they become quite large, they should be traced. For example, an unusually large inventory of finished goods may be thought of by the production head as strike insurance, while the marketing manager sees these same goods as a lot of white elephants. That is, this large inventory might mean an unexpected continuity of earnings during the shutdown, or it might mean an equally unexpected year-end write-off of unsalable goods. For this reason, occasionally pursue facts which on their own merit might not be of primary investment significance. If a contradiction is developing, pursuing it may lead you to a better understanding of the company.

14. HOW DOES THE COMPANY DEVELOP NEW PEOPLE?

We plan to be investors in a company over the long term, or at least to own the stock during certain periods and continue to follow the company even when we have temporarily sold out. Therefore, we want to know what provisions are being made to attract people who can replace key managers as this inevitably becomes necessary.

Again, the extremes are more illustrative than the middle-of-the-road situations. For instance, some companies bring in completely inexperienced trainees and then point to them as their source of future management potential. This is complete nonsense for companies other than the great monoliths, such as IBM and General Motors. Important openings are very likely to occur in almost any company during the next three or four years. Clearly, inexperienced young people fresh out of the M.B.A. mills are not going to fill these spots. The really key spots will have to be filled either from today's middle-management ranks or through outside connections which the company already will have pretty much in place.

The fact that a company is a good place for a trainee to be is probably more negative than positive. It means the company may be spending an inordinate amount of time working with people who are not carrying their own weight. It is far more helpful to look at the way the treasurer works with the financial vice president, for example, to see whether the treasurer is being given a fair chance at the senior person's job. Is the financial vice president going to be ready someday to succeed the president? Do middle managers generally have the access and exposure to the top people that will develop their real understanding of the business?

This is not so mysterious a process as some believe. It really comes down to some pretty simple questions: Why do people work there? What do they like about the job? What do they dislike? What new job would cause them to move on? How do they really spend their time on and off the job?

15. WHAT ARE YOUR INTUITIVE FEELINGS AND REACTIONS?

This is something you can use with every company you research. Sit back and reflect on the feelings which are arising in reaction to your various conversations. Did the key people convey a sense of energy and excitement? Did they directly answer your questions, or were they evasive? Did they volunteer information, or did you have to pry it out an inch at a time? Would you like to work for them or hire them to work for you? Could you get along with them over a long period of time? In short, would you buy a common stock from these people?

Suspend your disbelief, so to speak, and take off your skeptical accountant's green eyeshade. We all process a great deal of information unconsciously all the time. We can take advantage of this mental facility if we allow it to poke its head up past the steel traps of our own logical analysis!

This does not mean that final investment decisions are made at this point. You can, however, just slip into this mental set or attitude purposely, even while recognizing that your impressions and feelings are perhaps unreliable and will have to be evaluated more critically later on. This process occurs normally in any human being, and all that we are advocating is that instead of suppressing these valuable reactions, you allow them to move into your consciousness, where they can become a source of useful insight. While this suggestion is included in our discussion of top-management evaluation, it is, of course, equally applicable to every aspect of stock market research.

DECISIONS

The decision process pulls together all our research work into a consistent, logical framework. Here all the pieces are put back together so that we can come up with a final buy or sell decision.

Chapters 18 to 21 will lead you step by step through this decision process. Since the future price of a stock will be determined by the market's consensus estimate of the company's earnings, our first step is to forecast those earnings. Next we will look at some other quantitative indicators of company quality. In Chapters 21 and 22 the stock is appraised, and a specific Stock Price Forecast is developed. Your buy and sell points are based on that price prediction.

HOW TO FORECAST
A COMPANY'S
EARNINGS

The preceding chapters have prepared you to form many valuable new impressions of a company. These qualitative judgments will now provide the background for the more specific job of forecasting earnings per share (EPS). The main purpose of this chapter is to show you how to develop your own estimates. As you will see in the next few chapters, EPS estimates are a key part of predicting a stock's price and setting your buy and sell points. Also, the methods used here in EPS forecasting will come in handy later for your price work.

You can do a "first-cut" or preliminary EPS forecast fairly early in your research. Just don't get wedded to it until you complete your fieldwork as well. Even after that, keep an open mind. The most thorough estimate should always be thought of as a best approximation and subject to change as you get new information and develop new insights.

There are dozens of specialized books covering the subject of earnings forecasts. Here, especially, professionals will try to tell you that an individual private investor just cannot hope to get meaningful ideas from the maze of statistics which are now publicly available. Once again you will be told to stay back and let the pros digest and interpret the facts for you.

Don't be scared off. You do not need a lot of training. You do not need a whole alphabet of professional designations at the end of your name. You can get what you need out of the numbers with a few simple tools and your good common sense.

THE FORECASTING WORKSHEET

We will start with a forecasting worksheet, shown in Figure 6. Its purpose is to put the figures into one compact format so that you can spot the major trends and relationships.

The worksheet starts with sales (and/or total revenues), deducts all the expenses to show pretax earnings, applies the tax rate to give earnings after taxes, and finally divides by total shares outstanding to produce the EPS figure.

There are financial services which will give you something similar already done. Why not use their work? Because much of the value of the analysis comes from doing it yourself. You will spend a few extra hours per year grinding out your own work, but you will also get a far better feel for the data in the process. Many top professional analysts still do a lot of their own "number crunching" for this very reason. Try it yourself for a while, and if you still don't agree, then go buy a statistical service.

First, some general comments. This worksheet is only a sample. You will want to use somewhat different items for each individual company. In selecting items for the worksheet, each one should refer to a major aspect of the company's operations or condition. Is it a large enough part of the picture? Would a variation in the figure really have any meaning? Do you have a regular source for the information?

If you keep your worksheet as simple as possible, you will be able to develop and maintain it more easily, and you will focus your attention on the truly key determinants of earnings. Even if you have some knowledge of accounting or finance, don't get carried away with statistical analysis. You may get some satisfaction from a very elaborate worksheet, but that is not really helpful in making money from your stock selections. If you are spending more than an hour or two per week just on statistical analysis, the chances are pretty good that you are doing more than is really required for the business research. Desk work has an important place in finding uncommon stocks, but you also have to leave time to get out and talk with the people who can bring life and perspective to the numbers.

Forecasting Worksheet: Elliptical Feebleblitzer Corporation (EFC)

(All dollar figures in thousands except per share data)

Note # (See text for discussion)		5 Years Ago	Last Year	Compound Annual % Change	Estimated Current Year	% Change	Estimated Next Year	% Change
1.								
2.	Sales &/or Revenues	18,310	35,250	+14%	42,300	+20%	48,600	+15%
3.	Major Expenses:							
	Cost of Goods Sold	11,599	21,583	+13%	25,455	+18%	29,350	+15%
	(% of Revenues)	63.3%	61.2%		60.2%		60.4%	
	Selling & Administrative	4,293	7,325	+13%	9,765	+25%	11,025	+13%
	(% of Revenues)	23.4%	22.2%		23.1%		22.7%	
	Research & Development	282	1,400	+38%	1,480	+5%	1,800	+22%
	(% of Revenues)	1.5%	4.0%		3.5%		3.7%	
	All Other Expense, Net	594	1,199	+15%	1,440	+20%	1,500	+4%
	(% of Revenues)	3.2%	3.4%		3.4%		3.1%	
	Total Expenses	16,768	32,007	+14%	38,140	+19%	43,675	+14%
4.	Pretax Earnings	1,542	3,243	+16%	4,160	+28%	4,925	+18%
5.	(% of Revenues)	8.4%	9.2%		9.8%		10.1%	
6.	Income Taxes	725	1,378	+14%	1,830	+33%	2,250	+23%
6.	(Tax Rate)	47%	42%		44%		46%	
7.	Earnings After Taxes	817	1,865	+18%	2,330	+25%	2,675	+15%
	(% of Revenues)	4.5%	5.3%		5.5%		5.5%	
8.	Shares Outstanding ('000)	730	805	+2%	845	+5%	845	0%
9.	Earnings per Share	1.12	2.32	+16%	2.76	+19%	3.17	+15%

FIGURE 6. FORECASTING WORKSHEET FOR EFC.

The example used on this worksheet is our favorite little fictional company, the Elliptical Feebleblitzer Corporation (EFC). We will follow EFC all the way through to a buy or sell decision in this chapter and the three that follow. If you have not already looked over the worksheet, please get acquainted with it now before reading further.

AN INTERLOCKING SET OF ASSUMPTIONS

Your estimates should form an interlocking set of assumptions. Each assumption, such as the percentage change in sales, will affect many other lines in the worksheet. Therefore, it is unlikely that you will get an internally consistent result on the first run-through. Start the process by entering on the worksheet those elements about which you have the greatest confidence.

For example, your research work up to this point may have indicated the following: a current-year sales gain of about 20 percent and another increase next year of 15 percent; cost of goods sold as a percentage of revenues moving down about 1 percent this year and going up slightly next year; and research and development at $1.5 million in the current year, but with a big jump planned for next year. Some figures will be best estimated first as percentage changes, while others will be easier to arrive at in dollar terms. When you have entered your most confident estimates, then fill in the other lines as best you can.

Check the relationships for internal consistency as you go along. For instance, the major expense categories when subtracted from total sales must of course equal the income figure. Another illustration: A percentage estimate of research and development expense must be consistent with dollar figures derived separately. Fill in as much of the worksheet as possible. The more complete it is, the better you will be able to compare actual results when they are released.

Making this comparison and continually updating your forecast are two of the major ways you learn about a company. Make the best estimate you can, discuss it with your sources, and then analyze the "variances," or the differences between your worksheet and the final published results.

Don't expect to be very accurate. The whole process is inherently uncertain to begin with, and even full-time professional analysts make inaccurate forecasts. It is great when you come very close, but you are striving mostly to define your expectations so that you can compare them with the market consensus expectations. As you gain experience with estimating and as you become more familiar with the company, your accuracy will improve.

THE DETAILS OF THE FORECAST

Now let's get into some details. The numbers below refer to "Note #" over the left-hand column of the worksheet in Figure 6.

NOTE #1. YEARS SELECTED

You will of course want the last full fiscal year, as well as space for esti-mates for this year and the next. The fifth year back is usually a good base period for reference. If that year is abnormal, pick another. Just scan the annual reports and find some good reference point against which to measure longer-term results. (If you can run the numbers quickly, do each of the last five years.)

Quarterly data can be put on a cut-down version of this same work-sheet. Use only five to seven lines, though, to avoid excessive desk work. You won't get good, detailed data on a quarterly basis, but your contacts may give you some guidance. Also, quarterly data are often erratic and misleading, so just keep track of them and calculate a few major figures like profit margins (total pretax income as a percentage of total revenues). Don't get too absorbed in it unless there appear to be major divergences from the annual data and/or from your estimates. When that happens, turn off your calculator, get in your car, and go out to the company in person to ask what is going on.

NOTE #2. SALES AND/OR REVENUES

All kinds of nonsense is written about how to estimate a company's sales. As a practical matter, however, you should start with any indica-tions offered by management. Then add or subtract to reflect what other sources tell you and to adjust for management's tendency to be either conservative or optimistic.

Most firms are still very skittish about showing competitors and customers how well or poorly certain separate parts of the business are doing. However, a breakdown of sales (or revenues or whatever the company calls its "top line") by line of business is required by law to be disclosed. If it isn't clear in the annual report to shareholders, dig it out of the 10-K report. (See Chapter 10 if you haven't yet read about the SEC reports.)

While overall growth may be good, the breakdown by line of business will often show a really big loser or winner. Now you have a good topic to discuss with your sources. What caused this situation? What is being done now, either to remedy it or to keep it going well? Is the trend likely to reverse, as a result of either a decision to go out of a bad business or a return to normal after an unsustainable success? Some review of these components of sales by line of business will help you make an overall estimate of sales for the worksheet.

A company which has been growing at less than 10 percent per year in sales has one strike against it. This is because inflation alone is running at around 6 percent, leaving only 4 percent or less in real terms for the slower growers. The past record is no guarantee of the future, of course, but it gives you a point of departure for your field discussions. If the company plans to grow faster, ask the management people what they plan to do differently and why they think their plan will work.

NOTE #3.   MAJOR EXPENSE CATEGORIES

Major expense categories come right from the annual statement of income. Expense items equaling as little as 5 percent of revenues are often worth following even on this "big-picture" worksheet.

The worksheet in Figure 6 shows four of the most common categories of expense. Cost of goods sold is those expenses which are directly attributed to the manufacture of the goods. It is the best way to judge efficiency of production. Selling and administrative expense is the cost of moving the goods to market and keeping the business running, as opposed to the direct cost of the product. Research and development is any expense not connected with current sales. (For a discussion of the main business functions, see Chapter 15.)

Each major expense category has below it a line for calculating that expense as a percentage of revenues. This is a major ratio. It is useful both in absolute level and in the changes it exhibits. Why are these ratios what they are? Can they be reduced as sales expand, or is there some reason why they must stay the same? If one item makes up most of the expenses, try to break it down a bit more. Companies love to lump together offsetting trends to produce the appearance of stability.

When management publicly indicates a goal, such as a doubling of profits in three years, ask how these expense ratios are going to have to change and how that is to be achieved. The great value of even this brief worksheet is that it lets you see the main interconnections between future hope and past reality. Unless good evidence appears, never accept the assumption that expense ratios are going to quickly improve. A ratio tends to continue on its own momentum until a new force intervenes to change it. Hope alone is not a force for such change.

NOTE #4.   PRETAX EARNINGS

Pretax earnings are equal to sales less total expenses. This is the "bottom line"—except that with improved disclosure rules, you now get several bottom lines. Income segments are broken down into the same lines of business which are used in the sales breakdown. While these categories conceal more than they reveal, you can get some idea about the real importance to profits of each part of the company's activities. Also, trends in profitability are at least hinted at, and these will suggest questions to ask your sources.

Be sure the earnings figure you use is before adjustments for such things as write-offs, special charges, and amounts attributable to discontinued operations. These adjustments are important, but they should be considered separately once you are satisfied they really are nonrecurring. Try to include in your worksheet the income figure most reflective or representative of the company's ongoing operations. Your goal is to estimate the future, not to make a perfect historical record.

NOTE #5.   PROFIT MARGIN

"Profit margin" is the more common term for pretax income as a percentage of total revenues. It is often considered the second most important indicator of a company's condition. (Return on equity is the only more significant figure.)

The absolute level of profit margins varies greatly from one type of business to another. For example, supermarket chains may show only a 2 percent profit margin, while drug manufacturers are bringing down 20 percent of every sales dollar to pretax income. The same issues are raised in both cases, though: What is there about the business that causes these characteristic profit margins? How do they compare with those of other companies in the same field (if there are any comparable companies)? What accounts for such differences? Are margins unsustainably high, locked in place, or reversibly low? Is it realistic to expect any major changes in profit margins? If not, then of course improved earnings must come solely from expanded sales volume with no "leverage" from better profits per dollar of sales.

NOTE #6.   THE TAX RATE

The tax rate is actually the "effective tax rate," determined by dividing taxes (actually paid or accrued) by pretax income. The unpredictable changes being made in tax laws, combined with the horrible complexity of existing rules, make it virtually impossible to forecast a company's effective tax rate without a lot of coaching or guidance from management. A 5-percentage-point shift is not unusual anymore for any size or type of company. As a result, changes in tax rates are now a major cause of uncertainty.

The presence of low rates (below 40 percent) is a caution flag. Read the footnotes in the annual report carefully to get the explanation and then discuss the subject with someone in the company's financial department. You may never quite see how the rate goes together, but don't worry because the chances are that no one else does either! Just try to get a reliable range of tax rates for the next year or two and a rough idea of when (if ever) a major change might be expected.

Don't bet on any company's maintaining very low rates for more than five years, no matter what you are told. The hatchet of tax reform is lurching randomly around the economy, and no tax shelter is secure anymore. Put a more normal rate (40 to 50 percent) in your long-term projections, and if that ruins the attractiveness of the stock, so be it.

Another reason to be wary of an unusually low tax rate is that it may be a sign of "aggressive" (as opposed to "conservative") accounting practices, which usually means that some major expenses which are deducted from income on the company's tax return are not deducted on the stockholder reports. While this is perfectly legal, it understates expenses and overstates profits.

For all these reasons you should be extra careful about investing in low tax rate companies.

NOTE #7.   EARNINGS AFTER TAXES

Earnings after taxes are just pretax earnings less income tax. That sounds simple enough, but these days you will often see two or even more figures given for earnings after taxes, depending on how nonrecurring events are treated. Don't get bogged down in an exhausting reconstruction of post nonrecurring events. If they were nonrecurring, you should spend your time understanding how they will affect management's future actions. That will not spring out of even the most elaborate worksheet, but will come from personal meetings with your sources. If instead you suspect that the company is chronically getting into nonrecurring situations, then you should probably stop following it and face the fact that the situation is just too unpredictable. In either case, you can't get much from sorting out an overly complex record. The best approach is to stay with earnings from continuing operations, excluding nonrecurring factors.

The aftertax profit margin is simply earnings after taxes as a percentage of total revenues. It appears right below the earnings line. Since your source will often talk in terms of profit margin rather than absolute earnings, you may be able to estimate this figure more easily first, and then calculate earnings.

NOTE #8. SHARES OUTSTANDING
Watch this like a hawk because changes in the number of shares outstanding directly affect your share in the company. When "shares issued and outstanding" are rising, find out what was received by the company in exchange for those shares. A rapidly growing company often needs to sell shares to raise capital. What price did the company get, and how?

Shares are also issued to provide for executive stock options. Who got them, and what are they worth? Were these options reasonable and necessary, or were they just a legal raid on the company's treasury?

Shares are issued for acquisitions of other companies. What did the company get in terms of added earning power or special talents? Was there a guarantee made on the stock price as part of the deal, and, if so, what is the maximum number of shares which have to be issued when the guarantee period expires? What would be the EPS impact?

Dilution of your interest in the company over the long run must be more than offset by increased earnings, or else the new shares should not have been issued. You can never know that for sure in advance, of course, but at least satisfy yourself that management is very careful about handing out new shares. If you sense a lack of concern or understanding about this, avoid the stock.

NOTE #9. EARNINGS PER SHARE (EPS)
Per-share calculations are another apparently simple subject which has grown complex in recent years. For example, which income figure gets divided by which number of shares? Income before or after extraordi-

nary items? Income before or after adjustment to reflect full tax rates instead of temporary shelters? Shares now outstanding or also shares which may be issued under different contingencies? Year-end shares or the average outstanding?

There is no one best answer. Our preference is income from continuing operations, excluding extraordinary items, and this figure divided by year-end shares actually outstanding. This (or something close to it) is usually available in the annual and quarterly reports, and it will save you a lot of arithmetic.

If you have to get involved in complex per-share calculations which also produce widely different results, it usually isn't worth it to continue with an analysis of the company. Companies with complex capital structures and a checkered history of going into and out of many businesses are often a bad bet. Sophisticated financial maneuvers are best left to giant conglomerates, which are really in the business of buying and selling companies all the time and which frequently float all kinds of securities to raise the necessary capital.

The big money in the stock market is made with clean, well-run operating companies which are working hard in a well-defined business and have room to grow 10 times larger. Such companies usually (although not always) have fairly simple capital structures and only one or two big adjustments in the record which are easy to understand. Consequently, your per-share calculations can usually come right out of the published report. Any adjustments you might take time to make (e.g., to year-end shares from average shares or to fully diluted from primary) will not really make or break your analysis or be important in your final decision. This is heresy to a professional analyst, but our job is to make money by investing in uncommon stocks rather than by selling long research reports on well-known companies. We've been in both businesses, and there is a world of difference.

RANGE ESTIMATES OF EPS

Up to now all of our estimates have been expressed as single figures. The "next-year" EPS estimate for our fictional company is $3.17 on the worksheet in Figure 6. This means that $3.17 is our central estimate and that the actual results are equally likely to be above that point or below it. We can greatly improve that single-figure earnings estimate, however, by translating it into a "range estimate," such as $2.85 to $3.50.

The concept is critical to your later price forecasts, and so we will cover it with some care.

"Range estimate" in our work is given a very specific meaning: It means you judge that there is a 90 percent probability (9 chances in 10) that the actual EPS results, when reported, will fall inside the boundaries of the range. In the example given ($2.85 to $3.50), the figures were selected so that we would be willing to bet 90 to 10 percent that the company's actual earnings, when reported, will be $2.85 or above up to $3.50. It follows that we would also take the other side of the bet, namely, that the odds are 10 to 90 percent that the actual results will fall outside the range of $2.85 to $3.50. Also, we select our range so that it is equally likely that the actual figure will fall below the lower end as it is that it will fall above the upper end. Thus the odds we would quote on earnings' being below $2.85 are the same as those for the area above $3.50. Since the probability of earnings' being anywhere outside the range is 10 percent, the probability of each alone is 5 percent. Finally, we use our original single-figure estimate ($3.17 in the EFC example) as the exact center of our range. Since it is the center of the range, the odds on the actual results' being above $3.17 are 50 percent, and the odds on the actual results' being below $3.17 are also 50 percent.

All this may sound complicated on first reading, but it is really not, once you get the idea. First, we know that it is 100 percent certain that some figure for EPS is going to be reported. What the range-estimate exercise does is simply allocate those 100 percentage points across all the possible outcomes. (We will discuss how to do this below; for now let's just be clear about the definition.)

The range estimate for EFC described above can also be shown in three other ways. First, it can be expressed in the form of a table, as shown below.

Range Estimate	Probability or Odds
Above $3.50	5%
$2.85–$3.50	90% (center point is $3.17)
Below $2.85	5%
	100%

The same information can be shown in a bar chart (Figure 7) in which each square represents 1 percentage point of probability.

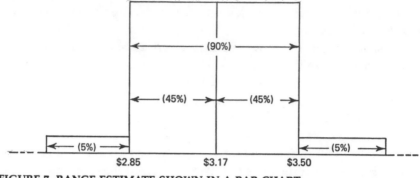

FIGURE 7. RANGE ESTIMATE SHOWN IN A BAR CHART.

Finally, the range estimate can be shown in a line diagram (Figure 8) in which the entire line represents 100 percentage points of probability.

How do you know what range is needed to produce "fair odds" of 90 percent? Why not a tighter range of $3.15 to $3.20 or a wider range of $1 to $4.35? First, you must know enough about the company to be able to form a knowledgeable opinion. Then you get to a range by a process of successive testing. The cardinal rule of range estimating is that you produce a fair bet in your own best judgment. This means that you must be willing to take either side of the bet implied by your range.

In the example of EFC, on the basis of everything we know about the company, we have said that there is a 90 percent chance that EPS will be reported between $2.85 and $3.50. This means we would be equally willing to bet $90 to $10 (90 to 10 percent) that actual EPS will be inside the range, or $10 to $90 (10 to 90 percent) that actual EPS will fall outside the range. If we had set the range closer together (say, $3.15 to $3.20), we wouldn't be willing to take the "inside" bet. If we had set the range very wide apart (say, $1 to $4.35), we wouldn't take the "outside" bet. You keep moving the range around in this successive testing fashion until you find the figures which seem to be a fair bet either way.

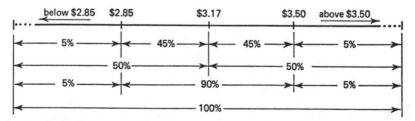

FIGURE 8. RANGE ESTIMATE SHOWN IN A LINE DIAGRAM.

The discipline is simple, and yet it can't be defeated. You set the range, and someone else gets to pick which side of the bet to take. Of course, in your work you are just trying to keep yourself honest. If you take it seriously and practice, though, you will make forecasts which are far more useful than conventional single-figure estimates.

USING SCENARIOS TO MAKE RANGE ESTIMATES

There is an easy mental exercise which we have used to help us decide just where to place the two ends of our range estimate of EPS. You may find it useful also.

You are probably familiar with the term "scenario." It is used in connection with moviemaking, politics, and economic forecasting. We use "scenario" to mean a careful educated guess about a company's future earnings under certain specified conditions. For example, we use three different "specified conditions":

1. Worst reasonable scenario. You are willing to bet that there is only about a 5 percent chance (1 in 20) that events will be worse than this description.

2. Most likely scenario. This careful educated guess about the company's future condition represents the center of the range of possible outcomes.

3. Best reasonable scenario. You think there is only a small chance (again, 5 percent, or 1 in 20) that events will be any better than this situation.

These scenarios can be very brief, as in the examples below, and in any case they should not take more than one page. (See the discussion of Winston Churchill's rule in Chapter 5.) The EPS range estimate for EFC was developed from judgments which can be summarized in these three scenarios for one year ahead.

1. WORST REASONABLE SCENARIO

Economic conditions worsen, with corporate profits generally off 10 to 15 percent and with unemployment up 1 full percentage point; EFC's industry trade association sees sales up 10 percent anyway, but it is optimistic, and a better guess is 0 to 5 percent industrywide; EFC has just completed an expensive R&D program and has several highly competitive new products coming out which will help it do slightly better than the industry, with sales up about 7 percent; EFC's expenses are under good control, and with tough times the company cuts or defers noncritical programs to help keep earnings just above the current year. Overall judgment under these conditions for next year is $2.85.

2. MOST LIKELY SCENARIO

This is our central estimate, as summarized in Figure 6. The EPS estimate is $3.17.

3. BEST REASONABLE SCENARIO

Economic conditions improve as inflation moderates temporarily and as corporate profits rise 15 to 20 percent; industry conditions permit EFC's new products to do better than expected; the ratio of selling and administrative expense to sales falls more than budgeted, while better overall sales volume helps keep the ratio of cost of goods sold to sales down slightly instead of up; some of the potential surge in earnings is disguised by accelerating purchases of expendable supplies and raising reserves for bad debt to help manage earnings. Thus earnings under these very good conditions are kept to $3.50.

In summary, our forecast for EFC's EPS is shown in Figure 9.

Worst reasonable scenario:　$2.85
Most likely scenario:　$3.17 (central estimate)
Best reasonable scenario:　$3.50
Range estimate:　$2.85–$3.50

FIGURE 9. EPS FORECAST FOR EFC.

In Chapter 19 we will look at some key indicators of a company's quality. In Chapter 20 we develop some specific bench marks for appraising the stock's price/earnings (P/E) ratio. The EPS forecast just developed is then combined with the P/E ratio to predict future stock prices (Chapter 21).

KEY INDICATORS OF COMPANY QUALITY

The subject of key quantitative indicators is endless, and for this reason you must settle on a few that help you keep track of the major issues for each individual company. Start with the issue, not the indicator. Once you know what you want to keep an eye on, it is far easier to settle on a few regular ratios or pieces of data to help you. You can be sure that a business researcher who claims to have dozens of key indicators and to be following everything that moves doesn't have any perspective on a company.

To get you started, we will look at three of the most important measures: return on equity (ROE), debt and its relationship to equity, and the current ratio. You may want to add others. The following are some examples of additional indicators to consider:

1. Sales per employee, which is a measure of efficiency and of labor intensity.

2. Cash flow, which is aftertax earnings plus depreciation; this indicates the cash available from operations.

3. Inventory turnover, which is cost of goods divided by inventory; this is an important test of inventory control.

4. Accounts receivable turnover, which is sales divided by accounts receivable; it measures credit management.

5. Capital intensity ratio, which is total assets divided by sales; this shows how critical a variable capital is to the success of the company.

RETURN ON EQUITY

Shareholders' equity is just the historical record of past additions to, and subtractions from, the "ownership account." These changes come mainly from annual earnings or losses. Important additions come from sale of stock, while reductions are also caused by dividend payouts and special charges. Equity is a good measure of financial strength and ability to do business. It is equivalent to an individual's net worth in that sense, although the accounting methods would differ.

Shareholders' equity per share is the "book value," and of course it has no necessary connection to stock prices in the open market. However, a book value per share which is several times higher or lower than current stock quotations is at least a warning to watch your assumptions more carefully.

ROE is the most important single indicator of a company's quality and level of achievement. It is calculated by dividing shareholders' equity into earnings after taxes. It neatly relates earnings to the historic accumulations of the ownership account. While you do not invest directly in the "equity" account, since of course you buy your shares in the open market, your return on investment in the long term is determined largely by how well the company does with its ROE.

A good rule of thumb is that an ROE of under 10 percent is anemic and that an ROE of over 20 percent is terrific. Think of it in basic terms as a return on your investment, even though you don't get that much spendable cash return in dividends or an immediate proportionate increase in stock prices to reflect the results. Would you put your money at risk for a 5 percent return? Of course not, since you can get a 5 percent cash return with no risk. Would 20 percent make you happy? If not, your greed is too great and will lead you to take reckless risks!

ROE can be used to compare companies in any industry. It is the one common denominator which cannot be excused because of special factors. A supermarket has very low profit margins (profit per dollar of sales) but has no excuse for an ROE below that of any other industry. Look at all the companies you are researching. How do they compare in ROE? Can you identify the real reasons for those differences? What changes in ROE are in the making, and why? All of your research work is in one sense aimed at an analysis of ROE, and so you should certainly keep close track of this key indicator.

DEBT AND ITS RELATIONSHIP TO EQUITY

The days are gone when absence of debt was a corporate virtue. Long-term debt is practically forced on management today because the interest payments are tax-deductible expenses and because of inflation. Under current conditions the money is nearly free, although eventually of course it must be repaid. This gives rise to the two main issues raised by this key indicator: the true cost of debt and the company's ability to repay without undue strain or interference with operations.

To illustrate the true cost of debt, let's look at the situation for a typical medium-sized company as of this writing:

Interest rate paid	12%
Effective tax deduction at 50%	(6%)
Aftertax cost of debt	6%
Inflation rate	(6%)
True economic cost of debt	0%

Isn't that remarkable? The true economic cost of debt is zero! How can this be? The explanation lies in the underlying assumptions of this calculation. The interest rate assumes that a bank or other lender will actually put money out for five years or longer at 12 percent. As of now, the lender is getting money in a flood, is paying 7 percent or less for it, and is very happy indeed to get 12 percent locked up from a good company.

Will the interest payments remain deductible in the future? Probably they will, and if changes do come, they will not be sudden or drastic. You can reasonably count on the government to pay half the interest cost of money, as long as the company stays profitable and has taxes to pay. That's critical: If the company slips into the red, its interest costs effectively double!

Why subtract the inflation rate? Because inflation is simply the process by which money becomes worth less in relation to goods and services. The current "depression rate" is about 6 percent, and a good bet is that inflation will continue at 4 to 8 percent per year for a long time to come. If it does, the company will pay back the debt with future dollars that are far "cheaper" than today's, i.e., with dollars that are easier to raise from business operations in the future.

This all may seem unreal to you. In economic terms it ought to be an unreal or unstable condition. However, it all rests on the willingness of ordinary savers and investors to accept 5 to 7 percent interest from banks, short-term trusts, or savings accounts; then be taxed on that meager interest; and finally watch inflation erode away the principal! Here is how the same calculation looks to the saver who provides these loan funds:

Interest received	7.0%
Tax at 40% rate	(2.8%)
Aftertax interest income	4.2%
Inflation rate	(6.0%)
True economic return	(1.8%)

Thus the true economic return to a saver is minus almost 2 percent per year! We can't pause now to dwell on this interesting bit of political economics, but the plain facts are that debt to a company is very low cost or free, and ordinary savers are actually losing money on the exercise! Eventually, if the public finally believes that inflation will continue at 4 to 8 percent per year, they may demand higher rates and some tax relief. Meanwhile, as a private investor you should make two observations: (1) Savings accounts are a very bad long-term investment, and (2) a reasonable load of debt on a company is a positive, not a negative.

What is a reasonable level of debt? Look at debt as a percentage of shareholders' equity. If it is much more than 100 percent (i.e., equal to, or greater than, equity), there may begin to be some question about the company's ultimate ability to repay it. Moreover, it may mean that future long-term financing will have to come from sale of stock instead, which may put pressure on the stock price for a while. If you are concerned about debt, look at the company's earnings before interest and taxes (EBIT) and compare that with annual debt service (interest and principal payments, shown in the footnotes in the annual report). If EBIT is two or more times greater than debt service and you can expect this situation to continue, the debt level is still comfortable.

THE CURRENT RATIO

The current ratio is current assets divided by current liabilities. It is good indication of a company's ability to pay its bills without any problems. Standards have changed as to what constitutes a proper current ratio. Without going into the whole debate, make up your mind on the basis of whether there is an extreme in either direction. If not, just watch the trend for tendencies toward extremes.

What is too low? A current ratio is too low when the company is having to borrow money at very high interest rates (twice prime rate or more) to pay its bills. This may begin at a current ratio of 1.2 or lower; however, the best indicator is not the ratio itself but the presence of high-cost short-term borrowings. These should be disclosed in the notes to the financial statements in the annual report. If they are not, just ask your financial contact what the company is paying for money these days. (There is no good reason not to tell you this.)

Why should you care? Not because the company is spending money on interest—it should be earning more than the cost of that money from sales which those borrowings make possible. The real issue is that long-term financing, or "permanent capital," is then becoming necessary. If the company realizes the need and if it has a realistic plan to raise more permanent capital, a low ratio is not worrisome. Otherwise, it is a major obstacle to growth.

Can a current ratio be too high? While it is uncommon, you may find a company with a current ratio of 3.0 or higher. This may indicate nothing at all, but here are three reasons why an excessively high ratio may be a sign of problems:

1. Money may be tied up in unsalable inventory or poorly managed receivables, causing a rise in current assets with no real rise in liquidity.

2. Cash sitting around in the bank year after year is a sure sign that management has no better ideas for using it than the bank does. Some managers are just insecure and like a lot of cash around, but if they can't use it, they should pay it out to the stockholders and let them reinvest it.

3. Business may be slow. If it is a seasonal slack, there is no problem. However, keep in mind that as business slows down, cash builds up from collected receivables and sales from inventory.

Unlike an individual, a company with a rising cash balance is more likely to be having problems than to be prospering.

We want to see evidence of a healthy pumping of funds through the business—from cash to inventory to sales and receivables and back to cash—not a stagnant hoarding of cash, decaying inventory, and delinquent receivables from inactive past customers. The current ratio will help you watch that process.

BENCH MARKS FOR
APPRAISING
A STOCK

By far the most common way of looking at the price of a stock is to divide its price by its EPS to produce a price/earnings (P/E) ratio. If a stock is selling at $30 per share and the company is estimated to earn $1.50 per share in the current year, then the stock is selling at a ratio of 20 times current earnings. This is expressed as "20X." There is nothing particularly revealing in this calculation by itself, but it has come to be a very convenient shorthand for comparing the prices at which stocks sell.

A P/E analysis is more art than science. There is no accepted or well-proved formula for relating the P/E ratio of a company to anything else. There are factors and there are influences, and we will discuss them below. But there doesn't seem to be any simple mathematical system which pulls it all together. You will see such systems often enough, but they just don't work. Formula price forecasting systems cannot include enough of what is really going on in the world, and they cannot handle complex shifts and changes. The systems are sometimes very elegant and reassuring, but they should be taken only as a point of departure in analysis and not as a shortcut to stock price forecasting.

COMPARISON SHOPPING FOR P/E RATIOS

The best way to keep informed about prevailing market conditions is to maintain current P/E ratios for "bench-mark companies." These are companies which are especially illustrative or typical of one segment of the stock market. Table 3 is only a brief sample and is not intended to provide a complete profile of all kinds of stocks. You should add

TABLE 3.   P/E RATIOS FOR 25 BENCH-MARK COMPANIES

Market: 114 (S&P 400)
Market EPS $10.30 (trailing 4 quarters)
Market P/E Ratio 11X   (114 ÷ 10.30)

Company	Concept or Market Segment	Recent Price	EPS	P/E Ratio	Relative P/E Ratio*
IBM	Growth	$271	$15.41	17.6X	1.6X
Merck	Growth	64	3.33	19.2X	1.7X
Xerox	Growth	59	4.30	13.7X	1.2X
Am. Home Products	Growth	29	1.71	17.0X	1.5X
Eastman Kodak	Growth	85	3.92	22.0X	1.8X
General Motors	Cyclical	71	9.45	7.5X	0.7X
General Electric	Cyclical	51	3.91	13.0X	1.2X
Du Pont	Cyclical	123	10.30	12.0X	1.1X
U.S. Steel	Cyclical	48	5.43	8.8X	0.8X
Caterpillar	Cyclical	57	4.78	11.9X	1.1X
Kresge	Consumer	42	2.08	20.2X	1.8X
Sears, Roebuck	Consumer	70	3.92	17.9X	1.6X
Avon Products	Consumer	47	2.74	17.1X	1.6X
Procter & Gamble	Consumer	94	5.21	18.0X	1.6X
Coca-Cola	Consumer	79	4.57	17.3X	1.6X
Exxon	Resources	51	5.81	8.8X	0.8X
Std. Oil (Ind.)	Resources	54	6.15	8.8X	0.8X
Weyerhauser	Resources	47	1.98	23.7X	2.2X
Texaco	Resources	26	3.17	8.2X	0.8X
Citicorp	Financial	29	3.00	9.7X	0.9X
Morgan (J.P.)	Financial	53	4.79	11.1X	1.0X
AT&T	Regulated	62	5.85	10.6X	1.0X
Gen. Telephone	Regulated	30	3.15	9.5X	0.9X
Pacific Telephone	Regulated	18	2.03	8.9X	0.8X
Tenneco	Regulated	34	4.26	8.0X	0.7X

* The stock P/E divided by the market P/E. A useful comparison scale.

stocks to this list to focus on areas of your special interest. In particular, you should add companies from specific industries which are directly related to your current research work. The information necessary to make up the table of bench-mark companies is all in the stock price pages of *The Wall Street Journal*. A more convenient source is Standard & Poor's *Stock Guide*, which gives all the EPS data in one place.

The 25 companies listed in Table 3 account for about one-third of the total value of all stocks traded on the New York Stock Exchange. Yet there are about 1,600 other listed companies, and there are many thousands more that are not on the Big Board. This fact, incidentally, points up dramatically the concentration of interest and power in a few huge companies and the open field of opportunity in the thousands of companies below this size.

The bench-mark list, expanded to include perhaps another 5 to 15 stocks which you select, will give you an excellent starting point for forecasting P/E ratios. Select established companies in areas comparable to the area of the stock you are working on. Then raise or lower the P/E ratio you assign to your company on the basis of these principal factors (we will discuss them below):

1. EPS growth rate

2. Predictability or quality of earnings

3. Image changes

4. Supply and demand

Keep working back and forth with your estimated P/E ratio until you have justified it from several angles. There really is not much theory to guide you. The best way to develop your ability to forecast P/E ratios is to practice. At the end of this chapter we illustrate the selection of a P/E range estimate for our fictional company, EFC. First, however, let's discuss the four principal factors you should consider in forecasting a P/E ratio.

EPS GROWTH RATE

The long-term rate of growth of EPS seems to have the strongest bearing on the P/E ratio. While even this correlation is imprecise and debatable, it is fairly easy to demonstrate how the relationship works. Under current conditions of interest rates and inflation, there seems to be a sort of "basic" P/E ratio of around 5 to 7 times earnings which applies to a company that can pay out in dividends about half of its earnings and continue to grow at about 5 to 7 percent per year. This growth rate will just about keep earnings even with inflation, and so the real growth rate is zero. Over the long term this will produce a total return of 12 to 15 percent if the "price" stays at 5 to 7 times earnings. Of course, if there is any question about the company's ability to grow at least at this small rate or if the suspicion arises that it may be stagnant and actually declining in earnings, the P/E ratio can dwindle down to as low as 2 to 4 times earnings and still be fairly valued.

There is good economic sense behind the higher (15X and up) multiples of earnings as well. One way of understanding this is to look at your potential return on investment if the company continues to grow at its predicted rate for 15 years, which is about as far as anyone can hope to see ahead. We will assume that at the end of 15 years the stock gradually becomes "ordinary" because the company's growth rate has dropped to 5 percent and the P/E ratio has dropped to 6 times earnings.

Using this oversimplified model of a growth stock investment (with no current dividends), we can then produce Table 4, which shows current P/E ratios each of which would still produce a 10 percent return despite the absence of dividends over the 15-year period of investment.

Naturally our model is unrealistically simple. But it is by this economic logic that high P/E ratios can come to be accepted for certain companies' stock. Therefore, it is not always true that a high P/E ratio stock is just a fad. Some investors prefer to obtain their long-term rate of return by the use of high P/E ratio stocks, with the thought that the

TABLE 4.   CURRENT P/E RATIOS THAT WOULD PRODUCE A
10 PERCENT RETURN EVEN WITHOUT DIVIDENDS OVER 15 YEARS

EPS Growth Rate	EPS in First Year	EPS in Fifteenth Year	Price of Stock in Fifteenth Year (at 6X EPS)	Current Price Required to Show 10% Gain in Price per Year	Current P/E Ratio Required
0%	1.00	1.00	6	1½	1½X
5%	1.00	2.07	12⅜	3	3X
10%	1.00	4.18	25⅛	6	6X
15%	1.00	8.12	48¾	11⅝	12X
20%	1.00	15.40	92⅜	22⅛	22X

future rate of growth is fairly reliable and that the total rate of return, while fairly modest, is at least very likely to be obtained. This is a variation of the "put-'em-away-forever" school of thought, and while there are better ways to invest, there are a lot worse ways as well!

We cannot give you a table showing growth rates and related P/E ratios which you can just use blindly. The relationship of earnings growth to P/E ratio is always shifting, and there is endless debate about it. The most important lesson for you to learn is that if you pay a lot more than a "market" P/E ratio (7 to 12X) for a stock, be very sure the growth rate is pretty high. Even then, don't rely for your profit on selling a stock at an unrealistic P/E ratio. Keep your feet on the ground (which for us is a P/E of under 15X) and don't pay up too much for an uncertain future. If a stock already sells at 20 or 30 times earnings, you usually (but not always) ought to accept the fact that everyone has already discovered its potential and that its price has been bid up to reflect this good outlook.

PREDICTABILITY OR QUALITY OF EARNINGS

A single-figure or single-point estimate (such as 12 percent) of the long-term earnings growth rate is still not enough to give us a clear handle on future P/E multiples. This becomes very obvious when we see two companies which have the same estimated future growth rate and the same present EPS, but which sell at dramatically different prices. The difference between them is what is commonly called "quality of earnings."

For example, in the early stages of an economic expansion an airline company could increase its EPS over the subsequent five years at a 15 percent compound annual rate. At the same time, a well-established growth stock might have the same prospect of around 15 percent growth per year. If both companies are presently earning $2 per share and if the long-term growth rate is the only factor in determining the P/E ratio, the two stocks should sell at the same price. In fact, the airline's stock might sell for $15 to $25 per share (7 to 12 times current earnings), while the established growth stock could easily be selling at $25 to $40 per share (12 to 20 times current earnings). The difference in predictability or quality of earnings encompasses a great deal, including fluctuation of results from year to year, accounting practices, and breakthrough potential.

Fluctuation of results from year to year around the long-term growth trend occurs even in the best and most established growth stocks. For example, a company might achieve 15 percent per year compound growth in earnings in an orderly pattern such as +17 percent, +14 percent, +16 percent, +12 percent, +16 percent. A more erratic record, still averaging the same 15 percent per year, might be a pattern such as +50 percent, −20 percent, +8 percent, +75 percent, −12 percent. While each company has the same 15 percent long-term compound annual rate of growth, the market is willing to pay a higher P/E ratio for a tight or predictable pattern, as opposed to extreme fluctuations. In the case of two otherwise equivalent growth situations, the one that shows predictability, or an orderly progression of earnings growth, can gain many P/E ratio points.

"Quality of earnings" is a term which usually connotes such factors as exposure to write-offs, capitalization of expenses, and other accounting-oriented concerns. For example, suppose we had two airlines which were identical in terms of estimated future growth, current EPS, and inherent predictability or fluctuation around the long-term trend line. There would still be plenty of room for differences in current stock price based on their "quality" factors. In this case specifically, the quality issue would focus on the airline's depreciation schedule for aircraft and ground equipment. The airline which was writing its equipment off fastest would be said to have a higher quality of earnings and would sell at a higher multiple of those more conservatively stated earnings. Of course, there are overly bullish times in the stock market when it seems that no one cares about earnings quality and accounting practices. However, over two to five years, which will normally encompass a complete market cycle, you can be pretty certain that these particular pigeons will come home to roost.

There is one apparent contradiction to the idea that higher predictability produces higher P/E ratios, and that is the company's breakthrough potential. Contrary to popular belief, investors do like surprises and are willing to pay for the chance to experience them—providing, of course, that they are in the form of breakthrough potential rather than disaster potential. This is especially true for those companies in which technology or exploration appears to be an important potential future source of sharply higher earnings.

It is surprising what high P/E ratios can be obtained by very mundane companies in frothy and exuberant markets. This is particularly true of electronic component manufacturers; the myth persists that such companies are capable of exciting fundamental breakthroughs in technology which will create entire new markets overnight. Their technology is very complex and moves in cycles of five years or less, and this seems to lend credence to the popular belief. In reality, electronic component manufacturers in most cases are in murderously competitive pricing situations. In addition, the apparently tremendous level of research spending is really just a continuing engineering cost of goods sold, not importantly different from the huge product engineering expense which goes into the annual model changes of automobile designs in Detroit. Certainly very few people believe that General Motors' expenditures on product design will produce any great revolutionary breakthroughs, and yet many are willing to ascribe breakthrough potential to economically similar cost being incurred by Fairchild Camera or Texas Instruments.

A legitimate example of breakthrough potential was provided by the unsuccessful joint venture between Syntex Corporation and Varian Associates called "SynVar." This jointly owned company was originally founded to do very fundamental research into the electrical properties of hydrocarbon materials. Its goal was the remote but exciting possibility that long-chain organic molecules could be created which would become superconductors of electricity at room temperature. If this program had been successful, it might have been possible to produce electric generators which could have powered an entire city and yet fit inside an ordinary room! It would have been possible to transmit power over extremely long distances with almost no loss of energy enroute. This would have opened up an industry fully comparable with the computer industry of the 1960s. There is really no way of telling where all the trails would have led. However, as we said, it didn't work.

A company with this sort of breakthrough potential ticking away in the background is very apt to have a few extra P/E ratio points tacked on, despite the extremely long odds involved. Similarly, if a company such as SynVar was set out on its own and its stock was sold separately in the public marketplace, it would of course have no earnings at the present time but would still have a very significant market price.

This game does not escape the attention of stockbrokerage firms, of course. In every period of feverish bull market activity one of the sure signs of an impending stock market top is the sudden mushrooming of new stock offerings in pure breakthrough-potential companies of this type.

IMAGE CHANGES

The subtle psychology behind company images and changes in image is another major determinant of the stock's P/E ratio. While changes are extremely difficult to predict, they are easy to analyze in hindsight. For example, very few people accurately foresaw that the trailer business would branch into the two growth areas of recreational vehicles and mobile homes, both of which have sold at multiples achieved only by companies like IBM. Even IBM itself underwent an image change to some extent during the great bear markets of 1969–1970 and 1973–1974, when computers were seen anew as just like any other capital goods. Order rates for computers fell off sharply, and many experts began to view the computer industry as a cyclical growth industry rather than a pure growth industry. While a lot of this is idle semantics, there was enough of a change of image to produce a sharp drop in P/E ratios.

You should be alert to the potential impact of image changes on P/E ratios. If a company making instruments for testing blood can suddenly blossom as a "medical electronics" company, the payoffs can be enormous. Even your local sewer digger or garbage collector can become a "pollution control" stock, and with no change in earnings the stock can double or triple. The trick, of course, is to get this potential change in image and in P/E ratio without paying up for it and then later to have enough sense to sell out if a "mania" happens to hit your stock.

SUPPLY AND DEMAND

We are now going to take a look at the supply-and-demand factors affecting P/E ratios and stock prices. The discussion contains more than you will use in practice. Select the ideas which will help you in any particular case, and certainly don't feel that you should be covering all these points in your work on any one stock.

The first step is to assess the actual current distribution of holdings in the stock, being as specific as possible. Management's holdings and transactions are a subject of public record and are available through the company's regular filings with the SEC (see Chapter 10) and also in a government publication called *Official Summary of Security Transactions and Holdings*. Usually the treasurer of the company will be willing to give you a rough outline also, and if the company has made an application to an exchange for listing, it might be willing to give you a copy of the application. Otherwise just write to the exchange for it. All these data should give you the first draft for a table of stock distribution similar to Table 5.

The next avenue of investigation involves what is commonly called "sponsorship." This term refers to the attitude of outsiders who have looked at the company for one reason or another and are in a position to influence public opinion concerning the stock. The two principal sources of sponsorship are brokerage houses and institutional holders such as mutual funds, banks, pension funds, and insurance companies.

The company's management people are usually willing to tell you which brokerage houses have been out to see them in the last year or so, and they will give you some indication of the depth of the work done by the analysts who made the visits. If the brokerage house is large and has many local offices for individual clients, as Merrill Lynch and Paine Webber do, for example, there should be little difficulty in obtaining a copy of its report through its local office.

Institutional reports (for banks, funds, etc.) are rarely written on smaller companies. If one is in circulation, you may be able to get it directly from the analyst who wrote it. It is in such analysts' own interest to deal with you if you convince them that you are knowledgeable about a company. It is in your interest, in turn, to have some idea of their attitudes toward a firm and of the depth of their knowledge and work on a company. Institutional analysts, in brokerage houses or banks or mutual funds, may be doing high-quality work; if so, they will be worth collaborating with.

You don't need to have any experience in dealing with brokerage houses in order to make a rough judgment as to the number of shares a particular house would be able to get its customers to buy. A regional

TABLE 5. STOCK DISTRIBUTION

Group	Shares Owned	Percent of Total	Notes on Changes
Management	350,000	35	Ex-treasurer only seller
Other insiders	50,000	5	Up 10,000 shares this year
Large institutions (banks, funds, insurance companies)	150,000	15	Two new owners who can own more
General public	450,000	45	Slow, steady decrease
Total outstanding	1,000,000	100	

brokerage house might do only 5,000 or 10,000 shares, while a major wire house could easily do several hundred thousand shares on a single recommendation. A very conservative insurance company or bank trust department or a small mutual fund might buy or sell 10,000 to 50,000 shares, while a major bank or growth fund could easily own up to 5 percent of a company's total stock.

You can get a good approximation of the buying power of a sponsor in another way. As to brokerage houses, the number of registered representatives (also known as "salesmen" or "account executives") is a good indicator of the amount of stock they can put away. A good rule of thumb is 100 shares per salesman, recognizing that there is a tremendous variability around this figure. Consequently, a small regional house with 50 salesmen might do only 5,000 shares, while Paine Webber, with its 2,000 salesmen, could do a quarter of a million shares in the same stock with the same set of facts and the same level of promotion. In assessing the buying power of institutions in your stock, look in the *Vickers Guide* (available in many libraries or at a well-equipped brokerage office). This will give you some idea of an institution's present portfolio and the scale of buying it normally does in any one stock.

Another important source of potential buying power is a company-controlled purchase plan, such as an employee stock purchase plan or a pension fund which purchases the company's securities. Occasionally, the company may have a policy of buying its own stock for its treasury. This does not create a floor under the stock's price, but it does give some indication of potential support and is widely regarded on Wall Street as a strong sign of confidence by management itself.

One of the major reasons for a particular pattern of ownership in a company's stock is often the company's own attitude. Who does the company want to own its stock? Some firms have one or more full-time people who do nothing but go around and talk to large institutional buyers and brokerage firms in the hope of generating substantial interest among these sources. Other firms are very reluctant even to grant interviews to potential large buyers, particularly those from the very aggressive growth funds. It is their view that these buyers are liable to be trading in and out on flimsy information and excuses and will destabilize the stock and cause more problems than their presence would be worth. Speculators might create volatility, which could even discourage more conservative investors. In addition, large blocks of stock can sharply accelerate a downward move in the price of a security, and the extreme depression of a stock under those circumstances can lead to a false impression of the severity of any problems. Such impressions can linger for years and interfere with financing or acquisition plans and with joint ventures, and they can even have an impact on the company's day-to-day operating business if customers are scared away.

Your position as an independent private investor is very different. There is a line of argument which you can use when necessary in introducing yourself to corporate management: Investors who are well enough informed about the company will act as a stabilizing influence on the price of the stock, rather than the opposite. They are less likely to be disturbed or surprised by events than uninformed speculators. As the company becomes extremely overvalued, they are likely to start selling carefully into the market, which will prevent extreme overvaluations, at least temporarily. On the other hand, if they do not already have a full position and the stock falls off sharply for the wrong reasons, they will step in and gradually accumulate the stock on the way down. This will tend to cushion the severe downside gyration. This is a good argument to bring up with management people if they seem reluctant to help you get to know their company.

On the supply or selling side of the supply-and-demand equation, look first at the insiders. Their past transactions are a good indication of their future leanings. A very large stock option program which is close to maturity may cause management to sell existing holdings to provide the funds for reinvestment in lower-cost optioned stock.

Of far more importance is the possibility of an outright sale of stock by major holders. If there is an individual or family which controls a substantial block of the stock, say, 10 percent or more, and the stock has a very low cost and has been in their hands for some time, you should inquire about the chance of a major selling program over the next couple of years.

This is not a negative or a positive in and of itself, however. If the company is doing well, an increase in the supply of stock can actually improve the liquidity and be more than compensated for by an increase in investor interest. This improved attention can arise either during the promotion preceding the stock offering itself or as the trading volume increases after the sale is completed.

However, if the fundamentals are at all shaky, an ill-timed major sale by insiders can completely collapse the stock, leaving you wondering how anyone could be so foolish as to put that kind of pressure on the company. This does happen with distressing frequency, and it is something you should be watching out for.

Some companies have developed "enemies" who can create a steady supply of selling by putting chronic pressure on the stock for several years. Foremost on this list would be security analysts for brokerage firms and newspaper columnists who successfully predicted the stock's fall in the past. The cynical view is that such analysts or writers have nothing to lose by continuing to be negative on the company. More often, however, they really are sincere in their belief. The result of their "self-advertising of past success," however, is that there develops a continuing negative drumbeat which only time and sharply improved fundamentals will ever overcome. This "chronic bear" problem can go beyond being simply a short-term market opportunity created by the chronic bear's faulty analysis. We like stocks to become cheap at times as well as anyone, but not when that "opportunity" persists over the period of a couple of years, leaving us with dormant capital in the meantime!

There is a way out of this situation. Once you are convinced of the value of the company (and have taken a position for yourself, or course), it may be worthwhile to spend some time trying to reeducate the chronic bear. If you are right, you will frequently be successful in moving this writer or analyst into a neutral position. If there is something wrong with your analysis, perhaps this person can help you see your mistake. Either way, you come out ahead.

THE P/E RANGE ESTIMATE

Now let's take all the preceding elements and put them together into the final P/E appraisal of a stock. Once again we will use the fictional Elliptical Feebleblitzer Corporation as an illustration. Our objective is to decide on a P/E range estimate. Just as we did in coming up with a range estimate of EPS, we will first work on a single central figure for the P/E and then translate that into a range with the help of three scenarios.

This is the procedure to follow:

1. If you have not already done so, make a current table of benchmark companies, as discussed at the beginning of this chapter.

2. Set up a P/E worksheet (see Figure 10) and start with the stock's current P/E ratio. Use the latest available stock price and the sum of the company's last four quarters' EPS.

3. Review each of the four principal factors affecting a P/E ratio and make any adjustments that seem warranted. Refer to your bench-mark list for guidance on how much to raise or lower the P/E. Adjusting and appraising P/Es is an art, so don't expect to be very precise. This whole process is aimed at making explicit your reasons for any assumption that the future P/E is likely to be different from the present P/E.

4. If you find it helpful, also look at the relative P/E (stock P/E divided by the market P/E; for market average we use the S&P 400 industrial average). Since the standards for P/E ratios rise and fall with the market, the relative P/E will be somewhat more stable.

Now let's go through the P/E analysis for EFC. To start, we review the bench-mark companies. See the beginning of this chapter for the basic 25 stocks; to these we add five others, shown in Table 6.

TABLE 6.   P/E RATIOS FOR FIVE ADDITIONAL BENCH-MARK COMPANIES

Company	Concept or Market Segment	P/E Ratio	Relative P/E Ratio
Octopus, Inc.	Largest competitor of EFC	8X	0.7X
PDQ Corp.	Only other public competitor	11X	1.0X
Silicon Gulch Co.	Company of same size in similar industry	12X	1.1X
Old Blue, Inc.	Major customer for EFC; also a well-recognized stock	17X	1.5X
Datacrunch Corp.	Already recognized uncommon stock of company with features similar to EFC's	19X	1.7X

These five bench-mark companies plus the 25 others will give us some guidance as we go through the P/E worksheet, shown in Figure 10. We start by calculating EFC's current P/E ratio. Then we look at each of the four principal factors and make any adjustments to reflect estimated future changes in EFC's P/E. In this analysis, we are focusing on the P/E one year ahead.

The remaining job is to translate this central estimate of an 11X P/E ratio into a range estimate. (Please review Chapter 18 if you are not familiar with the very specific meaning of this term.) We are making

P/E WORKSHEET	P/E Ratio	Relative P/E Ratio
EFC's CURRENT P/E		
Recent stock price = $22½		
Last four quarters' EPS = $2.50*		
Price divided by earnings = $22½ ÷ $2.50 =	9X	0.8X

* Note that this figure is the last four reported quarters, not last year ($2.32) or the estimate for this full calendar year ($2.76).

ADJUSTMENTS TO REFLECT PROJECTED
P/E ONE YEAR AHEAD

1. EPS GROWTH RATE. We expect EFC's earnings to be above trend this year but about in line with trend next year. We would make no adjustment for change in growth rate. However, the average P/E of our five established stocks (IBM, Merck, Xerox, American Home Products, and Eastman Kodak) is 18X, or 1.6 times the market. As EFC gets better recognized, a major P/E move is warranted on the basis of its well-above-average growth rate. In the near term, though, only a small plus adjustment is likely: **+1X**   **+0.1X**

2. PREDICTABILITY OR QUALITY OF EARNINGS. While EFC's overall growth rate is a respectable 16%, there were two bad years within the pattern. This explains in part why the stock's P/E is lower than that of its competitor, PDQ Corp. (11X), which has been more predictable and steady. EFC management is now more conscious of avoiding erratic earnings performance and can improve somewhat. We would not put heavy weight on this, though, because it still will not be possible for EFC to avoid bad years completely. Some upward adjustment is also warranted because EFC's accounting is more conservative than that of most firms. Finally, EFC has one truly exciting research program going which is not yet well known, and this could add some breakthrough-potential interest or attention. Overall conclusion on predictability factors: **+2X**   **+0.2X**

3. IMAGE CHANGES. The feebleblitzer industry is not now considered an unusually exciting segment of the stock market. Thus there does not appear to be much risk of a P/E drop as a result of image changes, and some increase is possible

	P/E Ratio	Relative P/E Ratio

since the industry acts as a supplier to such high P/E giants as Old Blue, Inc. (17X). However, the industry's image is still dominated by the mediocre Octopus, Inc. (8X), which shows no signs of change. The other public company, PDQ Corp., is at only 11X. Also, companies of similar size in other industries such as Silicon Gulch Co. (12X) have not yet attained higher P/Es. Therefore, it is probably too early to project a Datacrunch Corp. P/E (19X), although eventually we expect EFC to become equally well recognized as an uncommon stock. For the next year or two, however, we conclude that no P/E movement will come from image changes.

	P/E Ratio	Relative P/E Ratio
	No change	No change

4. SUPPLY AND DEMAND. The only significant fact we have found so far is that 75,000 shares belonging to the estate of EFC's late president will probably be sold over the next 18 months. This overhanging supply of stock must be expected to act as a damper on EFC's thinly traded shares. Over the long term (beyond two years) this will not matter, but for now we conclude it will:

	−1X	−0.1X
NET ADJUSTMENT:	+2X	+0.2X

CONCLUSION: Our single-figure estimate for EFC's P/E is that it will rise 2 points from its current 9X to 11X (1X relative P/E), with potential for further gains over the longer term.

	11X	1.0X

FIGURE 10. P/E WORKSHEET FOR EFC.

the best estimate we can, of course, but once again do not expect to achieve any real precision. Just by considering these issues and dealing explicitly with them, you will have a great advantage over most other investors. The tremendous value of these range estimates of EPS and of the P/E ratio will be evident in your improved stock price predictions. (See Chapter 21.)

To make our P/E range estimate, we look at the same three scenarios we used in Chapter 18 in developing the EPS range estimate of $2.85 to $3.50. To the business conditions projected under each of those scenarios we now add our best guess about the general stock market and about the factors which might affect this particular company's P/E ratio under the best and worst conditions.

Here are the three scenarios for EFC and our final P/E range estimates.

1. WORST REASONABLE SCENARIO

Under the economic conditions which could produce earnings of only $2.85 per share, we have to expect the stock market to be down sharply. The stock averages usually drop before industrial earnings actually turn down, and so the market P/E ratio will fall also, perhaps by 20 percent to about 9X. EFC's current relative P/E of 0.8X was expected to improve to 1X (that is, equal to the market) for the reason cited in the analysis above. Under adverse circumstances, however, a smaller, thinly traded stock like EFC would go down much more than the market. This should be cushioned somewhat by the company's relatively decent year (a modest gain in EPS while profits generally are falling). Even so, we should expect some small temporary erosion of EFC's relative P/E rather than a good gain. Therefore, if the market P/E falls from 11X to 9X, we expect EFC's relative P/E to slip temporarily from 0.8X to 0.7X. As a result, EFC's P/E moves to 0.7X (relative) times 9X (market), or about 6X.

2. MOST LIKELY SCENARIO

This is the central or single-figure estimate we did in Figure 10, where our conclusion was a relative P/E of 1X times a market P/E of 11X, producing the EFC estimated P/E of 11X.

3. BEST REASONABLE SCENARIO

With unusually good economic conditions the stock market would advance strongly. Since inflation is still expected to be high over the longer term, despite the temporary easing in this scenario, stock P/E valuations would not rise. Thus the market P/E would remain about 11X, and the market gain would be fueled entirely by the unexpectedly strong earnings. In this highly favorable climate, small companies are more readily accepted, and EFC's story becomes more widely known. Consequently, the relative P/E expansion goes well beyond what we foresaw one year ahead in the most likely scenario above, as EFC moves toward its long-term potential of a top-level valuation. Conclusion: EFC's relative P/E moves to about 1.5X, which, combined with the market P/E of 11X, gives the company a P/E under this scenario of 16X.

Worst reasonable scenario: 6X
Most likely scenario: 11X
Best reasonable scenario: 16X
Range estimate: 6–16X

FIGURE 11.   EFC'S P/E RATIO.

In summary, our appraisal of EFC's P/E ratio is as shown in Figure 11.

We now have all the ingredients for a prediction of future stock prices. In Chapter 21 we put together our range estimates of EPS and of the P/E ratio. The result is a Stock Price Forecast which combines in one place all our judgments about the company in a way which makes buy and sell decisions easy and profitable.

21

HOW TO PREDICT FUTURE STOCK PRICES

THE STOCK PRICE FORECAST

We are now ready to pull together our qualitative research work and our quantitative decisions. The final result will be a powerful and practical Stock Price Forecast, including predicted high and low prices plus buy and sell points. Because of the particular way we have made our underlying estimates of EPS and the P/E ratio, the Stock Price Forecast should be far more profitable for you than any conventional methods now in use by investors.

At this point in your work you have gone through all the factors affecting a stock's future price to isolate the key determinants. You have a well-thought-out range estimate of EPS, and through a similar process you have developed a good, defensible range estimate of the stock's P/E ratio. All the previous work was aimed at refining these basic conclusions. Now the Stock Price Forecast will enable you to put all these pieces back together again to come up with a final buy or sell decision.

It is vital to emphasize one point: The creation of a Stock Price Forecast presumes that enough of the fundamental research work has been done. The price prediction loses its usefulness if the required homework and fieldwork have not actually gone into it. The mechanics of predicting future stock prices are fairly simple, as you will see. Anyone could do it after a five-minute review of the company's annual report or at the end of a month-long study. An outside observer would have no way of knowing the difference. The difference would show up only over a period of time in the profit performance of the investments themselves.

With the right preparation, the Stock Price Forecast becomes a great discipline in day-to-day stock decisions. It is a handy condensation of all the pros and cons, all the technical judgments, and all the hunches and subtle intuitions. Anything you might use to make investment judgments is distilled in the ultimate form: a prediction of future price. It is no better than its inputs, of course, but it is far more helpful than a disorganized folder of unreconciled reports and notes. It is a reliable compass of self-discipline in a sometimes very stormy stock market.

THE FIRST TWO PRICE POINTS: HIGH AND LOW

The range estimates of EPS and the P/E ratio prepared earlier will be turned into solid, well-founded estimates of the stock's high and low prices one year ahead. Specific buy and sell prices which are wholly consistent with all the underlying investigations and analysis will then be determined.

The price of a stock simply recombines EPS and the P/E ratio, as shown in Figure 12. The high and low prices are put back together on the basis of the range estimates of EPS and the P/E ratio, each of which was derived from the three scenarios: the worst reasonable, the most likely, and the best reasonable. EPS and the P/E ratio in each scenario are multiplied together to produce the price estimated one year ahead under that set of circumstances. The predicted low is the price which would occur under your worst reasonable scenario. The central estimate, or "50/50 bet" price, one year ahead is based on your most likely scenario. The high price foreseen if everything goes unusually well is calculated from your best reasonable scenario.

$$\text{Price} = (\text{EPS})\left(\frac{\text{price}}{\text{earnings}}\right)$$

FIGURE 12. PRICE OF A STOCK.

TABLE 7.   RANGE ESTIMATES AND PRICE FORECASTS FOR EFC

Scenario	EPS	P/E Ratio	Price
Worst reasonable (low)	$2.85	6X	$17
Most likely	$3.17	11X	$35
Best reasonable (high)	$3.50	16X	$56
Full range estimate	$2.85–$3.50	6–16X	$17–$56

To illustrate this, we return to our fictional EFC. The range estimates and the resulting price forecasts are shown in Table 7.

Thus we have a full range estimate of the stock's price one year ahead: $17 to $56. It is made up of estimates which themselves have a very specific meaning, and that meaning is therefore carried into the price range estimate also, as shown in Figure 13.

This price range estimate can be displayed in a bar chart also. (See Figure 14.) The information is exactly the same; the chart is just an additional method of visualizing the concept. The bar chart was used also in Chapter 18 to display an EPS range estimate.

Note that the range estimate does not mean that we expect the stock to be everywhere within its boundaries of $17 to $56. Rather, we expect (that is, we are 90 percent sure) that the price in one year will be somewhere within this range. While we still recognize a small chance (10 percent, or 1 in 10) that it might end up outside our high and low limits, we don't know very well what the future will be like, and so we have

Price Point	Meaning
$17 (low)	We judge that there is only a 5% chance (1 in 20) that conditions will get so bad that the price will go below this point.
$35 (most likely)	This is the central or single-figure estimate—the point at which the odds are 50/50 that the stock will be higher or lower one year ahead.
$56 (high)	Only under very favorable conditions could the stock reach this point, and the odds are just 5% (1 in 20) that it will be above this price in one year.
$17–$56 (range estimate)	We are 90% sure (would bet 9 in 10) that the stock will be somewhere in this range one year from now. Also, we are 10% sure (would bet 1 in 10) that the price in one year will be outside this range.

FIGURE 13. PRICE RANGE ESTIMATE.

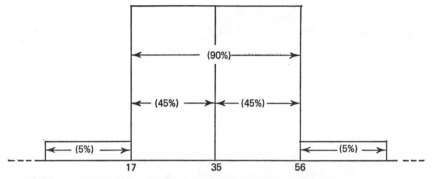

FIGURE 14. PRICE RANGE ESTIMATE SHOWN IN A BAR CHART.

projected the company's situation under both reasonable extremes as well as under the conditions which seem most likely.

You may be concerned that we are apparently trying to be too precise about something we all know is hard to forecast. Naturally we do not intend to imply that there is great precision in these predictions. The whole process is very uncertain. However, this method of predicting future stock prices forces you to place your bets somewhere. While the process is subjective, the estimates have the critical advantage of being completely explicit. All significant possibilities are assigned definite odds which reflect the best judgment possible under the prevailing conditions.

Less than this no wise investor will possess before risking hard-earned savings. More than this no mortal can foresee.

THE THIRD PRICE POINT: WHEN TO SELL

Our next step is to determine the highest price at which we would continue to hold the stock: our sell point. That decision is now very easy: Sell when the risks begin to equal or outweigh the rewards. That is, sell at the price at which the odds on higher prices one year away are equal to the odds on lower prices. From the price analysis already done, you can readily determine that the sell point is the same as the "most likely" price. In short, it is the 50/50 point within the range estimate. In the case of EFC the sell point is 35, since at that price the probabilities of gain and loss are both 50 percent. If you hold the stock in hopes that it will rise beyond that price, the risks begin to outweigh the rewards.

Does that mean we give up the tantalizing and still real chance that the stock might go on up to 40 or even 50? Yes, it most certainly does! Suppose you reach just a little higher, say, for a price of 40. What will happen? Your own best judgment, as we can see from the price forecast, is that the probability of EFC's hitting 40 or better is less than 50 percent, which means the odds are worse than could be obtained by just flipping coins. You might get lucky on this stock and squeak out a sell price of 40 or even higher. However, if you consistently keep your bet going after the odds pass 50/50, you will become a loser. Not knowing when to sell (or ignoring sell points) is a major cause of failure for investors. You must keep faith with your own best judgment or face the consequences of being in open ocean without a compass.

What if conditions have changed? What if the odds on various future events have really shifted? Then you should make up new range estimates for EPS, the P/E ratio, and the price of the stock. But be very careful that your judgment has changed for good reasons, and not just because the market is surging ahead and your stock "looks stronger." Only you can judge the extent to which you are being pulled along by the market. If things really are looking better, then go ahead and revise your estimates. If they are not, then recognize that the market is presenting you with a chance to sell while others are in the mood to buy.

Your price forecast will shift a little all the time, of course, as new information comes in. Also, every few months it will need revision anyway just because of the passage of time. Remember, the forecast is your estimate of prices one year ahead and is always supposed to be current or "good until canceled." So if you last made an estimate for the following January and it is now April, your chart is still supposed to be good for one full year ahead (i.e., until April of next year).

A good rule is to do a fresh Stock Price Forecast every quarter, usually after reviewing the latest quarterly report. Try drawing up the new forecast without looking at the old one first—just to help keep you from unconsciously shifting your estimates around to defend your old forecast.

THE FINAL PRICE POINT: WHEN TO BUY

Only by knowing when to sell can you know when to buy. You must know where you are trying to go before you can get started in the right direction. Your high, low, and sell points, together with your risk tolerance, will determine the maximum price you should be willing to pay for a stock. In the next few pages we will show you a system for setting a buy point in a way that is completely consistent with all these preceding assumptions. If you use this method, you will get the most possible profit from your investment time and money.

Our general approach is to calculate three different prospective buy prices and then use the one which is lowest. Each prospective buy price (X, Y, and Z) is the result of satisfying one of three essential requirements:

X: Buy only up to a price which does not violate your personal risk tolerance as expressed in your investment constitution. (See Chapter 9.)

Y: Buy only up to the point where the potential reward or gain exceeds the potential risk of loss by at least 2 to 1.

Z: Buy only up to a price which could give you a return of at least 30 percent.

The lowest price of the three will also satisfy the requirements of the other two, which is why we use this procedure. Let's look now at the reason for each of these requirements and the easiest way to determine their related prospective buy points.

Prospective buy price X is designed to ensure that you will not purchase stock at a level which would create more risk of loss than you had decided to take in your personal investment constitution. You decided first how much you could afford to lose in dollar terms and then expressed that as a percentage of your funds available for investment.

While a higher risk in one stock can be offset by a lower risk in another, let's assume that the overall risk tolerance (R) is also appropriate for this stock in particular. To calculate prospective buy price X, we need to find that price which would just produce the maximum loss allowable under the worst reasonable conditions. These conditions occur at the low (L) end of our price range estimate, since that is the way the forecasting process was arranged in the first place.

Thus we have three variables in our calculation: R, the risk tolerance expressed as a decimal (e.g., 40 percent is 0.40); L, the low; and X, the maximum buy price. These are related in the following way:

$$X = \frac{L}{1-R}$$

In our example, $L = 17$, and $R = 0.40$. Thus, $X = 17/(1 - 0.4) = 17/0.6 = 28$. This means we could buy EFC up to $28 per share while still keeping our risk at 40 percent or less. To check this answer, assume that you bought the stock at $28 and that everything did go wrong as foreseen in the worst possible scenario. The stock would then be at $17, showing a loss of $11. That $11 is just under 40 percent of the $28 original invest-ment. Therefore, $28 is in fact the highest price we could pay for EFC without violating our risk tolerance.

Prospective buy price Y is the highest price you can pay and still have the potential reward or gain be twice the potential loss. This guideline will ensure that the upside potential is enough to justify the risks, even if your risk tolerance would otherwise let you buy the stock.

Here we use three variables also: Y, the maximum buy price; L, the low; and S, the sell point, which also is the central figure in the price range estimate. The potential gain is $S - Y$, and the potential loss is $Y - L$. Since we want the gain to be at least twice the loss, then $(S - Y)/(Y - L) = 2$. Solving for Y, we find the general relationship

$$Y = \frac{S + 2L}{3}$$

Returning to our EFC example, $S = 35$, and $L = 17$. Thus, $Y = [35 + (2 \times 17)]/3 = 69/3 = 23$. Consequently, we could buy EFC up to $23 per share and still have a 2 to 1 ratio of gain to loss. To check this result, if you bought the stock at $23 and it went to $35, your gain would be $12. If instead the stock went to $17, your loss would be $6. The ratio of the $12 gain to the $6 loss is, of course, 2 to 1.

Prospective buy price Z ensures that you have a potential gain of at least 30 percent even if your risk tolerance and the reward-to-risk-ratio criteria are met. Why set a minimum gain of 30 percent for an individual stock? There are several reasons. A 30 percent move as a target or most likely return on an individual stock over a one-year period gives you a comfortable margin for error in attaining your long-term goals. Also, brokerage commissions and taxes have not been included, and these will reduce your gross gains somewhat.

The most important reason, though, is just plain experience. We have found through trial and error in owning hundreds of stocks that if we can't see at least a 30 percent move up to the sell price, then it is better to stay away. Naturally you can set any minimum percentage gain you feel right about, but it is a good idea to use one somewhere around 25 to 35 percent.

To calculate prospective buy price Z, we need only S, the sell point.

We know that a move up from Z to S must equal at least 30 percent. Thus, $Z + 0.3Z = S$. Putting this relationship into a formula for finding Z, we have $1.3Z = S$, or

$$Z = \frac{S}{1.3}$$

Applying this equation to EFC, our sell price is $35, and $Z = 35/1.3 = 27$. Therefore, our last prospective buy point is $27 per share. To verify this, a purchase at $27 and a sale at $35 would produce a gain of $8, which is just about 30 percent on the original investment.

Now we have all three prospective buy points, as shown in Table 8.

Obviously, the lowest of the three is $23 per share, and so this becomes our maximum purchase price or buy point (B). That is the most we can pay for EFC stock and still satisfy all three essential requirements.

Under different circumstances, any of the three (X, Y, or Z) could prove to be the limiting factor, and so each should be calculated. Once you get used to the procedure, you can plug in your assumptions and get the answer in a couple of minutes. For convenience, Figure 15 shows all three equations.

SUMMARY OF THE STOCK PRICE FORECAST

We have now completed the Stock Price Forecast, having worked through to our best judgment of the high (H), the low (L), the sell point (S), and the maximum buy point (B). In the example of EFC, we can summarize as shown in Figure 16.

This forecast stands as long as you think that the underlying analysis is unchanged. As changes occur in the company, the economy, or the market, you will be watching them. When these changes have become significant enough to make you feel that your price forecast is getting a bit ragged, then make any new adjustments necessary. Once the basic work is done, revisions do not take long. Meanwhile, between

TABLE 8. PROSPECTIVE BUY POINTS AND CALCULATED PRICES

Prospective Buy Point	Calculated Price
X: risk tolerance limits buy price to	$28 per share
Y: 2 to 1 or better gain/loss ratio at	$23 per share
Z: at least 30% return from	$27 per share

DEFINITIONS:

X: prospective buy price to avoid exceeding risk tolerance
Y: prospective buy price to have at least a 2 to 1 gain/loss ratio
Z: prospective buy price which offers at least a 30% gain
B: the final maximum buy point (the lowest of X, Y, and Z)
H: the high end of the range estimate
S: the middle of the range estimate and therefore the sell point
L: the low end of the range estimate

RELATIONSHIPS:

$$X = \frac{L}{1 - R}$$

$$Y = \frac{S + 2L}{3}$$

$$Z = \frac{S}{1.3}$$

FIGURE 15. CALCULATIONS FOR X, Y, AND Z.

revisions, gradually gather more knowledge about the company as you keep up to date with current events. In this way you will be continuously improving your underlying research in preparation for the next revised Stock Price Forecast.

TRADING TACTICS

One of the most fascinating parts of investing in uncommon stocks is watching their price movements. Now that you have done all your homework and fieldwork, you have the discipline necessary to keep the market in perspective. The daily jiggles should not bother you, and weekly price readings are certainly frequent enough. You need to watch prices more closely only while actually buying or selling.

PERIOD: ONE YEAR AHEAD
HIGH: $56
SELL: $35
BUY: $23
LOW: $17

FIGURE 16. STOCK PRICE FORECAST FOR EFC.

The price chart shown in Figure 17 is a handy way to post weekly prices and compare them with the four points of your Stock Price Forecast. You do not need to go to the trouble of posting a chart unless you get some fun out of it, since the main purpose is just to keep alert to current prices when they approach your buy and sell points. This could be done in one minute per week by just looking up the prices of your stocks in the financial pages.

Let's use the price chart on EFC to illustrate a few ideas about buy-

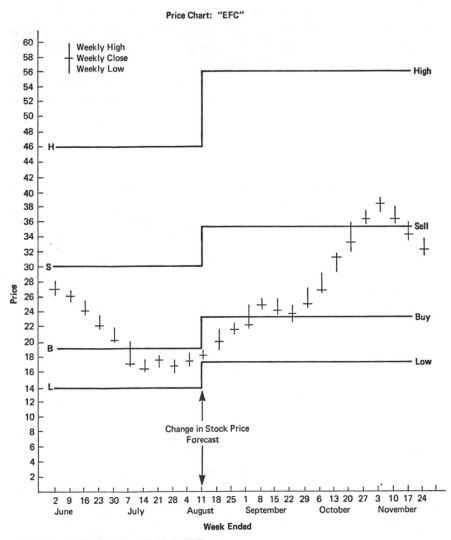

FIGURE 17. PRICE CHART FOR EFC.

ing and selling uncommon stocks. Notice that on August 11 we changed our Stock Price Forecast to its current points. We did this on the basis of the analysis described in this chapter and in chapters 18 to 20. Before that time we were carrying somewhat lower estimates. The change might have been a routine reappraisal based on a review of the June quarterly report, or perhaps it was triggered by some uncertainty felt as the stock dropped in June and early July. In any case, we confirmed our thinking that the stock had fallen into a buy range, and if we did not already own the stock, we would have begun buying in July.

Whenever you are ready to put in an order to buy or sell (see Chapter 12), don't suddenly abandon your perspective. Stick to your buy and sell points and try to ignore all the short-term chatter. In our example, if you can buy at 23 or less, do it. If you start getting cute and try to shave it to 22½ or 22, as often as not you will get whipsawed. If the stock is 18 or 20, be grateful and step in to buy. Don't look for bottoms. And don't start trading for halves and quarters. You are trying to make several hundred percent over several years and not 5 percent in one day, only to lose it the next.

Move in and out in an orderly way, following your discipline of price limits. If the stock is thinly traded, as it often will be, let your broker work at it. *Don't* push the broker to bid up the stock (or knock it down) too aggressively. If the stock is actively traded, you should make it clear that you expect to get your executions done within that traffic and that the broker is not delegated to play his or her own short-term trading tactics. In short, buy and sell within the flow of activity so that you will influence price movements as little as possible and still get in or out smoothly.

Sometimes the stock will move away before your order can be completed. If so, be patient. Markets change, and we've seldom had only one chance to buy or sell an uncommon stock. In the price chart in Figure 17, if you didn't fill your position below 23 between July 7 and the end of August, you had another chance during the week ending September 22. Similarly, the selling range was entered in the week of October 20. If you began selling around late October as you saw a weekly close over 35, you had until mid-November to finish selling.

The sharp price moves shown here are not unusual for uncommon stocks, although the time periods are longer. Such changes normally take several quarters and sometimes several years, but we shortened the price action to complete the illustration.

As the stock price moves around, you will be adjusting your own forecast. In some cases, as a result you may find that an uncommon stock stays for years in the hold range between your buy and sell points. For example, we held one stock over three years without a trade, from 15 down to 10 and back to 40. While we could wish to have done better, the results were still quite acceptable. In another situation, it would not be unreasonable to have bought and sold the stock a couple of times during those three years.

The extent of your trading activity is really a function of your buy and sell points, which in turn are determined by all your research and decision work. You just can't be sure in advance whether you will need to trade a lot or a little in any one year. At the outer limits, though, a complete turnover of your investments more than once a year is getting excessive; if you are not trading at all, maybe you should have another look at your one-year Stock Price Forecast to see whether the points are unrealistically far apart.

THE LONG-TERM GOAL

With all this emphasis on the one-year outlook and on trading, we should not lose sight of the extraordinary gains which are possible in uncommon stocks over the long term. Our Stock Price Forecast is necessarily focused just one year ahead. This is essential to our buy and sell discipline, which is designed as much to keep us from hanging on too long as to prevent us from selling out too early or near the lows. However, the same price forecasting process can be applied to the outlook for five or more years in the future.

Your level of confidence in a price forecast must drop as the forecasting period lengthens, but it is occasionally good to at least gaze off to the horizon. Let's look way out with our fictional EFC to illustrate the remarkable long-term profit potential of an uncommon stock.

On the basis of all our research to date, we can foresee an earnings growth rate of about 16 percent per year. (See Chapter 18.) This would take EPS from $2.76 this year to almost $6 in five years. With that record, plus the other factors cited in our analysis of the P/E ratio (see Chapter 20), we expect the P/E relative to the market to move from 0.8X to almost 1.5X. Even with no improvement in the market P/E (a reasonable working assumption), this would carry EFC's P/E up to about 16X. Thus EFC's most likely price five years from now is about $95, 400 percent above its present price.

This is only our best guess, of course, and a full range estimate would be very wide, as you might expect. The actual results could be a lot lower or even a lot higher. The important thing is that this kind of gain is a real practical possibility, and that is what makes uncommon stocks the most exciting investment vehicle of the 1980s.

We cannot conclude our discussion of uncommon stocks without a final, more personal look at our long-term goal. In the most direct sense, we are just trying to make as much money as possible within our ability to withstand risk. An important and continually stressed theme of this book has been that this path to wealth is directly within your control. There is a tremendous opportunity open to you in uncommon stocks. You need to be willing and able to put in several hours per week indefinitely, and you must take the risk of losing some of your hard-earned cash. But if you use these practical and direct methods of prospecting, researching, and decision making, you really can become financially independent. If you truly have the will to be wealthy, the path is here before you.

COMMON QUESTIONS ABOUT UNCOMMON STOCKS

Q: What is an uncommon stock?

A: An uncommon stock is one which has not yet been discovered by the crowd. It is a company of unusual quality and potential, distinctly superior to the many thousands of ordinary common stocks. The uncommon stock is capable of doubling and redoubling over the years, rather than just flying around and ending up nowhere.

Q: Where can I find such an uncommon stock? Are they rare?

A: They are located right in your own backyard. Within easy driving distance of almost everyone there are dozens of publicly traded companies. A few of those, perhaps one in ten or twenty, will be good enough to warrant your interest and maybe your investment.

Q: How do I recognize an uncommon stock?

A: You can recognize it by investigating its earning potential and the quality of its management. Then you estimate the stock's future price to see whether it has been discovered yet by the market.

Q: How can I do the work involved? I have a full-time occupation and have no training in this field.

A: You can do it in your spare time and without any specialized background. There is no mystique in learning to spot uncommon stocks.

People who tell you how hard it is are usually either trying to sell you something or attempting to justify their own carelessness in stock selection. Once you know what to look for, an uncommon stock stands out like a racehorse in a pack of mules.

Q: I've heard that you can't make money in stocks because the market price already reflects all the facts. How can you beat such an efficient market?

A: For the largest companies, which are closely watched by hundreds of professionals, this is probably true. However, there are thousands of companies which are just not well understood, and their stock prices usually are out of touch with what is really happening. In the case of uncommon stocks, the market can be just plain stupid at times, and you can buy some exceptional bargains.

Q: How much can I make? What are the chances of getting rich?

A: You can make a lot of money. Whether you get rich or not depends on what "rich" means to you, but you can raise your level of wealth 10 or 20 times higher over the long term. It also depends on your ability to take the right amount of risk, since you can be taking too much or too little risk in relation to these opportunities.

Q: How much money do I need to start?

A: You should have a few thousand dollars invested to make the returns worthwhile. People own uncommon stocks in odd lots to get started and then add to their positions from savings and profits. Just get started and learn to invest on your own; as your skills grow, so will the size of your investment account. There are accounts of every conceivable size, and so that is just not a consideration in getting started. What you need most to begin your trip down the path to wealth is the will to really do it.

Q: Do I need all kinds of expensive special services and information sources?

A: You need a subscription to *The Wall Street Journal*, some information about the Securities and Exchange Commission, and a large list of prospective stocks to begin researching. Everything except *The Wall Street Journal* is in your hands right now. This book shows you how to plug in to the original sources at very low cost. In this way, you avoid the information middlemen and their fees and their distortions.

Q: Even if uncommon stocks are good, haven't other investments done better lately, like real estate, antiques, and commodities?

A: Yes, the stock market in general has done poorly over the last decade, while purchases of "real things" have gone way up. Both these huge changes were caused by a dramatic increase in the rate of inflation. Now this movement has swung too far, and a reaction back is already beginning.

All kinds of investments have high and low periods lasting many years. The important question is: Which area has the best realistic opportunity for the next 10 years? You should want to know which horse is going to win the next race, not which one is already standing exhausted in the winner's circle. You can't make money on yesterday's results. Even without a move in the overall stock market, there are great bargains lying around in carefully selected uncommon stocks. In comparison with the grossly inflated real estate market, for example, uncommon stocks are outrageously undervalued.

APPENDIX

PROSPECT LIST
OF 7,200 STOCKS

(See Chapter 3 for a full explanation of this list.)

S. ZUCKER
STANLIFT CORP
36 RAMAH CIRCLE
AGAWAN, MA. 01001

C.L. POPEP
PAYSAVER CATALOG-SHOWROOMS
705 MEADOW ST
CHICOPEE, MA. 01014

BURKE A. WEISEND
PACKAGE MACHINERY CO
330 CHESTNUT ST
EAST LONGMEADOW, MA. 01028

R.G. DE CARLO
AMERICAN PAD & PAPER
75 APPLETON ST
HOLYOKE, MA. 01040

HARVEY J. FINISON
NORTHAMPTON CUTLERY
320 RIVERSIDE DR.
NORTHAMPTON, MA. 01060

ROBERT J. GAUDRAULT
FRIENDLY ICE CREAM CORP
1855 BOSTON ROAD
NORTH WILBRAHAM, MA. 01067

BERTRAM W. PERKINS,JR.
PERKINS MACHINE
WARREN, MA. 01083

ASHER NESIN
MICRO ABRASIVES
720 SOUTHAMPTON RD.
WESTFIELD, MA. 01085

JOHN I. SIMPSON
PECK LUMBER CO
S. BROAD ST
WESTFIELD, MA. 01085

EDWIN E. SMITH
H.B. SMITH CO
57 MAIN ST
WESTFIELD, MA. 01085

HOMER G. PERKINS
STANLEY HOME PRODUCTS
333 WESTERN AVE.
WESTFIELD, MA. 01085

G.M. STEVENS
WM. E. WRIGHT CO
SOUTH ST
WESTWARREN, MA 01092

JAMES J. SHEA, JR.
MILTON BRADLEY CO
P O BOX 3400
SPRINGFIELD, MA. 01101

BRIAN R. ROGERS
S. GELLIS & CO
95 STATE ST
SPRINGFIELD, MA. 01103

S. NATHANS, M.D.
LIFESTYLE COMPANIES
115 PROGRESS AVE
SPRINGFIELD, MA. 01104

J.D. CHAPIN
TAYLOR RENTAL CORP
570 COTTAGE ST
SPRINGFIELD, MA 01104

EDWARD K. WARD, JR.
CONIFER GROUP
54 NORTH ST
PITTSFIELD, MA. 01201

ROBERT E. O'CONNOR
RISING PAPER CO
PART ST
HOUSATONIC, MA. 01236

NEAL W. WELCH
SPRAGUE ELECTRIC CO
87 MARSHALL ST
NORTH ADAMS, MA. 01247

DOUGLAS R. STARRETT
THE L.S. STARRETT CO
121 CRESCENT ST
ATHOL, MA. 01331

WALKER J. HOSMER
MILLERS FALLS PAPER
MILL RD
MILLERS FALLS, MA. 01349

JOHN LAWLESS
MAYHEW STEEL PRODUCTS
SHELBURNE FALLS, MA 01370

MELVIN ROSENSAFT
GREAT AMERICAN CHEMICAL
650 WATER ST
FITCHBURG, MA. 01420

JOHN HEYWOOD
HEYWOOD-WAKEFIELD
206 CENTRAL ST
GARDNER, MA. 01440

HERMAN CATALUCCI
BURNS & TOWNE
20 MOHAWK DR
LEOMINSTER, MA 01453

LANGDON HOCKMEYER
VERTIPILE
SCOTT DR.
LEOMINSTER, MA. 01453

HOWARD HARDING,JR.
LODDING ENGINEERING CORP
BOX 269
AUBURN, MA. 01501

C.D. CASCIO
NYLACARB
PLAIN ST.
CLINTON, MA. 01510

FREDERICK WITZEL
THE FELTERS CO
22 WEST ST
MILLBURY, MA. 01527

LOUIS BROUGHTON
WESTWOOD INC
MILL ST
SOUTHBRIDGE, MA. 01550

J. ALDEN
ALDEN ELECTRONIC & IMPULSE
WASHINGTON ST
WESTBORO, MA. 01581

WILLIAM CADIGAN
MASSACHUSETTS ELECTRIC
20 TURNPIKE RD
WESTBOROUGH, MA. 01581

J.A. GODBEY
VALTEC CORP
99 HARTWELL ST
WEST BOYLSTON, MA. 01583

ROBERT C. McCRAY
WORCESTER CONTROLS CORP
125 HARTWELL ST
WESTBOYLSTON, MA 01583

JOSEPH R. CARTER
WYMAN-GORDON CO
105 MADISON ST
WORCESTER, MA. 01601

MERRILL WRIGHT
G.F. WRIGHT STEEL & WIRE
243 STAFFORD ST
WORCESTER, MA 01603

HENRY CUMMINGS, JR
LOWELL CORP
97 TEMPLE ST.
WORCESTER, MA. 01604

S.I. RECK
GODDARD INDUSTRIES INC
705 PLANTATION ST
WORCESTER, MA 01605

HOWARD G. FREEMAN
JAMESBURY CORP
640 LINCOLN ST
WORCESTER, MA 01605

OSCAR R. VAUDREUIL
REVA ENTERPRISES
705 NEW PLANTATION ST
WORCESTER, MA 01605

ROBERT CUSHMAN
NORTON CO
1 NEW BOND ST
WORCESTER, MA. 01606

JOHN ENGELSTED
O.S. WALKER CO
ROCKDALE ST
WORCESTER, MA 01606

JACOB HIATT
RAND-WHITNEY CORP
AGRAND ST
WORCESTER, MA. 01607

ALFRED R. LE BLANC
GEO. J. MEYER MFG.
P O BOX 866
WORCESTER, MA 01613

HOWARD WARREN
RILEY STOKER CORP
9 NEPONSET ST
WORCESTER, MA 01613

LEONARD M. JONES
BOSTON-WORCESTER CORP
855 WORCESTER RD
FRAMINGHAM, MA 01701

M.D. CIROLI
CHATEAU DE VILLE INC
220 WORCESTER RD
FRAMINGHAM, MA 01701

NELSON S. GIFFORD
DENNISON MFG.
300 HOWARD ST.
FRAMINGHAM, MA. 01701

DAVID B. PERINI
PERINI CORP
73 MOUNT WAYTE AVE
FRAMINGHAM, MA 01701

KENNETH FISHER
PRIME COMPUTER INC
145 PENNSYLVANIA AVE
FRAMINGHAM, MA. 01701

STANLEY FELDBERG
ZAYRE CORP
FRAMINGHAM, MA 01701

MARTIN A. ALLEN
COMPUTERVISION CORP
201 BURLINGTON RD
BEDFORD, MA. 01703

ARTHUR TANG
TANG INDUSTRIES, INC
4 AMY RD
FRAMINGHAM CENTER, MA 01704

SAMUEL J. PHILLIPS
ACTON CORP
P O BOX 407
ACTON, MA 01720

JOSEPH KRUY
CAMBRIDGE MEMORIES INC
12 CROSBY DR
BEDFORD, MA 01730

J.F. McCANN
CONTINENTAL LEASING CO
175 MIDDLESEX TURNPIKE
BEDFORD, MA 01730

M.J. FENNELL
ECRM INC
205 BURLINGTON RD
BEDFORD, MA 01730

FRANK BENSON
FANNY FARMER CANDY
4 PRESTON CT.
BEDFORD, MA 01730

MILTON GREENBERG
GCA CORP
BURLINGTON RD
BEDFORD, MA 01730

ROBERT B. KIMNACH
GENERAL AIRCRAFT CORP
HANSCOM FIELD
BEDFORD, MA 01730

DIMITRI D'ARBELOFF
MILLIPORE CORP
P O BOX F
BEDFORD, MA 01730

ARNOLD McCALMONT
TECHNICAL COMMUNICATIONS CORP
56 WINTHROP ST P O BOX STA 1
CONCORD, MA 01742

ARA AYKANIAN
BOSTON DIGITAL CORP
P O BOX 201
HOPKINTON, MA 01748

AARON KNOPPING
SMD INDUSTRIES INC
65 SOUTH ST
HOPKINTON, MA 01748

HARRY HOLZWASSER
ARROW AUTOMOTIVE INDUSTRIES
555 MAIN ST
HUDSON, MA. 01749

LESTER J. JOHNSEN
ATLANTIC BUSINESS FORMS
577 MAIN ST
HUDSON, MA. 01749

GORDON GRAVES
DATATROL INC
KANE INDUSTRIAL DR
HUDSON, MA. 01749

H.I. CORKIN
ENTWISTLE CO
BEGELOW ST
HUDSON, MA 01749

K.H. OLSEN
DIGITAL EQUIPMENT CORP
146 MAIN ST
MAYNARD, MA 01754

ROBERT L. LENINGTON
HYCOMP INC
146 MAIN ST. P O BOX 250
MAYNARD, MA 01754

FRANCIS H. ZENIE
WATERS ASSOCIATES, INC
MAPLE ST
MILFORD, MA 01757

W.L. ALDEN
ALDEN SELF-TRANSIT SYSTEMS
2 MERCER RD
NATICK, MA. 01760

P.D. GRINDLE
EALING CORP
22 PLEASANT ST
SOUTH NATICK, MA 01760

CHARLES LENHARD
ILIKON CORP
11 MERCER RD
NATICK, MA. 01760

PETER W. ALLEN
NEW ENGLAND PRESSED STEEL
95 WASHINGTON AVE
NATICK, MA 01760

ARTHUR VASH
PHILIPS SCREW CO
8 MERCER RD
NATICK, MA 01760

T.S. SAAD
SAGE LABORATORIES
3 HURON DR
NATICK, MA 01760

EDSON DE CASTRO
DATA GENERAL CORP
RT. NO 9
SOUTHBORO, MA 01772

J.J. MARTIN, JR
AMDEK CORP
120 UNION AVE
SUDBURY, MA 01776

ROBERT A. WATERS
WATERS MANUFACTURING
BOSTON POST RD
WAYLAND, MA 01778

ANDREW KARIOTIS
ALPHA INDUSTRIES
20 SYLVAN RD
WOBURN, MA 01801

FARNHAM SMITH
ATLEE CORP
8 GILL ST
WOBURN, MA 01801

R.F. JASSE
CHOMERICS INC
77 DRAGON CT
WOBURN, MA 01801

ANTHONY R. CATALDO
GOLD RIBBON FOODS
20 INDUSTRIAL PKWY
WOBURN, MA 01801

JOSEPH HYMAN
HYCOR INC
1 GILL ST
WOBURN, MA 01801

J.S. GALBRAITH
KEVLIN MANUFACTURING
24 CONNECTICUT ST
WOBURN, MA 01801

B.N. GRAY
LIFE SUPPORT EQUIPMENT CORP
2 GILL ST
WOBURN, MA 01801

F.O. ANDRESEN
POLYCLON INC
15 SIXTH RD
WOBURN, MA 01801

CHARLES ADAMS
DATA SYNESTICS CORP
PO BOX 402
BURLINGTON, MA 01803

STANLEY ABKOWITZ
DYNAMET TECHNOLOGY INC
8 A ST
BURLINGTON, MA 01803

J.P. BARGER
DYNATECH CORP
12 NEW ENGLAND EXECUTIVE PARK
BURLINGTON, MA 01803

F.L. BRYANT
ELECTRONIZED CHEMICALS CORP
SO. BEDFORD ST
BURLINGTON, MA 01803

PASCAL LEVESQUE
HIGH VOLTAGE ENGINEERING CORP
SOUTH BEDFORD ST
BURLINGTON, MA 01803

T.C. CRONIN
INFOREX INC
21 NORTH AVE
BURLINGTON, MA 01803

LAWRENCE GOULD
MICROWAVE ASSOCIATES
NORTHWEST INDUSTRIAL PARK
BURLINGTON, MA 01803

P.J. BRIGHTON
PROGRAMS & ANALYSIS
21 RAY AVE
BURLINGTON, MA 01803

ROLLAND ROBISON
SEMICON INC
10 NORTH AVE PO BOX 131
BURLINGTON, MA 01803

MARVIN G. SCHORR
TECHNICAL OPERATIONS INC
ONE BEACON ST
BURLINGTON, MA 01808

R.A. REICHTER
DASA CORP
15 STEVENS ST
ANDOVER, MA 01810

E.H. KOHN
DOCTOR PET CENTERS
DUNDEE PARK
ANDOVER, MA 01810

WARREN COOPER
STANDEX INTERNATIONAL
166 NORTH MAIN ST
ANDOVER, MA 01810

L.D. BALDWIN
FREQUENCY SOURCES INC
16 MAPLE RD
CHELMSFORD, MA 01824

T.B. TANDEN
PACER CORP
80 TURNPIKE RD
CHELMSFORD, MA 01824

JAMES FRANCE
SILICON TRANSISTOR CORP
KATRINA RD
CHELMSFORD, MA 01824

E.C. DONNER, JR
DOONER LABORATORIES
PO BOX 909 WARD HILL
HAVERHILL, MA 01830

J.S. ANDEREGG, JR
DYNAMICS RESEARCH CORP
60 CONCORD ST
WILMINGTON, MA 01837

ROBERT GABLE
CRAIG SYSTEMS CORP
360 MERRIMACK ST
LAWRENCE, MA 01842

J.F. CONWAY, JR
COURIER CORP
165 JACKSON ST
LOWELL, MA 01852

PETER WEISS
PANDEL-BRADFORD INC
200 MARKET ST
LOWELL, MA 01852

A.B. DU MONT
GRAPHIC SYSTEMS INC
PO BOX 649
LOWELL, MA 01853

J.H. BECK
BTU ENGINEERING CORP
ESQUIRE RD
NO. BILLERICA, MA 01862

LEO KAHN
PURITY SUPREME INC
312 BOSTON RD
NORTH BILLERICA, MA 01862

J.J. FITZGERALD
CAMBRIDGE NUCLEAR CORP
575 MIDDLESE TURNPIKE
BILLERICA, MA 01865

V.V. BASMAJIAN
MEGATECH CORP
29 COOK ST
BILLERICA, MA 01866

DONALD HAMMONDS
ADDISON-WESLEY PUBLISHING
READING, MA 01867

N. DUBINSKY
ASTRO-TECHNOLOGY
540 MAIN ST
TEWKSBURY, MA 01876

CHESTER TWISS
CORENCO CORP
525 WOBURN ST
TEWKSBURY, MA 01876

DR. AN WANG
WANG LABORATORIES, INC
836 NORTH ST
TEWKSBURY, MA 01876

B.M. GORDON
ANALOGIC CORP
AUDUBON RD
WAKEFIELD, MA 01880

THOMAS COE
WAKEFIELD ENGINEERING
AUDUBON RD
WAKEFIELD, MA 01880

HENRY FOSTER
THE CHARLES RIVERS BREEDING LAB.
251 BALLARDVALE ST
WILMINGTON, MA 01887

CARL E. DANTAS
COMPUGRAPHIC CORP
INDUSTRIAL WAY
WILMINGTON, MA 01887

J.J. BIONDO
SOLID STATE TECHNOLOGY
11 UPTON DR.
WILMINGTON, MA 01887

WILLIAM MOORE, JR
RECREONICS
PO BOX 307
BEVERLY, MA 01915

JAMES BICKMAN
STOCKER & YALE
PO BOX 494
BEVERLY, MA. 01915

M.C. LAUENSTEIN
VENTRON CORP
12-24 CONGRESS ST.
BEVERLY, MA. 01915

INGVAR TORNBERG
GLOUCESTER ENGINEERING
BLACKBURN INDUSTRIAL PK.
GLOUCESTER, MA. 01930

RICHARD LAWRENCE
SONOLITE CORP
LAKESIDE INDUSTRIAL PK.
GLOUCESTER, MA 01930

EDWARD MULLIGAN
TOWLE MANUFACTURING
260 MERRIMAC ST
NEWBURY PORT, MA. 01950

RALPH MILLS
CRESSEY DOCKHAM & CO
1 IGA WAY
SALEM, MA 01970

R.C. BARBATO
McMILLAN RADIATION LABS
73 WASHINGTON ST
SALEM, MA 01970

OSCAR MILLER
CHADWICK-MILLER
PEQUOT INDUSTRIAL PK. 300 TPKE
CANTON, MA 02021

HAROLD HINDMAN
INSTRON CORP
2500 WASHINGTON ST
CANTON, MA 02021

LOUIS R. SHINDLER
MORSE SHOE
555 TURNPIKE
CANTON, MA 02021

DANIEL M. HAMILBURG
PLYMOUTH RUBBER
REVERE ST
CANTON, MA 02021

C.E. DEPHOUSE
HERSEY PRODUCTS
250 ELM ST
DEDHAM, MA 02026

MARSHALL BERKMAN
RUST CRAFT GREETING CARDS
DEDHAM, MA 02026

EARLE PITT
THE FOXBORO CO
38 NEPONSET AVE
FOXBORO, MA 02035

HARVEY WHITE
IDENTICON CORP
1 KENWOOD CIRCLE
FRANKLIN, MA 02038

J.G. MANWARING
RADIO FREQUENCY
50 PARK ST.
MEDFIELD, MA 02052

RAY STATA
ANALOG DEVICES
RTE 1 INDUSTRIAL PK. BOX 280
NORWOOD, MA 02062

J.ROBERT GLOMEAU
MASONEILAN INT'L
63 NAHATAN ST
NORWOOD, MA 02062

JOSEPH CARSIDE
E.W. WIGGINS AIRWAYS
NORWOOD MUNICIPAL AIRPORT
NORWOOD, MA 02062

I. GREENBLATT
SOUTH SHORE PUBLISHING
777 COUNTRY WAY, N
SCITUATE, MA 02066

CARLTON E. GRIFFIN
SYSTEMS ENGINEERING LABS
PO BOX 440
STOUGHTON, MA 02072

RALPH HEIM
BIRD & SON
WASHINGTON ST
EAST WALPOLE, MA 02081

ROBERT FRANCISCO
EPSCO INC
411 PROVIDENCE HIGHWAY
WESTWOOD, MA 02090

JOHN P. KENDALL
KENDALL CO
PO BOX 10
BOXTON, MA. 02101

F. FRANK VORENBERG
GILCHRIST CO
417 WASHINGTON ST
BOSTON, MA 02102

WILLIAM W. WOLBACH
THE BOSTON CO
ONE BOSTON PL.
BOSTON, MA 02106

L.C. PETERS
ENERGY VENTURES
1 BOSTON PL.
BOSTON, MA 02106

WILLIAM TAYLOR
AFFILIATED PUBLICATIONS
135 WILLIAM MORISSEY BLVD.
BOSTON, MA 02107

HAROLD MILLER
HOUGHTON MIFFLIN
2 PARK ST
BOSTON, MA 02107

JOHN WILSON
VANCE, SANDERS & CO
PO BOX 2277
BOSTON, MA 02107

H.T. SPENCE
COMPUTER SYSTEMS OF AMERICA
141 MILK ST
BOSTON, MA 02109

GERALD SCHUSTER
CONTINENTAL WINGATE CO
20 KILBY ST
BOSTON, MA 02109

F.C. WELCH
ESSEX CO
53 STATE ST
BOSTON, MA 02109

CARL BAREN
HOSPITALITY INT'L
84 STATE ST.
BOSTON, MA 02109

JOHN F. KEANE
KEANE ASSOCIATES
120 COMMERCIAL ST
BOSTON, MA 02109

QUINCY A. SHAW, JR
NORTH AMERICAN MINES
50 CONGRESS ST
BOSTON, MA 02109

J.R. HESSE
AMERICAN GARDEN PRODUCTS
99 HIGH ST
BOSTON, MA 02110

GEORGE A. HIBBARD
BAYSTATE CORP
77 FRANKLIN ST
BOSTON, MA 02110

ROBERT A. CHARPIE
CABOT CORP
125 HIGH ST
BOSTON, MA 02110

MERVYN PERRY
THE MASS. CO
100 FEDERAL ST
BOSTON, MA 02110

MORTON NARVA
MORTON'S SHOE STORES
647 SUMMER ST. BOSTON HAR.IND
BOSTON, MA 02210

JAMES C. WEMYSS, JR
PENOBSCOT CO
211 CONGRESS ST
BOSTON, MASS   02110

CHARLES H. ABBOTT
SAMSON OCEAN SYSTEMS INC
99 HIGH ST
BOSTON, MA 02110

THOMAS C. VIOLA
SCA SERVICES INC
99 HIGH ST 30th FL
BOSTON, MA 02110

C. CHARLES MARRAN
SPENCES COS
450 SUMMER ST
BOSTON, MA 02110

AVRAM J. GOLDBERG
STOP & SHOP CO
393 D ST
BOSTON, MA 02110

GORDON OSBORNE
WARWICK MILLS
234 CONGRESS ST.
BOSTON, MA 02110

G.F. BENNETT
STATE ST RESEARCH & MNGT
225 FRANKLIN ST RM. 2920
BOSTON, MA 02111

ALEXANDER D'ARBELOFF
TERADYNE INC
183 ESSEX ST
BOSTON, MA 02111

DEAN BOYLAN
BOSTON SAND & GRAVEL
150 CAUSEWAY ST
BOSTON, MA 01221

OTTO MORINGSTAR
DATA PACKAGING CORP
205 BROADWAY
CAMBRIDGE, MA 02114

CHARLES KAYE
XTRA CORP
150 CAUSEWAY ST
BOSTON, MA 02114

MARVIN MYER CYKER
HEALTHCARE CORP
1125 STUART ST
BOSTON, MA 02116

RICHARD SMITH
GENERAL CINEMA CORP
480 BOYLSTON ST
BOSTON, MA 02116

H.M. COHEN
TECHNOLOGY ASSOCIATES
759 BOYLSTON ST   STE 100
BOSTON, MA 02116

J.G. MAYER
GLADDING CORP
PO BOX 586 BACK BAY ANNEX
BOSTON, MA 02117

MARVIN STOLBERG
NEW ENGLAND NUCLEAR CORP
575 ALBANY ST
BOSTON, MA 02118

ARNOLD HIATT
STRIDE RITE CORP
960 HARRISON AVE
BOSTON, MA 02118

H.S. GOODMAN
UNIPAK INC
70 CEYLON ST
BOSTON, MA 02121

KALMAN SHMUELI
GILMAN SERVICES INC
20 FREEPORT ST
BOSTON, MA 02122

ROBERT D. KODIS
DI-AN CONTROLS INC
944 DORCHESTER AVE
BOSTON, MA 02125

SEYMOUR N. SCHWARTZ
U.N.A. CORP
383 DORCHESTER AVE
BOSTON, MA 02127

LEONARD FLORENCE
LEONARD SILVER INT'L
144 ADDISON ST
BOSTON, MA 02128

PHILIP ST. GERMAIN
DUDDY'S INC
50 TERMINAL ST
CHARLESTOWN, MA 02129

EDWARD GELSTHORPE
H.P. HOOD INC
500 RUTHERFORD AVE
BOSTON, MA 02129

DAVID CASTY
CHELSEA INDUSTRIES INC
1360 SOLDIERS FIELD RD
BOSTON, MA 02135

ROBERT GORIN
GORIN STORES
1400 SOLDIERS FIELD RD
BOSTON, MA. 02135

JOHN DEMPSEY, JR
BAIRD-ATOMIC INC
125 MIDDLESEX TURNPIKE
BEDFORD MA 02138

STEPHEN LEVY
BOLT,BERANEK & NEWMAN
50 MOULTON ST
CAMBRIDGE MA 02138

KENNETH LEDEEN
CSM MEDICAL DEVICES, INC
377 PUTNAM AVE
CAMBRIDGE MA 02138

PIERRE LAMOND
ADVENT CORP
195 ALBANY ST
CAMBRIDGE MA 02139

MARTIN ANNIS
AMERICAN SCIENCE & ENG.
955 MASSACHUSETTS AVE
CAMBRIDGE MA 02139

M.J. BLOCK
BLOCK ENGINEERING
19 BLACKSTONE ST
CAMBRIDGE, MA 02139

WARREN MAC PHERSON
CAMBRIDGE RUBBER
680 MAIN ST
CAMBRIDGE, MA 02139

FRANKLIN HOBBS
ELECTRO POWERPACS CORP
253 NORFOLK ST
CAMBRIDGE MA 02139

DR. GILBERT BEINHOCKER
NAT'L INFORMATION SERVICES
675 MASSACHUSETTS AVE
CAMBRIDGE, MA 02139

KYMUS GINWALA
NORTHERN RESEARCH & ENG.
219 VASSAR ST
CAMBRIDGE, MA 02139

J.H. RISEMAN
ORION RESEARCH
11 BLACKSTONE ST
CAMBRIDGE, MA 02139

ROBERT MURRAY
TAX MAN
639 MASSACHUSETTS AVE
CAMBRIDGE MA 02139

J.F. MAGEE
ARTHUR LITTLE INC
ACORN PARK
CAMBRIDGE, MA 02140

R.L. HYDE
HYDE ATHLETIC INDUSTRIES
432 COLUMBIA ST
CAMBRIDGE, MA 02141

JOSEPH LA BARBERA
RECLAMATION SYSTEMS
29 EAST ST
CAMBRIDGE MA 02141

ARTHUR METCALF
ELECTRONICS CORP OF AMERICA
1 MEMORIAL DR
CAMBRIDGE, MA 02142

G.S. BECKWITH GILBERT
METROPOLITAN GREETINGS
215 FIRST ST
CAMBRIDGE, MA 02142

S. ASANO
SHINTRON CO
144 ROGERS ST
CAMBRIDGE, MA 02142

EUGENE SCHUPAK
NATIONAL MEDICAL CARE
77 POND AVE
BROOKLINE MA 02146

DAVID W. BERNSTEIN
AMERICAN BILTRITE
22 WILLOW ST.
CHELSEA, MA 02150

JAMES MURDOCK
MURDOCK CORP
158 CARTER ST
CHELSEA,MA 02150

JOHN A KANEB
NORTHEAST PETROLEUN INDUSTRIES
295 EASTERN AVE
CHELSEA, MA 02150

PHILIP SEGAL
AMERICAN SNACKS
400 EASTERN AVE
CHELSEA MA 02150

C. WM. CAREY
TOWN & COUNTRY JEWELRY
25 UNION ST
CHELSEA, MA 02150

EDWARD M. GALLAGHER
REVERE RACING ASSOC
190 V F W PKWY.
REVERE, MA 02151

G.J. ADAMS
ADAMS RUSSELL CO
280 BEAR HILL RD
WALTHAM, MA 02154

B.B. FRUSZTAJER
BBF GROUP
42 4th AVE
WALTHAM, MA 02154

HENRY HARDY
COMPO INDUSTRIES
125 ROBERTS RD
WALTHAM, MA 02154

R.F. COLE
CRYOGENIC TECHNOLOGY
KELVIN PK.
WALTHAM, MA 02154

MARTIN COOPERSTEIN
DATA ARCHITECTS
460 TOTTEN POND RD
WALTHAM, MA 02154

HARVEY FOX
KELTRON CORP
225 CRESCENT ST
WALTHAM, MA 02154

HERBERT ROTH
LFE CORP
1601 TRAPELO RD
WALTHAM, MA 02154

GEORGE NADDAFF
LIVING & LEARNING CENTRES
764 MAIN ST
WALTHAM, MA 02154

JOHN B. REECE
REECE CORP
200 PROSPECT ST
WALTHAM, MA 02154

G.N. HATSOPOULOS
THERMO ELECTRON CORP
101 FIRST AVE
WALTHAM, MA 02154

JOSEPH GASIANO
TYCO LABORATORIES
16 HICKORY DR
WALTHAM, MA 02154

L.R. PANICO
XENON CORP
39 COMMERCIAL ST
MEDFORD MA 02155

P.R. TISCH
LOEW'S BOSTON THEATRES
299 WASHINGTON ST
NEWTON, MA 02158

WILLIAM KENNEY
KING'S DEPT. STORES
150 CALIFORNIA ST
NEWTON, MA 02158

HARRY B. McHUGH
LA TOURAINE-BICKFORD'S FOOD
1 GATEWAY CENTER
NEWTON CORNER, MA 02158

ARTHUR CARR
CODEX CORPORATION
15 RIVERDALE AVE
NEWTON, MASS 02158

ALFRED KLUGMAN
ALPHA MEDICAL
1032 COMMONWEALTH AVE
BOSTON, MA 02159

TIMOTHY X. CRONIN
CRAMER ELECTRONICS INC
85 WELLS AVE
NEWTON, MA 02159

SHELDON WOOLF
NAT'L HARDGOODS DISTRIBUTORS
1330 CENTRE ST
NEWTON CENTRE, MA 02159

R.M. MANDELL
R & R ASSOCIATES
181 WELLS AVE
NEWTON, MA 02159

ROBERT BUNSHAFT
UNITED-OVERTON CORP
19 NEEDHAM ST
NEWTON HIGHLANDS MA 02161

MARVIN COHEN
ARP INSTRUMENTS
320 NEEDHAM ST
NEWTON, MA 02164

R.L. WEINBERG
RIX CORP
84 ROWE ST
AUBURNDALE, MA 02166

MESHULAM RIKLIS
AITS INC
210 BOYLSTON ST
CHESTNUT HILL, MA 02167

ROBERT WALKER
AMERICAN PROGRAM BUREAU
850 BOULSTON ST
CHESTNUT HILL, MA 02167

H.H. BRESKY
SEABOARD ALLIED MILLING CORP
200 BOYLSTON ST
NEWTON, MA 02167

J.G. LANDRY
ASTRA CORP
45 FIELD ST
QUINCY, MA 02169

KENDALL DOBLE, JR
PNEUMATIC SCALE CORP
65 NEWPORT AVE
QUINCY, MA 02171

L.C. LERNER
MARINA INDUSTRIES
542 E. SQUANTUM ST
SQUANTUM, MA 02171

ERVIN PIETZ
BARRY WRIGHT CORP
680 PLEASANT ST
WATERTOWN, MASS 02172

ARTHUR GOLDSTEIN
IONICS INC
65 GROVE ST
WATERTOWN, MA 02172

L.E. DONEGAN, JR
KEYDATA CORP
108 WATER ST
WATERTOWN, MA 02172

P.C. RICKS, JR
SCIENTIFIC ENERGY SYST.
570 PLEASANT ST
WATERTOWN, MA 02172

PAUL ALLEN
SEABOARD PLYWOOD & LUMBER
17 BRIDGE ST
WATERTOWN, MA 02172

GEORGE BERMAN
UNITRODE CORP
580 PLEASANT ST.
WATERTOWN, MA 02172

THOMAS ROSSE
INSTRUMENTATION LABORATORY
113 HARTWELL AVE
LEXINGTON, MA 02173

ROBERT HENDERSON
ITEK CORP
10 MAGUIRE RD
LEXINGTON, MA 02173

EDWARD HOUSEMAN
AUTOMATIC RADIO MFG.
2 MAIN ST
MELROSE, MA 02176

T. WEISS
PLATED WIRES & ELECTRONICS
37 WASHINGTON ST
MELROSE, MA 02176

HENRY GREER
AUTEX INC
55 WILLIAM ST
WELLESLEY, MA 02181

BERNARD J. O'KEEFE
EG & G INC
45 WILLIAM ST
WELLESLEY, MA 02181

JAMES F. UPTON
INCOTERM CORP
65 WALNUT ST
WELLESLEY HILLS, MA 02181

EDWARD L. CHASE
COLUMBIA TECHNICAL CORP
128 OFFICE PLAZA BLDG.
BRAINTREE, MA 02184

RICHMOND HOLDEN
J.L. HAMMETT CO
HAMMETT PL.
BRAINTREE, MA 02184

SVEN VAULE
JONES & VINING INC
174 FORBES RD
BRAINTREE, MA 02184

ERIC SANDQUIST
AINSLIE CORP
531 POND ST
BRAINTREE, MA 02185

LEO FLYNN
SIGMA INSTRUMENTS INC
170 PEARL ST
SOUTH BRINATREE, MA 02185

HOYT ECKER
TECHVEN ASSOCIATION
30 COLPITTS RD
WESTON, MA 02193

LEO FEUER
WILLIAM CARTER CO
963 HIGHLAND AVE.
NEEDHAM HEIGHTS, MA. 02194

DAVID KOSOWSKY
DAMON CORP
115-4th AVE
NEEDHAM HEIGHTS, MA 02194

A.B. MASON
LUDLOW CORP
PO BOX 101
NEEDHAM HEIGHTS, MA 02194

C.L. BANKART
NEW ENGLAND LAUNDRIES INC
25 HOMESTEAD PK.
NEEDHAM, AM 02194

L. MICHELSON
LION PRECISION INC
60 BRIDGE ST
NEWTON, MA 02195

FREDERIC C. DUMAINE, JR.
AMOSKEAG CO
PRUDENTIAL CENTER
BOSTON, MA 02199

WILLIAM PRUYN
EASTERN GAS & FUEL ASSOCIATES
2900 PRUDENTIAL TOWER
BOSTON, MA 02199

RODERICK MAC DOUGAL
NEW ENGLAND MERCHANTS CO
PRUDENTIAL CENTER
BOSTON, MA 02199

JAMES WOOD
PNEUMO CORP
PRUDENTIAL TOWER
BOSTON, MA 02199

WILLIAM ANSBRO
ALLYN & BACON
470 ATLANTIC AVE
BOSTON, MA 02210

ROBERT BECKETT
ADAGE, INC
1079 COMMONWEALTH AVE
BOSTON, MA 02215

PHILIP TABER
GENERAL ELECTRONIC LABS
1085 COMMONWEALTH AVE
BOSTON, MA 02215

PAUL SONNABEND
SONESTA INTN'L HOTEL
390 COMMONWEALTH AVE
BOSTON, MA 02215

SID SHNEIDER
CHILD WORLD, INC
25 LITTLEFIELD ST
AVON, MA 02322

MORTON LADGE
HERMETITE CORP
100 LADGE DR
AVON, MA 02322

M.B. SIDMAN
KIDDIE PRODUCTS
ONE KIDDIE DR
AVON, MA 02322

HAROLD THORKILSEN
OCEAN SPRAY CRANBERRIES
MAIN ST
HANSON, MA 02341

ROBERT MARGULIES
LEVITT INDUSTRIES
9 MEAR RD
HOLBROOK MA 02343

R.E. TRAVIS
MEDI INC
27 MAPLE AVE
HOLBROOK, MA 02343

SUMNER SMITH, JR
ABINGTON TEXTILE MACHINERY
200 WALES ST
NORTH ABINGTON, MA 02351

A.R. RICHARD
RICHARDS MICRO-TOOL CO. INC
NICKS ROCK RD
PLYMOUTH, MA 02360

R.M. ROSENBERG
DUNKIN DONUTS
RANDOLPH, MA 02368

EDWARD BERNAT
GARLAND CORP
GARLAND PLAZA
BROCKTON, MA 02401

PAUL KLEVEN
GEO KEITH CO
100 PERKINS AVE
BROCKTON, MA 02403

ALBERT WILSON
OCEAN RESEARCH EQUIP.
FALMOUTH HEIGHTS RD
FALMOUTH, MA 02541

S.O. RAYMOND
BENTHOS INC
EDGERTON DR
NORTH FALMOUTH, MA 02556

RUSSELL MAKEPEACE
A.D. MAKEPEACE CO
266 MAIN ST
WAREHAM, MA 02571

ROGER WELLINGTON
AUGAT INC
PO BOX 779
ATTLEBORO, MA 02703

RICHARD YOUNG
ACUSHNET CO
BELLEVILLE AVE
NEW BEDFORD, MA 02715

THAYER FRANCIS
SIPPICAN CORP
7 BARNABAS RD
MARION, MA 02738

KENNETH CHACE
BERKSHIRE HATHAWAY
97 COVE ST
NEW BEDFORD, MA 02744

SAMUEL KATZ
MARS BARGAINLAND, INC
1 RIVERSIDE AVE
NEW BEDFORD, MA 02746

ROGERS N. FARR
PAYNE CUTLERY CORP
295 PHILLIPS AVE
NEW BEDFORD, MA 02746

D.A. ARANSKY
CERTIFIED CORP
23 WEST BACON
PLAINVILLE, MA 02762

COURT J. BEISINGER
BEISINGER INDUSTRIES
PO BOX 987
TAUNTON, MA 02780

MATTHEW SHUSTER
NEW ENGLAND BRASS CO
16 PARK ST
TAUNTON, MA 02780

DONALD ROACH
BROWN & SHARPE MFG.
PRECISION PK. BOX 456
NORTH KINGSTOWN, R.I. 02852

J.A. JENSEN
PRELUDE CORP
67 ESMOND AVE
NO. KINGSTOWN, R.I. 02852

DONALD SALMANSON
ADAMS DRUG CO
75 SABIN ST
PAWTUCKET, R.I. 02860

DAVID BERGER
POWER-DYNE VEHICLES
55 TOWER ST
PAWTUCKET, R.I. 02860

KENNETH WASHBURN
UNION WADDING CO
PAWTUCKET, R.I. 02860

J.ALDEN DOOLEY
NARRAGANSETT RACING ASSOC
49 MANTON ST
PAWTUCKET, R.I. 02861

STEPHEN HASSENFELD
HASBRO INDSUTRIES
1027 NEWPORT AVE
PAWTUCKET, R.I. 02862

DARIO BACCHIOCCHI
BURRILLVILLE RACING ASSOC
LINCOLN, R.I. 02865

BRADFORD BOSS
A.T. CROSS CO
1 ALBION RD
LINCOLN, R.I. 02865

ROBERT PAGE
LESSONA CORP
33 STRAWBERRY FIELD RD
WARWICK, R.I. 02886

ALFRED PETTERUTI
ODEC INC
25 GRAYSTONE ST
WARWICK, R.I. 02886

B.M. COLE
TECTRA INDUSTRIES
100 PULASKI ST WEST
WARWICK, R.I. 02886

WILLIAM MC CULLOUGH
YARDNEY ELECTRIC
82 MECHANIC ST
PAWCATUCK, CT. 02891

A. W. ONDIS
ATLAN-TOL INDUSTRIES
ATLAN-TOL INDUSTRIAL PK.
WEST WARWICK, R.I. 02893

GEORGE BOTVIN
ACS INDUSTRIES
71 VILLANOVA ST
WOONSOCKET, R.I. 02895

BRUCE SUNDLUN
OUTLET CO
176 WEYBOSSET ST
PROVIDENCE, R.I. 02902

JEROME OTTMAR
AMTEL, INC
40 WESTMINSTER ST.
PROVIDENCE, R.I. 02903

JOHN J. CUMMINGS, JR
INDUSTRIAL NATIONAL CORP
55 KENNEDY PLAZA
PROVIDENCE, R.I. 02903

B.P. HAGGERTY
RUMFORD STEEL INDSUTRIES
33 ACORN ST
PROVIDENCE, R.I. 02903

STUART BANDMAN
LAFAYETTE UNITED CORP
984 CHARLES ST
PROVIDENCE, R.I. 02904

HUGH C. NEVILLE
RICHMOND GRAPHIC SYSTEMS
123 GEORGIA AVE
PROVIDENCE, R.I. 02905

HAROLD OTTOBRINI
METALIZED CERAMICS CORP
100 NIANTIC AVE
PROVIDENCE, R.I. 02907

E.A. KERBER
MASTERCRAFT HOMES, INC
815 RESERVOIR AVE
CRANSTON, R.I. 02910

R.R. PAPITTO
NARTEK, INC
815 RESERVOIR AVE
CRANSTON, R.I. 02910

G.T. PARKOS
CPL CORP
KING PHILIP RD
EAST PROVIDENCE, R.I. 02914

EDWIN PRITCHART
WASHBURN WIRE CO
BOORNE AVE
EAST PROVIDENCE, R.I. 02916

ROBERT HOWARD
CENTRONICS DATA COMPUTER CORP
ONE WALL ST
HUDSON, N.H. 03051

JAMES DOWNING
THE COLUMBIA PRECISION
PO BOX 187
HUDSON, N.H. 03051

CHARLES MOODY, JR
EDGCOMB STEEL OF NEW ENGLAND
WEST HOLLIS ST
NASHUA, N.H. 03060

WILLIAM E. CONWAY
NASHUA CORP
44 FRANKLIN ST
NASHUA, N.H. 03060

W.W. ZECHEL
ROYAL BUSINESS FORMS
SIMON ST
NASHUA, N.H. 03060

HAROLD POPE
SANDERS ASSOCIATES
DANIEL WEBSTER HWY.S.
NASHUA, N.H. 03060

E.L. GRAYSON
R.C.L. ELECTRONICS
195 MC GREGOR ST
MANCHESTER, N.H. 03102

J.L. LOVETT
RAYTHEON-MANCHESTER OP
676 ISLAND POND RD
MANCHESTER, N.H. 03103

MILTON W. SHAER
SHAER SHOE CORP
PO BOX 216
MANCHESTER, N.H. 03105

DAVID WILLIAMS
INTERN'L PACKINGS CORP
PLEASANT ST
BRISTOL, N.H. 03222

ARTHUR C. STEWART
RICHARD D. BREW & CO
90 AIRPORT RD
CONCORD, N.H. 03301

WALTON STILES
MERRIMACK FARMER'S EXCHANGE
18-22 LOW AVE
CONCORD, N.H. 03301

JOHN T. BOATWRIGHT
NORTHEAST ELECTRONICS CORP
PO BOX 640
CONCORD, N.H. 03301

RAYMOND WATERFIELD
PAGE BELTING CO
26 COMMERCIAL ST
CONCORD, N.H. 03302

MELVIN GORDON
HAMPSHIRE-DESIGNERS
PO BOX 239
MANCHESTER, N.H. 03105

RICHARD CHERWIN
NEW HAMPSHIRE BALL BEARINGS
RTE 202 & GROVE ST
PETERSBOROUGH, N.H. 03458

RICHARD BUESCHEL
TIME SHARE CORP
PO BOX 683
HANOVER, N.H. 03755

F. FULLER RIPLEY
TROY MILLS
TROY, N.H. 03465

F.T. BEDFORD, III
PROFILE SPORTS CORP
1 PROFILE PLAZA, W
LEBANON, N.H. 03748

GLEN SWANSON
CLAROSTAT MFG. CO
WASHINGTON ST
DOVER, N.H. 03820

SIEGFRIED SUSSKIND
ELECTRO AUDIO DYNAMICS
385 CENTRAL AVE
DOVER, N.H. 03820

FRANKLIN HOLLIS
EXETER & HAMPTON ELECTRIC
225 WATER ST
EXETER, N.H. 03833

MICHAEL DINGMAN
WHEELABRATOR-FRYE
LIBERTY LN
HAMPTON, N.H. 03842

WM. H. BANKS, JR
MAC ALLEN
BAY RD
NEW MARKET, N.H. 03857

JOHN SHATTUCK
PLASMINE CORP
61 BISHOP ST
PORTLAND, ME 04103

R.D. VALLE
VALLE'S STEAK HOUSE
660 FOREST AVE
PORTLAND, ME 04103

JOHN DAIGLE
CASCO NORTHERN CORP
PO BOX 678
PORTLAND, ME 04104

J.L. MOODY, JR
HANNAFORD BROS CO
PO BOX 1000
PORTLAND, ME 04104

TURNER JONES, JR
COCO-COLA BOTTLING PLANTS
650 MAIN ST
SOUTH PORTLAND, ME 04106

IRVING KRAGAN
PENOBSCOT SHOE CO
NORTH MAIN ST
OLD TOWN, ME 04468

DR. HARRIS BIXLER
MARINE COLLOIDS
PO BOX 308
ROCKLAND ME 04841

WILLIAM DEWEY
A.G. DEWEY
QUECHEE, VT 05059

J.D. HORN
MULTIVISIONS CORP
PO BOX 369
BELLOWS FALLS, VT. 05101

H.M. TAFT
VERMONT RESEARCH CORP
PRECISION PK.
NO. SPRINGFIELD, VT. 05150

H.F. CLIFFORD
STRATTON CORP
STRATTON MT. ,VT 05155

J.E. BARBIER
FELLOWS GEAR SHAPER
78 RIVER ST
SPRINGFIELD, VT. 05156

GERRY ATTIDGE
LOVEJOY TOOL CO
133 MAIN ST
SPRINGFIELD, VT 05156

R.S. GILLETTE
ROCK OF AGES CORP
PO BOX 482
BARRE, VT. 05641

P.L. SMITH
SHERBURNE CORP
SHERBURNE, VT. 05751

M.H. RHOADES, JR
M.H. RHOADES
99 THOMPSON RD
AVON, CT. 06001

FRANCIS E. BAKER, JR
ANDERSEN LABS
1280 BLUE HILLS AVE
BLOOMFIELD, CT. 06002

RALPH MOON
CONNECTICUT PRINTERS
55 GRANBY ST
BLOOMFIELD, CT 06002

HAROLD KNELLER
CONNECTICUT TECHNICAL
522 COTTAGE GROVE RD
BLOOMFIELD, CT. 06002

FRANCIS E. BAKER, JR
DATALIGHT
77E DUDLEY TOWN RD
BLOOMFIELD, CT. 06002

CHARLES KAMAN
KAMAN CORP
OLD WINDSOR RD
BLOOMFIELD, CT. 06002

WORTHINGTON ADAMS
SMYTH MFG. CO
85 GRANBY ST
BLOOMFIELD, CT. 06002

WALLACE BARNES
BARNES GROUP
18 MAIN ST
BRISTOL, CT. 06010

ANSON C. FYLER
SUPERIOR ELECTRIC
383 MIDDLE ST
BRISTOL, CT. 06010

W. LESTER KILLEN
THE BRISTOL BRASS CORP
580 BROAD ST
BRISTOL, CT. 06011

KLAUS W. MOSES
SIMPLEX LOCK CORP
10 FRONT ST
COLLINSVILLE, CT. 06022

T. MITCHELL FORD
EMHART CORP
426 COLT HIGHWAY
FARMINGTON, CT. 06032

HICKS B. WALDRON, JR
HEUBLEIN, INC
FARMINGTON, CT. 06032

CHARLES GOSS
GOSS & DE LEEUW MACHINE CO
KENSINGTON, CT. 06037

PRENTICE TROUP
PRENTICE CORP
319 NEW BRITAIN RD
KENSINGTON, CT. 06037

NEIL H. ELLIS
FIRST HARTFORD CORP
685 PARKER ST
MANCHESTER, CT. 06040

DAVID ABRAMS
PIONEER SYSTEMS, INC
PIONEER INDUSTRIAL PK
MANCHESTER, CT. 06040

MILLARD PRYOR, JR
LYDALL, INC
615 PARKER ST
MANCHESTER, CT 06043

PAUL ROGERS, JR
SKINNER PRECISION INDUSTRIES
95 EDGEWOOD AVE
NEW BRITAIN, CT. 06051

JOSEPH HUGHES
ALLIED THERMAL
215 WARREN ST
NEW BRITAIN, CT. 06052

ALBERT CLEAR
THE STANLEY WORKS
195 LAKE ST
NEW BRITAIN, CT. 06052

JACK LOPES
LA POINTE INDUSTRIES
155 WEST MAIN ST
ROCKVILLE, CT. 06066

HERBERT GILMAN
AMES DEPT. STORES
2418 MAIN ST
ROCKY HILL, CT. 06067

ERNEST W. SMITH, JR
HARTFORD SPECIAL MACHINERY
COLLEGE HWY
SIMSBURY, CT. 06070

A.E. CAFFYN
INDUSTRONICS
489 SULLIVAN AVE PO DRAWER G
SOUTH WINDSOR, CT. 06074

H.J. GERBER
GERBER SCIENTIFIC INSTRUMENT
83 GERBER RD
WAPPING, CT. 06087

P.A. MONGERSON
STANADYNE INC
92 DEERFIELD RD
WINDSOR, CT. 06095

J.H. JOHNSON
TAYLOR & FENN
PO BOX 70
WINDSOR, CT. 06095

EDWARD RAPAPORT
WAITT & BOND
PO BOX 507
WINDSOR, CT. 06095

WORTH LOOMIS
DEXTER CORP
ONE ELM ST
WINDSOR LOCKS, CT. 06096

ALVIN LUKASH
HI-G INC
SPRING ST
WINDSOR LOCKS, CT. 06096

SPENCER MONTGOMERY, JR
MONTGOMERY CO
WINDSOR LOCKS, CT. 06096

RICHARD NEWFIELD
HARTMAN TOBACCO
114 GROVE ST
HARTFORD, CT. 06101

JORDON FRIEDMAN
MERSICK INDUSTRIES
PO BOX 1170
HARTFORD, CT. 06101

CHARLES CHAPIN
SECURITY CORP
1000 ASYLUM AVE
HARTFORD, CT. 06101

BERNARD ADAMS
THREE D DEPARTMENTS
PO BOX 1110
HARTFORD, CT. 06101

HENRY C. WHITE
THE CAPEWELL MFG. CO
60 GOVERNOR ST
HARTFORD, CT. 06102

BERNARD L. GLASS
H.B. DAVIS CORP
1177 MAIN ST
HARTFORD, CT. 06103

BENJAMIN HEATH
MAGELLAN PETROLEUM
37 LEWIS ST
HARTFORD, CT. 06103

ROBERT C. WILSON
PANCOASTAL, INC
37 LEWIS ST
HARTFORD, CT. 06103

JOHN W. BUCKLEY
PANTEPEC INTN'L
37 LEWIS ST
HARTFORD, CT. 06103

LAFAYETTE KEENEY
SAGE-ALLEN & CO
900 MAIN ST
HARTFORD, CT. 06103

ANSON FYLER
ARROW-HART
103 HAWTHORNE ST
HARTFORD, CT. 06105

ARNOLD GREENBERG
COLECO INDUSTRIES
945 ASYLUM AVE
HARTFORD, CT. 06105

EDWARD LITTLE
EXERCYCLE CORP
PO BOX U STA. A
HARTFORD, CT. 06106

ROBERT SWIGGETT
KOLLMORGEN CORP
60 WASHINGTON ST
HARTFORD, CT. 06106

HENRY NOZKO
ACMAT CORP
141 PRESTIGE PK. RD.
EAST HARTFORD, CT. 06108

STANFORD COHEN
MOTT'S SUPER MARKETS
59 LEGGETT ST
EAST HARTFORD, CT. 06108

I.I. KAHN
KAHN INDUSTRIES
885 WELLS RD
WETHERSFIELD, CT. 06109

R.W. EBERLY
WHITLOCK MFG.
99 SOUTH ST
ELMWOOD, CT. 06110

J.D. MURPHY
THE WIREMOLD CO
WOODLAWN
HARTFORD, CT. 06110

W.D. PUTT
HOLOGRAPH CORP
22 CULBRO DR.
WEST HARTFORD, CT. 06110

E. RUSSELL EGGERS
LOCTITE CORP
705 N. MOUNTAIN RD
NEWINGTON, CT. 06111

DONALD THOMPSON
SCAN-OPTICS INC
22 PRESTIGE PK. RD
EAST HARTFORD, CT. 06111

T.P. MC DONAGH, JR
COMPUTER ASSISTANCE INTN'L
200 PARK RD
WEST HARTFORD, CT. 06119

NORMAN GREENMAN
ROGERS CORP
ROGERS, CT. 06263

RALPH POWERS, JR
ROBERTSON PAPER BOX CO
MONTVILLE, CT. 06353

D.P. MILLER
POSI-SEAL INTN'L
RTE. 49 & U.S. 95
NORTH STONINGTON, CT. 06359

CHARLES ARNOLD
HOMER D. BRONSON CO
BEACON FALLS, CT. 06403

JOSEPH SCOTT
ECHLIN MFG
ECHLIN RD & U.S.1
BRANFORD, CT. 06405

DONALD DAVIS
BALL & SOCKET MFG.
493 W. MAIN ST
CHESHIRE, CT. 06410

A.J. BOZZUTO
BOZZUTO'S INC
SCHOOLHOUSE RD
CHESHIRE, CT. 06410

LOUIS RADLER
CHESSCO INDUSTRIES
1960 BRONSON RD
FAIRFIELD, CT. 06430

MARTIN COHEN
MARCON COMMUNICATIONS
1188 POST RD
FAIRFIELD, CT. 06430

JOHN MORALES
S.R.C. LABS, INC
1525 KINGS HIGHWAY
FAIRFIELD, CT. 06430

P.H. COMSTOCK
PRATT-READ CORP.
MAIN ST
IVORYTON, CT. 06442

CARROLL COONEY, JR
VAST, INC
1 MAIN ST
IVORYTON, CT. 06442

HARRIS RANDALL
CONNECTICUT CONSOLIDATED
36 CAMBRIDGE ST
MERIDEN, CT. 06450

DURAND BLATZ
INSILCO
1000 RESEARCH PKWY
MERIDEN, CT. 06450

W.F. SKILLIN
UNION MFG. CO
MERIDEN, CT. 06450

G.B. RAYMOND
RAYMOND PRECISION INDUSTRIES
SMITH ST
MIDDLETOWN, CT. 06457

FRANK RUDOLPH
RIPLEY CO
1 FACTORY ST
MIDDLETOWN, CT. 06457

HERMAN SHEPARD
ATI INC
OLD GATE LN
MILFORD,CT. 06460

ROBERT ADLER
BIC PEN CORP
WILEY ST
MILFORD, CT. 06460

WEEMS ESTELLE
GENERAL SCIENCES CORP
540 NEW HAVEN AVE
MILFORD,CT. 06460

STEPHEN ZIFF
THE SOUND SCRIBER
SIMM LN
NEWTOWN, CT. 06470

STEPHEN ZIFF
DUAL-LITE
SIMM LN.
NEWTOWN, CT. 06470

DAVID CHAFFIN
COMPUTER DATABANKS
33 BERNHARD RD
NORTH HAVEN, CT. 06473

A.J. SHAFTEL
UMC ELECTRONICS
460 SACKETT POINT RD
NORTH HAVEN, CT. 06473

R.W. DIXON
HARVEY HUBBELL
DERBY MULFORD RD
ORANGE, CT. 06477

DAVID POLUR
CHLORIDE CONNREX CORP
PO BOX 45
PLANTSVILLE, CT. 06479

NELSON CURTIS
S. CURTIS & SON
SANDY HOOK, CT. 06482

RALPH CRUMP
FRIGITRONICS
770 RIVER RD
SHELTON, CT. 06484

W.B. RUGER
STURM, RUGER & CO
LACEY PL.
SOUTHPORT, CT. 06490

C.D.CROSBY
BROOKLINE INSTRUMENT CO
845 N. COLONY RD
WALLINGFORD, CT. 06492

FRANCIS SHOWAJ
ALCON DATA CORP
2926 FAIRFIELD AVE
BRIDGEPORT, CT. 06497

B. SCHWARTZ
ALLIANCE MEDICAL INDUSTRIES
959 MAIN ST
STRATFORD,CT 06497

G.L. SCHOLLE
COMPUCOLOR
SNIFFEN LN
STRATFORD, CT. 06497

JAMES WALSH
ARMSTRONG RUBBER
500 SARGENT DR PO BOX 1651
NEW HAVEN, CT. 06507

ROLAND BIXLER
J.B. & T. CO
425 CHAPEL ST
NEW HAVEN, CT. 06511

OLIVER KIMBERLY, JR
NATIONAL APPAREL
130 HAMILTON ST
NEW HAVEN, CT. 06511

LEON J. SIMKIN
SIMKINS INDUSTRIES
259 EAST ST
NEW HAVEN, CT. 06511

HOWARD PHELAN
WELSBACH CORP
240 SARGENT DR.
NEW HAVEN, CT. 06511

HERBERT FRIEDLANDER
MICRO PRECISION CORP
35 FULTON ST
NEW HAVEN, CT. 06512

JOHN J. COTT
COTT CORP
197 CHATHAM ST
NEW HAVEN, CT. 06513

PAOLIP PEOLELLA
PLASTICRETE CORP
1883 DIXWELL AVE
HAMDEN, CT. 06514

H.C. RIPLEY
WHITNEY BLAKE
1565 DIXWELL AVE
HAMDEN, CT. 06514

LEO BRENCATO
MITE CORP
446 BLAKE ST
NEW HAVEN, CT. 06515

DAVID OLIPHANT
ACADEMIC INDUSTRIES
SAW MILL RD
WEST HAVEN, CT. 06516

ABE STRAHL
FLAVO-RITE FOODS
135 FRONT AVE
WEST HAVEN, CT. 06516

RUSSELL MONTGOMERY
WEST HAVEN BUCKLE
742 WASHINGTON AVE
WEST HAVEN, CT. 06516

E.M. MORAN
SANITAS SERVICE CORP
649 AMITY RD
BETHANY, CT. 06525

BARTON WELLER
VITRAMON
PO BOX 544
BRIDGEPORT, CT. 06601

PHILIP BURDETT
REMINGTON ARMS CO
939 BARNUM AVE
BRIDGEPORT, CT. 06602

JAMES WALKER
WARNACO
350 LAFAYETTE ST
BRIDGEPORT, CT. 06602

F.B. SILLIMAN
HYDRAULIC
835 MAIN ST
BRIDGEPORT, CT. 06603

ALLAN SANDBERG
TELEMODEM
23 ALLEN ST
BRIDGEPORT. CT. 06604

WILLIAM WATHEN
TERRY CORP
LAMBERTON RD
WINDSOR, CT. 06606

LEE BUNTING
BUNTING STERISYSTEMS
46 BEATRICE ST
BRIDGEPORT, CT. 06607

HENRY WHEELER
ACME UNITED CORP
100 HICKS ST
BRIDGEPORT, CT. 06608

JOHN P. FROUGE
FROUGE CORP
5065 MAIN ST
TRUMBULL, CT. 06611

ROBERT GORDON
RAYBESTOR-MANHATTAN
100 OAKVIEW DR
TRUMBULL, CT. 06611

ROGER SWAIN
INFODEX
7 CHERRY AVE
WATERBURY, CT. 06702

HAROLD LEEVER
MAC DERMID
50 BROOKSIDE RD
WATERBURY, CT. 06708

A. WM. HAYDON
HAYDON SWITCH & INSTRUMENT
1500 MERIDEN RD
WATERBURY, CT. 06716

VINCENT LARGAY
BUELL INDUSTRIES
PO BOX 2029
WATERBURY, CT. 06720

RICHARD CRANE
LEA MFG.
237 E. AURORA ST
WATERBURY, CT. 06720

HERBERT BLADH
SCOVILL MFG.
SCOVILL SQ.
WATERBURY, CT. 06720

JOHN BENSON
WATERBURY BUCKLE CO
952 S. MAIN ST
WATERBURY, CT. 06720

C.H. BUCKLEY
RISDON MFG. CO
RISDON ST.
NAUGATUCK, CT. 06770

R.G. MC MILLEN
EASTERN CO
112 BRIDGE ST
NAUGATUCK, CT. 06772

L.W. ELSTON
PETER PAUL, INC
NEW HAVEN RD
NAUGATUCK, CT. 06772

P.E. PRITCHARD
AUDIO DYNAMICS CORP
PICKETT DISTRICT RD
NEW MILFORD, CT. 06776

ALFRED STEWART
DATRON SYSTEMS
401 WATERTOWN RD
THOMASTON, CT. 06787

ELMER STICCO
INTERN'L CONTROLS
400 WATERTOWN RD
THOMASTON, CT. 06787

GERALD CAHILL
TORIN CORP
KENNEDY DR
TORRINGTON, CT. 06790

ALLEN SPERRY
TURNER & SEYMOUR MFG
100 LAWTON ST
TORRINGTON, CT. 06790

MONROE KELEMENCKY
BASIC SCIENCES
RFD 3
WOODBURY, CT. 06798

ANTHONY COBURN
COMPUTER-OPTICS
BERKSHIRE INDUSTRIAL PK.
BETHEL, CT. 06801

R.B. BACON
TIME SHARE PERIPHERALS CORP
RT. 6 R.D. 2 STONY HILL
BETHEL, CT. 06801

MURRAY KLEIMAN
ACOUSTICON SYSTEMS CORP
SHELTER ROCK LN.
DANBURY, CT. 06810

NORMAN ALPERT
ALPEX COMPUTER CORP
37 EXECUTIVE DR
DANBURY, CT. 06810

EMIL KARKUT
BARDEN CORP
200 PARK AVE
DANBURY, CT. 06810

RICHARD MAHLER
DATA-CONTROL SYSTEMS
COMMERCE DR.
DANBURY, CT. 06810

CLINTON WALKER
ETHAN ALLEN
ETHAN ALLEN DR
DANBURY, CT. 06810

R.K. DOMBROWSKI
GRAPHIC SCIENCES
CORPORATE DR
DANBURY, CT. 06810

JOHN BUTTERWORTH
HIDCO INTN'L
COMMERCE PARK
DANBURY, CT. 06810

CHARLES SNEAD, JR
CALLAHAN MINING CORP
1120 POST RD
DARIEN, CT. 06820

J.W. DUNLAP
DUNLAP & ASSOCIATES
ONE PARKLAND DR
DARIEN, CT. 06820

THOMAS HOWES
ESTERLINE CORP
CBT PLAZA 1120 POST RD
DARIEN, CT. 06820

J.T. HALL
PINNACLE EXPLORATION
CBT PLAZA
DARIEN, CT. 06820

ALFRED MULLIKEN
GILBERT & BENNETT MFG
GEORGETOWN, CT. 06829

PIERRE GOUSSELAND
AMAX INC
AMAX CENTER
GREENWICH, CT. 06830

B.D. GLENN, JR
ARROW ELECTRONICS
600 STEAMBOAT RD
GREENWICH, CT. 06830

GEORGE HOGEMAN
AVCO CORP
1275 KING ST
GREENWICH, CT. 06830

A.P. GATES
BEKER INDUSTRIES
124 WEST PUTNAM AVE
GREENWICH, CT. 06830

J.A. BOOK
CHASE BAG CO
2 GREENWICH PLAZA
GREENWICH, CT. 06830

HENRY CLARKE, JR
CLABIR CORP
145 MASON ST
GREENWICH, CT. 06830

LESTER GOTTLIEB
DATA DIMENSIONS
51 WEAVER ST
GREENWICH, CT. 06830

CHARLES MORCHAND
DATA-PLEX SYSTEMS, INC
164 MASON ST
GREENWICH, CT. 06830

ANDREW LOZYNIAK
DYNAMICS CORP OF AMERICA
475 STEAMBOAT RD
GREENWICH, CT. 06830

ROBERT DE MANE
ECOLOGICAL RECYCLING
289 GREENWICH AVE
GREENWICH, CT. 06830

ROBERT JENSEN
GENERAL CABLE CORP
500 W. PUTNAM AVE
GREENWICH, CT. 06830

ANDRE JACOMET
HOWMET CORP
475 STEAMBOAT RD
GREENWICH, CT. 06830

TERRY J. FOX
IROQUOIS BRANDS LTD
41 WEST PUTNAM AVE
GREENWICH, CT. 06830

E. CONESE
IRVIN INDUSTRIES
51 WEAVER ST
GREENWICH, CT. 06830

LEWIS ARMSTRONG
KEARNEY-NATIONAL
GREENWICH OFFICE PK. BLDG 6
GREENWICH, CT. 06830

ROBERT W. HUTTON
LONE STAR INDUSTRIES
ONE GREENWICH PLAZA
GREENWICH, CT. 06830

HENRY WYMAN
THE PANTASOLE CO
PO BOX 1800
GREENWICH, CT. 06830

MORRIS SOBIN
PILOT RADIO CORP
66 FIELD POINT RD
GREENWICH, CT. 06830

JOSEPH ANNIELLO
LOUIS SHERRY
18 WEST PUTNAM AVE
GREENWICH, CT. 06830

A. LELAND GLIDDEN
THE NEW CANAAN CO
NEW CANAAN, CT. 06840

JAMES ETTINGER
ELECTRIC REGULATOR CORP
PEARL ST
NORWALK, CT. 06850

H.E. HARRIS
HARREL, INC
16 FITCH ST
EAST NORWALK, CT. 06850

KENNETH RAY
WASTE WATER TREATMENT
28 MICHEAL ST
NORWALK, CT. 06850

M.H. MEHR
MEASUREMENT SYSTEMS
523 WEST AVE
NORWALK, CT. 06850

ROBERT E. WEISSMAN
NATIONAL CSS
300 WESTPORT AVE
NORWALK, CT. 06851

CARL BENNETT
CALDOR, INC
20 GLOVER ST
NORWALK, CT. 06852

ROBERT KATZ
KATZ CORP
163 EAST AVE
NORWALK, CT. 06852

ROBERT SORENSEN
PERKIN-ELMER CORP
MAIN AVE
NORWALK, CT. 06852

ROBERT J. AMMAN
WILTEK, INC
GLOVER AVE
NORWALK, CT. 06852

GEORGE BATTOCCHIO
XEXEX INDUSTRIES
3 DUKE PL
NORWALK, CT. 06854

RICHARD FARLEY
BURNDY CORP
RICHARDS AVE
NORWALK, CT 06856

R.G. BOWMAN
C.R. GIBSON
32 KNIGHT ST
NORWALK, CT. 06856

A.M. ZAIS
RAY PROOF CORP
50 KEELER AVE
NORWALK, CT. 06856

BRIAN MC CARTHY
CONTROLLED AUTOMATION
18 MARSHALL ST
SOUTH NORWALK, CT. 06856

ROBERT JOHNSON
NORWALK CO
N   WATER ST
SOUTH NORWALK, CT. 06856

RONALD BARLOW
MOREHOUSE-BARLOW CO
78 DANBURY RD
WILTON, CT. 06867

GERALD ROSENBERG
CONDEC CORP
1700 POST RD
OLD GREENWICH, CT. 06870

JEROME DAVIS
VARIFAB INC
1700 E. PUTNAM
OLD GREENWICH, CT. 06870

VICTOR KIAM, III
BENRUS CORP
BENRUS CENTER
RIDGEFIELD, CT. 06877

HUGH K. STEVENSON
CLARKSON INDUSTRIES
890 ETHAN ALLEN HIGHWAY
RIDGEWAY, CT. 06877

JOSEPH VENTURA
SURG-O-FLEX OF AMERICA
1154 E. PUTNAM AVE
RIVERSIDE, CT. 06878

HARLAN SMITH
ASPRO INC
RIVERSIDE BLDG
WESTPORT, CT. 06880

NAHUM RAND
BRANDON APPLIED SYSTEMS
22 IMPERIAL AVE
WESTPORT, CT. 06880

WILMER J. THOMAS, JR
F.A.S. INTERN'L
17 RIVERSIDE AVE
WESTPORT, CT. 06880

DAYTON CORNISH
2001, INC
47 RIVERSIDE AVE
WESTPORT, CT. 06880

R.M. ROSENCRANS
UA-COLUMBIA CABLEVISION
PO BOX 589
WESTPORT, CT. 06880

JOHN EMERY, JR
EMERY AIR FREIGHT CORP
WILTON, CT. 06897

CHARLES JOHNSON
GENERAL DATACOMM INDUSTRIES
131 DANBURY RD
WILTON, CT. 06897

A.H. MORGAN
T-BAR INC
141 DANBURY RD
WILTON, CT. 06897

RICHARD GRISAR
ANALYTICAL SYSTEMS
777 SUMMER ST.
STANFORD, CONN. 06901

SAMUEL A. CASEY
GREAT NOTHERN NEKOOSA
75 PROSPECT ST
STAMFORD, CONN 06901

WILLIAM A. ERALNICH
OPINION INC.
777 SUMMER ST.
STAMFORD, CONN. 06901

F.D. RICH, JR.
F.D. RICH HOUSING
101 BROAD ST.
STAMFORD, CONN. 06901

ROBERT B. BARNES, JR.
BARNES ENGINNERING CO.
30 COMMERCE RD.
STAMFORD, CONN. 06902

ARTHUR J. SANTRY, JR.
COMBUSTION ENGINEERING
900 LONG RIDGE RD.
STAMFORD, CONN. 06902

CARL H. FREYER
CIG INTERNATION CAPITAL
65 WASHINGTON AVE.
STAMFORD, CONN. 06902

ABRAHAM BLUMERFELD
LANCER GRAPHIC INDUSTRIES
200 HENRY ST.
STAMFORD, CONN. 06902

JOHN O. BEATTIE
THE POLYCAST
69 SOUTHFIELD AVE.
STAMFORD, CONN. 06902

MARVIN BELSKY
GEOS
420 FAIRFIELD AVE.
STAMFORD, CONN. 06902

STANLEY M. WECKSLER
DATAPAX COMPUTER SYSTEMS
180 MOUNTAINWOOD RD.
STAMFORD, CONN. 0690

DENNIS N. CAULDFIELD
THERMO MAGNETICS
280 FAIRFIELD AVE.
STAMFORD, CONN. 06902

JOHN E. KIRCHER
CONTINENTAL OIL
HIGH RIDGE PARK
STAMFORD, CONN. 0690

DANIEL G. GILLESPIE
DORR-OLIVER
HAVEMEYER LANE
STAMFORD, CONN. 06904

HAROLD A. STRICKLAND, JR.
GENERAL SIGNAL
HIGH RIDGE PARK
STAMFORD, CONN. 06904

FRED T. ALLEN
PITNEY-BOWES
WALNUT & PACIFIC STS.
STAMFORD, CONN. 06904

H.R. BULLOCK
UMC INDUSTRIES
HIGH RIDGE PARK, BOX 1090
STAMFORD, CONN. 06904

ALAN E. SHALOV
ALANTHUS CORP.
111 HIGH RIDGE RD.
STAMFORD, CONN. 06905

J.B. LOVE
AMERICAN THREAD CO.
HIGH RIDGE PARK
STAMFORD, CONN. 06905

JEROME W. ROBBINS
HMW INDUSTRIES
HIGH RIDGE PARK
STAMFORD, CONN. 06905

STEVEN A. BURN
ROYAL GENERAL
1234 SUMMER ST. #500
STAMFORD, CONN. 06905

HAROLD A. THAU
ROYALTY CONTROLS
1234 SUMMER ST. #500
STAMFORD, CONN. 06905

L. W. MILES
UNIVERSITY PATENTS
2777 SUMMER ST.
STAMFORD, CONN. 06905

D. H. SHEPARD
COGNITRONICS
25 CRESCENT ST.
STAMFORD, CONN. 06906

FRANCIS A. GOVAN
YORK RESEARCH
ONE RESEARCH DR.
STAMFORD, CONN. 06906

ANDREW C. SIGLER
CHAMPION INTERNATIONAL
ONE LANDMARK SQ.
STAMFORD, CONN. 06921

FRANK GRYL
CONTINENTAL PLASTICS
10 PRODUCTION WAY
AVENEL, N.J. 07001

SHELDON FEINBERG
CADENCE INDUSTRIES
21 HENDERSON DR.
WEST CALDWELL, N.J. 07002

WILLIAM G. REMINGTON
PEERLESS TUBE CO.
58 LOCUST AVE.
BLOOMFIELD, N.J. 07003

SAMUEL WEINERSHEIMER
U.S. MAGNET & ALLOY
266 GLENWOOD AVE.
BLOOMFIELD, N.J. 07003

EDWIN S. SEABURY
RADIO FREQUENCY LAB.
POWERVILLE RD.
BOONTON, N.J. 07005

M.C. THOMPSON, JR.
AUTOMATED INFORMATION
1275 BLOOMFIELD AVE.
FAIRFIELD, N.J. 07006

EDGAR UDINE
BIO-MED. SCIENCES
140 NEW DUTCH LANE
FAIRFIELD, N.J.　07006

EMILE N. BERNARD
CHARVOZ-CARSEN
5 DANIEL RD.
FAIRFIELD, N.J.　07006

ARTHUR RUSH
DIGITAL COMPUTERCONTROLS
12 INDUSTRIAL RD.
FAIRFIELD, N.J.　07006

ARTHUR BRUKHARDT
ECLIPSE SYSTEMS
28 KULICK RD.
FAIRFIELD, N.J.　07006

VINCENT V. ABAJIAN
ELECTO-NUCLEONICS
368 PASSAIC AVE.
FAIRFIELD, N.J.　07006

P.J. PETROU
INTERNATIONAL PROTEINS
123 FAIRFIELD RD.
FAIRFIELD, N.J.　07006

T.L. MONACO, JR.
NORTHERN PRECISION LABS.
202 FAIRFIELD RD.
FAIRFIELD, N.J.　07006

ARNOLD L. PALMIERE
PRE CAST CONCRETE
62 CLINTON RD.
FAIRFIELD, N.J.　07006

ROBERT J. O'BRIEN
RAPIDATA, INC.
20 NEW DUTCH LANE
FAIRFIELD, N.J.　07006

R.R. BODD
RECREATIONAL & ED.
1275 BLOOMFIELD AVE.
FAIRFIELD, N.J.　07006

SOL INSPECTOR
SMUGGLERS ATTIC
1275 BLOOMFIELD AVE.
FAIRFIELD, N.J.　07006

EUGENE STARR
TYCOM CORP.
26 JUST RD.
FAIRFIELD, N.J. 07006

ARNOLD SMOLLER
HUDSON PHARMACEUTICAL
21 HENDERSON DR.
WEST CALDWELL, N.J.　07006

E.E. FINNEY
PANELGRAPHIC
10 HENDERSON DR.
WEST CALDWELL, N.J. 07006

M.S. GORDON
PERMANENT FILTER
P.O. BOX 1087
WEST CALDWELL, N.J.　07006

LARRIE S. CALVERT
POLLUTION CONTROL INDUST.
ONE FAIRFIELD CRESCENT
WEST CALDWELL, N.J.　07006

L.J. POLITE, JR.
PAULSBORO CHEM. INDUST.
1401 BROAD ST.
CLIFTON, N.J. 07011

ARMANDO D. MOTA
A.D.M. CORP.
820 BLOOMFIELD AVE.
CLIFTON, N.J.　07012

FRANK G. HICKEY
GENERAL INSTRUMENT
255 ALLWOOD RD. BOX 1201
CLIFTON, N.J. 07012

GEORGE F. BLASIUS
BLASIUS INDUSTRIES
1373 BROAD ST.
CLIFTON, N.J. 07013

PETER E. SIMON
PRIME MOTOR INNS
1030 CLIFTON AVE.
CLIFTON, N.J. 07013

H.G. SHELTON
TRYLON CHEM.
1200 RT. 46
CLIFTON, N.J.　07013

ALBERT SPITZ
MAJOR POOL EQUIPMENT
200 ENTIN RD.
CLIFTON, N.J.　07014

FRANK LAUTENBERG
AUTOMATIC DATA PROCESSING
405 ROUTE 3
CLIFTON, N.J. 07015

L. JOHN POLITE, JR.
ESSEX CHEMICAL
1401 BROAD ST.
CLIFTON, N.J. 07015

H. ATWOOD, JR.
I.T.I. ELECTRONICS
369 LEXINGTON AVE.
CLIFTON, N.J. 07015

W.G. LUCAS
MANAGEMENT DATA PROCESSING
385 LAKEVIEW AVE.
CLIFTON, N.J.　07015

MILTON PERLMUTTER
SUPERMARETS GENERAL
301 BLAIR RD.
WOODBRIDGE, N.J.　07015

HAROLD SCHWARZ
FOOD & DRUG REASEARCH
60 EVERGREEN PL.
EAST ORANGE, N.J. 07018

DR. MARTIN PRINCE
SYNTHATRON
150 RIVER RD.
EDGEWATER, N.J. 07020

ALPHONSE P. THIELE
AQUARIUS ARTS
101 BROAD AVE.
FAIRVIEW, N.J. 07022

IRVING LEVINES
BRISTOL SOUND CENTER
2125 CENTER AVE.
FORT LEE, N.J.   07024

ROBERT EDWARDS
RADIOFONE CORP.
2125 CENTER AVE.
FORT LEE, N.J. 07024

ALFRED ZASLOFF
VORNADO INC.
174 PASSAIC
CARFIELD, N.J.   07026

THOMAS L. CASALE
CASALE INDUSTRIES
50 CENTER ST.
GARWOOD, N.J.   07027

J. KASS
MAGNETAX
301 MAIN ST. BOX 473
CHATHAM, N.J. 07028

FRANK L. DRIVER, III
DRIVER-HARRIS
201 MIDDLESEX ST.
HARRISON, N.J. 07029

LEONARD N. STERN
HARTZ MOUNTAIN
700 S. 4TH. ST
HARRISON, N.J. 07029

SOL SKOLER
TRI-CHEM
ONE CAPE MAY ST.
HARRISON, N.J. 07029

R.M GUINN
COMPUCOMP
70 HUDSON ST.
HOBOKEN, N.J. 07030

HERBERT M. BLOCK
U.S. TESTING
1415 PARK AVE.
HOBOKEN, N.J. 07030

ANTHONY J. DAVANZO
ECONOMY BOOKBINDING
234 SCHUYLER ST.
KEARNY, N.J. 07032

I.L. LOPATA
RAGEN PRECISION INUSTRIES
9 PORETE AVE.
NORTH ARLINGTON, N.J. 07032

WALTER GOLDBERG
ASTOR HANDPRINTS
85 LINCOLN HIGHWAY
SOUTH KEARNY, N.J. 07032

M.C. TEMKIN
AMERICAN ALL-SERVUS
504 WASHINGTON AVE.
KENILWORTH, N.J. 07033

NELSON PELTZ
COFFEE-MAT
251 - 31 ST ST..
KENILWORTH, N.J.   07033

WILLIAM ZEUS, SR.
NATIONAL TOOL & MFG.
100 NORTH TWELFTH ST.
KENILWORTH, N.J. 07033

JERRY TURCO
INTERCARE NUSING
521 PINE BROOK RD.
LINCOLN PARK, N.J.   07035

BERNARD WECHSLER
COMSIP CUSTOMLINE
1418 E. LINDEN AVE.
LINDEN, N.J. 07036

LOUIS KAHN
FREOPLEX
240 E. ST. GEORGE AVE.
LINDEN, N.J.   07036

CHARLES P. COVINO
GENERAL MAGNAPLATE
1331 EDGAR RD. RT.1
LINDEN, N.J.   07036

J.R. PALUMBO
PLATRONICS
301 COMMERCE RD.
LINDEN, N.J.   07036

MAURICE FRIEDMAN
SCIENTIFIC COMPONENTS
350 HURST ST.
LINDEN, N.J. 07036

WILLIAM W. MOORE
BELCO POLLUTION CONTROL
P.O. BOX 412
LIVINGSTON, N.J. 07039

LEE CHERENSON
CHERENSON, CARROLL & HOLZER
508 S. LIVINGSTON AVE.
LIVINGSTON, N.J. 07039

FRANK A. LEE
FOSTER WHEELER CORP.
110 SOUTH ORANGE AVE.
LIVINGSTON, N.J.   07039

H.A. AUGENBLICK
MICROLAB-FXR
TEN MICROLAB RD.
LIVINGSTON, N.J. 07039

HERBERT MAXWELL
WINPORT MANUFACTURING
8 DEVONSHIRE RD.
LIVINGSTON, N.J. 07039

W.M. VOGEL, JR.
STANDARD CONTAINER
205 CLAREMONT AVE
MONTCLAIR, N.J. 07042

ROBERT T. COPPOLETTA
DATA ACCESS SYSTEMS
100 RT. 46
MOUNTAIN LAKES, N.J.07046

ARNOLD CHAIT
AMBASSADOR GROUP
8400 RIVER RD.
NORTH BERGEN, N.J. 07047

WALTER H. SIMSON
DURO-TEST
2321 KENNEDY BLVD.
NORTH BERGEN, N.J. 07047

RICHARD J. SCHWARTZ
JONATHAN LOGAN
3901 LIBERTY AVE.
NORTH BERGEN, N.J. 07047

EDWARD L. STERN
KREISLER MANUFACTURING
9015 BERGENLINE AVE.
NORTH BERGEN, N.J. 07047

JOHN J. PETILLO
NATCONTAINER
8101 TONNELLE AVE.
NORTH BERGEN, N.J, 07047

ALVIN J. GOREN
ORGANICS CORP. OF AMERICA
1615 51 ST ST..
NORTH BERGEN, N.J. 07047

IRVING ALPERT
REGAL ACCESSORIES
7500 WEST SIDE AVE.
NORTH BERGEN, N.J. 07047

JOSEPH SCHEIDER
SCOTTI COMMERCIAL
7700 MARINE RD.
NORTH BERGEN, N.J. 07047

ROBERT O. HALL
COOPER-JARRETT
23 S. ESSEX AVE.
ORAGNE, N.J. 07051

R.A. HIRSCHFIELD
COMPUTER AUDIT SYSTEMS
80 MAIN ST.
WEST ORANGE, N.J. 07052

H.J. MILLER
ATHLONE INDUSTRIES
200 WEBRO RD.
PARSIPPANY, N.J. 07054

MALCOLM F. BAKER
BAKER INDUSTRIES
199 CHERRY HILL RD.
PARSIPPANY, N.J. 07054

JACK FRUCHT
BOONTON ELECTRONICS
RT. 287 AT SMITH RD.
PARSIPPANY, N.J. 07054

ROBERT C. O'NEILL
COOPER LABORATORIES
1259 RT. 46
PARSIPPANY, N.J. 07054

FREDDIE SCHNELL
ELECTRO-PROTECTIVE
25 EASTMANS RD.
PARSIPPANY, N.J. 07054

WILLIAM R. HARTMAN
INTERPAGE
P.O. BOX 1111
PARSIPPANY, N.J. 07054

CHARLES I. SHANOK
SHIRE NATIONAL
199 CHERRY HILL RD.
PARSIPPANY, N.J. 07054

MICHAEL DOROTA
APEX ELECTRONICS
100 EIGHTH ST.
PASSAIC, N.J. 07055

M.A. MURRAY
DYNATION
P.O. BOX 1659, 3 CANAL ST.
PASSAIC, N.J. 07055

JOSEPH M. MILITELLO
NEW JERSEY ENGINEERING
577 MAIN AVE.
PASSAIC, N.J. 07055

ALFRED M. KATZ
RELIABLE CHEMICAL
85 LIBERTY ST.
PASSAIC, N.J. 07055

E.F. HANSEN
DRICO INDUSTRIAL
480 MAIN AVE.
WALLINGTON, N.J. 07057

ALBERT S. MILLMAN
SENECA FALLS MACHINE
BOX 2845
PLAINFIELD, N.J. 07062

ALBERT S. MILLMAN
SFM
900 NORTH AVE.
PLAINFIELD, N.J. 07062

ARNOLD SEMENOFF
AQUATERM PRODUCTS
1582 HART ST.
RAHWAY, N.J. 07065

R.L. CAMPBELL
AUTOMATED DATA ASSOC.
1333 LAWRENCE ST.
RAHWAY, N.J. 07065

BERNARD ACKERMAN
ELECTRO-CATHETER
2100 FELVER CT.
RAHWAY, N.J. 07065

PAUL A. CAMERON
PUROLATOR
970 NEW BRUNSWICK AVE.
RAHWAY, N.J. 07065

SPYROS PAPALEXIOU
AERONIX
P.O. BOX 917, 19 WALNUT ST..
CLARK, N.J. 07066

JOSEPH M. GENTILE
RESISTOFLEX
WOODLAND RD.
ROSELAND, N.J. 07068

D.A. DE STEFANO
INITIO
P.O. BOX 5000
RUTHERFORD, N.J. 07070

J.E. BERTOLI
JERSEY PATENTS
27 ORIENT WAY
RUTHERFORD, N.J. 07070

EDMUND ENTIN
POWER COMPUTER SYSTEMS
RTE. 3 & MEADOW RD.
RUTHERFORD, N.J. 07070

E.W. BRINKERHOFF
TEL-INSTRUMENT
728 GARDEN ST.
CARLSTADT, N.J. 07070

GEORGE FRIER
FRIER INDUSTRIES
P.O. BOX 307
CARLSTADT, N.J. 07072

STANLEY CELLER
ON-GUARD CORP.
350 GOTHAM PARKWAY
CARLSTADT, N.J. 07072

LAWRENCE REISMAN
SCIENTIFIC TEXTILE
55 TRIANGLE BLVD.
CARLSTADT, N.J. 07072

EDWARD ANDRIOLA
TEC TORCH CO.
611 INDUSTRIAL RD.
CARSTADT, N.J. 07072

GILBERT G. DAVIS
TRANS GRAPHICS
640 DELL RD.
CARLSTADT, N.J. 07072

MILTON MODELL
COSMO BOOK DISTRIBUTING
33-49 WHELAN RD.
EAST RUTHERFORD, N.J. 07073

GREGORY PAPALEXIS
MARATHON ENTERPRISES
66 E. UNION AVE.
EAST RUTHERFORD, N.J. 07073

JOSEPH R. STARITA
STAR-GLO INDUSTRIES
2 CARLTON AVE.
EAST RUTHERFORD, N.J. 07073

C.L. WELLINGTON
WELLINGTON TECH.
33-49 WHELAN RD.
EAST RUTHERFORD, N.J. 07073

IRVING RIFKIN
CREST-FOAM
100 CAROL PL.
NOONACHIE, N.J. 07074

D.D. GRIEG
ELECTRONIC RESEARCH
311 E. PARK ST.
MOONACHIE, N.J. 07074

LAWRENCE HERBERT
PANTONE
55 KNICKERBOCKER RD.
MOONACHIE, N.J. 07074

T. ROLAND BERNER
CURTISS-WRIGHT
ONE PASSAIC ST.
WOODBRIDGE, N.J. 07075

C.A. MAROTTA
COMPUTERS & RAILROADS
4400 S. CLINTON AVE.
SO. PLAINFIELD, N.J. 07080

E. GOLDSTEIN
DILLY MANUFACTURING
105 SYLVANIA PL.
SOUTH PLAINFIELD, N.J. 07080

A.I. DRANETZ
DRANETZ ENGINEERING
BOX E,
SOUTH PLAINFIELD, N.J. 17080

ROBERT W. CARRY
THE ENGINEER CO.
FOOT OF TEEPLE PL.
SOUTH PLAINFIELD, N.J. 07080

LUCIEN D. YOKANA
STERLING EXTRUDER
901 DURHAM AVE.
SOUTH PLAINFIELD, N.J. 07080

LESTER G. KAUFMAN
SUPRONICS
104 NEW ERA DR.
S. PLAINFIELD, N.J. 07080

H.J. FALLON
FEDERATED PURCHASER
155 NEW ERA DR.
SPRINGFIELD, N.J. 07081

A.M. LERNER
QUINDAR ELECTRONICS
60 FADEM RD.
SPRINGFIELD, N.J. 07081

LEO V. STAVENICK
REPUBLIC METAL PRODUCTS
33 COMMERCE ST.
SPRINGFIELD, N.J. 07081

PERRY SUMAS
VILLAGE SUPER MARKET
733 MOUNTAIN AVE.
SPRINGFIELD, N.J. 07081

L.J. SCHOENBERG
AGS COMPUTERS
2005 RTE. 22
UNION, N.J. 07083

JOHN L. DE ZERGA
ALLEN OIL CO.
P.O. BOX 447
UNION, N.J. 07083

JOSEPH J. MASCUCH
BREEZE CORP.
700 LIBERTY AVE.
UNION, N.J. 07083

MEYER BURGSTEIN
MAYFAIR SUPER MARKETS
1441 MORRIS AVE.
UNION, N.J. 07083

S.F. PESKIN
POLYPLASTEX UNITED
870 SPRINGFIELD RD.
UNION CITY, N.J. 07083

LOUIS RUDNICK
SANDERS CAREER SCHOOLS
1416 MORRIS AVE.
UNION, N.J. 07083

S.S. SCHIFFMAN
TENNEY ENGINEERING
1090 SPRINGFIELD RD.
UNION, N.J. 07083

CHESTER KOBY
TOWN & CAMPUS
1040 MORRIS AVE.
UNION, N.J. 07083

J.J. WILK
TRANSNET
2005 RTE. 22
UNION, N.J. 07083

MEYER BURGSTEIN
UNITED MARKETS
1441 MORRIS AVE.
UNION, N.J. 07083

PETER GOLDSTEIN
ACRODYNE
1217 SUMMIT AVE
UNION CITY, N.J. 07087

CARL OLLA
OLLA INDUSTRIES
4810 BROADWAY
UNION CITY, N.J. 07087

B.W. GIMBEL
U.C.F. INDUSTRIES
3908 BERGENLINE AVE.
UNION CITY, N.J. 07087

C.A. SMYLIE
Y & S CANDIES
45 CARINAL DR.
WESTFIELD, N.J. 07091

MARVIN A. ROSENBLUM
PRECISION POLYMER
1136 RTE. 22
MOUNTAINSIDE, N.J. 07092

SOL ZAUSNER
ZAUSNER FOODS CORP.
P.O. BOX 1146
MOUNTAINSIDE, N.J. 07092

ABE GINSBURG
JACLYN
635 - 59TH. ST..
WEST NEW YORK, N.J. 07093

HARRY ERIKSSON
FACIT-ADDO
501 WINSOR DR.
SECAUCUS, N.J. 07094

JEROME A. BARRER
GAYLORDS NATIONAL
10 ENTERPRISE AVE
SECAUCUS, N.J. 07094

HERBERT FISHER
JAMESWAY
40 HARTZ WAY
SECAUCUS, N.J. 07094

JULIUS H. GEWIRTZ
JOYCE LESLIE
20 ENTERPRISE AVE
SECAUCUS, N.J. 07094

LYLE STUART
LYLE STUART, INC.
120 ENTERPRISE AVE.
SECAUCUS, N.J. 07094

WILLIAM A. NELSON, JR.
NELSON RESOURCE
20 ENTERPRISE AVE.
SECAUCUS, N.J. 07094

HILDA KIRSCHBAUM GERSTEIN
PETRIE STORES
70 ENTERPRISE AVE.
SECAUCUS, N.J. 07094

FRED P. ROBIN
EASTCO MEDICAL EQUIPMENT
572 AMBOY AVE.
WOODBRIDGE, N.J. 07095

LOUIS V. ARONSON, II
RONSON
1 RONSON RD.
WOODBRIDGE, N.J. 07095

ISADOR CANDEUB
CANDUEB, FLEISSIG & ASSOC.
11 HILL ST.
NEWARK, N.J. 07102

BERNARD MANISCHEWITZ
B. MANISCHEWITZ
9 CLINTON ST.
NEWARK, N.J. 07102

ROBERT KISBERG
PRIVATE & COMPUTER SCHOOLS
790 BROAD ST.
NEWARK, N.J. 07102

JAMES C. KOSTELNI
GEORGIA BONDED FIBERS
NUTTMAN, NEW & WILSEY STS.
NEWARK, N.J. 07103

EDWARD FRIELING
ELECTRONIC ENTERPRISES
65 SEVENTH AVE.
NEWARK, N.J. 07104

MICHAEL T. GASPARIK
GENERAL ELECTRONICS
42 SPRING ST.
NEWARK, N.J. 07104

P.J. KURENS
HILLSIDE METAL PRODUCTS
300 PASSAIC ST.
NEWARK, N.J. 07104

JOHN DASEN
LITTLE CHEF FOOD PRODUCTS
100 SYLVAN AVE.
NEWARK, N.J. 07104

DONALD L. EPSTEIN
NU VU CORP.
2145 McCARTER HIGHWAY
NEWARK, N.J. 07104

PAUL A. FERTELL
SETON
849 BROADWAY
NEWARK, N.J. 07104

CARL KRIGER
CANRAD-HANOVIA
100 CHESTNUT ST.
NEWARK, N.J. 07105

J.E. GILBERT, JR.
CHASE CHEMICAL
280 CHESTNUT ST.
NEWARK, N.J. 07105

GERALD GARE
EUREKA PRODUCTS
135 JACKSON ST.
NEWARK, N.J. 07105

CALMAN J. KISH
FAIRMOUNT CHEMICAL
117 BLANCHARD ST.
NEWARK, N.J. 07105

ROBERT B. WINKEL
PPD
574 FERRY ST.
NEWARK, N.J. 07105

HERBERT DOBKIN
THERMO NATIONAL INDUST.
108-34 JOHNSON ST.
NEWARK, N.J. 07105

DONALD GREGG
FABER, COE & GREGG
231 JOHNSON AVE.
NEWARK, N.J. 07108

ANTHONY M. PETACCIO
ED. SYSTEM & PUBLICATIONS
83 VALLEY ST.
BELLESVILLE, N.J. 07109

M. BRUCKER
FARADYNE ELECTRONICS
140 LITTLE ST.
BELLESVILLE, N.J. 07109

STANLEY R. GOLDBERG
ALLEGRI TECH
141 RIVER RD.
NUTLEY, N.J. 07110

NORMAN ROCKWELL
METROPOLITAN MAINTENANCE
43 RIVER RD.
NUTLEY, N.J. 07110

W.C. WILLNER
WILLNER INDUSTRIES
580 CHANCELLOR AVE.
IRVINGTON, N.J. 07111

MAURICE BICK
AURIC
470 FRELINGHUYSEN AVE.
NEWARK, N.J. 07114

DAVID W. GOLDMAN
EVANS-ARISTOCRAT INDUSTRIES
768 FRELINGHUYSEN AVE.
NEWARK, N.J. 07014

MAURICE BICK
SURIC
470 FRELINGHUYSEN AVE.
NEWARK, N.J. 07114

LAURENCE A. TISHLER
THE   THRIFTWAY LEASING
157 HAYNES PL.
NEWARD, N.J. 07114

J.B. THARPE
VISUAL ELECTRONICS
285 EMMET ST.
NEWARK, N.J. 07114

DAVID GREEN
MOTOR CLUB OF AMERICA
484 CENTRAL AVE.
NEWARK, N.J. 07117

SEYMOUR HASPEL
MARVA INDUSTRIES
545 DOWD AVE.
ELIZABETH, N.J. 07201

EDWARD M. KAYE
BORNE CHEMICAL
632 SOUTH FRONT ST.
ELIZABETH, N.J. 07202

ADOLPH D. STORCH
PUREPAC LABORATORIES
200 ELMORA ST.
ELIZABETH, N.J. 07202

WALTER E. PUDNEY
CHATHAM
235 E. 11TH AVE.
ROSELLE, N.J. 07203

A.M. ROTHBARD
NATIONAL COLOR LABORATORIES
306 W. FIRST AVE.
ROSELLE, N.J. 07203

ARNOLD SURESKY
FARADAY LABORATORIES
100 HOFFMAN PL.
HILLSIDE, N.J. 07205

NATHANIEL COHEN
SERVISCO •
470 MUNDET PL.
HILLSIDE, N.J. 07205

OSCAR DAVIS
HAYWARD MANUFACTURING
900 FAIRMOUNT AVE.
ELIZABETH, N.J. 07207

JOHN F. BROBST
PHARMACAPS
1111 JEFFERSON AVE.
ELIZABETH, N.J. 07207

J. DAVID PARKINSON
THOMAS & BETTS
36 BUTLER ST.
ELIZABETH, N.J. 07207

BENJAMIN LEVY
MONTE CHRISTI
1145 KIPLING RD.
ELIZABETH, N.J. 07208

ELLIOT BERNSTEIN
FEL FUSE INC.
198 VAN VORST ST.
JERSEY CITY, N.J. 07302

J.A. BLOCK
BLOCK DRUG
257 CORNELISON AVE.
JERSEY CITY, N.J. 07302

ELY E. ASHKENZAI
REALTONE ELECTRICONS
34 EXCHANGE PL.
JERSEY CITY, N.J. 07302

ELY ASHKENAZI
SOUNDESIGN
34 EXCHANGE PL.
JERSEY CITY, N.J. 07302

WARREN A. ZIMMER
JOSEPH DIXON CRUCIBLE
167 WAYNE ST.
JERSEY CITY, N.J. 07303

A. KAUFMAN
ARMIN
301 WEST SIDE AVE.
JERSEY CITY, N.J. 07305

PHILIP F. MILLER
KRAFTWARE
675-683 GARFIELD AVE
JERSEY CITY, N.J. 07305

WILLIAM F. BLITZER
LIGHTOLIER
346 CLAREMONT AVE.
JERSEY CITY, N.J. 07305

PETER DE CARLO
BLIMPIE CORP.
26 JOURNAL SQ.
JERSEY CITY, N.J. 07306

J.A. EDWARDS
TUJAX INDUST.
420 HOBOKEN AVE.
JERSEY CITY, N.J. 07306

FRANK POWELL
FINANCIAL LEISURE
457 CENTRAL AVE.
JERSEY CITY, N.J. 07307

T.J. DERMOT DUNPHY
SEALED AIR
19-01 STATE HIGHWAY
FAIR LAWN, N.J. 07401

BERNARD A. ROSS
VIBRATION MOUNTINGS
P.O. BOX 776
BUTLER, N.J. 07405

JAMES WOOD
THE GRAND UNION
100 BROADWAY
EAST PATERSON, N.J. 07407

HAROLD L. SELBY
NAUTILOID
10 BUSHES LN.
ELMWOOD PARK, N.J. 07407

G.E. SPAULDING
RETENTION COMMUNICATION
5 PAUL KOHNER PL.
ELMWOOD PARK, N.J. 07407

KARABET SIMONYAN
CODI
POLLIIT DR. SOUTH
FAIR LAWN, N.J. 07410

ALLEN J. HOWARD
COPY-DATA SYSTEMS
12-20 RIVER RD.
FAIR LAWN, N.J. 07410

C.J. FLETCHER
AEROSYSTEMS TECHNOLOGY
WILDCAT RD.
FRANKLIN, N.J. 07416

PIERCE M. WELPTON
ATCO IND.
93 MAIN ST.
FRANKLIN, N.J. 07416

RONALD L. KIRK
HETEROTECH
668 HIGH MOUNTAIN RD.
FRANKLIN LAKES, N.J. 07417

MELVIN EISENBERG
NATIONAL BERYLLIA
GREENWOOD AVE.
HASKELL, N.J. 07420

JOHN T. BLOETJES
QUALITY DATA PROCESSING
199 LACKAWANNA AVE. W.
PATERSON, N.J. 07424

W.K. LEDGARD,JR.
AMERICAN PET
380 FRANKLIN TURNPIKE
MAHWAH, N.J. 07430

JOHN W. PIKE
ENVIRINMENTAL SERVICES
140 GRAND AVE.
MIDLAND PARK, N.J. 07432

ALBERT L. ROLTSCH
AMOR TECH INTL.
439 RAMAPO VALLEY RD.
OAKLAND, N.J. 07436

CARL BRYNKO
REPROGRAPHIS MATERIALS
112 CANNONBALL RD.
POMPTON LAKES, N.J. 07442

RAY C. EDWARDS
EDWARDS ENGINEERING
101 ALEXANDER AVE.
POMPTON PLAINS, N.J. 07444

A.S. GUNAR
HOAN PRODUCTS
615 E. CRESCENT AVE.
RAMSEY, N.J. 07446

SAM JACOBSSON
POLYSYSTEMS
185 ARCH ST.
RAMSEY, N.J. 07446

JOHN H. ZEEMAN
BREWSTER IND.
776 GRAND AVE.
RIDGEFIELD, N.J. 07457

F. BELL JR.
SONIC DEVELOPMENT
3 INDUSTRIAL AVE.
UPPER SADDLE RIVER, N.J.07458

W.A. HAWKINS
CHEMPLAST
150 DEY RD.
WAYNE, N.J. 07470

R.F. DUNSHEATH
FUTURISTIC APPLICATIONS
30 GALESI DR.
WAYNE, N.J. 07470

SETH HARRISON
R.E.D.M.
70 OLD TURNPIKE RD.
WAYNE, N.J. 07470

PETER J. MC LAUGHLIN
UNION CAMP
1600 VALLEY RD.
WAYNE, N.J. 07470

H.G. JACOBS
AMERICAN POLYMERS
50 CALIFORNIA AVE.
PATERSON, N.J. 07503

WILLIAM S. CUTTENBERG
BOGUE ELECTRIC MFG.
52 IOWA AVE.
PATERSON, N.J. 07503

ERNEST GELLES
KAYSAM CORP.
27 KENTUCKY AVE.
PATERSON, N.J. 07503

DON GUSTIN
PATINOS
253 CROOKS AVE.
PATERSON, N.J. 07503

DANIEL P. LIEBLICH
UNITED BOWLING CENTERS
140 MARKET ST.
PATERSON, N.J. 07505

J.J. TERRITO
TECH-AMERICAN RESOURCES
P.O. BOX BD
PATERSON, N.J. 07509

LIONEL M. LEVEY
THE FELSWAY
994 RIVERVIEW DR.
TOTOWA, N.J. 07512

ANTHONY NAJJAR
FILIGREE FOODS
TAFT RD.
TOTOWA, N.J. 07512

GILBERT RAFF
LITTLEFIELD, ADAMS
81 ADAMS DR.
TOTOWA, N.J. 07512

PHILIP GANGUZZA
VALLEY FAIR
15 JACKSON RD.
TOTOWA, N.J. 07512

DANIEL P. LIEBLICH
TREADWAY
140 MARKET ST.
PATERSON, N.J. 07570

S.R. CALABRO
AUTOMATED TECHNOLOGY
300 HUDSON ST.
HACKENSACK, N.J. 07501

S.D. FIRE
COMMUNITY CHARGE PLAN
395 MAIN ST.
HACKENSACK, N.J. 07601

NORMAN I. NELSON
CONSUMERS MARKETING
44 ESSEX ST..
HACKENSACK, N.J. 07601

SURAHAM SUHAMI
ELSCINT
P.O. BOX 832
HACKENSACK, N.J. 07601

IRA SILVERMAN
NATEK
190 MOORE ST.
HACKENSACK, N.J. 07601

KAZMIER WYSOCKI
PMC. IND.
293 HUDSON ST.
HACKENSACK, N.J. 07601

MARVIN CHARTER
POWER-MATE
514 S. RIVER ST.
HACKENSACK,N.J. 07601

MURRAY L. BEER
FINANCIAL RESOURCES
110 MAIN ST.
HACKENSACK, N.J. 07602

SEYMOUR PEARLMAN
HOUSE OF CHROME
65 RTE. 17
HASBROUCK HEIGHTS, N.J. 07604

E. KANAREK
UNIVERSAL LIGHTING
P.O. BOX 333
HASBROUCK HEIGHTS, N.J. 07604

ROBERT A. BURNS
METPATH
60 COMMERCE WAY
HACKENSACK, N.J. 07606

NORMAN SHAIFER
COLOR REPRODUCTIONS
CUSTOM BLDG.
SOUTH HACKENSACK, N.J. 07606

NORMAN SHAIFER
CUSTOM COMMUNICATIONS
30 RUTA CT.
SOUTH HACKENSACK, N.J. 07606

HARRY HOROWITZ
ELECTRO-MINIATURES
600 HUYLER ST.
SO. HACKENSACK, N.J. 07606

ROBERT JACOBSON
READING IND.
236 GREEN ST.
SO. HACKENSACK, N.J. 07606

WAYNE S. DODDS
TRONCHEMICS RESEARCH
480 U.S. RTE. 46
SO. HACKENSACK, N.J. 07606

HAROLD S. CAPLIN
TUDOR INDUSTRIES
P.O. BOX 2032
SO. HACKENSACK, N.J. 07606

R.A. LEONARD
COMPUSCAN
900 HUYLER ST.
TETERBORO, N.J. 07608

SEYMOUR L. GRODNER
TELEBEAM
32 HENRY ST.
TETERBORO, N.J. 07608

ROLAND KOLOGRIVOV
TRANSAMERICAN INSTRUMENT
85 KINDERAMACK RD.
EMERSON, N.J. 07630

LOUIS A. MASON
AIR POLLUTION IND.
95 CEDAR LN.
ENGLEWOOD, N.J. 07631

J. J. GRAHAM
DCL INC.
177 N. DEAN ST.
ENGLEWOOD, N.J. 07631

BARRY YAMPOL
DIGITAL PAGING SYSTEMS
99 W. SHEFFIELD AVE.
ENGLEWOOD,N.J. 07631

BARRY YAMPOL
GRAPHIC SCANNING
99 W. SHEFFIELD AVE.
ENGLEWOOD, N.J. 07631

SAM SHARKO
INTERCONTINENTAL DYNAMICS
170 COOLIDGE AVE.
ENGLEWOOD, N.J. 07631

JERALD J. JACOLOW
OROMONT DRUG & CHEMICAL
520 S. DEAN ST.
ENGLEWOOD, N.J. 07631

R.H. WEISINGER
ULTRA DYNAMICS
80 WEST ST.
ENGLEWOOD, N.J. 07631

EDWARD F. MANNING
WELLS TP SCIENCES
99 W. SHEFFIELD AVE.
ENGLEWOOD, N.J. 07631

A.A. ROMEO
B-G FOODS
120 AYLVAN AVE.
ENGLEWOOD CLIFFS, N.J. 07632

DR. EUGENE R. JOLLY
BIOMETRIC TESTING
661 PALISADES AVE.
ENGLEWOOD, N.J. 07632

S.A. JACOBS
CAREER GUIDANCE
29 SKYLINE DR.
ENGLEWOOD CLIFFS, N.J. 07632

JAMES W. MC KEE, JR.
CPC INTERNATIONAL
INTERNATIONAL PLAZA
ENGLEWOOD CLIFFS, N.J. 07632

JOSEPH DELLA MONICA
CREATIVE FOODS
333 SYLVAN AVE.
ENGLEWOOD CLIFFS, N.J. 07632

GEORGE H. HEILBORN
IPS COMPUTER MARKETING
467 SYLVAN AVE.
ENGLEWOOD CLIFFS, N.J. 07632

STEVEN L. MARKS
KETTERING IND.
570 SYLVAN AVE.
ENGLEWOOD CLIFFS, N.J. 07632

LESTER A. PROBST
NUMERAX
550 SYLVAN AVE.
ENGLEWOOD CLIFFS, N.J. 07632

FRANK J. DUNNIGAN
PRENTICE-HALL
ENGLEWOOD CLIFF, N.J. 07632

M.A. SALITAN
REX-NORECO
616 PALISADE AVE.
ENGLEWOOD CLIFFS, N.J. 07632

IRVING RUZAN
TCR SERVICE
140 SYLVAN AVE.
ENGLEWOOD CLIFF,N.J. 07632

C.J. TRAINOR
CONESCO IND.
214 GATES RD.
LITTLE FERRY, N.J. 07643

HENRY WILKENS
FLOWTRON IND.
2 ALSAN WAY
LITTLE FERRY, N.J. 07643

JAY FEDER
BARCLAY IND.
65 INDUSTRIAL RD.
LODI, N.J. 07644

LOUIS OSTROWE
FABIEN
P.O. BOX 176
LODI, N.J. 07644

NICHOLAS M. MOLNAR
FINE ORGANICS
P.O. BOX 248
LODI, N.J. 07644

K.H. BREFORD
PANACOLOR
P.O. BOX 303
LODI, N.J. 07644

RICHARD V. GIORDANO
AIRCO
85 CHESTNUT RIDGE RD.
MONTVALE, N.J. 07645

JOHN R. KENNEDY, JR.
FEDERAL PAPER BOARD
75 CHESTNUT RIDGE RD.
MONTVALE, N.J. 07645

WILSON W. CROSS
KEYES FIBRE CO.
160 SUMMIT AVE.
MONTVALE, N.J. 07645

MURRAY J. STEINFELD
MEDFAX
P.O. BOX 424
MONTVALE, N.J. 07645

FRANK G. LOHNES
ARWOOD
ROCKLEIGH IND. PARK
ROCKLEIGH, N.J. 07647

JACQUES KOHN
BALTER
10 FAIRWAY CT.
NORTHVALE, N.J. 07647

EDWIN A. COHEN
BARR LABORATORIES
265 LIVINGSTON ST.
NORTHVALE, N.J. 07647

MARVIN MILLER
IDENTIMATION
408 PAULDING AVE.
NORTHVALE, N.J. 07647

STEPHEN H. MAYER
MEM CO.
NORTHVALE, N.J. 07647

MARVIN MILLER
SIBANY MFG.
408 PAULDING AVE.
NORTHVALE, N.J. 07647

B.H. DE SANDRE
ALPHINE GEOPHYSICAL
70 OAK ST.
NORWOOD, N.J. 07648

EDWARD SILVER
COMPUTER SPECIALTIES
544 TENTH ST.
PALISADES PARK, N.J. 07650

N. HABER
HABER INSTRUMENTS
434 BERGEN BLVD.
PALISADES PARK, N.J. 07650

JOSEPH SPONTAK
TECH. LAB"S.
BERGEN AT EAST EDSALL
PALISADES PARK, N.J. 07650

J.R. RYAN
TEKOLOGY
BERGEN & EDSALL BLVD.
PALISADES PARK, N.J. 07650

FRANK MARTIN
BUTLER INTERNATIONAL
E81 STATE HIGHWAY NO. 4
PARAMUS, N.J. 07652

ALLAN G. JACOBSON
COMPUTER TRANSCEIVER
P.O. BOX 15
PARAMUS, N.J. 07652

LAWRENCE SAPER
DATASCOPE
580 WINTERS AVE.
PARAMUS, N.J. 07652

C.C. DEWEY
DEWEY ELECTRONIS
11 PARK PL.
PARAMUS, N.J. 07652

HERMAN E. ANSTATT
EAC IND.
80 E. RIDGEWOOD AVE.
PARAMUS, N.J. 07652

FRED JAROSLOW
ED. IND.
193 HIGHWAY 17
PARAMUS, N.J. 07652

MELVIN S. COOK
HOLOBEAM
560 WINTERS AVE.
PARAMUS, N.J. 07652

MURRAY HERSH
STATE DESIGNERS
GALLERY OFFICES, BERGEN MALL
PARAMUS, N.J. 07652

ROBERT J. FRANKEL
TITAN GROUP
EAST 81, STATE HIGHWAY 4
PARAMUS, N.J. 07652

ANTHONY J. FENNELLI, JR.
TRANSPORT DATA
615 WINTERS AVE.
PARAMUS, N.J. 07652

LOUIS LERNER
OFFICIAL IND.
776 GRAND AVE.
RIDGEFIELD, N.J. 07657

J.S. MULHOLLAND
HAYDEN PUBLISHING
50 ESSEX ST.
ROCHELLE PARK, N.J. 07662

DON MICHAEL
SEREX
116 BRIDGE ST.
ROSELLE PARK, N.J. 07662

E.A. HAMMERLE
CAMBRIDGE COMPUTER
PK. 80 PLAZA W.
SADDLE BROOK, N.J. 07662

IRVING SOLOMON
KINZEE IND.
259 SECOND ST.
SADDLE BROOK, N.J. 07662

MORTON G. MILLSTEIN
NATIONAL COMPUTER
P.O. BOX 432-361 MIDLAND AVE.
SADDLE BROOK, N.J. 07662

ABRAHAM BOSMAN
QUAKER CITY IND.
P.O. BOX 556
SADDLE BROOK, N.J. 07662

J. ROY MORRIS
CYBERMATICS
241 CEDAR LN.
TEANECK, N.J. 07666

THOMAS T. LENK
GARCIA
329 ALFRED AVE.
TEANECK, N.J. 07666

THOMAS A. HOLMES
INGERSOLL-RAND
200 CHESTNUT RIDGE RD.
WOODCLIFFE LAKE, N.J. 07675

J.C. HOAGLAND
DE TOMASO IND.
P.O. BOX 856
RED BANK, N.J. 07701

J. II. VAN KIRK
NORTH EUROPEAN OIL
P.O. BOX 456
RED BANK, N.J. 07701

MERRILL BRAVERMAN
BIO-SCIENCE RESOURCES
1200 RAILROAD AVE.
ASBURY PARK, N.J. 07712

WALTER F. RUPINSKI
CRG
2333 SUNSET AVE
ASBURY PARK, N.J. 07712

PAUL JACOBS
INTERNATION COMPONENTS
ASBURY AVE. & BOWNE RD.
ASBURY PARK, N.J. 07712

HAROLD T. SHER
UNITED TELECONTROL
3500 SUNSET AVE.
ASBURY PARK, N.J. 07712

EMANUEL M. TERNER
MIDLAND GLASS CO.
CLIFFWOOD AVE.
CLIFFWOOD, N.J. 07721

HARVEY CONNOR
ATLANTIC APPLIANCE
980 SHREWSBURY AVE.
NEW SHREWSBURY, N.J. 07724

EDWARD MALONEY
POWER PHYSICS
542 INDUSTRIAL WAY W.
EATONTOWN, N.J. 07724

WALTER A. MERKL
PRECISION OPTICS
612 INDUSTRIAL WAY W.
EATONTOWN, N.J. 07724

A.M. LIPPENS
PVC CONTAINER
556 INDUSTRIAL WAY W.
EATONTOWN, N.J. 07724

L.J. WINSLOW
WINSLOW TECHNOLOGY
607 INDUSTRIAL WAY W.
EATONTOWN, N.J. 07724

L.S. FRIEDMAN
METALLURGICAL INTERNATION
1 GOLDSTREAM WAY
NEW SHREWSBURY, N.J. 07724

D.T. BUCK
BUCK ENGINEERING
P.O. BOX 686
FARMINGDALE, N.J. 07727

EDWARD I. BROWN
MONMOUTH AIRLINES
P.O. BOX 126
FARMINGDALE, N.J. 07727

H.L. SCHWARTZ
PRECISION CIRCUITS
BOX 605
FARMINGDALE, N.J. 07727

VINCENT SHANNI
CAMPION
200 RTE. 9
FREEHOLD, N.J. 07728

C.A. CULLEY, JR.
COLONIAL FOODS
400 BROADWAY
FREEHOLD, N.J. 07728

J.J. SAKER
FOODARAMA SUPERMARKETS
303 W. MAIN ST.
FREEHOLD, N.J. 07728

J. J. RAYMOND
RAYCOMM INDUSTRIES
RTE. 33
FREEHOLD, N.J. 07728

EDWARD J. SIMMONS
TRANGLE IND.
P.O. BOX 850
HOLENDEL, N.J. 07733

H.J. BLACK
KING JAMES EXTENDED CARE
400 HIGHWAY 36
MIDDLETOWN, N.J. 07748

STEPHEN D. LAVOIE
LAVOIE LABORATORIES
MATAWAN-FREEHOLD RD.
MORGANVILLE, N.J. 07751

WILBURN W. SMITH
INTERNATION COMPUTER
1701 STATE HIGHWAY 35
OAKHURST, N.J. 07755

SHELDON GUNSBERG, JR.
WALTER READE ORGANIZATION
DEAL RD.
OAKHURST, N.J. 07755

DANIEL SINNOTT
INTERDATA
2 CRESCENT PL.
OCEANPORT, N.J. 07757

P.H. ISELIN
MONMOUTH PARK JOCKEY CLUB
OCEANPORT AVE. & RAILROD TRACKS
OCEANPORT, N.J. 07757

EDWARD A. PETKO
ELECTRONIC ASSOC.
185 MONMOUTH PK. HIGHWAY.
WEST LONG BRANCH, N.J. 07764

A.F. AMBIELLI
CUSTOM ALLOY
RTE. 513
CALIFON, N.J. 07830

JOHN F. DICKINSON
COMPAC
OLD FLANDERS RD.
NETCONG, N.J. 07857

R.M. BERBURG
ANKEN
1 HICKS AVE.
NEWTON, N.J. 07860

M.A. WELT
RADIATION TECHNOLOGY
LAKE DENMARK RD.
ROCKAWAY, N.J. 07866

JOHN J. CAHILL
ROCKAWAY
21 PINE ST.
ROCKAWAY, N.J. 07866

J.P. VERHALEN
UNITED STATES MINERAL PRODUCTS
STANHOPE, N.J. 07874

CHARLES F. BELL
OAKITE PRODUCTS
50 VALLEY RD.
BERKELEY HEIGHTS, N.J. 07922

A.J. KESSELHAUT
UNIVERSAL GRAPHICS
ONE SADDLE RD.
CEDAR KNOLLS, N.J. 07927

J. KASS
TECHNOLOGY LEASING
301 MAIN ST.-BOX 473
CHATHAM, N.J. 07928

DONALD S. RICH
INFLO SYSTEMS
FAIRMONT AVE.
CHESTER, N.J. 07930

JANE S. MUTAF
REALDATA
P.O. BOX 703
FAR HILLS,N.J. 07931

W.F. HAURLBURT, JR.
AUTOMATIC SWITCH CO.
50-56 HANOVER RD.
FLORHAM PARK, N.J. 07932

B. KRUTH
FLORHAM PK. COUNTRY CLUB
RIDGEDALE AVE.
FLORHAM PARK, N.J. 07932

BERNARD KRUTH
NATIONAL MODULAR CONCEPTS
236 RIDGEDALE AVE.
FLORHAM PARK, N.J. 07932

THOMAS J. CORBETT
CARMER INDUSTRIES
P.O. BOX 54
HANOVER, N.J. 07936

G.P.T. WILENIUS
ELECTRO GAS DYNAMICS
LITTELL RD. & RTE. 10
HANOVER, N.J. 07936

T.A. ZAPPA
ALASKA OIL & MINERALS
22 STONEHEDGE
MADISON, N.J. 07940

DR. J. BLAIR HOWKINS
INSPIRATION CONSOLIDATED
P.O. BOX 2247 R.
MORRISTOWN, N.J. 07960

THOMAS R. NYE
KEUFFEL & ESSER
20 WHIPPANY RD.
MORRISTOWN, N.J. 07960

W. PARSON TODD
QUINCY MINING
93 MADISON AVE.
MORRISTOWN, N.J. 07960

R.C. SORENSEN
UNITED STATES RADIUM
P.O. BOX 246
MORRISTONW, N.J. 07960

EDWARD E. SAYETTE
PRACTICE TENNIS CENTERS
P.O. BOX 334
MOUNT FREEDOM, N.J. 07970

ROBERT H. McCAFFREY
C.R. BARD INC.
731 CENTRAL AVE.
MURRAY HILL, N.J. 07971

LEON BRAUN
MOLECULAR ENERGY
132 FLORAL AVE.
MURRAY HILL, N.J. 07974

LOUIS SLATER
CHANNEL CO.
945 RTE. 10
WHIPPANY, N.J. 07981

STANLEY WOLFSON
CLINICAL SCIENCES
30 TROY RD.
WHIPPANY, N.J. 07981

M.J. ANTON
SUBURBAN PROPANE GAS
MT. PLEASANT AVE.
WHIPPANY, N.J. 07981

M.A. POLLACK
VAN DYK RESEARCH
45 SOUTH JEFFERSON RD.
WHIPPANY, N.J. 07981

MICHAEL J. DESIDERIO
WHIPPANY PAPER BOARD
10 N. JEFFERSON RD.
WHIPPANY, N.J. 07981

J.J. ELKINS
ELKINS-SINN
2 EASTERBROOK LN.
CHERRY HILL, N.J. 08002

DENNIS W. BROADMAN
HORVEL IND.
3 OLNEY AVE.
CHERRY HILL, N.J. 08002

IRA M. INGERMAN
MAGIC MARKER
ONE MAGIC MARKER LN.
CHERRY HILL, N.J. 08003

GILBERT N. ZITIN
MDC CORP.
26 SPRINGDALE RD.
CHERRY HILL, N.J. 08003

ROBERT A. LUCHT
LOGISTICS INDS.
GLOUCESTER PIKE
BARRINGTON, N.J. 08007

M. SAEPOFF
DYNASIL CORP.
P.O. BOX D
BERLIN, N.J. 08009

ROBERT STOELKER
FORMIGLI
P.O. BOX F
BERLIN, N.J. 08009

E.J. SEGAL
VOGART CRAFTS
50 CARROL ST.
CLIFTON, N.J. 07014

IRA M. INGERMAN
DIMENSIONAL COMMUNICATIONS
INTERSTATE IND. PARK
BELLMAWR, N.J. 08030

JEAN-PAUL C. RENOIR
CCA ELECTRONICS
716 JERSEY AVE.
GLOUCESTER CITY, N.J. 08030

CHARLES H. EVANS
LAUREL OAK
120 KINGS HWY. W.
HADDONFIELD, N.J. 08033

RICHARD E. OTT
SGL IND.
76 EUCLID AVE.
HADDONFIELD, N.J. 08033

ALEX EGYED
BASCO
RTE. 38 & WOODE AVE.
CHERRY HILL, N.J. 08034

JEROME FARBER
ELECTRO-ENT
120 HADDONTOWNE CT.
CHERRY HILL, N.J. 08034

W.C. MORRIS
MEDICIENCE TECHNOLOGY
12 SPRINGDALE RD.
CHERRY HILL, N.J. 08034

MARTIN SHULMAN
SHULMAN TRANSPORT
20 OLNEY AVE.
CHERRY HILL, N.J. 08034

WILLIAM A. GEMMEL
S. JERSEY IND.
ONE SOUTH JERSEY PLAZE,RTE.54
FOLSOM, N.J. 08037

JOHN H. THEE
DEER PARK BAKING
SOUTH EGG HARBOR RD.
HAMMONTON, N.J. 08037

ANTHONY COLASURDO
PAKCO COM.
BELLEVUE & THIRD
HAMMONTON, N.J. 08037

D.W. BOARDMAN
HARVEL IND.
TWO ECHELON PLAZA
VOORHEES, N.J. 08043

WILLIAM J. DOYLE
GENERAL ENERGY SYSTEMS
P.O. BOX 577
WILLINGBORO, N.J. 08046

ALLEN LANGMAN
ENFLO
FELLOWSHIP RD. & RTE. 73
MAPLE SHADE, N.J. 08052

JAMES A. SKIDMORE, JR.
SCIENCE MANAGEMENT
FELLOWSHIP RD.
MORRESTOWN, N.J. 08057

FRED COHEN
TELESCIENCES
351 NEW ALBANY RD.
MOORESTOWN, N.J. 08057

G.R. SEARLE
MOBILE HOMES-MULTIPLEX
RTE. 206
MOUNT HOLLEY, N.J. 08060

H. STIFEL
ARMOTEK IND.
701 PUBLIC RD.
PALMYRA, N.J. 08065

JOHN S. BAER
PRECISION SPECIALTIES
PITMAN, N.J. 08071

J.G. GUTTMAN
FIMACO
1911 ROWLAND ST.
RIVERTON, N.J. 08077

THOMAS MARTIN
THRESHOLD TECHOLOGY
RTE. 130 & UNION LANDING RD.
CINNAMINSON, N.J. 08077

SIDNEY H. PERLMAN
OPT-SCIENCES
U.S. HIGHWAY 130
RIVERTON, N.J. 08077

ALBERT J. ZURZOLO
ASSOC. LEISURE
17 OSAGE AVE.
SOMERDALE, N.J. 08083

SANFORD MILLER
MYSTIC DEVELOPMENT
RADIO RD., MYSTIC ISLANDS
TUCKERTON, N.J. 08087

JOSEPH B. VAN SCIVER III
J.B. VAN SCIVER
DELAWARE AVE.,FED. & ARCH ST.
CAMDEN, N.J. 08102

JOSEPH L. NICHOLSON
CAMDEN REFRIGERATING
KAIGHN & DELAWARE RIVER
CAMDEN, N.J. '08103

WILLIAM T. FESSLER
FROSTIE
1420-32 CRESTMONT AVE.
CAMDEN, N.J. 08103

BERNARD COHEN
STATE AUTOMOTIVE
DAVIS & COPEWOOD STS
CAMDEN, N.J. 08103

HERBERT S. WACHTEL
URETHANE FABS.
HADDON AVE. & LINE ST.
CAMDEN, N.J. 08103

HARVEY LAMM
SUBARU OF AMERICA
7040 CENTRAL HIGHWAY
PENNSAUKEN, N.J. 08109

CHARLES E. MARGOLIN
DATA SYSTEMS ANALYSTS
COOPER PARKWAY & N. PARK DR.
PENNSAUKEN, N.J. 08110

J.D. DE PAUL
LEHIGH PRESS
7001 N. PARK DR.
PENNSAUKEN, N.J. 08110

LEROY A. BONDY
SCHAEVITZ ENGINEERING
U.S. RTE. 130, SCHAEVITZ BLVD.
PENNSAUKEN, N.J. 08110

C.D. CASCIO
VIDEO SYSTEMS
7300 N. CRESCENT BLVD.
PENNSAUKEN, N.J. 08110

B. DEBLASIO
RENAULT WINERY
P.O. BOX 364
EGG HARBOR CITY, N.J. 08215

HARRY MELTON
RESIDEX
215 S. SHORE RD.
MARMORA, N.J. 08273

E.L. WATERMAN
STEEL CREST HOMES,
215 N. SHORE RD.
MARMORA, N.J. 08273

ALBERT H. FUNKE, JR.
P.J. RITTER
QUALITY LN.
BRIDGETON, N.J. 08302

FRANK E. DOUGHERTY
DOUGHERTY BROS.
PINE & TUCKAHOE
BUENA, N.J. 08310

JACK L. FOYIL
MAUL BROS.
111 S. 15 ST.
MILLVILLE, N.J. 08332

R.C. SHIVE
CIRCLE CONTROLS
204 S. WEST BLVD.
VINELAND, N.J. 08360

C.C. BALDERSTON
LEED & LIPPINCOTT
CHALFONTE-HADDON HALL
ATLANTIC CITY, N.J. 08401

R.P. LEVY
ATLANTIC CITY RACING
P.O. BOX 719
ATLANTIC CITY, N.J. 08404

GEORGE E. FIELDHOUSE
ATLANTIC CITY SEWERAGE
GUARANTEE TRUST BLDG.
ATLANTIC CITY, N.J. 08404

C.B. YATES
YATES IND.
23 AMBOY RD.
BORDENTOWN, N.J. 08505

J.F. GILLIGAN
DATARAM
PRINCETON,HIGHTSTOWN RD.
CRANBURY, N.J. 08512

LESTER H. ALLEN
ALLEN COMMUICATIONS
WARREN PLAZA W. RTE.130
HIGHTSTOWN, N.J. 08520

LEWIS A. BONDON
PRODELIN
P.O. BOX 131
HIGHTSTOWN, N.J. 08520

RAYMOND J. RIDOLFI
ADVANCED COMPUTER SUPPLIES
P.O. BOX 482
PRINCETON, N.J. 08540

DR. SOLOMON MAROLIN
AFFILIATED MED. RESEARCH
PRINCETON PIKE
PRINCETON, N.J. 08540

JOHN R. BENNETT
APPLIED DATA RESEARCH
RTE. 206
PRINCETON, N.J. 08540

MARTIN T. MOBACH
APPLIED LOGIC
900 STATE RD.
PRINCETON, N.J. 08540

D. JERARD AMAN
DELOS INTERNATIONAL
1101 STATE RD.
PRINCETON, N.J. 08540

THEODORE SPERRY
FIFTH DIMENSION
P.O. BOX 384
PRINCETON, N.J. 08540

J.F. BRINSTER
GENERAL SERVICES
P.O. BOX 050
PRINCETON, N.J. 08540

ROBERT B. BRUNS
INTERNATIONAL HYDRONICS
BOX 910 , R-4
PRINCETON, N.J. 08540

DR. TIBOR FABIAN
MATHEMATICA
P.O. BOX 2392
PRINCETON, N.J. 08540

JOHN C. CUGINI
METROMATION
1101 STATE RD.
PRINCETON, N.J. 08540

J.J. SHEEHAN
NATIONAL COMPUTER ANALYSTS
HIGHWAY 1 & LYNWOOD DR.
PRINCETON, N.J. 08540

GERAL HELLER
OPTEL
P.O. BOX 2215
PRINCETON, N.J. 08540

MARTIN A. CHOOLJIAN
PENN CORP.
ONE PALMER SQ.
PRINCETON, N.J. 08540

EMIL W. LEHMANN
PRINCETON APPLIED RESEARCH
P.O. BOX 2565
PRINCETON, N.J. 08540

LEONARD BLANK
PRINCETON ASSOCS FOR HUMAN.
575 EWING ST.
PRINCETON, N.J. 08540

C.N. WOLF
PRINCETON CHEM. RESEARCH
P.O. BOX 652
PRINCETON, N.J. 08540

WILLIAM P. KRAUSE
SYSTEMEDICS
PRINCETON AIR RESEARCH PARK
PRINCETON, N.J. 08540

DR. NATHANIEL I. KORMAN
VENTURES RESEARCH & DEVELOPMENT
371 RIVERSIDE DR.
PRINCETON, N.J. 08540

DONALD D. IVERSON
INTERNATIONAL COMPUMEDICS
14 WASHINGTON RD.
PRINCETON JUNCTION, N.J. 08550

ELLWARD LASKIN
CIRCLE F. INDUSTRIES
720 MONMOUTH ST.
TRENTON, N.J. 08604

F.B. WILLIAMSON, III
GOODALL RUNNER CO.
572 WHITEHEAD RD.
TRENTON, N.J. 08604

JOHN S. CHAMBERLIN
LENOX
PRINCE & MEAD
TRENTON, N.J. 08605

MONROE J. WEINTRAUB
ACME-HAMILTON MFG.
1437 E. STATE ST.
TRENTON, N.J. 08609

M.M. KRANZLER
BASE TEN SYSTEMS
3828 QUAKERBRIDGE RD.
TRENTON, N.J. 08619

NATHAN ZUCKER
CREST ULTRASONICS
MERCER COUNTY AIRPORT
TRENTON, N.J. 08628

IRVING FLICKER
HOMASOTE
LOWER FERRY RD.
WEST TRENTON, N.J. 08628

JOHN C. FARLEY
MAINE SUGAR INDUSTRIES
ROBBINSVILLE, N.J. 08691

MICHAEL L. TENZER
LEISURE TECHNOLOGY
ONE AIRPORT RD.
LAKEWOOD, N.J. 08701

EUGENE FRIEDMAN
TOWNCO MEDICAL ENTERRISES
14 HOSPITAL DR.
TOMS RIVER, N.J. 08753

JOHN E. SCHORK
RESEARCH-COTTRELL
P.O. BOX 750
BOUND BROOK, N.J. 08805

E.H. WAGNER
BOOKS MOBILE
HAY PRESS RD.
DAYTON, N.J. 08810

R.F. EVANS
INNOVATIVE COMMUNICATIONS
530 STATE HIGHWAY 18
EAST BRUNSWICK, N.J. 08816

E.M. GORMAN
CASCADE INDUSTRIES
TALMADGE RD.
EDISON, N.J. 08817

EDWARD L. SAMEK
CHILDCRAFT ED.
20 KILMER RD.
EDISON TOWNSHIP, N.J. 08817

L.P. RIZZUTO
CONAIR
11 EXECUTIVE AVE.
EDISON, N.J. 08817

DOUGLAS N. BROOKS
EASTECH
P.O. BOX 594, 308 TALMADGE RD.
EDISON, N.J. 08817

LEO W. WEISS
FDI
191 TALMADGE RD.
EDISON,N.J. 08817

H.A. BRAUN
LEE FILTER
191 TALMADGE RD.
EDISON, N.J. 08817

A. COHEN
METEX
970 NEW DURHAM RD.
EDISON, N.J. 08817

FRANK M. GRIPPO
OPCOA
330 TALMADGE RD.
EDISON, N.J. 08817

RENO D. SANSONE
WADELL EQUIPMENT
P.O. BOX 989
EDISON, N.J. 08817

ALLEN J. BALDWIN
NIXON-BALDWIN CHEMICALS
NIXON, NEW JERSEY 08818

KURT GOLDMAN
BONNIEBROOK MINERAL
P.O. BOX 272
FLEMINGTON, N.J. 08822

L.B. HERRMANN
BUXTON'S COUNTRY SHOPS
P.O. BOX 178
JAMESBURG, N.J. 08831

HUGO C. PRIBOR
CENTER FOR LAB. OF MED.
16 PEARL ST.
METUCHEN, N.J. 08840

A.J. MITTELDORF
SPEX INDUSTRIES
P.O. BOX 798
METUCHEN, N.J. 08840

ROBERT PHILLIPS
WARBERN PACKAGING
326 SMITH ST.
KEASBEY, N.J. 08832

WALTER F. GIPS, JR.
GULTON INDUSTRIES
212 DURHAM AVE.
METUCHEN, N.J. 08841

NORMAN KANTOR
ECONETICS
P.O. BOX 26
MIDDLESEX, N.J. 08846

ROD L. WHITE
KNICERBOCKER TOY
207 POND AVE.
MIDDLESEX, N.J. 08846

DANIEL MC COLLEY
WOOD INDUSTRIES
P.O. BOX 1112
MIDDLESEX, N.J. 08846

ROY Y. NAKAGAWA
BROTHER INTERNATIONAL
EIGHT CORPORATE PL.
PISCATAWAY, N.J. 08854

E.R. MEMOLY
MO-BILE INDUSTRIES
244 N. RANDOLPHVILLE RD.
PISCATHAWAY, N.J. 08854

KAREL SOKOLOFF
PROSPECT INDUSTRIES
600 PROSPECT AVE.
PISCATAWAY, N.J 08854

M. SIEGAL
WELDOTRON
1532 S. WASHINGTON AVE.
PISCATAWAY, N.J. 08854

P. MEISEL
CHEMICAL & POLLUTION SCIENCES
P.O. BOX 162
OLD BRIDGE, N.J. 08857

KURT T. BOROWSKY
METROCARE
P.O. BOX 819
PARLIN, N.J. 08859

WALTER NACHTIGALL
FANON/COURIER
175 E. WILLIAM ST.
HOPELAWN, PERTH AMBOY, N.J.08861

MARVIN S. FLOWERMAN
FLOCK INDUSTRIES
259 CENTER ST.
PHILLIPSBURG, N.J. 08865

RONALD ROSENZWEIG
MICROWAVE SEMICONDUCTOR
100 SCHOOL HOUSE RD.
SOMERSET, N.J. 08873

EDWARD F. EGAN
EGAN MACHINERY
40 SOUTH ADAMSVILLE RD.
SOMERVILLE, N.J. 08876

P.V. BOLLENBACHER
UNIMED
35 COLUMBIA RD.
SOMERVILLE, N.J. 08876

H.B. ERDMAN
NEW JERSEY ALUMINUM
JERSEY AVE.
NEW BRUNSWICK, N.J. 08901

JOHN C. TRACKMAN
BROWN BOVERI
1460 LIVINGSTON AVE.
NORTH BRUNSWICK, N.J. 08902

S.R. HOFSTEIN
PRINCETON ELECTRONIC
P.O. BOX 101
NORTH BRUNSWICK, N.J. 08902

SPENCER J. ETTMAN
CRYSTALOGRAPHY
303 GEORGE ST.
NEW BRUNSWICK, N.J. 08903

DAVID FREEDMAN
NEW BRUNSWICK SCIENTIFIC
1130 SOMERSET ST.
NEW BRUNSWICK, N.J. 08903

D.S. DOUGAN
LITHOID
318 CLEVELAND AVE.
HIGHLAND PARK, N.J. 08904

ARTHUR J. BROWN
ABC FRIGHT FORWARDING
201 11TH AVE.
NEW YORK, N.Y. 10001

D.H. MC CAMPBELL
ALLIED MAINTENANCE
2 PENN PLAZA
NEW YORK, N.Y. 10001

ROBERT WASSNER
ARNAV INDUSTRIES
31 W. 27TH. ST.
NEW YORK, N.Y. 10001

CALVIN J. KOHLER
AUTOMATED PROCEDURES
236 FIFTH AVE.
NEW YORK, N.Y. 10001

JULIUS TRUMP
BOND INDUSTRIES
FIFTH AVE. AT 35TH.ST.
NEW YORK, N.Y. 10001

J.E. SAUL
BROOKS FASHION STORES
370 SEVENTH AVE.
NEW YORK, N.Y. 10001

SEYMOUR ZIMBERG
CHESA INTERNATIONAL
366 5TH. AVE.
NEW YORK, N.Y. 10001

D.C. MINTON
CHURCH & DWIGHT
TWO PENN PLAZA
NEW YORK, N.Y. 10001

MORRIS GOLDSTEIN
CITY STORES
500 FIFTH AVE.
NEW YORK, N.Y. 10001

SAUL L. STOCKMAN
COLLAGEN
350 FIFTH AVE.
NEW YORK, N.Y. 10001

JOSEPH SHORE
COMMUNICATION CHANNELS
461 EIGHTH AVE.
NEW YORK, N.Y. 10001

T.T. CONNORS
DATAMATION SERVICE
461 EIGHTH AVE.
NEW YORK, N.Y. 10001

RICHARD B. LOYND
ELTRA
2 PENNSYLVANIA PLAZA
NEW YORK, N.Y. 10001

I. COHEN
FIFTH AVE. CARDS
18 WEST 34TH. ST.
NEW YORK, N.Y. 10001

SOL WALDEN
FOX-KNAPP
1 WEST 34TH. ST.
NEW YORK, N.Y. 10001

SEYMOUR LICHTENSTEIN
GARAN
350 FIFTH AVE.
NEW YORK, N.Y. 10001

BERNARD GOLDSTEIN
G.M.S. STORES
19 WEST 34TH. ST.
NEW YORK, N.Y. 10001

MORRIS BAILEY
GOODY'S FOOD
366 FIFTH AVE.
NEW YORK, N.Y. 10001

B. TANKEL
GRAFCO IND.
350 FIFTH AVE. RM. 1827
NEW YORK, N.Y. 10001

JOHN B. HANDAL
VICTOR B. HANDAL & BROS.
277 FIFTH AVE.
NEW YORK, N.Y. 10001

EDWARD D. SOLOMON
HARTFIELD-ZODY
441 NINTH AVE.
NEW YORK, N.Y. 10001

P.R. ANDREWS, JR.
HELIX MARKETING
264 W. 35TH. ST.
NEW YORK, N.Y. 10001

IRVING PAPARO
THE HOUSE OF RONNIE
1 PENN PLAZA
NEW YORK, N.Y. 10001

SIDNEY ZIPPER
JAYS IND.
222 W. 40TH. ST.
NEW YORK, N.Y. 10001

SAMUEL ROSENBLATT
JULYN SPORTSWEAR
213 WEST 35 ST.
NEW YORK, N.Y. 10001

HAROLD M. LANE, JR.
LERNER STORES
460 W. 33RD. ST.
NEW YORK, N.Y. 10001

LEONARD BEREN
LINK ENTERRISES
325 FIFTH AVE.
NEW YORK, N.Y. 10001

IRVING HEIBERGER
LIVING IND.
350 FIFTH AVE. SUITE 8015
NEW YORK, N.Y. 10001

ARTHUR FLACKS
LORTOGS
112 W. 34TH. ST. SUITE 1501
NEW YORK, N.Y. 10001

ALAN N. COHEN
MADISON SQ.GARDEN
2 PENN. PLAZA
NEW YORK, N.Y. 10001

ADOLF EBENSTEIN
MAJESTIC ELECTRO
230 FIFTH AVE.
NEW YORK, N.Y. 10001

T. LEDER
MULTICOM
225 W. 34TH. ST.
NEW YORK, N.Y. 10001

E.L. MARKS
NATCO IND.
19 W. 34TH. ST.
NEW YORK, N.Y. 10001

R.A. MONOHAN
NATIONAL COMPUTER
ONE PENN PLAZA
NEW YORK, N.Y. 10001

THEODORE LE SAVOY
NEWPORT GENERAL
EMPIRE STATE BLDG.
NEW YORK, N.Y. 10001

LEON RUCHLAMER
NOEL IND.
350 FIFTH AVE.
NEW YORK, N.Y. 10001

JOSEPH J. HOCHMAN
OCEANIC RESOURCES
362 FIFTH AVE.
NEW YORK, N.Y. 10001

C.R. MARTIN
ONEITA KNITTING MILLS
350 FIFTH AVE.
NEW YORK, N.Y. 10001

E.E. WELBORN
PIEDMONT IND.
1250 BROADWAY
NEW YORK, N.Y. 10001

HERBERT C. JACOBS
REGAL APPAREL
14 W. 33RD. ST.
NEW YORK, N.Y. 10001

SCOTT C. LEA
REXHAM
350 FIFTH AVE.
NEW YORK, N.Y. 10001

ISAAC RINKEWICH
RINKO IRRIGATION
290 9TH. AVE.
NEW YORK, N.Y. 10001

R.A. RUSSO
ROANNA TOGS
112 W. 34TH ST.
NEW YORK, N.Y. 10001

HYMAN SANDBERG
ROJEAN
213 W. 35TH. ST.
NEW YORK, N.Y. 10001

GEORGE HERMAN
SALANT
320 FIFTH AVE.
NEW YORK, N.Y. 10001

M.P. BERMAN
SAXON IND.
450 SEVENTH AVE.
NEW YORK, N.Y. 10001

HERBERT J. KIRSHNER
THE SEAGRAVE
350 FIFTH AVE.
NEW YORK, N.Y. 10001

L.J. BAUNSTEIN
SPACE & LEISURE TIME
254 W. 31ST. ST.
NEW YORK, N.Y. 10001

ROBERT ROSANES
TTI IND.
1271 BROADWAY
NEW YORK, N.Y. 10001

BURTON B. BROUS
UPS 'N DOWNS
461 EIGHTH AVE.
NEW YORK, N.Y. 10001

LELIE VIRANY
VIRANY CREATIONS
366 FIFTH AVE.
NEW YORK, N.Y. 10001

SEYMOUR FINKELSTEIN
AMERICAN YVETTE
120 E. 16TH. ST.
NEW YORK, N.Y. 10003

HARVEY BERKEY
BERKEY PHOTO
842 BROADWAY
NEW YORK, N.Y. 10003

WALTER SMALL
COMMERCIAL PROGRAMMING
853 BROADWAY
NEW YORK, N.Y. 10003

WALTER SMALL
CPU INTERNATIONAL
853 BROADWAY
NEW YORK, N.Y. 10003

NATHAN KATZ
FELCOSPORTS
113-119 4TH. AVE.
NEW YORK, N.Y. 10003

MERVYN SILVER
FRIGITEMP
121 E. 18th. ST.
NEW YORK, N.Y. 10003

STEPHEN LEFKOWITZ
GBC CLOSED CIRCUIT TV
74 FIFTH AVE.
NEW YORK, N.Y. 10003

B.L. ROSSET, JR.
GROVE PRESS
53 E. 11TH. ST.
NEW YORK, N.Y. 10003

SAUL LAPIDUS
INTELECTRON
115 FIFTH AVE.
NEW YORK, N.Y. 10003

RUBENSTEIN
I.O.A. DATA
383 LAFAYETTE ST.
NEW YORK, N.Y. 10003

WARREN KELLNER
KITTY KELLY SHOE
233 PARK AVE. SOUTH
NEW YORK, N.Y. 10003

CHARLES WENDEROTH
KENNEDY CONCEPTS
19 UNION WEST
NEW YORK, N.Y. 10003

RICHARD SHAPIRO
LEISURE TIME INNOVATION
7 EAST 17TH. ST.
NEW YORK, N.Y. 10003

ARTHUR CHAPNIK
ARTHUR RICHARDS
79 FIFTH AVE. 12TH. FL.
NEW YORK, N.Y. 10003

W.L. SCHIEFFELIN, III
SCHIEFFELIN
30 COOPER SQ.
NEW YORK, N.Y. 10003

STANLEY P. LEE
TECHNOLOGY TRANSFER
115 E. 9TH. ST.
NEW YORK, N.Y. 10003

E.E. PINTER
ZWICKER ELECTRIC
200 PARK AVE. SOUTH
NEW YORK, N.Y. 10003

JAMES P. HORN
AMERICAN EXPORT LINES
17 BATTERY PL.
NEW YORK, N.Y. 10004

EMANUEL NADLER
ENVIRONMENTAL SPECTRUM
126 E. 61ST. ST.
NEW YORK, N.Y. 10004

C.L. GLEAVES
HABANERO
ONE STATE ST. PLAZA
NEW YORK, N.Y. 10004

S.H. SCHEUER
LONDON TERRACE
50 BROADWAY
NEW YORK, N.Y. 10004

ARTHUR W. STOUT, JR.
TODD SHIPYARDS
1 STATE ST. PLAZA
NEW YORK, N.Y. 10004

STUART M. BERKMAN
WICHITA IND.
29 BROADWAY
NEW YORK, N.Y. 10004

TOM DUNLEAVY
WUI TAF
26 BROADWAY
NEW YORK, N.Y. 10004

JOSE A. RIVERO
AQUIRRE CO.
110 WALL ST.
NEW YORK, N.Y. 10005

ALBERT VAN DE MAELE
ANGLO
120 BROADWAY
NEW YORK, N.Y. 10005

MICHAEL S. SINGER
BEBETAX COMPUTER
120 WALL ST.
NEW YORK, N.Y. 10005

ROBERT H. BETHKE
DISCOURT CORP.
58 PINE ST.
NEW YORK, N.Y. 10005

CARL H. TIEDEMANN
DONALDSON, LUFKIN & JENRETTE
140 BROADWAY
NEW YORK, N.Y. 10005

ALBERT J. TAHMOUSH
FRANK B. HALL
88 PINE ST.
NEW YORK, N.Y.10005

JOHN GIANNETTI
MARINE PROTEIN
P.O. BOX 967, WALL ST. STA.
NEW YORK, N.Y. 10005

T.A. SNEDDEN
NEPTUNE MINING CO.
120 BROADWAY
NEW YORK, N.Y. 10005

HARRY A. DURNEY
PACIFIC TIN CONSOLIDATED
120 BROADWAY
NEW YORK, N.Y. 10005

R.C. JANNEN
SUBSCRIPTION TV
77 WATER ST.
NEW YORK, N.Y. 10005

ROBERT M. RAPAPORT
SUCREST
120 WALL ST.
NEW YORK, N.Y. 10005

J.W. KAUFMANN
COAST TO COAST
111 BROADWAY
NEW YORK, N.Y. 10006

J.V. MC. ADAMS
ALBERT FRANK-GUENTHER LAW
61 BROADWAY
NEW YORK, N.Y. 10006

R.J. ARMSTRONG
GENEVE
39 BROADWAY
NEW YORK, N.Y. 10006

STANLEY BERGER
PCS DATA PROCESSING
140 CEDAR ST.
NEW YORK, N.Y. 10006

NORMAN GREIF
RANDY INTERNATIONAL
90 WEST ST.
NEW YORK, N.Y. 10006

RICHARD JUI
AMERICAN TREAT
233 BROADWAY
NEW YORK, N.Y. 10007

ROBERT L. NOLAND
AMETEK
233 BROADWAY
NEW YORK, N.Y. 10007

F.D. MC. DONALD
MC DONALD MICRODATA
259 BROADWAY
NEW YORK, N.Y. 10007

EDWARD J. BEDNARZ
PINKERTON'S
100 CHURCH ST.
NEW YORK, N.Y. 10007

F.M. POWER,JR.
WILLIAM H. SADLIER
11 PARK PL.
NEW YORK, N.Y. 10007

CARL ROSEN
PURITAN FASHIONS
1400 BROADWAY
NEW YORK, N.Y. 10008

MILTON D. SKURKA
THAYER INTERNATIONAL
498 SEVENTH AVE.
NEW YORK, N.Y. 10008

H.D. OSTBERG
AD-MAR RESEARCH
300 PARK AVE. S.
NEW YORK, N.Y. 10010

NORMAN STEINBERG
ALLEN DENTAL-MEDICAL
289 THIRD AVE.
NEW YORK, N.Y. 10010

BENJAMIN C. ZITRON
ALLIED MANAGEMENT
P.O. BOX 525
NEW YORK, N.Y. 10010

JEROME FARMER
AMERICAN RECREATION GROUP
200 FIFTH AVE. N.
NEW YORK, N.Y. 10010

HERBERT ZLOTNICK
CRO-MED BIONICS
160 FIFTH AVE.
NEW YORK, N.Y. 10010

CHARLES F. LENHARD
DIVERSA-GRAPHICS
51 MADISON AVE.
NEW YORK, N.Y. 10010

L. CLARK
ESSES SYSTEM
15-19 EAST 26TH. ST.
NEW YORK, N.Y. 10010

A.M. BLOOM
FACSIMILE COMMUNICATIONS
300 PARK AVE. SOUTH-11TH FL.
NEW YORK, N.Y. 10010

MORTON J. LEVY
GABRIEL IND.
200 FIFTH AVE.
NEW YORK, N.Y. 10010

ALAN EMERICK
GREAT BEAR SPRING
51 MADISON AVE.
NEW YORK, N.Y. 10010

SEYMOUR HYMAN
HEALTH-CHEM. IND.
1107 BROADWAY
NEW YORK, N.Y. 10010

BURTON ADELMAN
M.H. LAMSTON
212 FIFTH AVE.
NEW YORK, N.Y. 10010

ISADORE MIZRAH
LITTLE RUFFY TOGS
71 WEST 23RD. ST.
NEW YORK, N.Y. 10010

EUGENE L. YOUNG
MEDALLION GROUP
1107 BROADWAY
NEW YORK, N.Y. 10010

MARTIN ABRAMS
MEGO INTERNATIONAL
1 MADISON SQ. PLAZA
NEW YORK, N.Y. 10010

ISRAEL TURITZ
MILES-SAMUELSON
15 EAST 26TH. ST.
NEW YORK, N.Y. 10010

BERNARD WALTZER
MINER IND.
200 FIFTH AVE.
NEW YORK, N.Y. 10010

MILTON M. SHAW
NEW YORK MERCHANDISE
32 WEST 23RD. ST.
NEW YORK, N.Y. 10010

MILTON SHAW
SEVERAL SLIDE FASTENERS
32-46 WEST 23RD. ST.
NEW YORK, N.Y. 10010

MARTIN R. LEWIS
WILLIAMHOUSE-REGENCY
28 W. 23RD. ST.
NEW YORK, N.Y. 10010

G.S. BERBER
ASKIN SERVICE
459 WEST 15TH. ST.
NEW YORK, N.Y. 10011

MORRIS KASS
ASTREX
150 FIFTH AVE.
NEW YORK, N.Y. 10011

RONALD DE FUSCO
ATLANTIC DEPT. STORES
111 EIGHTH AVE.
NEW YORK, N.Y. 10011

MARVIN F. BURTEN
BRANCH IND.
114 FIFTH AVE.
NEW YORK, N.Y. 10011

DONN MOSENFELDER
EDUCATIONAL DESIGN
47 WEST 13TH. ST.
NEW YORK, N.Y. 10011

IRVING SACHS
JAIN-SAX IND.
22 W. 19TH. ST.
NEW YORK, N.Y. 10011

E.M. COLEMAN
PLENUM PUBLISHING
227 W. 17TH. ST.
NEW YORK, N.Y. 10011

J.J. MONOTAGUE, JR.
RETRIEVAL CONTROL
211 WEST 19TH. ST.
NEW YORK, N.Y. 10011

M. KLEIN
SAV-ON
75 9TH. AVE.
NEW YORK, N.Y. 10011

EDGAR BERGMAN
SUPPLY RESOURCES
85 TENTH AVE.
NEW YORK,N.Y. 10011

PHILIP WISE
VOLUME MERCHANDISING
75 NINTH AVE.
NEW YORK, N.Y. 10011

SEYMOUR OFFERMAN
IND. ELECTRONIC
109 PRINCE ST.
NEW YORK, N.Y. 10012

JOSEPH DELMAN
SPLENTEX
632 BROADWAY
NEW YORK, N.Y. 10012

MICHAEL F. WEINBERG
AD PRESS
21 HUDSON ST.
NEW YORK, N.Y. 10013

JOHN CALICCHIO
ARGO INTERNATIONAL
140 FRANKLIN ST.
NEW YORK, N.Y. 10013

GEORGE G. GELLERT
ATLANTA
17-25 VARICK ST.
NEW YORK, N.Y. 10013

EDWARD AVILDSEN
AVILDSEN TOOLS
100 LAFAYETTE ST.
NEW YORK, N.Y. 10013

W.J. KAPLAN
CERTIFIED CREATIONS
75 VARICK ST.
NEW YORK, N.Y.10013

P.L. KOHNSTAMM
H. KOHNSTAMM
161 AVE. OF THE AMERICAS
NEW YORK, N.Y. 10013

J.M. MEYER
LATHAM PROCESS
200 HUDSON ST.
NEW YORK, N.Y. 10013

EDWIN R. MASBACK, JR.
MASBACK
330 HUDSON ST.
NEW YORK, N.Y. 10013

HUGH BARNES
RAYNE IND.
233 SPRING ST.
NEW YORK, N.Y. 10013

VICTOR SIMONTE, JR.
BOWNE & CO.
345 HUDSON ST.
NEW YORK, N.Y. 10014

R.W. RETTERER
COMPUTER MICROFILM
70 CHARLTON ST.
NEW YORK, N.Y. 10014

ROBERT E. ANSLOW
ROANWELL
180 VARICK ST.
NEW YORK, N.Y. 10014

JOHN FRANCIS ADAMS
UNION TERMINAL
525 WEST ST.
NEW YORK, N.Y. 10014

EDWARD B. ORY
U.S. BANKNOTE
345 HUDSON ST.
NEW YORK, N.Y. 10014

JUD R. LOBER
ABERDEEN MFG.
16 EAST 34TH. ST.
NEW YORK, N.Y. 10016

ABE OBERLIN
AILEEN
331 EAST 38TH. ST.
NEW YORK, N.Y. 10016

JAMES M. JENKS
ALEXANDER HAMILTON INST.
605 THIRD AVE.
NEW YORK, N.Y. 10016

LEON WEISBURG
ANSTAT
605 THIRD AVE.
NEW YORK, N.Y. 10016

MERWIN BAYER
ARNOLD CONSTABLE
453 FIFTH AVE.
NEW YORK, N.Y. 10016

DAVID E. LEWIS
BLESSING
4 PARK AVE.
NEW YORK, N.Y. 10016

ALBERT LAUGHEY
COLLINS & AIKMAN
210 MADISON AVE.
NEW YORK, N.Y. 10016

EDGAR M. CULLMAN
CULBRO
605 THIRD AVE.
NEW YORK, N.Y. 10016

MICHAEL RAPPAPORT
DAMON CREATIONS
16 EAST 34TH. ST.
NEW YORK, N.Y. 10016

MARVIN COOPER
DYNAMIC CLASSICS
307 FIFTH AVE.
NEW YORK, N.Y. 10016

SAMSON BITENSKY
FAB IND.
200 MADISON AVE.
NEW YORK, N.Y. 10016

A.I. SHERR
FOWNES BROS.
411 FIFTH AVE.
NEW YORK, N.Y. 10016

JOEL FINKLE
GROUND WATER IND.
10 EAST 40TH. ST.
NEW YORK, N.Y. 10016

LAWRENCE JOSEPH
HATTIE CARNEGIE JEWELRY
10 EAST 38TH. ST.
NEW YORK, N.Y. 10016

RICHARD FARKAS
JEFF-CRAIG ASSOC.
40 E. 34TH. ST., NO. 803
NEW YORK, N.Y. 10016

HAROLD M. ALTSHUL
KETCHUM & CO.
16 EAST 40TH. ST.
NEW YORK, N.Y. 10016

HARRY BERGER
LCI IND.
261 FIFTH AVE.
NEW YORK, N.Y. 10016

T.M. LEY
FRED T. LEY
30 EAST 40TH, ST.
NEW YORK, N.Y. 10016

MICHAEL GOTTLIEB
LIBERTY FABRICS
295 FIFTH AVE.
NEW YORK, N.Y. 10016

SALVATORE VANASCO
LMC DATA
116 EAST 27TH. ST.
NEW YORK, N.Y. 10016

BERNARD L. SCHWARTZ
LORAL
600 THIRD AVE.
NEW YORK, N.Y. 10016

J.M. SHAHEEN
MACMILLAN RING-FREE
90 PARK AVE.
NEW YORK, N.Y. 10016

EDWIN B. KRAUSE
MADISON IND.
279 FIFTH AVE.
NEW YORK, N.Y. 10016

STEPHEN KATZ
MATERIAL SCIENCES
P.O. BOX 449
NEW YORK, N.Y. 10016

A.J. KREIZEL
MOHICAN
200 MADISON AVE.
NEW YORK, N.Y. 10016

GEORGE SHUMSKY
NATIONAL PARAGON
385 FIFTH AVE.
NEW YORK, N.Y. 10016

MILTON BERNSTEIN
NATIONAL SILVER
241 FIFTH AVE.
NEW YORK, N.Y. 10016

JOSEPH LEFF
NATIONAL SPINNING CO.
183 MADISON AVE.
NEW YORK, N.Y. 10016

CLAY FELKER
NEW YORK MAGAZINE
207 EAST 32ND. ST.
NEW YORK, N.Y. 10016

WILBERT F. BOYCE
OPTIMUM COMPUTER
135 MADISON AVE.
NEW YORK, N.Y. 10016

JEFFREY BRITZ
PACESETTER IND..
295 FIFTH AVE.
NEW YORK, N.Y. 10016

EDWARD SILVERSTEIN
PARAMOUNT LEASING
303 FIFTH AVE.
NEW YORK, N.Y. 10016

J.H. HAMBERSTONE
PATENT MANAGEMENT
475 PARK AVE. SOUTH 10TH. FL.
NEW YORK, N.Y. 10016

ROGER SHASHOUA
PATENTS INTERNATIONAL
99 PARK AVE. 21ST. FL.
NEW YORK, N.Y. 10016

IRVING J. WOLF
THE PAY-O-MATIC
6 E. 39TH. ST.
NEW YORK, N.Y. 10016

LAWRENCE S. PHILLIPS
PHILLIPS-VAN HEUSEN
1290 AVE. OF AMERICAS
NEW YORK, N.Y. 10016

JACK YENTIS
PHOTO-MARKER
271 MADISON AVE.
NEW YORK, N.Y. 10016

ARTHUR REIS, JR.
ROBERT REIS
EMPIRE STATE BLDG.
NEW YORK, N.Y. 10016

MORTON SPAR
SHERIDANE DESIGNS
315 FIFTH AVE.
NEW YORK, N.Y. 10016

JESSE S. SIEGEL
HENRY I. SIEGAL
16 EAST 34TH. ST.
NEW YORK, N.Y. 10016

LILYAN H. AFFINITO
SIMPLICITY PATTERN
200 MADISON AVE.
NEW YORK, N.Y. 10016

S.E. HARWOOD
SQUARE IND.
10 EAST 40TH. ST.
NEW YORK, N.Y. 10016

JOEL SEIFF
STARDUST
145 MADISON AVE.
NEW YORK, N.Y. 10016

GLENN W. JOHNSTON
STERLING DRUG
90 PARK AVE.
NEW YORK, N.Y. 10016

ROBERT A. SOLOF
SUMMIT ORGANIZATION
385 FIFTH AVE.
NEW YORK, N.Y. 10016

MARSHALL TULIN
SWANK
90 PARK AVE.
NEW YORK, N.Y. 10016

MURRY ROSENBLATT
TEMCO SERVICE
ONE PARK AVE.
NEW YORK, N.Y. 10016

HAROLD POLCHTAR
TOSCANY IMPORTS
245 FIFTH AVE.
NEW YORK, N.Y. 10016

H. WEISS
VAN WYCK INTERNATIONAL
10 E. 40TH ST.
NEW YORK, N.Y. 10016

MARTIN H. SKOLNIK
WASKO GOLD PRODUCTS
112 MADISON AVE.
NEW YORK, N.Y. 10016

ANDREW H. NEILLY, JR.
JOHN WILEY & SONS
605 THIRD AVE.
NEW YORK, N.Y. 10016

IRWIN WINSTON
WINSTON NETWORK
275 MADISON AVE.
NEW YORK, N.Y. 10016

JOSEPH WOLF
WOLF CORP.
10 EAST 40TH. ST.
NEW YORK, N.Y. 10016

MANUEL KITROSSER
YOLANDE
16 EAST 34TH. ST.
NEW YORK, N.Y. 10016

ALAN SIDNAM
ALL AMERICAN SPORTS
555 FIFTH AVE.
NEW YORK, N.Y. 10017

GEORGE S. DEUTSCH
AMERACE
245 PARK AVE.
NEW YORK,N.Y. 10017

PAUL E. RAMSTAD
AMERICAN MAIZE-PRODUCTS
250 PARK AVE.
NEW YORK, N.Y. 10017

ARTHUR A. KATZ
ARTRONIC INFORMATION SYSTEMS
420 LEXINGTON AVE. SUITE 2835
NEW YORK, N.Y. 10017

JACK FLANAGAN
AUTHENTICOLR
227 EAST 45TH. ST.
NEW YORK, N.Y. 10017

J.H. NORWOOD
BARTELL MEDIA
205 EAST 42nd. ST.
NEW YORK, N.Y. 10017

BRUCE E. CRAWFORD
BBDO INTERNATIONAL
383 MADISON AVE.
NEW YORK, N.Y. 10017

LAWRENCE ELLMAN
BEEFSTEAK CHARLIE'S
230 PARK AVE.
NEW YORK, N.Y. 10017

ROBERT A. BELFER
BELCO PETROLEUM
1 DAG HAMMARSKJOLD PLAZA
NEW YORK, N.Y. 10017

JOHN W. HARTMAN
BILL BROS.
630 THIRD AVE.
NEW YORK, N.Y. 10017

C.C. LANDEGGER
BLACK-CLAWSON
200 PARK AVE.
NEW YORK, N.Y. 10017

LEO BOHN
BOHN BENTON
305 E. 46TH. ST.
NEW YORK, N.Y. 10017

EDWARD E. FITZGERALD
BOOK-OF-THE-MONTH CLUB
280 PARK AVE.
NEW YORK, N.Y. 10017

GERALD ROTHENBERG
BUN & BURGER
41 EAST 42ND. ST. 16TH. FL.
NEW YORK, N.Y. 10017

PETER M. NISSELSON
CABLE INFORMATION
230 PARK AVE.
NEW YORK, N.Y. 10017

T.F. LATIMER
CHICAGO PNEUMATIC TOOL
6 EAST 44TH. ST.
NEW YORK, N.Y. 10017

LEONARD WEITZ
CHIEF CONSOLIDATED
747 THIRD AVE.
NEW YORK, N.Y. 10017

SEYMOUR S. MINDEL
CHOCK FULL O'NUTS
425 LEXINGTON AVE.
NEW YORK, N.Y. 10017

RONALD FINEGOLD
COMPUTER HORIZONS
747 THIRD AVE.
NEW YORK, N.Y. 10017

DONALD PUTNAM
CONRAC
330 MADISON AVE.
NEW YORK, N.Y. 10017

PAUL A. FUND
CONVALESCENT CENTER
250 PARK AVE.
NEW YORK, N.Y. 10017

BARRIE DAMSON
DAMSON OIL
366 MADISON AVE.
NEW YORK, N.Y. 10017

RICHARD J. WALTERS
DIAMON INTERNATIONAL
733 THIRD AVE.
NEW YORK, N.Y. 10017

JOHN T. SARGENT
DOUBLEDAY
277 PARK AVE.
NEW YORK, N.Y. 10017

THOMAS C. SUTTON
DOVER
277 PARK AVE.
NEW YORK, N.Y. 10017

HAROLD AIBEL
DREW NATIONAL
555 FIFTH AVE.
NEW YORK, N.Y. 10017

JACOB L. GREEN
DYNA-LEASE
101 PARK AVE.
NEW YORK, N.Y. 10017

DOUBLAS BILLIAN
EDUCATION SYSTEMS
360 LEXINGTON AVE.
NEW YORK, N.Y. 10017

WILLIAM K. FERNIM
ELECTROGRAPHIC
227 EAST 45TH. ST.
NEW YORK, N.Y. 10017

MONROE GREENBAUM
ENCORE SALES
507 5TH. AVE.
NEW YORK, N.Y. 10017

MILTON F. ROSENTHAL
ENGELHARD MINERALS
299 PARK AVE.
NEW YORK, N.Y. 10017

FREDERICK W. PETERSON
FEDERAL HOUSING
866 UNITED NATIONS PLAZA
NEW YORK, N.Y. 10017

LYNN WALKER
FELMONT OIL
6 EAST 43RD. ST.
NEW YORK, N.Y. 10017

F.S. KELLSTROM
FISCHBACK & MOORE
485 LEXINGTON AVE.
NEW YORK, N.Y. 10017

PHILIP ORZECK
FLEXI-VAN
330 MADISON AVE.
NEW YORK, N.Y. 10017

ALBERT P. BRODAX
FOLIO ONE PRODUCTIONS
240 EAST 46TH. ST.
NEW YORK, N.Y. 10017

JOHN E. O'TOOLE
FOOTE, CONE & BELDING
200 PARK AVE.
NEW YORK, N.Y. 10017

EDWIN A. MALLOY
FRED F. FRENCH
551 FIFTH AVE.
NEW YORK, N.Y. 10017

W. MASON SMITH, JR.
FRESILLO
200 PARK AVE.
NEW YORK, N.Y. 10017

MALCOLM B. SMITH
GENERAL AMERICAN
330 MADISON AVE.
NEW YORK, N.Y. 10017

HARRIS J. ASHTON
GENERAL HOST
245 PARK AVE.
NEW YORK, N.Y. 10017

FRANCIS M. GERLT
GERLT & CO.
155 E. 44TH. ST.
NEW YORK,N.Y. 10017

W.B. WHALEY
GRAYBAR ELECTRIC
420 LEXINGTON AVE.
NEW YORK, N.Y. 10017

EDWARD H. MEYER
GREY ADVT.
777 THIRD AVE.
NEW YORK, N.Y. 10017

WILLIAM JOVANOVICH
HARCOURT BRACE JOVANOVICH
757 THIRD AVE.
NEW YORK, N.Y. 10017

H.R. SIEGEL
HARWYN IND.
800 SECOND AVE.
NEW YORK, N.Y. 10017

T.J. HOLT
T.J. TOLT & CO.
277 PARK AVE.
NEW YORK, N.Y. 10017

THEODORE W. ECKELS
HOWMEDICA
235 EAST 42ND. ST.
NEW YORK, N.Y. 10017

IZHAK BLANK
HYDROPHILICS
200 PARK AVE.
NEW YORK, N.Y. 10017

ANDRES MUTUTE
IBERIA INTERNATIONAL
475 FIFTH AVE.
NEW YORK, N.Y. 10017

ARTHUR H. GOLDBERG
INTEGRATED RESOURCES
295 MADISON AVE.
NEW YORK, N.Y. 10017

R.E. LUDT
INTERCONTINENTAL ENERGY
299 PARK AVE.
NEW YORK, N.Y. 10017

R.E. LUNT
INTERCONTINENTAL OIL
299·PARK AVE. RM. 2323
NEW YORK, N.Y. 10017

EDWARD H. WEITZEN
INTERNATIONAL BANKNOTE
230 PARK AVE.
NEW YORK, N.Y. 10017

P.H. O'NEILL
INTERNATIONAL MINING
200 PARK AVE.
NEW YORK, N.Y. 10017

PAUL A. GOLDNER
INTERNATIONAL SYSTEMS
50 EAST 42ND. ST.
NEW YORK, N.Y. 10017

MARTIN TUCKMAN
INTERPOOL
630 THIRD AVE.
NEW YORK, N.Y.

HILTON SCHWARTZ
JOREMI ENTERPRISES
6 EAST 43RD. ST.
NEW YORK, N.Y. 10017

HERMANN ROGGE
KENRICH
777 THIRD AVE.
NEW YORK, N.Y. 10017

BENJAMIN OSHER
KLEER-VU IND.
666 THIRD AVE.
NEW YORK, N.Y. 10017

E.A. MALLOY
KNICKERBOCKER VILLAGE
551 5TH. AVE.
NEW YORK, N.Y. 10017

HERMANN ROGGE
LARIBEE WIRE
777 THIRD AVE.
NEW YORK, N.Y. 10017

JEROLD NABRIDGE
LECTRO MANAGEMENT
215 E. 49TH. ST.
NEW YORK, N.Y. 10017

HOWARD S. LEVIN
LEVIN COMPUTER
224 EAST 49TH. ST.
NEW YORK, N.Y. 10017

MAXWELL M. POWELL
LIFE SCIENCES
230 PARK AVE.
NEW YORK, N.Y. 10017

P.A. SALBATING
LIQUID AIR
405 LEXINGTON AVE.
NEW YORK, N.Y. 10017

LAWRENCE ELLMAN
LONGCHAMPS
230 PARK AVE.
NEW YORK, N.Y. 10017

DAVID B. ROSENBLOOM
MALLORY RANDALL
122 E. 42ND. ST.
NEW YORK, N.Y. 10017

RAYMOND P. KURSHAN
MANAGEMENT ASSISTANCE
300 E. 44TH. ST.
NEW YORK, N.Y. 10017

W. ROBERT KOBELT
MAXWELL IND.
155 EAST 44TH. ST.
NEW YORK, N.Y. 10017

CHARLES D. ALKMAN
MC CALL
277 PARK AVE.
NEW YORK, N.Y. 10017

A.B. SHEPARD
MEDIA CORP.
747 THIRD AVE.
NEW YORK, N.Y. 10017

JOEL W. HARNETT
MEDIA HORIZONS
750 3RD. AVE.
NEW YORK, N.Y. 10017

JOHN W. KLUGE
METROMEDIA
277 PARK AVE.
NEW YORK, N.Y. 10017

ARNOLD KAISER
MPO VIDEOTRONICS
820 SECOND AVE.
NEW YORK, N.Y. 10017

MARC STRAUSBERG
MSS INFORMATION
655 MADISON AVE.
NEW YORK, N.Y. 10017

JOSEPH S. LINDEMANN
NESTLE LE-MUR
529 FIFTH AVE.
NEW YORK, N.Y. 10017

HERMANN ROGGE
NEWTON ELKIN SHOES
777 THIRD AVE.
NEW YORK, N.Y. 10017

ANDREW G. KERSHAW
OGILVY & MATHER
2 EAST 48TH. ST.
NEW YORK, N.Y. 10017

DR. CHARLES M. WEISS
ORATRONICS
405 LEXINGTON AVE. SUITE 5600
NEW YORK, N.Y. 10017

MORTON P. HYMAN
OVERSEAS SHIPHOLDING
511 FIFTH AVE.
NEW YORK, N.Y. 10017

ARTHUR SMADBECK
PARK-LEXINGTON CO.
52 VANDERBILT AVE.
NEW YORK, N.Y. 10017

E.M. LANG
REFAC TECH. DEVELOPMENT
122 EAST 42ND. ST.
NEW YORK, N.Y. 10017

DON REID
DON REID PRODUCTIONS
420 MADISON AVE.
NEW YORK, N.Y. 10017

DAVID A. SEGAL
ROYAL ATLAS
342 MADISON AVE.
NEW YORK, N.Y. 10017

ALLEN P. LUCHT
SERVOMATION
777 THIRD AVE.
NEW YORK, N.Y. 10017

DAVID SINGER
DAVID SINGER ASSOC.
400 MADISON AVE.
NEW YORK, N.Y. 10017

ARTHUR LEVEY
SKIATRON ELECTRONIS
30 EAST 42ND. ST.
NEW YORK, N.Y. 10017

MORTIMER D. MORIARTY
SOUTHPORT COMM.
277 PARK AVE.
NEW YORK, N.Y. 10017

F.A. COLLINS, JR.
SPERRY & HUTCHINSON
330 MADISON AVE.
NEW YORK, N.Y. 10017

A.E. ABRAMSON
SPORTS UNDERWRITERS
235 EAST 45TH. ST.
NEW YORK, N.Y. 10017

G. RUBIN
STAFF BUILDERS
122 EAST 42ND. ST.
NEW YORK, N.Y. 10017

EZRA J. ENERSTEIN
STANDARD PRUDENTIAL
277 PARK AVE.
NEW YORK, N.Y. 10017

LAWRENCE ELLMAN
STEAK & BREW
230 PARK AVE.
NEW YORK, N.Y. 10017

HANSJOERG SCHUDEL
HUGO STINNES
750 THIRD AVE.
NEW YORK, N.Y. 10017

EDWARD E. BARR
SUN CHEMICAL
200 PARK AVE.
NEW YORK, N.Y. 10017

K. FRED NITTER
SUPRADUR MFG.
122 EAST 42ND. ST.
NEW YORK, N.Y. 10017

DOUBLAS P. FIELDS
TDA IND.
122 EAST 42ND. ST.
NEW YORK, N.Y. 10017

R.E. RIEDEL
TELETAPE
708 THIRD AVE.
NEW YORK, N.Y. 10017

DON JOHNSTON
J. WALTER THOMPSON
420 LEXINGTON AVE.
NEW YORK, N.Y. 10017

GERALD DUNNE
TIZON CHEM.
330 MADISON AVE.
NEW YORK, N.Y. 10017

GEORGE MYRETUS
TOTAL ENERGY LEASING
330 MADISON AVE.
NEW YORK, N.Y 10017

A.HOFFMANN
TOWNE MINES
551 FIFTH AVE.
NEW YORK, N.Y. 10017

C. EDWARD ACKER
TRANSWAY
747 THIRD AVE. 37TH. FL.
NEW YORK, N.Y. 10017

JOHN V. BALLARD
TRIBUNE OIL
230 PARK AVE.
NEW YORK, N.Y. 10017

WALTER B. SHAW
TURNER CONST.
150 EAST 42ND. ST.
NEW YORK, N.Y. 10017

MORLEY P. THOMPSON
THE UNITED CORP.
250 PARK AVE.
NEW YORK,N.Y. 10017

H. STRAVE HENSEL
UNIVERSAL GAS & OIL
122 EAST 42ND. ST.
NEW YORK, N.Y. 10017

ARNOLD E. ABRAMSON
UNIVERSAL PUBLISHING
235 EAST 45TH. ST.
NEW YORK,N.Y. 10017

RICHARD E. MC CONNELL
VALLEY METALLURGICAL
280 PARK AVE.
NEW YORK, N.Y. 10017

MURRAY J. KING
VIDATA INTERNATIONAL
60 EAST 42ND. ST.
NEW YORK, N.Y. 10017

CHARLES V. MYERS
WALLACE-MURRAY
299 PARK AVE.
NEW YORK, N.Y. 10017

R.R. DANN
WATER IND.
469 FIFTH AVE.
NEW YORK, N.Y. 10017

D.P. FIELDS
WESTCALIND
122 EAST 42ND. ST.
NEW YORK, N.Y. 10017

DAVID L. LUKE
WESTVACO
299 PARK AVE.
NEW YORK, N.Y. 10017

SIGGI B. WILZIG
WILSHIRE OIL
250 PARK AVE.
NEW YORK, N.Y. 10017

HENRY SONNEBORN
WITCO CHEM.
277 PARK AVE.
NEW YORK. N.Y. 10017

A.F. SILBERT
YUBA, GODFIELDS
277 PARK AVE.
NEW YORK, N.Y. 10017

L. ROBERTS
YORKTOWN PRODUCTS
P.O. BOX 272
NEW YORK, N.Y. 10017

C.P. LECHT
ADVANCED COMPUTER
437 MADISON AVE.
NEW YORK, N.Y. 10022

R.C. MILLER
A F A PROTECTIVE
519 EIGHTH AVE.
NEW YORK, N.Y. 10018

ALEXANDER FARKAS
ALEXANDER'S
500 7TH. AVE.
NEW YORK, N.Y. 10018

SEYMOUR STERN
ALISON AYERS
1400 BROADWAY
NEW YORK, N.Y. 10018

WILLIAM A. MARQUARD
AMERICAN STANDARD
40 WEST 40TH. ST.
NEW YORK, N.Y. 10018

IRVING SCHECHTER
ANN STEVENS
134 WEST 37TH. ST.
NEW YORK, N.Y. 10018

JEROME REIKEN
APPLIEDHEALTH SERVICES
134 WEST 37TH. ST.
NEW YORK, N.Y. 10018

JOSEPH E. ROBBINS
ARCS IND.
1431 BROADWAY
NEW YORK, N.Y. 10018

R.T. KROPF
BELDING HEMINWAY
1430 BROADWAY
NEW YORK, N.Y. 10018

R.V. CANCRO
BI STATE IND.
1400 BROADWAY
NEW YORK,N.Y. 10018

IVAN MARKS
BRETMAR FABRICS
469 SEVENTH AVE.
NEW YORK, N.Y. 10018

E.R. HYMAN
CABOT KNITTING MILLS
1410 BROADWAY
NEW YORK, N.Y. 10018

H.C. COLE
CHARTER FABRICS
1001 AVE. OF AMERICAS
NEW YORK, N.Y. 10018

HAROLD STEINBERG
CHELSEA HOUSE ED.
70 W. 40TH. ST.
NEW YORK, N.Y. 10018

DAVID CAPLAN
CONCORD FABRICS
1411 BROADWAY
NEW YORK, N.Y. 10018

A.T. GIFFORD
COUNTRY MISS
1407 BROADWAY
NEW YORK, N.Y. 10018

HOWARD RICHMOND
CROMPTON CO.
1071 AVE. OF AMERICAS
NEW YORK, N.Y. 10018

CHARLES WEINSTEIN
CWC IND.
512 SEVENTH AVE.
NEW YORK, N.Y. 10018

HARVEY TAUMAN
DENTO-MED IND.
134 W. 37TH. ST.
NEW YORK, N.Y. 10018

OWEN ALPER
DEVONBROOK
498 7TH. AVE.
NEW YORK, N.Y. 10018

MURRAY NADLER
DONNKENNY
1411 BROADWAY
NEW YORK, N.Y. 10018

MURRAY LEVY
DON SOPHISTICATES
530 SEVENTH AVE.
NEW YORK, N.Y. 10018

MARVIN ROSEN
FASHION-IN-PARTS
525 SEVENTH AVE.
NEW YORK, N.Y. 10018

GEORGE FELDMAN
FINDERHOOD
15 WEST 38TH. ST.
NEW YORK, N.Y. 10018

MORTON GROPPER
FOXCO IND.
1412 BROADWAY
NEW YORK, N.Y. 10018

MICHAEL GOODSTEIN
GAYNOR-STAFFORD IND.
1450 BROADWAY
NEW YORK, N.Y. 10018

JAY GALIN
G & G SHOPS
229 WEST 36TH. ST.
NEW YORK, N.Y. 10018

ARTHUR HURVITZ
HEALTH-TEX
1411 BROADWAY
NEW YORK, N.Y. 10018

MARTIN WITKOFF
HERS APPAREL IND.
247 WEST 38TH. ST.
NEW YORK, N.Y. 10018

FRED HOWARD
HOWARD INTERNATIONAL
500 TENTH AVE.
NEW YORK, N.Y. 10018

HERB PHILLIPS
JARMEL FABRICS
229 WEST 36TH. ST.
NEW YORK, N.Y. 10018

MARK HOROWITZ
JAYMARK KNIT IND.
71 WEST 23RD.ST.
NEW YORK,N.Y. 10018

JEROME MANN
JUNIOR SPICE
463 SEVENTH AVE.
NEW YORK, N.Y. 10018

HYMAN TURK
KAPPA FROCKS
463 SEVENTH AVE.
NEW YORK, N.Y. 10018

IRWIN MOSKOWITZ
KENWIN SHOPS
505 8TH. AVE.
NEW YORK, N.Y. 10018

LAWRENCE GORDON
LEHIGH VALLEY IND.
119 WEST 40TH.ST.
NEW YORK, N.Y. 10018

JOHN J. POMERANTZ
LESLIE FAY
1400 BROADWAY
NEW YORK, N.Y. 10018

ROBERT BENDHEIM
M. LOWENSTEIN & SONS
1430 BROADWAY
NEW YORK, N.Y. 10018

ROBERT GIDDINS
LYNNWEAR
1400 BROADWAY
NEW YORK, N.Y. 10018

CHARLES MELTZER
MARLENE IND.
1372 BROADWAY
NEW YORK, N.Y. 10018

MATHEW MATLUCK
JO MATHEWS
525 SEVENTH AVE.
NEW YORK, N.Y. 10018

IRVING GOLDBERGER
KATE GREENAWAY IND.
1333 BROADWAY
NEW YORK, N.Y. 10018

PHILIP BROUS
MILLER-WOHL
112 W. 38TH.ST.
NEW YORK, N.Y. 10018

LYNN STUART
MISTER PANTS
1441 BROADWAY
NEW YORK, N.Y. 10018

IRWIN GOLDBERGER
MOVIE STAR
392 FIFTH AVE.
NEW YORK, N.Y. 10018

MANFRED BRECKER
S.E. NICHOLS
500 EIGHTH AVE.
NEW YORK, N.Y. 10018

ARTHUR ASCH
OAK HILL SPORTSWEAR
1407 BROADWAY
NEW YORK, N.Y. 10018

IRVING BADER
ORIGINALA
512 SEVENTH AVE.
NEW YORK, N.Y. 10018

MILTON L. REITER
ORIGINIT FABRICS
115 WEST 40TH. ST.
NEW YORK, N.Y. 10018

SOL COOPER
PAT FASHIONS IND.
1370 BROADWAY
NEW YORK, N.Y. 10018

GEORGE LIPPMAN
PUTNAM-GELLMAN
21 WEST 38TH. ST.
NEW YORK, N.Y. 10018

EDWARD P. MANDEAU
QUORUM IND.
119 WEST 40TH. ST.
NEW YORK, N.Y. 10018

AARON J. GROSS
QUOTE ME
1407 BROADWAY
NEW YORK, N.Y. 10018

ELI L. ROUSSO
RUSS TOGS
1411 BROADWAY
NEW YORK, N.Y. 10018

M.J. SCHRADER
ABE SCHRADER
530 SEVENTH AVE.
NEW YORK, N.Y. 10018

NORMAN EMBER
THE SEW-IN
501 7TH. AVE.
NEW YORK, N.Y. 10018

PETER G. SCOTESE
SPRING MILLS
104 WEST 40TH. ST.
NEW YORK, N.Y. 10018

MALCOLM STARR
MALCOLM STARR INC.
550 SEVENTH AVE.
NEW YORK, N.Y. 10018

E.M. STERN, JR.
STERN & STERN TEXTILES
1359 BROADWAY
NEW YORK, N.Y. 10018

SIDNEY H. KOSANN
STEVCOKNIT
1450 BROADWAY
NEW YORK, N.Y. 10018

IRVING SCHECHTER
ANN STEVENS
134 WEST 37TH. ST.
NEW YORK, N.Y. 10018

ARMIN GOLD
SWEATER BEE BY BANFF
1410 BROADWAY
NEW YORK, N.Y. 10018

LAWRENCE G. TANENBAUM
TAN-TEX IND.
1450 BROADWAY
NEW YORK, N.Y. 10018

HAROLD C. SUMMERFORD
UNITED PIECE DYE WORKS
111 WEST 40TH. ST.
NEW YORK, N.Y. 10018

AL PARIS
VENICE IND.
1412 BROADWAY
NEW YORK, N.Y. 10018

HENRY WARSHOW
H. WARSHOW & SONS
45 W. 36TH. ST.
NEW YORK,N.Y. 10018

HOWARD I. SIMON
WESTONS SHOPPERS CITY
505 EIGHTH AVE.
NEW YORK, N.Y. 10018

MANNY C. ROBERTS
WOLLFOAM
1 WEST 37TH. ST.
NEW YORK, N.Y. 10018

ALLEN KLEIN
ABKCO IND.
1700 BROADWAY
NEW YORK, N.Y. 10019

MITCHELL E. GOLDSTONE
ALPHANUMERIC
1345 AVE.OF AMERICAS
NEW YORK, N.Y. 10019

SAUL JEFFEE
MOVIELAB INC.
619 WEST 54TH. ST.
N.Y, N.Y. 10019

VICTOR POSNER
NATIONAL PROPANE
768 FIFTH AVE
N.Y., N.Y. 10019

BURTON ROBBINS
NATIN'L. SCREEN SERVICE
1600 BROADWAY
N.Y., N.Y. 10019

GEDALIO GRINBERG
NORTH AMERICAN WATCH
1345 SIXTH AVE.
N.Y,, N.Y. 10019

CHESTER ROSS
NOVO CORP
31 WEST 53
N.Y., N.Y. 10019

E.E. ERDMAN
OCG TECHNOLOGY
110 WEST 57th. ST.
N.Y., N.Y. 10019

C. AHTO
OPTICO
619 W. 54TH. ST.
N.Y., N.Y. 10019

ELMER WARD, JR.
PALM BEACH CO.
1290 AVE. OF AMERICAS
N.Y., N.Y. 10019

JEROME CASTEL
PENN-DIXIE INDUSTRIES
1345 AVE. OF AMERICAS
N.Y.,NY. 10019

G. LANGNAS
PROGRAMMING METHODS
1301 AVE OF AMERICAS
N.Y., N.Y. 10019

IRWIN MAUTNER
PROGRAMMING & SYSTEMS
151 WEST 51 ST.
N.Y., N.Y. 10019

SAMUEL WYMAN
RDR ASSOC.
1345 AVE. OF AMERICAS
N.Y., N.Y. 10019

RICHARD A. BLUMENTHAL
RESTAURANT ASSOC.
1540 BROADWAY
N.Y., N.Y. 10019

FRANC M. RICCIARDI
RICHTON INTERNATIONAL
1345 AVE. OF AMERICAS
N.Y., N.Y. 10019

ARTHUR BRANDON
ROYALPAR IND.
1345 AVE. OF AMERICAS
N.Y., N.Y. 10019

EDWIN VAN PELT
SEABOARD ASSOC.
1776 BROADWAY
NEW YORK, N.Y. 10019

MALCOLM A. SELIGMAN
SELIGMAN & LATZ
666 FIFTH AVE.
N.Y., N.Y. 10019

JAMES A. RICHTER
STAGE IND.
850 SEVENTH AVE.
N.Y., N.Y. 10019

ROBERT GRANT
TALCOTT NATIONAL CORP.
1290 AVE. OF AMERICAS
N.Y., N.Y. 10019

ROBERT SEIDELMAN
TELEWORLD
10 COLUMBUS CIRCLE
NEW YORK, N.Y. 10019

HERBERT M. PEARLMAN
THE UNIMAX GROUP
1740 BROADWAY
N.Y., N.Y. 10019

SALA HASSANEIN
UNITED ARTIST THEATRE
1700 BROADWAY
N.Y., N.Y. 10019

HERMAN GIMBEL
AUDIO FIDELITY ENTERPRISES,
221 WEST 57th ST
N.Y, N.Y. 10019

RADLEY METZGER
AUDUBON FILMS
850 SEVENTH AVE
N.Y., N.Y. 10019

H.B. STERNBERG
AUTOMATED REFERENCE
200 CENTRAL PK. S.
N.Y., N.Y. 10019

J.P. CROXTON
AUXTON COMPUTER ENTERPRISES
1345 AVE. OF AMERICAS
N.Y., N.Y. 10019

FRANK PATREY
BOURJOIS INC
9 WEST 57th St.
N.Y., N.Y. 10019

JAMES TAYLOR
BRADFORD NATN'L
1700 BROADWAY
N.Y., N.Y. 10019

N.O. WAGNER
CASTLE CAPITAL
1345 AVE. OF AMERICAS
N.Y., N.Y. 10019

ROBERT NAVIN
CAVITRON CORP
1290 AVE OF AMERICAS
N.Y., N.Y. 10019

JERRY GROSS
CINEMATION INDUS. INC
888 8th AVE. NO. 10W
N.Y., N.Y. 10019

FREDDIE FIELD
CREATIVE MANAGEMENT ASSOC
40 W. 57th ST.
N.Y., N.Y. 10019

E.M. WEBER
CUSTODIAL GUIDANCE SYSTEMS
157 WEST 57th ST.
N.Y., N.Y. 10019

GERALD YASS
DATATAB, INC.
888 SEVENTH AVE.
N.Y., N.Y. 10019

RUDOLPH BOYKO
DESERT DEVELOPMENT CORP
10 COLUMBUS CIRCLE
N.Y., N.Y. 10019

PAUL KAUFMAN
DU-ART FILM LABS
245 WEST 55th ST.
N.Y., N.Y. 10019

STANLEY GOLDMAN
EAGLE CLOTHES, INC
1290 AVE. OF AMERICAS
N.Y., N.Y. 10019

HAROLD SIGMAN
EAGLE GENERAL
1721 BROADWAY
N.Y., N.Y. 10019

RICHARD BARRIE
FABERGE
1345 AVE. OF AMERICAS
N.Y., N.Y. 10019

LOUIS RUDOLPH
FIRE FLY ENTERPRISES
1301 AVE OF AMERICAS
N.Y., N.Y. 10019

GORDON GREENFIELD
FRANCHARD CORP
640 FIFTH AVE.
N.Y., N.Y. 10019

JESSE WERNER
GAF CORP
140 WEST 51st ST.
N.Y., N.Y. 10019

BILL THOMPSON
HARDWICKE COMPANIES
9 WEST 57th
N.Y., .N.Y. 10019

SEYMOUR MORROW
THE HARWOOD COMPANIES
666 FIFTH AVE.
N.Y., N.Y. 10019

EUGENE CHINERY
INTAROME FRAGRANCE
429 W. 53 ST
N.Y., N.Y. 10019

IRVING SELBST
INTERCONTINENTAL APPAREL
888 SEVENTH AVE
N.Y., N.Y. 10019

Z. SITCHIN
INTERCONTINENTAL TRAILSEA
1290 AVE. OF AMERICAS
N.Y., N.Y. 10019

RICHARD HEITMEYER
IOTA INDUSTRIES
888 SEVENTH AVE   25th FL.
N.Y., N.Y. 10019

DON KIRSHNER
KIRSHNER ENTERTAINMENT
1370 AVE. OF AMERICAS
N.Y., N.Y. 10019

LEO KAPLAN
LAZARE KAPLAN INTERN'L
666   FIFTH AVE.
N.Y., N.Y. 10019

ALVIN DWORMAN
LEE NATIONAL
640 FIFTH AVE.
N.Y., N.Y. 10019

S. WESTON
LEISURE CONCEPTS
116 CENTRAL PK. S.
N.Y., N.Y. 10019

DONALD PELS
LIN BROADCASTING
1370 AVE OF AMERICAS
N.Y., N.Y. 10019

RONALD SAYPOL
LIONEL CORP
9 WEST 57th
N.Y., N.Y. 10019

WARNER LOEB
LISTFAX CORP
1370 AVE OF AMERICAS
N.Y., N.Y. 10019

MARSHALL NAIFY
MAGNA PICTURES
1700 BROADWAY'
N.Y., N.Y. 10019

SHEPARD FOREST
MASTON CO
640 FIFTH AVE.
N.Y., N.Y. 10019

STANLEY GILLETTE
MC GREBOR-DONIGER
666 FIFTH AVE.
N.Y., N.Y. 10019

J.D. GOEKEN
MCI TELECOMMUNICATIONS
1301 AVE OF AMERICAS
N.Y., N.Y. 10019

RICHARD FULSZ
MEDCOM
1633 BROADWAY
N.Y., N.Y. 10019

MORRIS SHMIDMAN
MEDIC-HOME ENTERPRISES
1700 BROADWAY
N.Y., N.Y. 10019

PETER BURGARD
MICRO THERAPEUTICS
330 WEST 58th
N.Y., N.Y. 10019

GEORGE HORVATH
MOUNT CLEMENS CORP
41 WEST 58th ST
N.Y. , N.Y. 10019

F.B. TARTER
UNIVERSAL COMMUNICATIONS
40 W. 57TH. ST.
N.Y., N.Y. 10019

CHARLES PETTIJOHN
VERCO ENERGY CORP.
151 WEST 51 ST.
N.Y., N.Y. 10019

BARRY BURNSTEIN
VIDEO TECHNIQUES
39 WEST 55TH. ST.
N.Y., N.Y. 10019

ANDREW GALEF
VIEWLEX INC.
1290 AVE. OF AMERICAS
N.Y., N.Y. 10019

ROBERT L. PURVIN
BARBER OIL CORP.
30 ROCKEFELLER PLAZA
N.Y., N.Y. 10020

J.A. STUART
CERVECERIA CORONA
1270 AVE.OF AMERICAS
N.Y., N.Y. 10020

S.C. PODORAS
EQUITABLE PETROLEUM
50 ROCKEFELLER PLAZA
N.Y., N.Y. 10020

H.E. GOODMAN
FRANKLIN CORP.
ONE ROCKEFELLER PLAZA
N.Y., N.Y. 10020

DONALD D. GEARY, JR.
GREENE CANANEA COPPER
1271 AVE. OF AMERICAS
N.Y., N.Y. 10020

WILLIAM H. ASHPLANT
HALCO PRODUCTS
ONE ROCKEFELLER PLAZA
N.Y., N.Y. 10020 #1602

PETER F. MATHEWS
LORD ELECTRIC CO.
45 ROCKEFELLER PLAZA
NEW YORK, N.Y. 10020

HARRY J. GLASER
MANAGEMENT TV SYSTEMS
1271 AVE. OF AMERICAS
N.Y., N.Y. 10020

LAURENCE C. LEEDS, JR.
MANHATTAN IND.
1271 AVE. OF AMERICAS
NEW YORK, N.Y. 10020

BENJAMIN PARRILL
MILLER BROS. IND.
135 W. 50TH. ST.
N.Y., N.Y. 10020

ANDREW J. FRANKEL
NATIONAL KINNEY CORP.
75 ROCKEFELLER PLAZA
NEW YORK, N.Y. 10020

ALAN W. DREW
PEABODY INTERNATIONAL
450 PARK AVE.
N.Y., N.Y. 10020

FREDERICK PAPERT
PKL COMPANIES
ONE ROCKEFELLER PLAZA
N.Y., N.Y. 10020

J.E. REEVES, JR.
REEVES BROS.
1271 AVE. OF AMERICAS
N.Y., N.Y. 10020

JAMES H. SHEILS
SIBONEY CORP.
1 ROCKEFELLER PLAZA
N.Y., N.Y. 10020

S.C. DAVIDSON
SOVEREIGN AMERICAN ARTS
50 ROCKEFELLER PLAZA   RM. 928
N.Y., N.Y. 10020

JOHN C. WALLACE
STRUTHERS SCIENTIFIC
630 FIFTH AVE.
N.Y., N.Y. 10020

JOHN C. WALLACE
STRUTHERS WELLS CORP.
630 FIFTH AVE.
N.Y., N.Y. 10020

JAMES D. O'DONNELL
STUTZ MOTOR CAR OF AMERICA
TIME & LIFE BLDG.
N.Y., N.Y. 10020

WILLIAM SHAW
VOLT INFORMATION SERVICE
1221 AVE. OF AMERICAS
N.Y., N.Y. 10020

C.B. HAYWORTH
WORLD PATENT DEVELOPMENT
1 ROCKEFELLER PLAZA
N.Y., N.Y. 10020

ALLAN GRANT
ANGLO-AMERICAN STAMP CO.
130 EAST 62ND. ST.
N.Y., N.Y. 10021

J.L. GOLDWATER
ARCHIE ENTERPRISES
1116 FIRST AVE.
N.Y., N.Y. 10021

SOL SINGER
CAMELOT ENTERPRISES
203 EAST 72ND. ST. #14E
N.Y., N.Y. 10021

ROBERT KROPP
CAPEHART CORP.
770 LEXINGTON AVE.
N.Y., N.Y. 10021

SEARS FARRINGTON
CASSETTE PLAYER CORP.
245 EAST 72ND. ST.
N.Y., N.Y. 10021

F.L. WILLIAMS, JR.
ESCALADE INCORPORATED
301 EAST 79TH. ST.#33L
N.Y., N.Y. 10021

MARTIN I. ISENBERG
GENIMAR INC.
11 E. 68TH. ST.
N.Y., N.Y. 10021

DR. MICHAEL A. ROSENBLUTH
HEALTH SURVEYS
912 FIFTH AVE.
N.Y., N.Y. 10021

C. BRUCE NEWBERY
INFLIGHT SERVICES
485 MADISON AVE.
N.Y., N.Y. 10021

DAVID HANANIA
INTERNATIONAL MODULEX
815 FIFTH AVE.
N.Y., N.Y. 10021

RAYMOND SPECTOR
C.F. KIRK LABORATORIES
655 MADISON AVE.
N.Y., N.Y. 10021

DANIEL C. HICKEY
KNOTT HOTELS
840 MADISON AVE.
N.Y.,N.Y. 10021

WILLIAM WURTZEL
LAMPERT COMMUNICATIONS
770 LEXINGTON AVE.
N.Y., N.Y. 10021

VINCENT E. DE SOUSA
MPS INTERNATIONAL
660 MADISON AVE.
N.Y., N.Y. 10021

JOSEPH PARIS
PARIS ENTERPRISES
750 LEXINGTON AVE.
N.Y., N.Y. 10021

G. GREGORY BRYAN
SILVER EUREKA
660 MADISON AVE.
N.Y., N.Y. 10021

BERNARD FEIN
UNITED INDUSTRIAL CORP.
660 MADISON AVE.
N.Y., N.Y. 10021

EDWARD GROPPER
UNIVERSAL CIGAR
660 MADISON AVE.
N.Y., N.Y. 10021

JOHN GALICCHIO
AERO-FLOW DYNAMICS
345 PARK AVE.
NEW YORK, N.Y. 10022

MICHAEL LEIBLE
AMERICAN COMPLEX INC.
375 PARK AVE.
N.Y., N.Y. 10022

J.H. GRUBMAN
AMERICAN MULTIMEDIA
745 5TH. AVE.
N.Y., N.Y. 10022

DAVID SEILER
A.J. ARMSTRONG CO.
850 THIRD AVE.
N.Y., N.Y. 10022

MARTIN BREGMAN
ARTISTS ENTERTAINMENT
641 LEXINGTON AVE.
N.Y., N.Y. 10022

RALPH GUILD
ASI COMMUNICATIONS
400 PARK AVE.
N.Y., N.Y. 10022

EDWARD R. FARLEY, JR.
ATLAS CORP.
485 MADISON AVE.
N.Y., N.Y. 10022

L.J. APPIGNANI
BARBIZON INTERNATIONAL
689 5TH. AVE
N.Y., N.Y. 10022

PHILIP S. SASSOWER
BATES MFG. CO.
850 THIRD AVE.
N.Y., N.Y. 10022

B.R. PAYN
BIOREX CORP.
505 PARK AVE.
N.Y., N.Y. 10022

JACK W. FRITZ
JOHN BLAIR & CO.
717 FIFTH AVE.
N.Y., N.Y. 10022

J.L. STERN
BRENNAND-PAIGE IND.
745 FIFTH AVE.
N.Y., N.Y. 10022

JOSEPH AXLER
BUECHE-GIROD CORP.
665 FIFTH AVE.
N.Y., N.Y. 10022

FELIX RANKIN
CAMIN IND.
505 PARK AVE.
N.Y., N.Y. 10022

CHRISTOPHER C. DEWEY
THE CANNON GROUP
405 PARK AVE.
N.Y., N.Y. 10022

DANIEL B. BURKE
CAPITAL CITIES
24 EAST 51ST. ST.
N.Y., N.Y. 10022

HERBERT J. SIEGEL
CHRIS-CRAFT IND.
600 MADISON AVE.
N.Y., N.Y. 10022

DONALD S. RUGOFF
CINEMA 5 LTD.
595 MADISON AVE.
N.Y., N.Y. 10022

DONALD S. RUGOFF
CINEVEST PRODUCTIONS
595 MADISON AVE.
N.Y., N.Y. 10022

DANTE C. FABIANI
CRANE CO.
300 PARK AVE.
N.Y., N.Y. 10022

ERNEST BOGEN
CREATIVE CINE-TEL
919 3RD. AVE.
NEW YORK, N.Y. 10022

FRANK J. GRAZIANO
CROMPTON & KNOWLES
345 PARK AVE.
N.Y., N.Y. 10022

M.E. DAVID
DAXOR CORP.
645 MADISON AVE.
N.Y., N.Y. 10022

GEORGE PRATT
DIEBOLD VENTURE
430 PARK AVE.
N.Y., N.Y. 10022

BARBARA BELLE
DIMENSIONAL ENTERTAINMENT
445 PARK AVE. SUITE 1001
N.Y., N.Y. 10022

A. EDWARD MILLER
DOWNE COMMUNICATIONS
641 LEXINGTON AVE.
N.Y., N.Y. 10022

A.L. BLINDER
ESQUIRE
488 MADISON AVE.
N.Y., N.Y. 10022

LEROY GREENSPAN
FLAGSTAFF CORP.
600 MADISON AVE
N.Y., N.Y. 10022

HOWARD SOLOMON
FOREST LABORATORIES
919 THIRD AVE.
N.Y., N.Y. 10022

PAUL GAYNOR
GAYNOR & CO.
575 MADISON AVE.
N.Y., N.Y. 10022

I. BURTON KOFFMANN
GREAT AMERICAN IND.
645 FIFTH AVE.
N.Y., N.Y. 10022

ROBERT B. CLARKE
GROLIER INC.
575 LEXINGTON AVE.
N.Y., N.Y. 10022

RUSSELL BANKS
GROW CHEM. CORP.
345 PARK AVE.
N.Y., N.Y. 10022

M. WILBUR TOWNSEND
HANDY & HARMAN
850 THIRD AVE.
N.Y., N.Y. 10022

WINTHROP KNOWLTON
HARPER & ROW PUBISHERS
10 E. 53RD. ST.
N.Y., N.Y. 10022

ARTHUR STELOFF
HERITAGE ENTERPRISES
445 PARK AVE.
N.Y., N.Y. 10022

RAPHAEL D. SILVER
HODGSON HOUSES
10 EAST 53RD. ST.
N.Y., N.Y. 10022

DAVID MAZER
HUDSON PULP & PAPER
477 MADISON AVE.
N.Y., N.Y. 10022

S.R, ROBINS
HYDROPONIC SCIENCES
625 MADISON AVE.
N.Y., N.Y. 10022

DAVID DUBOW
I.M.S. INTERNATIONAL
800 THIRD AVE.
N.Y., N.Y. 10022

NOAH FLESCHNER
INFORMATIVE COMPUTER
404 PARK AVE.
N.Y., N.Y. 10022

GILBERT E. KAPLAN
INSTITUTIONAL INVESTOR
488 MADISON AVE.
N.Y., N.Y. 10022

FRANCIS J. DONLEAVY
INTERNATIONAL TELEPHONE
320 PARK AVE.
N.Y., N.Y. 10022

ROBERT J. CARNEY
JET CAPITAL CORP.
800 THIRD AVE.
N.Y., N.Y. 10022

GLENN W. BAILEY
KEENE CORP.
345 PARK AVE.
N.Y., N.Y. 10022

MICHAEL R. GREEN
KENAI DRILLING
477 MADISON AVE.
N.Y., N.Y. 10022

B.J. BLANEY
KENTON CORP.
711 FIFTH AVE.
N.Y., N.Y. 10022

PIERRE SCHOENHEIMER
LEWIS TOTALMARKETING
375 PARK AVE.
N.Y., N.Y. 10022

FRANK C. PRINCE
LION MATCH CORP.
60 SUTTON PL. SOUTH #10G
N.Y., N.Y. 10022

G. FRANK SHEDIVY
LOMAS & NETTLETON
375 PARK AVE.
N.Y., N.Y. 10022

DAVID B. McCALL
LO ROCHE,McCAFFREY,McCALL
575 LEXINGTON AVE.
N.Y., N.Y. 10022

ROBERT A. BARTON
MACMILLAN
866 THIRD AVE.
N.Y., N.Y. 10022

WAYNE H. BURT
MAGMA COPPER
300 PARK AVE.
N.Y., N.Y. 10022

S.L. WANE
MARLINE OIL CORP.
767 FIFTH AVE.
N.Y., N.Y. 10022

D.B. McCALL
McCAFFREY& McCALL
575 LEXINGTON AVE.
N.Y., N.Y. 10022

JAMES C. MARLAS
MICKELBERRY CORP.
405 PARK AVE.
N.Y., N.Y. 10022

A. FRED MARCH
M.P.C. INC.
425 PARK AVE. 26TH. FL.
N.Y., N.Y. 10022

J.I. FELDMAN
NATIONAL PATENT DEVELOPMENT
375 PARK AVE.
N.Y., N.Y. 10022

JACK E. THOMPSON
NEWMONT MINING
300 PARK AVE.
N.Y., N.Y. 10022

GERALD COHEN
NEXUS IND.
950 THIRD AVE.
N.Y., N.Y. 10022

IRA V. GUILDEN
NORTH RIVER SECURITIES
595 MADISON AVE. SUITE 900
N.Y., N.Y. 10022

LOIS H. MULLER
NUTRIENT COSMETIC
595 MADISON AVE.
N.Y., N.Y. 10022

A.M. ZLOTNICK
OLD FLORIDA RUM
717 FIFTH AVE.
N.Y., N.Y. 10022

IRVING JAHRE
ON-SITE ENERGY SYSTEMS
919 THIRD AVE.
N.Y., N.Y. 10022

D.O. PEARCE
O'OKIEP COPPER CO.
300 PARK AVE.
N.Y., N.Y. 10022

JAMES P. MAC PHERSON
PARTY TIME PRODUCTS
375 PARK AVE.
N.Y., N.Y. 10022

D.J. SULLIVAN
PLASTOID CORP.
633 THIRD AVE.
N.Y., N.Y. 10022

ALBERT HERSH
PLY-GEM IND.
919 THIRD AVE.
N.Y., N.Y. 10022

NORMAN BLOCK
PROCESS PLANTS
135 E. 55TH. ST.
N.Y., N.Y. 10022

SOL ROSEN
PRO-TECH PROGRAMS
1010 THIRD AVE.
N.Y., N.Y. 10022

EMANUEL L. WOLF
PSP INC.
425 PARK AVE.
N.Y., N.Y. 10022

GEORGE TOPEL
PUEBLO INTERNATIONAL
375 PARK AVE.
N.Y., N.Y. 10022

ROBERT M. REININGER
ROSARIO RESOURCES
375 PARK AVE. STE. 310
N.Y., N.Y. 10022

WILLIAM J. SCHOEN
THE F. & M. SCHAEFER CORP.
485 MADISON AVE.
N.Y., N.Y. 10022

RICHARD GERSHON
SIMERA CORP.
600 MADISON AVE.
N.Y., N.Y. 10022

L. MAROLDA
SIMPLICITY COMPUTER
345 PARK AVE.
N.Y., N.Y. 10022

HOWARD OTT
SPIRAL METAL CO.
515 MADISON AVE.
N.Y., N.Y. 10022

BORIS GRESOV
STANDARD METALS
645 FIFTH AVE.
N.Y., N.Y. 10022

HENRY BENACH
STARRETT HOUSING
909 THIRD AVE.
N.Y., N.Y. 10022

IRA GUILDEN
JOHN B. STETSON CO.
595 MADISON AVE.
N.Y., N.Y. 10022

A.S. COWLEY
STEWART INT'L. PRODUCTIONS
405 PARK AVE.
N.Y., N.Y. 10022

JEFFREY J. STEINBERG
STONEHILL COMMUNICATIONS
38 EAST 57TH. ST.
N.Y., N.Y. 10022

G.K. GOULD
TELETRONICS
220 EAST 51ST. ST.
N.Y., N.Y. 10022

HENRY B. PLATT
TIFFANY & CO.
727 FIFTH AVE.
N.Y., N.Y. 10022

RICHARD BRANDT
TRANS-LUX CORP.
625 MADISON AVE.
N.Y., N.Y. 10022

RONALD GOLD
UNISYSTEMS
155 EAST 55TH ST.
N.Y., N.Y. 10022

LOUIS PERLMUTTER
U.S. COLSOLIN
515 MADISON AVE.
N.Y., N.Y. 10022

DAVID YARNELL
U.S. INTERNATIONAL NETWORK
375 PARK AVE.
N.Y., N.Y. 10022

LEON C. HIRSCH
UNITED STATES SURGICAL
919 THIRD AVE.
N.Y., N.Y. 10022

LEWIS MASLOW
UNIVERSAL CONTAINER
540 MADISON AVE.
N.Y., N.Y. 10022

ANDREW J. FRANKEL
URIS BLDG. CORP.
10 EAST 53RD. ST.
N.Y., N.Y. 10022

EDWIN JACOBSON
UV IND.
437 MADISON AVE.
N.Y., N.Y. 10022

C. HARTWELL
VELCRO IND.
681 FIFTH AVE.
N.Y., N.Y. 10022

R.M. BARUCH
VIACOM INT'L.
345 PARK AVE.
N.Y., N.Y. 10022

PAUL D. SCHURGOT, JR.
WALCO NATIONAL
743 FIFTH AVE.
N.Y., N.Y. 10022

WILLIAM C. SCOTT III
WESTERN PACIFIC IND.
345 PARK AVE.
N.Y., N.Y. 10022

WILLIAM COHEN
WORLD WIDE WEALTH
919 THIRD AVE.
NEW YORK, N.Y. 10022

FRANK L. MARX
ABTO INC.
1926 BROADWAY
N.Y., N.Y. 10023

HOWARD W. FRIEDMAN
AMREP CORP.
16 WEST 61ST ST.
N.Y., N.Y. 10023

JOHN MALONE
ATHENA COMMUNICATIONS
1 GULF & WESTERN PLAZA
N.Y., N.Y. 10023

P.D. BLACKMAN
THE POLLY BERGEN CO.
ONE GULF & WESTERN PLAZA
N.Y., N.Y. 10023

LOEBE JULIE
JULIE RESEARCH LABS
211 W. 61ST ST.
N.Y., N.Y. 10023

DAVID ROSEN
SEGA ENTERPRISES
1 GULF & WESTERN PLAZA
N.Y., N.Y. 10023

DAVID JORDON
VTR. INC.
ONE LINCOLN PLAZA
N.Y., N.Y. 10023

CYRUS ADLER
OFFSHORE SEA DEVELOPMENT
241 W. 97TH. ST.
N.Y., N.Y. 10025

LAWRENCE OLECK
BEEP COMMUNICATIONS
210 E. 86TH ST.
N.Y., N.Y. 10028

HERBERT J. SILBERMAN
LIBERTY CIRCLE
180 EAST END AVE. APT.19G
N.Y., N.Y. 10028

EDWARD PORTNOY
RECORD SHACK
2132 SECOND AVE.
N.Y., N.Y. 10029

ARTHUR SCHUTZMAN
PLASTIC ASSOC.
60 INIP DR.,INWOOD STA.
N.Y., N.Y. 10034

ARNOLD B. FUCHS
ARNEX IND.
48 WEST 48TH ST.
N.Y.,N.Y. 10036

SIMON SHEIB
AVNET INC.
767 FIFTH AVE.
N.Y., N.Y. 10036

JAMES H. HOLLYER
BALDT CORP.
1185 AVE. OF AMERICAS
N.Y., N.Y. 10036

GEORGE FREDERICK
BRIARCLIFF CANDY
500 5TH AVE. SUITE 3200
N.Y., N.Y. 10036

GLEN J. HATFIELD, JR.
COHEN-HATFIELD IND.
1140 AVE. OF AMERICAS
N.Y., N.Y. 10036

GEORGE SALTZMAN
DENTAL SCIENCES
36 WEST 47th. ST.
N.Y., N.Y. 10036

JAMES R. HEEKIN
DOYLE DANE BERNBACH
20 WEST 43RD. ST.
N.Y., N.Y. 10036

ARTHUR FLORMAN
F & B CECO IND.
315 WEST 43RD, ST.
N.Y., N.Y. 10036

RUEBEN BERMAN
FAIR-TEX MILLS
1460 BROADWAY
N.Y., N.Y. 10036

ANTHONY ROSATO
FULTON NAT'L.GROUP
25 WEST 43RD. ST.
N.Y., N.Y. 10036

JAMES W. KEEFE
TRUTH VERIFICATION
55 WEST 42ND. ST.
N.Y., N.Y. 10036

JEROME GINSBURG
GREAT EASTERN MANAGEMENT
1350 AVE.OF AMERICAS
N.Y., N.Y. 10036

FREDERICK M. PEYSER, JR.
GRUEN IND.
20 WEST 47TH. ST.
N.Y., N.Y. 10036

FREDERIC H. GUTTERMAN
HORN & HARDART CO.
1163 AVE. OF AMERICAS
N.Y., N.Y. 10036

WILLIAM R. BARRETT, SR.
INMONT CORP.
1133 AVE. OF AMERICAS
N.Y., N.Y. 10036

MARTIN COHEN
INTERNATIONAL STRETCH
1133 AVE. OF AMERICAS
N.Y., N.Y. 10036

JAMES P. THRASHER
INTERWAY CORP.
522 FIFTH AVE.
N.Y., N.Y. 10036

SAM LAKE
LAKE INTERNATIONAL
630 9TH. AVE.
N.Y., N.Y. 10036

ARTHUR MALSIN
LANE BRYANT
1501 BROADWAY
N.Y., N.Y. 10036

GEORGE MANN
LAWRENCE SERVES IND.
136 W. 42ND. ST.
N.Y., N.Y. 10036

JACK GOLDSTEIN
LOREN IND.
62 WEST 47TH. ST.
N.Y., N.Y. 10036

STANLEY BLUMSTEIN
LUCIEN PICCARD IND.
P.O. BOX 308
N.Y., N.Y. 10036

STEPHEN J. SCHULTE
MICROBIOLOGICAL SCIENCES
113 W. 42ND. ST.
N.Y., N.Y. 10036

MARTIN SANDERS
MID-CENTRAL PROPERTIES
1501 BROADWAY
N.Y., N.Y. 10036

J.J. MACALUSO
NAT'L. SHOWMANSHIP
115 WEST 45TH ST.
N.Y., N.Y. 10036

GEORGE J. GREEN
THE NEW YORKER MAGAZINE
25 WEST 43RD ST.
N.Y., N.Y. 10036

JERRY L. SHULMAN
PASCO INC.
530 FIFTH AVE.
N.Y., N.Y. 10036

JERRY MASON
THE RIDGE PRESS
25 WEST 43RD. ST.
N.Y., N.Y. 10036

JACK ROTHSCHILD
R-T-W COMPUTER NETWORK
1212 AVE. OF AMERICAS
N.Y., N.Y. 10036

RICHARD ROBINSON
SCHOLASTIC MAGAZINES
50 WEST 44TH. ST.
N.Y., N.Y. 10036

ERY KEHAYA
STANDARD COMMERCIAL
500 FIFTH AVE.
N.Y., N.Y. 10036

ALBERT H. SANDERS
STATE-O-MAINE, INC.
1 ASTOR PLAZA
N.Y., N.Y. 10036

M. LEE
TBS COMPUTER CENTER
1212 AVE. OF AMERICAS
N.Y., N.Y. 10036

DON TOWNSEND
TAD'S ENTERPRISES
119 W. 42ND. ST.
N.Y., N.Y. 10036

RUSSELL KARP
TELEPROMPTER CORP.
50 WEST 44TH ST.
N.Y., N.Y. 10036

R.I. LANDY
VISION CABLE COMM. INC.
501 MADISON AVE.
N.Y., N.Y. 10036

J. CARL CLAMP
UNITED STATES FILTER
522 FIFTH AVE.
N.Y., N.Y. 10036

ADOLPH LEBOVIC
WENDY JEWELRY
1200 AVE. OF AMERICAS
N.Y., N.Y. 10036

JOHNK. ZIEGLER
WILLCOX & GIBBS
1114 AVE. OF AMERICAS
N.Y., N.Y. 10036

MELVIN BIRNS
COORDINATED COMPUTER
15 MAIDEN LANE 19TH. FLR.
N.Y., N.Y. 10038

FRANK M. HOGAN
CORROON & BLACK CORP.
150 WILLIAM ST.
N.Y., N.Y. 10038

WILLIAM CASS
FANNING ENTERPRISES
180 BROADWAY
N.Y., N.Y. 10038

ALEX MILLMAN
FORWARD TIME
150 BROADWAY
N.Y.,N.Y. 10038

D.M. SULIVAN
FROST & SULLIVAN
106 FULTON ST.
N.Y., N.Y. 10038

JOSEPH T. CASCARELLA
NATIONWIDE THOROUGHBREDS
151 WILLIAM ST.
N.Y., N.Y. 10038

MYRON CHEFETZ
WELLS MANAGEMENT
170 BROADWAY
N.Y., N.Y. 10038

RAYMOND B. CAREY, JR.
AMERICAN DISTRICT TELEGRAPH
1 WORLD TRADE CENTER
N.Y., N.Y. 10048

JAMES B. SHERWOOD
SEA CONTAINERS
1 WORLD TRADE CENTER   SUITE 2841
N.Y., N.Y. 10048

ANTHONY SEDUTTO
SEDUTTO IND.
2000 RICHMOND TERRACE
STATEN ISLAND, N.Y. 10302

MAURICE DENENBERG
LOUIS DE JONGE & CO.
330 TOMPKINS AVE.
STATEN ISLAND, N.Y. 10304

LEONARD KLEIMAN
MODULAR CITIES
1306 ROCKLAND AVE.
S.I., N.Y. 10314

FRED K. SIEGEL
JOHN IRVING STORES
595 GERARD AVE.
BX., N.Y. 10451

SHERMAN N. BAKER
NATIONAL SHOES
595 GERARD AVE.
BX., N.Y. 10451

MILTON SIMON
SIMCO STORES
385 GERARD AVE.
BX., N.Y. 10451

RONALD RUBIN
THE BALTRONIC CORP.
120 EAST 144TH ST.
BX., N.Y. 10451

LEO M. WEINS
H.W. WILSON CO.
950 UNIVERSITY AVE.
BX., N.Y. 10452

H.W. LA MORTE
HICO CORP.
600 E. 132ND. ST.
BX., N.Y. 10454

MARTIN ROSENGARTEN
SHOPWELL
400 WALNUT AVE.
BX., N.Y. 10454

WILLIAM WEISSMAN
E & B SUPERMARKETS
564 SOUTHERN BLVD.
BX., N.Y. 10455

JACK RUDNICK
PANIFLEX
430 E. 165TH ST.
BX., N.Y. 10456

BARRY G. BERGER
MOGEN DAVID KOSHER MEATS
968 LONGFELLOW AVE.
BX., N.Y. 10459

MARTIN HIRSCHORN
IND. ACCOUSTICS
1160 COMMERCE AVE.
BX., N.Y. 10462

A.A. FINK
RMS ELECTRONICS
50 ANTIN PL.
BX., N.Y. 10462

B.A. JACKSON
U.S. COMPONENTS
1320 ZEREGA AVE.
BX., N.Y. 10462

A. GALERNE
INT'L. UNDERWATER
264 FORDHAM PL.
CITY ISLAND, N.Y. 10464

DARIO CIOTI
THE DE FOE CORP.
3966 MERRITT AVE.
BX., N.Y. 10466

MARIO MACCAFERRI
MASTRO IND.
3040 WEBSTER AVE.
BX., N.Y. 10467

L. STEUER
KAPNER,INC.
4234 VIREO AVE.
BX., N.Y. 10470

LEONARD H. APTMAN
COMPUMATRICS   INT'L.
BX., N.Y. 10471

IRA B. KRISTEL
COMM. ENVELOPE MFG.
2350 LAFAYETTE AVE.
BX., N.Y. 10472

HARRY PREVOR
PREVOR-MAYRSOHN INT'L.
UNIT 123-HUNTS POINT MARKET
BX., N.Y. 10474

GEORGE J. GREENBERG
LOEHMANN"S INC.
3450 BAYCHESTER AVE.
BX., N.Y. 10499

BERTRAM J. COHN
DPF INC.
141 CENTRAL AVE.
HARTSDALE, N.Y. 10503

RAYMOND KLEMMER
BY-WORD CORP.
530 MAIN ST.
ARMONK, N.Y. 10504

STANLEY G. PESCHEL
HIPOTRONICS INC.
RTE. 22
BREWSTER, N.Y. 10509

EDWARD W. HYDE
BURNS INTL. SECURITY
320 OLD BRIARCLIFF RD.
BRIARCLIFF MANOR, N.Y. 10510

E.L. ADELMAN
SAUCY SUSAN PROD.
104 WOODSIDE AVE.
BRIARCLIFF MANOR,N.Y. 10510

DONALD J. NOLAN
GUENTHER SYSTEMS
REYNOLDS LN.
BUCHANAN, N.Y. 10511

SVEND E. HARTMANN
COMPUTER MERCHANTS
75 SO. GREELEY AVE.
CHAPPAQUA,N.Y. 10514

P.W. SCHAAPHOK
CONTROLEX CORP.
TOWN OF NORTH SALEM
CROTON FALLS, N.Y. 10519

P.A. MITTELMAN
MATH APPLICATIONSS
3 WESTCHESTER PL.
ELMSFORD, N.Y. 10523

D.L. GROSS
MINI COMPUTER SYSTEMS
525 EXECUTIVE BLVD.
ELMSFORD, N.Y. 10523

J.E. TOWNSEND
ROCKWOOD NATIONAL
33 W. TARRYTOWN RD.
ELMSFORD, N.Y. 10523

MICHAEL SCHILLER
SEQUENTIAL INFORMATION
66 SAW MILL RIVER RD.
ELMSFORD, N.Y. 10523

F.C. RONEY, JR.
MELVILLE CORP.
P.O. BOX 677 EXEC.PK.
HARRISON, N.Y. 10528

DAVID HANANIA
POLORON PROD'S.
550 MAMARONECK AVE.
HARRISON, N.Y. 10528

A.J. BABBONI
ABSCOA IND. INC.
25 WEST HARTSDALE AVE.
HARTSDALE, N.Y. 10530

J.C. FLANNERY
FOODWAYS NATIONAL
140 BROADWAY
HAWTHORNE, N.Y. 10532

JOHN W. MURRAY, JR.
BURNHAM CORP.
2 MAIN ST.
IRVINGTON,N.Y. 10533

Z.E. HARVEY
HARVEY HOUSE
5 SOUTH BUCKHOUT ST.
IRVINGTON, N.Y. 10533

M.M. CASS
CONSOLIDATED REFINING
115 HOYT AVE.
MAMARONECK, N.Y. 10543

FRANK RADOCY
MAGNETIC MEDIA
616 FAYETTE AVE.
MANARONECK, N.Y. 10543

WILLIAM SILBERSTEIN
SEALECTRO CORP.
225 HOYT ST.
HAMARONECK, N.Y. 10543

W.J. WILSON
STARCH-INRA-HOOPER
566 E. BOSTON POST RD.
MAMARONECK , N.Y. 10543

R.H. DE PASQUALE
TECH. MATERIEL
700 FENIMORE RD.
MAMARONECK, N.Y. 10543

EMANUEL STERN
RESPONSIVE DATA
RADIO CIRCLE
MT. KISCO, N.Y. 10549

J.M. POLTS
UNIVERSAL VOLTRONICS
27 RADIO CIRCLE DR.
MT. KISCO, N.Y. 10549

HARRY GANTZ
AMERICAN TECH. IND.
29-31 ELM AVE.
MT. VERNON, N.Y. 10550

JOSEPH KAPPEL
COAST PHOTO MFG.
118 PEARL ST.
MT. VERNON, N.Y. 10550

C.K. SILVERSTEIN
COMM. DECAL INC.
650 SOUTH COLUMBUS AVE.
MT. VERNON, N.Y. 10550

RAYMOND KAUFMAN
DEL ELECTRONIS
250 SANFORD BLVD.
MT. VERNON, N.Y. 10550

BRUCE JAGID
POWER CONVERSION
70 MAC QUESTEN PK'WAY S.
MT. VERNON, N.Y. 10550

S. GOLDBERG
SIRCO INTL. CORP.
700 S. FULTON AVE.
MT. VERNON, N.Y. 10550

THOMAS H. GEORGE
TEXTURED PROD!S.
524 S. COLUMBUS AVE.
MT. VERNON, N.Y. 10550

R.J. KROHN
WARD LEONARD ELECTRIC
31 SOUTH ST.
MT. VERNON, N.Y. 10550

D.J. WHITE
TORK INC.
ONE GROVE ST.
MT. VERNON, N.Y. 10551

I.D. SWAWITE
MEDIATRICS INC.
200 N. COLUMBUS AVE.
MT. VERNON, N.Y. 10553

G.R. KNIGHT
STERNDENT CORP.
320 WASHINGTON ST.
MT. VERNON, N.Y. 10553

GENE FELDMAN
DENTAL COMMUNICATIONS
P.O. BOX 70
OSSINING, N.Y. 10562

GENE FELDMAN
WOMBAT PROD'S. INC.
P.O. BOX 70
OSSINING, N.Y. 10562

SAMUEL P. PUNER
EDUCATIONAL AUDIO
PLEASANTVILLE, N.Y. 10570

LEONARD KARDON
PREMIER MICROWAY
33 NEW BROAD ST.
PORT CHESTER, N.Y. 10573

MORRIS LEVINE
URANUS ELECTRONICS
531 BOSTON POST RD.
PORTCHESTER, N.Y. 10573

JOSEPH ALFREDO
SERVO SYSTEMS
80 LINCOLN AVE.
PURCHASE,N.Y. 10577

E. LAWRENCE TABAT
DICTAPHONE CORP.
120 OLD POST RD.
RYE,N.Y. 10580

JERALD GREENBERG
WORLDWIDE COMMERCE
22 PURCHASE ST.
RYE, N.Y. 10580

GEORGE H. McCLOUGHAN
CENTURY LABORATORIES
14 RECTORY LN.
SCARSDALE, N.Y. 10583

MORRIS FRIEDMAN
JOHNNY-ON-THE SPOT CENTRAL
1075 CENTRAL AVE.
SCARSDALE,N.Y. 10583

RICHARD G. TERKER
TERRY IND. INC.
14 OLD LYME RD.
SCARSDALE, N.Y. 10583

DANIEL KANE
KANE-MILLER
555 WHITE PLAINS RD.
TARRYTOWN, N.Y. 10591

JOHN A. MC KENNA
SIMMONDS PRECISION PROD.
150 WHITE PLAINS RD.
TARRYTOWN, N.Y. 10591

GUY CHARLAP
TECHNICON CORP.
511 BENEDICT AVE.
TARRYTOWN, N.Y. 10591

ROBERT K. LOW
SAVIN BUSINESS MACHINE
COLUMBUS AVE.
VALHALLA, N.Y. 10595

ALLAN W. STEERE
EDP RESOURCES
ONE NORTH BROADWAY
WHITE PLAINS, N.Y. 10601

H.D. BLANK
NAT'L. IND. SERVICES
34 SOUTH BROADWAY
WHITE PLAINS, N.Y.10601

PETER J. FASS
REICHHOLD CHEM. INC.
RCI BLDG.
WHITE PLAINS, N.Y. 10602

JOHN S. PECKHAM
PECKHAM IND. INC.
50 HAARLEM AVE.
WHITE PLAINS, N.Y. 10603

RAYMOND E. CARLEDGE
CLEVEPAK CORP.
925 WESTCHESTER AVE.
WHITE PLAINS, N.Y. 10604

ROBERT SCHWARTZ, JR.
HEALTH ADVANCEMENT
4 CORPORATE PK. DR.
WHITE PLAINS, N.Y. 10604

JOHN N. WILLMAN
IPCO HOSPITAL SUPPLY
1025 WESTCHESTER AVE.
WHITE PLAINS, N.Y. 10604

W.R. KUNTZ
MOLYCORP
6 CORPORATE PK.
WHITE PLAINS, N.Y. 10604

LUCA CAPPELLI, JR.
LUNA IND. INC.
66 FULTON ST.
WHITE PLAINS, N.Y. 10606

THOMAS CARVEL
CARVEL CORP.
430 NEPPERHAN AVE.
YOUKERS, N.Y. 10701

I.J. KERN
DELLWOOD FOODS
170 SAW MILL RIVER RD.
YONKERS, N.Y. 10701

FRANCIS MASSIE
DUGGAN'S DISTILLER
20 SOUTH BROADWAY
YONKERS, N.Y. 10701

HARRY E. SCHACTER
MICA PRODUCTS
FOOT OF MAIN ST.
YONKERS, N.Y. 10701

GREGORY HALPERN
POLYCHROME CORP.
ON THE HUDSON
YONKERS,N.Y. 10702

ROBERT WALKER
WALKER COLOR
955 YONKERS AVE.
YONKERS, N.Y. 10704

FRED LORGE
KINGS ELECTRONICS
40 MARLEDALE RD.
TUCKAHOE, N.Y. 10707

R.I. MENDELS
ELECTRONIC DEVICES
21 GRAY OAKS AVE.
YONKERS, N.Y. 10710

RAYMOND J. O'NEILL
GRATTEN MARINE RESEARCH
475 TUCKSHOE RD.
YONKERS, N.Y. 10710

R.I. MENDELS
RECTISEL CORP.
21 GREY OAKS AVE.
YONKERS, N.Y. 10710

ARNOLD BLYE
BLYE INTERNATIONAL
27 HORTON AVE.
NEW ROCHELLE, N.Y. 10801

ROCCO SCAPPATURA
EMERGENCY BEACON CORP.
15 RIVER ST.
NEW ROCHELLE, N.Y. 10801

DR. HARVEY J. ENGELSHER
HORIZON IND. LTD.
406 MAIN ST.
NEW ROCHELLE, N.Y. 10801

MILTON R. COHEN
HYDRA-POWER
10 PINE CT.
NEW ROCHELLE, N.Y. 10801

DR. KENNETH J. SILVERMAN
ORTHO IND.
49 LAWTON ST.
NEW ROCHELLE, N.Y. 10801

ROBERT S. BRINKER
R.E.C. CORP.
47 CEDAR ST.
NEW ROCHELLE, N.Y. 10801

GERALD A. SAULER
TECHNICAL TAPE
LE FEVRE
NEW ROCHELLE, N.Y. 10801

THOMAS J. ROTANELLI
ROTANELLI FOODS
924 WEST ST.
PELHAM, N.Y. 10803

ROBERT E. GOEBEL
SANBORN MAP CO.
629 FIFTH AVE.
PELHAM, N.Y. 10803

A.J. SCHEINE
LCS IND. INC.
10 PELHAM PKWAY
PELHAM MONOR,N.Y. 10803

H.L. SCHAFFER
FANESS IND.
27 WEYMAN AVE.
NEW ROCHELLE, N.Y. 10805

WILLIAM CORNELIUS
CHEMTREE CORP.
CHEMTREE PARK
CENTRAL VALLEY, N.Y. 10917

SHELDON S. GOLDSTEIN
BON-AIRE IND.
P.O. BOX 578
CHESTER, N.Y. 10918

E. ABBO
SAXTON PRODUCTS
215 N. RTE. 303
CONGERS, N.Y. 10920

A. RICHARD ROSENBERG
BIG V. SUPERMARKETS
176 NORTH MAIN ST.
FLORIDA, N.Y. 10921

LESLIE L. BALASSA
LESCARDEN LTD.
27 ST. JOHN ST.
GOSHEN, N.Y. 10924

WALTER JANKOWSKI
ARBOREAL ASSOC.
GROVE ST.
HARRIMAN, N.Y. 10926

EDWARD DOWNEY
LLOYD'D SHOPPING CENTERS
MIDDLETOWN, N.Y. 10940

CHARLES E. BYRNE
LOGOS DEVELOPMENT
2 WEST MAIN ST.
MIDDLETOWN, N.Y. 10940

SHELDON WEINIG
MATERIALS RESEARCH
RTE. 303
ORANGEBURG, N.Y. 10962

N.A. BRUML
WESPAK
400 RTE. 303
ORANGEBURG, N.Y. 10962

PAUL MARCUS
GOMAR IND.
85 PASCACK RD.
PEARL RIVER, N.Y. 10965

ARTHUR HERSHAFT
PACKAGING SYSTEMS
275 NO. MIDDLETOWN RD.
PEARL RIVER,N.Y. 10965

HERBERT D. WEID
BALCHEM CORP.
SLATE HILL, N.Y. 10973

VITO CASTELLANO
JETA POWER
RTE. 17
SLOATSBURG, N.Y. 10974

DEAN B. SEIFRIED
ORANGE & ROCKLAND
75 W. RTE. 59
SPRING VALLEY, N.Y. 10977

B. FRIEDMAN
SOLITRON DEVICES
256 OAK TREE RD.
TAPPAN, N.Y. 10983

H.E. SCHUELER, JR.
AMERICAN CADUCEUS IND.
46 CARNATION AVE.
FLORAL PARK, N.Y. 11001

GUSTAVE BARDFELD
GERIATRIC PHARM. CORP.
397 JERICHO TPKE.
FLORAL PARK, N.Y. 11002

MARTIN ROCHMAN
RANCHERS PACKING
10 CHARLES ST.
FLORAL PARK, N.Y. 11001

P.T. RUSSO
RYNCO SCIENTIFIC
31 STEWART ST.
FLORAL PARK, N.Y. 11002

STEPHEN KISS
THE MARFRANK CORP.
481 HEMPSTEAD TPKE.
ELMONT, N.Y. 11003

NATHAN FEDER
WORLDWIDE POLLUTION
481 HEMPSTEAD TURNPIKE
ELMONT, N.Y. 11003

A. HARRY FISHMAN
APL CORP.
L LINDEN PL.
GREAT NECK, N.Y. 11021

MORRIS GALANT
AUTOMATED BUSINESS
525 NORTHERN BLVD. SUITE 121
GREAT NECK, N.Y. 11021

MARSHALL D. BUTLER
AVX CORP.
98 CUTTER MILL RD.
GREAT NECK, N.Y. 11021

EDWARD ROSENSTOCK
BRIGGS LEASING
777 NORTHERN BLVD.
GREAT NECK, N.Y. 11021

NATHAN PINSLEY
ESPEY MFG.
445 NORTHERN BLVD.
GREAT NECK, N.Y. 11021

A.A. BLANCK
FUTURONICS
122 CUTTER MILL RD.
GREAT NECK, N.Y. 11021

FREDRIC H. GOULD
GOULD INVESTORS
245 GREAT NECK RD.
GREAT NECK, N.Y. 11021

JAY B. LANGNER
HUDSON GENERAL
ONE LINDEN PL.
GREAT NECK, N.Y. 11021

G. KOGEL
KOGEL, INC.
467 GREAT NECK RD.
GREAT NECK, N.Y. 11021

DR. KENNETH COLMEN
P & F IND.
98 CUTTER MILL RD.
GREAT NECK, N.Y. 11021

NORMAN HELLMAN
TEMTECH DESIGNS
17 BARSTOW RD.
GREAT NECK, N.Y. 11021

JAY R. THALHEIM
THALHEIM EXPOSITION MGMT.
98 CUTTER MILL RD.
GREAT NECK, N.Y. 11021

J.F. HUGHES
TIME SHARING RESOURCES
777 NORTHERN BLVD.
GREAT NECK, N.Y. 11021

BRUCE GORDON
THE TODD GROUP
9 CHELSEA PL.
GREAT NECK, N.Y. 11021

ROBERT M. MELTZER
TRIANGLE PACIFIC CORP.
9 PARK PL.
GREAT NECK, N.Y. 11021

HERMAN S. NATHANSON
VERNITRON CORP.
LAKE SUCCESS PK. COMM. DR.
GREAT NECK, N.Y. 11024

GEORGE E. HOWELL
PAY TV. CORP.
390 PLANDOME RD.
MANHASSET, N.Y. 11030

DAVID EASTON
AGARD ELECTRONICS
40 NASSAU TERMINAL RD.
NEW HYDE PK., N.Y. 11040

SEYMOUR BARTH
ASTROSYSTEMS
6 NEVADA DR.
NEW HYDE PK., N.Y. 11040

WILLIAM L. WESTERMAN
CELLU-CRAFT
1401 FOURTH AVE.
NEW HYDE PARK, N.Y. 11040

H. BIRMAN
CONAIR CORP.
246 BROADWAY
GARDEN CITY PK.,N.Y.11040

SOL SCHWARTZ
DESIGNATRONICS
55 S. DENTON AVE.
NEW HYDE PK., N.Y.11040

MARTIN KOLEN
EMPRESS INT'L. LTD.
3000 MARCUS AVE.
LAKE SUCCESS, N.Y.11040

DOMINIC MARANO
EXECUT. EQUIP. CORP.
3000 MARCUS AVE.
NEW HYDE PK.,N.Y. 11040

MARTIN B. BLOCH
FREQUENCY ELECTRONICS
3 DELAWARE DR.
NEW HYDE PK., N.Y.11040

SIDNEY HARMAN
HARMAN INT'L. INDUSTRIES
3000 MARCUS AVE.
NEW HYDE PK.,N.Y. 11040

IRVING L. BERNSTEIN
LINCOLN AMERICAN CORP.
410 LAKEVILLE RD.
LAKE SUCCESS, N.Y. 11040

MILTON PAULENOFF
MACROSE IND.
2060 JERICHO TPKE.
NEW HYDE PK., N.Y. 11040

MELVIN P. EHRLICH
NUCLEAR RESEARCH ASSOC.
12 NAVADA DR.
NEW HYDE PK., N.Y. 11040

ROBERT S. SCHLANGER
POLARAD ELECTRONICS
5 DELAWARE DR.
LAKE SUCCESS, N.Y. 11040

JEROME L. REINITZ
ROYAL ZENITH CORP.
2101 JERICHO TURNPIKE
NEW HYDE PK.,N.Y. 11040

BERNARD KUSHNER
BERNARD SCREEN PRINTING
2300 MARCUS AVE.
NEW HYDE PK., N.Y.11043

RICHARD A. OTTO
COURTESY DRUG STORES
83 HARBOR RD.
PORT WASHINGTON, N.Y. 11050

ALBERT LIPPERT
WEIGHT WATCHERS INT'L.
800 COMMUNITY DR.
MANHASSET, N.Y. 11050

ORLANDO TRASORRAS
ALARM PRODUCTS
24-02 40TH. AVE.
LONG ISLAND CITY, N.Y. 11101

FRANK A. D. ANDREA, JR.
ANDREA RADIO CORP.
2701 BRIDGE PLAZA NORTH
L.I.C., N.Y. 11101

HOWARD STERNBERG
AURIUM RESEARCH
47TH. ST & VERNON BLVD.
L.I.C., N.Y. 11101

H. RUBINSTEIN
BELVAC INT'L. IND.
45-10 CT. SQ.
L.I.C., N.Y. 11101

KARL KUSSY
THE CONTINENTAL GOURMET
37-10 CRESCENT ST.
L.I.C., N.Y. 11101

W.B. HANSEN
DEJUR-AMSCO CORP.
45-01 NORTHERN BLVD.
L.I.C., N.Y. 11101

EDWARD BRODY
EXECUTONE
29-10 THOMSON AVE.
L.I.C., N.Y. 11101

DANIEL A. PORCO
INTERPHOTO CORP.
23-20 JACKSON AVE.
L.I.C., N.Y. 11101

MORTON G. MEYER
METROPOLITAN TABACCO
45-20 33RD. ST.
L.I.C., N.Y. 11101

DAVID C. ROCKOLA
PEERLESS WEIGHING
29-28 41ST AVE.
L.I.C., N.Y. 11101

HAROLD PACHT
PRINTOGS
29-10 THOMPSON AVE.
L.I.C., N.Y. 11101

RICHARD A. SLOSS
PURO FILTER CORP.
21-01 51ST AVE.
L.I.C., N.Y. 11101

HERBERT BORCHARDT
RECOTON CORP.
46-23 CRANE ST.
L.I.C., N.Y. 11101

HAROLD L. OSHRY
SANDGATE CORP.
42-11 NORTHERN BLVD.
L.I.C., N.Y. 11101

THEODORE KAISH
SCIENTIFIC POLLUTION
47-01 VERNON BLVD.
L.I.C., N.Y. 11101

BERNARD FIFE
STANDARD MOTOR PRODUCTS
37-18 NORTHERN BLVD.
L.I.C., N.Y. 11101

EDWARD M. BEAGAN
TELTRONICS SERVICES
48-40 34TH. ST.
L.I.C., N.Y. 11101

M. PETER SCHWEITZER
WEST CHEM. PRODUCTS
42-16 WEST ST.
L.I.C., N.Y. 11101

LOUIS KAPLAN
CECILWARE CORP.
43-05 20TH. AVE.
L.I.C., N.Y. 11102

NORTON BERNSTEIN
MASTERCRAFT LITHOGRAPHERS
39-01 QUEENS BLVD.
L.I.C., N.Y. 11104

ROBERT STIEFEL
SUPERIOR MFG.
19-36 38TH. ST.
L.I.C., N.Y. 11105

JAY B. SHAPIRO
ANCHOR PLASTICS
36-36 36TH. ST.
L.I.C., N.Y. 11106

CHARLES SCHMALL
ASHLAND OPTICAL
35-40 30TH. ST.
L.I.C., N.Y. 11106

SAM KLEINHAUT
BAGPRINT LTD.
11-11 BROADWAY
L.I.C., N.Y. 11106

DALTON DAVIS
HUNTER MFG. CORP.
12-04 31ST. AVE.
L.I.C., N.Y. 11106

HAROLD MILLER
ESTER MILLER CREATIONS
36-46 33RD. ST.
L.I.C., N.Y. 11106

GEORGE KLEIN
BARTON'S CANDY
80 DE KALB AVE.
BROOKLYN, N.Y. 11201

JOHN E. McPARTLIN
BOORUM & PEASE
84 HUDSON AVE.
BROOKLYN, N.Y. 11201

H. GOODMAN
COSMOS IND. INC.
45 WASHINGTON ST.
BROOKLYN, N.Y. 11201

NICHOLAS ANTON
EON CORP.
175 PEARL ST.
BROOKLYN, N.Y. 11201

MORRIS GLUCK
HOUSE OF KNITTING
45-55 WASHINGTON ST.
BKLYN., N.Y. 11201

MARCEL WEISS
HOWARD STORES
40 FLATBUSH AVE. EXT.
BKLYN., N.Y. 11201

M.L. SHULMAN
J.W. MAYS INC.
510 FULTON ST.
BKLYN., N.Y. 11201

ROBERT MICHAELS
J. MICHAELS, INC.
182 SMITH ST.
BKLYN., N.Y. 11201

S. KAMINS
C & P IND. INC.
1019 EAST 46TH. ST.
BKLYN., N.Y. 11203

V.N. VULCANO
COMPU-SORT SYSTEMS
1080 UTICA AVE.
BKLYN., N.Y. 11203

M.HOFFMAN
VICTOR KELLERING CORP.
955 EAST 51ST. ST.
BKLYN., N.Y. 11203

RICHARD SOLOMON
R.H. COSMETICS
4848 FARRAGUT RD.
BKLYN., N.Y. 11203

GEORGE FUCHS
SPEED-WAY FOOD STORES
847 E. NEW YORK AVE.
BKLYN., N.Y. 11203

ALBERT WEINSTOCK
ALLE PROCESSING
502 FLUSHING AVE.
BKLYN., N.Y. 11205

HARRY STEIN
FANCY IND. INC.
BLDG.5 BKLYN. NAVY YARD
BKLYN., N.Y. 11205

ARNOLD W. WONSEVER
CAR-PUTER INT'L. CORP.
1603 BUSHWICK AVE.
BKLYN., N.Y. 11207

HARRY R. ASHLEY
EICO ELECTRONIC
283 MALTA ST.
BKLYN., N.Y. 11207

MARTIN HOFFINGER
LOMART PERFECTED DEVICES
980 ALABAMA AVE.
BKLYN., N.Y. 11207

STANLEY EISENBERG
ROYAL LAND
400 STANLEY AVE.
BKLYN. N.Y. 11207

J. BABKES
SONAR RADIO
73 WORTMAN AVE.
BKLYN., N.Y. 11207

STANLEY EISENBERG
SUNNYDALE FARMS
400 STANLEY AVE.
BKLYN., N.Y. 11207

JAY MONROE
TENSOR CORP.
333 STANLEY AVE.
BKLYN.,N.Y. 11207

ALBERT NOCELLA
MEATS & TREATS
1226 LIBERTY AVE.
BKLYN., N.Y. 11208

NAT SCHLESINGER
COMPUKNIT IND. INC.
50 WALLABOUT
BKLYN., N.Y. 11211

JEFF FREIRICH
REGAL CHEF
98 NORTH 3RD. ST.
BKLYN., N.Y. 11211

IRVING RUBIN
RUEBRO MFG. CO.
1002 GRAND ST.
BKLYN., N.Y. 11211

WILLIAM S. VERNON
CAMP AFFILIATES
170 2ND. AVE.
BKLYN., N.Y. 11215

DANIEL UDELL
DELDAN INC.
65 NINTH ST.
BKLYN., N.Y. 11215

BASIL B. BARWELL
EX-LAX
423 ATLANTIC AVE.
BKLYN., N.Y. 11217

W.K. MC MANUS
ATLANTIC SERVICE
711 CATON AVE
BKLYN., N.Y. 11218

MICHAEL M. SOMMA
METRA ELECTRONICS
660 MC DONALD AVE.
BKLYN., N.Y. 11218

SOL FRIEDMAN
ATLANTIC CONTROL SYSTEMS
1333 -60TH ST.
BKLYN., N.Y. 11219

A.R. LIEBERMAN
ESQUIRE RADIO
6201 15TH AVE.
BKLYN., N.Y. 11219

S.L. LANE
MAJOR ELECTRONICS
5802 3RD. AVE.
BKLYN., N.Y. 11220

H.B. OSTHEIMER
LIVERPOOL IND. INC.
162 57TH. ST.
BKLYN., N.Y. 1221

MARTIN SILVER
AMERICAN KOSHER
39 NORMAN AVE.
BKLYN., N.Y. 11222

CARL BAUM
VANGUARD DIVERSIFIED
10 JAVA ST.
BKLYN., N.Y. 11222

MAURICE ZALTA
MONICA SIMONE COSMETICS
2478 McDONALD AVE.
BKLYN., N.Y. 11223

BERNARD SCHWARTZ
WALDORF AUTO LEASING
1712 EAST 9TH. ST.
BKLYN., N.Y. 11223

H.J. ACCARINO
GENERAL IRON
2715 WEST 15TH. ST.
BKLYN., N.Y. 11224

MURRAY HANDWERKER
NATHAN'S FAMOUS
1310 SURF AVE.
BKLYN., N.Y. 11224

E.P. WHITNEY
ENTRON INC.
70-31 84TH. ST.
GLENDALE, N.Y. 11227

WILLIAM JOHENNING
UNITED GROCERS CO.
1630 CODY ST.
BKLYN., N.Y. 11227

FRANK MARINO
ACE TROPHIES
996 OCEAN PARKWAY
BKLYN., N.Y. 11230

M.E. COLLETON
NORTHEREAST POLLUTION
77 COMMERCE ST.
BKLYN., N.Y. 11231

GEORGE TASSONE
ATREO MFG. CO.
168 39TH ST.
BKLYN., N.Y. 11232

ABRAHAM WEINER
COLONIAL MIRROR
142 19TH ST.
BKLYN., N.Y. 11232

MAX HOUSS
INTERSTATE COMPUTER
754 4TH AVE.
BKLYN., N.Y. 11232

LOUIS B. MOSS
MASTER WOODCRAFT
FIRST AVE & 39TH ST.
BKLYN., N.Y. 11232

JOSEPH KLEIN
PHOENIX CANDY CO.
151-65 35TH ST.
BKLYN., N.Y. 11232

P. FREDERICK
SUPREME EQUIPMENT
170- 53RD. ST.
BKLYN., N.Y. 11232

JOEL J. SHORIN
TOPPS CHEWING GUM
254 36TH. ST.
BKLYN., N.Y. 11232

ALEXANDER, MARCUS
HALSEY DRUG
1827 PACIFIC ST.
BKLYN., N.Y. 11233

G. KNAUER
K.B. ELECTRONICS
5801 FOSTER AVE.
BKLYN., N.Y. 11234

SHELDON WYMAN
MICRO MED. IND.
1860 UTICA AVE.
BKLYN., N.Y. 11234

CARL HOROWITZ
POLYMER RESEARCH CORP.
2186 MILL AVE.
BKLYN, N.Y. 11234

N. FENSTER
FORWARD IND.
106-15 FOSTER AVE.
BKLYN., N.Y. 11236

J. MARANDO
JODMAR IND.
1790 E. 93RD. ST.
BKLYN., N.Y. 11236

MARTIN H. DUBILIER
MORSE ELECTRO PROD.
101-10 FOSTER AVE.
BKLYN., N.Y. 11236

SAM ZEMSKY
ZEMCO IND.
8608 FOSTER AVE
BKLYN., N.Y. 11236

IRVIN SCHWARTZ
MECHANICS BLDG. MATERIALS
1150 METROPOLITAN AVE.
BKLYN., N.Y. 11237

JACK A. MELTZER
A.K. ELECTRIC CORP.
384 CLASSON AVE.
BKLYN., N.Y. 11238

LEONARD H. SOBEL
COLLISION DEVICES
1302 60TH. ST.
BKLYN., N.Y. 11238

ALAN SPIEGEL
DETECTO SCALES
103-00 FOSTER AVE.
BKLYN., N.Y. 11238

LEON LAUFER
CRY-PLEX IND.
2800 COLLEGE PAINT CAUSEWAY
FLUSHING, N.Y. 11354

A.E. DENSEN
EASTCO IND.
26-15 123RD. ST.
FLUSHING, N.Y. 11354

ALBERT OSBORNE
ELECTRONIC TRANSISTORS
153-13 NORTHERN BLVD.
FLUSHING, N.Y. 11354

JOSEPH B. LOESING, JR.
PARK ELECTROCHEMICAL
33-37 FARRINGTON ST.
FLUSHING, N.Y. 11354

SAMUEL BAKER
AMERICAN BEVERAGE
117TH. ST. & 15TH. AVE.
COLLEGE POINT, N.Y. 11356

WILLIAM R. RYAN
EDO CORP.
14-04 111TH ST.
COLLEGE POINT, N.Y. 11356

JOSEPH J. SILVERSTEIN
ENGINE POWER
P.O. BOX 80
COLLEGE POINT, N.Y. 11356

S.J. RYMAN
ROYAL UNITED
13-15 131ST ST., BOX 413
COLLEGE POINT, N.Y. 11356

MORRIS SANDERS
KENT IND.
17-45 CLINTONVILLE ST.
WHITESTONE, N.Y. 11357

ALVIN M. MARKS
MARKS POLARIZED
153-16   10TH AVE.
WHITESTONE, N.Y. 11357

W.J. FOX
WHITLOCK CORP.
42-40 BELL BLVD.
BAYSIDE, N.Y. 11360

SEYMOUR MANN
ACETO CHEM. CO.
126-02 NORTHERN BLVD.
FLUSHING, N.Y. 11368

STANLEY LEWIN
CONTINENTAL HOSTS
111TH. ST. & 52ND. AVE.
FLUSHING, N.Y. 11368

R. MARK BOWRQUIN
BULOVA WATCH
BULOVA PARK
FLUSHING, N.Y. 11370

ALBERT L. UELTSCHI
FLIGHTSAFETY INT'L.
MARINE AIR TERMINAL
FLUSHING, N.Y. 11371

WARREN A. FUCIGNA
NEW YORK AIRWAYS
P.O. BOX 426
FLUSHING, N.Y. 11371

JACQUELINE SHER
MADJAC DATA
74-09 37TH. AVE.
JACKSON HEIGHTS, N.Y. 11372

ED HEIMBERG
ALUMINUM & CHEMICAL
116-55 QUEENS BLVD.
FOREST HILLS, N.Y. 11375

SIDNEY BERGER
BERGER IND.
74-16 GRAND AVE.
MASPETH, N.Y. 11375

JERRY GOLDBERG
PAN-AMERICAN DYNAMIC
118-21 QUEENS BLVD.
FOREST HILLS, N.Y. 11375

MURRAY KLEIN
AID AUTO STORES
34-36 65TH. ST.
WOODSIDE,QUEENS,N.Y.11377

A.J. EISENBERG
MEBCO IND.
24-01 BKLYN.-QUEENS EXPRESS. W.
WOODSIDE, N.Y. 11377

BENJAMIN SCHUR
PLASTOMETRICS
33-52   62ND ST.
WOODSIDE, N.Y. 11377

GEORGE LEVY
SAM GOOD
46-35 54TH RD.
MASPETH, N.Y. 11378

IRVING BRODY
ION IND.
59-31 56TH DR.
MASPETH, N.Y. 11378

L.S. STRAUSS
STRAUSS STORES
53-06 GRAND AVE.
MASPETH, N.Y. 11378

HARVEY E. PITTLUCK
PBA
150-15 183RD. ST.
SPRINGFIELD GARDENS, N.Y.11413

MARTIN SCHWARTZ
NATPAC
105-32 CROSS BAY BLVD.
OZONE PK., L.I.,N.Y. 11417

M.D. KANTOR
CVR IND.
89-25 130TH. ST.
RICHMOND HILL, N.Y. 11418

LIONEL WEINTRAUB
IDEAL TOY
184-10 JAMAICA AVE.
HOLLIS, N.Y. 11423

LEONARD A. KISSIN
MALLEN AUTOMATED FOOD
226-12 JAMAICA AVE.
BELLEROSE,N.Y. 11428

JOSEPH N. BERG
AIR EXPRESS INT'L.
JOHN F. KENNEDY AIRPORT
JAMAICA,N.Y. 11430

RICHARD M. JACKSON
SEABOARD WORLD AIRLINES
SEABOARD BLDG.,KENNEDY AIRPORT
JAMAICA, N.Y. 11430

BERNARD H. GREEN
EASTERN NEWSSTAND
90-10 MERRICK BLVD.
JAMAICA, N.Y. 11432

JOHN C. MALLON
IBI SECURITY
89-31 161ST ST.
JAMAICA, N.Y. 11432

ROBERT GLICK
MARTIN PAINT
153-22 JAMAICA AVE.
JAMAICA, N.Y. 11432

FELDMAN
HI-TECH IND.
180-08 LIBERTY AVE.
JAMAICA, N.Y. 11433

JEROME M. FELDMAN
SINTERAL
103-10 178TH ST.
JAMAICA, N.Y. 11433

JOSEPH M. KATZ
THE ODELL CO.
132-20 MERRICK BLVD.
JAMAICA, N.Y. 11434

J.W. BAILEY
OVERSEAS, NT'L.AIRWAYS
147-27 175TH ST.
JAMAICA, N.Y. 11434

IRA ROSENBERG
CHEMOLD
91-15 144 PL.
JAMAICA, N.Y. 11435

STANLEY B. ESSNER
LAWN-AT-MAT CHEM.& EQUIP.
153 JEFFERSON AVE.
MINEOLA, N.Y. 11501

H.C. LINDEMANN
LINDLY & CO.
248 HERRICKS RD.
MINEOLA,N.Y. 11501

CHARLES R. PIERCE
L.I. LIGHTING CO.
250 OLD COUNTRY RD.
MINEOLA, N.Y. 11501

STANLEY BURTON
POLY REPRO INT'L.
P.O. BOX 630
MINEOLA,N.Y. 11501

E.C. HOROWITZ
PROGRAMMED BOOKKEEPING
223 JERICHO TURNPIKE
MINEOLA, N.Y. 11501

SYDNEY JACOFF
GREAT NECK SAW MFG.
165 EAST 2ND ST.
MINEOLA, N.Y. 11502

C.G. PAFFENDORF
COAP SYSTEMS
175 I.U. WILLETS RD.
ALBERTSON, N.Y. 11507

VICTOR SILVERMAN
AIC PHOTO
168 GLEN COVE RD.
CARLE PL., N.Y. 11514

CHARLES E. BECK
AMBAC IND.
ONE OLD COUNTRY RD.
CARLE PL., N.Y. 11514

JAMES M. JACOBSON
HARVEY ED.
174 GLEN COVE RD.
CARLE PL., N.Y. 11514

LAWRENCE A. HARRIS
MICAMATIX CORP.
110-A VOICE RD.
CARLE PL., N.Y. 11514

HERMAN GLASSER
NUCLEAR ASSOC.
100 VOICE RD.
CARLE PL., N.Y. 11514

HERMAN GLASSER
RADIATION-MED. PRODUCTS
100 VOICE ROAD
CARLE PL., N.Y. 11514

LOUIS BENSON
MO-PARK IND.
P.O. BOX 375
CEDARHURST, N.Y. 11516

S.P. KONECKY
FOREMOST IND.
131 MAIN ST.
EAST ROCKAWAY, N.Y. 11518

WILLIAM H. BENSON
WHITEHALL IND.
WHITEHALL BLDG.
EAST ROCKAWAY,N.Y. 11518

EDWARD J. WARNKE
FLAGSHIP MARINE
149 SOUTH MAIN ST.
FREEPORT, N.Y. 11520

B.D. OSTROW
LEA-RONAL
272 BUFFALO AVE.
FREEPORT, N.Y. 11520

HERBERT S. DAVIDSON
MILGRAY ELECTRONICS
191 HANSE AVE.
FREEPORT, N.Y. 11520

ALVIN MARKS
WEKSLER INSTRUMENTS
80 MILL RD.
FREEPORT, N.Y. 11520

A.A. GENTILE
AAG, CORP.
666 FRANKLIN AVE
GARDEN CITY, N.Y. 11530

C.P. RYAN
CHARAN IND.
1122 FRANKLIN AVE. BOX 74
GARDEN CITY,, N.Y. 11530

H.M. YAFFE
DALE SYSTEMS
200 GARDEN CITY PLAZA
GARDEN CITY, N.Y. 11530

JOSEPH EHRENREICH
EHRENREICH PHOTO-OPTICAL
623 STEWART AVE.
GARDEN CITY, N.Y. 11530

FRANK SILVERMAN
HAMPTON SALES
750 STEWART AVE.
GARDEN CITY, N.Y. 11530

WILLIAM A. LEVINE
JOUET
330 WHITEHALL BLVD.
GARDEN CITY, N.Y. 11530

ARTHUR HUG, JR.
LITCO
P.O. BOX 1
GARDEN CITY, N.Y. 11530

D. MC GRAW
MANHATTAN INTERIORS
46 FIRST ST.
GARDEN CITY, N.Y. 11530

HARVEY GRANAT
MIDLAND RESOURCES
500 OLD COUNTRY RD.
GARDEN CITY, N.Y. 11530

JACK SILVERMAN
MODERN MAID FOOD
200 GARDEN CITY PLAZA
GARDEN CITY, N.Y. 11530

HOWARD L. BIEN
OPTRONICS
840 FRANKLIN AVE.
GARDEN CITY, N.Y. 11530

W.I. THOMPSON
OXFORD PENDALFLEX
33 CLINTON RD.
GARDEN CITY, N.Y. 11530

JACK P. JORDAN
PEPCOM IND.
ROOSEVELT FIELD
GARDEN CITY, N.Y. 11530

JOHN ALOGNA
PHILLIPS/ALOGNA ASSOC.
GARDEN CITY, N.Y. 11530

S.J. REED
REED, ROBERTS ASSOC.
118 SEVENTH ST.
GARDEN CITY, N.Y. 11530

R.S. SCHLANGER
RODALE ELECTRONICS
603 CHESTNUT ST.
GARDEN CITY, N.Y. 11530

CHARLES P. RYAN
SEAWAYS SHOPPING
1122 FRANKLIN-BOX 74
GARDEN CITY, N.Y. 11530

W.B. SPIELMAN
GRUMMAN ALLIED IND.
600 OLD COUNTRY RD.
GARDEN CITY, N.Y. 11532

HOWARD FERN
CECO SYSTEMS
37 COTTAGE ROW
GLEN COVE, N.Y. 11542

EDWARD MOSKOWITZ
EDMOS
GARVIES POINT RD.
GLEN COVE, N.Y. 11542

MILTON SCHEHR
FABRIC LEATHER
40 GARVIES POINT RD.
GLEN COVE, N.Y. 11542

LEO STASCHOVER
NORTH HILLS ELECTRONICS
ALEXANDER P.
GLEN COVE, N.Y. 11542

LEONARD OSROW
O S R CORP.
HAZEL ST.
GLEN COVE, L.I., N.Y. 11542

ABRAHAM KRASNOFF
PALL CORP.
30 SEA CLIFF AVE.
GLEN COVE, N.Y. 11542

HERBERT A. SLATER
SLATER ELECTRIC
45 SEA CLIFF AVE.
GLEN COVE, N.Y. 11542

ROBERT C. BARBATO
LUNDY ELECTRONICS
ROBERT LN.
GLEN HEAD, L.I., N.Y. 11545

MELVIN DUBLIN
SLANT-FIN
100 FOREST DR.
GREENVALE, N.Y. 11548

J.G. CORTALE
APPLIED SYSTEMATICS
393 FRONT ST.
HEMPSTEAD, N.Y. 11550

D.R. ALT
DON ALT-GAMUT
79 WASHINGTON ST.
HEMPSTEAD, N.Y. 11550

LOUIS KELLER
COMPONENT SPECIALTIES
393 S. FRANKLIN ST.
HEMPSTEAD, N.Y. 11550

HENRY BECKER
COMBINE CAMERA
225 HEMPSTEAD TURNPIKE
WEST HEMPSTEAD, N.Y. 11552

HERBERT H. ADISE
COMPUTER INTRUMENTS
92 MADISON AVE.
HEMPSTEAD, N.Y. 11550

DAVID EDWARDS
EMPIRE APPAREL
269 FULTON AVE.
HEMPSTEAD, N.Y. 11550

IRWIN SELINGER
SURGICOT
73-75 SEALY AVE.
HEMPSTEAD, N.Y. 11550

RALPH SENA
RELIANCE PET
90 W. GRAHAM AVE.
HEMPSTEAD, N.Y. 11551

HARRY FRIEDMAN
LAUREL COLOR
447 HEMPSTEAD AVE.
HEMPSTEAD, N.Y. 11552

QUIDO A. CAPPELLI
DANKER & WOHLK
635 NASSAU RD.
UNIONDALE, N.Y. 11553

W.A. STEFEN
NORTHFIELD PRECISION
4400 AUSTON BLVD.
ISLAND PK., N.Y. 11558

VICTOR PLAVIN
VEC-TREK
186 MAIN ST.
ELMSFORD, N.Y. 10523

HERBERT GOTTFRIED
REFRIG. FOR SCIENCE
31 ALABAMA AVE.
ISLAND PK., N.Y. 11558

BERNARD GUTMAN
DELCO
534 MERRICK RD.
LYNBROOK, N.Y. 11563

ROBERT BORNE
WILLOW IND.
8 FREER ST.
LYNBROOK, N.Y. 11563

GEORGE SILBER
REK-O-KUT
12 KEVIN CT.
MALVERNE, L.I., N.Y. 11565

ALBERT J. NASH
EDUCATIONAL TECH.
2224 HEWLETT AVE.
MERRICK, N.Y. 11566

H.A. GOTTLIEB
HYGRADE PACKAGING
P.O. BOX 148
OLD WESTBURY, N.Y. 11568

MARTIN SAVARICK
BEACON PHOTO
482 SUNRISE HIGHWAY
ROCKVILLE CENTRE, N.Y. 11570

B.H. DOWNEN
DOWNEN ZIER KNITS
80 BANKS AVE.
ROCKVILLE CENTRE, N.Y. 11570

MURRAY GROBMAN
ROCKVILLE IND.
315 SUNRISE HWY.
ROCKVILLE CENTRE, N.Y. 11570

B.P. ELKIN
BOSTON PNEUMATICS
P.O. BOX 292
ROCKVILLE CENTRE, N.Y. 11571

JOHN FELDMAN
BENEFICIAL LAB'S.
3959 SALLY LN.
OCEANSIDE, N.Y. 11572

M.D. KANTOR
SERVINATIONAL
100 MERRICK RD. STE.132
ROCKVILLE CENTRE, N.Y. 11572

ROBERT BARBOUR
CRYTON OPTICS
7 SKILLMAN ST.
ROSLYN, N.Y. 11576

F.W. LUNDGREN
DIAGNOSTIC RESEARCH
25 LUMBER RD.
ROSLYN, N.Y. 11576

HAROLD N. SAPHIN
COMPUTER INTERACTIONS
P.O. BOX 1354
ROSLYN HEIGHTS, N.Y. 11577

M.O. SCHULTZ
GUARDIAN COMM.
2 LAMBERT ST.
ROSLYN HEIGHTS, N.Y. 11577

PAUL BERGER
WATCHDOG PATROLS
99 POWERHOUSE RD.
ROSLYN HEIGHTS, N.Y. 11577

ARMAND FERRANTI
BERYLLIUM MFG.
253 W. MERRICK RD.
VALLEY STREAM, N.Y. 11580

CHARLES RACHELSON
COOKY'S-STEAK PUBS
107 SOUTH CENTRAL AVE.
VALLEY STREAM, N.Y. 11580

BERTRAM SAYER
CYBERMARK SYSTEMS
118 SOUTH FRANKLIN AVE.
VALLEY STREAM, N.Y. 11580

DAVID SCHEINMAN
HEALTH DELIVERY
65 ROOSEVELT AVE.
VALLEY STREAM,N.Y. 11580

KENNETH S. ROTH
HYDRO OPTICS
139 NO. CENTRAL AVE.
VALLEY STREAM, N.Y. 11580

HARRY BOGOVE
REMEMBER WHEN SWEET SHOPPE
39 STRINGHAM AVE.
VALLEY STREAM, N.Y. 11580

BERNARD KORN
COLONIAL COMM.
COLONIAL COMM. BLDG.
VALLEY STREAM, N.Y. 11581

MURRAY A. SPITZER
BARTH SPENCER
270 W. MERRICK RD.
VALLEY STREAM, N.Y. 11582

DANIEL BERLIN
ARKWIN IND.
WESTBURY, N.Y. 11590

KALUS P. BRINKMANN
BRINKMANN INSTRUMENTS
CANTIAGUE RD.
WESTBURY, N.Y. 11590

JACK DUBLER
CHURCHILL STEREO
123 FROST ST.
WESTBURY, N.Y. 11590

BERNARD KRAVITZ
DIONICS
65 RUSHMORE ST.
WESTBURY, N.Y. 11590

FRANK PERLOFF
FRIENDLY FROST
123 FROST ST.
WESTBURY, L.I. 11590

SIMON SARETZKY
IMC MAGNETICS
570 MAIN ST.
WESTBURY, L.I., N.Y. 11590

WALTER H. MILLER
KING KULLEN GROCERY
1194 PROSPECT AVE.
WESTBURY, N.Y. 11590

JESSE BIBLOWITZ
MASTERS
725 SUMMA AVE.
WESTBURY, N.Y. 11590

JEFF HARVEY
N.Y. TESTING LAB'S.
81 URBAN AVE.
WESTBURY, N.Y. 11590

WILLIAM OLSTEN
OLSTEN CORP.
ONE MERRICK AVE.
WESTBURY, N.Y. 11590

HERBERT ROTH
POWER DESIGNS
1700 SHAMES DR.
WESTBURY, L.I., N.Y. 11590

LEO LIEBOWITZ
POWER TEST
67 BOND ST.
WESTBURY, N.Y. 11590

ANTONIO CIFARELLI
PROGRESSIVE COMMUNICATIONS
1800 SHAMES DR.
WESTBURY, N.Y. 11590

ALBERT HANAN
SEW SIMPLE
710 SUMMA AVE.
WESTBURY, N.Y. 11590

B. REIFLER
UNIFLEX
474 GRAND BLVD.
WESTBURY, N.Y. 11590

ROBERT C. SCHWARTZ
MOTIVA
P.O. BOX 315
WOODMERE, N.Y. 11598

LEOPOLD LAPIDUS
TOTAL COMPUTER
789 SHERWOOD ST.
NORTH WOODMERE, N.Y. 11598

GEORGE E. MEYERS
EXTRUDYNE
45 RANICK DR.
AMITYVILLE, N.Y. 11701

EUGENE F. MURPHY
GEOTEL
185 DIXON AVE.
AMITYVILLE, N.Y. 11701

MIFTAR BEIO
SBD ELECTRONIC
275 DIXON AVE.
AMITYVILLE, N.Y. 11701

JOSEPH BAUMOEL
CONTROLOTRON
111 BELL ST.
W. BABYLON, N.Y. 11704

CHARLES ENTENMANN
ENTENMANN'S INC.
1724 FIFTH AVE.
BAYSHORE, N.Y. 11706

J. GROSS
SOLIDYNE
60 SPENCE ST.
BAYSHORE, N.Y. 11706

C.E. MURCOTT
LUMEX
100 SPENCE ST.
BAY SHORE, N.Y. 11707

WILLIAM J. BAKER
DALIN PHARMACEUTICALS
2647 GRAND AVE.
BELLMORE, N.Y. 11710

TIMOTHY R. CUTLER
MIRACLE ADHESIVES
250 PETTIT AVE.
BELLMORE, N.Y. 11710

JOSEPH G. GAVIN JR.
GRUMMAN CORP.
SOUTH OYSTER BAY RD.
BETHPAGE, N.Y. 11714

ARTHUR RUDOLPH
ARCO PHARMACEUTICALS
105 ORVILLE DR.
BOHEMIA, N.Y. 11716

JACK G. ANDERSON
ILC IND.
AIRPORT INTL. PLAZA
BOHEMIA, N.Y. 11716

R.R. RICHARDS
MEGADATA
35 ORVILLE DR.
BOHEMIA, N.Y. 11716

GEORGE KLEIMAN
SCIENTIFIC IND.
70 ORVILLE DR.
BOHEMIA, N.Y. 11716

ELLIOT I. BAUM
QUASAR MICROSYSTEMS
448 SUFFOLK AVE.
BRENTWOOD, N.Y. 11717

DAVID H. POLINGER
SUBURBAN BROADCASTING
S. SERVICE RD.,L.I. EXWAY.
CENTRAL ISLIP, N.Y. 11722

JAMES SHERIDAN
VICTOR GRAPHIC
95F HOFFMAN LN. SOUTH
CENTRAL ISLIP, N.Y. 11722

IRA WALDBAUM
WALBAUM INC.
HEMLOCK & BLVD.
CENTRAL ISLIP, N.Y. 11722

FREDERICK J. BENDER
JEROME UNDERGROUND
87 MODULAR AVE.
COMMACK, N.Y. 11725

DAVIDGE WARFIELD
RETREADING INTERNATIONAL
63 AUSTIN BLVD.
COMMACK, N.Y. 11725

H.P. POST
ROBIN IND.
75 AUSTIN BLVD.
COMMACK, N.Y. 11725

R. SHULMAN
BOLAR PHARMACEUTICAL
130 LINCOLN ST.
COPIAGUE, N.Y. 11726

LEWIS GOLDSTONE
CARE-FREE SWIMMING
1270 SUNRISE HIGHWAY
COPIAGUE, N.Y. 11726

HAROLD ROGGEN
NAPCO SECURITY
6 DI TOMAS CT.
COPIAGUE, N.Y. 11726

JACK I. GREEN
NORTHERN STAR
700 CHETTIC AVE.
COPIAGUE, N.Y. 11726

MARTIN KAPEKER
THERMOVAC IND.
41 DECKER ST.
COPIAGUE, N.Y. 11726

H. KORNAHRENS
GARSITE
10 GRAND BLVD.
DEER PARK, N.Y. 11729

R.B. HIRSCH
RHG ELECTRONICS
161 IND. CT.
DEER PARK, N.Y. 11729

FRANK D. PALOPOLI
SANITARY CONTROLS
225 MARCUS BLVD.
DEER PARK, N.Y. 11729

LOUIS GROSSMAN
SOUTHERN CONTAINER
140 WEST IND. CT.
DEER PARK, N.Y. 11729

CHARLES G. LEONHARDT
ARTEK SYSTEMS
275 ADAMS BLVD.
FARMINGDALE, N.Y. 11735

JEROME FISHEL
CIRCUIT TECHNOLGY
160 SMITH ST.
EAST FARMINGDALE, N.Y. 11735

IRVING BECKER
COMSPAGE
350 GREAT NECK RD.
FARMINGDALE, N.Y. 11735

D.K. WASSONG
DEL LAB'S.
565 BROAD HOLLOW RD.
FARMINGDALE, N.Y. 11735

ARTHUR LEWIS
FAIRFIELD-NOBLE
333 SMITH ST.
FARMINGDALE, N.Y. 11735

CHARLES GINGOLD
FIRELITE
280 RTE. 109
FARMINGDALE, N.Y. 11735

MAURICE MINUTO
FIBROTHANE
21-21 BROAD HOLLOW RD.
FARMINGDALE, N.Y. 11735

MAX FINE
GEM ELECTRONIC
34 HEMPSTEAD TPKE.
FARMINGDALE, N.Y. 11735

S.A. RINKEL
GENERAL MICROWAVE
155 MARINE ST.
FARMINGDALE, N.Y. 11735

BERNARD GREENMAN
GREENMAN BROS.
105 PRICE PARKWAY
FARMINGDALE, N.Y. 11735

ROB'T. L. NEEDHAM
INFRA-RED CIRCUITS
215B CENTRAL AVE.
EAST FARMINGDALE, N.Y. 11735

ELSTON H. SWANSON
INSTRUMENTS FOR IND.
151 TOLEDO
FARMINGDALE, N.Y. 11735

ARTHUR R. SZEGLIN
KINEMOTIVE
222 CENTRAL AVE.
FARMINGDALE, N.Y. 11735

HERBERT L. FISCHER
LOGITEK
42 CENTRAL AVE.
FARMINGDALE, N.Y. 11735

DAVID SHICHMAN
PHOENIX IND.
144 MILBAR BLVD.
FARMINGDALE, N.Y. 11735

F.R. BARLOW
POLYMER MATERIALS
100 ADAMS BLVD.
FARMINGDALE, N.Y. 11735

DANIEL ALROY
QI CORP.
6 DUBON CT.
FARMINGDALE, N.Y. 11735

FRED HABER
TRANSMAGNETICS
210 ADAMS BLVD.
FARMINGDALE, N.Y. 11735

DONALD N. HORN
VICON IND.
130 CENTRAL AVE.
FARMINGDALE, N.Y. 11735

LEONARD GENOVESE
GENOVESE DRUG STORES
80 MARCUS DR.
MELVILLE, N.Y. 11740

DAVID WESTERMANN
HAZELTINE CORP.
GREENLAWN, N.Y. 11740

JOHN I. NESTEL
CONSOLIDATED AIRBORNE
895 WAVERLY AVE.
HOLTSVILLE, N.Y. 11742

DOMONIC R. CIANCIULLI
BUILDEX
789 PARK AVE.
HUNTINGTON. N.Y. 11743

G.M. BENSTOCK
SUPERIOR SURGICAL MFG.
63 NEW YORK AVE.
HUNTINGTON, N.Y. 11743

BERNARD R. GARRETT
INSTRUMENTS SYSTEMS
789 PARK AVE.
HUNTINGTON, N.Y. 11743

WALTER B. KISSINGER
ALLEN GROUP
534 BROAD HOLLOW RD.
MELVILLE, N.Y. 11746

LOUIS F. LINDAUER
AUTOMATED PROCESSES
80 MARCUS DR.
MELVILLE, N.Y. 11746

WILLIAM M. ARNOWITZ
BECK-ARNLEY
548 BROAD HOLLOW RD.
MELVILLE, N.Y. 11746

PAUL DE MATTEO
DYNELL
75 MAXESS RD.
MELVILLE, N.Y. 11746

DANIEL JACOBSON
FILTER FLOW
260 BETHPAGE-SPAGNOLI RD.
MELVILLE, N.Y. 11746

PHILIP M. GETTER
GENERICS
75 MARCUS DR.
MELVILLE, N.Y. 11746

CLARK F. GALEHOUSE
GOLDEN CREST RECORDS
220 BROADWAY
HUNTINGTON STA.,L.I.N.Y.11746

E.J. PORTO
INT'L. ELECTRONICS
316 SOUTH SERVICE RD.
MELVILLE, N.Y. 11746

PHILIP KIRSCHNER
MOTOR PARTS IND.
540 BROAD HOLLOW RD.
MELVILLE, N.Y. 11746

JEROME YAEGER
NOBLE LUMBER
ONE HUNTINGTON QUADRANGLE
MELVILLE, N.Y. 11746

CHARLES W. OLSON
OLSON RESEARCH
42 LEWIS CT.
HUNTINGTON STA., N.Y. 11746

WILBUR MARKS
POSEIDON SCIENTIFIC
9 PASHEN PL.
DIX HILLS, N.Y. 11746

K.H. MORGANSTERN
RADIATION DYNAMICS
316 SOUTH SERVICE RD.
MELVILLE, N.Y. 11746

MARTIN TOLCHIN
TOLCHIN INSTRUMENTS
55 MARCUS DR.
MELVILLE, N.Y. 11746

FRANK J. DI SANTO
VISUAL SCIENCES
900 WALT WHITMAN RD.
HUNTINGTON STA., N.Y. 11746

BENJAMIN B. GROSSMAN
INT'L. ELECTRONICS
316 SO. SERVICE RD.
MELVILLE, N.Y. 11749

KARL STANLEY
CUT & CURL
125 SOUTH SERVICE RD.
JERICHO, N.Y. 11753

W.F. KENNY
MEENAN OIL
375 N. BROADWAY
JERICHO, N.Y. 11753

DAVID J. GRUTMAN
TAX COMPUTER
2923 HEMPSTEAD TURNPIKE
LEVITTOWN, N.Y. 11756

ROBERT ENCH
FLOWER TIME
1178 RTE. 109
LINDENHURST, N.Y. 11757

GERALD EHRLICH
LIECO
80 MONTAUK HIGHWAY
LINDENHURST, N.Y. 11757

ALFRED ROBBINS
PERFECT LINE MFG.
80 E. GATES AVE.
LINDENHURST, N.Y. 11757

ALFRED W. RUSSELL
RUSSELL REINFORCED PLASTICS
521 W. HOFFMAN AVE.
LINDENHURST, N.Y. 11757

A.J. ROACH
TII CORP.
P.O. BOX 622
LINDENHURST, N.Y. LL&%&

MARVIN COHEN
STELBER IND.
P.O. BOX 388
MEDFORD, N.Y. 11763

ROBERT D. HAWKINS
SEA-SPACE
P.O. BOX 295
OYSTER BAY, N.Y. 11771

PETER J. PAPADKOS
GYRODYNE
PARKSIDE AVE.
ST. JAMES, L.I., N.Y. 11780

G.M. SWEET
AMERICAN FLAVOR
110 KENNEDY DR.
SMITHTOWN, N.Y. 11787

ROBERT K. STERN
APPLIED DEVICES
60 PLANT AVE.
HAUPPAUGE, N.Y. 11787

WM. J. CATACOSINOS
APPLIED DIGITAL DATA
100 MARCUS BLVD.
HAUPPAUGE, N.Y. 11787

WALTER STEINBERG
AUTO NUMERICS
90 PLANT AVE.
HAUPPAUGE, N.Y. 11787

P. ALTEHANDO
COMPUTER CIRCUITS
143 MARCUS BLVD.
HAUPPAUGE, N.Y. 11787

JACK C. GREENE
COMTECH LAB'S.
135 ENGINEERS RD.
SMITHTOWN, N.Y. 11787

WILLIAM GLASSER
DYNAMIC INSTRUMENTS
933 MOTOR PKWAY.
HAUPPAUGE, N.Y. 11787

P.B. GROVEMAN
CREATIVE ENVIRONMENTS
85 HOFFMAN LN. SOUTH
HAUPPAUGE, N.Y. 11787

J.J. LANGFORD
GAP INSTRUMENT
110 MARCUS BLVD.
HAUPPAUGE, N.Y. 11787

ALFRED R. GLOBUS
GUARDIAN CHEM. CORP.
230 MARCUS BLVD.
HAUPPAUGE, N.Y. 11787

C.B. GIRSKY
JACO ELECTRONICS
195 ENGINEERS RD.
HAUPPAUGE, N.Y. 11787

ALAN S. HAYS
MAGNETIC HEAD
250 MARCUS BLVD.
HAUPPAUGE, N.Y. 11787

JOSEPH SALTZMAN
MULTIVOX CORP.
370 VANDERBILT MOTOR PKWY.
HAUPPAUGE, N.Y. 11787

DR. RICHARD T. DALY
QUANTRONIX
225 ENGINEER RD.
SMITHTOWN, N.Y. 11787

S.J. ARDITTI
RAI RESEARCH
225 MARCUS BLVD.
HAUPPAUGE, N.Y. 11787

EVELYN BEREZIN
REDACTRON
100 PARKWAY DR. S.
HAUPPAUGE, N.Y. 11787

M.I. ROTH
SPORTSOTRON
85 ENGINEERS RD.
HAUPPAUGE, N.Y. 11787

KLOCKENBRINK, CHRMN.
UPPSTER CORP.
110 MARCUS BLVD.
HAUPPAUGE, N.Y. 11787

SHELDON O. NEWMAN
ALGOREX
6901 JERICHO TURNPIKE
SYOSSET, N.Y. 11791

L.N. BLATT
HERLEY IND.
160 EILEEN WAY
SYOSSET , N.Y. 11791

ARTHUR H. BLACKBURN
LAFAYETTE ELECTRONICS
111 JERICHO TPKE.
SYOSSET, N.Y. 11791

MAXWELL NADLER
METALLURGICAL PROCESSING
180 MICHAEL DR.
SYOSSET, L.I.,N.Y. 11791

JACK RUDMAN
NATIONAL LEARNING
212 MICHAEL DR.
SYOSSET, N.Y. 11791

MAX REISSMAN
ORBIT INSTRUMENT
131 EILEEN WAY
SYOSSET, N.Y. 11791

P. V. DE LUCA
PORTA SYSTEMS
6901 JERICHO TURNPIKE
SYOSSET, N.Y. 11791

MORTON D. BROZINSKY
STANDARD MICROSYSTEMS
35 MARCUS BLVD.
HAUPPAUGE, N.Y. 11791

HARRY KIERNAN
VIATECH
1 AERIAL WAY
SYOSSET, N.Y. 11791

JEROME MARDER
WORLDWIDE FLEET
21 ELLIS DR.
SYOSSET, N.Y. 11791

RONALD W. HART
THE AMERICAN PLAN
100 CROSSWAY PK. WEST
WOODBURY, N.Y. 11797

LIONEL PHILLIPS
DIPLOMAT ELECTRONICS
303 CROSSWAY PARK DR.
WOODBURY, N.Y. 11797

R.S. EVANS
GENERAL TRAINING
175 CROSSWAYS PARKWEST
WOODBURY, N.Y. 11797

ROBERT L. BARBANELL
GEON IND.
80 CROSSWAY PARK DR.
WOODBURY, N.Y. 11797

HARVEY E. SAMPSON,JR.
THE HARVEY GROUP
60 CROSSWAY PARK WEST
WOODBURY, N.Y. 11797

CLYDE SKEEN
MAGNUS INT'L.
311 CROSSWAY PARK DR.
WOODBURY, N.Y. 11797

MICHAEL C. PASCUCCI
NAT'L. MERIDIAN
175 CROSSWAY PARK WEST
WOODBURY, N.Y. 11797

AMOS HEILICHER
PICKWICH INT'L.
135 CROSSWAY PARK DR.
WOODBURY, N.Y. 11797

BERNARD D. LANDAU
PROFESSIONAL DATA
CROSSWAYS IND. PARK
WOODBURY, N.Y. 11797

IRWIN KATZ
SOMERSET CONST. CO.
20 CROSSWAYS PARK
WOODBURY,N.Y. 11797

HOWARD E. THOMPSON
LUNN LAMINATES
STRAIGHT PATH RD.
WYANDANCH, L.I., N.Y. 11798

HARRY LIPMAN
JAMECO IND. INC.
248 WYANDANCH AVE.
WYANDANCH, N.Y. 11798

GEORGE KOGEL
CHEMSTAT
65 BLOOMINGDALE RD.
HICKSVILLE, N.Y. 11801

RICHARD GOLDSTEIN
DORSON SPORTS
5-09 BURNS AVE. BOX 606
HICKSVILLE, N.Y. 11801

ARTHUR J. MINASY
KNOGO
100 TEC ST.
HICKSVILLE, N.Y. 11801

JOSEPH LAZAR
LAD ELECTRO-SYSTEMS
102 NEW SOUTH RD.
HICKSVILLE, N.Y. 11801

M.C. PRESNICK
METATRONICS MFG.
111 BLOOMINGDALE RD.
HICKSVILLE, N.Y. 11801

A.MESHBANE
SAVANT INSTRUMENTS
221 PARK AVE.
HICKSVILLE, N.Y. 11801

HENRY BLACKSTONE
SERVO
111 NEW SOUTH RD.
HICKSVILLE, N.Y. 11801

ALBERT FRIEDMAN
UNITY BUYING
810 SOUTH BROADWAY
HICKSVILLE, N.Y. 11802

HERBERT K.KOLBER
DORSET COMPUTYPE
347 W. JOHN ST.
HICKSVILLE, N.Y. 11802

P. FEUER
Y.E. ENTERPRISES
108 NEW SOUTH RD.
HICKSVILLE, N.Y. 11802

MILTON BRENNER
AEROFLEX LAB'S.
SOUTH SERVICE RD.
PLAINVIEW, N.Y. 11803

LOUIS DE LALIO
THE ALUMET CORP.
201 E. ETHPAGE RD.
PLAINVIEW, N.Y. 11803

DAVID GREENBLATT
AMFESCO
2 AMFESCO DR.
PLAINVIEW, N.Y. 11803

HERBERT JUDIN
AREOPTIX
25 NORTH MALL
PLAINVIEW, N.Y. 11803

PAT MIOLA
ATOMIC DEVELOPMENT
7 FAIRCHILD CT.
PLAINVIEW, N.Y. 11803

FRED MARGULIES
AVIONICS
221 FAIRCHILD AVE.
PLAINVIEW, N.Y. 11803

MICHAEL CASH
BFL COMMUNICATION
ONE DUPONT ST.
PLAINVIEW, N.Y. 11803

SHELDON GARDNER
BINARY SYSTEMS
88 SUNNYSIDE BLVD.
PLAINVIEW, N.Y. 11803

LEON WEISSMAN
CHYRON CORP.
223 NEWTON RD.
PLAINVIEW, N.Y. 11803

JOSEPH GROSS
COMPUTER TERMINAL
52 NEWTOWN PLAZA
PLAINVIEW, N.Y. 11803

ROBERT CRANE
CRANE BIO-MED. IND.
21 CYNTHIA LN.
PLAINVIEW, N.Y. 11803

CHARLES CUMELLA
FED. CASTERS
120 EXPRESS ST.
PLAINVIEW, N.Y. 11803

FRED H. FELLOWS
FIBRE MATERIALS
40 DUPONT ST.
PLAINVIEW, N.Y. 11803

GARY SCHLEIMER
GAMAR ELECTROOMATIC
75 SHEER PLAZA
PLAINVIEW, N.Y. 11803

HERBERT LINDO
KENILWORTH RESEARCH
245 NEWTON RD.
PLAINVIEW, N.Y. 11803

J.D. FRANCIS
LIQUIDONICS
45 SOUTH SERVICE RD.
PLAINVIEW, N.Y. 11803

F.J. SPOSATO
LOGIMETRICS
121 DUPONT ST.
PLAINVIEW, N.Y. 11803

D.R. MAZZIOTA
MICROWAVE POWER
ADAMS CT.
PLAINVIEW, N.Y. 11803

WILLIAM A. BOURKE
NARDA MICROWAVE
75 COMMERCIAL ST.
PLAINVIEW, N.Y. 11803

PHILIP HAMERSLOUGH
NEW DIMENSIONS
160 DUPONT ST.
PLAINVIEW, N.Y. 11803

MALCOLM D. WIDENOR
NORTH ATLANTIC IND.
200 TERMINAL DR.
PLAINVIEW,N.Y. 11803

DR. PAUL KAPLAN
OCEANICS
TECH. INDUSTRIAL PK.
PLAINVIEW, N.Y. 11803

JAMES G. BECKERLEY
RADIOPTICS
10 DUPONT ST.
PLAINVIEW, N.Y. 11803

LAWRENCE M. RHEINGOLD
TEMPLET IND.
201 E. BETHPAGE RD.
PLAINVIEW, N.Y. 11803

GEORGE J. SBORDONE
TEMPO DEVICES
E. BETHPAGE RD.
PLAINVIEW, N.Y. 11803

J.P. LANFEAR
THREE DIMENSIONAL
31 COMMERCIAL ST.
PLAINVIEW, N.Y. 11803

BERNARD HERMAN
TRIO LAB'S.
80 DUPONT ST.
PLAINVIEW, N.Y. 11803

RICHARD PROJAIN
VEECO
TERMINAL DR.
PLAINVIEW, N.Y. 11803

DON HIRSCHHORN
DON HIRSCHHORN INC.
185 BETHPAGE SWEET HOLLOW RD.
OLD BETHPAGE, N.Y. 11804

VICTOR REICHENSTEIN
LEISURECRAFT
P.O. BOX 250
OLD BETHPAGE, N.Y. 11804

STANLEY I. LANDGRAF
MOHASCO
57 LYON ST.
AMSTERDAM, N.Y. 12010

B.H. FREED
FLAH'S
878 ALBANY-SHAKER RD.
LATHAM, N.Y. 12110

E.B. STRINGHAM
PENETRYN INT'L.
424 NISKAYUNA RD.
LATHAM, N.Y. 12110

A.J. MARCELLE
CALLANAN IND.
SOUTH BETHLEHEM, N.Y. 12161

ROBERT H. SLOAN
ALBANY INT'L.
1373 BROADWAY
ALBANY, N.Y. 12201

FRANK W. MC CABE
WYTEX
66 STATE ST.
ALBANY, N.Y. 12201

ALAN V. ISELIN
AMADAC IND.
18 COMPUTER DR. E.
ALBANY, N.Y. 12205

HUBERT M. ARONS
CENTRAL WAREHOUSE
COLONIE & MONTGOMERY
ALBANY, N.Y. 12207

JOHN E. STRYKER
C M P IND.
413 PEARL ST.
ALBANY, N.Y. 12207

JOHN L. MATRONE
ENVIRONMENT-ONE
2773 BALLTOWN RD.
SCHENECTADY, N.Y. 12309

NED W. BUOYMASTER
NAT'L. MICRONETICS
U.S. RTE. 28
WEST HURLEY, N.Y. 12491

C.J. LAWSON, JR.
ROTRON INC
7-9 HASBROUCK LN.
WOODSTOCK, N.Y. 12498

L.O. WARD
BIO. PRESERVATION
44-62 JOHNES ST.
NEWBURGH, N.Y. 12550

F.L. DAVENPORT
COMPUTER CAREERS
UNION AVE.
NEWBURGH, N.Y. 12550

WALTER A. RHULEN
ELECTRONIC TAB.
P.O. BOX 728
NEWBURGH, N.Y. 12550

MELVIN FINKELSTEIN
HOUSE OF WESTMORE
PIERCES RD.
NEWBURGH, N.Y. 12550

GERALD E. GRUENHAGEN
MAGNETIC CORE
JOHN ST.
NEWBURGH, N.Y. 12550

LEWIS OTT WARD
OVITRON
44 JOHNES ST.
NEWBURGH, N.Y. 12550

D.G. DUTTON
A.C. DUTTON LUMBER
8 CATHERINE ST.
POUGHKEEPSIE, N.Y. 12601

A.F. BROOK
WIRE-O CORP.
205 COTTAGE ST.
POUGHKEEPSIE, N.Y. 12601

WILLIAM C. KINSINGER
METAGRAPHIC
COMMERCE ST.
POUGHKEEPSIE, N.Y. 12603

L. GREENBERG
SULLIVAN COUNTY HARNESS
MONTICELLO RACEWAY
MONTICELLO, N.Y. 12701

R.B. STEVENS
STEVENS & THOMPSON PAPER
GREENWICH, N.Y. 12834

J.W. JUCKETT
SANDY HILL
27 ALLEN ST.
HUDSON FALLS, N.Y. 12839

L.R. HOLE
COLUMBIAN ROPE
309 GENESEE ST.
AUBURN, N.Y. 13021

RICHARD B. SANDERS
CORTLAND LINE CO.
67 EAST CT. ST.
CORTLAND, N.Y. 13045

R.L. McLAUGHLIN
MICROWAVE SYSTEMS
1 ADLER DR.
EAST SYRACUSE, N.Y. 13057

HENRY A. PANASCI, JR.
FAY'S DRUG
7327 7TH., NORTH
LIVERPOOL, N.Y. 13088

ROBERT J. SIRACUSA
OPTIVISION
441 BEECHWOOD AVE.
LIVERPOOL, N.Y. 13088

ROBERT L. TARNOW
GOULDS PUMPS
240 FALL ST.
SENECA FALLS, N.Y. 13148

GEORGE G. SOUHAN
VERMONT HOSIERY & MACH.
SENECA FALLS, N.Y. 13148

THEODORE PIERSON
ONONDAGA SUPPLY
344 W. GENESEE ST.
SYRACUSE, N.Y. 13201

PAUL A. BRUNNER
CROUSE-HINDS
WOLF & 7TH STS.
SYRACUSE, N.Y. 13201

EARL M. EDEN
P & C FOOD MARKETS
P.O. BOX 1365
SYRACUSE, N.Y. 13201

STEWART DAVIS
SYRACUSE SUPPLY
P.O. BOX 1044
SYRACUSE, N.Y. 13201

HARRY E. GOETZMANN, JR.
CONTINENTAL INFORMATION
600 MONY PLAZA
SYRACUSE, N.Y. 13202

H.N. SLOTNICK
CARROLS DEVELOPMENT
968 JAMES ST.
SYRACUSE, N.Y. 13203

L.W. AFFOLTER
A.E. NETTLETON
313 E. WILLOW ST.
SYRACUSE, N.Y. 13203

H.A. HAIR
ANAREN MICROWAVE
185 AINSLEY DR.
SYRACUSE, N.Y. 13205

H. FOLLETT HODGKINS, JR.
LIPE-ROLLAWAY
806 EMERSON AVE.
SYRACUSE, N.Y. 13214

FRED JUER
ADIRONDACK IND.
S/S MC KINLEY AVE.
DOLGEVILLE, N.Y. 13329

JOHN D. READON
DANIEL GREEN CO.
1 MAIN ST., M.
DOLGEVILLE, N.Y. 13329

JOSEPH M. WENTZELL
HOMOGENEOUS METALS
W. CANADA BLVD.
HERKIMER, N.Y. 13350

RALPH H. O'BRIEN
MOHAWK DATA
P.O. BOX 652
HERKIMER, N.Y. 13350

THOMPSON H. BILLINGTON
DUOFOLD
P.O. DRAWER A.
MOHAWK, N.Y. 13407

PIEREPONT T. NOYES
ONEIDA LTD.
KENWOOD STA.
ONEIDA, N.Y. 13421

JOHN A. FRINK
DIGIMETRICS
COMMERCIAL DR.
YORKVILLE, N.Y. 13495

MUNSON H. PARDEE
HAMILTON DIGITAL
2118 BEECHGROVE PL.
UTICA, N.Y. 13501

ROBERT E. REID
UTICA RADIATOR
2201 DWYER AVE.
UTICA, N.Y. 13501

A.E. ALLEN JR.
UTICA CUTLERY
820 NOYES ST.
UTICA, N.Y. 13502

GILBERT H. JONES
UTICA DUXBAK
815 NOYES ST.
UTICA, N.Y. 13502

WALTER J. MATT
WEST END BREWING
811 EDWARD ST.
UTICA,N.Y. 13503

FRANK A. AUGSBURY JR.
RUTLAND
P.O. BOX 629
OGDENSBURG, N.Y. 13669

GEORGE G. RAYMOND JR.
RAYMOND CORP.
GREENE, N.Y. 13778

HARRISON F. EDWARDS
SIMMONDS PRECISION ENGINE
17 E. MIDLAND DR.
NORWICH, N.Y. 13815

DARRYL R. GREGSON
VICTORY MARKETS
54 E. MAIN ST.
NORWICH, N.Y. 13815

ROBERT L. NEVIN
KEITH CLARK
UNION & DIVISION STS.
DISNEY, N.Y. 13838

R.R. KAUFMAN
JAYARK CORP.
P.O. BOX 656
BINGHAMTON,N.Y. 13902

FLOYD H. LAWSON
UNIVERSAL INSTRUMENTS
P.O. BOX 825
BINGHAMTON, N.Y. 13902

FRANCIS E. CROWLEY
CROWLEY FOODS
145 CONKLIN AVE.
BINGHAMTON, N.Y. 13903

FRANK H. MC INTOSH
MC INTOSH LAB. INC.
2 CHAMBERS ST.
BINGHAMTON, N.Y. 13903

CHARLES STRUBLE
SPAULDING BAKERIES
120 PLAZA DR.
BINGHAMTON, N.Y. 13903

ALEXANDER L. NAYLOR
FAIRBANKS CO.
10 GLENWOOD AVE.
BINGHAMTON, N.Y. 13905

F.D. BERKELEY III
GRAHAM MFG.
26 HARVESTER AVE.
BATAVIA, N.Y. 14020

PHILIP STRAUSS
KAYAK RECREATIONAL
5460 TRANSIT RD.
DEPEW, N.Y. 14043

MALCOLM C. REED
DUNKIRK RADIATOR
85 MIDDLE RD.
DUNKIRK, N.Y. 14048

K.T. KEANE
ASTRONICS CORP.
77 OCEAN RD.
EAST AURORA, N.Y. 14052

WILLIAM C. MOOG JR.
MOOG INC.
PRONER AIRPORT
EAST AURORA, N.Y. 14052

DARWIN READ
PETER COOPER CORP.
PALMER ST.
GOWANDA, N.Y. 14070

JAMES J. UPSON
UPSON CO.
UPSON POINT
LOCKPORT, N.Y. 14094

CHARLES R. CM ELROY
METAL CLADDING
NIAGARA & MILLER
NORTH TONAWANDA, N.Y. 14120

P.H. TAYLOR
TAYLOR DEVICES
NORTH TONAWANDA, N.Y. 14120

MILES D. BENDER
SYNCOM
ONE SYNCOM PL.
ORCHARD PL., N.Y. 14127

WILLIAM A. HARTY JR.
THE EXOLON CO.
1000 EAST NIAGARA ST.
TONOWANDA, N.Y. 14150

BEN W. PAPERMASTER
ASSOC. BIOMEDIC
872 MAIN ST.
BUFFALO, N.Y. 14202

DANIEL A. ROBLIN JR.
ROBLIN IND.
290 MAIN ST.
BUFFALO, N.Y. 14202

LEONARD ROCHWARGER
FIRSTMARK CORP.
107 DELAWARE AVE.
BUFFALO, N.Y. 14202

JACK A. KEENAN
CONNOHIO
1031 ELLICOTT SQ.
BUFFALO, N.Y. 14203

C.S. FIELDING
HOBAM
50 BROADWAY
BUFFALO, N.Y. 14203

GERALD C. SALTARELLI
HOUDAILLE IND.
1 M & T PLAZA
BUFFALO, N.Y. 14203

HENRY E. JONES
PIERCE & STEVENS
710 OHIO ST.
BUFFALO, N.Y. 14203

R. JOHN OSHEI
TRICO
817 WASHINGTON ST.
BUFFALO, N.Y. 14203

CHARLES J. PALISANO
BOSS-LINCO LINES
226 OHIO ST.
BUFFALO, N.Y. 14204

DAVID R. NEWCOMB
BUFFALO FORGE
490 BROADWAY
BUFFALO, N.Y. 14204

WILLIAM SHERMAN
LOBLAW
P.O. BOX 941
BUFFALO, N.Y. 14205

F.E. MUNSCHAUER JR.
NIAGARA MACHIN
P.O. BOX 475
BUFFALO, N.Y. 14205

SAVINO P. NANULA
NIAGARA FRONTIER
60 DINGENS ST.
BUFFALO, N.Y. 14206

E. J. BURKE JR.
BURKE SECURITY
1555 MAIN ST.
BUFFALO, N.Y. 14209

WILLIAM M. E. CLARKSON
GRAPHIC CONTROLS
189 VAN RENSSELAER ST.
BUFFALO, N.Y. 14210

WILLIAM K. SIMON
WILLIAM SIMON BREWERY
705 CLINTON ST.
BUFFALO, N.Y. 14210

S.J. ROSEN
BISON MFG.
35 ROETZER ST.
BUFFALO, N.Y. 14211

GEORGE H. HYDE
THE MENTNOLATUM CO.
1360 NIAGARA ST.
BUFFALO, N.Y. 14213

CLEMENT R. ARRISON
GLAR-BAN
388 EVANS ST.
BUFFALO, N.Y. 14215

R.C. JENDRON
HARD MFG.
230 GRIDER ST.
BUFFALO, N.Y. 14215

ROBERT S. KELSO
CALSPAN
4455 GENESEE ST.
BUFFALO, N.Y. 14221

R.A. MARKS
COMPUTER TASK
5501 MAIN ST.
BUFFALO, N.Y. 14221

ROBERT D. WHITE
PELOREX
120 GARDENVILLE PKWAY. WEST
WEST SENECA, N.Y. 14224

ROBERT J. FIERLE
AMERICAN PRECISION IND.
2777 WALDEN AVE.
BUFFALO, N.Y. 14225

W. W. BIRD
BIRDAIR
2015 WALDEN AVE.
BUFFALO, N.Y. 14225

F.G. BEDDICK
MUNRO GAMES
3901 UNION RD.
BUFFALO, N.Y. 14225

NICHOLAS D. TRBOVICH
SERVOTRONICS
3901 UNION RD.
BUFFALO, N.Y. 14225

SHERWOOD H. CALHOUN
SIERRA RESEARCH
P.O. BOX 222
BUFFALO, N.Y. 14225

W.L. HUMSTON
STANDARD ELECTRONICS
3519 UNION RD.
CHEEKTOWAGA, N.Y. 14225

R.J. ADAMS
R.P. ADAMS CO.
225 EAST PARK DR.
BUFFALO, N.Y. 14240

ROBERT F. NORRIS
S.M. FLICKINGER CO.
P.O. BOX 1086
BUFFALO, N.Y. 14240

S. SHEPHARD WILSON
LISK -SAVORY
901 FUHRMANN BLVD.
BUFFALO, N.Y. 14240

RAYMOND D. STEVENS JR.
PRATT & LAMBERT
P.O. BOX 22
BUFFALO, N.Y. 14240

ABRAHAM LEVIN
REGAL
P.O. BOX 861
BUFFALO, N.Y. 14240

HAROLD A. EGAN JR.
TWIN FAIR
ONE TWIN FAIR CORP.
BUFFALO, N.Y. 14240

WILLIAM H. WENDEL
CARBORUNDUM
CARBORUNDUM CENTER
NIAGARA FALLS, N.Y. 14302

PAUL E. HAAS
CONBOW
880 MILITARY RD.
NIAGARA FALLS, N.Y. 14304

DAVID POLUR
ELECTRO NETWORKS
MAPLE ST.
CALEDONIA, N.Y. 14423

FREDERICK W. SARKIS
BRISTOL
R.D. NO. 3
CANANDAGUA, N.Y. 14424

MARVIN SANDS
CANANDAIGUA WINE
116 BUFFALO ST.
CANANDAIGUA, N.Y. 14424

L.A. MORRIS JR.
CLIFTRONICS
2 SOUTH ST.
CLIFTON SPRINGS, N.Y. 14432

DAVID G. GOLDSTEIN
DYNAMIC OPTICS
317 E. CHESTNUT ST.
EAST ROCHESTER, N.Y. 14445

ROGER WOODWARD
FERRONICS
60 N. LINCOLN RD.
EAST ROCHESTER, N.Y. 14445

ARTHUR J. BRAUER
ROBINEX INT'L.
P.O. BOX 207
EAST ROCHESTER, N.Y. 14445

K.H. KOSTUSIAK
DETECTION SYSTEMS
400 MASON RD.
FAIRPORT, N.Y. 14450

JR.R. COSTELLO
PURFICATION
75 EAST NORTH ST.
GENEVA, N.Y. 14456

EDWARD B. HATTON
INFORMATION TRANSFER
235 MURRAY ST.
NEWARD, N.Y. 14513

JACK T. HAMMER
HOUSING SYSTEMS
2135 FIVE MILE LINE RD.
PENFIELD, N.Y. 14526

ROBERT L. INSON
PENN YAN EXPRESS
100 W. LAKE RD.
PENN YAN, N.Y. 14527

R.A. FURMAN
INFODATA
30 A STATE ST.
PITTSFORD, N.Y. 14534

JOSEPH C. TOLLEY
VOLPEX CORP.
1100 PITTSFORD-VICTOR RD.
PITTSFORD, N.Y. 14534

WILLIAM FLEMING
STYLEX HOMES
1864 SCOTTSVILLE-MUMFORD RD.
SCOTTSVILLE, N.Y. 14546

E.G. STRASENBURGH
R.D. PROD.
6132 RTE. 96
VICTOR, N.Y. 14564

WALLACE J. WOLF
BASTIAN BROS.
1600 CLINTON AVE. N.
ROCHESTER, N.Y. 14601

R.H. GUTKIN
DYNALAB
350 COMMERCE DR.
ROCHESTER, N.Y. 14601

HUGH E. CUMMINGS
CURTICE-BURNS
P.O. BOX 681
ROCHESTER,N.Y. 14602

FRED R. SILVERSTEIN
NEISNER BROS.
49 EAST AVE.
ROCHESTER, N.Y. 14602

EDWARD H. CARSON
TOBIN PACKING
900 MAPLE ST.
ROCHESTER, N.Y. 14602

WILLIAM E. CUTLER
DOLLINGER
ONE TOWNLINE CIRCLE
ROCHESTER, N.Y. 14603

ISAAC GORDON
I. GORDON RLTY. CORP.
16 EAST MAIN ST.
ROCHESTER. N.Y. 14604

GILBERT G. MC CURDY
MC CURDY & CO.
285 EAST MAIN ST.
ROCHESTER, N.Y. 14604

GORDON S. PRESENT
THE PRESENT CO.
82 ST. PAUL ST.
ROCHESTER , N.Y. 14604

WILLIAM G. VONBERG
SYBRON
1100 MIDTOWN TOWER
ROCHESTER, N.Y. 14604

ROBERT H. HURLBUT
VARI-CARE
814 MEDICAL ARTS BLDG.
ROCHESTER, N.Y. 14604

ANTHONY H. YONDA JR.
YONDATA
40 ST. PAUL ST.
ROCHESTER, N.Y. 14604

W.J. HOOT
GENESEE BREWING
445 ST. PAUL ST.
ROCHESTER, N.Y. 14505

KURT ENSLEIN
GENESEE COMPUTER
20 UNIVERSITY AVE.
ROCHESTER, N.Y. 14605

C.H. CLARRIDGE
ROCHESTER INSTRUMENTS
275 NORTH UNION ST.
ROCHESTER, N.Y. 14605

HOWARD A. BEACHNER
HYDRAULIC REFUSE
101 LOUISE ST.
ROCHESTER, N.Y. 14606

A.J. GOLDSTEIN
OPIC
571 LYELL AVE.
ROCHESTER, N.Y. 14606

M.S. STILES
SCIENTIFIC RADIO
367 ORCHARD ST.
ROCHESTER, N.Y. 14606

R.F. SYKES
SYKES DATATRONICS
375 ORCHARD ST.
ROCHESTER, N.Y. 14606

W.J. BERK
TRANSMATION
977 MT. READ BLVD.
ROCHESTER, N.Y. 14606

HENRY D. CARHART JR.
CARHART PHOTO
105 COLLEGE AVE.
ROCHESTER, N.Y. 14607

JOSEPH P. FOX
CHAMPION PRODUCTS
115 COLLEGE AVE.
ROCHESTER, N.Y. 14607

ALFRED J. MURRER
GLEASON WORKS
1000 UNIVERSITY AVE.
ROCHESTER, N.Y. 14607

DOUGLAS M. JOHNSON
STECHER-TRAUNG-SCHMIDT
274 NORTH GOODMAN ST.
ROCHESTER, N.Y. 14607

ROBERT A. LANG
INTERSTATE
33 CANAL ST.
ROCHESTER, N.Y. 14608

S.J. ALBANO
TEL-PAGE
74 LAKE AVE.
ROCHESTER, N.Y. 14608

H.A. AFFEL JR.
COMPUTER CONSOLES
97 HOMBOLDT ST.
ROCHESTER, N.Y. 14609

ALFRED N. WATSON
LIVING CARE CENTER
45 CROUCH ST.
ROCHESTER, N.Y. 14609

A.F. TADDEO
TADDEO CONST.
873 MERCHANTS RD.
ROCHESTER, N.Y. 14609

D.H. GOLDMAN
RELTRON
45 GOULD ST.
ROCHESTER, N.Y. 14610

WILLIAM J. STILZE
RF COMMUNICATIONS
1680 UNIVERSITY AVE.
ROCHESTER, N.Y. 14610

THEODORE LEVINSON
STAR SUPERMARKETS
175 HUMBOLDT ST.
ROCHESTER, N.Y. 14610

LEWIS G. LYNN
TRI-AID SCIENCES
161 NORRIS DR.
ROCHESTER, N.Y. 14610

AMIEL J. MOKHIBER
AMIEL'S ENTERPRISES
854 MAIN ST. WEST
ROCHESTER, N.Y. 14611

H. B. DORREN
STELLEX IND.
380 COTTAGE ST.
ROCHESTER, N.Y. 14611

STANLEY FULWILER
TAPECON
P.O. BOX 4741
ROCHESTER, N.Y. 14612

DONALD L. CLARK
BERNZ-OMATIC
740 DRIVING PARK AVE.
ROCHESTER, N.Y. 14613

NEIL O. BRODERSON
CAP-ROC.
300 STATE ST.
ROCHESTER, N.Y. 14614

WILLIAM A. LANG
ROCHESTER TRANSIT
103 HIGHLAND PARKWAY
ROCHESTER, N.Y. 14620

HARRY C. MILLER
SARGENT & GREENLEAF
24 SENECA AVE.
ROCHESTER, N.Y. 14621

D.L. DECKER
TECHTRAN IND.
580 JEFFERSON RD.
HENRIETTA, N.Y. 14623

G.H. McNEIL
BUNNINGTON
60 SAGINAW DR.
ROCHESTER, N.Y. 14623

GOODMAN SALZMAN
DECKER-MOHN
71 SAGINAW DR.
ROCHESTER, N.Y. 14623

S.J. MAVES
MAVES COFFEE
60 MUSHROOM BLVD.
ROCHESTER, N.Y. 14623

SEYMOUR TESLER
PANTS 'N STUFF
38 SAWINAW DR.
ROCHESTER, N.Y. 14623

N.A. DE MARE
PK. MANAGEMENT
2805 W. HENRIETTA RD.
ROCHESTER, N.Y. 14623

BERNARD KOZEL
KAYEX
1000 MILLSTEAD WAY
ROCHESTER. N.Y. 14624

GERALD G. WILMOT
PAGE AIRWAYS
1265 SCOTTSVILLE RD.
ROCHESTER, N.Y. 14624

HARRY TURNER
A.D. DATA
830 LINDEN AVE.
ROCHESTER, N.Y. 14625

S.J. REFERMAT
LASER ENERGY
320 NORTH WASHINGTON ST.
ROCHESTER, N.Y. 14625

ROBERT E. NAUM
NAUM BROS.
2373 RIDGE RD. WEST
ROCHESTER, N.Y. 14626

HAROLD J. RUTTENBERG
AVM CORP.
JONES & GIFFORD
JAMESTOWN, N.Y. 14701

W.E. RECTOR
CRESCENT NIAGARA
200 HARRISON ST.
JAMESTOWN, N.Y. 14701

ANDERSON, PRESIDENT
DAHLSTROM CORP.
111 WEST 2ND. ST.
JAMESTOWN, N.Y. 14701

E.W. CAFLISCH
PENNINSULA RESOURCES
P.O. BOX 100
CLYMER, N.Y. 14724

JAMES McLAUGHLIN
ACME ELECTRIC
20 WATER ST.
CUBA, N.Y. 14727

WILLIAM D. BARRY
MESSER OIL
101 N. UNION ST.
OLEAN, N.Y. 14760

ARTHUR S. WOLCOTT
SENECA FOODS
74 SENECA ST.
DUNDEE, N.Y. 14837

BRUCE M. BABCOCK
BABCOCK IND.
P.O. BOX 280
ITHACA, N.Y. 14850

LYNN CARTER
SHEPARD NILES CRANE
SCHUYLER AVE.
MONTOUR FALLS, N.Y. 14865

STUART KOMER
ARTISTIC GREETINGS
1575 LAKE ST.
ELMIRA, N.Y. 14901

D.G. ANDERSON
HARDINGE BROS.
1420 COLLEGE AVE.
ELMIRA, N.Y. 14901

JOHN H. FASSETT
HILLIARD CORP.
100 WEST FOURTH ST.
ELMIRA, N.Y. 14901

T.R. ALLEN JR.
BOLLINGER
1001 DUSS AVE.
AMBRIDGE, PA. 15003

RICHARL L. SHAW
MICHAEL BAKER
P.O. BOX 280
BEAVER, PA. 15009

S.B. BUCHWACH
ACTION IND.
460 NIXON RD.
CHESWICK, PA. 15024

ROBERT W. OSTERMAYER JR.
PENNSYLVANIA IND.
120 STATE ST.
CLAIRTON, PA. 15025

L.H. MAJOR
SOUTHERN PIPE
LOCK BOX G.
FREEDOM, PA. 15042

R.S. MERRICK, SR.
STANDARD HORSE NAIL
14TH. ST. & 5TH. AVE.
NEW BRIGHTON, PA. 15066

RALPH C. LAURO
MOTOR COILS
100 TALBOT AVE.
BRADDOCK,PA. 15104

L.A. WIBLE
UNION ELECTRIC
P.O. BOX 465
CARNEGIE, PA. 15106

F.E. SCHUCHMAN JR.
HOMESTEAD IND.
P.O. BOX 348
CARAPOLIS, PA. 15108

JOSEPH A. SCIOSCIA
ROFFLER IND.
400 CHESS ST.
CORAPOLIS, PA. 15108

WILLIAM T. WITHERS
G.C. MURPHY
531 FIFTH AVE.
MC KEESPORT, PA. 15131

C.T. MARSHALL
EDGEWATER CORP.
OAKMONT, PA. 15139

FRANK J. PIZZUTO
KELLY & COHEN
3820 WILLIAM PENN HIGHWAY
MONROEVILLE, PA. 15146

S.W. SAMPSON
SAMPSON MILLER ASSOC.
2620 MOSSIDE BLVD.
MONROEVILLE, PA. 15146

BERNARD C. SABEL
THE UNION CORP.
JONES ST.
VERONA, PA. 15147

ROBERT G. MC ILROY
ROBROY IND.
P.O. BOX 97
VERONA, PA. 15147

ANTHONY MEROLA
AMEROLA PROD.
5258 BUTLER ST.
PITTSBURGH, PA. 15201

ROBERT C. EAZOR
EAZOR EXPRESS
EAZOR SQ.
PITTSBURGH, PA. 15201

PAUL H. DALY
HEPPENSTALL
4620 HATFIELD ST.
PITTSBURGH, PA. 15201

HENRY E. HALLER JR.
NAT'L. VALVE
158   49TH. ST.
PITTSBURGH, PA. 15201

WALTER SIECKMAN
PENN. ENGINEERING
P.O. BOX 4055
PITTSBURGH, PA. 15201

LOUIS J. SLAIS
PITTSBURGH BREWING
3340 LIBERTY AVE.
PITTSBURGH, PA. 15201

C.J. RAMSBURGE JR.
PITTSBURGH GAGE
3000 LIBERTY AVE.
PITTSBURGH, PA. 15201

MILTON G. HULME JR.
CATALYST RESEARCH
201 N. BRADDOCK AVE.
PITTSBURGH, PA. 15208

HARRY T. GARDNER
WILLIAM G. JOHNSTON CO.
1130 RIDGE AVE.
PITTSBURGH, PA. 15212

HARRY GURRENTZ
CURB-PAC
200 S. CRAIG ST.
PITTSBURGH, PA. 15213

MELVIN H. LETCHINGER
DECORATOR IND.
4615 FORBES AVE.
PITTSBURGH, PA. 15213

OLIVER J. STERLING
PITTSBURGH FAIRFAX
4614 FIFTH AVE.
PITTSBURGH, N.Y. 15213

LOUIS BERKMAN
AMPCO-PITTSBURGH CORP.
700 PORTER BLDG.
PITTSBURGE, PA. 15219

PHILLIP H. SMITH
COPPERWELD
FRICK BLDG.
PITTSBURGH, PA. 15219

MELVIN H. LETCHINGER
DECORATOR IND.
4615 FORBES AVE.
PITTSBURGH, PA. 15219

ROBERT C. TYO
DISSTON INC.
601 GRANT ST.
PITTSBURGH, PA. 15219

EDWARD G. PERKINS
FISHER SCIENTIFIC
711 FORBES ST.
PITTSBURGH, PA. 15219

KENTON E. McELHATTAN
NAT'L. MINE SERVICE
3000 KOPPER BLDG.
PITTSBURGH, PA. 15219

J.S. MORROW
H.K. PORTER CO.
PORTER BLDG.
PITTSBURGH, PA. 15219

ALAN AMPER
STEELMET
1204 GRANT BLDG.
PITTSBURGH, PA 15219

HENRY M. ALTMAN JR.
COMPUTER RESEARCH
7 PARKWAY CENTER
PITTSBURGH, PA. 15220

JAMES L. LA FLUER
GTI CORP.
1910 COCHRAN RD.
PITTSBURGH, PA. 15220

ROBERT C.EMMETT
PITTSBURGH TESTING LABS.
850 POPLAR ST.
PITTSBURGH, PA. 15220

D.H. WEIS
THERMAL IND.
301 BRUSHTON AVE.
PITTSBURGH, PA. 15221

ADALBERT SCHULZ
DEFENSIVE INSTRUMENTS
925 PENN AVE.
PITTSBURGH, PA. 15222

ROBERT DICKEY III
DRAVO CORP.
ONE OLIVER PLAZA
PITTSBURGH, PA. 15222

W.E. BIERER
EQUIMARK
OLIVER PLAZA
PITTSBURGH, PA. 15222

EDWARD F. DAVIDSON
HOVERMARINE
THREE GATEWAY CENTER
PITTSBURGH,PA. 15222

FURMAN SOUTH, III
LAVA CRUCIBLE-REFRIG.
OLIVER BLDG.
PITTSBURGH, PA. 15222

JEROME N. LEHMAN
MYLAN LABS.
ONE OVIVER PLAZA
PITTSBURGH, PA. 15222

WILLIAM H. REA
OLIVER TYRONE CORP.
ONE OLIVER PLAZA
PITTSBURGH, PA 15222

AUREL F. SAROSDY
PITTSBURGH FORGINGS
401 LIBERTY AVE.
PITTSBURGH, PA. 15222

DOUGLAS A. JONES
H. H. ROBERTSON IND.
TWO GATEWAY CENTER
PITTSBURGH, PA. 15222

PAUL M. HICKOX
THRIFT INVESTMENT
GATEWAY 3 - 18TH. FLR.
PITTSBURGH, PA. 15222

WILLIAM G. BLESSING
THOMAS MACHINE CO.
BUTLER PLANK RD.
PITTSBURGH, PA. 15223

WILLIAM H. KNOELL
CYCLOPS CORP.
650 WASHINGTON RD.
PITTSBURGH, PA. 15228

M. J. GREENE
KINCAID IND.
615 WASHINGTON RD.
PITTSBURGH, PA. 15228

JACK ROSEMAN
ON-LINE SYSTEMS
115 EVERGREEN HEIGHTS DR.
PITTSBURGH, PA. 15229

JOHN D. IVERSEN
MESTA MACHINE
P.O. BOX 1466
PITTSBURGH, PA. 15230

H. R. HEARD
SALEM CORP.
P.O. BOX 2222
PITTSBURGH, PA. 15230

C.C. KLEINSCHMIDT
WILLIAMS & CO.
901 PENN. AVE.
PITTSBURGH, PA. 15233

NEAL H. HOLMES
ALLIED SECURITY
2840 LIBRARY RD.
PITTSBURGH, PA. 15234

E. W. MERRY
MINE SAFETY
400 PENN CENTER BLVD.
PITTSBURGH, PA. 15235

JOSEPH M. KATZ
THE PAPERCRAFT CORP.
PAPERCRAFT PARK
PITTSBURGH, PA. 15238

WALTER J. KAUFMAN
WATSON-STANDARD
P.O. BOX 11250
PITTSBURGH, PA. 15238

NATHAN N. TYSON
TYSON METAL
1909 NEW TEXAS RD.
PITTSBURGH, PA. 15239

MALCOLM M. PRINE
RYAN HOMES
100 NORTH WREN DR.
PITTSBURGH, PA. 15243

GEORGE P. BAUMUNK
WASHINGTON STEEL
WOODLAND & GRIFFITHS
WASHINGTON, PA. 15301

DELVIN MILLER
WASHINGTON TROTTING ASSN.
P.O. BOX 417
MEADOWLANDS, PA. 15347

MARK B'. SILVERBURG
JEANNETTE CORP.
BULLITT AVE.
JEANNETTE, PA. 15644

ALEX G. MC KENNA
KENNAMETAL
P.O. BOX 346
LATROBE, PA. 15650

J.C. NEWCOMER
NEWCOMER PROD.
P.O. BOX 272
LATROBE, PA. 15650

R.A. DOMIN
YOUNGWOOD ELECTRONIC
4060 NORBATROL AVE.
MURRYSVILLE, PA. 15668

B.J. ERENSTEIN
JIFFY FOODS
RTE. 286
SALTSBURG, PA. 15681

G.P. REMEY
ROCHESTER & PITT. COAL
655 CHURCH
INDIANA, PA. 15701

FRANK GORELL
SEASON ALL IND.
RTE. 119 S.
INDIANA, PA. 15701

D.H. ERICKSON JR.
ERICKSON CORP.
P.O. BOX 527
DUBOIS, PA. 15801

JOHN A. WINFIELD
BROCKWAY GLASS
MC CULLOGH AVE.
BROCKWAY, PA. 15824

LEONARD J. BLACK
GLOSSER BROS.
FRANKLIN Y LOCUST STS.
JOHNSTOWN, PA. 15901

G. FESLER EDWARDS
PENN TRAFFIC
319 WASHINGTON ST.
JOHNSTOWN, PA. 15901

GERALD N. POTTS
VULCAN
AVE. E.
LATROBE, PA. 15950

CHARLES G. BRAZIL
PENN METAL FABRICATORS
1002 RAILROAD ST.
WINDBER, PA. 15963

UMBERTO MONAGELLI
INT'L. STAPLE
EAST BUTLER RD.
BUTLER, PA. 16001

J. ROBERT BROWN
SPANG IND.
P.O. BOX 751
BUTLER, PA. 16001

ROBERT E. IRR
SUN DRUG
P.O. BOX 751
BUTLER, PA. 16001

WARREN E. HOEFFNER
REX-HIDE
EAST BRADY, PA. 16028

J. W. SANT
UNIVERSAL-RUNDLE
P.O. BOX 960
NEW CASTLE, PA. 16101

IRWIN M. YANOWITZ
SHARON TUBE
134 MILL ST.
SHARON, PA. 16146

CHARLES D. FAGAN JR.
SHARPSVILLE STEEL
SHARPSVILLE, PA. 16150

W. SANTINI JR.
PHOENIX MATERIALS
833 BUTLER RD.
KITTANNING, PA. 16201

QUENTIN E. WOOD
QUAKER STATE OIL
QUAKER STATE BLDG.
OIL CITY, PA. 16302

BRUCE TAYLOR
PENN AIRE AVIATION
PENN AIRE OFFICE BLDG. RTE. 8
FRANKLIN, PA. 16323

JOHN L. BLAIR
NEW PROCESS
220 HICKORY ST.
WARREN, PA. 16365

HARRY A. LOGAN, JR.
UNITED REFINING
BOX 780
WARREN, PA. 16365

JOHN E. BRITTON
TANNETICS
700 FIRST NATIONAL BANK BLDG.
ERIE, PA. 16501

ROBERT D. WALKER
HIGH PRESSURE EQUIP.
1222 LINDEN AVE.
ERIE, ·PA. 16506

HENRY E. FISH
AMERICAN STERLIZER
P.O. BOX 620
ERIE, PA. 16512

JAMES J. WALSH
ERIE TECH. PROD.
P.O. BOX 961
ERIE, PA. 16512

ALBERT F. DUVAL
HAMMERMILL PAPER
P.O. BOX 1440
ERIE, PA. 16512

D.C. STROUD
PRESCOTECH INC.
859 EAST 8TH. ST.
ERIE, PA. 16512

R.T. MOSHER
TECHNO
P.O. BOX 1416
ERIE, PA. 16512

R.E. ROGERS
WHITE EAGLE
P.O. BOX 6177
ERIE, PA. 16512

DAVID M. ZURN
ZURN IND.
2214 W. 8TH. ST.
ERIE, PA. 16512

EDWARD A. OLIPHANT
SMALL TUBE
SPRING MEADOWS
ALTOONA, PA. 16603

DONALD G. EVERHART
REEVES PARVIN
IND. PARK
HUNTINGDON, PA. 16652

H.C. O'CONNOR JR.
CHEMCUT CORP.
500 SCIENCE PK. RD.
STATE COLLEGE, PA. 16801

ROBERT H. WECKER
NEASE CHEM. CO.
P.O. BOX 221
STATE COLLEGE, PA. 16801

EUGENE E. COSTELLO
COTY'S ENTERPRISES
P.O. BOX 114
CAMP HILL, PA. 17011

J.T. SIMPSON
HARSCO CORP.
CAMP HILL, PA. 17011

WILLIAM S. MASLAND
C.H. MASLAND & SONS
SPRING RD.
CARLISLE, PA. 17013

JACOB J. MYERS JR.
AMALGAMATED AUTOMOTIVE
320 MARKET ST. BOX 17
LEMOYNE, PA. 17043

JOHN A. WADDELL
MANN EDGE TOOL
LEWISTOWN, PA. 17044

JOHN N. HALL
HALL'S MOTOR
6060 CARLISLE PIKE
MECHANICBURG, PA. 17055

JOHN C. REDMOND JR.
WILCOX FORGING
E. ALLEN ST.
MECHANICSBURG, PA. 17055

JOSEPH P. DECHERT
DECHERT DYNAMICS
713 W. MAIN ST.
PALMYRA, PA. 17078

LEWIS E. LEHRMAN
RITE AID
TRINDLE & RAILROAD
SHIREMANSTOWN, PA. 17091

ROCCO A. ORTENZIO
REHAB
1511 N. FRONT ST.
HARRISBURGE, PA. 17102

GEORGE H. HOLDER
HERSHEY CREAMERY
P.O. BOX 1821
HARRISBURG, PA. 17105

JAMES V. RAPAGNA
TERRYPHONE
P.O. BOX 4038
HARRISBURG, PA. 17111

EUGENE C. CLARKE JR.
CHAMBERSBURGE
DERBYSHIRE ST.
CHAMBERSBURG, PA. 17201

J.L. GROVE
JLG IND.
P.O. BOX 695
MC CONNELSBURG, PA. 17233

J. MARTIN BENCHOFF
GROVE MFG.
P.O. BOX 21
SHADY GROVE, PA. 17256

ALBERT EICHNER
DOE SPUN
CONNELLY RD.
EMIGSVILLE, PA. 17318

GORDON P. KING
HANOVER SHOE
118 CARLISLE ST.
HANOVER, PA. 17331

E. J. CAUGHLIN
AMERICAN INSULATOR
NEW FREEDOM, PA. 17349

P. H. GLATEFELTER III
P.H. GLATEFELTER CO.
228 S. MAIN ST.
SPRING GROVE, PA. 17362

B.J. RAYBURN
CAMPBELL CHAIN
3990   E. MARKET ST.
YORK, PA. 17402

ROBERT GROSSMAN
EMONS IND.
490 E. MARKET ST.
YORK, PA. 17403

JOHN U. WISOTZKEY
MAPLE PRESS CO.
210-234 E. YORT ST.
YORK, PA. 17403

ROBERT J. DE TREY
DENTSPLY IT'L.
500 WEST COLLEGE AVE.
YORK, PA. 17404

EDWARD R. MC DONALD
FECOR IND.
P.O. BOX 1602
YORK, PA. 17405

LOUIS D. ROOT JR.
NEW YORK WIRE
441 E. MARKET ST.
YORK, PA. 17405

L. DOYLE ANKRUM
P.A. & S. SMALL
1100 N. SHERMAN ST.
YORK, PA. 17405

G. COOPER
THERM-AIRE
630 LOCKS MILL RD.
YORK, PA. 17405

PAUL C. RAUB
YORK CORRUGATING
P.O. BOX 70
YORK, PA. 17405

H. DIETZ KELLER
YORK-HOOVER
LINDEN & BELVIDERE AVE.
YORK, PA. 17405

H.E. ROHRBACK
EBY SHOE
136 N. STATE ST.
EPHRATA, PA. 17522

A.Y. JOHNSON
PENN. SCALE
21 GRAYBILL RD.
LEOLA,PA, 17540

R.G. WOOLWORTH
WOODSTREAM CORP.
FRONT & LOCUST STS.
LITITZ,PA. 17543

JOHN F. GARBER JR.
PENN DAIRIES
1801 HEMPSTEAD RD.
LANCASTER, PA. 17601

D.R. BAKER
CONESTOGA TRANSPORTATION
825 E. CHESTNUT ST.
LANCASTER, PA. 17602

H.W. LORIN
CYTON IND.
208 CENTERVILLE RD.
LANCASTER, PA. 17603

R.K. DODGE
DODGE CORK
11 LAUREL ST.
LASCASTER, PA. 17603

W.W. POSEY II
POSEY IRON
560 SO. PRINCE ST.
LANCASTER, PA. 17603

JAMES W. LIDDELL
AC & S CORP.
120 N. LIKE ST.
LANCASTER, PA. 17604

J. H. BINNS
ARMSTRONG CORK
LIBERTY & CHARLOTTE STS.
LANCASTER, PA. 17604

JAMES W. HART
SCHICK
216 GREENFIELD RD.
LANCASTER, PA. 17604

GEORGE BONSALL
BRO-DART
1609 MEMORIAL AVE.
WILLIAMSPORT, PA. 17701

HAROLD J. STROHMANN
STROHMANN BROS.
1685 FOUR MILE DR.
WILLIAMSPORT, PA. 17701

LESTER F. WIDMANN
L.F. WIDMANN INC.
738 BELLEFONTE AVE.
LOCK HAVEN, PA. 17745

E.A. ROBB
SUNBURY MILK
178 LENKER AVE.
SUNBURY, PA. 17901

SIGFRIED WEIS
WEIS MARKETS
1000 S. SECOND ST.
SUNBURY, PA. 17801

G.L. COHN
AG-MET
P.O. BOX 216
FRACKVILLE, PA. 17931

L. ROSEN
YANKEE PLASTICS
RINGTOWN, PA. 17967

JAMES J. CONWAY
THE BETHLEHEM CORP.
P.O. BOX 348
EASTON, PA. 18017

T.R. ANDERSON
LEHIGH COAL
528 N. NEW ST.
BETHLEHEM,PA. 18018

P.A. LENTZ
COPLAY CEMENT
COPLAY, PA. 18037

BERNARD RICHARDS
ALPHA PORTLAND IND.
15 SOUTH THIRD ST.
EASTON, PA. 18042

RUSSELL J. MC CHESNEY
BINNEY & SMITH
P.O. BOX 431
EASTON, PA. 18042

E.P. HARTNETT
FURNTEC IND.
430 LINCOLN ST.
EASTON, PA. 18042

RAYMOND A. BARTOLACCI
LANECO
1720 BUTLER ST.
EASTON, PA. 18042

MICHAEL E. HEISLEY
SI HANDLING SYSTEMS
P.O. BOX 70
EASTON, PA. 18042

RAYMOND G. PERELMAN
BELMONT IND.
FOURTH & FURNACE STS.
EMMAUS, PA. 18049

R.H. FOSTER
WHITEHALL CEMENT MFG.
5160 MAIN ST.
WHITEHALL, PA. 18052

JEROME MARKOWITZ
ALLEN ORGAN CO.
MACUNGIE, PA. 18062

M.R. BULLOCK
CASA INT'L.
1132 HAMILTON ST.
ALLENTOWN, PA. 18101

P.I. BERMAN
HESS'S
9TH. & HAMILTON STS.
ALLENTOWN, PA. 18101

HENRY A. LUBSEN JR.
NATURE'S PRODUCTS
COMMONWEALTH BLDG. RM. 607
ALLENTOWN, PA. 18101

ROBLEE B. MARTIN
KEYSTONE PORTLAND
2280 HAMILTON ST.
ALLENTOWN, PA. 18105

WILLIAM J. YOUNG
LEHIGH PORTLAND CEMENT
YOUNG BLDG.
ALLENTOWN, PA. 18105

J. B. WILLS
EASTERN IND. INC.
WESCOSVILLE, PA. 18106

R.C. GENNARO
UNITED RESEARCH
P.O. BOX 307
HAZELTON, PA. 18201

JOHN G. HORSMAN
BUCK HILL FALLS CO.
BUCK HILL FALLS, PA. 18323

WILLIAM S. WYCKOFF
E.W. IND.
1410 SPRUCE ST.
STROUDSBURG, PA. 18360

GURDON W. WATTLES
AMERICAN MFG.
206 WILLOW AVE.
HONESDALE, PA. 18431

GERALD J. SOUTHERTON
SOUTHERTON CORP.
214 NINTH ST.
HONESDALE, PA. 18431

JOHN R. THOMAS
WESEL MFG.
1141 N. WASHINGTON AVE.
SCRANTON, PA. 18501

S.H. ALFIERO
MARK IV HOMES
HAMPTON IND. PARK
TAYLOR, PA. 18504

HARRY KANOFF
TEN-DA BRAND
BIRNEY AVE.
MOOSIC, PA. 18507

D. FIEGLEMAN
ASSOC. SCRANTON IND.
2000 ROSANNA AVE.
SCRANTON, PA. 18509

IRVING GROSSMAN
SCRANTON CORP.
1313 MEYLERT AVE.
SCRANTON, PA. 18509

RICHARD W. KISLIK
INTEXT
OAK & PAWNEE STS.
SCRANTON, PA. 18515

MARVIN SHILLER
SHILLER CHEM. INC.
YATESVILLE, PA. 18640

E.P. BERG
ATLAS CHAIN
P.O. BOX 27
WEST PITTSTON, PA. 18643

SEYMOUR HOLTZMAN
JEWELCOR
50 ANN ST.
WEST PITTSON, PA. 18643

ROSS V. SWAIN
ELECTRONICS, MISSILES
P.O. BOX 116
WHITE HAVEN, PA. 18661

V.C. DIEHM
POCONO DOWNS
RTE. 315
WILKES-BARRE, PA. 18702

JAMES B. POST
POST COACH
730 CASEY AVE.
WILKES-BARRE,PA. 18702

ADRIAN M. PEARSALL
CRAFT ASSOC.
1212 SCOTT ST.
WILKES-BARRE, PA. 18705

SIGMUND W. FRIEDMAN
RECORD CLUB
P.O. BOX 22
YORK, PA. 18705

DAVID F. HANSEN
PENN. ENTERPRISES
33 PUBLIC SQ.
WILES-BARRE, PA. 18711

EMIL MIHALKO
INERTIAL MOTORS
280 N. BROAD ST.
DOYLESTOWN, PA. 18901

J. HOWARD FOOTE
PENN. ENG. & MFG.
P.O. BOX 311
DOYLESTON, PA. 18901

A. PASSERIN
PROFESSIONAL CARE
BOX 447
BUCKINGHAM, PA. 18912

HAROLD ISEN
PARAMOUNT PACKAGING
202 OAK AVE.
CHALFONT, PA. 18914

L.P. KEDSON
SOLID STATE SCIENTIFIC
MONTGOMERY,IND. CENTER
MONTGOMERVILLE, PA. 18936

JOHN N. VEALE
OPTICAL SCANNING
P.O. BOX 40
NEWTOWN, PA. 18940

P.G. BOSTOCK
AMERICAN BIOCULTURE
P.O. BOX 100
PLUMSTEADVILLE, PA. 18949

HARRIS N. HOLLIN
LEMMON PHARMACAL
P.O. BOX 30
SELLERSVILLE, PA. 18960

WM. F. MITCHELL
ENVIRONMENTAL TECT. CORP.
COUNTY LINE IND. PK.
SOUTHAMPTON, PA. 18966

LESTER R. VOID
ELECTRO-MECH. INSTRUMENT
8TH. & CHESTNUT
PERKASIE, PA. 18944

JAY H. TOLSON
FISCHER & PORTER
COUNTY LINE RD.
WARMINSTER, PA. 18974

WILLIAM M. KAY
HURST PERFORMANCE
50 WEST ST. RD.
WARMINSTER, PA. 18974

EARL J. SERFASS
MILTON ROY CO.
201 IVYLAND RD.
E. IVYLAND, PA. 18974

ALAN B. MILLER
AMERICAN MEDICORP.
1 DECKER SQ.
BALA CYNWYD, PA. 19004

HENRY C. BISCHOFF
REFRESHMENT MACH.
300 JACKSONVI LE RD.
WARMINISTER, PA. 18974

G.B. STOLLSTEIMER
FLEXIBLE CIRCUITS
PAUL VALLEY IND. PK.
WARRINGTON, PA. 18976

CONSTANTINE STEPHANO
NEW COMMUNITIES
968 EASTON RD.
WARRINGTON, PA. 18976

GARY E. ERLBAUM
PANELRAMA
44 W. LANCASTER AVE.
ARDMORE, PA. 19003

S.W. ANGEL
AID
TWO DECKER SQ.
BALA CYNWYD, PA. 19004

NORMAN M. KRANZDORF
AMTERRE DEVELOPMENT
2 DECKER SQ.
BALA CYNWYD, PA. 19004

J.M. BENJAMIN JR.
BIONIC INSTRUMENTS
221 ROCKHILL RD.
BALA CYNWYD, PA. 19004

RALPH J. ROBERTS
COMCAST
ONE BELMONT AVE. STE.227
BALA CYNWYD, PA. 19004

JOSEPH J. DONAHUE
CONNELLY CONTAINERS
RIGHTERS FERRY RD.
BALA CYNWYD, PA. 19004

J.E. MORAN
GEN. REFRACT. CO.
50 MONUMENT RD.
BALA CYNWYD,PA. 19004

SHELDON H. GROSS
MUSIC FAIR
ONE BALA AVE. BLDG.
BALA CYNWYD, PA. 19004

WILLIAM SENNETT
TRANSPORT POOL
2 DECKER SQ.
BALA-CYNWYD, PA. 19004

HERBERT KURTZ
ROCKOWER BROS.
3103 PHILMONT AVE
HUNTINGDON VALLEY, PA. 19006

K. DE WITT
SONEX INC.
2337 PHILMONT AVE.
BETHAYRES, PA. 19006

JOSEPH WEXELBAUM
RED ROPE IND.
WOOD AVE.
BRISTOL, PA. 19007

R.A. SAMANS
SCANFORMS
181 RITTENHOUSE CIRCLE
BRISTOL, PA. 19007

ROBERT E. DAVIS
THIOKOL
EXECUTIVE OFFICES
BRISTOL, PA. 19007

ARNO E. KRUMBIEGEL
FIEDELCO
1200 E. LANCASTER AVE.
ROSEMONT, PA. 19010

JAMES T. BOLAN
KEWANEE IND.
P.O. BOX 591
BRYN MAWR, PA. 19010

JAMES M. BALLENGEE
PHILIDELPHIA SUBURBAN
762 LANCASTER AVE.
BRYN MAWR, PA. 19010

JOHN KUC
UPLAND
115 SIXTH ST.
UPLAND, PA. 19015

R. BARRY BORDEN
DELTA DATA
1765 WOODHAVEN DR.
CORNWELLS HEIGHTS, PA. 19020

LEONARD KLINGSBERG
UNITED PUBLISHING
3399 FORREST RD.
CORNWELLS HTS., PA. 19020

ERNEST A. SIEMSSEN
SELAS CORP.
DRESHER, PA. 19025

EUGENE ZEPKIN
LEARNING AIDS
1 NOWBOLO RD.
FAIRLESS HILLS, PA. 19030

HERBERT S. LOTMAN
KEYSTONE FOODS
600 KAISER DR.
FOLCROFT, PA. 19032

AYHAN HAKIMOGLU
AYDIN CORP.
401 COMMERCE DR.
FORT WASHINGTON, PA. 19034

ALDO J. DE FRANCESCO
NARCO SCIENTIFIC
COMMERCE DR.
FORT WASHINGTON, PA. 19034

JOHN W. ECKMAN
ROGER-AMCHEM
500 VIRGINIA DR.
FORT WASHINGTON, PA. 19034

F.A. NEUBAUER
EANCO
400 S. WARMINSTER RD.
HATBORO, PA. 19040

WILLIAM WATERMAN
WATERMAN INSTRUMENT
400 S. WARMISTER RD.
HATBORO, PA. 19040

WERNER THIESSEN
DELSTAR
551 W. LANCASTER AVE. STE. 202
HAVERFORD, PA. 19041

DAVID COHEN
PENNSTAR CO.
551 W. LANCASTER AVE. STE. 202
HAVERFORD, PA. 19041

WINFIELD SHIROS
DECISION DATA COMPUTER
100 WITMER RD.
HORSHAW, PA. 19044

RONALD G. MOYER
DIGI-LOG
BABYLON RD.
HORSHAM, PA. 19044

A.R. SEITEL
DREXEL IND.
MAPLE AVE.
HORSHAM, PA. 19044

ROBERT E. REYNOLDS
GLOVE TICKET
680 BLAIR MILL RD.
HORSHAM, PA. 19044

FREDERICK W. KULICKE JR.
KULICKE & SOFFA
507 PRUDENTIAL RD.
HORSHAM, PA. 19044

MORRIS YOFFE
AMERICAN MED.
THE BENJAMIN FOX-FOXCROFT SQ.
JENKINTOWN, PA. 19046

ARNOLD ROSENFELD
ROTEX
BENJAMIN FOX PAVILION STE.416
JENKINTOWN, PA. 19046

JOHN L. GARDE
SPECTRO
JENKINTOWN PLAZA
JENKINTOWN, PA. 19046

JOHN R. SELBY JR.
STANDARD PRESSED STEEL
TOWNSHIP LINE &OLD YORK RD.
JENKINTOWN, PA. 19046

EMANUEL GOREN
THOMAS HOLMES
TOWNSHIP & OLD YORK RD.
JENKINTOWN, PA. 19046

ROBERT B. MARSH
BETZ LABS.
4636 SOMERTON RD.
TREVOSE, PA. 19047

J.J. SITKIN
SITKIN SMELTING
P.O. BOX 708
LEWISTOWN, PA. 19053

STUART BOROCHANER
INT'L. WATERPURE
5 HEADLEY PL.
FALLSINGTON, PA. 19054

RICHARD M. BERMAN
ALPHAMEDICS MFG.
P.O. BOX 521
LEVITTOWN, PA. 19058

BRIAN G. HARRISON
FRANKLIN MINT
FRANKLIN CENTER, PA. 19063

ROBERT J. DOBUSKI
VULCANIZED RUBBER
5 S. PENN. AVE.
MORRISVILLE, PA. 19067

JOHN F. CRAMP
BRYN MAWR CAMP
69TH. ST. TERMINAL
UPPER DARBY, PA. 19082

H.R. LOCKE
ECKOL CONTAINER
1728 HAWTHORNE AVE.
HAVERTOWN, PA. 19083

ROBERT S. GOLDFIELD
CGS SCIENTIFIC
5 VALLEY FORGE EXECUTIVE MALL
WAYNE, PA. 19087

THEODORE A. BURTIS
SUN CO.
240 RADNOR-CHESTER RD.
ST. DAVIDS, PA. 19087

WILLIAM A. BABBOUR
CHILTON CO.
CHILTON WAY
RADNOR, PA. 19089

A.N. BECKMAN
KELLETT
P.O. BOX 35
WILLOW GROVE, PA. 19090

B.R. DRILL
TRANSDUCER
710 DAVISVILLE RD.
WILLOW GROVE, PA. 19090

H.S. GLICK
CONTINENTAL COMPUTER
CEDAR BROOK MALL
WYNCOTE, PA. 19095

MARVIN ORLEANS
FPA CORP.
P.O. BOX 176
WYNCOTE, PA. 19095

EARL T. McCUTCHEON
DRUG HOUSE
1011 W. BUTLER ST.
PHILA., PA. 19101

ROBERT R. SALYARD
A.V.C.
THREE GIRARD PLAZA
PHILA., PA. 19102

PATRICK R. FISCHETTI
AMERICAN VISUAL LIBRARY
1212 PENNWALT BLDG.
PHILA., PA. 19102

GEORGE BARTOL
HUNT MFG.
1405 LOCUST ST.
PHILA., PA. 19102

EDWIN E. TUTTLE
PENNWALT
PENNWALT BLDG.
PHILA., PA. 19102

A.E. LANG
PUBLICKER IND.
1429 WALNUT ST.
PHILA., PA. 19102

FRANK R. WALLACE JR
RESE ENGINEERING
2 PENN CENTER
PHILA., PA. 19102

JAMES SILL MORGAN
VESTAUR SECURITIES
1500 CHESTNUT ST. RM. 404
PHILIDELPHIA, PA. 19102

SAMUEL RUDOFKER
AFTER SIX
N.E. CORNER 22ND. & MARKET STS.
PHILA., PA. 19103

SIDNEY H. ELLIS
ATLANTIC GENERAL
1737 CHESTNUT ST.
PHILA., PA. 19103

HERBERT COOK
BLUEBIRD INC.
2000 MARKET ST.
PHILA., PA. 19103

W.R. GARRISON
CDI
5 PENN CENTER PLAZA
PHILA., PA. 19103

WILLIAM J. LEVITT JR.
DISC INC.
1825 WALNUT ST.
PHILA., PA. 19103

RONALD RUBIN
PAN AMERICAN
1700 MARKET ST.
PHILA., PA. 19103

ROBERT A. FOX
WARNER
1721 ARCH ST.
PHILA., PA. 19103

RAMSEY G. DI LIBERO
WASTE RESOURCES
1721 ARCH ST.
PHILA., PA. 19103

RAYMOND ROSENBERG
YARDIS
1922 SPRUCE ST.
PHILA., PA. 19103

JACK M. FRIEDLAND
FOOD FAIR
3175 JOHN F. KENNEDY BLVD.
PHILA., PA. 19104

JOSEPH W. LIPPINCOTT JR.
J.B. LIPPINCOTT CO.
EAST WASHINGTON SQ.
PHILA., PA. 19105

V.L. GREGORY
ROHM & HAAS
IND. MALL WEST
PHILA., PA. 19105

RANDALL E. COPELAND
STRAWBRIDGE & CLOTHIER
801 MARKET ST.
PHILA., PA. 19105

WILLIAM S. FISHMAN
ARA
INDEPENDENCE SQ.
PHILA., PA. 19106

PAUL RIMMEIR
LEISURE EXPOSITIONS
117 MARKET ST.
PHILA., PA. 19106

MC BEE BUTCHER
PHILA. BOURSE
21 S. FIFTH ST.
PHILA., PA. 19106

MAYLIN H. GREASER
AMERICAN DREDGING
12 SOUTH 12TH. ST.
PHILA., PA. 19107

S.J. ALESI
LPI DATA
146 N. 13TH. ST.
PHILA., PA. 19107

LAWRENCE KATZ
MAC ANDREWS & FORBES
1339 CHESTNUT ST.
PHILA., PA. 19107

WILLIAM H. SYLK
PENROSE IND.
107 N. JUNIPER ST.
PHILA., PA. 19107

E. B. LEISENRING JR.
WESTMORELAND COAL
123 S. BROAD ST.
PHILA., PA. 19109

BENJAMIN BROADSKY
PROGRESSIVE
RHAWN ST. AT WHITAKER AVE.
PHILA., PA. 19111

T.J. WHITAKER
EDGCOMB STEEL
P.O. BOX 6055
PHILA., PA. 19114

MORRIS GOLDWASSER
MOTIVATIONAL SYSTEMS
P.O. BOX 14383
PHILA., PA. 19115

ROBERT SHAY
MORLAN INT'L.
PHILMONT AVE. & BYBERRY BLVD.
PHILA., PA. 19116

HARVEY SALIGMAN
QUEEN CASUALS
10175 NORTHEAST AVE.
PHILA., PA. 19116

JOHN J. ROONEY
WILLIAM PENN RACING
LIBERTY BELL PARK-WOODHAVEN RD.
PHILA., PA. 19116

PAUL KANDEL
BAYNTON
2709-11 N. BROAD ST.
PHILA., PA. 19117

B.B. ROTKO
R.H. MEDICAL
60 E. TOWNSHIP RD.
ELKINS PARK, PA. 19117

BENJAMIN P. BOODMAN
AMERICAN-ED.
1400 E. WILLOW GROVE AVE.
PHILA., PA. 19118

BERNARD PAUL
GEN. HOBBIES
621 E. CAYUGA ST.
PHILA., PA. 19120

NEAL KOSMIN
CONVENIENCE FOODS
4563 TORRESDALE AVE.
PHILA., PA. 19124

E.J. CAHILL
DECO IND.
4250 ADAMS AVE.
PHILA., PA. 19124

ROBERT E. LINCK
WARREN-EHRET-LINCK
LUZERNE & E. STS.
PHILA., PA. 19124

MAURICE J. COOPER
CHARLES JACQUIN ET CIE
2633 TRENTON AVE.
PHILA., PA. 19125

AARON A. GOLD
OXFORD FIRST
6701 N. BROAD ST.
PHILA., PA. 19126

DANIEL R. KURSMAN
JETRONIC IND.
MAIN & COTTON STS.
PHILA., PA. 19127

JOSEPH PAUL
WALLACE LEISURE
31ST. & JEFFERSON STS.
PHILA., PA. 19127

DAVID FIELDS
CONSULTING TECH.
3824 TERRACE ST.
PHILA., PA. 19128

PHILIP J. BAUR JR.
TASTY BAKING
2801 HUNTING PK. AVE.
PHILA., PA. 19129

A.J. DE MARCO
DE MARCO BUSINESS
3747 RIDGE AVE.
PHILA., PA. 19132

M.E. STERNBERG
MOYCO IND.
21ST. & CLEARFIELD STS.
PHILA., PA. 19132

BENJAMIN STRAUSS
PEP BOYS
32 ND. & ALLEGHENY
PHILA., PA. 19132

ALBERT H. VOIGT
VOIGT IND.
17TH. & CAMBRIA
PHILA., PA. 19132

LYNMAR BROCK JR.
BROCK & CO.
420 EAST ERIE AVE.
PHILA., PA. 19134

WILLIAM FORMAN
DEVON APPAREL
3300 FRANKFORD AVE.
PHILA., PA. 19134

E. W. MUNZ
ROSELON IND.
C. ST. & INDIANA AVE.
PHILA., PA. 19134

BARNEY BERNSTEIN
SIM-KAR LIGHTING
D & TIOGA STS.
PHILIADELPHIA, PA. 19134

ROY E. HOCK
TECH. INC.
1952 EAST ALLEGHENY AVE.
PHILIDELPHIA, PA. 19134

JOHN A. BALDINGER
DEVAL AERO DYNAMICS
TULIP ABOVE COTTMAN
PHILA., PA. 19135

SAMUEL GRATZ
LANNETT CO.
9000 STATE RD.
PHILA., PA. 19136

THOMAS G. RITTENHOUSE
PRECISION GRINDING WHEEL
8301 TORRESDALE AVE.
PHILA., PA. 19136

DANIEL VELORIC
GERIATRIC MED. CENTER
63RD. & WALNUT ST.
PHILA., PA. 19139

BERNARD GITLOW
RENTEX SERVICES
2006 W. HUNTING PK. AVE.
PHILA., PA. 19140

J.R. LEWIS
KEYSTONE CABLE
18TH. & WINDRIM AVE.
PHILA., PA. 19141

JOSEPH L. NICHOLSON
QUAKER CITY
2204 SOUTH DELAWARE
PHILA., PA. 19142

HARRY G. MAZUR
DCA ED. PROD.
4865 STENTON AVE.
PHILA., PA. 19144

ARTHUR BROWN
VISUAL ART IND.
WAYNE & WINDRIM AVES.
PHILA., PA. 19144

EARL PERLOFF
PERLOFF BROS.
BOX 6499
PHILA., PA. 19145

JOSEPH GIUFFRIDA
FREDA CORP.
1334 S. FRONT ST.
PHILA., PA. 19147

LOUIS BAILIS
WELDED TUBE
SHUNK & VANDALIA STS.
PHILA., PA. 19148

F.N. PIASECKI
PIASECKI AIRCRAFT
ISLAND RD. INT'L. AIRPORT
PHILA., PA. 19153

BERNARD KANT
SILO INC.
800 PENROSE AVE.
PHILIDELPHIA, PA. 19153

STEPHEN D. RUDMAN
ELECTRO-NITE
COMLY & DECATUR RDS.
PHILA., PA. 19154

BENJAMIN LEVY
MAJESTIC PENN STATE
COMLY & CARLINE
PHILA., PA. 19154

MARTIN J. FARBER
FILM CORP.
CAROLINE & CHARTER RDS.
PHILA., PA. 19176

R.O. SNELLING SR.
SNELLING & SNELLING
2 INDUSTRIAL RD.
PAOLI, PA. 19301

CHARLES A. CARLSON JR.
LUKENS STEEL
SOUTH FIRST AVE.
COATESVILLE, PA. 19320

W.W. GIBB
INTERSTATE AMIESITE
P.O. BOX 8
CONCORDVILLE, PA. 19331

THOMAS R. GREELEAF
CHEM. LEAMAN TANK
520 EAST LANCASTER AVE.
DOWNINGTOWN, PA. 19335

G.T. HADDEN
HADDEN SAFETY
P.O. BOX 208
DOWNINGTOWN, PA. 19335

WAYNE T. BARRETT
FOOTE MINERAL
RTE. 100
EXTON, PA. 19341

JOHN H. MC COY
NAT'L. ROLLING MILLS
MOREHALL RD.
MALVERN, PA. 19355

LEON RESNICOW
REON REISTOR
420 LINCOLN HIGHWAY
FRAZIER, PA. 19355

DR. FELIX ZANDMAN
VISHAY INTERTECH.
63 LINCOLN HWAY.
MALVERN, PA. 19355

D.L. PEIRCE
DENNY-REYBURN
30 W. BARNARD
WESTCHESTER, PA. 19380

ALVIN BARG
DYNAFAB
7-11 BOLMAR ST.
WEST CHESTER, PA. 19380

DONALD F. U. GOEBERT
VESCO
9 S. HIGH ST.
WESTCHESTER, PA. 19380

PAUL H. WOODRUFF
ROY F. WESTON
WESTON WAY
WESTCHESTER, PA. 19380

MORRIS SIDEWATER
CHARMING SHOPPES
8 E. MAIN ST.
NORRISTOWN, PA. 19401

T.A. RAYMOND
GEN. DEVICES
P.O. BOX 667
NORRISTOWN, PA. 19401

R.R. BURNS
SCAN DATA
800 E. MAIN ST.
NORRISTOWN, PA. 19401

MORRIS GREENBURG
ELECTRONICS SENSING
4TH. & DEPOT STS.
BRIDGEPORT, PA. 19405

J.J. CAVELLA
DATADYNE
VALLEY FORGE CENTER BLDG. 37A
KING OF PRUSSIA, PA. 19406

L.S. SOMERS III
EXTRACORPOREAL MED.
ROYAL & ROSS RDS.
KING OF PRUSSIA, PA. 19406

ROBERT K. SCRIVENER
GINO'S
215 WEST CHURGH RD.
KING OF PRUSSIA, PA. 19406

G.M. LEADER
INTERMEDIATE NURSING
VALLEY FORGE TWS., STE. 120
KING OF PRUSSIA, PA. 19406

VINCENT G. BELL JR.
SAFEGUARD IND.
P.O. BOX 323
KING OF PRUSSIA, PA. 19406

R. J. MAC ALEER
SHARED MED. SYSTEMS
650 PARK AVE.
KING OF PRUSSIA, PA. 19406

BURTON RAND
AUTOSONICS
P.O. BOX 300
CONSHOHOCKEN,PA. 19428

PETER A. BENOLIEL
QUAKER CHEM.
ELM & LEE STS.
CONSHOHOCKEN, PA. 19428

HARLESTON R. WOOD
ALAN WOOD STEEL
P.O. BOX 112
CONSHOHOCKEN, PA. 19428

DR. LEON RIEBMAN
AMERICAN ELECTRONIC
P.O. BOX 552
LANSDALE, PA. 19446

W.A. EVERETT
MET-PRO
5TH. & MITCHELL STS.
LANSDALE, PA. 19446

V.G. BELL JR.
SAFEGUARD BUSINESS
1114 N. BROAD ST.
LANSDALE, PA. 19446

DONALD ATWELL
ULTRACOM
RICHARDSON RD.
LANSDALE, PA. 19446

DAVID T. KIMBALL
LEED & NORTHRUP
SUMNEYTOWN PIKE
NORTH WALES, PA. 19454

L.K. BLACK
TELEFLEX
CHURCH RD.
NORTH WALES, PA. 19454

WILLIAM S. WEST
WEST CO.
WEST BRIDGE ST.
PHOENIXVILLE, PA. 19460

TERRY A. HALPERN
ROBINSON-HALPERN
1 APOLLO RD.
PLYMOUTH MEETING, PA. 19462

ROBERT C. SMITH
MRS. SMITH'S PIE
SOUTH & CHARLOTTE STS.
POTTSTOWN, PA. 19464

F. WM. HEILMAN JR.
SANDERS & THOMAS
GRIFFITH TOWERS
POTTSTOWN, PA. 19464

W.A. SANDERS
STV. INC.
GRIFFITH TOWERS
POTTSTOWN, PA. 19464

WILLIAM T. BEAVER
U.S. AXLE CO.
WATER ST.
POTTSTOWN, PA. 19464

E.G. RORKE
MOORE PRODUCTS
SUMNEYTOWN PIKE
SPRING HOUSE, PA. 19477

JAMES JORDAN JR.
NAYADIC SCIENCES
VILLAGE OF EAGLE UWCHLAND,
PA. 19480

GEORGE J. HAUFLER
CERTAIN-TEED
VALLEY FORGE, PA. 19481

C.G. SEMPIER
NT'L. INFORMATION
150 ALLENDALE RD.
VALLEY FORGE, PA. 19481

ARTHUR E. BONE
UGI CORP.
P.O. BOX 858
VALLEY FORGE, PA. 19482

JOHN H. BYRNE
COLORCON
MOYER BLVD.
WEST POINT, PA. 19486

A.F. McLEAN
BIRDSBORO CORP.
BIRDSBORO, PA. 19508

RAY H. CLARKE
BOYERTOWN BURIAL
23 NORTH WALNUT ST.
BOYERTOWN, PA. 19512

ALBERT P. COSTELLO
KOOLY KUPP
P.O. BOX 8
BOYERTOWN, PA. 19512

JACK BRIER
KLEINERT'S
191 WILLOW ST.
KUTZTOWN, PA. 19530

PAUL M. HERRING
KUTZTOWN FOUNDRY
KUTZTOWN, PA. 19530

WOODROW R. ESHENAUR
GLEN GERY
227 N. 5TH.
READING, PA. 19601

LAWRENCE B. KELLEY
WYOMISSING
7TH. & READING
READING, PA. 19602

F. RUCCIUS JR.
B.O.P. CORP.
50 NORTH 5TH. ST.
READING, PA. 19603

J. R. STOUDT
GILBERT ASSOC.
525 LANCASTER AVE.
READING, PA. 19603

WALTER R. LOWRY
KAWECKI-BERYLCO
P.O. BOX 1462
reading, pa. 19603

VINCENT D. HOFMANN
HOFMANN IND.
3145 SHILLINGTON RD.
SINKING SPRINGS, PA. 19608

JOHN W. CLINE
V.F. CORP.
1047 N. PARK RD.
WYOMISSING, PA. 19610

ELLIS D. TAYLOR
ARTESIAN WATER
191 CHURCHMANS RD.
NEWARK, DEL. 19711

ALBERT HEISLER
REYBOLD HOMES
UNIVERSITY OFFICE PLAZA STE. 102
NEWARD, DEL. 19711

W.R. POWERS
SPECIALTY COMPOSITES
DELAWARE IND. PARK
NEWARK, DEL. 19711

W.E. GREGG
NVF CO.
YORKLYN RD.
YORKLYN, DEL. 19736

FRED J. YOUNG
CENTRAL WEST
100 W. 10TH. ST.
WILMINGTON, DEL. 19801

L.R. SCHWARTZ
CENTURY CIRCUIT
100 W. 10TH. ST.
WILMINGTON, DEL. 19801

W. FRED ANDERSON
ELECTRIC HOSE
12TH. & DURE ST.
WILMINGTON, DEL. 19801

GEORGE R. JORDAN JR.
GREAT SOUTHERN
1105 N. MARKET ST.
WILMINGTON, DEL. 19801

JOHN M. SEABROOK
IU INT'L.
1105 N. MARKET ST.
WILMINGTON, DEL. 19801

JAMES C. LOVELL
MERCANTILE STORES
100 W. 10TH. ST.
WILMINGTON, DEL. 19801

WILLIAM R. DEELEY
AMERICAN STORES
ONE ROLLINS PLAZA
WILMINGTON, DEL. 19803

JAMES I. PRICE
IRON MOUNTAIN
LANCASTER PIKE & DUPONT RD.
WILMINGTON, DEL. 19803

HENRY W. VAN BALLEN
ARISTAR
P.O. BOX 4140
WILMINGTON, DEL. 19807

JEROME C. BERLIN
ROBINO-LADD
ONE PIKE CREEK CENTER
WILMINGTON, DEL. 19808

DONALD E. PARADIS
CHAPPAQUA OIL
100 W. 10TH. ST.
WILMINGTON, DEL. 19810

ALEXIS TARUMIANZ
RETIREMENT LIVING
3600 SILVERSIDE RD.
WILMINGTON, DEL.19810

ELMER A STICCO
ALL AMERICAN IND.
P.O. BOX 1247/801 S. MADISON
WILMINGTON, DEL. 19899

JOHN W. ROLLINS JR.
RLC CROP.
ONE ROLLINS PLAZA
WILMINGTON, DEL. 19899

ERNST DANEMANN
DANNEMANN FABRICS
326 LOOCKERMAN ST.
DOVER, DEL. 19901

PAUL CURTIS
ANDERSON-STOKES
48 REHOBOTH AVE.
REHOBOTH BEACH, DEL. 19971

EDWIN I. COLODNY
ALLEGHENY AIRLINES
NATIONAL AIRPORT
WASHINGTON, D.C. 20001

J.W. HECHINGER
HECHINGER CO.
901 17TH. ST., N.E.
WASHINGTON, D.C. 20002

S.W. FANTLE
PEOPLES DRUG
60 FLORIDA AVE. N.E.
WASHINGTON, D.C. 20002

M.C. MULLIGAN
WASHINGTON TERMINAL
UNION STA.
WASHINGTON, D.C. 20002

M.R. COHEN
SOLON AUTOMATED
115 L ST. S.E.
WASHINGTON, D.C. 20003

M.S. MARSHALL
M.S. GINN
919 E. ST. N.W.
WASHINGTON, D.C. 20004

RICHARD C. WILSON
NT'L. PRESS BLDG.
1346 F ST. N.W.
WASHINGTON, D.C. 20004

K.B. LUDWIG
PHOTO DATA
419 SEVENTH ST. N.W. STE. 500
WASHINGTON, D.C. 20004

MILTON LYONS
GOLD & MINERALS CO.
1522 K ST., N.W.
WASHINGTON, D.C. 20005

W. GRAHAM CLAYTOR JR.
NEW ORLEANS TERMINAL
920 15TH. ST. N.W.
WASHINGTON, D.C. 20005

STANLEY Z. SIEGEL
ECOLOGY DEVEL. CORP.
1700 PEEN. AVE., N.W.
WASHINGTON, D.C. 20006

DAVID R. WATERS
GARFINCKEL, BRRKS BROS.
1629 K. ST., N.W.
WASHINGTON, D.C. 20006

PHILIP E. LOITERSTEIN
GROUP OPERATIONS
2025 L ST., N.W.
WASHINGTON, D.C. 20006

B. FRANK TAYLOR
INT'L. GENERAL
1701 PENN. AVE., N.W.
WASHINGTON, D.C. 20006

O. ROY CHALK
D.C. TRANSIT
3600 M. ST., N.W.
WASHINGTON, D,C, 20007

R.J. DONOHOE
DONOHOE CONST.
2139 WISCONSIN AVE., N.W.
WASHINGTON, D.C. 20007

A.L. WHEELER
PIONEER IND.
1522 WISCONSIN AVE., N.W.
WASHINGTON, D.C. 20007

MORTON GERBER
DISTRICT THEATRES
4301 CONNECTICUT AVE. N.W.
WASHINGTON, D.C. 20008

H.S. KILLGORE
TELE-BROADCASTERS
SHOREHAM HOTEL STE. 101A
WASHINGTON, D.C. 20008

PHILIP L. GORE
SECURITY STORAGE
1701 FLORIDA AVE., N.W.
WASHINGTON, D.C. 20009

MAX SILVERMAN
WAXIE MAXIE
5772 SECOND ST., N.W.
WASHINGTON, D.C. 20011

W. JARVIS MOODY
AMERICAN SECURITY
734 15TH. ST., N.W.
WASHINGTON, D.C. 20013

J.B. DANZANSKY
GIANT FOOD
P.O. BOX 1804
WASHINGTON, D.C. 20013

E.K. HOFFMAN
WOODWARD & LOTHROP
11TH. F & G. STS., NW.
WASHINGTON, D.C. 20013

WILLIAM P. GONDON JR.
AVEMCO
7315 WISCONSIN AVE.
BETHESDA, MARYLAND 20014

E.D. COXEN
AUTOCOMP
7910 WOODMONT AVE.
BETHESDA, MARYLAND 20014

L.R. SANCHEZ
RESOURCE MANAGEMENT
7910 WOODMONT AVE.
BETHESDA, MARYLAND 20014

B.H. DOVEY
SURVIVAL TECH.
7801 WOODMONT AVE.
BETHESDA, MARYLAND 20014

J.W. CROWLEY
SYSTEM SCIENCES
4720 MONTGOMERY LN.
BETHESDA,MARYLAND 20014

CLIFFORD M. KENDALL
COMPUTER DATA
7315 WISCONSIN AVE.
WASHINGTON, D.C. 20014

CHRIS A. CLARK II
ARIES
8401 CONNECTICUT AVE.
CHEVY CHASE, MARYLAND 20015

J.E. NAHRA
DASI
5454 WISCONSIN AVE.
CHEVY CHASE, MARYLAND 20015

JACOB R. FISHERMAN
AMERICAN HEALTH
5530 WISCONSIN AVE., N.W.
WASHINGTON, D.C. 20015

J.I. BREGMAN
WAPORA
6900 WISCONSIN AVE., N.W.
WASHINGTON, D.C. 20015

LEE JOHNSON
COMPUTER NETWORK
2185 MAC ARTHUR BLVD. N.W.
WASHINGTON, D.C. 20016

J.W. MARRIOTT JR.
MARRIOTT CORP.
5161 RIVER RD.
WASHINGTON, D.C. 20016

W.H. COLSTON
BEITZELL & CO.
707 EDGEWOOD ST., N.W.
WASHINGTON, D.C. 20017

C.M. LEVINSON
AUTOSCOPE
3188 BLADENBURG RD. N.E.
WASHINGTON, D.C. 20018

MURRAY KAYE
CAPITAL RECLAMATION
2115 BRYANT ST., N.E.
WASHINGTON, D.C. 20018

JAMES SCHWARTZ
SCHWARTZ BROS.
2146 24TH. PL., N.W.
WASHINGTON, D.C. 20018

GEORGE A. TOTTEN III
TRIANGLE AIRWAYS
100 RIVER FOREST LN.
TANTALON, MD. 20021

LAWRENCE M. BRENEMAN
WASHINGTON HOMES
6192 OXON HILL RD. STE. 400
OXON HILL, MD. 20021

BURTON J. REINER
BRESLER & REINER
401 M ST., S.W.
WASHINGTON, D.C. 20024

PETER BOYKO
CAPITAL FILM
470 E. ST., S.W.
WASHINGTON, D.C. 20024

LOUISE A. McCARTHY
DATA ASSOC.
400 TWELFTH ST., S.W.
WASHINGTON, D.C. 20024

J.L. NEWBOLD
MERCHANTS TRANSFER
1616 FIRST ST.,SW.
WASHINGTON, D.C. 20024

C.H. HOFFBERGER
TERMINAL REFRIG.
4TH. & D STS., S.W.
WASHINGTON, D.C. 20024

IRWIN S. MONSEIN
LEARNING CORP.
7405 HADDINGTON
BETHESDA, MD. 20034

WILLIAM J. McCORMICK
CHECCHI
1730 RHODE ISLAND AVE.
WASHINGTON, D.C. 20036

JOHN A. MARTIN
E.C. ERNST
2000 L ST., N.W.
WASHINGTON, D.C. 20036

TED STANWICK
STANWICK CORP.
1735 K. ST., N.W.
WASHINGTON, D.C. 20036

LYMAN H. TREADWAY
UNION COMMERCE
21 DU PONT CIRCLE, N.W.
WASHINGTON, D.C. 20036

WILLIAM G. MC COWAN
MCI TELECOMMUNICATIONS
1150 17TH. ST., NW.
WASHINGTON, D.C. 20056

SAMUEL SCHALKOWSKY
EXOTECH
1200 QUINCE ORCHARD BLVD.
GAITHERSBERG, MD. 20160

A. ANTON
PARGAS
WASHINGTON RD., BOX 67
WALDORF, MD. 20601

FRANK L. GOODWIN JR.
TECH SERV.
5301 HOLLAND DR.
BELTSVILLE, MD. 20705

MELVIN S. COHEN
DIST. PHOTO
10619 BALTIMORE AVE.
BELTSVILLE, MD. 20715

R.J. SAKS
U.S. VINYLE
6707 POPLAR HILL LN.
CLINTON, MD. 20735

B.O. WEINSCHEL
WEINSCHEL ENGINEERING
P.O. BOX 577
GAITHERSBURG, MD. 20760

JOHN F. DEALY
FAIRCHILD IND.
SHERMAN FAIRCHILD TECH. CTR.
GERMANTOWN, MD. 20767

CHARLES W. LOCKYER
PUBCO
11200 PROSPECT HILL RD.
GLENN DALE, MD. 20769

JOSEPH P. KINGSLY
THE MACKE CO.
ONE MACKE CIRCLE
CHEVERLY, MD. 20781

JOHN A. MARTIN
E.C. ERNST
2000 L ST., NW.
WASHINGTON, D.C. 20036

ERNEST L. MARKS
GOV. EMPLOYEES
1705 L ST., N.W.
WASHINGTON, D.C. 20036

TED STANWICK
STANWICK CORP.
1735 K ST., N.W.
WASHINGTON, D.C. 20036

WILLIAM G. MC COWAN
MCI TELECOMMUNICATIONS
1150 17TH. ST., N.W.
WASHINGTON, D.C. 20056

HERBERT H. HAFT
DART DRUG
3301 PENNSY DR.
LANDOVER, MD. 20784

FRANK L. GOODWIN JR.
TCH. SERV.
5301 HOLLAND DR.
BELTSVILLE, MD. 20705

STEPHEN E. SILVERMAN
COMPUTER OPERATIONS
9700 B. GEORGE PALMER HWY.
LANHAM, MD. 20801

R.H. HUTCHISON JR.
LAUREL HARNESS RACING
P.O. BOX 111
LAUREL, MD. 20810

C.D. GORDON
PLAIN N' FANCY DONUTS
816 2ND. ST.
LAUREL, MD. 20810

LEONARD BROWN
MIFFLIN, MC CAMBRIDGE
6400 RHODE ISLAND AVE.
RIVERDALE, MD. 20840

JOSEPH K. WINEKE
COMRESS
2 RESEARCH CT.
ROCKVILLE, MD. 20850

PAUL GRAFTON
CONSTELLATION CORP.
P.O. BOX 512
ROCKVILLE, MD. 20850

LOUIS H. WOLCOTT
MICRODYNE
P.O. BOX 1527
ROCKVILLE, MD. 20850

C.F. JONES
NUS CORP.
4 RESEARCH PL.
ROCKVILLE, MD. 20850

RALPH F. BLASEY JR.
WESTON INT'L.
2351 SHADY GROVE RD.
ROCKVILLE, MD. 20850

J.F. HORTY
ASPEN SYSTEMS
11600 NEBEL ST.
ROCKVILLE, MD. 20852

WALTER BELL
W. BELL & CO.
12401 TWINBROOK PKWAY.
ROCKVILLE, MD. 20852

BERNARD J. CRAVATH
DIVERSITRON
10500 ROCKVILLE PIKE
ROCKVILLE, MD. 20852

R.W. GABBE
EMERSON LTD.
11790 PARKLAWN DR.
ROCKVILLE, MD. 20852

W.L. ANDERSON
GENERAL KINETICS
12300 PARKLAWN DR.
ROCKVILLE, MD. 20852

ROBERT A. MALLET
INFORMATION & COMM. APPL.
6110 EXECUTIVE BLVD.
ROCKVILLE, MD. 20852

MORDECAI K. KATZ
MULTRONICS
12307 WASHINGTON AVE.
ROCKVILLE, MD. 20852

K.M. MILLER
PENRIL
5520 RANDOLPH RD.
ROCKVILLE, MD. 20852

HAROLD A. TIMKEN JR.
QUANTA SYSTEMS
979 ROLLING AVE.
ROCKVILLE, MD. 20852

G.V. LEVIN
BIOSPHERICS
4928 WYACONDA RD.
ROCKVILLE, MD. 20853

MAURICE P. FOLEY
MODULE SYSTEMS
10500 ROCKVILLE PIKE
ROCKVILLE, MD. 20853

CARL M. FREEMAN
CARL M. FREEMAN ASSOC.
1400 SPRING ST.
SILVER SPRING,MD. 20901

ERIC WALDBAUM
GREENBELT CONSUMER SERVICES
8547 PINEY BRANCH RD.
SILVER SPRING,MD. 20901

STEWART BAINUM
QUALITY INNS
10750 COLUMBIA PIKE
SILVER SPRING, MD. 20901

JACK RUBENSTEIN
BAGEL MASTER
2646 UNIVERSITY BLVD.
SILVER SPRING, MD. 20902

BRIAN T. CUNNINGHAM
COMPUTER ENTRY SYSTEMS
2141 IND. PKWAY.
SILVER SPRING, MD. 20904

B. HOUSTON MC CENEY
MANOR-CARE
10800 LOCKWOOD DR.
SILVER SPRING, MD. 20904

M.L. GOEGLEIN
AMERICAN FINANCE
1320 FENWICK LN.
SILVER SPRING, MD. 20910

JULIAN LAZRUS
BOWLES FLUIDICS
9347 FRASER AVE.
SILVER SPRING, MD. 20910

RALPH M. JOHNSON JR.
CHESAPEAKE IND.
818 ROEDER RD.
SILVER SPRING, MD. 20910

RALPH V. GUGLIEMI
COMPUTER BUSINESS
1220 E. WEST HIGHWAY
SILVER SPRING, MD. 20910

R.D. ROSENTHAL
NEOTEC
2431 LINDEN LN.
SILVER SPRING, MD. 20910

D.W. ORDUN
ELECTRONIC MODULES
MC CORMICK R.D
COCKEYSVILLE, MD. 21030

H.K. WELLS
MC CORMICK & CO.
11350 MC CORMICK RD.
COCKEYSVILLE, MD. 21030

JOHN C. QUINN JR.
BALTIMORE BUSINESS FORMS
EXECUTIVE PLAZA STE. 400
HUNT VALLEY, MD. 21031

JEROME W. GECKLE
PETERSON, HOWELL, HEATHER
11333 MC CORMICK RD.
HUNT VALLEY, MD. 21031

FRED HITTMAN
HITTMAN CORP.
9190 RED BRANCH RD.
COLUMBIA, MD. 21043

MATHIAS J. DEVITO
THE ROUSE CO.
COLUMBIA, MD. 21043

JAMES P. RYAN
THE RYLAND GROUP
10221 WINCOPIN CIRCLE
COLUMBIA, MD. 21043

R.L. SPANGLER
LEWRON TV.
FOREST HILL INDUSTRIAL PK.
FOREST HILL, MD. 21050

M.B. RUFFIN
ALLIED RESEARCH
P.O. BOX 1000
GLEN BURNIE,MD. 21061

S.H. COHAN
NAT'L. CHECK CORP.
91 AQUAHART RD.
GLEN BURNIE, MD. 21061

MORRIS KAY
UNITED CONSOLIDATED IND.
7225 PARKWAY DR.
HANOVER, MD. 21076

HENRY SHAPIRO
MARYLAND CUP
OWINGS MILLS, MD. 21117

NORMAN J. ALFIN
MERLIN IND.
RAILROAD AVE.
WESTMINSTER, MD. 21157

JEROME MARKMAN
COMPUTER CENTER
423 W. MONUMENT ST.
BALTIMORE, MD. 21201

R.M. GOLDMAN
DIVERSIFIED RETAILING
2 HOPKINS PLAZA
BALTIMORE, MD. 21201

W.D. MAC CALLAN
PETROLEUM CORP.
201 N. CHARLES ST.
BALTIMORE, MD. 21201

JEROLD C. HOFFBERGER
NAT'L. BREWING
225 N. CALVERT ST.
BALTIMORE, MD. 21202

HYMAN MARCUS
TRANS-UNITED IND.
300 ST. PAUL PL.
BALTIMORE , MD. 21202

WILLIAM M. PASSANO JR.
WAVERLY PRESS
428 E. PRESTON ST.
BALTIMORE, MARYLAND 21202

PHILIP L. KLING
CHARG-IT OF BALTIMORE
P.O. BOX 1013
BALTIMORE, MD. 21203

A.J. MORRIS
CROWN CENTRAL
ONE N. CHARLES ST.
BALTIMORE, MD. 21203

A.P. MC ILWAIN
MARYLAND SHIPBUILDING
P.O. BOX 537
BALTIMORE, MD. 21203

GEORGE L. BUNTING JR.
NOXELL CORP.
11050 YORK RD.
BALTIMORE, MD. 21203

W.G. HUPFELDT
SCHLUDERBERG-KURDLE
3800 EAST BALTIMORE ST.
BALTIMORE, MD. 21203

MARVIN J. KAHN
AAI
P.O. BOX 6767
BALTIMORE, MD. 21204

FRANCIS X. KNOTT
ARUNDEL
110 WEST RD.
BALTIMORE, MD. 21204

FRANCIS P. LUCIER
THE BLACK & DECKER MFG.
701 E. JOPPA RD.
TOWSON,MD. 21204

SETH H. BAKER
CHC
EQUITABLE-TOWSON BLDG.
TOWSON, MD. 21204

FRANK BOND
HOLIDAY UNIVERSAL
300 E. JOPPA RD.
TOWSON,MD. 21204

E.J. LINEHAN
MED. SERVICES
409 WASHINGTON AVE.
TOWSON, MD. 21204

OLIVER S. TRAVERS JR.
SCHENUIT IND.
7800 YORK RD.
BALTIMORE, MD. 21204

JOHN L. KNOTT
KNOTT IND.
1726 WHITEHEAD RD.
BALTIMORE, MD. 21207

CHARLES M. MATHEWS
FALCONER CO.
6001 ERDMAN AVE.
BALTIMORE, MD. 21205

S. MEYER BARNETT
RELIABLE STORES
3002 DRUID PARK DR.
BALTIMORE, MD. 21215

BENNETT S. ROBIN
CANNON SHOE CO.
LAFAYETTE & DICKSON
BALTIMORE, MD. 21217

MORTON M. LAPIDES
ALLEGHENY BEVERAGE
2216 N. CHARLES ST.
BALTIMORE, MD. 21218

HARRY R. SHRIVER
BALTIMORE RADIO SHOW
13 E. 20TH.ST.
BALTIMORE, MD. 21218

S. KIRK MILLSPAUGH
KIRK CORP.
2400 KIRK AVE.
BALTIMORE, MD. 21218

J.M. CURLEY JR.
EASTMET
ROLLING MILL RD., COLGATE
BALTIMORE COUNTY, MD. 21224

JOSEPH SCHWABER JR.
MONARCH RUBBER
3500 PULASKI HWAY.
BALTIMORE, MD. 21224

MICHAEL KOVENS
UNIVERSAL SECURITY
2829 POTEE ST.
BALTIMORE, MD. 21225

CHARLES N. ANDERSON JR.
ALCOLAC
3440 FAIRFIELD RD.
BALTIMORE, MD. 21226

JOSEPH J. MARTIN
RPS PRODUCTS
1700 S. CATON AVE.
BALTIMORE, MD. 21227

EDMUND F. HOEY
FAIR LANES
1112 N. ROLLING RD.
BALTIMORE, MD. 21228

PAUL ISAACS
FIVE STAR FOODS
6630 BALTIMORE NAT'L. PIKE
BALTIMORE, MD. 21228

PHILIP H. KNITZ
BALTIMORE PAINT
2325 HOLLINS FERRY RD. M.
BALTIMORE, MD. 21230

R.E. BOWE
ELLICOTT MACH.
1611 BUSH ST.
BALTIMORE, MD. 21230

RAYMON V. HAYSBERT DR.
H.G. PARKS
501 WEST HAMBURG ST.
BALTIMORE, MD. 21230

HOWARD C. JACOBS
AUTOLINE OIL
CAROLINE & DOCK
BALTIMORE, MD. 21231

CARL F. WEBER JR.
REPUBLIC VAN
9219 HARFORD RD.
BALTIMORE, MD. 21234

E.A. COONS
POLY-SEAL
8303 PULASKI HIGHWAY
BALTIMORE, MD. 21237

DR. ROBERT O. TEEG
DUROLITH CORP.
AIRPARK DR.
EASTON, MD. 21601

FLETCHER HANKS
HANKS SEAFOOD
P.O. BOX 70
EASTON, MD. 21601

ALVA T. BLADES
PRESTON TRUCKING
151 EASTON BLVD.
PRESTON, MD. 21655

FRANKLIN M. THOMAS JR.
CENTRAL CHEM.
P.O. BOX 918
HAGERSTOWN, MD. 21740

GARY J. KELLOFF
BIOMEDICAL SERVICES
8301 ARLINGTON BLVD.
FAIRFAX, VIRGINIA 22030

T.G. WALKINSHAW
SIMULATION ENGINEERING
2724 DORR AVE.
FAIRFAX, VA. 22030

D.A. JOSEPH
CERBERONICS
5600 COLUMBIA PIKE
FALLS CHURCH, VA. 22041

G.E. GAUTNEY
DATRONICS
2922 TELESTAR CT.
FALLS CHURCH, VA. 22042

BERNARD FARKAS
SYSTEMATICS
2922 TELESTAR CT.
FALLS CHURCH, VA. 22042

KEITH A. CUNNINGHAM
UNITED NUCLEAR
7700 LEESBURG PIKE
FALLS CHURCH, VA. 22043

RALPH A. BEETON
FIRST VA. BANKSHARES
FIRST VA. PLAZA
FALLS CHURCH, VA. 22046

J.P. CHAMERS
MELPAR
7700 ARLINGTON BLVD.
FALLS CHURCH, VA. 22046

G. WOODARD
WOODARD RESEARCH
P.O. BOX 405
HERNDON, VA. 22070

ROBERT M. TYBURSKI
OPTICAL RECOGNITION
1928 ISSAC NEWTON SQ. W.
RESTON, VA. 22070

WILLIAM C. SCHAUB
SCOPE INC.
1860 MICHAEL FARADEY DR.
RESTON, VA. 22072

ARTHUR B. LAWRENCE JR.
IND. MICRONICS
RD. 2, BOX 120
LEESBURG, VA. 22075

EDWARD K. O'CONNOR
COLUMBIA COMPUTER
1224 DALESVIEW DR.
MC LEAN, VA. 22101

EDWARD K. O'CONNOR
CONSOLIDATED SOFTWARE
1224 DALEVIEW DR.
MC LEAN, VA. 22101

CHARLES G. GULLEDGE
DYNALECTRON CORP.
1313 DOLLEY MADISON BLVD.
MC LEAN, VA. 22101

DR. HARRY LETAW JR.
RADIATION SYSTEMS
1755 OLD MEADOW RD.
MC LEAN, VA. 22101

JAMES H. DUGGAN
SERVAIR INC.
1313 DOLLEY MADISON BLVD.
MC LEAN, VA. 22101

J.D. SCHROTT
VORTEX CORP.
P.O. DRAWER M.
MC LEAN, VA. 22101

W.C. KRAUSER
POTOMAC IND.
P.O. BOX 38
MERRIFIELD, VA. 22116

F.E. WILLIAMS JR.
WILLIAMS IND.
2931 GALLOWS RD., P.O. BOX 325
MERRIFIELD, VA. 22116

GORDON O. F. JOHNSON
LOG ETRONICS
7001 LOISDALE RD.
SPRINGFIELD, VA. 22150

R. H. TWYFORD
MECHANICAL ENTERPRISES
8000 FORBES PL.
SPRINGFIELD, VA. 22151

E.G. GOLDBERG
BOWL AMERICA
P.O. BOX 1288
SPRINGFIELD, VA. 22151

R.E. STREETS
GEN. ENVIRONMENTS
6840 IND. ROAD
SPRINGFIELD, VA. 22151

MILTON J. FIVEL
ISOMET CORP.
5414 PORT ROYAL RD.
SPRINGFIELD, VA. 22151

D.P. NIELSEN
HAZELTON LAB'S.
9200 LEESBURG TURNPIKE
VIENNA, VA. 22180

D.M. KRUCHKO
VEGA PRECISION
800 FOLLIN LAND
VIENNA, VA. 22180

R. DARE CLIFTON
REALM CORP.
14205 TELEGRAPH RD.
WOODBRIDGE, VA. 22191

STEPHEN HARTWELL
COLCHESTER CORP.
P.O. BOX 73
WOODBRIDGE, VA. 22194

JOHN H. SMITH
COMPUTER LEASING
2001 JEFFERSON DAVIS H'WAY.
ARLINGTON, VA. 22202

G.A. FREED
PARAMOUNT COMMUNITIES
313 NORTH GLEBE RD.
ARLINGTON, VA. 22203

JOHN E. ALEXANDER
NVDH CORP.
601 SOUTH CARLIN SPRINGS RD.
ARLINGTON, VA. 22204

DR. WILLIAM W. FAIN
CACI INC.
1815 N. FORT MYER DR.
ARLINGTON, VA. 22209

JAMES H. CONNORS JR.
KAPPA SYSTEMS
1815 N. FORT MYER DR.
ARLINGTON, VA. 22209

RAYMOND W. HARMON
FIRST FOTO
515 MT. VERNON AVE.
ALEXANDRIA,VA. 22301

J.B. TOOMEY
VALUE ENG. CO.
2550 HUNTINGTON AVE.
ALEXANDRIA, VA. 22303

CHARLES A. WEBB JR.
HALIFAX ENG. INC.
5309 CHEROKEE AVE.
ALEXANDRIA, VA. 22312

MILTON L. ELSBERG
DRUG FAIR
6295 EDSALL RD.
ALEXANDRIA, VA. 22314

ARTHUR C. ANGELOS
THE ELECTRONICS & MFG.
840 N. HENRY ST.
ALEXANDRIA, VA. 22314

ANTHONIE C. VAN EKRIS
KAY CORP.
320 KING ST.
ALEXANDRIAM VA. 22314

J.C.H. BRYANT
O'SULLIVAN CORP.
P.O. BOX 603
WINCHESTER, VA. 22601

C.N. BROADDUS
CASSCO CORP.
125 WEST BRUCE ST.
HARRISONBURG, VA. 22801

JAMES E. CARSON
RELIANCE OIL
P.O. BOX 1014
CHARLOTTESVILLE,VA. 22902

LAWRENCE H. CAMP
THE CHESAPEAKE CORP.
WEST POINT, VA. 23181

KENNETH G. GENTIL
OVERNITE TRANSPORTATION
P.O. BOX 1216
RICHMOND, VA. 23209

J. LOUIS REYNOLDS
ESKIMO PIE
530 EAST MAIN ST.
RICHMOND, VA. 23212

HORACE B. FABER JR.
STANDARD PAPER MFG.
FIRST & HULL STS.
RICHMOND, VA. 23212

A.S. DONNAHOE
MEDIA GENERAL
333 EAST GRACE ST.
RICHMOND, VA. 23213

ROBERT C. WILLIAMS
JAMES RIVER CORP.
TREDEGAR ST.
RICHMOND, VA. 23217

WARREN M. PACE
RICHMOND CORP.
914 CAPITOL ST.
RICHMOND, VA. 23219

CHARLES G. THALHEIMER
THALHEIMER BROS.
615 E. BROAD ST.
RICHMOND, VA. 23219

ANDREW M. LEWIS
BEST PRODUCTS
P.O. BOX 26320
RICHMOND, VA. 23220

R. LARRY SNIDER
MERIDIAN ELECTRONICS
1001 WEST BROAD ST.
RICHMOND, VA. 23220

WILLIAM L. ZIMMER III
A.H. ROBINS CO.
1407 CUMMINGS DR.
RICHMOND, VA. 23220

SAM KORNBLAU
RLTY. IND.
2512 W. CARY ST.
RICHMOND, VA. 23220

EDWARD M. O'NEAL JR.
TOMLINSON CO.
1312 W. MARSHALL ST.
RICHMOND, VA. 23220

HYMAN MYERS
HEILIG-MEYERS
3228 W. CARY ST.
RICHMOND, VA. 23221

G. F. NOLDE JR.
NOLDE BROS.
2520 E. BROAD ST.
RICHMOND, VA. 23223

RALPH S. THOMAS
ROBERTSHAW CONTROLS
1701 BYRD AVE.
RICHMOND, VA. 23226

C.T. HUGHES JR.
CONSUMAT SYSTEMS
P.O. BOX 9379
RICHMOND, VA. 23227

JAMES A. BARGATZE
GENERAL MEDICAL CORP.
8741 LANDMARK RD.
RICHMOND, VA. 23228

S.A. CARMINE III
CARMINE FOODS
2004 DABNEY RD.
RICHMOND, VA. 23230

RICHARD W. WILTSHIRE
HOME BENEFICIAL
3901 WEST BROAD ST.
RICHMOND, VA. 23230

J.T. ANTONELLI
MAJOR LEAGUE BOWLING
6308 W. BROAD ST.
RICHMOND, VA. 23230

G.G. MINOR JR.
OWENS, MINOR & BODEKER
4825 BETHLEHEM RD.
RICHMOND, VA. 23230

GORDON L. CRENSHAW
UNIVERSAL LEAF
HAMILTON ST. AT BROAD
RICHMOND, VA. 23230

WILLIAM THOMPSON, III
SPOTLESS CO.
WESTWOOD AVE. & TOMLYNN ST.
RICHMOND, VA. 23230

ALAN WURTZEL
WARDS CO.
2040 THALBRO ST.
RICHMOND, VA. 23230

R.H. BUNZLE
AMERICAN FILTRONA
8401 JEFFERSON DAVIS H'WAY.
RICHMOND, VA. 23234

ROBERT W. HOUSER
WM. P. POYTHRESS & CO.
16 N. 22 ND. ST.
RICHMOND, VA. 23261

W.R. POLLARD
UNITED TRANSIT
P.O. BOX 27386
RICHMONT, VA. 23261

E.V. THOMPSON
NEWPORT BUSINESS FORMS
PEMBROKE & G. STS.
HAMPTON, VA. 23361

JOSEPH W. LUTER
SMITHFIELD FOODS
P.O. BOX 447
SMITHFIELD, VA. 23430

CHARLES L. CLEAVES
AMERICAN LAND
3113 PACIFIC AVE.
VIRGINIA BEACH, VA. 23451

JESSEE BLOODWORTH
ECONO-TRAVEL
3 KOGER EXECUTIVE
NORFOLK, VA. 23502

T.J. BROECKER
STEWART SANDWICHES
5732 CURLEW DR.
NORFOLK, VA. 23502

WILLIAM B. CLOE JR.
VIRGINIA DATA CENTER
888 NORFOLK SQ.
NORFOLK, VA. 23502

CHARLES F. BURROUGHS JR.
ROYSTER CO.
ROYSTER BLDG.
NORFOLK, VA. 23510

GERALD J. FRIEDMAN
TIDEWATER GROUP
217 E. MAIN ST.
NORFOLK, VA. 23510

R.F. OUREDNIK
NOLAND CO.
2700 WARWICK BLVD.
NEWPORT NEWS. VA. 23607

VERNON W. MULES
DOUGHTIE'S FOODS
2410 WESLEY ST.
PORTSMOUTH, VA. 23707

HARRY W. BUCHANAN
VA. CHEM. INC.
3340 W. NORFOLK RD.
PORTSMOUTH, VA. 23703

W.S. JOHNSON
BRENCO
PRINCE GEORGE IND. PK.
PETERSBURG, VA. 23803

WILLIAM P. MC PHILAMY
DATAMAC
121 W. CAMPBELL AVE.
ROANOKE, VA. 24004

KOSSEN GREGORY
GEN. STONE & MATERIALS
P.O. BOX 1198
ROANOAKE, VA. 24006

J.H. HILL
JOHNSON-CARPER FURNITURE
HOLLINS RD.
ROANOKE, VA. 24006

JOEL KIRSCH
AMERICAN MOTOR INNS
P.O. BOX 1410
ROANOKE, VA. 24007

DAVID W. REED JR.
JOHN W. HANCOCK INC.
P.O. BOX 8305
ROANOKE, VA. 24014

ROBERT H. SPILMAN
BASSETT FURNITURE IND.
BASSETT, VA.

J. CLYDE HOOKER JR.
HOOKER FURNITURE
MARTINSVILLE, VA. 24112

JULIUS HERMES
MARTIN PROCESSING
P.O. BOX 5068
MARTINSVILLE, VA. 24112

JAMES W. SEVERT
NAT'L. HOMES INC.
P.O. BOX 5511
MARTINSVILLE, VA. 24112

WI LIAM G. PANNILL
PANNILL KNITTING CO.
CLEVELAND & WATER
MARTINSVILLE, VA. 24112

WILLIAM F. FRANCK
TULTEX CORP.
P.O. BOX 519A
MARTINSVILLE, VA. 24112

H.C. GRAVELY
GRAVELY FURNITURE
RIDGEWAY, VA. 24148

GERALD M. BIRNBACH
ROWE FURNITURE
239 ROWAN ST.
SALEM, VA. 24153

CABELL BRAND
STUART MC GUIRE CO.
115 BRAND RD.
SALEM, VA. 24153

T.B. STANLEY JR
STANLEY FURNITURE
STANLEYTOWN, VA. 24168

JOHN C. BOLINGER JR.
COLONIAL NAT. GAS
P.O. BOX 1590
PULASKI, VA. 24301

BERNARD C. WAMPLER
PULASKI FURNITURE
BOX 1371
PULASKI, VA. 24301

DENNIS B. DRAPER
CLIFTON FORGE-WAYNESBORO
P.O. BOX 2008
STAUNTON, VA. 24401

JOSEPH GILBERT
SMITH'S TRANSFER
P.O. BOX 1000
STAUNTON, VA. 24401

ARCHIBALD A. SPROUL
VA. INT'L. CO.
P.O. BOX 2006
STAUNTON, VA. 24401

THOMAS J. LENNON
VA. HOT SPRINGS
HOT SPRINGS, VA. 24445

ROBERT S. LOCKRIDGE
CRADDOCK-TERRY
3100 ALBERT LANKFORD DR.
LYNCHBURG, VA. 24505

J.C. KLEIN
STROTHER DRUG CO.
9221 TIMBERLAKE RD.
LYNCHBURG, VA. 24505

BERNARD B. LANE
LANE CO.
ALTAVISTA, VA. 24517

W.O. THOMAS
PIEDMONT LABEL CO.
311 W. DEPOT ST.
BEDFORD, VA. 24523

R.B. BRIDGFORTH JR.
DIBRELL BROS. INC.
512 BRIDGE ST.
DANVILLE, VA. 24541

G.W. DEHOFF
RICHMONT CEDAR WORKS
400 BRIDGE ST.
DANVILLE, VA. 24541

CHAPMAN I. JOHNSTON JR.
BLUEFIELD SUPPLY
BLUEFIELD, W. VA. 24701

WILLIAM W. WALKER
MAJESTIC COLLIERIES
WEST VA. HOTEL BLDG.
BLUEFIELD, WEST VA. 24701

R.E. BOWLBY
BURKE-PARSONS-BOWLBY
P.O. BOX 231
RIPLEY, W. VA. 25143

GARY LASHINSKY
NAT'L. SHOWS
CHARLESTON NAT'L. PLAZA BLDG.
CHARLESTON, W. VA. 25301

J.P. CLARK
MED-PAK CORP.
912 PENN. AVE.
CHARLESTON, W. VA. 25302

RUSSELL L. ISAACS
HECK'S INC.
P.O. BOX 2233
CHARLESTON, W. VA. 25328

HALE E. ANDREWS
PENN. GLASS SAND
BERKELEY SPRINGS, W. VA. 25411

A.F. GOOD
SHENANDOAH CORP.
P.O. BOX 551
CHARLES TOWN, W. VA. 25414

ROY A CUNNINGHAM
ELK HORN COAL
P.O. BOX 1894
BACKLEY, W. VA. 25801

SYDNEY S. GOOD JR.
L.S. GOOD & CO.
1134 MARKET ST.
WHEELING, W. VA. 26003

CHARLES J. STEIN
ROBERTS LUMBER CO.
2715 MARKET ST.
WHEELING, W. VA. 26003

ROBERT E. MICHENER
M. MARSH & SON
915 MARKET ST.
WHEELING, W. VA. 26003

ARTHUR EICHELKRAUT
WHEELING MACHINE
KRAUSE & NAT'L.
WHEELING, W. VA. 26003

DAVID B. DALZELL
FOSTORIA GLASS
1200 FIRST ST.
MOUNDSVILLE, W. VA. 26041

DOUGLAS E. COCHRAN
MC DONOUGH CO.
P.O. BOX 1774
PARKERSBURG, W. VA. 26101

LLOYD A. COOK
RAVENS-METAL
RTE. 2 NORTH,
PARKERSBURG, W. VA. 26102

JOHN C. WRIGHT
PETROLEUM EXPLORATION
TRICO BLDG.
SISTERVILLE, W. VA. 26175

J.N. RYAN
PETROLEUM DEVELOPMENT
103 E. MAIN ST.
BRIDGEPORT, W. VA. 26330

JOHN W. WEIMER
SENECA GLASS
709 BEECHURST AVE.
MORGANTOWN, W. VA. 26505

MICHAEL E. BASILE
ELECTRONIC CONTROL
WESTCHESTER ADDITION
FAIRMONT, W. VA. 26554

J.E. WOLTZ
QUALITY MILLS
US 52 SOUTH
MOUNT AIRY, N.C. 27030

L.A. STADLER
PEXTILE CORP.
STONEVILL, N.C. 27048

T.H. DAVIS
PIEDMONT AVIATION
SMITH-REYNOLDS AIRPORT
WINSTON-SALEM, N.C. 27101

MORRIS BRENNER
BRENNER IND.
P.O. BOX 76
WINSTON-SALEM,N.C. 27102

J. EDWIN COLLETTE
INTEGON
420 N. SPRUCE ST.
WINSTON-SALEM, N.C. 27102

CHARLES G. REAVES
WACHOVIA RLTY.
P.O. BOX 3174
WINSTON-SALEM, N.C. 27102

JAMES R. GILLEY
WASHINGTON GROUP
P.O. BOX 1015
WINSTON-SALEM, N.C. 27102

G. DONALD EBERT
ELECTRONIC DATA
P.O. BOX 5565
WINSTON-SALEM, N.C. 27103

ROBERT E. ELBERSON
HANES CORP.
P.O. BOX 5416
WINSTON-SALEM, N.C. 27103

DUDLEY L. SIMMS III
PIECE GOODS SHOPS
280 CHARLOIS BLVD.
WINSTON-SALEM, N.C. 27103

HUBERT L. SHORTT
TECHNOGRAPH
P.O. BOX 5376
WINSTON-SALEM, N.C. 27103

JOHN WOODS
WOODS COMMUNICATION
P.O. BOX 5129
WINSTON-SALEM, N.C. 27103

ROBERT E. HALBY
AMERICAN PEPSI-COLA
P.O. BOX 4746
WINSTON-SALEM, N.C. 27107

AMORY MELLEN JR.
MC LEAN TRUCKING
617 WAUGHTOWN ST.
WINSTON SALEM, N.C. 27107

W. DOUGLAS FOSTER
SALEM CARPET MILLS BX.4537
1-40 EAST AT LINVILLE RD.
WINSTON-SALEM, N.C. 27107

ALBERT A. HARRELSON JR.
HARRELSON RUBBER
P.O. BOX 1167
ASEBORO, N.C. 27203

M.R. WILLIAMS
B.B. WALKER CO.
P.O. BOX 1167
ASHEBORO, N.C. 27203

H.A. WEEKS
WEEKS CONSTRUCTION
P.O. BOX 1,
ASHEBORO, N.C. 27203

J.L. BULL JR.
SOUTHERN FILM EXTRUDERS
2327 ENGLISH RD.
HIGH POINT, N.C. 27260

W.B. NEWBORNE JR.
ADAMS-MILLIS
P.O. BOX 2650
HIGH POINT, N.C. 27261

JOHN P. HAILEY
PHILLIPS-FOSCUE CORP.
2222 SURRETT DR.
HIGH POINT, N.C. 27261

RICHARD J. SNIKER
AUTOMATION BUSINESS
P.O. BOX 190
EDEN, N.C. 27288

WILLIAM C. BATTLE
FIELDCREST MILLS
326 EAST STADIUM DR.
EDEN, N.C. 27288

O.T. SLOAN
MACK STORES
P.O. BOX 2010
SANFORD, N.C. 27330

HUGH E. CARR
TRION INC.
P.O. BOX 760
SANFORD, N.C. 27330

J.W. JOHNSON
REX PLASTICS
P.O. BOX 948
THOMASVILLE, N.C. 27360

L.W. FLIPPO
WELLINGTON HALL LTD.
500 CAROLINA AVE.
THOMASVILLE, N.C. 27360

BRUCE E. BEAMAN
BEAMAN CORP.
800 W. SMITH ST.
GREENSBORO, N.C. 27401

L. KIMSEY MANN
BLUE BELL
335 CHURCH ST.
GREENSBORO, N.C. 27401

ROBERT BRUCE MACRAE
COLONIAL IND.
P.O. BOX 779
GREENSBORO, N.C. 27402

CHARLES A. HAYES
GUILFORD MILLS
P.O. BOX U-4
GREENSBORO, N.C. 27402

JOHN E. FIELD
CONE MILLS
FOURTH & MAPLE STS.
GREENSBORO, N.C. 27405

JACK W. WORSHAM
SOUTHERN PLASTICS
P.O. BOX 6428
GREENSBORO, N.C. 27405

W. BARNHARDT
SOUTHERN WEBBING MILLS
P.O. BOX 6245, SUMMIT STA.
GREENSBORO, N.C. 27405

GILBERT M. DORLAND
CAROLINA STEEL
1451 S. ELM ST.
GREENSBORO, N.C. 27406

JAMES E. LAVASQUE
OAKWOOD HOMES
P.O. BOX 7386
GREENSBORO, N.C. 27407

LAWRENCE M. COHEN
JEWEL BOX STORES
P.O. BOX 21768
GREENSBORO, N.C. 27420

W.G. SMITH
KEY CO.
P.O. BOX 20207
GREENSBORO, N.C. 27420

JOSEPH HAMILTON
TEXFI IND.
P.O. BOX 20348
GREENSBORO, N.C. 27420

G.A. McBANE
UNIFI
7201 W. FRIENDLY RD.
GREENSBORO,N.C. 27420

R.F. HALL JR.
WYSONG & MILLS
P.O. BOX 21168
GREENSBORO, N.C. 27420

LEE P. SHAFFER
KENAN TRANSPORT
P.O. BOX 2729
CHAPEL HILL, N.C. 27514

GEORGE A. CRALLE
DURHAM HOSIERY MILLS
BOX 476
FRANKLINTON, N.C. 27525

SAMUEL R. GOANS
EAGLE STORES
P.O. BOX 468
FUQUAY-VARINA, N.C. 27526

LUCIUS H. HARVIN JR.
ROSE'S. STORES
P.O. BOX 51
HENDERSON, N.C. 27536

DONALD H. GRUBB
HUYCK CORP.
WAKE FOREST, N.C. 27587

GEORGE P. KOURES
ATHEY PRODUCTS
P.O. BOX 669
RALEIGH, N.C. 27602

JAMES M. PEDEN JR.
PEDEN STEEL
1815 NORTH BLVD.
RALEIGH, N.C. 27604

L.M. MELVIN
SUPER DOLLAR STORES
3401 GRESHAMS LAKE RD.
RALEIGH, N.C. 27604

WILLIAM A. PRIOR
AEROTRON
P.O. BOX 6527
RALEIGH, N.C. 27608

W.J. SMITH JR.
CAMERON-BROWN
4300 SIX FORKS RD.
RALEIGH, N.C. 27609

WILLIAM A. GRANBERRY
AMIC CORP.
3984 BROWNING PL.
RALEIGH, N.C. 27611

D.K. APPLETON
NAT'L. NURSING
P.O. BOX 25487
RALEIGH, N.C. 27611

R. WALKER MARTIN
SOUTHERN FRONTIER
P.O. BOX 26627
RALEIGH, N.C. 27611

J.R. MAYNARD
TELERENT LEASING
4209 FAYETTEVILLE RD.
RALEIGH, N.C. 27611

RAYMOND J. MULLIGAN
LIGGETT GROUP
4100 ROXBORO RD.
DURHAM, N.C. 27702

D. BULLARD
WRIGHT MACH. CO.
1600 MIST LAKE DR.
DURHAM, N.C. 27702

T.W. TYSINGER
TRIANGLE BRICK
RTE. 4
DURHAM, N.C. 27703

CRAIG M. BLACK
BLACK IND.
2816 ROXBORO RD.
DURHAM, N.C. 27704

LEON A. DUNNE JR.
GUARDIAN CORP.
3801 SUNSET AVE. WEST.
ROCKY MOUNT, N.C. 27801

JACK A. LAUGHERY
HARDEE'S FOOD SYSTEMS
1233 N. CHURCH ST.
ROCKY MOUNT, N.C. 27801

THOMAS B. BATTLE
ROCKY MOUNT MILLS
1151 FALLS RD.
ROCKY MOUNT, N.C. 27801

C.D. GARRETT
LITTLE MINT INC.
P.O. BOX 3455
GREENVILLE, N.C. 27834

J.H. LINEBERGER
PIEDMONT PROCESSING
P.O. BOX 1006
BELMONT, N.C. 28012

J.L. FRALEY
CAROLINA FREIGHT CARRIERS
BOX 697
CHERRYVILLE, N.C. 28021

SAM R. MAY JR.
CHINA GROVE COTTON MILLS
CHINA GROVE, N.C. 28023

C.E. WARNER
ELOX INC.
P.O. BOX 2227
DAVIDSON, N.C. 28036

JAMES H. MARTIN JR.
TEXTILES INC.
GASTONIA, N.C. 28052

FRED E. MYERS
WIX CORP.
P.O. BOX 1967
GASTONIA, N.C. 28053

HAROLD P. HORNADY
CANNON MILLS
P.O. BOX &
KANNAPOLIS, N.C. 28081

WAYNE BURRIS
BURRIS IND.
P.O. BOX 698
LINCOLNTON, N.C. 28092

T.E. COCHRANE
COCHRANE FURNITURE
402 EDWARDS ST.
LINCOLNTON, N.C. 28092

ROBERT LEHRER
WYNDMOOR IND.
P.O. BOX 818
LINCOLNTON, N.C. 28092

CARL L. MOSACK
CONSOLIDATED BRASS
P.O. BOX 247
MATTHEW, N.C. 28105

LEON LEVINE
FAMILY DOLLAR STORES
P.O. BOX 1276
MATTHEWS, N.C. 28005

ALVIN E. LEVINE
PIC'N PAY STORES
P.O. BOX 745
MATTHEWS, N.C. 28105

JOSEPH VITALE
PRF CORP.
201 CUTHBERTSON ST.
MONROE, N.C. 28010

RALPH W. KETNER
FOOD TOWN STORES
P.O. BOX 1330
SALISBURY, N.C. 28144

HENRY A. LINEBERGER
ROWAN COTTON MILLS
CHARLOTTE HWY.
SALISBURY, N.C. 28144

CHARLES H. REYNOLDS
SPINDALE MILLS
P.O. BOX 217
SPINDALE, N.C. 28160

ADIN H. RUCKER
STONECUTTER MILLS
SPINDALE, N.C. 28160

K.W. HORNE
HORNWOOD INC.
HIGHWAY 52 SOUTH
WADESBORO, N.C. 28170

F.A. HUNTLEY
WEST KNITTING
514 N. WASHINGTON ST.
WADESBORO, N.C. 38170

EDWIN P. LATIMER
AMERICAN DISCOUNT CO.
122 E. STONEWALL ST. BOX 2665
CHARLOTTE, N.C. 28201

JOHN T. FIELDER
J.B. IVEY
127 N. TRYON ST.
CHARLOTTE, N.C. 28201

A.F. SLOAN
LANCE INC.
P.O. BOX 2389
CHARLOTTE, N.C. 28201

THOMAS N. ROBOZ
STANWOOD CORP.
P.O. BOX 1891
CHARLOTTE, N.C. 28201

BLAND W. WORLEY
AMERICAN CREDIT
P.O. BOX 2665
CHARLOTTE, N.C. 28204

SHELTON GORELICK
C.M.C. GROUP
P.O. BOX 4229
CHARLOTTE, N.C. 28204

CALVIN J. HARRIS
ERVIN CO.
4037 E. INDEPENDENCE BLVD.
CHARLOTTE, N.C. 28205

RICHARD G. NOLTE
ENVIRONMENTAL CONTROL
P.O. BOX 15753
CHARLOTTE, N.C. 28210

GEORGE I. RAY JR.
THERMO PLASTICS
P.O. BOX 15694
CHARLOTTE, N.C. 28210

F. KENNETH IVERSON
NUCOR CORP.
4425 RANDOLPH RD.
CHARLOTTE, N.C. 28211

LAWRENCE J. SPEIZMAN
SPEIZMAN IND.
P.O. BOX 927
CHARLOTTE, N.C. 28231

T.J. NORMAN JR.
ENGRAPH
P.O. BOX 1888
CHARLOTTE, N.C. 28233

WAYLAND H. CATO JR.
CATO CORP.
P.O. BOX 2416
CHARLOTTE, N.C. 28234

ALAN T. DICKSON
RUDDICK CORP.
2000 JEFFERSON FIRST PLAZA
CHARLOTTE, N.C. 28282

JEROME SCHOTTENSTEIN
CORVAIR FURNITURE MFG.
1524 16TH. ST. N.E.
HICKORY, N.C. 28501

DAVID FUCHS
HAMPTON IND.
501 E. CASWELL ST.
KINSTON, N.C. 28501

WALLACE J. CONNER
CONNER HOMES
U.S. HIGHWAY 70
NEWPORT, N.C. 28570

HUBERT D. FRY SR.
HICORY-FRY FURNITURE
P.O. BOX 818
HICKORY, N.C. 28601

J.H. JOHNSON
HICKORY FURNITURE
P.O. BOX 998
HICKORY, N.C. 28601

JAMES L. ROBB
SUPERIOR CABLE
1928 MAIN ST.
HICKORY, N.C. 28601

ROGER HARD
CAROLINA CARIBBEAN CORP.
P.O. BOX 277
BANNER ELK, N.C. 28604

M.E. DIGH
MON'N' POP'S HAM HOUSE
BOX 399
CLAREMONT, N.C. 28610

RICHARD T. CHATHAM
CHATHAM MFG.
ELKIN, N.C. 28621

O. LEONARD MORETZ
CAROLINA MILLS
MAIDEN, N.C. 28650

JOHN COLLETT
HENREDON FURNITURE
MORGANTON, N.C. 28655

JOHN A. WALKER
LOWE'S CO. INC.
BOX 1111
NORTH WILKESBORO, N.C. 28659

LOUIS W. GARROU
ALBA-WALDENSIAN
VALDESE, N.C. 28690

C. FRANK GADLY JR.
BURKYARNS INC.
VALDESE, N.C. 28690

PHIFE C. ROSS
VALDESE MFG.
VALDESE, N.C. 28690

ROBERT W. TWITTY
MARION MFG.
BALDWIN AVE.
MARION, N.C. 28752

BRADLEY E. RAGAN
BRAD RAGAN INC.
112 GREENWOOD RD.
SPRUCE PINE, N.C. 28777

ROLF KAUFMAN
WELLCO ENTERPRISES
P.O. BOX 188
WAYNESVILLE, N.C. 28786

HERBERT J. BRONER
UNAGUSTA
WELCH RD.
WAYNESVILLE, N.C. 28786

WILLARD F. FOSTER
C.H. HEIST CORP.
1701 NORTHWESTERN BANK BLDG.
ASHVILLE, N.C. 28801

CLAUDE RAMSEY
AKZONA INC.
P.O. BOX 2930
ASHEVILLE, N.C. 28802

T. JOHN SCHILLEREFF
RONDESICS LEISURE HOMES
527 McDOWELL ST.
ASHEVILLE, N. C. 28803

JACK W. ROBINSON
MINERAL MINING CORP.
KERSHAW, S.C. 29067

H.A. BELLOWS
TRIANGLE CORP.
P.O. BOX 1807
ORANGEBURG, S.C. 29115

W.L. GANTE
COLITE IND.
229 PARSON ST.
WEST-COLUMBIA, S.C. 29169

STEPHEN W. TREWHELLA
SHAKESPEARE CO.
P.O. BOX 246
COLUMBIA, S.C. 29202

J.L. CROWDER
GIANT PORTLAND CEMENT
P.O. BOX 5907
COLUMBIA, S.C. 29205

E.M. BROOME
GENE BROOME SYSTEMS
806 BUSH RIVER RD.
COLUMBIA, S.C. 29210

J.S. BROADY
ATLANTIC PEPSI-COLA
P.O. BOX 4480
COLUMBIA, S.C. 29240

CLEVELAND S. HARLEY
HARLEY CORP.
P.O. BOX 5497
SPARTANBURG, S.C. 29301

J.J. RICHARDSON
SPARTAN FOOD SYSTEMS
INTERSTATE H'WAY. 85
SPARTANBURG, S.C. 29201

W.A. COLEMAN II
SYNALLOY CORP.
P.O. BOX 5627
SPARTANBURG, S.C. 29301

WALTER S. MONTGOMERY
SPARTAN MILLS
463 HOWARD ST.
SPARTANBURG, S.C. 29303

J.M. HAMRICK
MUSGROVE MILLS
515 WEST BUFORD ST.
GAFFNEY,S.C. 29340

STEVEN SONDOV
REPUBLIC MOBILE HOMES
P.O. BOX 401
LAURENS, S.C. 29260

ROBERT D. MALLIET
AMERICAN MICRO DEVICES
PEOPLES BLDG. STE. 809
CHARLESTON, S.C. 29401

I.H. JACOBSON
OCEAN HARVESTER INTERATIONAL
P.O. BOX 373
CHARLESTON, S.C. 29402

A.A. BURRIS JR.
BURRIS CHEM. INC.
P.O. BOX 4944
CHARLESTON, S.C. 29405

PAUL ALCON BELKNAP
CHARLESTON RUBBER CO.
P.O. BOX 4367
CHARLESTON, S.C. 29405

J.D. HASTIE
REEVES TELECOM
615 WESLEY DR.
CHARLESTON, S.C. 29407

MELVIN SOLOMON
SAM SOLOMON CO.
5935 RIVER AVE
CHARLESTON HEIGHTS, S.C. 29411

W.R. HERMAN
HERMIES INC.
P.O. BOX 832
FLORENCE, S.C. 29501

M.J. FOURTICO
STEM IND.
HIGHWAY 41
JOHNSONVILLE, S.C. 29555

R.B. SOPKIN
WENTWORTH MFG.
P.O. BOX 939
LAKE CITY, S.C. 29560

CHARLES W. COX
DANIEL IN'L. CORP.
DANIEL BLDG.
GREENVILLE, S.C. 29602

THOMAS M. BANCROFT
MOUNT VERNON MILLS
DANIEL BLDG.
GREENVILLE, S.C. 29602

WILSON C. WEARN
MULTIMEDIA INC.
P.O. BOX 1688
GREENVILLE, S.C. 29602

WADE H. STEPHENS JR.
ROSS BUILDERS
P.O. BOX 3056
GREENVILLE, S.C. 29602

J.W. BURNETT JR.
SOUTHERN WEAVING CO.
P.O. BOX 367
GREENVILLE, S.C. 29602

F.H. KAUFMANN
STEEL HEDDLE MFG.
P.O. BOX 1867
GREENVILLE, S.C. 29602

DAVID W. JOHNSTON JR.
DAN RIVER INC.
P.O. BOX 6126, STA. B.
GREENVILLE, S.C. 29606

E.E. MADDREY II
RIEGEL TEXTILE
P.O. BOX 6807
GREENVILLE, S.C. 29606

DONALD D. GREER
ROYAL SCOTSMAN INNS
P.O. BOX 6721, STA. B.
GREENVILLE, S.C. 29606

HAROLD A. KELLY
BI-LO INC.
DRAWER 99
MAULDIN, S.C. 29662

RONALD KLIMER
HER MAJESTY IND.
BON AIR ST.
MAULDIN, S.C. 29662

R.M. TREWHELLA
GLASSMASTER
P.O. BOX 788
LEXINGTON, S.C. 29702

C.G. MALMGREN
HUNTLEY OF YORK
P.O. BOX 419
YORK, S.C. 29745

ROBERT P. TIMMERMAN
GRANITEVILLE CO.
GRANITEVILLE, S.C. 29829

JAMES W. LIGHT
SEA PINES CO.
SEA PINES CIRCLE
HILTON HEAD ISLAND, S.C. 29928

CHARLES E. SELEGMAN
E.T. BARWICK IND.
NEW PEACHTREE RD.
CHAMBLEE, GEORGIA 30005

NED HEYWARD
WOODMAN CO.
113 NEW ST.
DECATUR, GEORGIA 30030

EDWARD A. ROLLOR JR.
ADVANCED RESEARCH CORP.
641 DE KALB IND. WAY.
DECATUR, GEORGIA 30033

DAVID A. CUNNINGHAM JR.
CUNNINGHAM ART PROD.
1555 ROADHAVEN DR.
STONE MOUNTAIN, GEORGIA 30038

RICHARD A. BEAUCHAMP
REFRIGERATED TRANSPORT CO.
P.O. BOX 308
FOREST PARK, GA. 30050

JOHN E. PIPPIN
ELECTOMAGNETIC SCIENCES
125 TECHNOLOGY PK.
ATLANTA, GA. 30071

JAMES R. HEWELL JR.
PEACHTREE DOORS INC.
P.O. BOX 700
NORCROSS, GA. 30071

GEORGE E. SMITH
J.M. TULL IND.
BLUE RIDGE IND. PK.
NORCROSS, GA. 30071

PETER H. STARR
R. T. SYSTEMS
1280 WINCHESTER PARKWAY
SMYRNA, GA. 30080

FRANK L. POIRIER
TREND IND.
ROME, GA. 30161

ROBERT J. FREEMAN
LITONIA LIGHTING INC.
CONYERS, GA. 30207

WILMER B. THOMPSON
DODGE WIRE CORP.
P.O. BOX 1017
COVINGTON, GA. 30209

WILLIAM M. LENDMAN
GLASROCK PRODUCTS
7380 BOHANNON RD.
FAIRBURN, GA. 30213

J.E. BARROW
JEBCO INC.
148 S. MAIN ST.
JONESBORO, GA. 30236

WILLIAM H. HIGHTOWER JR.
THOMASTON COTTON MILLS
115 E. MAIN ST.
THOMASTON, GA. 30286

EDWARD M. ABRAMS
ABRAMS IND.
P.O. BOX 1969
ATLANTA, GA. 30301

CARL J. REITH
OXFORD IND.
P.O. BOX 1618
ATLANTA, GA. 30301

R. RANDALL ROLLINS
ROLLINS INC.
P.O. BOX 647
ATLANTA, GA. 30301

W.L. BURGE
EQUIFAX INC.
P.O. BOX 4081
ATLANTA, GA. 30302

S.A. DAY
SCRIPTO INC.
423 HOUSTON ST. N.E.
ATLANTA, GA. 30302

R. CRAIG MURRAY
ATLANTIC AMERICAN CORP.
90 FAIRLIE ST., N.W.
ATLANTA, GA. 30303

CARL L. PATRICK
FUQUA IND.
FIRST NATIONAL BANK
FIRST NAT'L. BANK BLDG.
ATLANTA, GA. 30303

R.W. COURTS II
GREAT SOUTHERN ENTERPRISES
HURT BLDG.
ATLANTA, GA. 30303

PIERCE E. MARKS JR.
IVY CORP.
100 PEACHTREE ST.
ATLANTA, GA. 30303

A. H. FRYE
M & F GRAPHIC ARTS
220 KUCKIE ST. N.W.
ATLANTA, GA. 30303

JOEL GOLDBERG
RICH'S INC.
BROAD, ALABAMA, FORSYTH
ATLANTA, GA. 30303

J.B. SKONE
WORLD-WIDE COIN INVESTMENTS
2970 PEACHTREE RD. N.W.
ATLANTA, GA. 30305

T.G. GERMANY
CRAWFORD & CO.
131 PONCE DE LEON AVE., N.E.
ATLANTA, GA. 30308

L.D. PATTON
REDFERN FOODS
600 W. PEACHTREE ST. NW.#1604
ATLANTA, GA. 30308

F.S. RYAN
REID-PROVIDENT LABS.
25 FIFTH ST. N.W.
ATLANTA, GA. 30308

CLIFFORD M. KIRTLAND
COX BROADCASTING
1601 W. PEACHTREE ST. NE.
ATLANTA, GA. 30309

H.W. HARRIS
COX CABLE COMM. INC.
1601 W. PEACHTREE ST. NE.
ATLANTA, GA. 30309

W. BENNETT COLLETT
GENERAL RESOURCES
1409 PEACHTREE ST. N.E.
ATLANTA, GA. 30309

HIRAM F. GRIFFIES
UUNFORD INC.
68 BROOKWOOD DR. N.E.
ATLANTA, GA. 30309

ERWIN ZABAN
NAT'L. SERVICE IND.
P.O. BOX 7158
ATLANTA, GA. 30309

R.E. WILGUS
RHODES INC.
1100 SPRING ST.
ATLANTA, GA. 30309

R.E. TURNER
TURNER COMM. CORP.
1018 PEACHTREE ST. NW.
ATLANTA, GA. 30309

W.J. GILLELAND
XACRON CORP.
1409 PEACHTREE ST.
ATLANTA, GA. 30309

WILLIAM C. BARTHOLOMAY
ATLANTA BRAVES
521 CAPITOL AVE. S.E.
ATLANTA, GA. 30312

W.C. HATCHER
GENUINE PARTS CO.
299 PIEDMONT AVE. N.E
ATLANTA, GA. 30312

BENNETT N. OXMAN
ALLIED FOODS
P.O. BOX 2928 STA. D
ATLANTA, GA. 30318

L.G. DEWBERRY JR.
ATLANTIC STEEL
1300 MECASLIN ST.
ATLANTA, GA. 30318

J.D. CAGLE
CAGLE'S INC.
2000 HILLS AVE. N.W.
ATLANTA, GA. 30318

MICHAEL C. CARLOS
NAT'L. DISTRIBUTING
1455 ELLSWORTH IND. DR. NW.
ATLANTA, GA. 30318

T.P. ROTH
ANDERSON 2000, INC.
P.O. BOX 20769
ATLANTA, GA. 30320

ROBERT WEISTEIN
ELLMAN'S
2489 CHESHIRE BRIDGE RD.
ATLANTA, GA. 30324

D.A. SELLERS
DONUT KASTLE
6343 ROSWELL RD.
ATLANTA, GA. 30328

C.C. WORKMAN
MANAGEMENT SERVICES
3 CORPORATE SQ. N.E.
ATLANTA, GA. 30329

GEORGE W. THORPE
NAT'L. DATA CORP.
1 NATIONAL DATA PLAZA
ATLANTA, GA. 30329

ALLEN V. CROOM
SOVEREIGN IND.
1644 TULLIE CIRCLE N.E.STE.108
ATLANTA, GA. 30329

ISIDORE ALTERMAN
ALTERMAN FOODS
600 SELIG DR. S.W.
ATLANTA, GA. 30336

WM. H. WILKERSON
AUTO-SOLER CO.
5101 FULTON IND. BLVD.
ATLANTA, GA. 30336

S.A. MAKOVER
SHIRLEY OF ATLANTA
4200 SHIRLEY DR.
ATLANTA, GA. 30336

C. STEPHENSON
STEPHENSON CHEM. CO.
P.O. BOX 87188
COLLEGE PARK, GA. 30337

W.J. BIGGERS
AMERICAN BUSINESS PROD.
2690 CUMBERLAND PKWAY. STE.500
ATLANTA, GA. 30339

SIDNEY TOPOL
SCIENTIFIC-ATLANTA INC.
3845 PLEASANTDALE RD.
ATLANTA, GA. 30340

FRANK A. ARMSTRONG
THE MOXIE-MONARCH-NUGRAPE
3742 NORTHEAST FREEWAY
DORAVILLE, GA. 30340

ROBERT P. TYLER
SIMMONS CO.
P.O. BOX 4900
ATLANTA, GA. 30340

THOMAS S. CHEEK
VINTAGE ENTERPRISES
3825 NORTHEAST EXPRESSWAY
ATLANTA, GA. 30340

STEPHEN A. FURBACHER
NEPTUNE INT'L. CORP.
30 PERIMETER PARK
ATLANTA, GA. 30341

ERNEST F. BOYCE
COLONIAL STORES INC.
2251 N. SYLVAN RD.
EAST POINT, GA. 30344

STUART V. BOWEN
AUTOMATIC SERVICE
2175 PARKLAKE DR. N.E.
ATLANTA, GA. 30345

NEAL SCHACHTEL
GABLE IND.
41 PERIMETER CENTER E. STE. 660
ATLANTA, GA. 30346

DONALD A. McMAHON
ROYAL CROWN COLA CO.
41 PERIMETER CENTER EAST
ATLANTA, GEORGA 30346

ALVIN W. VOGTLE JR.
THE SOUTHERN CO.
64 PERIMETER CENTER E., BOX
ATLANTA, GA. 30346   720071

J. WILLIAM ROBINSON
JOHN H. HARLAND CO.
P.O. 105250
ATLANTA, GA. 30348

F.R. DICKERSON
ROPER IND.
BOX 269
COMMERCE, GA. 30529

GEORGE E. MC GRIFF JR.
MOBILE HOME SALES
P.O. BOX 6088
ATHENS, GA. 30604

GEORGE W. FELKER III
WALTON MILL CO.
MONROE, GA. 30655

BERNARD S. BARG
ALDON IND.
NORTH IND. BLVD.
CALHOUN, GA. 30701

MICHAEL BERNSTEIN
CROWN CRAFTS INC.
P.O. BOX 371
CALHOUN, GA. 30701

DAVID D. HAMILTON
GROWNAMERICA INC.
P.O. BOX 1127
DALTON, GA. 30720

ROBERT E. SHAW
SHAW IND. INC.
EAST FRANKLIN ST.
DALTON, GA. 30720

J.A. HUTCHINSON   JR.
BRIGARDIER IND.
P.O. DRAWER 954
THOMSON, GA. 30824

H.I. GILBERT
AUGUSTA CHEM. CO.
GLASS FACTORY AVE.
AUGUSTA, GA. 30901

W.E. LASSITER
FINE PRODUCTS CO.
823-31 TELFAIR ST.
AUGUSTA, GA. 30902

R.E. BROWN
DAISY CORP.
P.O. BOX 2206
AUGUSTA, GA. 30903

P.S. KNOX III
MERRY CO. INC.
P.O. BOX 1474
AUGUSTA, GA. 30903

GUY S. LEWIS
RIVERSIDE MILLS
P.O. BOX 2387
AUGUSTA, GA. 30903

WILLIAM R. MILLS
STYLECRAFT
P.O. BOX 1028
DUBLIN, GA. 31021

WILLIAM A. FICKLING JR.
CHARTER MED. CORP.
P.O. BOX 209
MACON, GA. 31202

WILLIAM S. MANNING
BIBB CO.
237 COLISEUM DR. BX.4207
MACON, GA. 31208

WILLIAM W. SPRAGUE JR.
SAVANNAH FOODS
P.O. BOX 339
SAVANNAH, GA. 31402

WILLIAM MULLIS
NEPTUNALIA SEAFOOD CO.
P.O. BOX 3776,STA. B.
SAVANNAH, GA. 31404

RICHARD PHILLIPS
LAND O'FABRICS
P.O. BOX 190
BRUNSWICK, GA. 31520

ROBERT D. CONNER
MODERN DIVERSIFIED IND.
P.O. BOX 1728
VALDOSTA, GA. 31601

JAMES H. GRAY
GRAY COMM. SYSTEMS
P.O. BOX 3130
ALBANY, GA. 31706

W.C. WEREEN JR.
MOULTRIE COTTON MILLS,
FIRST AVE. & 11TH. ST. SW.
MOULTRIE, GA. 31768

JASPER DAVIS
DAVIS WATER & WASTE
1828 METCALF AVE.
THOMASVILLE, GA. 31792

AMOS R. MC MULLAN
FLOWERS IND.
236 S. MADISON ST.
THOMASVILLE, GA. 31792

J.L. LANIER JR.
WEST POINT-PEPPERELL
P.O. BOX 71
WEST POINT, GA. 31833

A.B. EDGE III
COLUMBUS MILLS INC.
P.O. BOX 1560
COLUMBUS, GA. 31902

W.H.G. FRANCE
INT'L. SPEEDWAY
1801 VOLUSLA AVE.
DAYTONA BEACH, FLA. 32015

DR. JACKSON B. BRAGG
DAYTONA BEACH GEN. HOSPITAL
U.S. HIGHWAY 1
HOLLY HILL, FLA. 32017

M.C. WHATMORE
COWLES COMM. INC.
444 SEABREEZE BLVD.
DAYTONA BEACH, FLA. 32018

FRANK E. HERRERA
ECONO-CAR INT'L.
P.O. BOX 5765
DAYTONA BEACH, FLA. 32020

F. MONACO
MASTERCRAFT MED. & IND.
P.O. BOX 117
DELEON SPRINGS, FLA. 32023

KENT ROGERS
GENERAL ALLOYS CO.
150 SOUTH NOVA RD. BOX 337
ORMOND BEACH, FLA. 32074

GEORGE W. GIBBS JR.
GIBBS CORP.
BOX 89
SATSUMA, FLA. 32089

ROBERT H. PAUL III
CANADA DRY BOTTLING
711 MARGARET ST.
JACKSONVILLE, FLA. 32201

D.S. WEINSTEIN
DAYLIGHT IND.
P.O. BOX 52687
JACKSONVILLE, FLA. 32201

EDWARD L. BAKER
FLORIDA ROCK IND.
744 RIVERSIDE AVE.
JACKSONVILLE, FLA. 32201

WALLACE F. E. KIENAST
KOGER PROPERTIES
P.O. BOX 4520
JACKSONVILLE, FLA. 32201

W.R. LOVETT
PIGGLY WIGGLY CORP.
P.O. BOX 149
JACKSONVILLE, FLA. 32201

J.C. BELIN
ST. JOE PAPER CO.
P.O. BOX 1380
JACKSONVILLE, FLA. 32201

JOHN A. GILLILAND
STOCKTON, WHATLEY, DAVIN
100 WEST BAY ST.
JACKSONVILLE, FLA. 32202

PAUL STEWART
BAKER BROS.
558 STUART LN.
JACKSONVILLE, FLA. 32203

M.G. LEWIS
LEWIS BUSINESS FORMS
P.O. DRAWER M.
JACKSONVILLE, FLA. 32203

JACK H. QUARITIUS
McMILLEN CORP.
645 RIVERSIDE AVE.
JACKSONVILLE, FLA. 32203

BRUCE DOUGLAS
SAV-A-STOP INC.
7660 GAINESVILLE AVE.
JACKSONVILLE, FLA. 32203

BERT L. THOMAS
WINN-DIXIE STORES
5050 EDGEWOOD CT.
JACKSONVILLE, FLA. 32203

DONALD M. BISPLINGHOFF
ADCOM METALS CO.
925 N. LN. AVE.
JACKSONVILLE, FLA. 32205

FRED RUBIN
NATL. COMPACTOR
P.O. BOX 6922
JACKSONVILLE, FLA. 32205

JOHN R. SHAW
SOUTHERN BELLE FROZEN FOODS
P.O. BOX 3823
JACKSONVILLE, FLA. 32206

O.F. MATSON
HARRELL INTL. INC.
4161 CARMICHAEL AVE.
JACKSONVILLE, FLA. 32207

R.R. BOWEN
IND-AMERICA
1955 GULF LIFE TOWER
JACKSONVILLE, FLA. 32207

ALLAN J. MC CORKLE
MOBILE AMERICA CORP.
2118 GULF LIFE TOWER
JACKSONVILLE, FLA. 32207

W.L. DURDEN
SERVAMERICA INC.
1851 EXECUTIVE CENTER DR.
JACKSONVILLE, FLA. 32207

JULIAN E. JACKSON
LIL'CHAMP FOOD STORES
P.O. BOX 8987
JACKSONVILLE, FLA. 32211

J. DONALD FUFFKIN
MOTOR HOMES OF AMERICA
10360 BEACH BLVD.
JACKSONVILLE, FLA. 32216

JOSEPH G. POQUETTE
CITY COACH LINES
3733 UNIVERSITY BLVD. W. STE.212
JACKSONVILLE, FLA. 32217

SIDNEY RALPH
TOTAL SUPPLY
3733 UNIVERSITY BLVD. W.
JACKSONVILLE, FLA. 32217

WILLIAM S. SMITH JR.
UNIVERSAL ENVIRONMENTAL
P.O. BOX 1407
JACKSONVILLE BEACH, FLA. 32250

ROBERT A. RIEDEL
CONSURGICO CORP.
P.O. BOX 1509
TALLAHASSE, FLA. 32302

W.C. SMITH
SOUTHEASTERN SURGICAL
P.O. BOX 1509
TALLAHASSEE, FLA. 32302

D.C. PRICE
CAMPTOWN IND.
P.O. BOX 3187
TALLAHASSEE, FLA. 32303

J.T. WILLIAMS JR.
KILLEARN PROPERTIES
P.O. BOX 3635
TALLAHASSEE, FLA. 32303

JULIAN LARAMORE
MOBILE HOME IND.
P.O. BOX 2253
TALLAHASSEE, FLA. 32304

ALVIN L. DICKERSON JR.
GRO-PLANT IND.
765 EAST WASHINGTON ST.
MONTICELLO, FLA. 32344

J.R. CHESHIRE
MARIFARMS
P.O. BOX 2239
PANAMA CITY, FLA. 32401

JAMES E. LEWIS JR.
SUNSHINE-JR. STORES
P.O. BOX 2498
PANAMA CITY, FLA. 32401

HOWARD HUBBARD
ANTENNAS FOR COMM. INC.
486 CYPRESS RD.
OCALA, FLA. 32670

TERRY E. TREXLER
NOBILITY HOMES
P.O. BOX 1652
OCALA, FLA. 32670

R.L. WEBER
JOHNSON ELECTRONICS
P.O. BOX 7
CASSELBERRY, FLA. 32707

W.L. ROSE
ROSE INT'L. INC.
231 S. LIZ HOWELL RD.
CASSELBERRY, FLA. 32707

J.P. BRODERRICK
CONTINENTAL TESTING
763 HWY. 17-92
FERN PARK, FLA. 32730

R.L. BAKER
ELECTONE
110 ATLANTIC DR.
FERN PARK, FLA. 32730

F.R. HILL
MARINE RESOURCES
755 HIGHWAY 17
FERN PARK, FLA. 32730

T.C. EDWARDS
ROVAC CORP.
109 BLDG. CANDACE DR.
MAITLAND, FLA. 32751

EUGENE KERIK GARFIELD
AUTO-TRAIN
P.O. BOX 2159
SANFORD, FLA. 32771

RAYMOND D. SHAFFNER
ELECTRON-MACHINE
P.O. BOX M.
UMATILLA, FLA. 32784

A.R. KILBEY
ORTRONIX INC.
1870 BAKER DR.
WINTER PARK, FLA. 32789

DARRELL G. HAASS
AMERICAN PIONEER
P.O. BOX 3509
ORLANDO, FLA. 32802

DAVID H. HUGHES
HUGHES SUPPLY
521 W. CENTRAL BLVD.
ORLANDO, FLA. 32802

PAUL J. SPELLMAN
SPELLMAN ENGINEERING
P.O. BOX 6037
ORLANDO, FLA. 32803

TERRANCE W. MC LAUGHLIN
TROPICANNA POOLS
3600 E. COLONIAL DR.
ORLANDO, FLA. 32803

E.J. ELLIOTT
MECHTRON INT'L. CORP.
2140 W. WASHINGTON ST.
ORLANDO, FLA. 32805

D.C. BROWN
DBA SYSTEMS
1135 W. NASA BLVD.
MELBOURNE, FLA. 32901

JAMES SOTTILE III
THE GOLDFIELD CORP.
65 E. NASA BLVD.
MELBOURNE, FLA. 32901

H.H. MORGAN
ELECTRA-TRONICS
P.O. BOX 3306
COCOA, FLA. 32922

FREDRIC E. HELFAND
SCAN SYSTEMS
P.O. BOX 102
COCOA BEACH, FLA. 32931

H.E. CANNON
REAL EIGHT CO.
763 PINE TREE DR.
INDIAN HARBOUR BEACH, FLA. 32937

C. SHUMWAY
SHUMWAY OPTICAL INSTRUMENTS
104 TOMAHAWK DR.
INDIAN HARBOUR BEACH, FLA. 32937

E.H. BROOME
SYMETRICS IND.
1227 SOUTH PATRICK DR.
SATELLITE BEACH, FLA. 32937

R.C. DELANO
INT'L. CABELVISION
P.O. BOX 2500
VERO BEACH, FLA. 32960

DANIEL E. CHAIFETZ
INT'L. CITRUS CORP.
811 26TH. AVE.
VERO BEACH, FLA. 32960

MORRIS MARDER
AMERICAN URBAN
3149 W. HALLANDALE BEACH BLVD.
HALLANDALE, FLA. 33009

R.C. OTT
BROS. TWO INT'L.
1385 S.E. 9TH. AVE.
HIALEAH, FLA. 33010

ALBERT GOODSTEIN
DADE ENGINEERING
558 W. 18TH. ST.
HIALEAH, FLA. 33010

D.E. COURTNEY
ECO ELECTRICAL MFG.
445 W. 26TH. ST.
HIALEAH, FLA. 33010

E.S. CHRISTIANSEN
EQUIPMENT CO. OF AMERICA
1075 HIALEAH DR.
HIALEAH, FLA. 33010

ROWLAND SHAEFER
F.T. IND.
750 W. 18TH. ST.
HIALEAH, FLA. 33010

DAVID GOLDBERG
J.D. GRAMM INC.
461 HIALEAH DR.
HIALEAH, FLA. 33010

ALBERT GOODSTEIN
PERFECTO MFG.
558 W. 18TH. ST.
HIALEAH, FLA. 33010

ALBERT H. HAHMD
WATSCO INC.
1800 W. 4TH. AVE.
HIALEAH, FLA. 33010

ROWLAND SCHAEFER
FASHION TRESS
P.O. BOX 1210
HIALEAH, FLA. 33011

ZELIG L. BASS
UNIVERSAL JET IND.
P.O. BOX 70
HIALEAH, FLA. 33011

MORT ADLER
ADLER-BUILT IND.
2861 W. 14TH. CT.
HIALEAH, FLA. 33012

LEONARD BINDLER
COSMETICALLY YOURS
3320 W. 17TH. CT.
HIALEAH, FLA. 33012

EDWARD B. CAHEN
JOHN ALLMAND BOATS
6969 W. 20TH. AVE.
HIALEAH, FLA. 33013

I.E. EFEROFF
BENTLEY NAT'L. CORP.
1090 EAST 23RD. ST.
HIALEAH, FLA. 33013

ROBERT J. BRAUN
ALLIED LEISURE IND.
245 W. 74TH. PL.
HIALEAH, FLA. 33014

MURRAY GURMAN
ED. AIDS
8205 W. 20TH. AVE.
HIALEAH, FLA. 33014

R.M. ROSENBLOOM
LUMIDOR IND.
5360 N.W. 167TH. ST.
HIALEAH, FLA. 33014

KLEBER E. DUNKLIN
ROYAL CASTLE SYSTEM
6000 N.W. 153RD. ST.
HIALEAH, FLA. 33014

BELVIN FRIEDSON
SAVE-WAY BARBER
5300 N.W. 163RD. ST.
HIALEAH, FLA. 33014

A. BRENNER
SUPERIOR WINDOW CO.
540 W. 83RD. ST.
HIALEAH, FLA. 33014

NORMAN H. COHAN
SECURITY PLASTICS
14427 N.W. 60TH. AVE.
MIAMI LAKES, FLA. 33014

GERALD GREENBLATT
SUAVE SHOE CORP.
14100 N.W. 60TH. AVE.
MIAMI LAKES, FLA. 33014

ALLAN WOLK
URT IND.
9880 N.W. 77TH. AVE.
HIALEAH GARDENS, FLA. 33016

JOHN F. BENNETT
ADOBE BLDG.
2056 SCOTT ST.
HOLLYWOOD, FLA. 33020

JOHN P. CHRISTOPHER
NEPTUNIAN MARICULTURE
1942 HOLLYWOOD BLVD.
HOLLYWOOD, FLA. 33020

RONALD G. ASSAF
SENSORMATIC ELECTRONICS
2040 SHERMAN ST.
HOLLYWOOD, FLA. 33020

E.N. EDE
MEDCOR INC.
5920 RODMAN ST.
HOLLYWOOD, FLA. 33023

JACK FINEBERG
THE MINI MART CORP.
2991 S.W. 32ND. AVE.
HOLLYWOOD, FLA. 33023

JOHN M. RICHARDSON
RSC IND.
BLDG. 102 OPA LOCKS AIRPORT
OPA LOCKS, FLA. 33054

E.J. MANNING
NEW INDUSTRIAL TECH.
12325 W. SAMPLE RD.
CORAL SPRINGS, FLA. 33060

FREDERICK VAN LENNEP
CASTLETON IND.
1800 S.W. 3RD. ST.
POMPANO BEACH, FLA. 33060

MICHAEL IVASHUK
CONTROL LASER CORP.
1800 S.W. 7TH. AVE.
POMPANO BEACH, FLA. 33060

N.L. CHRISTOPHER
FILL-R-UP SYSTEMS
1025 S.W. 13TH. CT.
POMPANO BEACH, FLA. 33060

DONALD L. SMITH JR.
DEVCON INT'L.
1125 S.W. THIRD ST.
POMPANO BEACH, FLA. 33061

JACK B. NUDELMAN
LYNMAR LUMBER IND.
P.O. BOX 1360
POMPANO BEACH, FLA. 33061

PAUL H. ZIMMER
ZIMMER HOMES
P.O. BOX 1147
POMPANO BEACH, FLA. 33061

JANIS RISBERGS
GENERAL BUILDERS CORP.
P.O. BOX 2915
POMPANO BEACH, FLA. 33062

RICHARD D. LEVY
ORIOLE HOMES CORP.
450 N.W. 65TH. TERRACE
MARGATE, FLA. 33063

B.N. BATZER
PLASTILINE INC.
1251 N.E. 48TH. ST.
POMPANO BEACH, FLA. 33064

HARRISON M. LASKY
LEADERSHIP HOUSING
6006 UNIVERSITY DR.
TAMARAC, FLA. 33065

JOSEPH KLEIN
CAVANAGH COMM. CORP.
P.O. BOX 3580
MIAMI, FLA. 33101

WES MOFFATT
CRESTLINE IND.
P.O. BOX 3005
MIAMI, FLA. 33101

ALVAH H. CHAPMAN JR.
KNIGHT-RIDDER NEWSPAPERS
1 HERALD PLAZA
MIAMI, FLA. 33101

TED BODIN
BODIN APPAREL
3500 N.W. 79TH. ST.
MIAMI, FLA. 33110

JAMES H. KEEGAN JR.
ADVENTURE EXPLORATIONS
1901 N.W. SOUTH RIVER DR.
MIAMI, FLA. 33125

T.L. WATKINS JR.
MARINE EXPLORATION
2995 N.W. SOUTH RIVER DR.
MIAMI, FLA. 33125

J. GERALD MAYER
PEARCE-SIMPSON
4701 N.W. 77TH. AVE.
MIAMI, FLA. 33125

MILTON N. FISHER
PANELAB INT'L.
1600 N.E. LE JEUNE RD.
MIAMI, FLA. 33126

BERNARD BIELER
SOUTHERN DIVERSIFIED IND.
1650 N.W. 70TH. AVE.
MIAMI, FLA. 33126

ISADORE HERSKOWITZ
AMERICAN SERVICE CORP.
2159 N.W. FIRST CT.
MIAMI, FLA. 33127

P. DASH
DAVID & DASH INC.
2445 N. MIAMI AVE.
MIAMI, FLA. 33127

IRVING GOLDSTEIN
CHARRON-WILLIAMS SYSTEMS
255 S.W. 8TH. ST.
MIAMI, FLA. 33128

MITCHELL WOLFSTON
WOMETCO ENTERPRISES
316 N. MIAMI AVE.
MIAMI, FLA. 33128

FRANK E. MACKLE JR.
THE DELTONA CORP.
3250 S.W. 3RD. AVE.
MIAMI, FLA. 33129

CHARLES E. COBB JR.
ARVIDA CORP.
2020 ONE BISCAYNE TOWER
MIAMI, FLA. 33131

A.P. O'HARA
BACARDI CORP.
200 S.E. 1ST. ST. STE. 905
MIAMI, FLA. 33131

CHARLES DE MENZES
XIOX INT'L.
14 N.E. FIRST AVE.
MIAMI, FLA. 33131

H.N. MOSS
OTX INC.
444 BRICKELL AVE. STE. 1025
MIAMI, FLA. 33131

MS. NEIMAN
SUN CITY IND.
1111 S. BAYSHORE DR.
MIAMI, FLA. 33131

GUY B. BAILEY
UNITED RESOURCES
1000 RICKWELL AVE.
MIAMI, FLA. 33131

L.L. FINE
ADVANCE METAL
2424 S. DIXIE HIGHWAY
MIAMI, FLA. 33133

DANIEL BAITCHER
AMERDYNE IND.
30 SAMANA DR.
MIAMI, FLA. 33133

D.W. MATSON JR.
MATSON INT'L. CORP.
2600 S.W. 27TH. AVE.
MIAMI, FLA. 33133

D.W. MATSON JR.
MY NATIONAL CORP.
2600 S.W. 27TH. AVE.
MIAMI, FLA. 33133

JOHN B. SCOGGINS
AMCOURT SYSTEMS
1550 MADURA AVE.
CORAL CABLES, FLA. 33134

CLARENCE DAUPHINOT
DELTEC INT'L.
2801 PONCE DE LEON BLVD.
CORAL GABLES, FLA. 33134

GEORGE R. WACKENHUT
WACKENHUT CORP.
3280 PONCE DE LEON BLVD.
CORAL GABLES, FLA. 33134

CASTLE W. JORDAN
AEGIS CORP.
250 CATALONIA AVE. 705
MIAMI, FLA 33134

DONALD W. THAYER
BASIC FOOD IND.
7600 RED RD. 300
MIAMI, FLA. 33134

M.M. KRAUS
JERRY'S INC.
215 ZAMORA AVE.
MIAMI, FLA. 33134

JACK LASONDER
LAND & LEISURE
P.O. BOX BIN-C, 350 LINCOLN RD.
MIAMI BEACH, FLA. 33134

MARTIN OSMAN
ATLANTIC IND.
P.O. BOX 350637
MIAMI, FLA. 33135

JEROME BIENENFIELD
FLA. GLASS IND.
1601 N.W. 7TH. AVE.
MIAMI, FLA. 33136

DR. W.P. MURPHY JR.
CORDIS CORP.
125 N.E. 40TH. ST.
MIAMI, FLA. 33137

EGMONT SONDERLING
SONDERLING BROADCASTING
3050 BISCAYNE
MIAMI, FLA. 33137

D.S. DUBBIN
CANAVERAL INT'L. CORP.
7100 BISCAYNE BLVD.
MIAMI BEACH, FLA. 33138

S.H. WILLS
GAC CORP.
7880 BISCAYNE BLVD.
MIAMI, FLA. 33138

BARNEY B. LEE
MIAMI TILE & TERRAZZO
6454 N.E. 4TH. AVE.
MIAMI, FLA. 33138

GERALD ROBINS
ROLAND INT'L.
8101 BISCAYNE BLVD.
MIAMI, FLA. 33138

HERBERT L. KAPLAN
ROYAL PALM BEACH
8080 N.E. FIFTH AVE.
MIAMI, FLA. 33138

JACK TAYLOR
TAYLOR RLTY.
941 N.E. 79TH. ST.
MIAMI, FLA. 33138

ROBERT BIRENBAUM
VIKING GEN. CORP.
123 N.E. 79TH. ST.
MIAMI, FLA. 33138

PHILIP E. SIMON
WCA INT'L. INC.
238 N.E. 79TH. ST.
MIAMI, FLA. 33138

BARBARA DUBBIN
CASA BELLA IMPORTS
1801 BAY RD.
MIAMI BEACH, FLA. 33139

BERNARD H. HOROWITZ
EQUITABLE DEVELOPMENT
546 LINCOLN RD.
MIAMI, FLA. 33139

IRWIN H. MASON
FOTO IND.
1252 WASHINGTON AVE.
MIAMI BEACH, FLA. 33139

LES KERN
IMEX CORP.
320 SO. HIBISCUS DR.
MIAMI, FLA. 33139

BENJAMIN CHAVES
PROPERTY LEASING
407 LINCOLN RD.
MIAMI BEACH, FLA. 33139

LEE RATNER
COMPUTER COLLEGE
800 71ST. ST.
MIAMI BEACH, FLA. 33141

VICTOR POSNER
D.W.G. CORP.
6917 COLLINS AVE.
MIAMI BEACH, FLA. 33141

ROGER STAKE
UNIVERSAL HOUSING
6917 COLLINS AVE.
MIAMI BEACH, FLA. 33141

VICTOR POSNER
WILSON BROS.
6917 COLLINS AVE.
MIAMI BEACH, FLA. 33141

LEONARD L. TAICHER
CARESSA
3601 N.W. 54TH. ST.
MIAMI, FLA. 33142

LEONARD A. SOLOMAN
DIVERSIFIED SERVICES
2601 N.W. LE JEUNE RD.
MIAMI, FLA. 33142

VICTOR REITER
THE LAWNLITE CO.
3789 N.W. 46TH. ST.
MIAMI, FLA. 33142

J.D. OLSHEN
OLSHEN OVERSEAS
3595 N.W. 46TH. ST.
MIAMI, FLA. 33142

LEWIS I. SERBIN
SERBIN FASHIONS
3480 NORTH WEST 41ST ST.
MIAMI, FLA. 33142

R.P. DONOVAN
WORLD JA-ALAI INC.
3500 N.W. 37TH. AVE.
MIAMI, FLA. 33142

JOHN HOUGHTALING
MAGIC FINGERS
7800 RED RD. STE. 213
MIAMI, FLA 33143

M.R. RUSSINOF
BARRY-MARTIN PHARMACEUTICALS
5792 S.W. 8TH. ST.
MIAMI, FLA. 33144

PHILIP TASHMAN
PRECISION IND.
7500 N.W. 41ST ST.
MIAMI, FLA. 33144

W.S. BARKETT SR.
ROCKET IND.
P.O. BOX 608
MIAMI, FLA. 33144

WILLIAM M. PORTER
CONTEXT IND.
3010 CORAL WAY
MIAMI, FLA. 33145

ROBERT D. GROSSMAN
FORWARD IND.
3491 N.W. 79TH.ST.
MIAMI, FLA. 33147

ROBERT RUSSELL
MIAMI EXTRUDERS
3775 N.W. 77TH.ST.
MIAMI, FLA. 33147

CHARLES M. LEAVY
NAT'L. LITHOGRAPHERS
7700 N.W. 37TH. AVE.
MIAMI, FLA. 33147

W.H. HEGAMYER
PIONEER METALS
3611 N.W. 74TH. ST.
MIAMI, FLA. 33147

AL WEINER
RENARD MFG.
3131 N.W. 79TH AVE.
MIAMI, FLA. 33147

JACK MASSAR
RICHFORD IND.
6250 N.W. 35TH AVE.
MIAMI, FLA. 33147

THOMAS H. GERARD
TIF INSTRUMENTS
3661 N.W. 74TH. ST.
MIAMI, FLA. 33147

PAUL J. FINAZZO
AIRLIFT INT'L.
MIAMI INT'L. AIRPORT
MIAMI, FLA. 33148

NICOLAS STERN
CARIBBEAN SHOE CORP.
P.O. BOX 480397
MIAMI, FLA. 33148

JAMES W. SMITH SR.
WOLLARD AIRCRAFT SERVICE
6950 N.W. 77TH. AVE.
MIAMI, FLA. 33148

JOSEPH STEIN
MAXITRON CORP.
1121 GRANDON BLVD.
KEY BISCAYNE, FLA. 33149

RICHARD H. SWESNIK
THOR CORP.
801   41ST ST.
MIAMI BEACH, FLA. 33150

J. LINDHEIMER
WHITECRAFT IND.
7350 N.W. MIAMI CT.
MIAMI, FLA. 33150

EDWIN H. HILL JR.
HILL BROS.
P.O. BOX 765
MIAMI, FLA. 33152

LEO A. CHAIKIN
SHELL'S CITY
P.O. BOX 763
MIAMI, FLA. 33152

PETER STORER
STORER BROADCASTING
1177 KANE CONCOURSE
MIAMI BEACH, FLA. 33154

LEONARD MILLER
LENNAR CORP.
9555 N. KENDALL DR.
MIAMI, FLA. 33156

S.W. FREEDMAN
PTC. IND.
708 DADELAND TOWERS
MIAMI, FLA. 33156

WALTER B. HARVEY JR.
WALTER HARVEY CORP.
9501 COLONIAL DR.
MIAMI, FLA. 33157

L.L. GARBETT
ALSON IND.
2690 N.E. 191ST ST.
MIAMI, FLA. 33160

JAY M. TISCHENKEL
CONTINENTAL DRUG
13000 N.W. 47TH. AVE.
MIAMI, FLA. 33161

MORTON D. WEINER
NORIN CORP.
12100 N.E. 16TH. AVE.
NORTH MIAMI, FLA. 33161

I.G. DAVIS JR.
RESORTS INT'L.
915 N.E. 125TH. ST.
NORTH MIAMI, FLA. 33161

LEONARD DUBLIN
DUBLIN ENGINEERING
18500 N.E. FIFTH AVE.
NORTH MIAMI BEACH, FLA. 33162

H.A. KELLER
KELLER IND.
1800 STATE RD. 9
MIAMI, FLA. 33162

S.G. GREENSTEIN
STERLING GENERAL
1345 N.E. 163RD ST.
N. MIAMI BEACH, FLA. 33162

STANLEY FRIEDMAN
SMART-PAK IND.
19401 W. DIXIE HIGHWAY
MIAMI, FLA. 33163

R.G. HOLMES
AERO SYSTEMS
5700 N.W. 36TH ST.
MIAMI SPRINGS, FLORIDA 331166

LLOYD ROTHENBERG
AUTOMATED MED. LABS.
7501 N.W. 66ST.
MIAMI, FLA. 33166

EUGENE C. FERRI JR.
IMPERIAL IND.
8600 N.W. SOUTH RIVER DR.
MIAMI, FLA. 33166

LAWRENCE P. PUCKETT JR.
PRESTRESSED SYSTEMS
5601 N.W. 72ND AVE.
MIAMI, FLA. 33166

LESLIE O. BARNES
RYDER SYSTEM
3600 N.W. 82ND AVE.
MIAMI, FLA. 33166

ROBERT J. SHELLEY
SHELLEY MFG. CO.
4225 N.W. 72ND AVE.
MIAMI, FLA. 33166

I.J. WOLLOWICK
BEVERAGE CANNERS
3550 N.W. 110TH ST.
MIAMI, FLA. 33167

RICHARD FIRST
REAL ESTATE DATA
2398 N.W. 119TH ST.
MIAMI, FLA. 33167

CHARLES E. TENNESSON
AMICOR
20215 N.W. SECOND AVE.
MIAMI, FLA. 33169

ROCCO TARANTINO
ANODYNE
1270 N.W. 165TH ST.
NORTH MIAMI BEACH, FLA. 33169

MARTIN ROTHMAN
AUTOMATED BUSINESS CONTROLS
P.O. BOX 3514
MIAMI, FLA. 33169

JOSEPH G. FLANIGAN
BIG DADDY'S LOUNGES
16565 NORTHWEST 15TH. AVE.
MIAMI, FLA. 33169

W.C. RUNNSTROM
DATATYPE CORP.
1050 N.W. 163RD DR.
MIAMI, FLA. 33169

E.R. SCHARPS
DECRAFORM
1251 N.W. 165TH. ST.
MIAMI, FLA. 33169

MICHAEL JAHARIS JR.
KEY PHARMACEUTICALS
50 N.W. 176 TH ST.
MIAMI, FLA. 33169

JULIUS MUFSON
JEFFERSON STORES
15800 N.W. 13TH AVE.
MIAMI, FLA. 33169

ROBERT M. ELLIOTT
LEVITZ FURNITURE
1400 N.W. 167TH ST.
MIAMI, FLA. 33169

ALEXANDER MILLER
MILLER IND.
16295 N.W. 13TH. AVE.
MIAMI, FLA. 33169

R. ROSENBERG
NORTH AMERICAN BIOLOGICALS.
15960 N.W. 15TH. ST.
MIAMI, FLA. 33169

G.J. KOTLER
SUN-GLO PRODUCTS
1130 N.W. 159TH. DR.
MIAMI, FLA. 33169

JOSEPH L. GREENWELL
ALLIED GENERAL
14200 S.W. 256TH ST.
PRINCETON, FLA. 33171

DR. MICHAEL SOSSIN
SOSSIN SYSTEM
11750 BIRD RD.
MIAMI, FLA. 33175

E.P. THAL
BUNING THE FLORIST
144 E. LAS OLAS BLVD.
FORT LAUDERDALE, FLA. 33301

GERRY LUPO
RICHARDS AIRCRAFT SUPPLY
P.O. BOX 278
FORT LAUDERDALE, FLA. 33302

DOV DUNAEVSKY
RAPIDEK IND.
P.O. BOX 2366
FORT LAUDERDALE, FLA. 33303

ROBERT C. RADICE
AMERICAN COMMUNITY
2601 E. OAKLAND PK. BLVD.
FORT LAUDERDALE, FLA. 33306

ROBERT C. RADICE
AMERICAN MODULAR COMM.
2601 EAST OAKLAND PARK BLVD.
FORT LAUDERDALE, FLA. 33306

DAVID C. YODER
COMPUTER PRODUCTS
P.O. BOX 23849
FORT LAUDERDALE, FLA. 33307

HAROLD N. MORRIS
DATACRAFT CORP.
P.O. BOX 23550
FORT LAUDERDALE, FLA. 33307

E.A. COSENTINO
ARCHITECTUAL MARBLE CO.
4425 N.E. 6TH. TERRACE
FORT LAUDERDALE, FLA. 33308

ALAN GORDICH
ATLAS AMERICAN CORP.
721 N.E. 42ND. ST.
FORT LAUDERDALE, FLA. 33308

CY J. CASE
BAIRD-CASE FUNERAL HOMES
4343 N. FEDERAL HIWHWAY
FORT LAUDERDALE, FLA. 33308

WILLIAM SELEWACZ
DIGITAL PRODUCT.
4030 N.E. SIXTH AVE.
FORT LAUDERDALE, FLA. 33308

T.S. KLISTON
BIOMEDICAL IND.
3501 POWERLINE RD.
FORT LAUDERDALE, FLA. 33309

JORN JENSEN
JENSEN CORP.
1101 N.W. 69TH ST.
FORT LAUDERDALE, FLA. 33309

KENNETH G. HARPLE
MODULAR COMPUTER
1650 W. McNAB RD.
FORT LAUDERDALE, FLA. 33309

R.L. SJOSTROM
SJOSTROM AUTOMATIONS
1101 N.W. 69TH ST.
FORT LAUDERDALE, FLA. 33309

RICHARD W. STEPHAN
THE STEPHAN CO.
1850 W. McNAB RD.
FORT LAUDERDALE, FLA. 33309

ALEC R. FABERMAN
ALOE CREME LABS.
P.O. BOX 9477
FORT LAUDERDALE, FLA. 33310

E. ARCHIE MISH
BAYUK CIGARS
2150 S. ANDREWS AVE.
FORT LAUDERDALE, FLA. 33310

CRAIG A. NALEN
STP CORP.
1400 W. COMMERCIAL BLVD.BX.9828
FORT LAUDERDALE, FLA. 33310

STANLEY R. ROSENTHAL
ALL-STATE PROPERTIES
4200 N.W. 16TH ST.
LAUDERHILL, FLA. 33313

JACK KORY
U.S. DYNAMICS
4740 S.W. 82ND. AVE.
DAVIE, FLA. 33314

JAMES C. FLOYD
PEC IND.
P.O. BOX 22873
FORT LAUDERDALE, FLA. 33315

EVERETT A. COOPER
SUNAIR ELECTRONICS
3101 S.W. THIRD AVE.
FORT LAUDERDALE, FLA. 33315

JOSEPH C. MACKEY
MACKEY INT'L.
3116 S. ANDREWS AVE.
FORT LAUDERDALE, FLA. 33316

HOWARD H. MILLER
H. MILLER & SONS
7421 NW 4TH.
FORT LAUDERDALE, FLA. 33317

HUGH E. McQUIRE
GROUND-DATA CORP.
P.O. BOX 15337
P.LANTATION, FLA. 33318

E.L. SLATER
VISUAL GRAPHICS
5701 N.W. 94TH AVE.
TAMARAC, FLA. 33321

HENRY EPSTEIN
GULFSTREAM LAND & DEVELOPMENT
8751 W. BROWARD BLVD.
FORT LAUDERDALE, FLA. 33324

NICK A. CAPORELLA
BURNUP & SIMS
4047 OKEECHOBEE RD.
WEST PALM BEACH, FLA. 33401

H. IRWIN LEVY
CENVILL COMM. INC.
CENTURY VILLAGE
WEST PALM BEACH, FLA. 33401

M.E. CARROLL
STERLING PRECISION
319 CLEMATIS ST.,STE. 900
W. PALM BEACH, FLA. 33401

A. KENNETH PINCOURT JR.
TODHUNTER INT'L.
P.O. BOX O,
W. PALM BEACH, FLA. 33402

W.L. CARGILL
MRI PROPERTIES
4176 BURNS RD.
PALM BEACH GARDENS, FLA. 33403

GEORGE LEWSON
KEY LEARNING SYSTEMS
301 BROADWAY
RIVIERA BEACH, FLA. 33404

GEORGE LEWSON
OCEANOGRAPHY DEVELOPMENT
301 BROADWAY
RIVIERA BEACH, FLA. 33404

R.W. TALMO
DATA LEASE FINANCIAL
618 N. FED. H'WAY.
NORTH PALM BEACH, FLA. 33408

H.M SYLVESTER JR.
FASCO IND.
601 N. FED. H'WAY.
BOCA RATON, FLA. 33432

A.L. GUTERMA
UNITED COMMUNITIES
499 EAST PALMETTO PK. RD.
BOCA RATON, FLA. 33432

JOHN B. BOY
U.S. SUGAR
P.O. BOX 1207
CLEWISTON, FLA. 33440

R. MATTSON
SCOTT-MATTSON FARMS
211 PROFESSIONAL BLDG.
FORT PIERCE, FLA. 33450

ROBERT A. JAEB
SHOP & CO.
P.O. BOX 428
MANGO, FLA. 33550

A. STANLEY TAYLOR
AMERICAN FOODS INC.
RTE. 1, P.O. BOX 1005
LAKE WORTH, FLA. 33460

S.K. ELLENBOGEN
COMET INT'L. CORP.
178 NORTH COUNTY RD.
PALM BEACH, FLA. 33480

MAC D. HOY
MOAMCO CORP.
P.O. BOX 2465
PALM BEACH, FLA. 33480

DAVID H. JONES
ELECTRONIC DATA
5315   14TH ST., WEST
BRADENTON, FLA. 33505

ANTHONY T. ROSSI
TROPICANA PRODUCTS
P.O. BOX 338
BRADENTON, FLA. 33505

H.J. FRANK
AEROSONIC
1212 N. HERCULES AVE.
CLEARWATER, FLA. 33515

CHARLES RUTENBERG
U.S. HOME
2536 COUNTRYSIDE BLVD. STE.471
CLEARWATER, FLA. 33515

JOHN R. VICKERY JR.
MED. SCIENTIFIC INTL.
1425 S. BELCHER RD.
CLEARWATER, FLA. 33516

WILLIAM D. CALLAGHAN JR.
PIONEER WESTERN CORP.
301 PIERCE ST.
CLEARWATER, FLA. 33516

STEWART TURLEY
JACK ECKERD CORP.
P.O. BOX 4689
CLEARWATER, FLA. 33518

JUNE E. BAUMGARDNER
KAPOK TREE INNS
923 NORTH HAINES RD.
CLEARWATER, FLA. 33519

M.E. LEVINSON
OCEAN PROD. INC.
RTE. 574 & GALLAGHER RD.
DOVER, FLA. 33527

M.E. LEVINGSON
TREASURE ISLE
RTE. 574 & GALLAGHER RD.
DOVER, FLA. 33527

FRANKLIN T. SCHULTZ
PHARMACARE
7111 ULMERTON RD.
LARGO, FLA. 33540

EARL M. SLOSBERG
PLASTICS DEVELOPMENT
3914 McKAY CREEK DR.
LARGO, FLA. 33546

R.E. WEST
SUNSHINE PARK RACING
OLDSMAR, FLA. 33557

A.K. ANDERSON
A.B.A. IND.
P.O. BOX 517
PINELLAS PARK, FLA. 33565

FRED L. CHASE
PACEMASTER
801 EAST BAKER ST.
PLANT CITY, FLA. 33566

MELVIN S. GORDON
PARADISE FRUIT CO.
P.O. DRAWER Y
PLANT CITY, FLA. 33566

IRA KAMEN
THE LASER LINK CORP.
101 BENJ. FRANKLIN DR. APT. 72
SARASOTA, FLA. 33577

GEORGE R. O'DAY
HUPSI CORP.
1847 S. JAMIAMI TRAIL
VENICE, FLA. 33593

T.E. BRONSON
FLA. MINING & MATERIALS
P.O. BOX 1050
TAMPA, FLA. 33601

W.L. VAN DYKE
HAVATAMPA CORP.
500 S. FALKENBURG RD.
TAMPA, FLA. 33601

MARIO R. CABERA
REDWING CARRIERS
P.O. BOX 426
TAMPA, FLA. 33601

JORDON L. LARSON
TOWER CREDIT
P.O. BOX 1215
TAMPA, FLA. 33601

W.A. KRUSEN
CHEMEX IND.
P.O. BOX 5072
TAMPA, FLA. 33605

ROBERT DRESSLER
CROWN IND.
P.O. BOX 18125
TAMPA, FLA. 33609

M.P. HAYMAN
DATA DYNAMICS
5422 BAY CENTER
TAMPA, FLA. 33609

BOB JACOBSON
DIBBS ALUMINUM PROD.
P.O. BOX 18125
TAMPA, FLA. 33609

E.H. HOORNSTRA
LI'L. GEN. STORES
P.O. BOX 13198
TAMPA, FLA. 33611

G.L. FINCH JR.
ALDERMAN INTERIOR
4511 W. BUFFALO AVE.
TAMPA, FLA. 33614

HAROLD HOLDER
AMERICAN AGRONOMICS
P.O. BOX 24247
TAMPA, FLA. 33622

RALPH EUBANKS
AUTOMATIC MERCHANDISING
P.O. BOX 23088
TAMPA, FLA. 33622

E.L. FLOM
FLORIDA STEEL CORP.
P.O. BOX 23328
TAMPA, FLA. 33622

JULIAN LEMUS
LEEDS SHOES INC.
P.O. BOX 23687
TAMPA, FLA. 33622

JOE B. CORBELL
THE JIM WALTER CORP.
P.O. BOX 22601
TAMPA, FLA. 33622

DANA M. GROFF
GROFF IND.
P.O. BOX 15056
TAMPA, FLA. 33684

MICHAEL J. PAOLINI
DIGITAL COMM. INC.
310 14TH AVE. SOUTH
ST. PETERSBURG, FLA. 33701

THEODORE SINGELIS
METROCARE INC.
2100 62ND. AVE. N.
ST. PETERSBURG, FLA. 33702

ABRAHAM LEVINE
DATA RESEARCH
4910 1ST AVE. NORTH
ST. PETERSBURG, FLA. 33710

M.A. ROTHMAN
KANE FURNITURE
3390 46TH AVE., NORTH
ST. PETERSBURG, FLA. 33714

CHARLES K. CHEEZEM
CHEEZEM DEVELOPMENT
P.O. BOX 237
ST. PETERSBURG, FLA. 33731

E. REX SMYTH
CONCEPT
AIRPORT STA.
ST. PETERSBURG, FLA. 33732

G.L. ALBIN
MEDFIELD
P.O. BOX 15207
ST. PETERSBURG, FLA. 33733

WILLIAM L. COBB
PINELLAS IND.
P.O. BOX 11869
ST. PETERSBURG, FLA. 33733

ALAN HENRY
RAHALL COMM. CORP.
P.O. BOX 14000
ST. PETERSBURG, FLA. 33733

J. STANLEY SARGEANT
ORANGE BLOSSOM PRODUCT.
P.O. BOX 433
LAKELAND, FLA. 33802

JAMES W. SIKES
SIKES CORP.
P.O. BOX 447
LAKELAND, FLA. 33802

JOHN H. McKNIGHT
CUTLER-FED. INC.
P.O. DRAWER M.
EATON PARK, FLA. 33840

T.C. FLOYD
FLOYD ENTERPRISES
P.O. BOX 367
HAINES CITY, FLA. 33844

JAMES FENTRESS
CONSOLIDATED TOMOKA
P.O. BOX 1907
SEBRING, FLA. 33870

R.D. POPE JR.
FLA. CYPRESS GARDENS
P.O. BOX 1
CYPRESS GARDENS, FLA. 33880

RAY H. COONEY
SCOTTY'S
P.O. BOX 939
WINTER HAVEN, FLA. 33880

WILBUR H. COLE
PUNTA GORDA ISLES
1769 W. MARION AVE.
PUNTA GORDA, FLA. 33950

K.W. SCHWARTZ
AMERICAN DEPT. STORES
3333 CLEVELAND AVE.
FT. MEYERS, FLA. 33901

ISADORE HECHT
SOUTHWEST FLA. ENTERPRISES
3333 CLEVELAND AVE.
FORT MYERS, FLA. 33902

J.R. SPRATT
ALICO INC.
P.O. BOX 338
LA BELLE, FLA. 33935

GERALD H. GOULD
LEHIGH ACRES
201 E. JOEL BLVD.
LEHIGH ACRES, FLA. 33936

E.C. GWALTNEY
RUSSELL CORP.
ALEXANDER CITY, AL. 35010

S.P. KIMERLING
ALABAMA OXYGEN CO.
P.O. BOX 309
BESSEMER, AL. 35020

J.R. SCHILLER
SCHILLER IND.
2000 HIGHWAY 157 W. BX. 1088
CULLMAN, AL. 35055

WILLIAM L. BAGGET
SPRING VALLEY FOODS
EMPIRE, AL. 35063

DONALD COMER JR.
AVONDALE MILLS
SYLACAUGA, AL. 35150

JOSEPH BRUNO
BRUNO'S INC.
P.O. BOX 2486
BIRMINGHAM, AL. 35201

K.G. ROBINSON III
COMPUTER SERVICENTER
P.O. BOX 1536
BIRMINGHAM, AL. 35201

J.A. WILLIAMSON
COMPUTERIZED AUTO
12 OFFICE PK.CIRLCE, BX.235
BIRMINGHAM, AL. 35201

J.W. NALL
GOLDEN FLAKE
P.O. BOX 2447
BIRMINGHAM, AL. 35201

J.G. WALLER
KENPLASCO
BOX 1332
BIRMINGHAM, AL. 35201

CALDWELL MARKS
MOTION IND.
P.O. BOX 1477
BIRMINGHAM, AL. 35201

F.G. KOENIG JR.
ALABAMA BY-PRODUCTS
P.O. BOX 10246
BIRMINGHAM, AL. 35202

JOHN S. SHAW JR.
SOUTHERN NAT'L. RESOURCES
P.O. BOX 2563
BIRMINGHAM, AL. 35202

EMORY O. CUNNINGHAM
PROGRESSIVE FARMER CO.
820 SHADES CREEK PARKWAY
BIRMINGHAM, AL. 35209

N.L. ANDREWS JR.
PASQUALE FOOD
19 W. OXMOOR RD.
BIRMINGHAM, AL. 35219

JEFFERSON W. DAVIS
EXPEDITER SYSTEMS
200 OFFICE PK. DR.
BIRMINGHAM, AL. 35223

J.H.R. CROMWELL
KARDAR CANADIAN OILS
P.O. BOX 7603-A
BERMINGHAM, AL. 35223

ROBERT W. ARNOLD
POLLUTION CONTROL
200 OFFICE PK. DR.
MOUNTAIN BROOK, AL. 35223

BERNARD A. MONAGHAN
VULCAN MAT. CO.
P.O. BOX 7497
BIRMINGHAM, AL. 35223

JOHN V. JONES
BESSEMER COAL
P.O. BOX 7800
BIRMINGHAM, AL. 35228

T. MORRIS HACKNEY
HACKNEY CORP.
P.O. BOX 7887
BIRMINGHAM, AL. 35228

HENRY C. CHEEK
DELWOOD FURNITURE
701 S. 20TH. ST.
BIRMINGHAM, AL. 35233

HARRIS SAUNDERS JR.
SAUNDERS LEASING
P.O. BOX 43000
BIRMINGHAM, AL. 35243

DON N. TIDWELL
TIDWELL IND.
P.O. BOX 679
HALEYVILLE, AL. 35565

N.J. KEMP
CONTINENTAL CONVEYOR
P.O. BOX 400
WINFIELD, AL. 35594

PETER D. PETROFF
CARE ELECTRONICS
4102 PIEDMONT DR.
HUNTSVILLE, AL. 35802

OLIN B. KING
SCI SYSTEMS
8620 SOUTH MEMORIAL PKWAY
HUNTSVILLE, AL. 35802

HUGH H. AIKEN
GEN. COMPUTER SERVICE
P.O. BOX 5148
HUNTSVILLE, AL. 35805

KENNETH J. FOWLER
DANMONT CORP.
110 WYNN DR., N.W.
HUNTSVILLE, AL. 35806

F.H. MARTIN JR.
MARTIN IND.
P.O. BOX 1527
HUNTSVILLE, AL. 35807

JAMES D. MURPHY JR.
AMERICAN BLDG.
STATE DOCKS RD.
EUFAULA, AL. 36027

WINSTON M. BLOUNT
BLOUNT INC.
P.O. BOX 949
MONTGOMERY, AL. 36101

CHARLES W. JONES
RING AROUND PRODUCTS
P.O. BOX 589
MONTGOMERY, AL. 36101

PERRY MENDEL
KINDER-CARE LEARNING
P.O. BOX 2151
MONTGOMERY, AL. 36103

WILLIAM A. WILLIAMSON JR.
DURR-FILLAUER MEDICAL INC.
2061 W. FAIRVIEW AVE.
MONTGOMERY, AL. 36108

J.R. MAUMENEE
ALABAMA DRY DOCK
P.O. BOX 1507
MOBILE, AL. 36601

DAVID A. STICKELBER
MARION CORP.
P.O. BOX 16006 BEL AIR STA.
MOBILE, AL. 36606

RICHARD L. REINER
SUPER STORES INC.
1310 TELEGRAPH RD.
PRICHARD, AL. 36611

D.R. COWART
MORRISON INC.
P.O. BOX 2608
MOBILE, AL. 36625

WILLIAM M. HANNON
MURRAY OHIO MFG.
P.O. BOX 606
BRENTWOOD, TENN. 37027

PETER W. LUFKIN
WINNER CORP.
19T. & PICKERT STS.
DICKSON, TENN. 37055

JACK DALTON
KOLPAK IND.
P.O. BOX 428
LOBELVILLE, TENN. 37097

LOUIS FIELD
FLC CORP.
301 FOURTH AVE. S.
NASHVILLE, TENN. 37201

JOEL C. GORDON
GEN. CARE CORP.
6213 CHARLOTTE AVE.
NASHVILLE, TENN. 37201

C. STROHM JR.
BREEKO IND.
P.O. BOX 1247
NASHVILLE, TENN. 37202

JACK C. MASSEY
HOSPITAL CORP.
ONE PARK PLAZA
NASHVILLE, TENN. 37202

ERNEST L. WAINSCOTT
MINERVA INTERNAT'L. INC.
P.O. BOX 1014
NASHVILLE, TENN. 37202

T.L. CUMMINGS JR.
CUMMINGS SIGN SERVICE
200 12TH. AVE. SOUTH
NASHVILLE, TENN. 37203

FRANKLIN M. JARMAN
GENESCO INC.
111 SEVENTH AVE. NORTH
NASHVILLE, TENN. 37203

THOMAS L. BUSH
IRELAND'S RESTAURANTS
1701 WEST END AVE.
NASHVILLE, TENN. 37203

P.F. OSBORN
NASHVILLE & DECATUR RR.
UNION STA.
NASHVILLE, TENN. 37203

SAM MOORE
THOMAS NELSON
405 - 7TH. AVE. SO.
NASHVILLE, TENN. 37203

JACK W. KUHN
KUHN'S-BIG K STORES
P.O. BOX 40587
NASHVILLE, TENN. 37204

ARTHUR DURFEE
NATIONAL GLASS
P.O. BOX 40543
NASHVILLE, TENN. 37204

RAYMOND ZIMMERMAN
SERVICE MERCHANDISE CO.
P.O. BOX 40787
NASHVILLE, TENN. 37204

BEN C. CAVALIER
CAVLIER IND.
P.O. BOX 50257
NASHVILLE, TENN. 37205

GEORGE P. VAN
HOSPITAL AFFILIATES INTERNAT'L.
P.O. BOX 50444
NASHVILLE, TENN. 37205

R. KIRKPATRICK
ROGER MILLER'S KING OF RD.
211 N. FIRST ST.
NASHVILLE, TENN. 37207

RAYMOND L. DANNER
SHONEY'S BIG BOY
1727 ELM HILL PIKE
NASHVILLE, TENN. 37210

R.F. SMITH
McDOWELL ENTERPRISES
301 PLUS PARK BLVD.
NASHVILLE, TENN. 37217

WALTER L. SHELTON
HIGHLAND INNS
P.O. BOX 3165
NASHVILLE, TENN. 37219

JOHN L. CHAMBERS
PERFORMANCE SYSTEMS
P.O. BOX 2584
NASHVILLE, TENN. 37219

JOHN H. MAXHEIM
UNITED CITIES GAS
404 JAMES ROBERTSON PKWAY.
NASHVILLE, TENN. 37219

SETH M. SMITH
COSMOPOLITAN SPA.
P.O. BOX 228
BRENTWOOD, TENN. 37227

S.B. RYMER JR.
MAGIC CHEF
740 KING EDWARD AVE.
CLEVELAND, TENN. 37311

N.E. WELCH
LASER SYSTEMS
P.O. BOX 248
TULLAHOMA, TENN. 37388

R.C. THATCHER JR.
STANDARD-COOSA THATCHER
18TH. & WATKINS STS.
CHATTANOOGA, TENN. 37401

H. CLAY EVENS JOHNSON
INTERSTATE CORP.
540 MC COLLIE AVE.
CHATTANOOGA, TENN. 37402

R.B. DAVENPORT III
THE KRYSTAL CO.
SEVENTH & CHERRY STS.
CHATTANOOGA, TENN. 37402

J.M. TUCKER
PROGROUP
99 TREMONT ST.
CHATTANOOGA,TENN. 37405

RICHARD SIGNORELLI
HERITAGE QUILTS
P.O. BOX 1810
CHATTANOOGA, TENN. 37407

JACK L. FROST
TUFTCO CORP.
2318 HOLTZCLAW AVE.
CHATTANOOGA, TENN. 37408

ALEXANDER GUERRY JR.
CHATTEM DRUG.
1715 38TH. ST.
CHATTANOOGA, TENN. 37409

HERBERT L. OAKES
THE DORSEY CORP.
P.O. BOX 7037
CHATTANOOGA, TENN. 37410

DONALD L. BLEVINS
RED FOOD STORES,INC.
5901 SHALLOWFORD RD.
CHATTANOOGA, TENN. 37421

G.C. SELLS
GEN. SHALE PRODUCTS
P.O. BOX 3547 CRB
JOHNSON CITY, TENN. 37601

ROY H. HAISLEY
TPI CORP.
135 WESLEY ST.
JOHNSON CITY, TENN. 37601

FRANCIS M. HERNAN
ASG IND.
P.O. BOX 929
KINGSPORT, TENN. 37662

J.L. LINDBERG
TENN. FORGING
P.O. BOX 237
HARRIMAN, TENN. 37748

LAWRENCE W. WHALEN JR.
BERKLINE CORP.
ONE BERKLINE DR.
MORRISTOWN, TENN. 37814

GEORGE P. MOONEY
MOONEY BROADCASTING
HAMILTON BANK BLDG.
KNOXVILLE, TENN. 37901

G.B. LAXER
CAMEL MFG.
329 S. CENTRAL AVE.
KNOXVILLE, TENN. 37902

C.A. TERRELL
STERCHI BROS.
114 S. GAY ST.
KNOXVILLE, TENN. 37902

J.W. HOFFMAN
BLUE DIAMOND COAL
P.O. BOX 10008
KNOXVILLE, TENN. 37919

D.A. STUBBLEFIELD
SCOTTISH INNS
104 BRIDGEWATER RD.
KNOXVILLE, TENN. 37919

J.O. TANKERSLEY
UNITED FOODS
100 DAWSON AVE.
BELLS, TENN. 38006

HARRY BLOOMFIELD
BBI INC.
9991 MACON RD.
CORDOVA, TENN. 38018

RICHARD M. TIMMS
TROXEL MFG. CO.
HWY. 57
MOSCOW, TENN. 38057

JOHN M. TULLY
ANDERSON-TULLY CO.
BOX 28,
MEMPHIS, TENN. 38101

WILLIAM M. ROSSON
CONWOOD CORP.
P.O. BOX 217
MEMPHIS, TENN. 38101

IRA A. LIPMAN
GUARDSMARK, INC.
P.O. BOX 45
MEMPHIS, TENN. 38101

L.J. HUDSON
RAIFORD'S INC.
P.O. BOX 97
MEMPHIS, TENN. 38101

SAMUEL B. HOLLIS
SOUTHWIDE INC.
STERICK BLDG. BOX 77
MEMPHIS, TENN. 38101

LEWIS K. MC KEE
FED. CO.
P.O. BOX 3623
MEMPHIS, TENN. 38103

JOHN E. MURDOCK DR.
MURDOCK ACCEPTANCE CORP.
400 UNION AVE.
MEMPHIS, TENN. 38103

SHELBY D. MASSEY
VALMAC IND.
P.O. BOX 3060
MEMPHIS, TENN. 38103

ROBERT B. WOOD
ADMIRAL BENBOW INN
29 SOUTH BELLEVUE BLVD.
MEMPHIS, TENN. 38104

JOHN A. DE CELL
MERIT CORP.
1331 UNION AVE.
MEMPHIS, TENN. 38104

ARTHUR BURING
BURING FOOD
P.O. BOX 13039
MEMPHIS, TENN. 38113

PAUL P. PIPER JR.
PIPER IND.
1175 HARBOR AVE.
MEMPHIS, TENN. 38113

J.R. HYDE III
MALONE & HYDE
1451 UNION AVE.
MEMPHIS, TENN. 38116

M.C. MURPHEY
WILLIAM BOND
2930 AIRWAYS
MEMPHIS, TENN. 38116

J.E. FREEMAN
AMERICAN FOODS
5384 POPLARSTE. 311
EAST MEMPHIS, TENN. 38117

EDWARD W. COOK
COOK IND.
855 RIDGE LAKE BLVD.
MEMPHIS, TENN. 38117

SIDNEY A. STEWART, JR.
E.H. CRUMP CO.
5350 POPLAR AVE. BX. 171377
MEMPHIS, TENN. 38117

O.O. BURKS
BURK-HALL CO.
4050 GETWELL RD.
MEMPHIS, TENN. 38118

FRANK JAMISON
AMCON INTL. INC.
P.O. BOX 30303
MEMPHIS, TENN. 38130

W. HAMILTON CRAWFORD
CRAWFORD CORP.
P.O. BOX 30185
MEMPHIS, TENN. 38130

LANCE McFADDIN
SERVICO
5100 POPLAR AVE.
MEMPHIS, TENN. 38137

DON W. COCKROFT
UNITED INNS
5100 POPLAR AVE.
MEMPHIS, TENN. 38137

ROBERT B. COLBERT JR.
WAYNE-GOSSARD
N. 22ND. ST.
HUMBOLDT, TENN. 38343

ROBERT A. KOLINSKI
TRANS-HYDRO
815 GILBREATH DR.
LAWRENCEBURG, TENN. 38464

BENJAMIN PIERCE
TYRONE HYDRAULICS
P.O. BOX 511
CORINTH, MISS. 38834

W. CALDWELL JR.
MAGNA AMERICAN CORP.
P.O. BOX 90
RAYMOND, MISS. 39154

J.D. COLE
ELPAC
P.O. BOX 1044
VICKSBURG, MISS. 39180

B.R. WENDROW
U.S. RUBBER RECLAIMING
P.O. BOX 54
VICKSBURG, MISS. 39180

R.M. HEARIN
SCHOOL PICTURES
1118 FIRST NATL. BANK.
JACKSON, MISS. 39201

J. KELLEY WILLIAMS
FIRST MISS. CORP.
P.O. BOX 1249
JACKSON, MISS. 39205

R.W. HYDE, JR.
MISS. VALLEY PORTLAND
P.O. BOX 22491
JACKSON, MISS. 39205

J.N. PALMER
MOBILE COMM. CORP.
1500 CAPITOL TOWER
JACKSON, MISS. 39205

C.M. DORCHESTER
SOUTHERN STATES OIL
P.O. BOX 1185
JACKSON, MISS. 39205

H.V. ALLEN JR.
VALLEY CEMENT IND.
P.O. BOX 22491
JACKSON, MISS. 39205

FRED ADAMS JR.
CAL-MAINE FOODS
3320 WOODROW WILSON
JACKSON, MISS. 39207

TYLOR G. HOLLAND
MISS. VALLEY GAS
P.O. BOX 3348
JACKSON, MISS. 39207

W.A. CALDWELL JR.
MAGNA CORP.
P.O. BOX 5780
JACKSON, MISS. 39208

DON R. GREEN
FERSON OPTICS
2006 GOVERNMENT ST.
OCEAN SPRINGS, MISS. 39564

GEORGE W. THOMPSON
ALTAMIL CORP.
P.O. BOX 206
FERNWOOD, MISS. 39635

L.J. RAUTIO
CLAYTON & LAMBERT MFG.
HIGHWAY 146
BUCKNER, KY. 40010

W.E. WEIGAND
OHIO VALLEY ALUMINUM
P.O. BOX 69
SHELBYVILLE, KY. 40065

HARLIN D. PEDEN
CONVENIENT IND.
P.O. BOX 660
LOUISVILLE, KY. 40201

JAMES THOMPSON
GLENMORE DISTILLERIES
P.O. BX. 900
LOUISVILLE, KY. 40201

H. WENDELL CHERRY
HUMANA INC.
P.O. BOX 1438
LOUISVILLE, KY. 40201

W.H. KING
LOUISVILLE DOWNS
SHERATON HOTEL
LOUISVILLE, KY. 40201

C.E. REDMEN
S & T IND.
P.O. BOX 1859
LOUISVILLE, KY. 40201

CHARLES P. BREWER
BELKNAP INC.
111 E. MAIN ST.
LOUISVILLE, KY. 40202

GENE P. GARDNER
LOUISVILLE CEMENT
501 S. SECOND ST.
LOUISVILLE, KY. 40202

JOSEPH A. GAMMON
NATL. IND. INC.
510 W. BROADWAY
LOUISVILLE, KY. 40202

JACK SEGELL
NATL. RECREATION PROD.
510 W. BROADWAY
LOUISVILLE, KY. 40202

J.J. SEALE
OHIO RIVER SAND CO.
129 RIVER RD.
LOUISVILLE, KY. 40202

T.R. FULLER
THOMAS IND.
207 E. BROADWAY
LOUISVILLE, KY. 40202

L.B. THOMAS JR.
VERMONT AMERICAN
500 E. MAIN ST.
LOUISVILLE, KY. 40202

GEORGE HUNT COLLINS
COLLINS CO.
945 S. FLOYD ST.
LOUISVILLE, KY. 40203

CLIFFORD PEARCE
BOURBON STOCK YARDS
1048 E. MAIN ST.
LOUISVILLE, KY. 40206

JESSE M. SHAVER
AMERICAN AIR FILTER
215 CENTRAL AVE.
LOUISVILLE, KY. 40208

LYNN STONE
CHURCHILL DOWNS
P.O. BOX 8427
LOUISVILLE, KY. 40208

W.L. LYONS BROWN JR.
BROWN FORMAN DISTILLERS
850 DIXIE H'WAY.
LOUISVILLE, KY. 40210

ROBERT E. GILL
ARMOR ELEVATOR CO.
P.O. BOX 14367
LOUISVILLE, KY. 40214

ROBERT B. WYLAND
SAFETRAN SYSTEMS
7721 NATL. TURNPIKE
LOUISVILLE, KY. 40214

ROBERT O. DENHAM
MOTHER'S COOKIE CO.
2287 RALPH AVE.
LOUISVILLE, KY. 40216

JAMES HENDERSHOT
RELIANCE UNIVERSAL
1930 BISHOP LN.
LOUISVILLE, KY. 40218

GEORGE E. FISCHER
METRIDATA COMPUTING
P.O. BOX 21099
LOUISVILL, KY. 40220

R.J. DOUBLASS
GAMBLE BROS.
P.O. BOX 21145
LOUISVILLE, KY. 40221

HARRY KLETTER
IND. SERVICES
P.O. BOX 21000
LOUISVILLE, KY. 40221

LEE J. PERME
LIQUID TRANSPORTERS
P.O. BOX 21395
LOUISVILLE, KY. 40221

J.M. BARNETT
MOBILE WASTE CONTROLS
7100 GRADE LAN. BOX 21100
LOUISVILLE, KY. 40221

SAMUEL J. KRASNEY
BANNER IND.
24500 CHAGRIN BLVD.
CLEVELAND, OHIO 44122

J.N. NEEL
NUCLEAR ENG. CO.
9200 SHELBYVILLE RD.
LOUISVILLE, KY. 40222

ROBERT J. BEGLEY
BEGLEY DRUG
EASTERN COLLEGE BY-PASS
RICHMOND, KY. 40475

WARREN W. ROSENTHAL
JERRICO
1949 NICHOLASVILLE RD.
LEXINGTON, KY. 40503

BYRON J. BEGLEY
SERV-QUIK
2039 REGENCY RD. STE. 2
LEXINGTON, KY. 40503

EARL S. WILSON
KY. FINANCE
200 E. MAIN ST.
LEXINGTON, KY. 40507

C.W. CLAY
KY. RIVER COAL CORP.
FIRST NATL. BANK BLDG.
LEXINGTON, KY. 40507

JOSEPH A. MILBURN
STEART-DECATUR SECURITY
P.O. BOX 38
COVINGTON, KY. 41014

RALPH E. VISCONTI
SPERTI DRUG
7 SPERTI DR.
FORT MITCHELL, KY. 41017

J.R. SMITH
CSI COMPUTER SYSTEMS
7390 EMPIRE DR.
FLORENCE, KY. 41042

ROBERT E. YANCEY
ASHLAND OIL
1409 WINCHESTER AVE.
ASHLAND, KY. 41101

RUSSELL S. SHELTON
SHELTON METROLOGY LAB.
2550 SOUTH BELTLINE HWY.
PADUCAH, KY. 42001

CHESTER GULICK
KY.-TENNESSEE CLAY CO.
P.O. BOX 449
MAYFIELD, KY. 42066

HOWARD HAWES
MERIT CLOTHING CO.
SOUTH FIFTH ST.
MAYFIELD, KY. 42066

CAL TURNER
DOLLAR GEN. CORP.
P.O. BOX 427
SCOTTSVILLE, KY. 42164

D.C. BENSON
ORBIT GAS CO.
P.O. BOX 950
OWENSBORO, KY. 42301

DENNIS R. HENDRIX
TEXAS GAS
P.O. BOX 1160
OWENSBORO, KY. 42301

O.U. GREEN
GRIEF BROS.
621 PENN. AVE.
DELAWARE, OHIO 43015

W.F. HILSMAN
HOOSIER ENG. CO.
5750 SHIER-RINGS RD.
DUBLIN, OHIO 43017

J.H. FISHER
BEASLEY IND. INC.
3500 LACON RD.
HILLIARD, OHIO 43026

C.C. WALDBILLIG
MEDEX INC.
4490 EDGEYN AVE.
HILLIARD, OHIO 43026

MAURICE H. HERRON JR.
O.M. SCOTT & SONS CO.
333 N. MAPLE ST.
MARYSVILLE, OHIO 43040

WILLIAM S. MOORE III
WILLIAM S. MOORE INC.
HEALTH RD.
NEWARD, OHIO 43055

J.W. STRAKER
NATL. GAS & OIL CORP.
1500 GRANVILLE RD.
NEWARK, OHIO 43056

WALTER T. KRUMM
LANDCO INC.
6820 HIGH ST.
WORTHINGTON, OHIO 43085

J.H. MC CONNELL
WORTHINGTON IND.
HUNTLEY & SCHROCK RD.
WORTHINGTON, OHIO 43085

GEORGE C. BARBER
ANCHOR HOCKING
109 N. BROD ST.
LANCASTER, OHIO 43130

BARTON A. HOLL
LOGAN CLAY
201 E. BOWEN ST.
LOGAN, OHIO 43138

D.L. AULD
APPLIED IND.
1209 N. FIFTH ST.
COLUMBUS, OHIO 43201

RICHARD J. GROSH
RANCH
601 WEST 5TH. AVE.
COLUMBUS, OHIO 43201

DAVID L. NELSON
IND. NUCLEONICS
650 ACKERMAN RD.
COLUMBUS, OHIO 43202

DANIEL DAWSON
HEALTH FOOD CENTER
2840A FISHER RD.
COLUMBUS, OHIO 43204

JAMES H. MURRAY
COLUMBUS DENTAL MFG.
634 WAGER ST.
COLUMBUS, OHIO 43206

R.L. EVANS
BOB EVANS FARMS
3776 S. HIGH ST. BX. 7863
COLUMBUS, OHIO 43207 STA.G.

HARRY CUTLER
RETAIL MERCHANT'S
3275 ALUCREEK DR.
COLUMBUS, OHIO 43207

C.D. HILL
SCIOTO DOWNS
6000 S. HIGH ST.
COLUMBUS, OHIO 43207

J. PAT ROSS
FOODPLEX INC.
524 N. CASSADY RD.
COLUMBUS, OHIO 43209

L.H. WEXNER
LIMITED STORES
4461 E. MAIN ST.
COLUMBUS, OHIO 43213

GORDON ZACKS
R.G. BARRY CORP.
78 E. CHESTNUT ST.
COLUMBUS, OHIO 43215

ROWLAND C.W. BROWN
BUCKEYE INTL. INC.
100 E. BROAD ST.
COLUMBUS, OHIO 43215

J.B. GERLACH
LANCASTER COLONY
37 N. BROAD ST.
COLUMBUS, OHIO 43215

HERBERT H. SCHIFF
SCOA IND.
35 N. 4TH. ST.
COLUMBUS, OHIO 43215

J. BREWSTER DAVIS
SUMMER & CO.
870 MICHIGAN AVE.
COLUMBUS, OHIO 43215

THOMAS L. PARKER
BIG DRUM
1183 ESSEX AVE.
COLUMBUS, OHIO 43216

K.S. KLAGES
COLUMBUS AUTO PARTS
HUDSON ST. & N. FREEWAY
COLUMBUS, OHIO 43216

S.A. SHENK
CONSOLIDATED INTL.
2020 CORVAIR AVE.
COLUMBUS, OHIO 43216

BEATON F. PETTENGILL
CORCO INC.
P.O. BOX 2439
COLUMBUS, OHIO 43216

IVAN GILBERT
GILBERT CO.
P.O. BOX 1120
COLUMBUS, OHIO 43216

J.S. HANNA
HANNA CHEM. COATING
1313 WINDSOR AVE.
COLUMBUS, OHIO 43216

JAMES D. ANDERSON
JAEGER MACHINE
550 WEST SPRING ST.
COLUMBUS, OHIO 43216

JOHN A. HAMMOND
MIDLAND GROCERY CO.
405 HIGH ST.
COLUMBUS, OHIO 43216

JOHN L. MARAKAS
NATL. CORP.
246 N. HIGH ST.
COLUMBUS, OHIO 43216

J.D. McGILL
UNITED McGILL CORP.
2400 FAIRWOOD AVE.
COLUMBUS, OHIO 43216

F.N. HANOVER
HANOVER MFG.
1825 JOYCE AVE.
COLUMBUS, OHIO 43219

J.M. WILKINS
COMPU-SERV NETWORK
5000 ARLINGTON CENTRE BLVD.
COLUMBUS, OHIO 43220

R.L. BARNEY
WENDY'S INTL. INC.
2066 W. HENDERSON RD.
COLUMBUS, OHIO 43220

ROY F. MITTE
ILEX CORP.
1670 FISHINGER RD.
COLUMBUS , OHIO 43221

S.R. DAVIS
ORANGE CO.
2011 RIVERSIDE DR.
COLUMBUS, OHIO 43221

A.E. SCHOTTENSTEIN
SCHOTTENSTEIN STORES
3521 WESTERVILLE RD.
COLUMBUS, OHIO 43224

R. GENE BROWN
MONTEREY LIFE SYSTEMS
1375 S. HAMILTON RD.
COLUMBUS, OHIO 43227

D.A. FREYTAG
BEVERAGE MANAGEMENT
1001 KINGSMILL PKWAY.
COLUMBUS, OHIO 43229

GEORGE SKESTOS
HOMEWOOD CORP.
6079 NORTHGATE RD.
COLUMBUS, OHIO 43229

E.W. BARNHART
ALLOY CAST STEEL
P.O. BOX 534
MARION, OHIO 43302

W.B. WARD
STANWARD CORP.
P.O. BOX 588
MARION, OHIO 43302

HUBERT H. MARSHALL
MERCHANTS IND.
BELLEFONTAINE, OHIO 43311

M.J. ANDERSON
ARO CORP.
BRYAN, OHIO 43506

W.C. KILLGALLON
OHIO ART
720 E. HIGH ST.
BRYAN, OHIO 43506

ELWOOD L. ELBERSON
DINNER BELL FOODS
DRAWER 388
DEFIANCE, OHIO 43512

WALLACE D. IOTT
SEAWAY FOOD TOWN
1020 FORD RD.
MAUMEE, OHIO 43537

GEORGE L. PILLIOD
PILLIOD CABINET CO.
105 WOODLAND AVE.
SWANTON, OHIO 43558

R.A. STRANAHAN JR.
CHAMPION SPARK PLUG
900 UPTON AVE.
TOLEDO, OHIO 43601

MARVIN KOBACKER
KOSTIN
408 SUMMIT ST.
TOLEDO, OHIO 43601

EDWIN D. DODD
OWEN-ILLINOIS INC.
OWEN-ILLINOIS BLDG.
TOLEDO, OHIO 43601

ARTHUR M. INGRAM
LAMB COMM. INC.
500 EDWARD LAMB BLDG.
TOLEDO, OHIO 43603

WILLIAM R. COBOURN
DOLPHIN PAINT & CHEM.
922 LOCUST ST.
TOLEDO, OHIO 43604

LOUIS M. ASHENBRENNER
GREAT LAKES TERMINAL
355 MORRIS ST.
TOLEDO, OHIO 43604

LE ROY W. SIEGLER
SEILON
EDWARD LAMB BLDG.
TOLEDO, OHIO 43604

WARD M. CANADAY
THE OVERLAND CORP.
SECUITY BLDG.
TOLEDO, OHIO 43604

WILLIAM E. LOUGHRAN
BISHOP & BABCOCK
1345 MIAMI ST.
TOLEDO, OHIO 43605

DONALD J. FRANCILL
NATL. RED. & DEVELOPMENT
3156 BELLEVUE RD.
TOLEDO, OHIO 43606

P.L. TREUHAFT
PET BAZAAR
1419 EXPRESSWAY DR. N.
TOLEDO, OHIO 43608

MYRON M. EICHER
HICKORY FARMS OF OHIO
1021 N. REYNOLDS RD.
TOLEDO, OHIO 43615

CHESTER DEVENOW
SHELLER-GLOBE CORP.
P.O. BOX 1270
TOLEDO, OHIO 43624

P.M. GRIEVE
QUESTOR CORP.
P.O. BOX 317
TOLEDO, OHIO 43691

GERALD MITCHELL
DANA CORP.
P.O. BOX 1000
TOLEDO, OHIO 43697

JAY F. SHAW
SHAW-BARTON
535 WALNUT ST.
COSHOCTON, OHIO 43812

ARTHUR M. EPSTEIN
EPKO SHOES
198 PENN ST.
BRILLIANT, OHIO 43913

P.C. HERRIED
KOBACKER STORES
198 PENN ST.
BRILLIANT, OHIO 43913

ERIC T. NORD
NORDSON CORP.
JACKSON ST.
AMHERST, OHIO 44001

R.S. MORRISON
MOLDED FIBER GLASS CO.
1315 WEST 47TH. ST.
ASHTABULA, OHIO 44004

JOHN FAZIO
FISHER FOODS
5300 RICHMOND RD.
BEDFORD HTS., OHIO 44014

C.C. TIPPIT
MOGUL CORP.
CHAGRIN FALLS, OHIO 44022

JAMES A. HORNER
STRUCTURAL FIBERS
FIFTH AVE.
CHARDON, OHIO 44024

HAROLD P. KOENIG
BROWN FINTUBE CO.
300 HURON ST.
ELYRIA, OHIO 44035

G.P. HOPKINS
EMTEC INC.
140 S. OLIVE ST.
ELYRIA, OHIO 44035

J.W. ZAJAC
THE PERRY-FAY
200 PERRY CT.
ELYRIA, OHIO 44035

B. WADE WHITE
FLUID CONTROLS
P.O. BOX 49
MENTOR, OHIO 44060

MORT MAURER
NATL. SCREW & MFG.
8100 TYLER BLVD.
MENTOR, OHIO 44060

J.J. LOHRMAN
RUSSELL, BURDSALL & WARD
8100 TYLER BLVD.
MENTOR, OHIO 44060

S.R. GILFORD
GILFORD INSTRUMENT
132 ARTINO ST.
OBERLIN, OHIO 44074

ROBERT V.D. BOOTH DR.
UNION SAND & SUPPLY
P.O. BOX 148
PAINESVILLE, OHIO 44077

JULIUS ZAJAC
INARCO
P.O. BOX 4444
TWINSBURG, OHIO 44087

SIDNEY DWORKIN
REVCO D.S.
1925 ENTERPRISE PKWAY.
TWINSBURG, OHIO 44087

WILLIAM BLOCK
AMERICAN LA FRANCE
4420 SHERWIN RD.
WILLOUGHBY, OHIO 44094

ALFRED V. GANGNES
A-T-O INC.
4420 SHERWIN RD.
WILLOUGHBY, OHIO 44094

MANNY SCHOR
CURTIS NOLL
34959 CURTIS BLVD.
EASTLAKE, OHIO 44094

L.R. WINSLOW
FEEDALL
38379 PELTON RD.
WILLOUGHBY, OHIO 44094

JEROME BENNETT
WHITE MOTOR
35129 CURTIS BLVD.
EAST LAKE, OHIO 44094

W. PAUL COOPER
ACME-CLEVELAND
P.O. BOX 5617
CLEVELAND, OHIO 44101

H.T. WATKINS
ALLEGHENY & WESTERN
P.O. BOX 6419
CLEVELAND, OHIO 44101

SCOTT A. ROGERS JR.
MEDUSA
P.O. BOX 5668
CLEVELAND, OHIO 44101

JAMES S. REID JR.
STANDARD PRODUCTS
2130 W. 110TH ST.
CLEVELAND, OHIO 44102

JOHN J. TANIS
UNITED SCREW & BOLT
3590 W. 58TH. ST.
CLEVELAND, OHIO 44102

EDWARD C. HILLS
WARREN REFINING & CHE.
5151 DENISON AVE.
CLEVELAND, OHIO 44102

SHELDON K. TOWSON JR.
ELWELL-PARKER
4205 ST. CLAIR AVE.
CLEVELAND, OHIO 44103

GEORGE A. BRICHMONT
PARK DROP FORGE
777 EAST 79TH ST.
CLEVELAND, OHIO 44103

ROBERT WARREN
PREMIER IND.
4415 EUCLID AVE.
CLEVELAND, OHIO 44103

J.M. OSBORNE
RAVENCLIFFS DEVELOPMENT
4614 PROSPECT AVE.
CLEVELAND, OHIO 44103

GEORGE H. RICHMAN
RICHMAN BROS.
1600 EAST 55TH ST.
CLEVELAND, OHIO 44103

LEIGH CARTER
TREMCO
10701 SHAKER BLVD.
CLEVELAND, OHIO 44104

L.C. JONES
VAN DORN
2700 E. 79TH ST.
CLEVELAND, OHIO 44104

C.H. CLAWSON
BROADHEAD-GARRETT
4560 E. 71ST ST.
CLEVELAND, OHIO 44105

NORTON W. ROSE
COLE NAT'L.
5777 GRANT AVE.
CLEVELAND, OHIO 44105

WILLIAM F. HAUSERMAN
HAUSERMAN INC.
5711 GRANT AVE.
CLEVELAND, OHIO 44105

FOSTER H. PETTAY
OHIO CRANKSHAFT
3800 HARVARD AVE.
CLEVELAND, OHIO 44105

G.A. BRICHMONT
PARK-OHIO IND.
3800 HARVARD AVE.
CLEVELAND, OHIO 44105

PRESTON B. HELLER JR.
PIONEER-STANDARD
4800 E. 131ST ST.
GARFIELD HTS., OHIO 44105

WILLIAM E. PAINTER
GIBSON-HOMANS
2366 WOODHILL RD.
CLEVELAND, OHIO 44106

CRAIG R. SMITH
WARNER & SWASEY
11000 CEDAR AVE.
CLEVELAND, OHIO 44106

RALPH SCHEY
SCOTT & FETZER
14600 DETROIT AVE.
CLEVELAND, OHIO 44107

JOHN H. MYERS
ENAMEL PRODUCTS
341 EDDY RD.
CLEVELAND, OHIO 44108

ROBERT D. HICKOK
HICKOK ELECTRICAL
10514 DU PONT AVE.
CLEVELAND, OHIO 44108

SIDNEY C. HOWELL
WEATHERHEAD
300 E. 131ST ST.
CLEVELAND, OHIO 44108

WILLIAM S. BECKENBACH
CLARK CONSOLIDATED
3184 WEST 32ND. AVE.
CLEVELAND, OHIO 44109

LESLIE E. WILES
BRUSH WELLMAN
17876 ST. CLAIR AVE.
CLEVELAND, OHIO 44110

ROBERT H. GROSSMAN
LINDSAY WIRE
14001 ASPINWALL AVE.
CLEVELAND, OHIO 44110

P.F. MITCHELL
UPSON-WALTON
12500 ELMWOOD AVE.
CLEVELAND, OHIO 44111

WARD SMITH
WHITE CONSOLIDATED IND.
11770 BEREA RD.
CLEVELAND, OHIO 44111

PATRICK S. PARKER
PARKER-HANNIFIN
17325 EUCLID AVE.
CLEVELAND, OHIO 44112

WILLIAM H. NORTH
FERRY CAP & SET SCREW
2151 SCRANTON RD.
CLEVELAND, OHIO 44113

JOSEPH A. BOYD
HARRIS CORP.
55 PUBLIC SQ.
CLEVELAND, OHIO 44113

HENRY G. BROWNELL
HIGBEE & CO.
100 PUBLIC SQ.
CLEVELAND, OHIO 44113

DONALD B. CAMPBELL
HOSPITALITY MOTOR
2100 TERMINAL TOWER
CLEVELAND, OHIO 44113

EUGENE K. ZYCHICK
INT'L. SEAWAY TRADING
1382 W. 9TH ST.
CLEVELAND, OHIO 44113

HENRY J. BOLWELL
MIDLAND-ROSS
2000 ILLUMINATING BLDG.
CLEVELAND, OHIO 44113

SHELDON B. GUREN
U.S. RLTY.
637 TERMINAL TOWER
CLEVELAND, OHIO 44113

MAURICE SALTZMAN
BOBBIE BROOKS
3830 KELLEY AVE.
CLEVELAND, OHIO 44114

S.M. LOVEMEN
BURDOX INC.
3300 LAKESIDE AVE.
CLEVELAND, OHIO 44114

JOHN A. GELBACH
CENTRAN
ONE CENTRAL NTL. BANK BLDG.
CLEVELAND, OHIO 44114

SAMUEL K. SCOVIL
CLEVELAND-CLIFFS IRON
UNION COMMERCE BLDG. STE.1460
CLEVELAND, OHIO 44114

W.H. BRICKER
DIAMOND SHAMROCK CORP.
1100 SUPERIOR AVE.
CLEVELAND, OHIO 44114

PAUL A. MILLER
EATON
100 ERIEVIEW PLAZA
CLEVELAND, OHIO 44114

CLIFFORD M. ANDREWS
FERRO CORP.
ONE ERIEVIEW PLAZA
CLEVELAND, OHIO 44114

JEROME A. WEINBERGER
GRAY DRUG STORES
666 EUCLID AVE.
CLEVELAND, OHIO 44114

JAMES W. PURSE
HANNA MINING CO.
100 ERIEVIEW PLAZA
CLEVELAND, OHIO 44114

RAMON S. PANETTI
INTERSERVICE CORP.
666 EUCLID AVE.
CLEVELAND, OHIO 44-14

JOSEPH C. FOGG
JUDSON-BROOKS CO.
1241 SUPERIOR AVE.
CLEVELAND, OHIO 44114

R.L. HULETTE
MC DOWELL-WELLMAN
113 ST. CLAIR AVE., N.E.
CLEVELAND, OHIO 44114

E.M. WULIGER
OHIO-SEALY MATTRESS MFG.
1300 E. 9TH. ST.
CLEVELAND, OHIO 44114

SAL F. MARINO
PENTON INC.
1111 CHESTER AVE.
CLEVELAND, OHIO 44114

ELTON HYT III
PICKANDS MATHER & CO.
1100 SUPERIOR AVE.
CLEVELAND, OHIO 44114

JOSEPH E. COLE
SHELTER RESOURCES
29001 CEDAR RD.
CLEVELAND, OHIO 44114

AUBREY H. MILNES
SIFCO IND.
970 EAST 64TH ST.
CLEVELAND, OHIO 44114

HARRY H. BISHOP
TRANSOHIO FINANCIAL
PENTON PLAZA BLDG.
CLEVELAND, OHIO 44114

J.J. BERNET
U.S. TRUCK LINES
UNION COMMERCE BLDG.
CLEVELAND, OHIO 44114

L.A. ROSENTHAL
WORK WEAR
1768 E. 25TH ST.
CLEVELAND, OHIO 44114

MAX MULLER
BASIC
845 HANNA BLDG.
CLEVELAND, OHIO 44115

JOSEPH M. BRUENING
BEARINGS
3634 EUCLID AVE.
CLEVELAND, OHIO 44115

R.J. BUCKLEY
BULKLEY BLDG.
520 BULKLEY BLDG.
CLEVELAND, OHIO 44115

MARVIN E. SHIFFMAN
LEADER NATL. CORP.
1001 EUCLID AVE.
CLEVELAND, OHIO 44115

J.J. DWYER
OGLEBAY NORTON CO.
P.O. BOX 6508
CLEVELAND, OHIO 44115

HERBERT S. RICHEY
VALLEY CAMP COAL
700 WESTGATE TOWER
CLEVELAND, OHIO 44116

N.C. MICHELS
LEE WILSON ENGINEERING
20005 LAKE RD.
ROCKY RIVER, OHIO 44116

L.E. COLEMAN
LUBRIZOL
P.O. BOX 17100
CLEVELAND, OHIO 44117

C.R. KUBIK
MOTCH & MERRYWEATHER
1250 E. 22ND ST.
EUCLID, OHIO 44117

HARRY SCHARF
PENTRON IND.
14055 CEDAR RD.
CLEVELAND, OHIO 44118

O. BENNET JR.
NORTH AMERICAN COAL
12800 SHAKER BLVD.
CLEVELAND, OHIO 44120

SIDNEY SIMON
THE AMBINA
23215 COMMERCE PK. BLVD.
BEACHWOOD, OHIO 44122

J.R. BORCOMAN
CBM
3690 ORANGE RD.
CLEVELAND, OHIO 44122

MARTIN ROSSKAMM
FABRI-CENTERS
23550 COMMERCE PK. RD.
BEACHWOOD, OHIO 44122

HARRY W. HOSFORD, JR.
GILMORE IND.
3355 RICHMOND RD.
CLEVELAND, OHIO 44122

HERBERT WAINER
HORIZONS RESEARCH
23800 MERCANTILE RD.
CLEVELAND, OHID 44122

W.D. ARMSTRONG
IMPERIAL PAPER
3645 WARRENSVILLE CENTER RD.
CLEVELAND, OHIO 44122

SHELDON R. RUBIN
LEASEPAC CORP.
23945 MERCANTILE RD.
CLEVELAND, OHIO 44122

W.J. O'NEILL JR.
LEASEWAY TRANSPORTATION
21111 CHARGRIN BLVD.
CLEVELAND, OHIO 44122

SIDNEY SIMON
MIDWEST PRESTRESSED
23215 COMMERCE PK. RD.
BEACHWOOD, OHIO 44122

EDWARD E. PARSONS JR.
PARSONS & CO.
24500 CHAGRIN BLVD.
CLEVELAND, OHIO 44122

B. CHARLES AMES
RELIANCE ELECTRIC
29325 CHAGRIN BLVD.
CLEVELAND, OHIO 44122

JEROME A. BARRER
GIANT TIGER STORES
22800 LAKE SHORE BLVD.
EUCLID, OHIO 44123

DAVID SKYLAR
COMPCORP.
5510 CLOVERLEAF PARKWAY.
VALLEY VIEW, OHIO 44125

FRANCIS W. THEIS
AMERICAN SHIPBUILDING
4211 W. 199TH ST.
CLEVELAND, OHIO 44126

R.A. KEMPE
METALPHOTO
18531 SOUTH MILES RD.
CLEVELAND,OHIO 44128

WALTER L. ABT
MOR-FLO IND.
18450 S. MILES RD.
CLEVELAND, OHIO 44128

RONALD L. WHITE
TENNA
19201 CRANWOOD PKWAY.
WARRENSVILLE,HTS., OHIO 44128

ALBERT B. RATNER
FOREST CITY
10800 BROOKPARK RD.
CLEVELAND, OHIO 44130

MARVIN L. LADER
CENTRAL DATA SYSTEMS
1215 VALLEY BELT RD.
CLEVELAND, OHIO 44131

RICHARD G. WIDMAN
ARTHUR G. MC KEE & CO.
6200 OAK TREE BLVD.
CLEVELAND, OHIO 44131

EDMUND L. FACHTMAN JR.
RUPP IND.
4569 SPRING RD.
CLEVELAND, OHIO 44131

M.H. EMMERLICH
COMPUTER RESOURCES, INC.
4650 W. 160TH ST.
CLEVELAND, OH. 44135

B.W. MANNING
THE HANSEN MFG. CO.
4031 W. 150TH ST.
CLEVELAND, OH. 44135

R.H. CROSSMAN
AMPOULES, INC.
14001 ASPINWALL AVE.
CLEVELAND, OH. 44236

MARTIN M. LEWIS
COOK UNITED, INC.
16501 ROCKSIDE RD., MAPLE HGTS.
CLEVELAND, OH. 44137

EDWARD RICHARD
MAGNETICS INT'L. INC.
5400 DUNHAM RD.
MAPLE HEIGHTS, OH. 44137

R.S. REITMAN
AAV COMPANIES
31100 SOLON RD.
SOLON, OH. 44139

JAMES D. KIGGEN
THE CYRIL BATH CO.
32400 AURORA RD.
SOLON, OH. 44139

THOMAS G. BRICK
KEITHLEY INSTRUMENTS, INC.
28775 AURORA RD.
CLEVELAND, OH. 44139

R.S. GRIMM
TECHNICARE CORP.
29100 AURORA RD.
CLEVELAND, OH. 44139

IRVING I STONE
AMERICAN GREETINGS CORP.
10500 AMERICAN RD.
CLEVELAND, OH. 44144

G.J. GRABNER
LAMSON & SESSIONS CO.
5000 TIEDEMAN RD.
CLEVELAND, OH. 44144

FRED RZEPKA
TRANSCON BUILDERS, INC.
25250 ROCKSIDE RD.
BEDFORD HGHTS., OH. 44146

ARMOND WAXMAN
WAXMAN INDUSTRIES INC.
24455 AURORA RD.
CLEVELAND, OH. 44146

ROGER V. GOCHNEAUR
FASHION TWO TWENTY, INC.
1263 S. CHILLICOTHE RD.
AURORA, OH. 44202

E.W. GASCOIGNE
FUNTIME, INC.
P.O. BOX 184
AURORA, OH. 44202

GORDON E. HEEFERN
SOCIETY CORP.
127 PUBLIC SQ.
CLEVELAND, OH. 44214

BLAKE H. HOOPER
MORGAN ADHESIVES CO.
4560 DARROW RD.
STOW, OH. 44224

HENRY M. FAWCETT
MOHAWK RUBBER CO.
50 EXECUTIVE PKWY.
HUDSON, OH. 44236

BRADFORD BURNHAM
SAMUEL MOORE & CO.
MAIN & ORCHARD
MANTUA, OH. 44255

NEIL R. GOWE
GOWE PRINTING CO.
620 E. SMITH RD.
MEDINA, OH. 44256

RICHARD H. SCHNELLSCHMIDT
PLASTI-KOTE, INC.
1000 LAKE RD.
MEDINA, OH. 44256

ALAN I. ROOT
A.I. ROOT CO.
623 W. LIBERTY ST.
MEDINA, OH. 44256

T.C. SULLIVAN
RPM INC.
2628 PEARL RD.
MEDINA, OH. 44256

LOUIS S. MYERS
MYERS IND., INC.
1293 S. MAIN ST.
AKRON, OH. 44301

JOHN L. TORMEY
ROADWAY EXPRESS INC.
P.O. BOX 471
AKRON, OH. 44309

RICHARD A. MICHELSON
MC NEIL CORP.
96 E. CROSIER ST.
AKRON, OH. 44311

ANDRE J. ANDREOLI
TRANSAIRCO, INC.
3200 W. MARKET ST.
AKRON, OH. 44313

ALEX GROSS
ALBEE HOMES
931 SUMMIT ST.
NILES, OH. 44446

R.W. McINTYRE
WARREN TOOL CORP.
CRISWOLD ST. EXT.,
WARREN, OH. 44481

R.J. WEAN, JR.
WEAN UNITED, INC.
347 N. PARK AVE.
WARREN, OH. 44481

JOHN A. LOGAN
AJAX MAGNETHERMIC CORP.
P.O. BOX 991
WARREN, OH. 44482

JOHN P. LYNN
AMERICAN WELDING & MFG.
100 DIETZ RD.
WARREN, OH. 44483

CHARLES B. CUSHWA, JR.
COMMERCIAL SHEARING INC.
P.O. BOX 239
YOUNGSTOWN, OH. 44501

T.L. HARSHBARGER
THOROFARE MARKETS INC.
P.O. BOX 120
YOUNGSTOWN, OH. 44501

W.F. ZARBAUGH
YOUNGSTOWN RESEARCH & DVLPMT, CO.
701 STAMBAUGH BLDG.
YOUNGSTOWN, OH. 44503

GEORGE B. MOSELEY
G.F. BUSINESS EQUIPMENT INC.
EAST DENNICK AVE.
YOUNGSTOWN, OH. 44505

P.J. RENNER
RENNER CO.
4020 SIMON RD.
YOUNGSTOWN, OH. 44512

WARREN W. BROWN
MASSILON STEEL CASTING CO.
577 OBERLIN AVE.
MASSILON, OH. 44646

PAUL H. SMUCKER
J.M. SMUCKER CO.
STRAWBERRY LN.
ORRVILLE, OH. 44667

WILLARD M. ARNOLD
ARNOLD GRAPHIC IND. INC.
10000 CARNEGIE AVE.
UNIONTOWN, OH. 44685

LESTER E. CIGAX
RUBBERMAID, INC.
1147 AKRON RD.
WOOSTER, OH. 44691

DAVID L. LAVIN
SUGARDALE FOODS, INC.
1600 HARMONT AVE., N.E.
CANTON, OH. 44701

J.S. RENKERT
METROPOLITAN INDUSTRIES, INC.
2185 BOLIVAR RD., S.W.
CANTON, OH. 44706

H.E. MARKLEY
THE TIMKEN CO.
1835 DUEBER AVE., S.W.
CANTON, OH. 44706

R.L. CUNNINGHAM
OHIO FERRO-ALLOYS CORP.
839 30TH ST., N.W.
CANTON, OH. 44709

RAYMOND KOONTZ
DIEBOLD INC.
818 MULBERRY RD.
CANTON, OH. 44711

JOHN HAGGARTY
SPARTEK, INC.
P.O. BOX 8049
CANTON, OH. 44711

W.K. RIEMENSCHNEIDER
UNION METAL MFG. CO.
1432 MAPLE AVE., N.E.
CANTON, OH. 44711

FRED TABACCHI
HOOVER CO.
101 E. MAPLE ST.
NORTH CANTON, OH. 44720

RICHARD H. CARTER
FOSTORIA CORP.
P.O. BOX 823
FOSTORIA, OH. 44830

ROBERT L. MUNGER, JR.
CEDAR POINT INC.
CEDAR POINT
SANDUSKY, OH. 44870

C.J. FULLER
UNIVERSAL CLAY PRODUCTS CO.
1528 FIRST ST.
SANDUSKY, OH. 44870

JOHN N. WILLMAN
PIONEER RUBBER CO.
P.O. BOX 367
WILLARD, OH. 44890

ROBERT R. HARBAUGH
RICHLAND BRICK CO.
P.O. BOX 328
MANSFIELD, OH. 44901

DONALD C. BLASIUS
TAPPAN CO.
TAPPAN PARK
MANSFIELD, OH. 44901

JAMES C. GORMAN
GORMAN-RUPP CO.
305 BOWMAN ST.
MANSFIELD, OH. 44902

JAMES H. HOFFMAN
MANSFIELD TIRE & RUBBER CO.
515 NEWMAN ST.
MANSFIELD, OH. 44902

WILLIAM R. CRESS
OHIO BRASS CO.
380 N. MAIN ST.
MANSFIELD, OH. 44902

HARRY HOLIDAY, JR.
ARMCO STEEL CORP.
703 CURTIS ST.
MIDDLETOWN, OH. 45042

S.H. REED
CRYSTAL TISSUE CORP.
MIDDLETOWN, OH. 45042

DE WITT M. YOST
SORG PAPER CO.
901 MANCHESTER AVE.
MIDDLETOWN, OH. 45042

WILLIAM H. DICKHONER
THE CINCINNATI GAS & ELECTRIC
FOURTH & MAIN STS.
CINCINNATI, OH. 45201

MR. W.D. ATTEBERRY
EAGLE-PICHER IND. INC.
P.O. BOX 779
CINCINNATI, OH. 45201

GENE D. HOFFMAN
THE KROGER CO.
1014 VINE ST.
CINCINNATI, OH. 45201

CARL H. LINDER
AMERICAN CONTINENTAL HOMES, INC.
ONE EAST FOURTH ST.
CINCINNATI, OH. 45202

J. HOWARD FRAZER
AMERICAN CONTROLLED IND. INC.
6 E. 4TH ST.
CINCINNATI, OH. 45202

M.P. THOMPSON
D.H. BALDWIN CO.
1801 GILBERT AVE.
CINCINNATI, OH. 45202

M.C. MYERS
CARLISLE CORP.
511 WALNUT ST.
CINCINNATI, OH. 45202

EDWARD L. HUTTON
CHEMED CORP.
DU BOIS TOWER
CINCINNATI, OH. 45202

JOHN R. BULLOCK
CINCINNATI TERMINAL WAREHOUSES
49 CENTRAL AVE.
CINCINNATI, OH. 45202

LOUIS BARTEL
COMPUTER MICROMATION SYSTEMS
307 DIXIE TERMINAL BLDG.
CINCINNATI, OH. 45202

D.R. HINKLEY
EMERY IND., INC.
4300 CAREW TOWER
CINCINNATI, OH. 45202

HAROLD KRENSKY
FEDERATED DEPT. STORES INC.
222 W. 7TH ST.
CINCINNATI, OH. 45202

J.P. HAYDEN JR.
THE MIDLAND CO.
FIRST NAT'L. BANK BLDG.
CINCINNATI, OH. 45202

J.P. HAYDEN, JR.
MIDLAND-GUARDIAN CO.
FIRST NAT'L. BANK BLDG.
CINCINNATI, OH. 45202

J.C. THOMPSON
RAPOCA ENERGY CORP.
1601 DU BOIS TOWER
CINCINNATI, OH. 45202

DONALD L. FERRIS
SCRIPPS-HOWARD BROADCASTING CO.
CENTRAL TRUST TOWER
CINCINNATI, OH. 45202

J. HOWARD FRAZER
VULCAN CORP.
6 E. 4TH ST.
CINCINNATI, OH. 45202

MARVIN WARNER
WARNER NATIONAL CORP.
136 E. 6TH ST.
CINCINNATI, OH. 45202

R.E. PRATT
EARLY & DANIEL CO.
525 CARR ST.
CINCINNATI, OH. 45203

PHILIP W. CASPER
F.H. LAWSON CO.
801 EVANS ST.
CINCINNATI, OH. 45204

JACK C. MAIER
FRISCH"S RESTAURANTS, INC.
3011 STANTON AVE.
CINCINNATI, OH. 45206

R.L. PAULSON
XYOVEST INC.
2181 VICTORY PKWY.
CINCINNATI, OH. 45206

STANLEY H. RUTSTEIN
U.S. SHOE CORP.
1658 HERALD AVE.
CINCINNATI, OH. 45207

JAMES A.D. GEIER
CINCINNATI MILACRON
4701 MARBURG AVE.
CINCINNATI, OH. 45209

F.G. SORENSEN, JR.
OHMART CORP.
4241 ALLENDORF DR.
CINCINNATI, OH. 45209

L.T. APPLEGATE
SURGICAL APPLIANCE IND. INC.
ERIE & ROSSLYN DR.
CINCINNATI, OH. 45209

W.D. WILDER
WILLIAMSON CO.
3500 MADISON RD.
CINCINNATI, OH. 45209

JOHN M. SHEPHERD
SHEPPERD CHEMICAL CO.
5000 POPLAR ST.
CINCINNATI, OH. 45212

EDWARD C. STUDER
CINCINNATI ECONOMY DRUG CO.
P.O. BOX 14179
CINCINNATI, OH. 45214

JOHN D. RAUH
CLOPAY CORP.
CLOPAY SQ.
CINCINNATI, OH. 45214

J. VINCENT SMYTH
LUNKENHEIMER CO.
BEEKMAN ST. & WAVERLY AVE.
CINCINNATI, OH. 45214

DARWIN C. YUNG
CAMBRIDGE TITLE MFG. CO.
P.O. BOX 15071
CINCINNATI, OH. 45215

J.E. LAWSON
CINCINNATI INDUSTRIES, INC.
514 STATION AVE.
CINCINNATI, OH. 45215

R.H. EGGLESTON
FOX PAPER CO.
LOCK & COOPER
CINCINNATI, OH. 45215

IVAN PERKINS
PERKINS FOODS, INC.
24 LANDY LN.
CINCINNATI, OH. 45215

A.R. MACK
MACK SHIRT CO.
333 W. SEYMOUR AVE.
CINCINNATI, OH. 45216

SANFORD M. BROOKS
THE TOOL STEEL GEAR & PINION
211 TOWNSHIP AVE.
CINCINNATI, OH. 45216

DUDLEY S. TAFT
TAFT BROADCASTING CO.
1906 HIGHLAND AVE.
CINCINNATI, OH. 45219

DAVID M. GANTZ
WILSON FREIGHT CO.
3636 FOLLETT AVE.
CINCINNATI, OH. 45223

MARTIN GLOTZER
CINCINNATI UNION STOCK YARD CO.
3129 SPRING GROVE AVE.
CINCINNATI, OH. 45225

WILLIAM L. DOLLE, JR.
THE LODGE & SHIPLEY CO.
3055 COLERAIN AVE.
CINCINNATI, OH. 45225

J.B. PLY, JR.
POLAR VAC IND.
4669 KELLOG AVE.
CINCINNATI, OH. 45226

G.J. PANDAPAS
ELECTRO-TEC CORP.
5721 DRAGON WAY
CINCINNATI, OH. 45227

L.W. METTHEY
KDI CORP.
5721 DRAGON WAY
CINCINNATI, OH. 45227

A.S. JOHNSON
VAN LUENSEN'S INC.
5574 WOOSTER PIKE
FAIRFAX, OHIO 45227

V.P. CHRONIS
ITI CORP.
660 NORTHLAND RD.
CINCINNATI, OH. 45240

JOSEPH LINDER
FIBRE GLASS-EVERCOAT CO., INC.
660 CORNELL RD.
CINCINNATI, OH. 45242

DURWOOD G. RORIE, JR.
UNITED AIR SPECIALISTS
6665 CREEK RD.
CINCINNATI, OH. 45242

C. LAWSON REED, JR.
XOMOX CORP.
4444 COOPER RD.
CINCINNATI, OH. 45242

FRANK KOEGEL
PRO DYN INC.
11703 CHESTERDALE RD.
CINCINNATI, OH. 45246

W.G. TANNER
UNIBRAZE CORP.
7502 W. STATE ROUTE 41
COVINGTON, OH. 45318

MAY J. HUMBERT
PARAMONT INT'L. COIN CORP.
PARAMONT BLDG.
ENGLEWOOD, OH. 45322

J.H. JOHNSON
STOP-N-GO FOODS, INC.
12 W. WENGER RD.
ENGLEWOOD, OH. 45322

WILLIAM E. HOLE
AMERICAN AGGREGATES CORP.
AVENUE B & GARST AVE.
GREENVILLE, OH. 45331

STUART J. NORTHRUP
HUFFMAN MFG. CO.
7701 BYERS RD.
MIAMISBERG, OHIO 45342

KARL W. MONSON
ALLEN-A CO.
803 N. DOWNING ST.
PIQUA, OHIO 45356

MATTHEW O. DIGGS, JR.
COPELAND CORP.
CAMPBELL RD.
SIDNEY, OH. 45365

KERMIT T. KUCK
MONARCH MACHINE TOOL CO.
N. OAK AVE.
SIDNEY, OH. 45365

D.F. ALDRICH
ALLIED TECHNOLOGY INC.
3245 S. COUNTRY RD.
TROY, OH. 45373

DAVID B. MEEKER
HOBART CORP.
WORLD HDQRTRS. AVE.
TROY, OH. 45373

N.G. McCALLISTER
HOOVEN & ALLISON CO.
677 CINCINNATI AVE
XENIA, OH. 45385

R.L. BATES
CHEMINEER, INC.
P.O. BOX 1123
DAYTON, OH. 45401

ROBERT F. SHARPE
DURIRON CO, INC.
425 N. FINDLAY ST.
DAYTON, OH. 45401

J.N. TAYLOR, JR.
KURZ-KASCH, INC.
1421 S. BROADWAY
DAYTON, OH. 45401

F.E. BURNHAM
MASTER CONSOLIDATED INC.
P.O. BOX 657
DAYTON, OH. 45401

THOMAS R. LOEMKER
MONARCH MARKING SYSTEMS, INC.
P.O. BOX 608
DAYTON, OHIO 45401

ROBERT H. BRETHEN
PHILIPS IND. INC.
4801 SPRINGFIELD ST.
DAYTON, OH. 45401

EDWIN F. STRASSER
REYNOLDS & REYNOLDS CO.
800 GERMANTOWN ST.
DAYTON, OH. 45401

DONALD F. WHITEHEAD
STANDARD REGISTER CO.
626 ALBANY ST.
DAYTON, OH. 45401

NICK G. HARRIS
UNITED AIRCRAFTS PRODUCTS INC.
1116 WEST STEWART ST.
DAYTON, OH. 45401

ERNEST F. DOURLET
DAYCO CORPORATION
333 W. FIRST ST.
DAYTON, OH. 45402

D.C. FREYTAG
EQUIDATA, INC.
606 HARRIS BLDG.
DAYTON, OH. 45402

R.E. MAC DONALD
E.F. MAC DONALD CO.
129 S. LUDLOW ST.
DAYTON, OH. 45402

WARREN L. BATTS
THE MEAD CORP.
TALBOTT TOWER
DAYTON, OH. 45402

M. KRUG
TECHNOLOGY, INC.
1115 DALBOTT TOWER
DAYTON, OH. 45402

C.W. WEPRIN
MAPI INC.
1628 SPRINGFIELD ST.
DAYTON, OH. 45403

MICHAEL ADLER
PROGRESSIVE INDUSTRIES CORP.
2030 KUNTZ RD.
DAYTON, OH. 45404

MAX GUTMAN
ELDER-BEERMAN STORES CORP.
153 HELENA ST.
DAYTON, OH. 45405

GERALD S. OFFICE, JR.
PONDEROSA SYSTEM, INC.
3661 SALEM AVE.
DAYTON, OH. 45406

JOSEPH H. MC CARTHY, JR.
LAU, INC.
2027 HOME AVE.
DAYTON, OH. 45407

PAUL S. RIEDEL
VINDALE CORP.
630 HAY AVE.
BROOKVILLE, OH. 45414

JOHN F. TORLEY
DAYTON MALLEABLE, INC.
3931 S. DIXIE HGWY.
KETTERING, OH. 45429

C. ELWOOD SHAFFER
SUPER FOOD SVCS., INC.
KETTERING BOX 2323
DAYTON, OH. 45429

HARLIN D. PEDER
INLAND SYSTEMS, INC.
P.O. BOX 1346
SPRINGFIELD, OH. 45501

R.R. FELVER
PORTAGE IND. CORP.
P.O. BOX 1346
SPRINGFIELD, OH. 45501

J. ROBERT GROFF
JAMES LEFFEL & CO.
426 EAST ST.
SPRINGFIELD, OH. 45501

FRED G. WALL
ROBBINS & MYERS, INC.
1345 LAGONDA AVE.
SPRINGFIELD, OH. 45501

R.T. BEEGHLY
STANDARD SLAG CO.
STAMBAUGH BLDG.
YOUNGSTOWN, OH. 45503

R.D. MARTING
MARTING BROS. CO.
515 CHILCOTHE ST.
PORTSMOUTH, OH. 45662

JOHN A. KAYE
ALBRO IND. CORP.
P.O. BOX 143
MARIETTA, OH. 45750

C.L. BROUGHTON
BROUGHTON'S FOODS CO.
210 N. 7TH ST.
MARIETTA, OH. 45750

R.L. BERGEN
FORMA SCIENTIFIC, INC.
P.O. BOX 649
MARIETTA, OH. 45750

W.H. HAAS
TITAN WELLS, INC.
WESTVIEW AVE.
MARIETTA, OH. 45750

W.E. DICKERSON
RANDALL BEARINGS
GREENLAWN AVE. & LAKE ST.
LIMA, OH. 45802

ARNOLD U. FRUMIN
RE-CON CORP
683 W. MARKET ST. C/O OAK PARK
LIMA, OH. 45802

D.W. MONTGOMERY
CELINA FINANCIAL CORP.
INSURANCE SQ.
CELINA, OH. 45822

WAYNE B. BREWER
COOPER TIRE & RUBBER CO.
LIMA & WESTERN AVES.
FINDLAY, OH. 45840

HAROLD D. HOOPMAN
MARATHON OIL CO.
539 S. MAIN ST.
FINDLAY, OH. 45840

R.R. MITCHELL
PENN-MICHIGAN MFG. CORP.
220 S. KIRK
WEST LAFAYETTE, OH. 45854

C.J. MCHUGH
COMMERCIAL FILTERS CORP
HGWY. 32 W.
LEBANON, IND. 46052

HAROLD W. MUTZ
MUTZ CORP.
1853 LUDLOW AVE.
INDIANAPOLIS, IND. 46201

ROBERT HAESLOOP
AMERICAN UNDERWRITERS, INC.
2105 N. MERIDIAN ST.
INDIANAPOLIS, IND. 46202

THOMAS W. MOSES
SHOREWOOD CORP.
1220 WATERWAY BLVD.
INDIANAPOLIS, IND. 46202

W.N. RODENBECK
JEFFERSON CORP.
1100 FIRST FED. BLDG.
INDIANAPOLIS, IND. 46204

OTTO N. FRENZEL, III
MERCHANTS NAT'L. CORP.
11 S. MERIDIAN ST.
INDIANAPOLIS, IND. 46204

ROBERT P. CRONIN
STEAK N SHAKE, INC.
ONE INDIANA SQ. STE. 2610
INDIANAPOLIS, IND. 46204

ROBERT A. DE ROSE
DE ROSE INDUSTRIES
4002 MEADOWS DR.
INDIANAPOLIS, IND. 46205

WALTER H. EDWARDS, JR.
WALTER H. EDWARDS ENGINEERING
2345 WINTHROP AVE.
INDIANAPOLIS, IND. 46205

BUERT R. SERVASS
THE CURTISS PUB. CO.
1100 WATERWAY BLVD.
INDIANAPOLIS, IND. 46206

MAX S. DANNER
DANNERS, INC.
6060 N. GUION RD., P.O. BOX 1146
INDIANAPOLIS, IND. 46206

WILLIAM P. COOLING
INDIANA GROUP, INC.
115 N. PA. ST.
INDIANAPOLIS, IND. 46204

H.C. GOODRICH
INLAND CONTAINER CORP.
151 N. DELAWARE ST.
INDIANAPOLIS, IND. 46206

FREDERICK A. ALDEN, III
INSLEY MFG. CORP.
801 OLNEY ST.
INDIANAPOLIS, IND. 46206

CLARK DAUGHERTY
P.R. MALLORY & CO., INC.
3029 E. WASHINGTON ST.,
INDIANAPOLIS, IND. 46206

ROBERT A. EFROYMSON
REAL SILK HOSIERY MILLS, INC.
BOX 956
INDIANAPOLIS, IND. 46206

HOWARD W. SAMS
HOWARD W. SAMS & CO., INC.
4300 W. 62ND ST.
INDIANAPOLIS, IND. 46206

ALFRED J. STOKELY
STOKELY-VAN CAMP, INC.
941 N. MERIDIAN ST.
INDIANAPOLIS, IND. 46206

HENRY L. DITHMER
INDIANA ICE AND FUEL CO.
2000 NORTHWESTERN AVE.
INDIANAPOLIS, IND. 46207

BILL C. DUNCAN
ALEXANDER NAT'L. GROUP, INC.
3333 N. MERIDIAN ST.
INDIANAPOLIS, IND. 46208

MERRIT W. SMITH
BALDWIN & LYONS, INC.
3100 N. MERIDIAN ST.
INDIANAPOLIS, IND. 46208

JOHN E. MAXWELL,
RANSBURG CORP.
3939 W. 56TH ST.
INDIANAPOLIS, IND. 46208

RICHARD C. LINDOP
UNAC INT'L CORP
3637 N. MERIDIAN ST.
INDIANAPOLIS, IND. 46208

CARL N. PEHLKE
TEXSCAN CORP.
2446 N. SHADELAND AVE.
INDIANAPOLIS, IND. 46219

R.D. PALAMARA
ANACOMP, INC.
6161 HILLSIDE AVE.
INDIANAPOLIS, IND. 46220

C. ROBERT HILES
LILLY INDUSTRIAL COATINGS
666 S. CALIFORNIA ST.
INDIANAPOLIS, IND. 46225

JAMES T. REILLY
BUEHLER CORP.
9000 PRECISION DR.
INDIANAPOLIS, IND. 46226

ELMORE H. RICE III
GENERAL AVIATION ELECTRONICS
4141 KINGMAN DR.
INDIANAPOLIS, IND. 46226

N.P. REAVES
HOOK DRUGS, INC.
2800 ENTERPRISE ST.
INDIANAPOLIS, IND. 46226

F.O. RITTER
REGENCY ELECTRONICS, INC.
7707 RECORDS ST.
INDIANAPOLIS, IND. 46226

W.T. MILLER
CAM-OR INC.
P.O. BOX 41271
INDIANAPOLIS, IND. 46241

J. KEATON LANDIS
BIO-DYNAMICS, INC.
6535 E. 82ND ST.
INDIANAPOLIS, IND. 46250

JOHN R. BENBOW
INDIANA NAT'L. CORP.
ONE INDIANA SQ.
INDIANAPOLIS, IND. 46226

G.V. ROCH
HURCO MFG. CO
P.O. BOX 68180
INDIANAPOLIS, IND. 46268

DAVID L. CHAMBERS, JR.
INDIANAPOLIS STOCKYARDS CO.
4040 W. 71ST ST.
INDIANAPOLIS, IND. 46268

GERALD PAUL
PAUL HARRIS STORES
6003 GUION RD.
INDIANAPOLIS, IND. 46268

RICHARD J. DYE
COMPONENTS, INC.
4400 HOMERLEE AVE.
EAST CHICAGO, IND. 46312

ROBERT D. LEWIS
QUEEN ANNE CANDY CO.
604 HOFFMAN ST.
HAMMOND, IND. 46320

JOHN CHALIK, JR.
AMERICAN RUBBER & PLASTICS CORP.
315 BRIGHTON ST.
LA PORTE, IND. 46350

P.H. STANTON
INFONICS, INC.
4333 S. OHIO ST.
MICHIGAN CITY, IND. 46360

DONALD C. HOODES
SULLAIR CORP.
3700 E. MICHIGAN BLVD.
MICHIGAN CITY, IND. 46360

A.B. WILLIAMSON
MC GILL MFG. CO. INC.
909 N. LAFAYETTE ST.
VALPARAISO, IND. 46383

GLENN R. BROWN
BRISTOL PRODUCTS, INC.
503 VISTULA ST.
BRISTOL, IND. 46507

RAYMOND BASSETT
PARKWOOD HOMES INC.
COUNTY ROAD 8
BRISTOL, INDIANA 46507

DREXELL SIMPSON
ADM INDUSTRIES, INC.
150 CHELSEA RD.
ELKHART, IND. 46514

ROY L. BECK
BECK CORP.
2930 LA RUE ST.
ELKHART, IND. 46514

JAMES E. COLEMAN
C-P PRODUCTS
1611 W. BRISTOL ST.
ELKHART, IND. 46514

GEORGE A. GOULET
ILC PRODUCTS CO.
1800 14TH ST.
ELKHART, IND. 46514

FREDERICK H. IDE
KELTIC, INC.
500 E. ST.
ELKHART, IND. 46514

ROWLAND G. ROSS
MILES LABS
1127 MYRTLE ST.
ELKHART, IND. 46514

DONALD E. CASTELLO
NEW YORKER HOMES CORP.
701 COLLINS RD.
ELKHART, IND. 46514

LEE MARTIN
NIBCO, INC.
500 SIMPSON AVE.
ELKHART, IND. 46514

M.D. LUNG
PATRICK IND. INC.
1800 S. 14TH ST.
ELKHART, IND. 46514

GEORGE PRICE
PRICE-MEYERS CORP.
1135 KENT ST.
ELKHART, IND. 46514

R.E. SUMMERS
RIBLET PRODUCTS CORP.
3601 CALIFORNIA RD.
ELKHART, IND. 46514

RONALD F. KLOSKA
SKYLINE CORP.
2520 BY-PASS RD.
ELKHART, IND. 46514

EDWARD J. HUSSEY
LIBERTY HOMES, INC.
P.O. BOX 46526
GOSHEN, IND. 46526

DAVID R. MILLER
TRAVEL EQUIPMENT CORP.
P.O. BOX 512
GOSHEN, IND. 46526

RICHARD C. MYNSBERGE
MONARCH IND. INC.
BOX 1
GOSHEN, IND. 46540

T.H. CORSON
COACHMEN IND. INC.
P.O. BOX 30
MIDDLEBURY, IND. 46540

ALFRED D. HUFFMAN
SHIPPERS DISPATCH, INC.
1216 W. SAMPLE ST.
S. BEND, IND. 46624

R.E. SOUTH
MESSENGER CORP.
318 E. 7TH ST.
AUBURN, IND. 46706

M.E. RIEKE
RIEKE CORP.
500 W. 7TH ST.
AUBURN, IND. 46706

CONRAD J. BALENTINE
FRANKLIN ELECTRIC CO.
400 E. SPRING ST.
BLUFFTON, IND. 46714

BRYAN S. REID, JR.
GENERAL COLOR GRAPHICS, INC.
P.O. BOX 329
FT. WAYNE, IND. 46801

DANIEL G. RUSS
TELCTRO-MEK, INC.
2700 NUTTMAN AVE.
FT. WAYNE, IND. 46801

JOSEPH J. GUIDRY
TOKHEIM CORP.
P.O. BOX 360
FT. WAYNE, IND. 46801

R.O. LOCKE
TOWN & COUNTRY FOOD CO.
P.O. BOX 1138
FT. WAYNE, IND. 46801

DOUGLAS G. FLEMING
CENTRAL SOYA CO.
FT. WAYNE BANK BLDG.
FT. WAYNE, IND. 46802

IAN M. ROLLAND
LINCOLN NAT'L. CORP
1301 S. HARRISON ST.
FT. WAYNE, IND. 46802

WARREN DALE SCHOUWEILER
OLD FORT IND. INC.
2013 S. ANTHONY BLVD.
FT. WAYNE, IND. 46803

N. RICHARD HUSER
TRANSPORT MOTOR EXPRESS INC.
MEYER RD.
FT. WAYNE, IND. 46803

R.O. LOCKE
KINGSFORD INDUSTRIES INC.
422 W. COLISEUM BLVD.
FT. WAYNE, IND. 46805

EDWARD A. WHITE
BOWMAR INSTRUMENT CORP.
8000 BLUFFTON RD.
FT. WAYNE, IND. 46807

W.A. MAC COMBER
FLINT & WALLING, INC.
INTERSTATE IND. PARK
FT. WAYNE, IND. 46808

HAROLD V. KOCH
BRYAN STEAM CORP
P.O. BOX 27
PERU, IND. 46970

WILLIAM F. BOYD
WABASH, INC.
P.O. BOX 708
WABASH, IND. 46992

DANIEL A. HILLENBRAND
HILLENBRAND IND. INC.
HGWY. 46
BATESVILLE, IND. 47006

EUGENE I. ANDERSON
ARVIN IND. INC.
1531 E. 13TH ST.
COLUMBUS, IND. 47201

ROBERT L. WENDLING
COSCO, INC.
STATE & GLADSTONE
COLUMBUS, IND. 47201

HENRY B. SCHACHT
CUMMINS ENGINE CO. INC.
1000 5TH ST.
COLUMBUS, IND. 47201

JOHN W. FISHER
BALL CORPORATION
1509 S. MACEDONIA AVE.
MUNCIE, IND. 47302

JOHN HARTMEYER
COMMAND HELICOPTERS INC.
109 E. MAIN ST.
MUNCIE, IND. 47302

JOHN G. MARHOEFER
MARHOEFER PACKING CO.
P.O. BOX 2487
MUNCIE, IND. 47302

ALLAN B. MC CREA
NAT'L. AUTOMATIC TOOL CO.
NAT'L. RD. W.
RICHMOND, IND. 47374

ARNOLD DIETZ
RICHMOND HOMES, INC.
N.W. L & SHERIDAN
RICHMOND, IND. 47375

PIERRE-GEORGE ROY
OVERMYER CORP.
117 W. RAILROAD AVE.
WINCHESTER, IND. 47394

DON. E. MARSH
MARSH SUPERMARKETS, INC.
YORKTOWN, IND. 47396

GEORGE REED, JR.
BLOOMINGTON LIMESTONE
P.O. BOX 250
BLOOMINGTON, IND. 47401

J.D. TUCKER
INDIANA LIMESTONE CO.
405 1 ST.
BEDFORD, IND. 47421

RODERIC M. KOCH
STANDARD IND. PRODUCTS
P.O. BOX 325
EVANSVILLE, IND. 47701

WENDALL L. DIXON
CREDITHRIFT FINANCIAL CORP.
601 N.W. 2ND ST
EVANSVILLE, IND. 47708

RICHARD D. CANNON
MEDCO CENTER INC.
947 BOND ST.
EVANSVILLE, IND. 47708

JOSEPH R. CLOUTIER
INDIANA GAS & CHEMICAL CORP.
13TH & HULMAN STS.
TERRE HAUTE, IND. 47802

J.H. MULLER, JR.
GENERAL HOUSEWARES CORP.
1536 BEECH ST.
TERRE HAUTE, IND. 47802

JOHN T. SABLA
TERRE HAUTE MALLEABLE & MFG.
P.O. BOX 4095
TERRE HAUTE, IND. 47804

LEE A. ROADS
SMITH-ALSOP & VARNISH CO.
630 N. THIRD ST.
TERRE HAUTE, IND. 47808

H.W. BOTTOMLY
DUNCAN ELECTRIC CO.
P.O. BOX 180
LAFAYETTE, IND. 47902

JAMES J. SHAW
NAT'L. HOMES CORP.
EARL AVE. & WALLACE ST.
LAFAYETTE, IND. 47904

T.R. HENDERSON
SCHWAB SAFE CO.
3000 MAIN ST.
LAFAYETTE, IND. 47904

EMERSEN KAMPEN
GREAT LAKES CHEMICAL
P.O. BOX 2200
W. LAFAYETTE, IND. 47906

VERNON L. WALDEN
INGRESS MFG. CO.
1001 E. COLLEGE ST.
CRAWFORDSVILLE, IND. 47933

FRED A. ERB
ERB LUMBER CO.
375 S. ETON RD.
BIRMINGHAM, MICH. 48008

ROBERT J. EVANS
LOCK THREAD CORP.
690 E. MAPLE RD.
BIRMINGHAM, MICH. 48011

HAROLD M. MARKO
SOS CONSOLIDATED
P.O. BOX 3500
BIRMINGHAM, MICH. 48011

FRED A. ERB
ERESBO, INC.
P.O. BOX 439
BIRMINGHAM, MICH. 48012

ARTHUR KAUFMANN
KUHLMAN CORP.
P.O. BOX 288
BIRMINGHAM, MICH. 48012

WILFRED O. DUNKEL
NAT'L. MOBILE DEVELOPMENT CO.
P.O. BOX 126
CLARKSTON, MICH. 48016

DAVID HANDELMAN
HANDELMAN CO.
1055 W. MAPLE
CLAWSON, MICH. 48017

RICHARD A. HEADLEE
HAMILTON INTERNATIONAL
33045 HAMILTON BLVD.
FARMINGTON HILLS, MICH. 48024

A.A. BLAY
MAGNETIC VIDEO CORP.
24380 INDOPLEX CIRCLE
FARMINGTON HILLS, MICH. 48024

HAROLD C. WARD
OMNI SPECTRA, INC.
24600 HALLWOOD CT.
FARMINGTON, MICH. 48024

ALBERT WEISS
WEISS POLLUTION CONTROL CORP.
30999 TEN MILE RD.
FARMINGTON, MICH. 48024

R.E. CROSS, SR.
CROSS CO.
17801 FOURTEEN MILE RD.
FRASER, MICH. 48026

C.H. JOHNSON
PULTE HOME CORP.
6400 FARMINGTON RD.
W. BLOOMFIELD, MICH. 48033

JACK A. ROBINSON
PERRY DRUG STORES
3720 LAPEER RD., BOX 4377
PONTIAC, MICH. 48057

N.L. GROSTICK
BIN DICTATOR CO.
1915 DOVE ST.
PORT HURON, MICH. 48060

GORDON MORSETH
PORT HURON PAPER CO.
PORT HURON, MICH. 48060

ROBERT BERSON, JR.
NAT'L. TWIST DRILL & TOOL CO.
ROCHESTER, MICH. 48063

J.N. KNIGHT
H.W. RICKEL & CO.
26711 WOODWARD AVE.
HINTINGTON WOODS, MICH. 48070

A.M. BEERBOHM
TWO B SYSTEMS
30105 STEPHENSON HGWY.
MADISON HEIGHTS, MICH. 48071

D.L. GOLDEN
ACRYLIC OPTICS CORP.
19800 W. EIGHT MILE RD.
SOUTHFIELD, MICH. 48075

J.D. LUPTAK
AMERICANADA LTD.
23999 W. 10 MILE RD.
SOUTHFIELD, MICH. 48075

R.L. LAMBERT
BIFF'S INC.
16900 W. 8 MILE RD.
SOUTHFIELD, MICH. 48075

EDWARD H. PERKINS, JR.
BROOKS & PERKINS
HONEYWELL CENTER BLDG.
SOUTHFIELD, MICH. 48075

A.C. BROWNELL
COMP-U-CHECK INC.
24400 NORTHWESTERN HGWY.
SOUTHFIELD, MICH. 48075

ROBERT W. OLSEN
THE COMPUTER SVCS. CORP.
23225 NORTHWESTERN HGWY.
SOUTHFIELD, MICH. 48075

J.P. BUKHAI
GREAT LAKES RECREATION CO.
24245 NORTHWESTERN HGWY.
SOUTHFIELD, MICH. 48075

HERBERT H. FREEDLAND
HOWELL INDUSTRIES
17515 W. 9 MILE RD., STE. 650
SOUTHFIELD, MICH. 48075

WILLIAM L. MULLEN
INDUSTRIAL FUELS CORP.
22255 GREENFIELD RD.
SOUTHFIELD, MICH 48075

HARRY C. OLSEN
F.L. JACOBS CO.
24500 NORTHWESTERN HGWY.
SOUTHFIELD, MICH. 48075

T.E. ADDERLEY
KELLY SVCS.
16130 NORTHLAND DR.
SOUTHFIELD, MICH. 48075

MERTON J. SEGAL
MEADOWBROOK, INC.
24370 NORTHWESTERN HGWY.
SOUTHFIELD, MICH. 48075

IRVING R. SELIGMAN
SELIGMAN & ASSOCS.
24315 NORTHWESTERN HGWY.
SOUTHFIELD, MICH. 48075

WILLIAM F. HIBNER
SILHOUETTE-AMERICAN HEALTH SPAS
3055 SOUTHFIELD RD.
SOUTHFIELD, MICH. 48075

W.B. WALKER, JR.
WALWAY CO.
SOUTHFIELD, MICH. 48075

DR. ROBERT MOSS
ALDEN CARE ENTERPRISES
30555 SOUTHFIELD RD.
SOUTHFIELD, MICH. 48076

RICHARD B. LUTZ, JR.
MICHIGAN MOBILE HOMES
26711 NORTHWESTERN
SOUTHFIELD, MICH. 48076

CHARLES D. CRONENWORTH
DIAMOND CRYSTAL SALT
916 S. RIVERSIDE AVE.
ST. CLAIR, MICH. 48079

S.S. GORDEN
REPUBLIC AUTOMOTIVE PARTS
20200 E. NINE MILE RD.
ST. CLARE SHORES, MICH. 48083

J.A. BACON, JR.
AMT CORP.
1225 E. MAPLE RD.
TROY, MICH. 48084

JAMES H. MC NEAL, JR.
THE BUDD CO.
2155 W. BIG BEAVER RD.
TROY, MICH. 48084

KAYE G. FRANK
D.A.B. INDS.
466 STEPHENSON HGWY.
TROY, MICH. 48084

S.R. OVSHINSKY
ENERGY CONVERSION DEVICES
1675 W. MAPLE RD.
TROY, MICH. 48084

J.E. ZITOMER
NATIONAL BRANDS, INC.
1210 E. MAPLE RD.
TROY, MICH. 48084

KENNETH D. McCLAIN
McCLAIN INDS.
6200 ELMRIDGE
UTICA, MICH. 48087

E.J. GIBLIN
EX-CELL-O CORP.
850 LADD RD.
WALLED LAKE, MICH. 48088

CHARLES F. TRAPP
FORMSPRAG CO.
23601 HOOVER RD.
WARREN, MICH. 48089

MICHAEL PINTO
LE MAIRE MACHINE TOOL CO.
2500 E. NINE MILE RD.
WARREN, MICH. 48089

T.M. CLARK
MICHIGAN RIVET CORP.
21221 HOOVER RD.
WARREN, MICH. 48089

T.M. CLARK
PRO SYSTEMS, INC.
13201 STEPHENS
WARREN, MICH. 48089

BERNARD WEISBERG
CHATHAM SUPER MARKETS
2300 E. TEN MILE RD.
WARREN, MICH. 48091

FRED ELIAS
ELIAS BROS. RESTS.
4199 MARCY ST.
WARREN, MICH. 48091

J.D. ADAIR
KENT-MORE CORP.
28635 MOUND RD.
WARREN, MICH. 48092

W.P. DONOHUE
TRANS-INDUSTRIES
3777 AIRPORT RD.
WATERFORD, MICH. 48095

CHARLES GELMAN
GELMAN INSTRUMENT
600 S. WAGNER RD., BOX 1448
ANN ARBOR, MICH. 48103

C.L. BIXBY
INTERFACE SYSTEMS
462 JACKSON PLAZA
ANN ARBOR, MICH. 48103

JOHN STRAND
LASER SYSTEMS
117 N. 1ST
ANN ARBOR, MICH. 48103

JAMES E. SAUTER
BOOTH NEWSPAPERS
3959 RESEARCH PARK DR.
ANN ARBOR, MICH 48104

J.W. EDWARDS
EDWARDS BROS.
2500 S. STATE ST.
ANN ARBOR, MICH. 48104

R.A. OLSEN
KMS INDUSTRIES
3941 RESEARCH DR.
ANN ARBOR, MICH. 48104

SAMUEL N. IRWIN
SYCOR INC.
100 PHOENIX DR.
ANN ARBOR, MICH. 48104

RONALD L. SARGENT
THETFORD CORP.
3000 S. STATE RD.
ANN ARBOR, MICH. 48104

DR. MAURICE J. DAY
ARGUS, INC.
2601 S. STATE ST.
ANN ARBOR, MICH 48106

R.L. CRANDALL
COMSHARE, INC.
P.O. BOX 1588
ANN ARBOR, MICH. 48106

ALAN K. PARKER
DAEDALUS ENTERPRISES
P.O. BOX 1869, 7101 JACKSON RD.
ANN ARBOR, MICH. 48106

HOWARD DIAMOND
TRANSIDYNE GENERAL
903 AIRPORT DR.
ANN ARBOR, MICH. 48106

JOHN F. DALY
HOOVER BALL & BEARING
P.O. BOX 1003
ANN ARBOR, MICH. 48107

F.R. GELLENBECK
FEDERAL ASPHALT PRODS.
P.O. BOX 44114
DEARBORN, MICH. 48126

DANIEL LE VINE
STEARNS MFG. CO.
WEST HURON RIVER DR.
FLAT ROCK, MICH. 48134

GREGORY C. SMITH
WOLVERINE-PENTRONIX
1650 HOWARD ST.
LINCOLN PARK, MICH. 48146

GENE HIRS
HYDROMATION FILTER
39201 ARMHEIN RD.
LIVONIA, MICH. 48150

W.G. FREDERICK, JR.
PHOTON SOURCES, INC.
37100 PLYMOUTH RD.
LIVONIA, MICH. 48150

D.J. THRONBER
SERVICE PRODUCING CO.
12263 MARKET ST.
LIVONIA, MICH. 48150

THOMAS I. KLEIN
VELVET-O'DONNELL CORP.
30111 SCHOOLCRAFT
LIVONIA, MICH. 48150

C.T. KNABUSCH
LA-Z-BOY CHAIR CO.
1284 N. TELEGRAPH RD.
MONROE, MICH. 48161

C.S. McINTYRE, III.
MONROE AUTO EQUIP.
INTERNATIONAL DR.
MONROE, MICH. 48161

W.M. DAVIDSON
GUARDIAN INDS.
43043 W. 9 MILE RD.
NORTHVILLE, MICH 48167

R.W. HUFFMAN
SOLVENTOL CHEMICAL PRODS.
13177 HURON RIVER DR.
ROMULUS, MICH. 48174

CARL E. PFEIFFER
QUANEX CORP.
WM. H. McNUNN ST.
SO. LYON, MICH. 48178

RICHARD A. MANOOGIAN
MASCO CORP.
21001 VAN BORN RD.
TAYLOR, MICH. 48180

S.J. LANG
BAGLEY BUILDING
910 FRANCIS PALMS BLDG.
DETROIT, MICH. 48201

JAMES VERNOR DAVIS
V.G.A. CO.
4501 WOODWARD AVE.
DETROIT, MICH. 48201

ANTHONY J. VINCI
WINKELMAN STORES
25 PARSONS ST.
DETROIT, MICH. 48201

ARTHUR ROSENSTEIN
BRASS-CRAFT MFG.
700 FISHER BLDG.
DETROIT, MICH. 48202

E. PAUL CASEY
MC CORD CORP.
2850 W. GRAND
DETROIT, MICH. 48202

MAXWELL GOLDSTEIN
FEDERAL'S INC.
1200 E. MC NICHOLS RD.
DETROIT, MICH. 48203

R.W. MONTGOMERY
H.A. MONTGOMERY CO.
17191 WALTER P. CHRYSLER HGWY.
DETROIT, MICH. 48203

M. HOENSHEID
COMMERCIAL STEEL TREATING
6100 TIREMAN AVE.
DETROIT, MICH. 48204

A.W. ARMOUR,III.
HUCK MFG. CO.
2500 BELLEVUE AVE.
DETROIT, MICH. 48207

HYMAN SAFRAN
SAFRAN PRINTING
3939 BELLEVUE
DETROIT, MICH. 48207

HOWARD N. MAYNARD
SNYDER CORP.
3400 E. LAFAYETTE AVE.
DETROIT, MICH. 48207

CHARLES R. WEIR
COMMONWEALTH INDS.
5900 COMMONWEALTH AVE.
DETROIT, MICH. 48208

HARRY A. LOMASON
DOUGLAS & LOMASON
5800 LINCOLN AVE.
DETROIT, MICH. 48208

WILLIAM P. YOUNG
DETROIT HARBOR TERMINALS
4461 W. JEFFERSON AVE.
DETROIT, MICH. 48209

W. TOM ZUR SCHMIEDE
FEDERAL SCREW WORKS
3401 MARTIN AVE.
DETROIT, MICH. 48210

ARTHUR M. ACKER
SHATTERPROOF GLASS
4815 CABOT AVE.
DETROIT, MICH. 48210

REUBEN T. BERGMAN
FREDERICK & HERRUD
1487 FARNSWORTH ST.
DETROIT, MICH. 48211

J.A. CORMACK
R.P. SCHERER CORP.
9425 GRINNELL AVE.
DETROIT, MICH. 48211

R.A. SHAPERO
CUNNINGHAM DRUG STORES
1927 12TH ST.
DETROIT, MICH. 48216

MAX J. PINCUS
HUGHES & HATCHER
1300 12TH ST.
DETROIT, MICH. 48216

HARRY MODELL
MOHAWK LIQUEUR CORP.
1965 PORTER ST.
DETROIT, MICH. 48216

WILLIAM H. HOLMAN
MC LOUTH STEEL
300 S. LIVERNOLIS AVE.
DETROIT, MICH. 48217

B.M. BOND
BROWN-MC LAREN MFG. CO.
195 CAMPBELL
RIVER ROUGE, MICH. 48218

JOSEPH R. DEANE
NICHOLSON TERMINAL & DOCK
GREAT LAKES AVE
ECORSE, MICH. 48218

D.C. RILEY
HYGRADE FOOD PRODS. CORP.
P.O. BOX 19170
DETROIT, MICH. 48219

W.B. KLINSKY
ALBERTS INC.
10811 N. END AVE.
FERNDALE, MICH. 48220

E.L. NICOLAY, JR.
SQUIRT-DETROIT BOTTLING CO.
515 WANDA AVE.
FERNDALE, MICH. 48220

JAMES J. SHEA
GAM RAD INC.
16825 WYOMING AVENUE
DETROIT, MICH. 48221

SAMUEL RICH
ACORN BUILDING COMPONENTS
12620 WESTWOOD
DETROIT, MICH. 48223

FREDERICK BRAUN
BRAUN ENGINEERING CO.
19001 GLENDALE AVE.
DETROIT, MICH. 48223

R.D. BAKER
AMERICAN MUSIC STORES
1515 WOODWARD AVE.
DETROIT, MICH. 48226

HERBERT S. EPSTEIN
ARMADA CORP.
1300 BUHL BLDG.
DETROIT, MICH. 48226

W.W. ANDERSON, JR.
BUNDY CORP.
333 W. FORT ST.
DETROIT, MICH. 48226

R.B. BURTON
BURTON SOHIGIAN, INC.
1400 PENOBSCOT BLDG.
DETROIT, MICH. 48226

ROBERT P. SYKE
COMMUNIDYNE CORP.
1800 1ST NAT'L. BLDG.
DETROIT, MICH. 48226

R.E. WINKEL
CROWLEY, MILNER & CO.
GRATIOT & FARMER
DETROIT, MICH. 48226

ELLIOTT PHILLIPS
DETROIT & CANADA TUNNEL
151 ATWATER ST.
DETROIT, MICH. 48226

WALTER E. HAINES
EVANS INDS.
2441 FIRST NAT'L. BLDG.
DETROIT, MICH. 48226

SPENCER REUBEN
JOSHUA DOORE INC.
2365 GUARDIAN BLDG.
DETROIT, MICH. 48226

P.A. REGER
SHELBY UNIVERSAL CORP.
1904 GUARDIAN BLDG
DETROIT, MICH. 48226

PAUL BORMAN
BORMAN'S INC.
12300 MARK TWAIN AVE.
DETROIT, MICH. 48227

ARBIE O. THALACKER
DETREX CHEMICAL INDS.
P.O. BOX 501
DETROIT, MICH. 48232

ROY G. LANCASTER
DETROIT INT'L. BRIDGE
P.O. BOX 447
DETROIT, MICH. 48232

ROBERT ROWAN
FRUEHAUF CORP.
10900 HARPER AVE.
DETROIT, MICH. 48232

R.A. MC CARROLL
ACME PRECISION PRODUCTS
3750 E. OUTER DRIVE
DETROIT, MICH. 48234

MAX WEINBERG
FRANK'S NURSERY SALES
6399 E. NEVADA
DETROIT, MICH. 48234

E.J. COLOSIMO
COMTEL, CORP.
17500 W. MC NICHOLS RD.
DETROIT, MICH. 48235

THOMAS F. RUSSELL
FEDERAL-MOGUL CORP.
P.O. BOX 1966
DETROIT, MICH. 48235

WARREN D. GREENSTONE
PUBLIC LOAN CO.
17700 MC NICHOLS ST.
DETROIT, MICH. 48235

H.L. GRAEBNER
TEMPCO BUSINESS SERVICES
16415 WEST MILE RD.
DETROIT, MICH. 48235

DELBERT E. GAINES
THE LYNCH CORP.
15322 FULLERTON AVE.
DETROIT, MICH. 48238

ROBERT M. WILLIAMS
GENOVA, INC.
300 RISING ST.
DAVISON, MICH. 48423

JOSEPH MORRIS
CHAMPION HOME BUILDERS
5573 E. NORTH ST.
DRYDEN, MICH. 48428

GEORGE McCOLLOUGH, JR.
VESELY CO.
2101 N. LAPEER RD.
LAPEER, MICH. 48446

PHILIP B. HARLEY
BAKER PERKINS
1000 HESS ST.
SAGINAW, MICH. 48601

ERNEST FLEGENHEIMER
MICHIGAN SUGAR CO.
SECOND NAT'L. BANK BLDG.
SAGINAW, MICH. 48601

RICHARD V. WOLOHAN
WOLOHAN LUMBER
1740 MIDLAND RD.
SAGINAW, MICH. 48603

A.S. BRENNAN
WATER WONDERLAND FIBER GLASS
400 WATER ST.
ST. CHARLES, MICH. 48655

DEAN KNIGHT
NEWCOR, INC.
1846 N. TRUMBULL ST.
BAY CITY, MICH. 48706

LEONARD E. NICHOLS
RESISTANCE WELDER CORP.
2105 S. EUCLID AVE.
BAY CITY, MICH. 48706

WALTER E. WALPOLE
WALBRO CORPORATION
6242 GARFIELD ST.
CASS CITY, MICH. 48726

J.P. McGOFF
PANAX CORP.
P.O. BOX 1860
EAST LANSING, MICH. 48823

J.R. WHITMAN
WHITMAN INDUSTRIES, INC.
331 N. CROSWELL RD.
ITHACA, MICHIGAN 48847

LOREN B. HANCHETT
MWA CO.
510 S. WASHINGTON ST.
OWOSSO, MICH. 48867

DAVID D. AREHART
PALACE CORP.
WILLIAMSTON, MICH. 48895

J.H. GROSS
GROSS TELECASTING, INC.
EAST SAGINAW ST.
LANSING, MICH. 48906

PATRICK J. CALLIHAN
PROVINCIAL HOUSE, INC.
4000 N. GRAND RIVER AVE.
LANSING, MICH. 48906

H.E. GUYSELMAN
TRANTER, INC.
735 E. HAZEL ST.
LANSING, MICH. 48909

H.N. HOLTZER
CLAUSING CORP.
2019 PITCHER ST.
KALAMAZOO, MICH. 49001

AL L. DIXON
MASTER-CRAFT CORP.
831 COBB AVE.
KALAMAZOO, MICH. 49001

DAVID R. MARKIN
CHECKER MOTORS CORP.
2016 N. PITCHER ST.
KALAMAZOO, MICH. 49002

DAN INT-HOUT, JR.
MICHIGAN CARTON CO.
79 E. FOUNTAIN ST.
BATTLE CREEK, MICH. 49014

J.B. FREED
UNION PUMP CO.
87 CAPITOL AVE, S.W.
BATTLE CREEK, MICH 49014

W. BRUCE BOWERS
U.S. REGISTER CO.
344 E. BURNHAM ST.
BATTLE CREEK, MICH. 49016

O.C. SCHULTZ
BENTON HARBOR MALLEABLE INDS.
GRAHAM AVE.
BENTON HARBOR, MICH. 49022

JOHN H. PLATTS
WHIRLPOOL CORP.
BENTON HARBOR, MICH. 49022

MR. JESSUP
JESSCO, INC.
P.O. BOX 468
DOWAGIAC, MICH. 49047

STEPHEN I. JOHNSON
HASTINGS MFG. CO.
325 N. HANOVER ST.
HASTINGS, MICH. 49058

DR. FRANCIS X. WAZETER
INT'L. RESEARCH & DVLPMT.
900 N. MAIN ST.
MATTAWAN, MICH. 49071

C.E. KIRSCH
KIRSCH CO.
309 N. PROSPECT ST.
STURGIS, MICH. 49091

F.C. HAGEMAN
NAT'L. MOBILE CONCRETE
P.O. BOX 225
BERRIEN SPRINGS, MICHIGAN 49103

BERT E. PHILLIPS
CLARK EQUIPMENT CO.
CIRCLE DR.
BUCHANAN, MICH. 49107

GEORGE HUSSEY, JR.
NATIONAL-STANDARD CO.
601 N. 8TH ST.
NILES, MICH. 49120

ROBERT E. COURTNEY
COURTHOUSE INDUSTRIES, INC.
P.O. BOX 1
UNION, MICH. 49130

U.E. PATRICK
PATRICK PETROLEUM
744 W. MICHIGAN AVE.
JACKSON, MI. 49201

CHARLES E. DRURY
HAYES-ALBION
1999 WILDWOOD AVE.
JACKSON, MI. 49202

J.R. FOWLER
JACOBSON STORES
1200 N. WEST AVE.
JACKSON, MI. 49202

L. JAMES BAILEY
RYERSON & HAYNES
2500 ENTERPRISE
JACKSOK, MI. 49202

JOHN J. SMITH
SPARTON CORP.
2400 E. GANSON ST.
JACKSON, MI. 49202

FRED C. JANKE
HANCOCK IND.
225 NORTH HORTON ST.
JACKSON, MI. 49204

R.B. WESTFALL
ADRIAN STEEL
906 JAMES ST.
ADRIAN, MI. 49221

PAUL C. MEECH
KEWAUNEE SCIENTIFIC
SOUTH CENTER ST.
ADRIAN, MI. 49221

WENDALL LADD
W.A.I.
BOX 593
ADRIAN, MI. 49221

H.R. KONKLE
DECKER MFG.
703 N. CLARK ST.
ALBION, MI. 49224

A.A. CALDERONE
CALDERONE-CURRAN RANCHES
4749 WILLIS RD.
GRASS LAKE,MI. 49240

ROBERT W. NAVARRE
SIMPSON IND.
917 ANDERSON RD.
LITCHFIELD, MI. 49252

ROBERT F. BELL
FARADAY, INC.
805 S. MAUMEE
TECUMSEH, MI. 49286

W.E. MAC BETH
TECUMSEH PROD.
OTTAWA & PATTERSON STS.
TECUMSEH, MI. 49286

THOMAS D. GLEASON
WOLVERINE WORLD WIDE
ROCKFORD, MI. 49341

PHILIP A. UZIELLI
LEIGH PROD.
COOPERVILLE, MI. 49404

ARTHUR J. FRENS
GERBER PROD.
445 STATE ST.
FREMONT, MI. 49412

JAMES R. SEYFERTH
WESTRAN
1148 W. WESTERN AVE.
MUSKEGON, MI. 49440

NORMAND PHANEUF
LAKE WAY CHEM.
5025 EVANSTON AVE.
MUSKEGON, MI. 49443

H.N. FORMAN
STORY CHEM. CORP.
500 AGARD RD.
MUSKEGON, MI. 49445

EDWARD I. SCHALON
SEALED POWER CORP.
2001 SANFORD ST.
MUSKEGON HTS., MI. 49444

HUGH DE PREE
HERMAN MILLER
140 W. McKINLEY
ZEELAND, MI. 49464

G.E. MILLS
CORDUROY RUBBER
FULLER AVE.
GRAND RAPIDS,MI. 49501

R.F. BRUSH
ROSPATCH
P.O. BOX 2738
GRAND RAPIDS, MI. 49501

DONALD H. FREEMAN
AGM IND.
450 UNION BANK BLDG.
GRAND RAPIDS, MI. 49502

PHILIP DE JOURNO
CARE
200 TRUST BLDG.
GRAND RAPIDS, MI. 49502

KENNETH S. CASE
CITATION CO.
648 MONROE AVE. N.W.
GRAND RAPIDS, MI. 49502

JOHN D. BOUWER
CONCORDIA
201 TRUST BLDG.
GRAND RAPIDS, MI. 49502

KEITH C. VANDER HYDE
GUARDSMAN CHEM.
1350 STEELE AVE. S.W.
GRAND RAPIDS, MI. 49502

CLARE F. JARECKI
JARECKI CORP.
320 HALL ST., S.W.
GRAND RAPIDS, MI. 49502

GORDON H. BUTER
ASSOC. FREIGHTWAYS
200 MONROE N.W.
GRAND RAPIDS, MI. 49503

W.W. PERKINS
R.C. ALLEN
678 FRONT AVE. N.W.
GRAND RAPIDS, MI. 49504

JOHN W. DWYER
AMERICAN SEATING
901 BROADWAY
GRAND RAPIDS, MI. 49504

DONALD J. KNAPE
KNAPE & VOGT MFG.
2700 OAK IND. DR. N.E.
GRAND RAPIDS, MI. 49505

R.W. WEBSTER
HOLLY'S INC.
255 COLRAIN ST., S.W.
GRAND RAPIDS, MI. 49508

RAYMOND A. WEIGEL
KYSOR IND.
ONE MADISON AVE.
CADILLAC, MI. 49601

MH. DENNOS
CHEF PIERRE
P.O. BOX 1009
TRAVERSE CITY, MI. 49684

J.R. BRISSON
LODAL
P.O. BOX 791
KINGSFORD, MI. 49802

MARILOU ENGLISH
INDIANHEAD SKI CORP.
WAKEFIELD, MI. 49968

C.C. HACH
HACH CHEM.
713 S. DUFF AVE.
AMES, IOWA 50010

T.W. TALBOT
EMMERT MFG.
AUDUBON, IOWA 50025

FLOYD G. VAN AUKEN
DEFLECTA-SHIELD
314 E. JEFFERSON
CORYDON, IOWA 50060

PAUL W. AHRENS
MIRACLE RECREATION
WEST HIGHWAY 6
GRINNELL, IOWA 50112

K.H. YINGST
MAN-AN-SQ. CORP.
820 B. 6TH. ST.
NEVADA, IOWA 50201

DANIEL J. KRUMM
MAYTAG CO.
403 W. 4TH. ST.
NEWTON, IOWA 50208

WILLIAM F. VERNON JR.
VERNON CO.
604 W. 4TH. ST. N.
NEWTON, IOWA 50208

JAMES MELTON
CONTRACT PACKAGING
1505 N. AVE.
NORWALK, IOWA 50211

ROBERT A. BURNETT
MEREDITH
1716 LOCUST ST.
DES MOINES, IOWA 50303

R.J. FLEMING
NATL. BY-PRODUCT
1020 LOCUST ST.
DES MOINES, IOWA 50303

F.A. DE PUYDT
DICO CORP.
200 S.W. 16TH. ST.
DES MOINES, IOWA 50305

REAVES E. PETERS
DEN-TAL-EZ
P.O. BOX 4686
DES MOINES, IOWA 50306

RICHARD S. LEVITT
DIAL FINANCE
207 NINTH ST.
DES MOINES, IOWA 50307

CHARLES DUCHEN
YOUNKERS BROS.
7TH. & WALNUT STS.
DES MOINES, IOWA 50307

W.L. BROWN
PIONEER HI-BRED INTL.
1206 MULBERRY ST.
DES MOINES, IOWA 50308

R.L. DAVIS
DAVIS THEATRES
311 11TH. ST.
DES MOINES, IOWA 50309

D.S. FREEMAN
FREEMAN DECORATING
P.O. BOX 130
DES MOINES, IOWA 50309

J.M. HOAK
HERITAGE COMM. INC.
2195 INGERSOLL AVE.
DES MOINES, IOWA 50312

ROBERT D. WILLIAMS
INTL. FUNERAL
2501 GRAND AVE.
DES MOINES, IOWA 50312

R.A. WESTCOTT
MID-CONTINENT IND.
1679 N.E. 51ST AVE.
DES MOINES, IOWA 50313

ROBERT SANDLER
U.S. HOMES
5390 SECOND AVE.
DES MOINES, IOWA 50313

W.A. JENNINGS
CONST. PRODUCTS
BOX D, EAST 14TH ST. STA.
DES MOINES, IOWA 50316

W.A. JENNINGS
ECONOMY FORMS
4301 N.E. 14TH ST.
DES MOINES, IOWA 50316

H.L. HANSEN
DIAMOND LAB.
2538 S.E. 43RD ST.
DES MOINES, IOWA 50317

E. HOWARD HILL
I D PACKING CO.
S.E. 18TH & SCOTT
DES MOINES, IOWA 50317

ARNOLD FLETCHER JR.
SEDALIA-MARSHALL-BOONVILLE
5805 FLEUR DR.
DES MOINES, IOWA 50321

J.D. KENT JR.
CONTINENTAL WESTERN
11201 DOUBLAS AVE.
DES MOINES, IOWA 50322

RICHARD L. CURRIE
CURRIES MFG.
251 NINTH ST., S.E.
MASON CITY, IOWA 50401

JACK MAC NIDER
NORTHERWESTERN STATES CEMENT
12 SECOND ST., N.E.
MASON CITY, IOWA 50401

J.H. THRELKELD
BRITT TECH
BRITT, IOWA 50423

JOHN V. HANSON JR.
WINNEBAGO IND.
P.O. BOX 152
FOREST CITY, IOWA 50436

F.A. FIELDER
ART'S-WAY MFG.
ARMSTRON, IOWA 50514

GERALD F. FISHER
CREST PAK
1513 15TH. ST. N. BX. 416
HUMBOLDT, IOWA 50548

R.W. VOORHEES
STANDARD MFG.
220 E. 4TH ST.
CEDAR FALLAS, IOWA 50613

W.C. DUDLEY
O'S GOLD SEED
PARKERSBURG, IOWA 50665

EMMET A. MC GUIRE
RATH PACKING
P.O. BOX 330
WATERLOO, IOWA 50704

L.C. FRENCH
AGRI-DYNAMICS
P.O. BOX 1043
CHEROKEE, IOWA 51012

WILLIAM T. DIBLE
TERRA CHEM.
507 SIXTH ST.
SIOUX CITY, IOWA 51101

W.C. HODGES
CM CORP.
211 GRAYSON BLDG.
SIOUX CITY, IOWA 51102

JERRY P. KOZNEY
SPENCER FOODS
SPENCER, IOWA 51301

ALVIN L. SCHLUTER
AMERICAN HEALTH FACILITIES
LAKE VIEW, IOWA 51450

D. ARCHIE
MID-AMERICAN PUBLISHING
BOX 130
SHENANDOAH, IOWA 51601

FRANK H. BERTSCH
FLEXSTEEL IND.
BRUNSWICK INC. BLOCK
DUBUQUE, IOWA 52001

MARTIN HOFFINGER
CLINTON ENGINES
CLARK & MAPLE STS
MAQUOKETA, IOWA 52060

SHELDON J. CLINTON
SUNNYCREST NURSING
303 AMERICAN BLDG.
CEDAR RAPIDS, IOWA 52401

G.P. NISSEN
NISSEN CORP.
930 27TH AVE. SW
CEDAR RAPIDS, IOWA 52404

CHARLES H. DYKENMAN
AMERICAN FUNERAL
613 2ND. AVE. SE
CEDAR RAPIDS, IOWA 52406

E.C. STRAZISHAR
HEALTH MANAGEMENT
P.O. BOX 1808
CEDAR RAPIDS, IOWA 52406

KENNETH A. WATTS
LE FEBURE-SARGENT
P.O. DRAWER 2028
CEDAR RAPIDS, IOWA 52406

D.H. MINER
NETWORK DATA
321 3RD. ST., S.E.
CEDAR RAPIDS, IOWA 52407

M.C. FORSYTHE
J.W. EDGERLY
120-124 W. MAIN ST.
OTTUMWA, IOWA 52501

L.F. CONRAD
CONRAD
HIGHWAY 16 WEST
HOUGHTON, IOWA 52631

ROBERT J. WUSTROW
HUBINGER
601 MAIN ST.
KEOKUK, IOWA 52632

HARKER COLLINS
BANDAG
1056 HERSHEY AVE.
MUSCATINE, IOWA 52761

S.M. HOWE
HON IND.
414 E. 3RD. ST.
MUSCATINE, IOWA 52761

LLOYD G. SCHERMER
LEE ENTERPRISES
130 E. 2ND. STE. 300
DAVENPORT, IOWA 52801

A.H. SHERMAN
ALLOY METAL PROD.
626 SCHMIDT RD.
DAVENPORT,IOWA 52802

H.G. MULLETT
BRADLEY WASHFOUNTAIN
W. 142 N9101 FOUNTAIN DR.
MENOMONEE FALLS, WISC. 53055

W.W. GALLAHER
MUSEBECK SHOE
FOREST & WESTOVER
OCONOMOWOC, WISC. 53066

HOWARD C. DICKELMAN
SCHULTZ SAV-O STORES
2215 UNION AVE.
SHEBOYGAN , WISC. 53081

R.D. ZIEGLER
ZIEGLER CO.
215 N. MAIN ST.
WEST BEND, WISC. 53095

STUART W. TISDALE
STR-RITE
234 S. EIGHT ST.
DELAVAN, WISC. 53115

JOHN E. KAISER
MAC WHYTE
2906 14TH. AVE.
KENOSHA, WISC. 53140

NORMAN E. LUTZ
SNAP-ON TOOLS
8028 28TH. AVE.
KENOSHA, WISC. 53140

CHARLES F. STEIN
NAPCO GRAPHIC ARTS
2601 SOUTH MOORLAND RD.
NEW BERLIN, WISC. 53151

JOSEPH CALABRIA
HYTEK INTL.
303 WEST MARQUETTE AVE.
OAK CREEK, WISC. 53154

L.A. COSTARELLA
NINO'S
2201 SOUTHBRANCH BLVD.
OAK CREEK, WISC. 53154

EUGENE P. BERG
BUCYRUS-ERIE CO.
SOUTH MILWAUKEE, WISC. 53172

JOHN A. GODFREY
GODFREY
1200 W. SUNSET DR. BX. 298
WAUKESHA, WISC. 53186

JOHN D. WATSON
HEIN-WERNER
1200 NATL. AVE.
WAUKESHA, WISC. 53186

LOREN D. BARRE
RTE. CORP.
1900 E. NORTH ST.
WAUKESHA, WISC. 53186

R.G. PIPER
WISCONSIN CENTRIFUGAL
WAUKESHA, WISCONSIN 53186

LAWRENCE R. KEM
AMERICAN APPRAISAL ASSOC.
525 E. MICHIGAN ST.
MILWAUKEE, WISC. 53201

EUGENE B. PETERS
JOS. SCHLITZ
235 W. GALENA ST.
MILAUKEE, WISC. 53201

CHESTER O. WANVIG JR.
GLOBE-UNION
5757 N. GREEN BAY AVE.
MILWAUKEE, WISC. 53201

W.S. PEARCE
HARCO HOLDINGS
P.O. DRAWER 8-B
MILWAUKEE, WISC. 53201

RICHARD T. LINDGREN
KOEHRING CO.
P.O. BOX 312
MILWAUKEE, WISC. 53201

WILLARD H. DAVIDSON
MARINE CORP.
1 MARINE PLAZA
MILWAUKEE, WISC. 53201

JOE E. DAVIS
NATL. HEALTH
P.O. BOX 351
MILWAUKEE, WISC. 53201

JAMES C. WINDHAM
PABST BREWING
917 W. JUNEAU AVE.
MILAUKEE, WISC. 53201

FRED J. SCHWERMAN
SCHWERMAN TRUCKING
P.O. BOX 1601
MILWAUKEE, WISC. 53201

FRANK H. ROBY
SOLAR BASIC IND.
P.O. BOX 753
MILWAUKEE, WISC. 53201

JOHN L. MURRAY
UNIVERSAL FOODS
433 E. MICHIGAN ST.
MILWAUKEE, WISC. 53201

V.F. NAST JR.
WESTERN LIME & CEMENT
125 E. WELLS ST.
MILWAUKEE, WISC. 53201

ROBERT FEITLER
WEYENBERG SHOE MFG.
234 E. RESERVOIR AVE.
MILWAUKEE, WISC. 53201

HAROLD NASH
AMERICAN MED. SERVICES
1301 N. FRANKLIN PL.
MILWAUKEE, WISC. 53202

EDDY G. NICHOLASON
CONGOLEUM
777 E. WISCONSIN AVE.
MILWAUKEE, WISC. 53202

D.E. RUNGE
FARM HOUSE FOODS
733 N. VAN BUREN ST.
MILWAUKEE, WISC. 53202

FRED L. BRENGEL
JOHNSON CONTROL
507 E. MICHIGAN ST.
MILWAUKEE, WISC. 53202

ROBERT V. KRIKORIAN
REXNORD
777 E. WISCONSIN AVE. STE. 3500
MILWAUKEE, WISC. 53202

J.W. CHECOTA
AMERICAN MED. BLDG.
515 W. WELLS ST.
MILWAUKEE, WISC. 53203

F.A. SHAPIRO
ENROC IND.
710 N. PLANKINTON AVE.#622
MILWAUKEE, WISC. 53203

HENRY G. HERZING
HERZING INSTITUTES
174 W. WISCONSIN AVE.
MILWAUKEE, WISC. 53203

BEN MARCUS
MARCUS CORP.
212 W. WISCONSIN AVE.
MILWAUKEE, WISC. 53203

REIMER A. PERKINS
MEDALIST IND.
735 N. 5TH ST.
MILWAUKEE, WISC. 53203

W.H. ALVERSON
MILWAUKEE PROFESSIONAL SPORTS
901 N. 4TH. ST.
MILWAUKEE, WISC. 53203

ALVIN A. STEIN
PILL AND PUFF
112 W. WISCONSIN AVE.
MILWAUKEE, WISC. 53203

FRANK W. NORRIS
TIME HOLDINGS
735 N. 5TH. ST.
MILWAUKEE, WISC. 53203

J.J. ZILBER
UNICARE SERVICES
105 W. MICHIGAN ST.
MILWAUKEE, WISC. 53203

W.C. SMITH
L.L. COOK
1830 N. 16TH. ST.
MILWAUKEE, WISC. 53205

DANIEL C. FERGUSON JR.
E.Z. PAINTR CORP.
4051 SOUTH IOWA AVE.
MILWAUKEE, WISC. 53207

A.A. SILVERMAN
VILTER MFG.
2217 SOUTH FIRST ST.
MILWAUKEE, WISC. 53207

D.G. PROSSER
AUTOROL CORP.
5855 NORTH GLEN PARK RD.
MILWAUKEE, WISC. 53209

DONNAL W. HANSEN
DELTA OIL PROD.
6263 NORTH TEUTONIA AVE.
MILWAUKEE, WISC. 53209

EDWARD NEUWIRTH
E.R. WAGNER MFG.
4611 N. 32ND. ST.
MILWAUKEE, WISC. 53209

ROBERT A. HERSCH
WINDSOR GROUP
3825 W. GREENTREE RD.
MILWAUKEE, WISC. 53209

J.A. WINTER
JACK WINTER INC.
8100 N. TEUTONIA AVE.
MILWAUKEE, WISC. 53209

GERALD S. PASHALLE
KOSS CORP.
4129 N. PORT WASHINGTON AVE.
MILWAUKEE, WISC. 53212

VINCENT R. SHIELY
BRIGGS & STRATTON
3300 N. 124 ST.
WAUWATOSA, WISC. 53213

HARRY F. PHILLIPS
BAUSH MACHINE
6800 WEST NATL. AVE.
WEST ALLIS, WISC. 53214

RUSSELL A. HEDDEN
KEARNEY & TRECKER
11000 THEODORE TRECKER WAY
WEST ALLIS, WISC. 53214

R.L. MANEGOLD
WEHR CORP.
10201 W. LINCOLN AVE.
WEST ALLIS, WISC. 53214

OSCAR J. REAK
CUTLER-HAMMER
4201 N. 27TH. ST.
MILWAUKEE, WISC. 53216

JOHN R. PARKER
A.O. SMITH CORP.
3533 NORTH 27TH. ST.
MILWAUKEE, WISC. 53216

MITCHELL S. FROMSTEIN
MANPOWER INC.
5301 N. IRONWOOD RD.
MILWAUKEE, WISC. 53217

CARL L. GOSEWEHR
OILGEAR CO.
2300 S. 51ST ST.
MILWAUKEE, WISC. 53219

ROBERT F. PFEFFER
BADGER METER INC.
4545 W. BROWN DEER RD.
MILWAUKEE, WISC. 53223

ROBERT E. MILLER
CURTIS IND.
8000 W. TOWER AVE.
MILWAUKEE, WISC. 53223

FRANK C. POWERS
CONTINENTAL RECREATION
6001 N. 91ST ST.
MILWAUKEE, WISC. 53225

RICHARD G. JACOBUS
INLAND HERITAGE
2323 N. MAYFAIR RD.
WAUWATOSA, WISC. 53226

D.G. PUNCHES
PAYCO AMERICAN
2401 N. MAYFAIR RD.
MILWAUKEE, WISC. 53226

PETER E. BARRY
THIEM CORP.
9800 W. ROGERS ST.
MILWAUKEE, WISC. 53226

GEORGE W. JANDACEK
CLARK OIL & REFINING
8530 W. NATL. AVE.
MILWAUKEE, WISC. 53227

DR. ALFRED BADER
SIGMA-ALDRICH
940 W. ST. PAUL AVE.
MILWAUKEE, WISC. 53233

HENRY HARNISCHFEGER
HARNISCHFEGER
4400 W. NATL. AVE.
WILWAUKEE, WISC. 53246

E.E. RICHTER
MODINE MFG.
1500 DE KOVEN AVE.
RACINE, WISC. 53403

GERALD SLADE
WESTERN PUBLISHING
1220 RACINE ST.
RACINE, WISC. 53404

J.E. MOHRHAUSER
VERSA TECH.
1914 INDIANA ST.
RACINE, WISC. 53405

J.G. BAKER
BAKER MFG.
133 ENTERPRISE ST.
EVANSVILLE, WISC. 53536

SCOTT MOORE
MORRE'S FOOD PRODUCTS
801 ROCKWELL AVE.
FORT ATKINSON, WISC. 53538

ARTHUR W. NESBITT
NASCO INTL.
901 JANESVILLE AVE.
FORT ATKINSON, WISC. 53538

GEORGE S. PARKER II
PARKER PEN CO.
219 E. COURT ST.
JANESVILLE, WISC. 53546

LEO VAN ERT
PATHFINDER MOBILEHOME
P.O. BOX 378
STOUGHTON, WISC. 53589

ROBERT M. BOLZ
OSCAR MAYER & CO.
910 MAYER AVE.
MADISON, WISC. 53701

DONALD D. HASELHORST
NICOLET INSTRUMENT
5225 VERONA RD.
MADISON, WISC. 53711

MARK J. SPLAINE
METALFAB
401 MADISON ST.
BEAVER DAM, WISC. 53916

JOHN A. ZERATSKY
SHALER CO.
WAUPUN, WISC. 53963

J.H. BUELL
DOMAIN IND.
215 N. KNOWLES AVE.
NEW RICHMOND, WISC. 54017

TERRELL L. RUHLMAN
ANSUL CO.
STANTON ST.
MARINETTE, WISC. 54143

EDWIN A. MEYER JR.
BADGER PAPER MILLS
PESHTIGO, WISC. 54157

JOHN D. WEST
MANITOWOC CO.
P.O. BOX 66
MANITOWOC, WISC. 54220

F.C. PRESCOTT
MIRRO ALUMINUM
P.O. BOX 49
MANITOWOC, WISC. 54220

PAUL J. SCHIERL
FORT HOWARD PAPER
1919 S. BROADWAY
GREEN BAY, WISC. 54304

E.R. WINDAHL
NORTHWEST ENG. CO.
201 W. WALNUT ST.
GREEN BAY, WISCONSIN 54305

W.V. ARVOLD
WAUSAU PAPER MILLS
BROKAW, WISC. 54417

JAMES C. PAGE
PAGE MILE CO.
MERRILL, WISC. 54452

CLARENCE SCHOLTENS
MOSINEE PAPER
MOSINEE, WISC. 54455

HAROLD MURTFELDT
CONSOLIDATED PAPERS
WISC. RAPIDS, WISC. 54494

A.W. CLARK
C.W. TRANSPORT
610 HIGH ST.
WISC. RAPIDS, WISC. 54494

M.F. BUSS
JOHNSON HILL'S
40 4TH. AVE. NORTH
WISCONSIN RAPIDS, WISC. 54494

WILLIAM THOMAS JR.
PREWAY
1430 2ND. ST. N.
WISCONSIN RAPIDS, WISC. 54494

J.E. MC LOONE
MC LOONE METAL GRAPHICS
75 SUMMER ST.
LA GROSSE, WISC. 54601

LA VERN G. SOPER
NATL. PRESTO IND.
1515 BALL ST.
EAU CLAIRE, WISC. 54601

JOHN A. MURPHY
GATEWAY TRANSPORTATION
2130 SOUTH AVE.
LA GROSSE, WISC. 54601

R.G. CLEARY
G. HEILEMAN BREWING
925 SOUTH THIRD ST.
LA GROSSE, WISC. 54601

R.P. ALEXANDER
LA CROSSE COOLER
2809 LOSEY BLVD. SOUTH
LA GROSSE, WISC. 54601

THOMAS HANCOCK
TRANE CO.
3600 PAMMEL CREEK RD.
LA GROSSE, WISC. 54601

HARVEY V. MASON
ITT THORP
THORP, WISC. 54771

C.F. HYDE JR.
OSHKOSH B'GOSH
112 OTTER ST.
OSHKOSH, WISC. 54901

JOHN P. MOSLING
OSHKOSH TRUCK
2307 OREGON ST.
OSHKOSH, WISC. 54901

PRESTON H. WILBOURNE
AIR WISCONSIN
P.O. BOX 888
APPLETON, WISC. 54911

V.I. MINAHAN
POST CORP.
P.O. BOX 559
APPLETON, WISC. 54911

JOHN E. LYNCH
PRESTO PROD.
1843 W. REEVE ST.
APPLETON, WISC. 54911

FRANK C. NELSON
FWD CORP.
CLINTONVILLE, WISC.54929

ALLAN L. MC KAY
GIDDINGS & LEWIS
142 DOTY ST.
FOND DU LAC, WISC. 54935

C. DAVID WILSON
FRED RUEPING LEATHER CO.
96 DOTY ST.
FOND DU LAC, WISC. 54935

WILLIAM D. STEENBERG
STEENBERG HOMES
RT. 1 HWAY. 41 NORTH
FOND DU LAC, WISC. 54935

WILLIAM H. FIEWEGER
GEORGE BANTA CO.
CURTIS REED PLAZA
MENASHA, WISC. 54942

H.R. MOORE
BERGSTROM PAPER CO.
BERGSTROM RD.
NEENAH, WISC. 54956

HARRY J. SHEERIN
KIMBERLY-CLARK
N. LAKE ST.
NEENAH, WISC. 54956

D.P. STERN
NORTHERN INSTRUMENTS
6680 N. HIGHWAY NO. 49
LINO LAKES, MINN. 55014

J.M. CALDWELL
DYNAMIC INFORMATION
AIRLAKE PK.
LAKEVILLE, MINN. 55044

JAMES S. WOMACK
SHELDAHL
P.O. BOX 170
NORTHFIELD, MINN. 55057

H. WILLIAM LURTON
JOSTENS
7851 METRO PARKWAY
OWOTONNA, MINN. 55060

NORMAN O. HILLEREN
TLC NURSING CENTERS
1400 W. FOURTH ST.
RED WING, MINN. 55066

C. BRUCE BROWN
NORTH STAR CHEM.
P.O. BOX 28
SOUTH ST. PAUL, MINN. 55076

D.W. GUSTAFSON
KROY IND.
6238 OASIS AVE.N.
STILLWATER, MINN. 55082

R. GILBERT
UNITED FABRICATORS
S. GREELEY ST.
STILLWATER, MINN. 55082

EVERETT F. CARTER
BUCKBEE-MEARS
245 E. 6TH ST.
ST. PAUL, MINN. 55101

F.T. WEYERHAEUSER
CONWED
332 MINNESOTA ST.
ST. PAUL, MINN. 55101

D.E. FEINBERG
EMC
180 E. 6TH ST.
ST. PAUL, MINN. 55101

W.W. WATSON
GREAT NORTHERN IRON
W-1481 FIRST NATL. BANK
ST. PAUL, MINN. 55101

JOHN W. LAMBERT
TWIN CITY BARGE
1303 RED ROCK RD.
ST. PAUL, MINN. 55101

F.T. LANNERS JR.
ECONOMICS LAB.
OSBORN BLDG.
ST. PAUL, MINN. 55102

G.V. HANSON
OLD HOME FOODS
370 UNIVERSITY AVE. W.
ST. PAUL, MINN. 55103

ROBERT P. FOX
AMERICAN HOIST & DERRICK
63 S. ROBERT ST.
ST. PAUL, MINN, 55107

SAM SINGER
APPLEBAUM'S FOOD
222 PLATO BLVD.
ST. PAUL, MINN. 55107

A.L. ANDERSEN
H.B. FULLER CO.
2400 KASOTA ST.
ST. PAUL, MINN. 55108

ARTHUR W. SCHWALM
CARIAC PACEMAKERS
1140 RED FOX RD.
ST. PAUL, MINN. 55112

L.W. REES
ENVIRONMENTAL RESEARCH
3725 N. DUNLAP ST.
ST. PAUL, MINN. 55112

R.H. BERG
MED. DEVICES
833 THIRD ST., S.W.
ST. PAUL, MINN. 55112

MICHAEL P. WARDWELL
BRIGGS TRANSPORTATION
3360 WEST COUNTY RD. C.
ST. PAUL, MINN. 55113

K.R. LARSON
SLUMBERLAND
2361 WEST HIGHWAY
ROSEVILLE, MINN. 55113

DONALD J. HERMAN
COMTEN
1950 W. COUNTY RD.
ST. PAUL, MINN. 55113

EUGENE R. OLSON
DE LUXE CHECK PRINTERS
2199 N. PASCAL AVE.
ST. PAUL, MINN. 55113

E.G. CHAMBERS
DIAGNOSTIC
1955 COUNTY RD.
ST. PAUL, MINN. 55113

R.W. REYNOLDS
HUCK FINN
2575 N. FAIRVIEW
ST. PAUL, MINN. 55113

EDWARD L. MURPHY JR.
MURPHY MOTOR FREIGHT LINES
2323 TERMINAL RD.
ST. PAUL, MINN. 55113

JEROME M. HALPER
NATL. PACKAGING
3075 LONG LAKE RD.
ST. PAUL, MINN. 55113

D.E. NUGENT
PENTAIR IND.
1700 W. HIGHWAY 65
ST. PAUL, MINN. 55113

L.M. FINGERSON
THERMO-SYSTEMS
2500 N. CLEVELAND AVE.
ST. PAUL, MINN. 5113

LAWRENCE PLATT
KNOX LUMBER
2233 UNIVERSITY AVE.
ST. PAUL, MINN. 55114

N.J. RAVICH
UNIVERSAL DISCOUNT
850 VANDALIA
ST. PAUL, MINN. 5114

RICHARD G. DONOVAN
DONOVAN CO.
1080 MONTREAL AVE.
ST. PAUL, MINN. 55116

JOHN F. MONAHAN
RESORT PROD.
790 S. CLEVELAND AVE.
ST. PAUL, MINN. 55116

ROBERT E. HAUGAN
WEBB CO.
1999 SHEPARD RD.
ST. PAUL, MINN. 55116

R. GILBERSTON
COPHER CONTAINER
3075 LONG LAKE RD.
ST. PAUL, MINN. 55117

R.L. SCHAAK
SCHAAK ELECTRONICS
1415 MENDOTA HEIGHTS RD.
ST. PAUL, MINN. 55120

R.E. MOORE
COCA-COLA BOTTLING
2750 EAGANDALE BLVD.
ST. PAUL, MINN. 55121

THOMAS H. WYMAN
GREEN GIANT CO.
HAZELTINE GATES
CHASKA, MINN. 55318

TERRENCE E. KLEFFMAN
INTL. TIMESHARING
ITS BLDG.
CHASKA, MINN. 55318

C.O. KALLESTAD
KALLESTAD LABS.
CHASKA, MINN. 55318

R.R. TAYLOR
MINETONKA LABS.
JOHNATHAN, MINN. 55318

H.B. BERMAN
CIRCLE RUBBER
6851 FLYING CLOUD DR.
EDEN PRAIRIE, MINN. 55343

M.A. YORK
CROWN AUTO STORES
7550 CORPORATE WAY.
EDEN FRAIRIE, MINN. 55343

RICHARD FULLER
FULLER LABS.
7900 FULLER RD.
EDEN PRAIRIE, MINN. 55343

R.G. FINKE
ADVANCE PACKAGING
21 HARRISON AVE., N.
HOPKINS, MINN. 55343

D.F. SCHEFF
CPT
1001 SOUTH 2ND. ST.
HOPKINS, MINN. 55343

ERWIN A. KELEN
ELECTRO-CRAFT
1600 SECOND ST. S.
HOPKINS, MINN. 55343

RICHARD L. McELHENY
FARMHAND
1011 FIRST ST. S.
HOPKINS, MINN. 55343

E.G. SCHATZ
MINNETONKA MILLS
810 FIRST ST. S.
HOPKINS, MINN. 55343

FRANK D. TRESTMAN
NAPCO IND.
1600 2ND. ST. S.
HOPKINS, MINN. 55343

L.F. MITCHELL
NATL. BEAUTY
1111 EXCELSIOR AVE. E.
HOPKINS, MINN. 55343

D. DEAN SPATZ
OSMONICS
15404 IND. RD.
HOPKINS, MINN. 55343

E.J. REUTER
REUTER INC.
410 11TH. AVE. S.
HOPKINS, MINN. 55343

MELVIN ROTH
RED OWL STORES
215 E. EXCELSIOR AVE.
HOPKINS, MINN. 55343

RICHARD A. WALTER
SCIENTIFIC COMPUTERS
10101 BREN RD. E.
MINNETONKA, MINN. 55343

E. GARY SCHATZ
STANDARD FABRICS
810 FIRST ST. S.
HOPKINS, MINN. 55343

JACK J. CROCKER
SUPER VALU STORES
101 JEFFERSON AVE.
HOPKINS, MINN. 55343

PETER M. WIMSATT
TONKA CORP.
10505 WAYZATA BLVD.
HOPKINS, MINN. 55343

BURTON J. LINDAHL
ADVANCE CIRCUITS
14901 MINETONKA IND. RD.
MINNETONKA, MINN. 55343

HAROLD D. KLETSCHKA
BIO-MEDICUS
15307 MINNETONKA IND. PK.
MINNETONKA, MINN. 55343

M.F. MYERS
ECONO THERM ENERGY
11321 K-TEL DR.
MINNETONKA, MINN. 55343

J.D. HUSBANDS JR.
FEI
11321 K-TEL DR.
MINNETONKA, MINN. 55343

TED DEIKEL
FINGERHUT
4400 BAKER RD.
MINNETONKA, MINN. 55343

R.D. MORANEY
THERADYNE
P.O. BOX 458
JORDAN, MINN. 55352

STEWART PFANNSTIEHL
WASHINGTON SCIENTIFIC IND.
LONG LAKE, MINN. 55356

D.A. ADLER
MAPLE PLAIN CO.
MAPLE PLAIN, MINN. 55359

W.F. FEYERSON
COMPONENT SYSTEMS
ROGERS, MINN. 55374

MELVYN BELL
POLLUTION CONTROLS
P.O. BOX 238 RR.1
SHAKOPEE, MINN. 55379

FRANK M. FEENEY
STERNER LIGHTING
WINSTED, MINN. 55395

HAROLD FISHMAN
CINEVIDEO
1050 MIDLAND BANK BLDG.
MINNEAPOLIS, MINN. 55401

C.T. DAHL
COSMETEX IND.
17 S. FIRST ST. A202
MINNEAPOLIS, MINN. 55401

PHILIP J. KRELITZ
KRELITZ IND.
900 N. 3RD. ST.
MINNEAPOLIS, MINN. 55401

S.R. COHEN
NORSTAN RESEARCH
524 N. 5TH. ST.
MINNEAPOLIS, MINN. 55401

GEORGE HOSSALLA
STEIN IND.
137 E. ISLAND AVE.
MINNEAPOLIS, MINN. 55401

RAYMOND PLANK
APACHE
1800 FOSHAY TOWER
MINNEAPOLIS, MINN. 55402

RICHARD A. YOUNG
BEMIS CO.
800 NORTHSTAR CENTER
MINNEAPOLIS, MINN. 55402

ROY H. JONES
CORNELIUS CO.
400 SHELARD PLAZA S.
MINNEAPOLIS, MINN. 55402

W.A. ANDRES
DAYTON-HUDSON
777 NICOLLET MALL
MINNEAPOLIS, MINN. 55402

DARRELL M. RUNKE
INTL. MULTIFOODS
1200 MULTIFOODS BLDG.
MINEAPOLIS, MINN. 55402

S.A. KELLER
KODICOR
800 MARQUETTE AVE.
MINNEAPOLIS, MINN. 55402

LYMAN D. WALTERS
MED. INVESTMENT
1600 DAIN TOWER
MINNEAPOLIS, MINN. 55402

PAUL R. CHRISTEN
MEI CORP.
733 MARQUETTE AVE.
MINNEAPOLIS, MINN. 55402

A.C. DORENFELD
MINERALS TECH.
1250 BUILDERS EXCHANGE
MINNEAPOLIS, MINN. 55402

W.G. STOCKS
PEAVEY CO.
PEAVEY BLDG. 730 2ND. AVE.S.
MINNEAPOLIS, MINN. 55402

RUSSELL BAUMGARDNER
APOGEE
1410 HARMON PL.
MINNEAPOLIS, MINN. 55403

M.P. HOLLERN
BROOKS-SCANLON
127 SOUTH 10TH. ST.
MINNEAPOLIS, MINN. 55403

GERALD SINGER
COMBINED
1616 PARK AVE.
MINNEAPOLIS, MINN. 55404

R.G. STILLMAN
FAVCO
2801 WAYZATA BLVD.
MINNEAPOLIS, MINN. 55405

RICHARD FINK
G & K
621 OLSON MEMORIAL H'WAY.
MINNEAPOLIS, MINN. 55405

REID JAPLING
INTL. GRAPHICS
2207 N. 2ND. ST.
MINNEAPOLIS, MINN. 55405

A. BYRON REED
MUNSINGWEAR
718 GLENWOOD AVE.
MINNEAPOLIS, MINN. 55405

H.L. DEMOREST
MODERN CONTROLS
3040 SNELLING AVE. S.
MINNEAPOLIS, MINN. 55406

W.L. KOSKI
SWENKO RESEARCH
2715 WASHINGTON AVE., N.
MINNEAPOLIS, MINN. 55411

R.W. ATWOOD
DURKEE
215 7TH. ST., N.E.
MINNEAPOLIS, MINN. 55413

J.B. GOETZ
GEN. TV.
2021 E. HENNEPIN AVE.
MINNEAPOLIS, MINN. 55413

P.B. HERMAN
INTERPLASTIC
2015 N.E. BROADWAY
MINNEAPOLIS, MINN. 55413

JAMES B. MASSIE
NORTHRUP, KING & CO.
1500 JACKSON ST., N.E.
MINNEAPOLIS, MINN. 55413

G.A. STUMPF
DESPATCH IND.
619 S.E. EIGHTH ST.
MINNEAPOLIS,MINN. 55414

BURTON M. JOSEPH
AMERICAN POLLUTION
FLOUR EXCHANGE BLDG.
MINNEAPOLIS, MINN. 55415

K.R. JOHNSON
DATA MANAGEMENT
1015 S. 6TH ST.
MINNEAPOLIS, MINN. 55415

E.G. BALASSIE
VALSPAR
1101 THIRD ST. S.
MINNEAPOLIS, MINN. 55415

JAMES H. CALLAN
CALLAN PUBLISHING
3033 EXCELSIOR BLVD.
MINNEAPOLIS, MINN. 55416

P.C. DECKAS
DEXON
3440 BELT LINE BLVD.
MINNEAPOLIS, MINN. 55416

NORMAN GROSSMAN
GELCO
P.O. BOX 16040,ELMWOOD BRANCH
MINNEAPOLIS, MINN. 55416

GERALD B. FREDERICK
NORTHWEST SYSTEMS
5922 EXCELSIOR BLVD.
MINNEAPOLIS, MINN. 55416

DALE R. OLSETH
MEDTRONIC
3055 HIGHWAY 8
MINNEAPOLIS, MINN. 55418

R.D. DALY
COMSERV
3050 METRO DR.
MINNEAPOLIS, MINN. 55420

WILLIAM F. REIMER
COUNTRY KITCHEN INTL.
7851 METRO PKWAY.
MINNEAPOLIS, MINN. 55420

S.R. CRAY
CRAY RESEARCH
7850 METRO PKWAY.
MINNEAPOLIS, MINN. 55420

E.W. SHIMEK
DATA SYSTEMS
3050 METRO DR.
MINNEAPOLIS, MINN. 55420

S.C. BROOKS
DYNAMIC MERCHANDISING
8711 LYNDALE S.
MINNEAPOLIS, MINN. 55420

E.S. WEBSTER
EDDIE WEBSTER'S
1500 E. 79TH. ST.
BLOOMINGTON, MINN. 55420

J.H. MAXWELL
MED. GENERAL
10800 LYNDALE AVE. S.
MINNEAPOLIS, MINN. 55420

DAVID H. BALDWIN
NORWESCO
7850 METRO PKWY.
MINNEAPOLIS, MINN. 55420

MYRON O. KIRKEBY
PURATRONICS
8200 GRAND AVE. S.
MINNEAPOLIS, MINN. 55420

R.M. SCHULZE
SOUND OF MUSIC
900 E. 80TH. ST.
BLOOMINGTON, MINN. 55420

DAVID T. MC LAUGHLIN
TORO
8111 LYNDALE AVE. S.
MINNEAPOLIS, MINN. 55420

ALLAN O. JOHNSON
VAN DUSEN AIR
2801 E. 78TH ST.
MINNEAPOLIS, MINN. 55420

ROBERT L. HALE
TENANT CO.
701 N. LILAC DR.
MINNEAPOLIS, MINN. 54422

WILLIAM J. BEGIN
SHELTER CORP.
155 E. 78TH. ST.
MINNEAPOLIS, MINN. 55423

G.N. BUTZOW
MTS. SYSTEMS
14041 W. 78TH. ST.
MINNEAPOLIS, MINN.   55424

A.E. ABRAMSON
RESEARCH
P.O. BOX 24064
MINNEAPOLIS, MINN. 55424

A.A. TILSEN
EAGLE IND.
3938 MEADOWBROOK RD.
MINNEAPOLIS, MINN. 55426

DUANE SWANSON
EL DORADO INL. INC.
SHELARD PLAZA, WAYZATA BLVD.
MINNEAPPLIS, MINN. 55426

D.J. KRUSKOPE
FLAME IND.
7317 W. LAKE ST.
MINNEAPOLIS, MINN. 55426

ZC. POSSIS
POSSIS CORP.
825 RHODE ISLAND AVE. S.
MINNEAPOLIS, MINN. 55426

A.J. PORTER
PRODUCT DESIGN
750 FLORIDA AVE.
MINNEAPOLIS, MINN. 55426

C.C. JENSCH
SUNSTAR FOODS
SHELAND PLAZA
MINNEAPOLIS, MINN. 55426

FRED RAPPAPORT
TAL-CAP
7600 WAYZATA BLVD.
MINNEAPOLIS, MINN. 55426

C.T. DAHL
TELMONT CORP.
7035 WAYZATA BLVD.
MINNEAPOLIS, MINN. 55426

HAROLD ROITENBERG
MODERN MERCHANDISING
6490 EXCELSIOR BLVD.
ST. LOUIS PK., MINN. 55426

MICHAEL R. HOFFMAN
GRAPHICS DIVERSIFIED
2468 LOUISIANA AVE. N.
GOLDEN VALLEY, MINN. 55427

K.H. DAHLBERG
DETECTION SCIENCES
7731 COUNTRY CLUB DR.
MINNEAPOLIS, MINN. 55427

D.M. HOUPT
J. GRUMAN STEEL
1605 N. COUNTY RD. 18
MINNEAPOLIS, MINN..55427

C.E.SKLAR
BIG-SAVE FURNITURE
5520 COUNTY RD. 18
MINNEAPOLIS, MINN. 55428

C.W. PETERS
MINNESOTA FABRICS
5600 N. COUNTY RD. 18
NEW HOPE, MINN. 55428

J.A. OCKEN
ALLSTATE LAW
5141 LAKELAND AVE. N.
CRYSTAL, MINN. 55429

E.E. KIRBY
COMTROL
5323 N. LAKELAND AVE.
MINNEAPOLIS, MINN. 55429

G.L. OXBOROUGH
PHOTO-CONTROL
5225 HANSON CT.
MINNEAPOLIS, MINN. 55429

W.P. STROUT
STROUT PLASTICS
9611 JAMES AVE. S.
BLOOMINGTON, MINN. 55431

R.H. HILDEN
DICOMED CORP.
9700 NEWTON AVE. S.
MINNEAPOLIS, MINN. 55431

WILLIAM A. HODDER
DONALDSON CO.
1400 W. 94TH. ST.
MINNEAPOLIS, MINN. 55431

CHARLES M. SLOCUM
UNISOURCE
7900 ZERZES AVE. S.
MINNEAPOLIS, MINN. 55431

THOMAS G. VALENTY
ONAN CORP.
1400 73RD. AVE. N.E.
MINNEAPOLIS, MINN. 55432

WILLIS K. DRAKE
DATA CARD
7625 PARKLAWN AVE.
EDINA, MINN. 55435

L.F. POLK JR.
LEISURE DYNAMICS
4400 W. 78TH. ST.
MINNEAPOLIS, MINN. 55435

R.C. ROSEN
NUTRITION WORLD
5270 W. 74TH.
EDINA, MINN. 55435

WAYNE FIELD
REMBRANDT ENTERPRISES
3434 HERITAGE DR.
EDINA, MINN. 55435

CHARLES DENNY
ADC PRODUCTS
4900 WEST 78TH. ST.
MINNEAPOLIS, MINN. 55435

F.W. LANG
ANALYST INTL.
7615 METRO BLVD.
MINNEAPOLIS, MINN. 55435

J.G. LINDELL
CAMBRIDGE CORP.
4444 W. 76TH. ST.
MINNEAPOLIS, MINN. 55435

T.D. SANFORD
CONTECH
7711 COMPUTER AVE.
MINNEAPOLIS, MINN. 55435

EDWARD D. ORENSTEIN
DATA 100 CORP.
7725 WASHINGTON AVE. S.
MINNEAPOLIS, MINN. 55435

SUMMER S. YOUNG
LARSON IND.
7400 METRO BLVD. STE. 460
MINNEAPOLIS, MINN. 55435

C.M. DENNY JR.
MAGNETIC CONTROLS
4900 W. 78TH. ST.
MINNEAPOLIS, MINN. 55435

H.R. WARD
NATL. COMPUTER
4401 W. 76TH. ST.
MINNEAPOLIS, MINN. 55435

V.H. HEATH
ROSEMOUNT INC.
4900 W. 78TH. ST.
MINNEAPOLIS, MINN. 55435

R.A. KOKESH
SOLID CONTROLS
6925 WASHINGTON AVE. S.
MINNEAPOLIS, MINN. 55435

VIC ROCCHIO
TECHNALYSIS CORP.
4640 W. 77 TH. ST.
MINNEAPOLIS, MINN. 55435

L.G. CHERNE
CHERNE IND.
5701 S. COUNTY RD. 18
EDINA, MINN. 55436

M.F. MICKELSON
FABRO-TEK INC.
5901 S. COUNTY RD. 18
MINNEAPOLIS, MINN. 55436

HARRIS COOPER
INTL. DAIRY QUEEN
5701 GREEN VALLEY DR.
MINNEAPOLIS, MINN. 55437

J. W. THAXTON
SPORTS FILMS & TALENTS
7625 BUSH LAKE RD.
MINNEAPOLIS, MINN. 55437

ARTHUR S. MOORE
TRAVELERS EXPRESS CO.
15 S. FIFTH ST.
MINNEAPOLIS, MINN. 55439

DENIS G. CSATHY
DELTAK CORP.
P.O. BOX 9496
MINNEAPOLIS, MINN. 55440

J.H. ADELMAN
EMPIRE-CROWN AUTO
P.O. BOX 1217
MINNEAPOLIS, MINN. 55440

D.A. KOCH
GRACO
P.O. BOX 1441
MINNEAPOLIS, MINN. 55440

RICHARD G. SPIEGEL
LA MAUR CO.
P.O. BOX 1221
MINNEAPOLIS, MINN. 55440

G.G. WORKINGER
MC QUAY-PERFEX
P.O. BOX 1551
MINNEAPOLIS, MINN. 55440

ROBERT R. BUCHANAN
NORTHWESTERN DRUG
2001 KENNEDY ST. N.E.
MINNEAPOLIS, MINN. 55440

BEN KNAZAN
NU-ERA
P.O. BOX 570
MINNEAPOLIS, MINN. 55440

ROBERT L. GALLOWAY
PAKO
6300 OLSEN MEMORIAL HIGHWAY
MINNEAPOLIS, MINN. 55440

R.J. BORDEN
CIRCUT SCIENCE
615 N. COUNTY RD. 18
MINNEAPOLIS, MINN. 55441

F.W. HETMAN
DE VAC
10130 HIGHWAY 55
MINNEAPOLIS, MINN. 55441

ROBERT F. STAHL JR.
WHEEL GOODS
14524 21ST. AVE. N.
MINNEAPOLIS, MINN. 55441

HENRY R. WEBER
MESABA SERVICE
HIGHWAY 169 E. & 13TH.
HIBBING, MINNESOTA 55746

T.A. BURTON
WATERS INSTRUMENTS
P.O. BOX 6117
ROCHESTER, MINN. 55901

ROY WATSON JR.
KAHLER CORP.
20 - 2ND. AVE. S.W.
ROCHESTER, MINN. 55902

I.J. HOLTON
GEO. A. HORMEL & CO.
501 -16TH. AVE. N.E.
AUSTIN, MINN. 55912

ROBERT W. BUNKE
CENCOM INC.
P.O. BOX 606
RUSHFORD, MINN. 55971

B.A. MILLER
FIBERITE
501-559 WEST 3RD. ST.
WINONA, MINN. 55987

JAMES J. JERSEK
PEERLESS CHAIN
1416 E. SANBORN ST.
WINONA, MINN. 55987

DENIS J. DALY
KAYOT
P.O. BOX 789
MANKATO, MINN. 56001

ROBERT K. ELSE
MIDTEX
P.O. BOX 1179
MANKATO, MINN. 56001

R.G. WADE
FAIRMONT RAILWAY MOTORS
415 N. MAIN ST.
FAIRMONT, MINN. 56031

C.E. WESTIN
SCHERR-TUMICO
301 ARMSTRONG BLVD. N.
ST. JAMES, MINN. 56081

RICHARD HORNER
E.F. JOHNSON CO.
299 TENTH AVE.
WASECA, MINN. 56093

PAUL C. SMITH
DYNASONICS
P.O. BOX 672
PIPESTONE, MINN. 51664

MACK M. EVANS
MARSHALL FOODS
103 N. 8TH. ST.
MARSHALL, MINN. 56258

E.G. BELZER
ROBEL BEEF PACKERS
14TH. & 3RD. AVE., S.
SAINT CLOUD, MINN. 56301

R.E. DE PALMA
BELLANCA AIRCRAFT
BOX 624, MUNICIPAL AIRPORT
ALEXANDRIA, MINN. 56308

L.E. ANDERSON
MANUFACTURERS SYSTEMS
BOX 703, 620 W. MAIN ST.
DETROIT LAKES, MINN. 56501

G.H. LUND
LUND AMERICAN
NEW YORK MILLS, MINN. 56567

JOHN C. PENN
ARCTIC
P.O. BOX 635
THIEF RIVER FALLS, MINN. 56701

J.L. MULLIGAN
AMERICAN WESTERN
BOYCE-GREELEY BLDG.
SIOUX FALLS, S.D. 57102

DAVID E. RAE
BIO-DEGRADABLE PLASTICS
BOYCE-GREELEY BLDG.
SOUIX FALLS, S.D. 57102

D.A. CHRISTENSEN
RAVEN IND.
205 E. 6TH. ST.
SIOUX FALLS, S.D. 57102

R.G. FOWLER
DAKOTA MINERALS
P.O. BOX 271
SPEARFISH, S.D. 57783

GORDON P. STREET JR.
NORTH AMERICAN ROYALTIES
P.O. BOX 1136
BISMARCH, N.D. 58501

H.S. ROBERTSON
ROBERTSON CO.
405 BRUCE AVE.
GRAND FORKS, N.D. 58201

R.W. ROVELSTAD
BAUKOL-NOONAN
P.O. BOX 248
MINOT, N.D. 58701

J.C. EGAN
WESTLAND OIL
504 E. CENTRAL AVE.
MINOT, N.D. 58701

R.C. VICKERS
GEORESOURCES, INC.
P.O. BOX 1505
WILLISTON, N.D. 58801

C.E. OSGOOD, JR.
AMARCO RESOURCES CORP.
611 MIDLAND NAT'L. BANK BLDG.
BILLINGS, MT. 59101

JAMES F. COLLINS
KAMPGROUNDS OF AMERICA
P.O. BOX 1138
BILLINGS, MT. 59103

JOHN C. LAWRENCE
UNITED STATES ANTIMONY CORP.
P.O. BOX 643
THOMPSON FALLS, MT. 59873

W.G. CORNETT III
RESPIRATORY CARE INC.
900 W. UNIVERSITY DR.
ARLINGTON HEIGHTS, IL. 60004

JORAM SASSOWER
SWINGLES FURNITURE RENTAL INC.
2461 E. OAKTON ST.
ARLINGTON HEIGHTS, IL. 60005

IRA A. EICHNER
AAR CORP.
2050 W. TOUHY AVE.
ELK GROVE VILL., IL. 60007

MITCHELL E. MORRIS
ADVANCED SYSTEMS, INC.
1601 TONNE RD.
ELK GROVE VILLAGE, IL. 60007

CHARLES E. WATERS
APPLICATION ENGINEERING CORP.
850 PRATT BLVD.
ELK GROVE VILLAGE, IL. 60007

IRWIN M. HARVEY
GALAXY CARPET MILLS, INC.
850 ARTHUR AVENUE
ELK GROVE VILLAGE, IL. 60007

STANLEY T. MANDELTORT
GLOBE-AMERADA CLASS CO.
2001 GREENLEAF AVE.
ELK GROVE, IL. 60007

ROBERT RITTMASTER
QONAAR CORPORATION
751 PRATT BLVD.
GROVE VILLÄGE, IL. 60007

JACK J. CULBERG
RONCO TELEPRODUCTS
1200 ARTHUR AVE.
ELK GROVE VILLAGE, IL. 60007

LEWIS M. LAWTON, JR.
U.I.P. CORP.
1970 ESTES AVE.
ELK GROVE VILLAGE, IL. 60007

DANIEL T. CARROLL
GOULD, INC.
10 GOULD CENTER
ROLLING MEADOWS, IL. 60008

EARL K. MANHOLD, JR.
REED CANDY CO.
ONE CROSSROADS OF COMMERCE
ROLLING MEADOWS, IL. 60008

EDWARD C. SAWYER
KEYSTONE INDUSTRIES INC.
1 CROSSROADS OF COMMERCE
ROLLING MEADOWS, IL. 60008

GEORGE CADAR
3H BUILDING CORP.
4902 TOLLVIEW RD.
ROLLING MEADOWS, IL. 60008

MARLIN E. BOURNS
CHICAGO AERIAL INDS.
550 W. NORTHWEST HGWY.
BARRINGTON, IL. 60010

WILL J. LEPESKA
HOSPITAL FINANCIAL CORP.
1300 GROVE AVE.
BARRINGTON, IL. 60010

JAMES B. TAFEL
TECHNICAL PUBLISHING
1301 S. GROVE AVE.
BARRINGTON, IL. 60010

GREGSON L. BARKER
UARCO, INC.
WEST COUNTY LINE RD.
BARRINGTON, IL. 60010

E.A. CARTER
OAK INDS.
CRYSTAL LAKE, IL. 60014

ROBERT SHERIDAN
NATIONWIDE INDS.
104 WILMONT RD.
DEARFIELD, IL. 60015

J.W. VAN GORKOM
TRANS UNION CORP.
90 HALF DAY RD.
LINCOLNSHIRE, IL. 60015

ROBERT L. SCHMITT
WALGREEN CO.
200 WILMONT
DEERFIELD, IL. 60015

GEORGE A. NICHOLS
DE SOTO, INC.
1700 S. MT. PROSPECT RD.
DES PLAINES, IL. 60016

R.M. LEFFEL
GENERAL BOX
1825 MINER ST.
DES PLAINES, IL. 60016

NORMAN L. ARROYO
KAR PRODS. INC.
461 N. 3RD AVE.
DES PLAINES, IL. 60016

JAMES V. CRAWFORD
UOP INC.
TEN UOP PLAZA
DES PLAINES, IL. 60016

K.N. PONTIKES
COMDISCO, INC.
2200 E. DEVON AVE.
DES PLAINES, IL. 60018

WILLIAM B. BASILE
RICHARDSON CO.
2400 E. DEVON AVE.
DES PLAINES, IL. 60018

HERBERT R. MOLNER
TFI COS.
1515 MT. PROSPECT RD.
DES PLAINES, IL. 60018

GORDON R. HJALMARSON
SCOTT, FORESMAN & CO.
1900 E. LAKE AVE.
GLENVIEW, IL. 60025

J.T. SCHANCK
SIGNODE CORP.
3600 W. LAKE AVE.
GLENVIEW, IL. 60025

E.L. OBERTO
BURGESS VIDEOCRAFTERS
GRAYSLAKE, IL. 60030

R.R. BAXTER
CF INDUSTRIES
SALAM LAKE DR.
LONG GROVE, IL. 60047

THOMAS HOLLINGSWORTH
ANCHOR COUPLING CO.
342 N. 4TH ST.
LIBERTYVILLE, IL. 60048

JAMES KEMPER, JR.
KEMPER CORP.
LONG GROVE, IL. 60049

J.H. MANGLE
COOK ELECTRIC
6201 OAKTON ST.
MORTON GROVE, IL. 60053

SCOTT HARROD
M.H. HARPER CO.
8200 LEHIGH AVE.
MORTON GROVE, IL. 60053

WILLIAM A. JENNETT
TRAVENOL LABS.
6301 LINCOLN AVE.
MORTON GROVE, IL. 60053

STUART R. SCHEYER
CONDECOR INC.
444 E. COURTLAND ST.
MUNDELEIN, IL. 60060

D.E. MAYWORM
TOWER PRODS.
1919 S. BUTTERFIELD RD.
MUNDELEIN, IL. 60060

JOHN A. GAVIN
CULLIGAN, INC.
1 CULLIGAN PKWY.
NORTHBROOK, IL. 60062

WARREN R. ROTHWELL
GENERAL BINDING CORP.
1101 SKOKIE BLVD.
NORTHBROOK, IL. 60062

D.J. TERRA
LAWTER CHEMICALS INC.
990 SKOKIE BLVD.
NORTHBROOK, IL. 60062

JAMES MILLS
MEDLINE INDS.
1825 SHERMER RD.
NORTHBROOK, IL. 60062

NORMAN E. HARDEN
A.C. NIELSEN CO.
NIELSEN PLAZA
NORTHBROOK, IL. 60062

NELSON HARRIS
PITTWAY CORP.
333 SKOKIE BLVD. BOX 602
NORTHBROOK, IL. 60062

ROBERT S. LA MONTIA
DANIEL WOODHEAD INC.
3411 WOODHEAD DR.
NORTHBROOK, IL. 60062

DAVID D. PETERSON
FANSTEEL, INC.
ONE TANTALUM PL.
NORTH CHICAGO, IL. 60064

DOUGLAS F. HUDSON
FIDELITONE
207 N. WOODWORK LN.
PALATINE, IL. 60067

JOHN H. BACHNER
CHICAGO MOLDED PRODUCTS
330 S. NORTHWEST HGWY.
PARK RIDGE, IL. 60068

DANIEL V. TALBOTT
MEDEQUIP CORP.
205 TOUHY AVE.
PARK RIDGE, IL. 60068

GEORGE DERDERIAN
TRANSWORLD CORP.
10 CIRCUIT DR.
ROUND LAKE BEACH, IL. 60073

ALLAN FRIEDMAN
ALPHATYPE CORP.
7500 McCORMICK BLVD.
SKOKIE, IL. 60076

A.B. ANIXTER
ANIXTER BROS. INC.
4711 GOLF RD. - 1 CONC. PLAZA
SKOKIE, IL. 60076

K.B. ABERNATHY
BRUNSWICK CORP.
ONE BRUNSWICK PLAZA
SKOKIE, IL. 60076

P.C. MILLER
HALLMARK DATA SYSTEMS
5500 W. TOUNY AVE.
SKOKIE, IL. 60076

MELVIN S. GANSKOW
POWERS REGULATOR
3400 OAKTON ST.
SKOKIE, IL. 60076

ANDREW McNALLY, IV.
RAND McNALLY & CO.
8255 CENTRAL PARK AVE.
SKOKIE, IL. 60076

HOWARD C. WARREN
THE RILEY CO.
7401 N. HAMLIN AVE.
SKOKIE, IL. 60076

T.M. MINTS, JR.
SARGENT-WELCH SCIENTIFIC CO.
7300 N. LINDER AVE.
SKOKIE, IL. 60076

H.E. WICKSTRA
SHERWOOD MEDICAL INDS.
1 BRUNSWICK PLAZA
SKOKIE, IL. 60076

CHARLES D. STRANG
OUTBOARD MARINE
100 SEA HORSE DR.
WAUKEGAN, IL. 60085

ALVIN L. ERLICK
WARD FOODS
1000 SKOKIE BLVD.
WILMETTE, IL. 60091

ROBERT P. KENO
ALLIED LEASING CO.
540 FRONTAGE RD.
NORTHFIELD, IL. 60093

S.H. LEVINSON
RAILWEIGHTS, INC.
1821 WILLOW RD.
NORTHFIELD, IL. 60093

F. QUINN STEPAN
STEPAN CHEMICAL
EDINS & WINNETKA
NORTHFIELD, IL. 60094

R.W. JINDRICH
CHICAGO RIVET & MACHINE
950 S. 25TH
BELLWOOD, IL. 60104

E.C. FREISENDORF
ST. CLAIR MFG.
120 25TH AVE.
BELLWOOD, IL. 60104

CHARLES E. NELSON
BEELINE FASHIONS
100 BEELINE DR.
BENSENVILLE, IL. 60106

FRANK FLICK
FLICK-REEDY CORP.
7015 YORK RD.
BENSENVILLE, IL. 60106

THOMAS H. ROBERTS, JR.
DEKALB AGRESEARCH, INC.
SYCAMORE ED.
DE KALB, IL. 60115

WILLIAM A. RICHMAN
ELGIN SWEEPER CO.
1300 W. BARTLETT RD.
ELGIN, IL. 60120

JACOB SALIBA
KATY INDS.
853 DUNDEE AVE.
ELGIN, IL. 60120

EDWARD J. WILLIAMS
MC GRAW EDISON CO.
333 W. RIVER RD.
ELGIN, IL. 60120

D.W. BRINCKMAN
SAFETY-KLEEN CORP.
655 BIG TOWER RD.
ELGIN, IL. 60120

ORVAL GRAENING
WOODRUFF & EDWARDS, INC.
119 N. STATE ST.
ELGIN, IL. 60120

J.P. SOMMERS
CHAMBERLAIN MFG. CORP.
845 LARCH AVE.
ELMHURST, IL. 60126

A.E. LARKIN, JR.
KEEBLER CO.
ONE HOLLOW TREE LANE
ELMHURST, IL. 60126

R.G. BROWN
KEYSTONE ALLOYS CO.
845 LARCH AVE.
ELMHURST, IL. 60126

N.C. VOJTA
ARI INDS.
9000 KING ST.
FRANKLIN PARK, IL. 60131

BURKE B. ROCHE
BINKS MFG. CO.
9201 W. BELMONT AVE.
FRANKLIN PARK, IL. 60131

ROBERT J. HEGGIE
A.M. CASTLE & CO.
3400 N. WOLD RD.
FRANKLIN PARK, IL. 60131

S.J. ANCEL
CHEMTRUST INDS.
11250 W. ADDISON
FRANKLIN PARK, IL. 60131

HOWARD M. DEAN
DEAN FOODS
3600 N. RIVER RD.
FRANKLIN PARK, IL. 60131

ROBERT MAYBEE
RIXSON-FIREMARK
9100 W. BELMONT
FRANKLIN PARK, IL. 60310

R.W. HAWKINSON
BELDEN CORP.
2000 S. BATAVIA AVE.
GENEVA, IL. 60134

E.L. MAKAR
CETRON ELECTRONIC CORP.
715 HAMILTON ST.
GENEVA, IL. 60134

JOHN. H. CONNOR
VARLEN CORP
477 E. BUTTERFIELD RD.
LOMBARD, IL. 60148

S.C. WERNHAM
MC GILL METAL PRODS. CO.
142 E. PRAIRIE ST.
MARENGO, IL. 60152

EDWARD F. ANIXTER
PEMCOR, INC.
2121 S. MANNHEIM RD.
WESTCHESTER, IL. 60153

EDWARD RIFKIN
TASKPOWER SVCS.
10001 DERBY LN.
WESTCHESTER, IL. 60153

L.G. MALANFANT
OAKRIDGE HOLDINGS
4410 W. ROOSEVELT RD.
HILLSIDE, IL. 60162

THEODORE DIMITRIOU
WALLACE BUSINESS FORMS, INC.
4600 ROOSEVELT RD.
HILLSIDE, IL. 60162

TED E. GATY
COLEMAN CABLE & WIRE CO.
1900 N. RIVER RD.
RIVER GROVE, IL. 60171

JACK HOFFMAN
HOFFMAN ROSNER CORP.
P.O. BOX 10
HOFFMAN ESTATES, IL. 60172

RICHARD J. SANDBERG
NUCLEAR DATA INC.
GOLF & MEACHAM RDS.
SCHAUMBURG, IL. 60172

JACK HENN
TELEMED CORP.
2345 PEMBROKE AVE.
HOFFMAN ESTATES, IL. 60172

D.W. HAWLEY
HAWLEY PRODS.
333 N. 6TH
ST. CHARLES, IL. 60174

L.A. FISH
BANK COMPUTER NETWORK
10561 DELTA
SCHILLER PARK, IL. 60176

C.L. PETERSON
DUPLEX PRODUCTS
228 W. PAGE ST.
SYCAMORE, IL. 60178

LEONARD A. KNOPF
THE MEYERCORD CO.
365 E. NORTH AVE.
CAROL STRM.WHEATON,IL 60187

ELLIOTT M. LYON
ODYSSEY, INC.
1603 ORRINGTON AVE.
EVANSTON, IL. 60201

STANLEY P. HUTCHISON
WASHINGTON NAT'L. CORP.
1630 CHICAGO AVE.
EVANSTON, IL. 60201

ARTHUR S. NICHOLAS
APECO CORP.
2100 W. DEMPSTER ST.
EVANSTON, IL. 60202

JOSEPH L. CASEY
MARK CONTROLS CORP.
1900 DEMPSTER ST.
EVANSTON, IL. 60202

MR. DAVID BRAMSON
BRAMSON, INC.
1132 LAKE ST.
OAK PARK, IL. 60301

S.A. CARIA
WEST TOWN BUS CO.
259 LAKE ST.
OAK PARK, IL. 60302

GEORGE P. SCELZO
PRT SYSTEMS CORP.
1020 CHICAGO RD.
CHICAGO HTS., IL. 60411

K.S. ARVANITAKIS
IDREX, INC.
P.O. BOX 367
FRANKFORT, IL. 60423

THOMAS R. ELMBALD
WHITING CORP.
157TH & LATHROP
HARVEY, IL. 60426

JOHN P. YOUNG
RICHARD D. IRWIN, INC.
1818 RIDGE RD.
HOMEWOOD, IL. 60430

W.R. SCHAUB
SCOT LAD FOODS
ONE SCOT LAD LANE
LANSING, IL. 60438

WILLIAM E. HOLLY
HOLLYMATIC CORP.
80 NORTH ST.
PARK FOREST, IL. 60466

GEORGE A. FISCHER
GOODHEART-WILLCOX CO.
123 W. TAFT DR.
SOUTH HOLLAND, IL. 60473

A.W. WHALEN
LYON METAL PRODS.
25 MADISON ST.
AURORA, IL. 60505

BENNETT ARCHAMBAULT
THOR POWER TOOL
175 N. STATE ST.
AURORA, TL. 60505

A.S. GREENE
BARBER-GREENE CO.
400 N. HIGHLAND AVE.
AURORA, IL. 60506

H.C. SCHWENK
HENRY PRATT CO.
401 S. HIGHLAND AVE.
AURORA, IL. 60507

MR. R. BUERGER
PICTORIAL PAPER PACK. CORP.
232 S. LAKE ST.
AURORA, IL. 60507

KENNETH T. WESSNER
SERVICEMASTER INDS.
2300 WARRENVILLE RD.
DOWNERS GROVE, IL. 60515

G.T. VAUGHAN
VAUGHAN-JACKLIN CORP.
5300 KATRINE AVE.
DOWNERS GROVE, IL. 60515

GEORGE S. TRIMBLE, JR.
BUNKER RAMO CORP.
900 COMMERCE DR.
OAK BROOK, IL. 60521

CHARLES P. SCHWARTZ, JR.
CHAMPION PARTS REBUILDERS, INC.
2000 SPRING RD.
OAKBROOK, IL. 60521

M.G. MITCHELL
CHICAGO BRIDGE & IRON
800 JORIE BLVD.
OAK BROOK, IL. 60521

RAYMOND G. RINEHART
CLOW CORP.
1211 W. 22ND ST.
OAK BROOK, IL. 60521

BERNARD L. MOSS
CMT INDS.
1301 W. 22ND - STE. 410A
OAKBROOK, IL. 60521

PATRICK W. RYAN
CONFARE RESTS.
P.O. BOX 22
OAK BROOK, IL. 60521

FRANK J. BURGERT
INTERLAKE INC.
2015 SPRING RD.
OAK BROOK, IL. 60521

ROBERT T. POWERS
NALCO CHEMICAL
2901 BUTTERFIELD RD.
OAK BROOK, IL. 60521

JOHN F. MC CULLOUGH
ORTON-MC CULLOUGH CRANE
1211 W. 22ND. ST.
OAK BROOK, ILL. 60521

JAMES A. MILLER
PORTEC
300 WINDSOR DR.
OAK BROOK, ILL. 60521

E.E. SCHULZE
STANDARD ALLIENCE IND.
1211 W. 22ND. ST.
OAK BROOK, ILL. 60521

HAROLD GERSHOWITZ, SR.
WASTE MANAGEMENT
900 JORIE BLVD.
OAK BROOK, ILL. 60521

EVAN T. COLLINSWORTH
BLISS & LAUGHLIN IND.
122 WEST 22ND. ST.
OAK BROOK, ILL. 60523

WILLIAM S. CONKLIN JR.
JACKSON STORAGE & VAN CO.
112 E. BURLINGTON
LA GRANGE, ILL. 60525

J.B. SEAMAN
SEAMAN PAPER
5331 S. DANSHER RD.
COUNTRYSIDE, ILL. 60525

JOHN H. KREHBIEL JR.
MOLEX INC.
2222 WELLINGTON CT.
LISLE, ILL. 60532

HERBERT W. DATES
OAKBROOK CONSOLIDATED
4242 SOUTH FIRST AVE.
LYONS, ILL. 60534

RICHARD E. BUROW
KROEHLER MFG.
222 E. FIFTH AVE.
NAPERVILLE, ILL. 60540

CHARLES F. SEBASTIAN
ADVANCE GROWTH
397 DOWNING RD.
RIVERSIDE, ILL. 60546

J.I. KANTER
ALLIED FARM
35 E. WACKER DR.
CHICAGO, ILL. 60601

WALLACE J. STENHOUSE, JR.
AMERICAN RESERVE CORP.
65 E. SOUTH WATER ST.
CHICAGO, ILL. 60601

GOFF SMITH
AMSTED IND.
PRUDENTIAL PLAZA
CHICAGO, ILL. 60601

HENRY G. PLITT
BALABAN & KATZ
CHICAGO THEATRE BLDG.
CHICAGO, ILL. 60601

WILLIAM W. WIRTZ
BISMARCK HOTEL
171 W. RANDOLPH ST.
CHICAGO, ILL. 60601

JOHN P. GALLAGHER
CHEMETRON
111 E. WACKER DR.
CHICAGO, ILL. 60601

RALPH W. APPLEGATE SR.
CIC FINANCIAL
222 N. MICHIGAN AVE.
CHICAGO, ILL. 60601

J.L. GIDWITZ
CONSOLIDATED PACKAGING
111 EAST WACKER DR.
CHICAGO, ILL. 60601

WILLIAM A. RYAN
CONTINENTAL MATERIALS
111 E. WACKER DR.
CHICAGO, ILL. 60601

H.A. FUENTE
CORTERRA
333 N. MICHIGAN AVE.
CHICAGO, ILL. 60601

CARL DEVOE
EXECUTIVE HOUSE
71 E. WACKER DR.
CHICAGO, ILL. 60601

JOHN A. DOWNS
GREAT LAKES DREDGE & DOCK
228 N. LA SALLE ST.
CHICAGO, ILL. 60601

FRANK C. CALLAHAN
HEALTH-MOR, INC.
203 NORTH WABASH AVE.#600
CHICAGO, ILL. 60601

EMIL B. VANDERVATE
ILLINOIS BRICK CO.
228 NORTH LA SALLE ST.
CHICAGO, ILL. 60601

J.H. JACOBS
IMOCO-GATEWAY
111 E. WACKER DR.
CHICAGO, ILL. 60601

ROBERT J. ZEDLER
INOLEX
PRUDENTIAL PLAZA
CHICAGO, ILL. 60601

EDWARD W. ROSS
JUPITER IND.
400 E. RANDOLPH
CHICAGO, ILL. 60601

ROBERT L. FLYNNE
SMITH INTL. INC.
P.O. BOX 1860
NEWPORT BEACH, CALIF. 92660

RICHARD B. BLACK
MAREMONT
200 E. RANDOLPH DR.
CHICAGO, ILL. 60601

ROBERT A. FRIED
F.W. MEANS & CO.
35 E. WACKER DR.
CHICAGO, ILL. 60601

ROGER W. STONE
STONE CONTAINER
360 N. MICHIGAN AVE.
CHICAGO, ILL. 60601

WALTER H. LENHARD JR.
UNICOA
ONE EAST WACKER DR.
CHICAGO, ILL. 60601

HOWARD R. ROSS
HOUSE OF VISION
137 NORTH WABASH AVE.
CHICAGO, ILL. 60602

A.K. MUENZE
WIEBOLDT STORES
1 NORTH STATE ST.
CHICAGO, ILL. 60602

H.E. CAMPBELL
ADVANCE ROSS CORP.
135 S. LA SALLE ST.
CHICAGO, ILL. 60603

N.H. HALVERSON
ATKINS
39 S. LA SALLE ST.
CHICAGO, ILL. 60603

JOHN C. BACKMAN
AUTOMATED MARKETING
104 S. MICHIGAN AVE.
CHICAGO, ILL. 60603

JOHN L. LESHER
BOOZ, ALLEN & HAMILTON
135 S. LA SALLE ST.
CHICAGO, ILL. 60603

MICHAEL F. MATHEWS
CAPITOL FOOD IND.
105 WEST ADAMS ST.
CHICAGO, ILL. 60603

HAROLD R. SPURWAY
CARSON PIRIE SCOTT
ONE SOUTH STATE ST.
CHICAGO, ILL. 60603

N.E. FRIEDMANN
CORDURA
10 S. LA SALLE ST.
CHICAGO, ILL. 60603

E.G. HUNT
DIVERSEY
100 WEST MONROE ST.
CHICAGO, ILL. 60603

DAVID MELTZER
EVANS
36 S. STATE ST.
CHICAGO, ILL. 60603

ROBERT A. PRITZKER
HAMMOND CORP.
39 S. LA SALLE ST.
CHICAGO, ILL. 60603

A. PETER DI TULLIO
HYATT INTL. CORP.
39 SOUTH LA SALLE ST.
CHICAGO, ILL. 60603

J.M. DUNLIN
IND. RESOURCES
135 S. LA SALLE ST.
CHICAGO, ILL. 60603

M.B. LEVINE
MANGOOD
105 W. ADAMS ST.
CHICAGO, ILL. 60603

ROBERT A. PRITZKER
MARMON GROUP
39 S. LA SALLE ST.
CHICAGO, ILL. 60603

T.A. STRUVE
MIDWEST MANAGEMENT
120 S. LA SALLE ST. STE. 1640
CHICAGO, ILL. 60603

EARL H. FORSTER
PAXALL
100 W. MONROE RM. 500
CHICAGO, ILL. 60603

JOHN A. McCONNELL JR.
ROXBURY CARPET
1 S. STATE ST.
CHICAGO, ILL. 60603

H.C. BUCKINGHAM
UTAH SHALE LAND & MINERALS
135 S. LA SALLE ST.
CHICAGO, ILL. 60603

W.N. HERLEMAN
WURLITZER CO.
105 W. ADAMS ST.
CHICAGO, ILL. 60603

JAMES FENTRESS JR.
BAKER, FENTRESS
208 S. LA SALLE ST.
CHICAGO, ILL. 60604

LESTER S. ABELSON
BARTON BRANDS
200 S. MICHIGAN AVE.
CHICAGO, ILL. 60604

ROBERT O. BASS
BORG-WARNER
200 S. MICHIGAN AVE.
CHICAGO, ILL. 60604

ALBERT B. GOLDSTEIN
COMPUMATICS
327 SOUTH LA SALLE ST.
CHICAGO, ILL. 60604

D.D. KUSAR
DARFIELD IND.
208 S. LA SALLE ST.
CHICAGO, ILL. 60604

THOMAS P. O'BOYLE
ECODYNE CORP.
111 WEST JACKSON BLVD.
CHICAGO, ILL. 60604

STANFORD J. GOLDBLATT
GOLDBLATT BROS.
333 S. STATE ST.
CHICAGO, ILL. 60604

H.H. HOWARD
EDWARD HINES LUMBER
200 S. MICHIGAN AVE.
CHICAGO, ILL. 60604

JOHN W. COLE
HENRY C. LYTTON
235 S. STATE ST.
CHICAGO. ILL. 60604

JACK JACOBSON
MERCANTILE IND.
111 W. JACKSON, NO. 2100
CHICAGO, ILL. 60604

SAMUEL B. CASEY JR.
PULLMAN INC.
200 S. MICHIGAN AVE.
CHICAGO, ILL. 60604

ROBERT E. HARRAH
STANRAY
200 S. MICHIGAN AVE.
CHICAGO, ILL. 60604

DAVID S. LEAVITT
UNARCO IND.
332 S. MICHIGAN AVE.
CHICAGO, ILL. 60604

M.H. BRONNER
G.R.I. CORP.
623 S. WABASH AVE.
CHICAGO, ILL. 60605

ANTHONY M. TORTORIELLO
TORCO OIL
624 S. MICHIGAN AVE.
CHICAGO, ILL. 60605

GEORGE P. TURCI
AMERICAN BAKERIES
10 S. RIVERSIDE PLAZA
CHICAGO, ILL. 60606

D.J. DONAHUE
ATLANTA/LA SALLE
150 S. WACKER DR. STE.575
CHICAGO, ILL. 60606

L.A. DREXLER
AURORA CORP.
10 S. RIVERSIDE PLAZA
CHICAGO, ILL. 60606

RAYMOND FRENCH
CANAL-RANDOLPH
150 S. WACKER DR.
CHICAGO, ILL. 60606

R.H. COHN
C.F.S. CONTINENTAL
100 SOUTH WACKER DR.
CHICAGO, ILL. 60606

D.E. RUTZ
CLINTON E. FRANK
120 S. RIVERSIDE PLAZA
CHICAGO, ILL. 60606

FRANK J. KELLY III
COMPUDYNE
100 S. WACKER DR.
CHICAGO, ILL. 60606

C.B. EDGAR
M.H. DETRICK
20 N. WACKER DR.
CHICAGO, ILL. 60606

R.G. MILLER JR.
ELGIN NATL. IND.
120 SOUTH RIVERSIDE PLAZA
CHICAGO, ILL. 60606

M.N. SANDLER
ERO IND.
1 SOUTH WACKER DR.
CHICAGO, ILL. 60606

KARL F. HOENECKE
FED. SIGNAL
120 S. RIVERSIDE PLAZA
CHICAGO, ILL. 60606

M.C. KUEHN
FULTON-CARROL CO.
222 W. ADAMS
CHICAGO,ILL. 60606

HERBERT F. IMHOFF
GENERAL EMPLOYMENT
150 S. WACKER DR.
CHICAGO, ILL. 60606

JEROME S. GORE
HART, SCHAFFNER & MARX
36 S. FRANKLIN ST.
CHICAGO, ILL. 60606

BRIAN P. MONIESON
INDECON
300 S. WACKER DR.
CHICAGO, ILL. 60606

JERRY STERGIOS
INTL. COURIERS
330 JEFFERSON ST.
CHICAGO, ILL. 60606

WILLIAM E. BURCH
FRED S. JAMES & CO.
230 W. MONROE
CHICAGO, ILL. 60606

JOSEPH W. RITTENHOUSE
JOSLYN MFG. & SUPPLY
2 N. RIVERSIDE PLAZA
CHICAGO, ILL. 60606

JACK ABRAMS
MARKET FACTS
100 S. WACKER DR.
CHICAGO, ILL. 60606

LESTER A. MC INTOSH
MC INTOSH CORP.
20 N. WACKER DR.
CHICAGO, ILL. 60606

PAUL F. HOFFMAN
MICHIGAN CHEM.
2 N. RIVERSIDE PLAZA
CHICAGO, ILL. 60606

JOHN W. SIMONS
MORTON-NORWICH PRODUCTS
110 N. WACKER DR.
CHICAGO, ILL. 60606

HARRY W. TODD
L.E. MYERS CO.
550 W. JACKSON BLVD.
CHICAGO, ILL. 60606

LEO GANS
NATL. BUSINESS
162 N. FRANKLIN ST.
CHICAGO, ILL. 60606

CHARLES H. MATHER
ROLLINS BURDICK HUNTER
10 S. RIVERSIDE PLAZA
CHICAGO, ILL. 60606

R.L. LALICH
SPECTOR IND.
205 W. WACKER DR.
CHICAGO, ILL. 60606

R.N. PAUL
TECHNOMIC RESEARCH
1 NORTH WACKER DR.
CHICAGO,ILL. 60606

F.B. WILLIAMS
TIME IND.
100 S. WACKER DR.
CHICAGO, ILL. 60606

K.H. ROBERTSON
UDYCO IND.
200 W. ADAMS
CHICAGO, ILL. 60606

GEORGE DIDISHEIM
WALTHAM WATCH
231 S. JEFFERSON ST.
CHICAGO, ILL. 60606

R.J. BRIDELL
AMERICAN TARA CORP.
1311 WEST LAKE ST.
CHICAGO, ILL. 60607

JOSEPH F. PALUCH
FULTON MARKET COLD STORAGE
1000 FULTON MARKET
CHICAGO, ILL. 60607

HAROLD PRICE
C-P MFG.
2364 S. ASHLAND AVE.
CHICAGO, ILL. 60608

SAMUEL J. POPEIL
POPEIL BROS.
2323 W. PERSHING RD.
CHICAGO, ILL. 60609

C.F. MURPHY JR.
INSURANCE EXCHANGE
4 W. BURTON PL.
CHICAGO,ILL..60610

ARTHUR BRAVER
MAYFAIR SOUND
666 W. KINZIE ST.
CHICAGO, ILL. 60610

DONALD P. COHEN
OPELINKA MFG.
361 W. CHESTNUT ST,
CHICAGO, ILL. 60610

D.L. SASLOW
D.L. SASLOW CO.
500 N. ORLEANS ST.
CHICAGO, ILL. 60610

WILLIAM H. SCHOLL
SCHOLL INC.
213 W. SCHILLER ST.
CHICAGO, ILL. 60610

J. GRANT BEADLE
UNION SPECIAL
400 N. FRANKLIN ST.
CHICAGO, ILL. 60610

LEE A. GOLDBOSS
AES TECH. SYSTEMS
625 N. MICHIGAN AVE.
CHICAGO, ILL. 60611

WILLIAM W. WIRTZ
AMERICAN FURNITURE
666 N. LAKE DR.
CHICAGO, ILL. 60611

BURTON WALL
ARTS & LEISURE
2 E. OAK ST.
CHICAGO, ILL. 60611

E.J. KLECKNER
BELSCOT RETAILERS
251 E. GRAND AVE.
CHICAGO, ILL. 60611

JAMES E. SNYDER
CLC OF AMERICA
401 N. MICHIGAN AVE.
CHICAGO, ILL. 60611

P.E. ROLLHAUS,JR.
ENERGY ABSORPTION SYSTEMS
ONE IBM PLAZA
CHICAGO. ILL. 60611

WALSTEIN FINDLAY JR.
WALLY F. FINDLAY GALLERIES
814 N. MICHIGAN AVE.
CHICAGO, ILL. 60611

G.N. GILLETT JR.
GLOBE BROADCASTING
ONE IBM PLAZA
CHICAGO, ILL. 60611

DAVID GILLESPIE
GRANT ADVERTISING
400 N. MICHIGAN AVE.
CHICAGO, ILL. 60611

H.L. FREUND
J-K IND.
39 S. LA SALLE ST.
CHICAGO, ILL. 60611

JOSEPH F. ROBINEAU
MUNISING WOOD
666 LAKE SHORE DR.
CHICAGO, ILL. 60611

W.W. HUGGETT
NATL. TERMINALS
444 N. LAKE SHORE DR.
CHICAGO, ILL. 60611

RICHARD M. JAFFEE
OIL-DRI CORP.
520 N. MICHIGAN AVE.
CHICAGO, ILL. 60611

DERICK J. DANIELS
PLAYBOY ENTERPRISES
919 N. MICHIGAN AVE.
CHICAGO, ILL. 60611

W. LEE PRYOR
PRYOR COMPUTER IND.
400 N. MICHIGAN AVE.
CHICAGO, ILL. 60611

PAUL J. FERRI
TELCO MARKETING
625 N. MICHIGAN AVE.
CHICAGO, ILL. 60611

L.H. ANGELOS
WALTON-VAIREK
8404 HANCOCK BLDG.
CHICAGO, ILL. 60611

WILLIAM WRIGLEY
WM. WRIGLEY JR. CO.
410 N. MICHIGAN AVE.
CHICAGO, ILL. 60611

ALVIN K. EATON
BRAND INSULATIONS
2350 W. FULTON ST.
CHICAGO, ILL. 60612

T.R. MILES
STRANGE CO.
342 N. WESTERN AVE.
CHICAGO, ILL. 60612

FRANK A. NELSON JR.
STRATEGIC MED. RESEARCH
1655 W. JACKSON BLVD.
CHICAGO, ILL. 60612

CARL KORN
DYNASCAN
1801 W. BELLE PLAINE AVE.
CHICAGO, ILL. 60613

S. SPARER
PRECISION APPARATUS
1801 W. BELLE PLAINE
CHICAGO, ILL. 60613

ABE SAMUELS
SPEED-O-PRINT
1801 W. LARCHMONT AVE.
CHICAGO, ILL. 60613

W.C. PETERSON
DIETZGEN
2425 N. SHEFFIELD AVE.
CHICAGO, ILL. 60614

B.E. PADORR
GENERAL PHOTOS
2717 N. LEHMANN ST.
CHICAGO, ILL. 60614

PHILIP SPERTUS
INTERCRAFT IND.
1840 N. CLYBOURN AVE.
CHICAGO, ILL. 60614

GEORGE E McKEWEN
LUDLOW IND.
2032 CLYBOURN AVE.
CHICAGO, ILL. 60614

HERBERT GRAETZ
PERFECTION ENTERPRISES
1800 N. CLYBOURN AVE.
CHICAGO, ILL. 60614

BENNETT ARCHAMBAULT
STEWART-WARNER
1826 DIVERSEY PARKWAY
CHICAGO, ILL. 60614

EDGAR A. JONES
BRINK'S INC.
234 E. 24TH ST.
CHICAGO, ILL. 60616

C.L. MC EVOY
CUNEO PRESS
2242 S. GROVE ST.
CHICAGO, ILL. 60616

C.W. LAKE JR.
R.R. DONNELLEY& SONS
2223 SOUTH PARKWAY
CHICAGO, ILL. 60616

S.M. BERNSTEIN
AIRKING CORP.
3065 N. ROCKWELL ST.
CHICAGO, ILL. 60618

W.T. O'DONNELL
BALLY MFG.
2640 WEST BELMONT AVE.
CHICAGO, ILL. 60618

KENNETH L. GLASSMAN
FABRIC MART DRAPERIES
1401 E. 95TH ST.
CHICAGO, ILL. 60619

JERRY GANZ
GATEWAY IND.
8825 S. GREENWOOD AVE.
CHICAGO, ILL. 60619

ARTHUR HERMAN
TRIANGLE HOME
945 E. 93RD. ST.
CHICAGO, ILL. 60619

J.J. GOODMAN
PRESTIGE PRODUCTS
1907 N. MENDALL ST.
CHICAGO, ILL. 60622

S.D. BRINSFIELD
CENCO
2600S. KOSTNER
CHICAGO, ILL. 60623

ROBERT G. ROWAN
WESTERN ACADIA
4115 W. OGDEN AVE.
CHICAGO, ILL. 60623

YALE A. BLANC
MARTIN YALE IND.
500 N. SPAULDING
CHICAGO, ILL. 60624

ROGER A. WEILER
SCHAWK GRAPHICS
4546 N. KEDZIE AVE.
CHICAGO, ILL. 60625

MORLAN E. FITERMAN
STAINLESS PROCESSING
1190 S. COTTAGE GROVE AVE.
CHICAGO,ILL. 60628

CHARLES S. LARMON
TOOTSIE ROLL IND.
7401 S. CICERO AVE.
CHICAGO, ILL. 60629

HARRY ONO
POWER - SKI CORP.
5500 NORTH NORTHWEST H'WAY.
CHICAGO, ILL. 60630

JOHN W. SULLIVAN
SKIL CORP.
5033 ELSTON AVE.
CHICAGO, ILL. 60630

SHELDON I. DORENFEST
COMPUCARE
8550 W. BRYN MAWR AVE.
CHICAGO, ILL. 60631

HAROLD BYRON SMITH JR.
ILLINOIS TOOL WORKS
8501 W. HIGGINS RD.
CHICAGO, ILL. 60631

WESTON R. CHRISTOPHERSON
JEWEL CO.
5725 E. RIVER RD.
CHICAGO, ILL. 60631

G.H. BOBEEN
LINDBERG CORP.
8501 W. HIGGINS RD.
CHICAGO, ILL. 60631

RUSSELL R. MALIK
SUN ELECTRIC
6323 AVONDALE
CHICAGO, ILL. 60631

N.T. ANTON
WEN PRODUCTS
5810 NORTHWEST HIGHWAY
CHICAGO, ILL. 60631

HERBERT V. DOUGLAS
CENTRAL STEEL & WIRE
3000 W. 51ST. ST.
CHICAGO, ILL. 60632

HARRY J. FAIR JR.
CALUMET IND.
13921 MACKINAW AVE.
CHICAGO, ILL. 60633

JAMES A. BOGGIS
GLOBE IND.
2638 E. 126TH ST.
CHICAGO, ILL. 60633

STANLEY HOWARD
CHICAGO BUILDERS
3701 N. HARTEM AVE.
CHICAGO, ILL. 60634

B,O, FKEVARUS
POLYTECHNIC DATA
4102 N. NASHVILLE AVE.
CHICAGO,ILL. 60634

JOHN S. GLEASON JR.
CHICAGO HELICOPTER
5240 W. 63RD. ST.
CHICAGO, ILL. 60638

HARRY BRODY
B. BRODY SEATING
5921 W. DICKINS
CHICAGO, ILL. 60639

R.S. KNOX
W.F. HALL PRINTING
4600 DIVERSEY AVE.
CHICAGO, ILL. 60639

WALTER KAPLAN
HELENE CURTIS IND.
4401 W. NORTH AVE.
CHICAGO, ILL. 60639

R.W. SELLECK
PEPSI-COLA BOTTLERS
1745 N. KOLMAR AVE.
CHICAGO, ILL. 60639

ALBERT S. WELLS JR.
WELLS-GARDNER
2701 N. KILDARE AVE.
CHICAGO, ILL. 60639

WM. HARRISON FETRIDGE
DARTNELL CORP.
4660 N. RAVENSWOOD AVE.
CHICAGO, ILL. 60640

R.E. WHITEFORD
MERCOID
4201 W. BELMONT AVE.
CHICAGO, ILL. 60641

J.J. MOJOHNNIER
MOJOHNIER BROS.
4601 W. OHIO ST.
CHICAGO, ILL. 60644

GEORGE CONTARSY
LIBCO
6699 N. LINCOLN AVE.
LINCOLNWOOD, ILL. 60645

PAUL GREVENDICK
OCE IND.
6500 N. LINCOLN AVE.
CHICAGO, ILL. 60645

GARRY BRAININ
ALTAIR
6200 HIAWATHA AVE.
CHICAGO, ILL. 60646

J.R. MORRILL
GOLCONDA
4201 W. PATTERSON AVE.
CHICAGO, ILL. 60646

ROBERT C. BARTLETT
COMMERCE CLEARING
4025 PETERSON AVE.
CHICAGO,ILL. 60646

RICHARD GOODMAN
GSC
4433 W. TOUHY
LINCOLNWOOD, ILL. 60646

GORDON C. ADAMS
LEATH
7111 NORTH LINCOLN AVE.
CHICAGO, ILL. 60646

WALLACE M. SCOTT JR.
MSL IND. INC.
7373 N. LINCOLN AVE.
LINCOLNWOOD, ILL. 60646

GERSON E. LEWIS
MEDIMARK GROUP
4433 S. TOUHY
LINCOLNWOOD, ILL. 60646

J.J. SKAHILL
ROBERTS & PORTER
4140 W. VICTORIA AVE.
CHICAGO, ILL. 60646

RICHARD D. GODDARD
WEIMAN & CO.
4801 W. PETERSON AVE.
CHICAGO, ILL. 60646

L.S. WILSON
WILSON LEASING
4747 WEST PETERSON AVE.
CHICAGO, ILL. 60646

E.C. FRIESENDORF
HANDSCHY CHEM.
2525 N. ELSTON AVE.
CHICAGO, ILL. 60647

J.C. STETSON
A.B. DICK
5700 W. TOUHY AVE.
CHICAGO, ILL. 60648

DAVID W. GRAINGER
W.W. GRAINGER
5959 W. HOWARD ST.
CHICAGO, ILL. 60648

CHESTER B. LYNN
LAWSON PRODUCTS
7711 N. MERRIMAC AVE.
NILES,ILL. 60648

EDWIN R. MOORE
E.R. MOORE
7230 N. CALDWELL AVE.
NILES, ILL. 60648

JAMES C. DANLY
DANLY MACHINE
2100 S. LARAMIE AVE.
CHICAGO, ILL. 60650

NED A. OCHITREE JR.
CECO CORP.
5601 W. 26TH. ST.
CHICAGO, ILL. 60650

EDWARD I. HORWICH
PROCESS
3450 S. 54TH. AVE.
CHICAGO, ILL. 60650

W.J. PFEIF
SUNBEAM
5400 W. ROOSEVELT RD.
CHICAGO, ILL. 60650

E. JOSEPH SEIFERT
PETTIBONE
4710 W. DIVISON ST.
CHICAGO, ILL. 60651

WILLIAM C. CROFT
PYLE NATL. CO.
1334 N. KOSTNER AVE.
CHICAGO, ILL. 60651

W.J. MC GINLEY
MEDICENTERS OF AMERICA
7447 W. WILSON AVE.
CHICAGO, ILL. 60656

WAYNE E. TOUSSAINT
VANCE IND.
7401 W. WILSON AVE.
CHICAGO, ILL. 60656

L.H. COHEN
CROWN SELF SERVICE
3138 N. LINCOLN AVE.
CHICAGO, ILL. 60657

D.C. ROCKOLA
ROCK-OLA MFG.
800 N. KEDZIE AVE.
CHICAGO, ILL. 60657

J. DAYTON FORD
ALLIED VAN LINES
P.O. BOX 4403
CHICAGO, ILL. 60680

JAMES A. WATSON
NATL. TEA
P.O. BOX 6970A
CHICAGO, ILL. 60680

JAMIE C. GIBSON
ROPER CORP.
1905 WEST CT. ST.
KANKAKEE, ILL. 60901

DANIEL C. FERGUSON
NEWELL CO.
916 S. ARCADE AVE.
FREEPORT, ILL. 61032

J.J. GALLAGHER
YATES-AMERICAN
ROSCOE, ILL. 61073

KENYON Y. TAYLOR
REGAL-BELOIT
P.O. BOX 38
SOUTH BELOIT, ILL. 61080

WILLIAM W. KEEFER
WARNER ELECTRIC
449 GARDNER ST.
S. BELOIT, ILL. 61080

H.B. MUSGROVE
FRANTZ MFG.
301 THIRD ST.
STERLING, ILL. 61081

W.M. DILLON
NORTHWESTERN STEEL
AVE. B & WALLACE ST.
STERLING, ILL. 61081

JOSEPH M. CVENGROS
REED IND.
340 BLACKHAWK PARK AVE.
ROCKFORD, ILL. 61101

CARL L. SADLER
SUNDSTRAND CORP.
4751 HARRISON AVE.
ROCKFORD, ILL. 61101

BRUCE M. LIVINGSTON
WOODWARD GOVERNOR
5001 N. 2ND. ST.
ROCKFORD, ILL. 61101

PALMER PRESIDENT
J.L. CLARK MFG.
2300 6TH ST.
ROCKFORD, ILL. 61108

V.J. LOHMAN
ILLINOISE BEEF
1039 S. OAKWOOD AVE.
GENESEO, ILL. 61254

FREDERICK L. CARUS
MATTHIESSEN & HEGELER
9TH. & STERLING STS.
LA SALLE, ILL. 61301

A.G. ENGLISH
BOSS MFG.
221 W. FIRST ST.
KEWANEE, ILL. 61443

J.R. MC GATH
DURA-PLEX IND.
3526 N. CALIFORNIA ST.
PEORIA, ILL. 61603

EDWARD B. HOERR
HEIGHTS FINANCE
4001 N. WAR MEMORIAL DR.
PEORIA, ILL. 61614

GERALD D. STEPHENS
RLI CORP.
9025 N. LINDERGH DR.
PEORIA, ILL. 61614

DELMAR D. WALKER
FUNK BROS.
1300 W. WASHINGTON ST.
BLOOMINGTON, ILL. 61701

WILLIAM W. WALKER
HONEGGER'S
201 W. LOCUST ST.
FAIRBURY, ILL. 61739

PHILIP D. GELVIN
CAP & GOWN
1000 N. MARKET ST.
CHAMPAIGN, ILL. 61821

F.C. BULLOCK
BULLOCK CO.
702 S. GILBERT ST.
DANVILLE, ILL. 61832

EVERETT FITZJARRALD
PROCESS IND.
400 E. PROGRESS ST.
ARTHUR, ILL. 61911

E.J. SPIEGEL JR.
ALTON BOX BOARD CO.
P.O. BOX 276
ALTON, ILL. 62002

GENE TUMBLESON
WALSTON ENTERPRISES
P.O. BOX 360
E. ALTON, ILL. 62024

HOWARD M. LOVE
GRANITE CITY STEEL
20TH. & STATE STS.
GRANITE CITY, ILL. 62040

G. NOVOTNY
ST. LOUIS NATL. STOCKYARDS
EXCHANGE BLDG.
NATL. STOCK YARDS, ILL. 62071

CARL H. TOTSCH
MIDWEST RUBBER
P.O. BOX 744
E. ST. LOUIS, ILL. 62203

J.A. STELLE
CAHOKIA DOWNS
RTE. NO. 460 & PICKET RD.
EAST ST. LOUIS, ILL. 62205

M.H. HESS
MARTHA MANNING CO.
1700 ST. LOUIS RD.
COLLINSVILLE, ILL. 62234

L.W. NIMMO
PUTNAM DYES
301 OAK ST.
QUINCY, ILL. 62301

JAMES R. RANDALL
ARCHER-DANIELS
4666 FARIES PARKWAY
DECATUR, ILL. 62525

D.E. NORDLUND
A.E. STALEY MFG.
P.O. BOX 151
DECATUR, ILL. 62525

E.D. HUNTER
AFSCO
726 S. COLLEGE ST.
SPRINGFIELD, ILL. 62708

B.D. HUNTER
AMEDCO
726 S. COLLEGE ST.
SPRINGFIELD, ILL. 62708

A.C. DAVIS
ALVA C. DAVIS PETROLEUM
P.O. BOX 480
FAIRFIELD, ILL. 62837

A.C. DAVIS
SKILES OIL
P.O. BOX 480
FAIRFIELD, ILL. 62837

EUGENE D. POWERS
COMPONENTS CORP.
MOUNT CARMEL, ILL. 62863

JOHN R. BORSANTI JR.
KELLWOOD CO..
600 KELLWOOD PARKWAY
ST. LOUIS, MO.   63017

T.C. WETTERAU JR.
WETTERAU
8400 PERSHALL RD.
HAZELWOOD, MO. 63042

H.B. ABRAMS
MYLEE DIGITAL
155 WELDON PARKWAY
HAZELWOOD, MO. 63043

J.C. O'NEAL JR.
O'NEAL, JONES & FELDMAN
2510 METRO BLVD.
MARYLAND HTS. MO. 63043

J. SIMPKINS
TIFFANY IND.
100 PROGRESS PKWAY. STE. 114
MARYLAND HTS, MO. 63043

JOSEPH A. VOLK
BETA
4328 BRIDGETON IN. DR.
BRIDGETON, MO. 63044

RALPH C. COOK
MOBILE ENTERPRISES
500 NORTHWEST PLAZA
ST. LOUIS, MO. 63074

GEORGE W. HALL
DEBRON
500 NORTHWEST PLAZA
ST. ANN, MO. 63074

W.W. KING
CURLEE CLOTHING
TENTH & WASHINGTON
ST. LOUIS, MO. 63101

W.W. ALLEN JR.
HYDRAULIC-PRESS BRICK CO.
705 OLIVE ST.
ST. LOUIS, MO. 63101

ROBERT J. MC DOWELL
LUDWIG MUSIC HOUSE
1004 OLIVE ST.
ST. LOUIS, MO. 63101

DONALD H. ZIEGLER
LA BARGE
500 BROADWAY BLDG.
ST. LOUIS, MO. 63102

PAUL B. AKIN
LACLEDE STEEL
10 BROADWAY
ST. LOUIƐ Ƭ MO. 63102

ELLIS L. BROWN
PETROLITE
100 N. BROADWAY
ST. LOUIS, MO. 63102

PATRICK J. GILLIGAN
VALLEY IND.
105 S. NINTH ST.
ST. LOUIS, MO. 63102

J.G. ROWAN
ELDER MFG.
703 NORTH 13TH ST.
ST. LOUIS, MO. 63103

BERNARD FEIN
AFFILIATED HOSPITAL
1920 S. JEFFERSON AVE.
ST. LOUIS, MO. 63104

RICHARD W. SHOMAKER
BROWN GROUP
8400 MARYLAND AVE.
ST. LOUIS, MO. 63105

IRVING A. SHEPARD
CHROMALLOY AMERICAN
120 S. CENTRAL AVE.
ST. LOUIS, MO. 63105

JOSEPH B. WOODLIEF
DIVERSIFIED IND.
7701 FORYTH BLVD.
CLAYTON, MO. 63105

JAMES A. VAN SANT
GEN. STEEL IND.
P.O. BOX 16000
ST. LOUIS, MO. 63105

STEPHEN M. FRIEDRICH
LIBERTY LOAN
7711 BONHOMME AVE.
ST. LOUIS, MO. 63105

LEO G. PECK
MEYER-BLANKE CO.
222 S. CENTRAL AVE.
ST. LOUIS, MO. 63105

M. MOSS ALEXANDER
MISSOURI-PORTLAND CEMENT CO.
7711 CARONDELET AVE.
ST. LOUIS, MO. 63105

A.S. LAPIN
CLAYTON CORP.
4205 FOREST PARK BLVD.
ST. LOUIS, MO. 63108

ROBERT A. CLABAULT
MALLINCKRODT INC.
3600 N. SECOND ST.
ST. LOUIS, MO. 63107

GEORGE S. ROSBOROUGH, JR.
MEASUREGRAPH CO.
4245 FOREST PARK BLVD.
ST. LOUIS, MO. 63108

PAUL KALMANOVITZ
FALSTAFF BREWING CORP.
5050 OAKLAND AVE.
ST. LOUIS, MO. 63110

BERNARD DUCHINSKY
INTERTHERM INC.
3800 PARK AVE.
ST. LOUIS, MO. 63110

CARL BAUER
MISSOURI ROLLING MILL CORP.
6800 MANCHESTER AVE.
ST. LOUIS, MO. 63110

R.H. SLOSBERG
RIPLEY INDS.
4067 FOLSOM AVE.
ST. LOUIS, MO. 63110

R.P. CONERLY
POTT INDUSTRIES
611 E. MARCEAU
ST. LOUIS, MO. 63111

EARL J. BEWIG
ST. LOUIS STEEL CASTING
100 MOTT ST.
ST. LOUIS, MO. 63111

JOHN D. LEVY
ANGELICA CORP.
700 ROSEDALE AVE.
ST. LOUIS, MO. 63112

R.F. ESON
HUTTIG SASH & DOOR
8900 PAGE BLVD.
ST. LOUIS, MO. 63114

A.M. CORNWELL, JR.
JACKES-EVANS MFG. CO.
4427 GERALDINE AVE.
ST. LOUIS, MO. 63115

JULIUS K. NEMETH
REARDON CO.
3616 SCARLET OAK BLVD.
ST. LOUIS, MO. 63122

FRANK J. NOVOSON
SOCIETY BRAND INDUSTRIES
10411 CLAYTON RD.
ST. LOUIS, MO. 63131

R.T. McCARTHY
BRODERICK & BASCOM
10440 TRENTON
ST. LOUIS, MO. 63132

FRANKLIN A. JACOBS
FALCON PRODS.
9387 DIELMAN INDUSTRIAL DR.
ST. LOUIS, MO. 63132

WALTER FUNK, JR.
MO. RESEARCH LABS.
10225 PAGE IND. BLVD.
ST. LOUIS, MO. 63132

V.T. GORGUZE
THE EMERSON ELECTRIC CO.
8100 FLORISSANT AVE.
ST. LOUIS, MO. 63136

J.A. SMITH
BANK BLDG. & EQUIP. CORP.
1130 HAMPTON AVE.
ST. LOUIS, MO. 63139

WILBURT J. SMITH
VICO CORP.
11975 WEST LINE DR.
ST. LOUIS, MO. 63141

STANLEY L. LOPATA
CARBOLINE
350 HANLEY IND. CT.
ST. LOUIS, MO. 63144

VICTOR M. HERMELIN
K-V PHARMACEUTICAL CO.
2503 S. HANLEY RD.
ST. LOUIS, MO. 63144

BERNARD A. EDISON
EDISON BROS. STORES
P.O. BOX 14020
ST. LOUIS, MO. 63178

ROBERT E. HARMON
HARMON INDS.
ROUTE #1
GRAIN VALLEY, MO. 64029

D.H. SIZEMORE
TOROTEL, INC.
13402 S. 71 HWY.
GRANDVIEW, MO. 64034

GUY L. CALDWELL
GUY'S FOODS
405 S. LEONARD
LIBERTY, MO. 64068

ROBERT M. ADDISON
U.S. SUPPLY
1315 W. 12TH ST.
KANSAS CITY, MO. 64101

CHARLES B. JENNINGS
K.C. STOCK YARDS
1600 GENESSEE ST.
KANSAS CITY, MO. 64102

JOHN S. HARROW
K.C. STRUCTURAL STEEL
21ST & METROPOLITAN
KANSAS CITY, MO. 64104

JAMES P. SUNDERLAND
ASH GROVE CEMENT
1000 TEN MAIN CENTER
KANSAS CITY, MO. 64105

RICHARD J. STERN
CENTRAL COAL & COKE
DWIGHT BLDG.
KANSAS CITY, MO. 64105

JOHN W. TUCKER
R.B. JONES CORP.
301 W. 11TH ST.
KANSAS CITY, MO. 64105

HENRY P. POINDEXTER
H.T. POINDEXTER & SONS
801 BROADWAY
KANSAS CITY, MO. 64105

L.L. WARD
RUSSEL STOVER CANDIES
1004 BALTIMORE AVE.
KANSAS CITY, MO. 64105

PAUL UHLMANN, JR.
STANDARD MILLING
1009 CENTRAL ST.
KANSAS CITY, MO. 64105

DUTTON BROOKFIELD
UNITOG CO.
1004 BALTIMORE AVE.
KANSAS CITY, MO. 64105

LEE REEDER
W.S.C. GROUP
1221 BALTIMORE AVE.
KANSAS CITY, MO. 64105

ROBERT F. BROZMAN
CENCOR, INC.
1003 WALNUT
KANSAS CITY, MO. 64106

STANFORD MILLER
ERC CORP
21 W. 10TH
KANSAS CITY, MO. 64106

C.M. HAYMAN, JR.
FORUM RESTS.
1500 BRYANT BLDG.
KANSIS CITY, MO. 64106

ROBERT L. SHAW
I.C.H. CORP.
906 GRAND AVE.
KANSAS CITY, MO. 64106

HELMUT VOGEL
PROM MOTOR HOTEL
6TH & MAIN
KANSAS CITY, MO. 64106

O.R. PINKERMAN
PURITAN-BENNETT
OAK AT 13TH
KANSAS CITY, MO. 64106

ALFRED H. LIGHTON
WOOLF BROS.
1020 WALNUT
KANSAS CITY, MO. 64106

RICHARD H. OREAR
COMMONWEALTH THEATRES
215 W. 18TH
KANSAS CITY, MO. 64108

RONALD JARVIS
OPPENHEIMER INDS.
1808 MAIN ST.
KANSAS CITY, MO. 64108

R.G. MARTIN
REALEX CORP.
2500 SUMMIT
KANSAS CITY, MO. 64108

JEROME S. KIVETT
REGAL PLASTIC CO.
1725 HOLMES ST.
KANSAS CITY, MO. 64108

CHARLES G. HANSON
STUART HALL CO.
2121 CENTRAL ST.
KANSAS CITY, MO. 64108

ARTHUR D. STEVENS
AUTOMATIQUE, INC.
3225 ROANOKE RD.
KANSAS CITY, MO. 64111

H.W. BLOCH
H. & R. BLOCH
4410 MAIN ST.
KANSAS CITY, MO. 64111

J.F. COLEMAN
COLEMAN AMERICAN CO.
3435 BROADWAY
KANSAS CITY, MO. 64111

ROBERT M. PATTERSON
C.J. PATTERSON & CO.
3947 BROADWAY
KANSAS CITY, MO. 64111

JAMES F. O'CROWLEY
GATEWAY SPORTING GOODS
P.O. BOX 11445
KANSAS CITY, MO. 64112

LOUIS B. GRESHAM
GENERAL ENERGY CORP.
231 W. 47TH
KANSAS CITY, MO. 64112

KENNETH D. HILL
GILBERT-ROBINSON
P.O. BOX 16000
KANSAS CITY, MO. 64112

RAYMOND M. ALDEN
UNITED TELECOMMUNICATION
P.O. BOX 11315
KANSAS CITY, MO. 64112

ROBERT V. PALAN
KING LOUIS INT'L.
311 W. 72ND ST.
KANSAS CITY, MO. 64114

THOMAS E. HUGUNIN
LMF CORP.
P.O. BOX 8725
KANSAS CITY, MO. 64114

HASKELL SOBEL
NEW PROD. DEVLPT. SVCS.
P.O. BOX 8424
KANSAS CITY, MO. 64114

C.F. HIGGINS
NAT'L BELLAS HESS INC.
715 ARMOUR RD.
N. KANSAS CITY, MO. 64116

JAMES E. WIDNER
ROBO CAR WASH
2330 BURLINGTON
KANSAS CITY, MO. 64116

C. CRAIG WHITAKER
WHITAKER CABLE CORP.
2801 ROCK CREEK PKWY.
KANSAS CITY, MO. 64116

ROBERT F. BROZMAN
CENTURY ACCEPTANCE CORP.
1003 WALNUT ST.
KANSAS CITY, MO. 64120

FRANK PAXTON,
FRANK PAXTON CO.
6311 ST. JOHN AVE.
KANSAS CITY, MO. 64123

WALTER C. GUMMERE
THE VENDO CO.
7400 E. 12TH ST.
KANSAS CITY, MO. 64126

A.N. BRUNSON
BRUNSON INST. CO.
8000 E. 23RD ST.
KANSAS CITY, MO. 64129

I.H. MILLER
RIVAL MFG. CO.
36TH & BENNINGTON
KANSAS CITY, MO. 64129

FORREST L. THOMPSON
BROOKS RESEARCH & MFG.
5612 BRIGHTON TERR.
KANSAS CITY, MO. 64130

LEE S. SIEBERT
MARK TWAIN MARINE
4800 BLUE PKWY.
KANSAS CITY, MO. 64130

F.L. THOMPSON
XEBEC CORP.
5612 BRIGHTON TERR.
KANSAS CITY, MO. 64130

LAMSON RHEINFRANK, JR.
STANDARD HAVENS
8800 E. 63RD ST.
KANSAS CITY, MO. 64133

E.M. KAUFFMAN
MARION LABS.
10236 BUNKER RIDGE RD.
KANSAS CITY, MO. 64137

GEORGE C. DILLON
BUTLER MFG. CO.
BMA TOWER-PENN VALLEY PK.
KANSAS CITY, MO. 64141

JOHN S. AYERS
COOK PAINT & VARNISH CO.
P.O. BOX 389
KANSAS CITY, MO. 64141

PAUL HAMILTON, JR.
LSC FINANCIAL
3430 BROADWAY
KANSAS CITY, MO. 64141

HAL S. HARDIN
NELLY DON
P.O. BOX 616
KANSAS CITY, MO. 64141

J.T. HOUSE
TOPSY'S INT'L.
P.O. BOX 1607
KANSAS CITY, MO. 64141

JERRY C. GREGOIRE
DEAN RESEARCH CORP.
8100 N.W. 97TH TERR.
KANSAS CITY, MO. 64153

ROBERT P. ORTLIP
GREAT MIDWEST CORP.
8300 N.E. UNDERGROUND DR.
KANSAS CITY, MO. 64161

DON K. SPALDING
ST. JOSEPH STOCK YARDS CO.
LIVE STOCK EXCHANGE BLVD.
S. ST. JOSEPH, MO. 64488

GEORGE F. BOYD
TRI-STATE MOTOR TRANSIT
P.O. BOX 113
JOPLIN, MO. 64802

HARRY M. CORNELL, JR.
LEGGETT & PLATT
600 W. MOUND ST.
CARTHAGE, MO. 64836

R.W. PLASTER
EMPIRE GAS CORP.
P.O. BOX 303
LEBANON, MO. 65536

WILLIAM G. ROLLER
G&R INDS. INC.
P.O. BOX 18
PURDY, MO. 65734

L.P. MUELLER
PAUL MUELLER CO.
P.O. BOX 828
SPRINGFIELD, MO. 65801

L.D. MANLEY
MANLEY INDS.
304 E. PERSHING
SPRINGFIELD, MO. 65806

G.E. WAINSCOTT
COMMERCE ACCEPTANCE CO.
215 N. 5TH ST.
ATCHISON, KS. 66002

MARVIN S. KIPLING
PALACE CLOTHING CO.
709-711 KANSAS AVE.
TOPEKA, KS. 66603

NAT N. NAST, JR.
NAT NAST, INC.
P.O. BOX 415
BONNER SPRINGS, KS. 66012

E.J. KING JR.
KING RADIO CORP.
400 N. ROGERS RD.
OLATHE, KS. 66061

MERLIN A. STICKELBER
STICKELBER & SONS
P.O. BOX 3116
KANSAS CITY, KS. 66103

JOSEPH E. GRINNAS
S.W. FREIGHT LINES
1400 KANSAS AVE.
KANSAS CITY, KS. 66105

ESTHER COSNER BERG
LADY BALTIMORE FOODS
1601 FAIRFAX TRAFFICWAY
KANSAS CITY, KS. 66115

L.G. GALAMBA, SR.
S.G. METALS INDS.
2ND & RIVERVIEW
KANSAS CITY, KS. 66118

WILLIAM J. MC KENNA
H.D. LEE CO.
JOHNSON DR. AT STATE LINE
SHAWNEE MISSION, KS. 66201

ROBERT L. MC FADEN
THE MARLEY CO.
5800 FOXRIDGE DR.
MISSION, KS. 66202

L.A. BEREY
SYNERGISTIC COMMUNICATIONS
6901 W. 63RD ST.
OVERLAND PK., KS. 66202

JEROME E. BAKER
INTER-CONTINENTAL SVCS.
2000 JOHNSON DR.
SHAWNEE MISSION, KS. 66205

D.J. LUND
COMMONWEALTH LOAN
9500 MISSION RD.
OVERLAND PARK, KS. 66206

E. CLAYTON GENGRAS
ADLEY CORP.
P.O. BOX 7268
SHAWNEE MISSION, KS. 66207

RICHARD GOLDMAN
MEDCO JEWELRY
10950 EL MONTE, BOX 7130
SHAWNEE MISSION, KS. 66207

DONALD L. McMORRIS
YELLOW FREIGHT SYSTEM
10990 ROE AVE.
SHAWNEE MISSION, KS. 66207

C.L. WILLIAM HAW
NAT'L. ALFALFA DEHYDRATING
4800 MAIN ST.
SHAWNEE MISSION, KS. 66212

R.S. ZIMMERMAN
BUTLER NAT'L. CORP.
8246 NIEMAN
SHAWNEE MISSION, KS. 66214

J.J. EKSTROM
GAY GIBSON INC.
8101 LENEXA DR.
LENEXA, KS. 66214

RICHARD M. LEVIN
JASON-EMPIRE
9200 CODY
OVERLAND PARK, KS. 66214

L. CHANDLER SMITH
CONCHEMCO
1000 MARSHALL DR.
LENEXA, KS. 66215

JACK FRIEDMAN
DOUGLAS PHARMACAL INDS.
8906 ROSEHILL RD.
LENEXA, KS. 66215

JEROME E. BAKER
INTER-CONT. COMPUTING
2000 JOHNSON DR.
MISSION WOODS, KS. 66222

J.V. ALLEN
DRUMMER BOY
P.O. BOX 208
TOPEKA, KS. 66601

H.A. MC COY
TWIN AMERICA'S AG. & IND. DVLPRS.
P.O. BOX 1516
TOPEKA, KS. 66601

LOUIS POZEZ
VOLUME SHOE
3515 E. 6TH ST.
TOPEKA, KS. 66607

STANLEY H. STAUFFER
STAUFFER PUBLICATIONS
6TH & JEFFERSON
TOPEKA, KS. 66607

DAVID C. FREEMAN
MIDWESTERN DIST. INC.
400 N. NATIONAL
FORT SCOTT, KS. 66701

WAYNE A. McMURTREY
KUSTOM ELECTRONICS, INC.
1010 W. CHESTNUT ST.
CHANUTE, KS. 66720

CHARLES L. FUSSMAN
MONARCH CEMENT CO.
P.O. BOX 187
HUMBOLDT, KS. 66748

P.W. FRILEY
W.S. DICKEY CLAY MFG. CO.
P.O. BOX 6
PITTSBURG, KS. 66762

A. SOLOMON
HARVEST BRAND INC.
101 N. ELM ST.
PITTSBURG, KS. 66762

EVAN L. HOPKINS
HOPKINS MFG. CORP.
P.O. BOX F
EMPORIA, KS. 66801

CAMERON FUNK
CANADIAN PROSPECTS
RFD BOX 130
AUGUSTA, KS. 67010

L.A. PAUL
INT'L. PLASTICS
10 INNOVATION LN.
COLWICH, KS. 67030

L.D. SAWYER
K.T. OIL CORP.
400 S. MAIN ST., BOX 981
EL DORADO, KS. 67042

HAROLD E. HARRIS
MC, INC.
127 W. 1ST
HALSTEAD, KS. 67056

HOWARD L. BRENNEMAN
HESSTON CORP.
P.O. BOX 545
HESSTON, KS. 67062

JOHN C. WALLACE
STRUTHERS THERMO-FLOOD
P.O. BOX 753
WINFIELD, KS. 67156

RUSSELL W. MEYER
CESSNA AIRCRAFT
P.O. BOX 1521
WICHITA, KS. 67201

L.M. JONES
COLEMAN, CO.
250 N. FRANCIS AVE.
WICHITA, KS. 67201

HARRY B. COMBS
GATES LEARJET CORP.
P.O. BOX 1280
WICHITA, KS. 67201

DONALD SBARRA
KANSAS STATE NETWORK
833 N. MAIN ST., BOX 333
WICHITA, KS. 67201

A.G. MC CORMICK
MC CORMICK-ARMSTRONG CO., INC.
P.O. BOX 1377
WICHITA, KS. 67201

M.J. KNOPF
RACON, INC.
P.O. BOX 198
WICHITA, KS. 67201

RICHARD W. VOLK
ENERGY RESERVES GROUP, INC.
217 N. WATER ST.
WICHITA, KS. 67202

O.A. SUTTON
OASIS PETROLEUM
SUTTON PL.
WICHITA, KS. 67202

WILLIAM M. RAYMOND
RAYMOND PETROLEUM CO., INC.
200 W. DOUGLAS, #800
WICHITA, KS. 67202

W.A. MICHAELIS, JR.
SIERRA PETROLEUM
211 N. BROADWAY
WICHITA, KS. 67202

M.L. CARTER
S.E. PETRO-CHEM, INC.
220 W. WATERMAIN ST.
WICHITA, KS. 67202

W.E. TOMLINSON
TOMLINSON OIL CO.
200 W. DOUGLAS, STE. 1030
WICHITA, KS. 67202

FRANK E. HEDRICK
BEECH AIRCRAFT CORP.
9709 E. CENTRAL AVE.
WICHITA, KS. 67206

FRANK L. CARNEY
PIZZA HUT
10225 E. KELLOGG
WICHITA, KS. 67207

R.D. LAWRENCE
AG. & IND. DEVLPT.
661 WETMORE
WICHITA, KS. 67209

M. EUGENE TORLINE
VARIANT CORP.
6235 W. KELLOGG DR.
WICHITA, KS. 67209

C.W. WIRTH
MID-AMERICA NURSING CENTERS
4510 W. CENTRAL
WICHITA, KS. 67212

E.L. YOST
DAVID'S, INC.
P.O. BOX 18008
WICHITA, KS. 67218

CLARK L. BRANDON
FARM & RANCH FINANCIAL
1069 PARKLANE
WICHITA, KS. 67218

E.L. YOST
MFY INDS.
P.O. BOX 18008
WICHITA, KS. 67218

S.A. HANN
MEDICALODGES, INC.
P.O. BOX 574
COFFEYVILLE, KS. 67337

WILLIAM H. GRAVES
GRAVES TRUCK LINE INC.
P.O. BOX 1387
SALINA, KS. 67401

ALBERT J. SCHWARTZ
THE LEE CO.
1648 W. MAGNOLIA
SALINA, KS. 67401

R.G. SANBORN
DUCKWALL STORES
OPALENA AT COTTAGE
ABILENE, KS. 67410

R.E. DILLON. JR.
DILLON CO'S.
2700 E. 4TH ST.
HUTCHISON, KS. 67501

R.H. SPENCER
HI-PLAINS ENTERPRISES
P.O. BOX 590
LEOTI, KS. 67861

R.B. DAUGHERTY
VALMONT INDS.
VALLEY, NE. 68064

ROBERT C. BYRNE
CARPENTER PAPER
815 HARNEY ST
OMAHA, NE. 68102

ALBERT SCHROEDER
WESTCENTRAL COOPERATIVE GRAIN
GRAIN EXCHANGE BLVD.
OMAHA, NE. 68102

PATRICK G. NIPP
CONT. CARE CENTER
8712 W. DODGE RD.
OMAHA, NE. 68114

JOHN E. CLEARY
DATA DOCUMENTS
4205 S. 96TH
OMAHA, NE. 68127

CHARLES SOPHIR
MORRIS INDS.
10200 L. ST.
OMAHA, NE. 68127

P.G. SCHRAGER
PACESETTER BUILDING SYSTEMS
4343 S. 96TH ST.
OMAHA, NE. 68127

LEE WEGENER
PAMIDA, INC.
8800 F ST.
OMAHA, NE. 68127

CHARLES M. HARPER
CONAGRA INC.
200 KIEWIT PLAZA
OMAHA, NE. 68131

JOE SHAVER
SHAVER FOOD MARTS
330 N. 114TH ST.
OMAHA, NE. 68154

P.A. KOSLOSKY
MAGNOLIA METAL
MAGNOLIA PK.
AUBURN, NE. 68305

A.A. ANDROS
HY-GAIN ELECTRONICS
N.E. HGWY. 6 AT STEVENS
LINCOLN, NE. 68502

C.W. OLSON
OLSON CONST. CO.
410 S. 7TH ST.
LINCOLN, NE. 68508

B.A. ROBBINS
FOOD HOST USA
P.O. BOX 30160
LINCOLN, NE. 68510

RONALD J. FAIRBAIRN
OPTIC SCIENCE INDS.
P.O. BOX 965
COLUMBUS, NE. 68601

DALE C. TINTSMAN
IOWA BEEF PROCESSORS
DAKOTA CITY, NE. 68731

ROBERT L. PETERSON
MADISON FOODS
1200 INDUSTRIAL PKWY.
MADISON, NE. 68748

GEORGE RISK
GEORGE RISK INDS.
802 SOUTH ELM ST.
KIMBALL, NE. 69145

FRED W. SCHNEIDER
LOCKWOOD CORP.
P.O. BOX 160
GERING, NE. 69341

DANIEL N. SILVERMAN
NAT'L. ENVIRONMENTAL CONTROLS
912 DAVID DRIVE
METAIRIE, LA. 70003

WILLIAM F. BUCKLEY, JR.
STARR BROADCASTING GROUP
3715 WILLIAMS BLVD.
KENNER, LA. 70062

RICHARD H. KRIETE, JR.
TACA INT'L. AIRLINES
P.O. BOX 428
KENNER, LA. 70062

T. ROBERT FIDDLER
D.H. HOLMES CO., LTD.
819 CANAL ST.
NEW ORLEANS, LA. 70103

L.E. BROCK
BROCK EXPLORATION CORP.
202 PERE MARQUETTE BLDG.
NEW ORLEANS, LA. 70112

R.L. GOODWIN
EXCHANGE OIL & GAS CORP.
1010 COMMON ST., 16TH FLR.
NEW ORLEANS, LA. 70112

J.B. STOREY
PELTO OIL
1010 COMMON ST.
NEW ORLEANS, LA. 70112

L.J. ROUSSEL
UNIVERSAL DRILLING
1500 AMERICAN BANK BLDG.
NEW ORLEANS, LA. 70112

WILLIAM B. BRU
DIAMONDHEAD CORP.
4450 GEN'L. DE GAULLE DR.
NEW ORLEANS, LA. 70114

C.J. CHARBONNET
AMERICAN RENT-ALL INC.
3940 TULANE AVE.
NEW ORLEANS, LA. 70119

JOHN P. LABORDE
TIDEWATER MARINE SERVICE
3308 TULANE AVE.
NEW ORLEANS, LA. 70119

DENNIS B. MULLEN
CHART HOUSE
4820 BRADLEY DR.
NEW ORLEANS, LA. 70121

R.L. SUGGS
PETROLEUM HELICOPTERS
P.O. BOX 23502
HARAHAN, LA. 70123

N. SIDNEY WIENER
WIENER CORP.
4725 POWELL ST.
NEW ORLEANS, LA. 70123

C.K. GORDON
TOTH ALUMINUM
5010 LEROY JOHNSON DR.
NEW ORLEANS, LA. 70126

MR. MAC WELSON
EDWARDS ENGINEERING
1170 CONSTANCE ST.
NEW ORLEANS, LA. 70130

J.M. HOLLADAY, JR.
GEOSCIENCE TECHNOLOGY
744 ST. CHARLES AVE.
NEW ORLEANS, LA. 70130

EADS POITEVENT
THE ICB CORP.
321 ST. CHARLES AVE.
NEW ORLEANS, LA. 70130

FRANK A. NEMEC
LYKES CORP.
100 POYDRAS ST.
NEW ORLEANS, LA. 70130

WILLIAM A. CARPENTER
WHITNEY HOLDING CORP.
228 ST. CHARLES AVE.
NEW ORLEANS, LA. 70130

E.B. INGRAM
INGRAM CORP.
4100 ONE SHELL SQUARE
NEW ORLEANS, LA. 70139

R.J. SHOPF
NEWPARK RESOURCES
4420 ONE SHELL SQUARE
NEW ORLEANS, LA. 70139

GEORGE H. TROXELL, JR.
OCEAN OIL & GAS CO.
P.O. BOX 61780
NEW ORLEANS, LA. 70160

HUGH J. KELLY
OCEAN DRILLING
1600 CANAL ST.
NEW ORLEANS, LA. 70161

EDGAR KEATS
STANDARD DREDGING
P.O. BOX 8092 GEN. STA.
NEW ORLEANS, LA. 70182

HAROLD C. HARSH
KALVAR
907 S. BROAD ST.
NEW ORLEANS, LA. 70185

BURT H. KEENAN
OFFSHORE LOGISTICS
P.O. BOX 5-C
LAFAYETTE, LA. 70501

AUGUSTIN CABRER
STERLING SUGARS
P.O. BOX 572
FRANKLIN, LA. 70538

RICHARD W. KRAJICEK
CESCO
P.O. BOX 3044
LAKE CHARLES, LA. 70601

CHARLES D. SYLVEST
LOUISIANA SUPPLY
P.O. DRAWER 1419
LAKE CHARLES, LA. 70604

TILLMAN CAVERT JR.
CALCASIEU PAPER
ELIZABETH. LA. 70638

H.J. WILSON
H.J. WILSON
5825 FLORIDA BLVD.
BATON ROUGE, LA. 70806

ANDREW H. PHILLIPS
POST AMERICAN
8149 FLORIDA BLVD.
BATON ROUGE, LA. 70815

W.R. BARRON
NUCLEAR SYSTEMS
P.O. BOX 2543
BATON ROUGE, LA. 70821

HARRIS J. CHUSTZ
UNITED CO. FINANCIAL
P.O. BOX 1591
BATON ROUGE, LA. 70821

HERBERT J. FRENSLEY
P & H TUBE
411 HAMILTON RD.
BOSSIER CITY, LA. 71010

SHEFFIELD NELSON
ARKASSAS LA. GAS
SLATTERY BLDG.
SHREVEPORT, LA. 71101

JAMES A. LATHAM
DIAMOND COAL
900 MID SOUTH TOWERS
SHREVEPORT, LA. 71101

J.A. LATHAM
TRANSCONTINENTAL OIL
900 MID SOUTH TOWERS
SHREVEPORT, LA. 71101

ROBERT F. ROBERTS
CRYSTAL OIL
P.O. BOX 1101
SHREVEPORT, LA. 71102

W.A. PEAVY JR.
PEAVY-WILSON LAND
P.O. BOX 1103
SHREVEPORT, LA. 71102

J.C. TRAHAN
RESOURCE EXPLORATION
P.O. BOX 4382
SHREVEPORT, LA. 71104

J.B. RUCKER
RUCKER PHARMACAL
6540 LINE AVE.
SHREVEPORT, LA. 71106

T.T. HAILEY
PETROL IND.
P.O. BOX 7941
SHREVEPORT, LA. 71107

MORTON H. KINZLER
BARNWELL IND.
P.O. BOX 4
SHREVEPORT, LA. 71161

E.M. KNIGHT
BERRY PETROLEUM CO.
P.O. BOX 1101
SHREVEPORT, LA. 71163

ALTON H. HOWARD
HOWARD BROTHERS DISCOUNT
3030 AURORA
MONROE, LA. 71201

STAFFORD G. KEES SR.
FEDERATED NUSING
1108 MAIN ST.
PINEVILLE, LA. 71360

MARJEN H. COLLET
OLINKRAFT
JONESBORO RD.
W. MONROE, LA. 71291

BEATRICE JOYCE KEAN
TREMONT LUMBER
JOYCE, LA. 71440

B. JERRY TANENBAUM JR.
UDS
HIGHWAY 54
DUMAS, ARK. 71639

ROBERT J. SWEENEY
MURPHY OIL
200 JEFFERSON AVE.
EL DORADO,ARK.. 71730

JAMES R. BEMIS
OZAN LUMBER
407 OZAN DR.
PRESCOTT, ARK. 71857

J.W. ALLISON
CASTLE IND.
P.O. BOX 1141
CONWAY, ARK. 72032

F.A. O'DANIEL
PIONEER FOOD
P.O. BOX 231
DE WITT, ARK. 72042

WILLIAM DILLARD
DILLARD DEPARTMENT STORES
313 MAIN ST.
LITTLE ROCK, ARK. 72201

C.R. WARNER JR.
FAIRFIELD COMMUNITIES LAND
1207 REBSAMEN PK. RD.
LITTLE ROCK, ARK. 72203

R.E. HORAN
JACUZZI BROS.
11511 NEW BENTON HWY.
LITTLE ROCK, ARK. 72203

K. J. BOWEN
MINUTE MAN OF AMERICA
P.O. BOX 828
LITTLE ROCK, ARK. 72203

LESTER BARNETT
PACESETTER
410 E. WASHINGTON, BOX 578
N. LITTLE ROCK, ARK. 72203

DABBS SULLIVAN JR.
SOUTHWEST SCOTTISH INNS
412 LOUISIANA ST. BX. 2379
LITTLE ROCK, ARK. 72203

DAVE GRUNDFEST JR.
STERLING STORES
6500 FORBING RD.
LITTLE ROCK, ARK. 72204

C.J. UPTON
SOUTHLAND RACING
WEST MEMPHIS, ARK. 72301

T.W. ROGERS JR.
MASS MERCHANDISERS
P.O. BOX 790
HARRISON, ARK. 72601

FEROLD G. AREND
WAL-MART STORES
P.O. BOX 116
BENTONVILLE, ARK. 72712

E.G. HEINRICH
CITATION MFG.
HIGHWAY 59 SOUTH
SILOAM SPRINGS, ARK. 72761

DON TYSON
TYSON FOODS
2210 W. OAKLAWN DR.
SPRINGDALE, ARK. 72764

R.A. YOUNG III
ARKANSAS BEST
1000 S. 21ST ST.
FORT SMITH, ARK. 72901

LARRY L. FLOCKS
LEISURE LODGES
P.O. BOX 1628
FORT SMITH, ARK. 72901

J.M. YANTIS
MID-AMERICA IND.
900 ROGERS AVE.
FORT SMITH, ARK. 72901

JOHN M. YANTIS
PARTS IND.
900 ROGERS AVE.
FORT SMITH, ARK. 72901

BOB L. MARSELL
PERDUE HOUSING IND.
215 S. FIRST
CHICASHA, OKLAHOMA 73018

D.R. ABEL
SENTRY MFG.
CRYSTAL PARK
CHICKASHA, OK. 73018

LOYD G. DORSETT
DORSETT ED. SYSTEMS
GOLDSBY AIRPORT
NORMAN, OK. 73069

N.A. PIERSON
NATURIZER
P.O. BOX 755
NORMAN, OK. 73069

J.W. MASON
AMAREX
P.O. BOX 1678
OKLAHOMA,CITY, OK. 73101

THOMAS W. DI ZEREGA
APCO OIL
P.O. BOX 1841
OKLAHOMA CITY, OK. 73101

BILL SWISHER
CMI CORP.
P.O. BOX 1985
OAKLAHOMA CITY, OK. 73101

JACK E. GOLSEN
LSB IND.
P.O. BOX 1149
OKLAHOMA CITY, OK. 73101

H. DALE JORDAN
SOUTHWEST FACTORIES
P.O. BOX 773
OKLAHOMA CITY, OK. 73101

R. TOLBERT III
ANTA
2400 FIRST NATIONAL CENTER W.
OKLAHOMA CITY, OK. 73102

JOHN W. NICHOLS
CALVERT-MID-AMERICA
1120 LIBERTY BANK BLDG.
OKLAHOMA CITY, OK. 73102

J.B. CRAWLEY
CONSOLIDATED PROD.
HIGHTOWER BLDG.
OKLAHOMA CITY, OK. 73102

T.K. HENDRICK
HADSON OHIO OIL
1125 FIDELITY PLAZA
OKLAHOMA CITY, OK. 73102

J.V. SMITH
SCRIVNER
1400 1ST. NATL. CENTER
OKLAHOMA CITY, OK. 73102

V.C. BRATTON
CENTRAL DAIRY PRODUCTS
101 E. MAIN ST.
OKLAHOMA CITY, OK. 73104

KENNETH J. GRIGGY
WILSON & CO.
4545 N. LINCOLN BLVD.
OKLAHOMA CITY, OK. 73105

HERB MEE JR.
BEARD OIL
2000 CLASSEN BLDG. STE.200
OKLAHOMA CITY,OK. 73106

F.H. STROTHMANN
CAP CORP.
3000 LIBERTY TOWER
OKAHOMA CITY, OK. 73107

JOHN MONSOUR
MAJOR BRANDS
4601 N.W. 3-BX. 75247
OKLAHOMA CITY, OK. 73107

MARVIN A. ASLEFELD
OKLAHOMA BRICK
4300 N.W. 10TH ST.
OKLAHOMA CITY, OK. 73107

W.J. PHILLIPS
PHIL - GOOD PROD.
3500 WEST RENO AVE.
OKLAHOMA,CITY, OK. 73107

M.S. LEE
LEE WAY MOTOR FREIGHT
P.O. BOX 82488
OKLAHOMA CITY, OK. 73108

M.D. JIROUS
SONIC IND.
6800 N. BRYANT ST.
OKLAHOMA CITY, OK. 73111

J.H. SHERBURN
ACADEMY COMPUTING
2601 N.W. EXPRESSWAY STE. 120
OKLAHOMA CITY, OK. 73112

T.C. FOWLER
SENECA OIL
3013 N.W. 59
OKLAHOMA CITY, OK. 73112

GEORGE PLATT
TEXAS INTL. CO.
3545 N.W. 58TH.
OKLAHOMA CITY, OK. 73112

JIM L. HURLEY
TIERCO
P.O. BOX 12702
OKLAHOMA CITY, OK. 73112

A.D. FRESHOUR
WOODS PETROLEUM
500-3555 N.W. 58TH. ST.
OKLAHOMA CITY, OK. 73112

H.F. SCHNITTGER
COMPUTER CONGENERICS
7301 N. BROADWAY STE. 225
OKLAHOMA CITY, OK. 73116

ALLEN G. POPPING
BENHAM-BLAIR & AFFILIATES
6323 N.W. GRAND BLVD.
OKLAHOMA,CITY, OK. 73118

ROBERT J. COLLINS
EASON OIL
P.O. BOX 9755
OKLAHOMA CITY, OK. 73118

GERALD G. BARTON
LANDMARK LAND
P.O. BOX 18901
OKLAHOMA CITY, OK. 73118

ROY E. TOWNSDIN
WOODS CORP.
4900 N. SANTA FE, BX. 18547
OKLAHOMA CITY, OK. 73118

E.J. HARDEBECK
TECOMA MINES
3004 ROBIN RIDGE RD.
OKLAHOMA CITY, OK. 73120

LEO MAXWELL
AMERICAN DYNAMIC IND.
530 S. BROADWAY
OKLAHOMA CITY, OK. 73125

C. WAYNE LITCHFIELD
PLANNED CREDIT
P.O. BOX 25276
OKALAHOMA CITY, OK. 73125

DOUGLAS G. FIFE
FIFE CORP.
P.O. BOX 26508
OKLAHOMA CITY, OK. 73126

R.D. HARRISON
FLEMING CO.
P.O. BOX 26647
OKLAHOMA CITY, OK. 73126

FLOYD BURNS
RENDEZVOUS TRAILS
12115 NORTHEAST EXPRESSWAY
OKLAHOMA CITY, OK. 73131

MAL GREENBERG
SERVICE COMPUTER
4500 S.E. 59TH ST.
OKLAHOMA CITY, OK. 73135

ROY BUTLER
NOBLE AFFILIATES
P.O. BOX 1967
ARDMORE, OK. 73401

HARRIS S. SMITH
TEXO OIL
P.O. BOX 308
ARDMORE, OK. 73401

SAM STONER
CUSTER CHANNEL WING
604 N. GRAND
ENID, OK. 73701

DONALD E. ADAMS
ADAMS HARD FACING
802 6TH. ST. N.E.
GUYON, OK. 73942

W.C. DOUCE
PHILLIPS PETROLEUM
18 PHILLIPS BLDG.
BARTLESVILLE, OK. 74004

JAMES E. BEEBE
BRADEN IND.
P.O. BOX 206
BROKEN ARROW, OK. 74012

DEAN B. KNIGHT
KNIGHT IND.
P.O. BOX 348
BROKEN ARROW, OK. 74012

A.A. KAMINSHINE
ELECTRONIC SYSTEMS
CUSHING, OK. 74023

M.O. MORRISON
AMERICAN WIND TURBINE
1016 E. AIRPORT RD.
STILLWATER, OK. 74074

ROBERT G. WALKER
KIN-ARK CORP.
P.O. BOX 1499
TULSA, OK. 74101

S.J. JATRAS
TELEX CORP.
6422 E. 41ST ST.
TULSA, OK. 74101

GENE W. SCHNEIDER
UNITED CABLE TV.
P.O. BOX 3423
TULSA, OK. 74101

H.E. RORSCHACH
COLONIAL ROYALTIES
KENNEDY BLDG.
TULSA, OK. 74103

BEN VOTH
G.F. IND.
2001 NATL. BANK OF TULSA
TULSA, OK. 74103

O. STROTHER SIMPSON
HOME STAKE ROYALTY
507 PHILTOWER BLDG.
TULSA, OK. 74103

R.L. PARKER
PARKER DRILLING
518 NATL. BANK OF TULSA
TULSA, OK. 74103

CHARLES E. THORTON
READING & BATES OFFSHORE
3800 FIRST PL.
TULSA, OK. 74103

BILL B. HILL
ED. DEVELOPMENT
4920 S. LEWIS
TULSA. OK. 74105

JERRY ENKICH
GENIE OIL & GAS
3015 E. SKELLY DR. STE. 200
TULSA, OK. 74105

JOSEPH R. ROSS
ROSS AVIATION
RIVERSIDE AIRPORT RTE.5
TULSA, OK. 74107

JOHN C. MC GRATH
CENTURY GEOPHYSICAL
P.O. BOX 15828
TULSA, OK. 74112

W.H. HELMERICH III
HELMERICH & PAYNE
1579 E. 21ST ST.
TULSA, OK. 74114

JAMES R. FIRESTONE
AIR CARGO
P.O. BOX 15630
TULSA, OKLA. 74115

J.D. METCALFE
STANDARD IND.
P.O. BOX 15670
TULSA, OK. 74115

D.M. FLYNN
FLYNN ENERGY
1602 FOURTH NATL. BANK. BLDG.
TULSA, OK. 74119

H.F. KINCAID
SOUTHLAND ENERGY
1201 PETROLEUM CLUB BLDG.
TULSA, OK. 74119

R.L. SCHULER
LOCKE-SCHULER
5200 S. HARVARD STE. 5D
TULSA, OK. 74135

JAMES M. DAVIS
PACER PHOENIX
3902 E. 51ST ST. STE. 600
TULSA, OK. 74135

B.G. WEBER
SELCO
4107 S. YALE
TULSA, OK. 74135

ROY W. WINTERS
TERRA RESOURCES
5416 S. YALE AVE. STE. 300
TULSA, OK. 74135

J.D. MC INTOSH
ATKINS & MERRILL
7700 E. 38TH ST.
TULSA, OK. 74145

J.M SCHMIDT
FLORAFAX INTL.
4219 S. MEMORIAL DR. BX. 45745
TULSA, OK. 74145

ROBERT L. ZELIGSON
CCI MARQUARDT
P.O. BOX 51191
TULSA, OK. 74151

W.H. JAMES JR.
STERLING OIL
P.O. BOX 52484
TULSA, OK. 74152

O.W. COBURN
COBURN OPTICAL IND.
1701 S. CHEROKEE
MUSKOGEE,OK. 74401

K. GEORGE PAGANIS
MINNEHOMA FINANCIAL
1901 N. SHERIDAN R.D BX. 51168
TULSA, OK. 74151

J. PRESTON AMMON
ELFAB CORP.
762 WILEY POST RD.
ADDISON, TEXAS 75001

H.H. AIKEN
GEN. COMPUTER
P.O. BOX 128
ADSISON, TEXAS 75001

JACK J. BOOTH
BOOTH INC.
1725 SANDY LAKE RD.
CARROLLTON, TEXAS 75006

L.J. SEVIN
MOSTEK
1215 W. CROSBY RD.
CARROLLTON, TX. 75006

LEWIS C. PAGE
GEN. ELECTRODYNAMICS
4430 FOREST LANE
GARLAND, TX. 75040

NICHOLAS NADOLSKY
MICROPAC IND.
905 E. WALNUT
GARLAND,TX. 75040

GREGG W. YOUNG
DIGITAL APPLICATIONS
2519 NATL. DR.
GARLAND, TX. 75041

JERRY O. ARMSTRONG
SALEM NTL. CORP.
3837 DIVIDEND ST.
GARLAND , TX. 75041

T. YANAGISAWA
VARO
O.O. BOX 1567
GARLAND, TX. 75041

W.M. CRAMER
SEACO COMPUTER
410 KIRBY ST.
GARLAND, TX. 75042

J.H. ALLEN
MODULAR AMBULANCE
1801 S. GREAT SOUTHWEST PKY.
GRAND PRAIRIE, TX. 75050

GEORGE BREMER JR.
TEXSTAR COPR.
P.O. BOX 685
GRAND PRAIRIE, TX. 75050

MICHAEL R. CORBOY
TOCOM
33o1 ROYALTY ROW
IRVING, TX. 75060

B.J. MEREDITH
DOCUTEL CORP.
2619 E. GRAUWYLER RD.
IRVING, TEXAS 75061

R.C. DAWE
MICROTRON IND.
P.O. BOX 3128
IRVING, TX. 75061

I.L. LEVY
NATL. CHEM. CORP.
P.O. BOX 217
IRVING, TX. 75061

JOHN L. COCKRILL
ALTEC
FIRST BANK& TRUST BLDG.
RICHARDSON,TX. 75080

JAMES A. LEIDICH
CHILDREN'S WORLD
408 S. CENTRAL EXPRESSWAY
RICHARDSON, TEXAS 75080

C.W. GRAY
REPUBLIC ALUMINUM CO.
708 GAYLEWOOD DR.
RICHARDSON, TX. 75080

G. WARD PAXTON JR.
SPECTRONICS
830 E. ARAPAHO RD.
RICHARDSON, TX. 75080

KENNETH A. McCRADY
ENNIS BUSINESS FORMS
107 N. SHERMAN ST.
ENNIS, TX. 75119

FRANK J. FRECH
NATL. CARE CENTERS
2231 HIGHWAY 80 , E.
MESQUITE, TX. 75149

J.A. CRICHTON
ARABIAN SHIELD DEVELOPMENT
900 EMPIRE LIFE BLDG.
DALLAS, TX. 75201

N.C. MILLER
BLUE CROWN
2900 FIDELITY UNION TOWER
DALLAS, TX. 75201

PAUL R. SEEGERS
CENTEX
4600 REPUBLIC NTL. BANK TOWER
DALLAS, TEXAS 75201

O.R. PRUITT
CHAMPION WINKLER OIL
1604 TOWER PETROLEUM BLDG.
DALLAS, TEXAS 75201

R. MAURICE STEWART
CHEM. EXPRESS.
1530 MAINST.
DALLAS, TX. 75201

CLAYTON E. NILES
COMM. IND.
511 N. AKARD ST.
DALLAS, TX. 75201

L.F. CORRIGAN
CORRIGAN JORDAN
1700 -211 N. ERVAY
DALLAS, TX. 75201

NORMAN C. MILLER
DELHI INTL. OIL
2900 FIDELITY UNION TOWER
DALLAS, TX. 75201

W.C. MC CORD
ENSERCH
301 S. HARDWOOD ST.
DALLAS, TX. 75201

LAMAR NORSWORTHY
HOLLY
2001 BRYAN TOWERS
DALLAS, TX. 75201

J.W. GRAY
LANDA IND.
2230 REPUBLIC BANK TOWER
DALLAS, TX. 75201

R.O. MC DONALD
PLANET OIL
1200 MERCANTILE BANK BLDG.
DALLAS, TEXAS 75201

ASHLEY H. PRIDDY
SABINE
MERCANTILE BANK BLDG.
DALLAS, TX. 75201

EDWIN L. COX
SEDCO
1901 N. AKARD
DALLAS, TX. 75201

JACK D. KNOX
SUMMIT ENERGY
1925 MERCANTILE DALLAS BLDG.
DALLAS, TX. 75201

J.E. UPFIELD
TEMTEX IND.
1516 LTV TOWER
DALLAS, TX. 75201

WILLIAM L. HUTCHINSON
TEXAS OIL
2520 FIDELITY UNION TOWER
DALLAS, TX. 75201

J.F. MC KINNEY
TYLER CORP.
SOUTHLAND CENTER
DALLAS, TX. 75201

HERMAN MARCUS
HERMAN MARCUS INC.
1709 N. MARKET ST.
DALLAS, TX. 75202

CHARLES P. ABERG
LANE WOOD
2020 DAVIS BLDG.
DALLAS, TEXAS 75202

NORMAN W. CAMPBELL
TRACY- LOCKE CO.
1407 MAIN ST.
DALLAS, TX. 75202

JOE CLICKMAN
MARGO'S LA MODE INC.
3909 LIVE OAK
DALLAS, TX. 75204

F.W. COLE
AMCO
521 MEADOWS BLDG.
DALLAS, TX. 75206

R.J. BROMELL
AUTOMATIC DRILLING MACH.
5646 MILTON AVE.
DALLAS, TX. 75206

EMIL V. HEGYI
BARUCH-FOSTER CORP.
4925 GREENVILLE AVE. #1160
DALLAS, TEXAS 75206

DONALD G. THOMASON
BONANZA INTL. INC.
1000 COMPBELL CENTRE
DALLAS, TX. 75206

WHEELER M. SEARS
CIMMARRON
1050 ONE ENERGY SQ.
DALLAS, TX. 75206

DAN M. KRAUSSE
EARTH RESOURCES
1200 ONE ENERGY SQ.
DALLAS, TX. 75206

E.E. MASON
ENERGY SOURCES
4925 GREENVILLE AVE.
DALLAS, TX. 75206

JACK CORMAN
FORUM CO.
144 MEADOWS BLDG.
DALLAS, TX. 75206

WILLIAM P. BARNES
GENERAL AMERICAN OIL
MEADOWS BLDG.
DALLAS, TX. 75206

JAMES R. REESE
HYDCO
1400 EXPRESSWAY TOWER
DALLAS, TX. 75206

W.L. KING
k-B IND.
605 MEADOWS BLDG.
DALLAS, TX. 75206

MAX W. WOODARD
LEAR PETROLEUM
950 ONE ENERGY SQ.
DALLAS,TX. 75206

C.E. RAMSEY JR.
MAY PETROLEUM
ONE ENERGY SQ. STE. 1000
DALLAS, TX. 75206

A.M. WIEDERKEHR
SOUTHERN UNION PROD.
8350 N. CENTRAL EXPRESSWAY
DALLAS, TX. 75206

JACK CORMAN
SURVEYOR CO.
144 THE MEADOWS BLDG.
DALLAS, TX. 75206

W.I. LEE
TRITON OIL & GAS
4925 GREENVILLE AVE.
DALLAS, TX. 75206

EDGAR O. WELLER
FROZEN FOOD EXPRESS IND.
318 CADIZ ST.
DALLAS, TX. 75207

J.W. JASPERSON
GEN. AUTOMOTIVE PARTS.
4600 HARRY HINES BLDG. BOX 10506
DALLAS, TX. 17207

V.L. EZELL
GIFFEN IND.
P.O. BOX 10821
DALLAS, TX. 75207

GEORGE N. SCHOONOVER
KING OPTICAL
1403 SLOCUM
DALLAS, TX. 75207

CLOYCE K. BOX
OKC
1949 N. STEMMONS FREEWAY
DALLAS, TX. 75207

F.J. DYKE JR.
SMC IND.
131 HOWELL ST.
DALLAS, TX. 75207

ME. MOORE
TCO IND.
315 CONTINENTAL AVE.
DALLAS, TX. 75207

W. RAY WALLACE
TRINITY IND.
4001 IRVING BLVD.
DALLAS, TX. 75207

LOUIS J. MAHER
TRANS-NATL. LEASING.
P.O. BOX 7246
DALLAS, TEXAS 75209

DONALD A. SILLERS JR.
PEERLESS MFG.
P.O. BOX 20657
DALLAS, TX. 75220

C.B. LANE
CAMPBELL TAGGART
P.O. BOX 2640
DALLAS, TX. 75221

C.E. MERRITT
COMMERCIAL METALS
P.O. BOX 1046
DALLAS, TX. 75221

V.A. SMITH
CHILTON
2819 N. FITZHURN AVE.
DALLAS, TEXAS 75221

JAMES B. LENDRUM
GENERAL PORTLAND
P.O. BOX 324
DALLAS, TX. 75221

HENRY NEUHOFF III
NEUHOFF BROS.
P.O. BOX 2338
DALLAS, TX. 75221

JOHN F. KNIGHT
REPUBLIC FINANCIAL
P.O. BOX 3000
DALLAS, TX. 75221

O MAX MONTIGOMERY
REPUBLIC HOUSING
P.O. BOX 750
DALLAS, TX. 75221

DONALD ZALE
ZALE CORP.
BOX 2219
DALLAS, TEXAS 75221

JOHN W. DIXON
E-SYSTEMS INC.
P.O. BOX 6030
DALLAS, TX. 75222

F.J. SPILLMAN
THE PIZZA INN
2930 STEMMONS FREEWAY
DALLAS, TX. 75222

J. RODNEY REESE
RECOGNITION EQUIPMENT
P.O. BOX 22307
DALLAS, TX. 75222

HOWARD M. MEYERS
RSR CORP
2823 N. WESTMORELAND
DALLAS, TX. 75222

DAN STRICKLIN
SHOP RITE FOODS
P.O. BOX 5055
DALLAS, TX. 75222

WILLIAM A. ROTH
SPACE CORP.
P.O. BOX 5175
DALLAS, TX. 75222

NORMAN BRINKER
STEAK & ALE RESTAURANTS
P.O. BOX 22102
DALLAS, TX. 75222

CHARLES J. WYLY, JR.
WYLY CORP.
P.O. BOX 6228
DALLAS, TX. 75222

ROBERT McKEE, III
WORLDCOM, INC.
11181 HARRY HINES BLVD.
DALLAS, TX. 75224

E.R. SLAUGHTER, JR.
SLAUGHTER BROS.
P.O. BOX 12148
DALLAS, TX. 75225

SHERMAN MARKMAN
TEXAS INT'L. EXPORT CO.
8333 DOUGLAS AVE.
DALLAS, TX. 75225

C.R. JOSEPHS
ALD INC.
4301 S. FITZHUGH
DALLAS, TX. 75226

WILSON C. DRIGGS
DALLAS TRANSIT
101 N. PEAK
DALLAS, TX. 75226

HOWARD B. WOLF
HOWARD B. WOLF, INC.
3809 PARRY AVE.
DALLAS, TX. 75226

JAMES K. DEVLIN
CANTERFONE COMM. CORP.
2639 WALNUT HILL LN.
DALLAS, TX. 75229

JOHN RANDOLPH
DAIRY QUEEN STORES
11261 SHADY TRAIL
DALLAS, TX. 75229

ALAN M. WEISS
INCOM, INC.
10005 MEADOWBROOK
DALLAS, TX. 75229

T.W. HANLEY
MAGNOLIA CHEMICAL CO.
2646 RODNEY LN.
DALLAS, TX. 75229

LEE POSEY
REDMAN INDS.
2550 WALNUT HILL LN.
DALLAS, TX. 75229

E.T. SUMMERS
SUMMERS ELECTRIC
P.O. BOX 20233
DALLAS, TX. 75229

H.C. SIMMONS
CONTREN CORP.
12880 HILLCREST
DALLAS, TX. 75230

M.A. HART III
ELECTRONIC DATA SYSTEMS
7171 FOREST LN.
DALLAS, TX. 75230

J.G. MAYNARD
MAYNARD OIL CO.
12900 PRESTON RD.
DALLAS, TX. 75230

L.D. WEBSTER
WHITEHALL CORP.
P.O. BOX 30128
DALLAS, TX. 75230

E.A. TRAPP
HALL-MARK ELECTRONICS
9333 FOREST LN.
DALLAS, TX. 75231

GUY M. FOOTE
WYLAIN INC.
10400 N. CENTRAL EXPRESSWAY
DALLAS, TX. 75231

GILBERT CUELLAR
EL CHICO CORP.
P.O. BOX 34025
DALLAS, TX. 75234

BYRON W. STUCKEY
NAT'L. DATA COMM.
2997 LBJ FREEWAY
DALLAS, TX. 75234

DOUGLAS OWEN BROWN
OWEN LABS
3737 BELT LINE RD.
DALLAS, TX. 75234

EDWARD D. MILLER, JR.
RODEWAY INNS OF AMERICA
P.O. BOX 34736
DALLAS, TX. 75234

GIFFORD K. JOHNSON
AMERICAN BIOMEDICAL CORP.
1525 VICEROY, SUITE 300
DALLAS, TX. 75235

M.H. EARP
BRITCO, INC.
P.O. BOX 35313
DALLAS, TX. 75235

C.P. WALLACE
CENTRAL ENERGY
2102 PROCTOR ST.
DALLAS, TX. 75235

BILLY BOB ELKINS
ELKINS INSTITUTE, INC.
2727 INWOOD RD.
DALLAS, TX. 75235

R.D. BUCKNER
SAM P. WALLACE
P.O. BOX 35828
DALLAS, TX. 75235

EDUARDO R. REDLHAMMER
MULTI-AMP CORP
4271 BRONZE WAY
DALLAS, TX. 75237

THOMAS L. ANDERSON
ANDERSON INDS.
13601 PRESTON RD.

JACK W. EVANS
COLLUM CO'S.
14303 INWOOD RD.
DALLAS, TX. 75240

EUGENE E. NEARBURG
GENERAL EXPLORATION
4219 SIGMA RD.
DALLAS, TX. 75240

JAMES R. MOFFETT
MC MORAN EXPLORATION
601 CARILLON TOWER EAST
DALLAS, TX. 75240

W.P. WILLIAMSON
OAKMONT MARINE
13740 MIDWAY RD.
DALLAS, TX. 75240

R.C. HAUGH
OVERHEAD DOOR
6250 LBJ FREEWAY
DALLAS, TX. 75240

RUSSELL A. STEPHENS
UNIVERSAL RESOURCES
1000 CARILLON TOWER E.
DALLAS, TX. 75240

RALEIG WRIGHT
ACS INVESTORS
1171 EMPIRE CENTRAL
DALLAS, TX. 75247

DONALD L. ROGERS
BURGESS IND.
P.O. BOX 47146
DALLAS, TX. 75247

H.P. CAMPBELL
CAMPBELL MFG.
1262 VICEROY DR.
DALLAS, TX. 75247

J.T. VERDESCA
COMPUTER DIMENSIONS
8585 N. STEMMONS FWY. STE.501
DALLAS, TEXAS 75247

M.F. SIVINSKI
COMPUTER TECHNOLOGY
7200 STEMMONS FREEWAY
DALLAS, TEXAS 75247

ROBERT SCHMIDT
CONSOLIDATED ACCESSORIES
3140 IRVING BLVD.
DALLAS, TX. 75247

JOHN D. WISENBAKER
CORE LABORATORIES
7501 STEMMONS FREEWAY
DALLAS, TX. 75247

T.E. BEACH
FINE INC.
1555 REGAL ROW
DALLAS,TX. 75247

HUMBERT C. COZZA JR.
CARDNER-DENVER
8585 STEMMONS FREEWAY
DALLAS, TX. 75247

J.R. HILL JR.
GIFFORD-HILL
8435 STEMMONS FREEWAY
DALLAS, TX. 75247

R.R. ROGERS
MARY KAY COSMETICS
8900 CARPENTER FREEWAY
DALLAS, TX. 75247

J.D. MILLER
MEDICAL COMPUTER
8585 N. STEMMONS FREEWAY
DALLAS, TX. 75247

JOHN B. TUTHILL
PIONEER TEXAS
1165 EMPIRE CENTRAL PL.
DALLAS, TX. 75247

R. BURKE STANDARD
RIVERSIDE PRESS
4901 WOODALL ST.
DALLAS, TX. 75247

C.C. HOPPER
SOUTHWESTERN DRUG
8000 JOHN W. CARPENTER FREEWAY
DALLAS, TX. 75247

RICHARD L. KOLLINGER
SUE ANN
1130 INWOOD
DALLAS, TX. 75247

D.H. MEENACH
SUPERIOR FOODS
9001 CHANCELLOR ST.
DALLAS, TX. 75247

ROBERT D. ROGERS
TEXAS IND.
8100 CARPENTER FREEWAY
DALLAS, TX. 75247

T.J. NORRIS
TRANSDATA
P.O. BOX 47762
DALLAS, TX. 75247

W.L. LINDGREN
OMEGA - ALPHA
P.O. BOX 50046
DALLAS, TX. 75250

JASPER S. HOWARD
HOWARD DISCOUNT CENTERS
SUMMERHILL PARK DR.
TEXARKANA, TX. 75501

H.T. WELLMAN
WELLMAN IND.
P.O. BOX 3144
LONGVIEW, TX. 75601

BURKE MATHES JR.
CURTIS MATHES
P.O. BOX 151
ATHENS, TX. 75751

JOE C. DENMAN JR.
TEMPLE IND.
101 N. FIRST, P.O. DRAWER N.
DIBOLL, TX. 75941

H.E. HARTON
FLORENCE MILLER COSMETICS
2016 E. RANDAL MILL RD.
ARLINGTON, TX. 76011

BRUCE C. JUELL
GREAT SOUTHWEST
P.O. BOX 5555
ARLINGTON, TX. 76011

J.M. HILL
RANGAIRE CORP.
CLEBURNE, TX. 76031

GEORGE S. WALLS JR.
WALLS IND.
1905 N. MAIN ST.
CLEBURNE, TX. 76031

L.C. MARTIN
AZTEC MFG.
P.O. BOX 668
CROWLEY, TX. 76036

E.P. MILES JR.
ECC
1010 PAMELA DR.
EULESS, TX. 76039

G.A. JAGGERS
GRAHAM MAGNETICS
GRAHAM, TX. 76046

EDGAR H. SCHOLLMAIER
ALCON LABS.
P.O. BOX 1959
FORT WORTH, TX. 76101

BILL N. NEWMAN
BEKLAND RESOURCES
P.O. BOX 2905
FORT WORTH, TX. 76101

WILLIAM C. O'NEIL
BIOMEDICAL RESOURCES
777 ROSEDALE, BX. 2547
FT. WORTH, TX. 76101

JACK N. GREENMAN
CHICKASHA COTTON OIL
P.O. BOX 511
FORT WORTH, TX. 76101

J.N. GREENMAN
FLOUR MILLS OF AMERICA
2109 S. MAIN ST.
FORT WORTH, TX. 76101

S.L. MALONE
FORT WORTH STEEL
3600 MC CART ST.
FORT WORTH, TX. 76101

H.D. OWEN
GEARHART-OWEN IND.
SOUTH EXPRESSWAY & EVERMAN RD.
FORT WORTH, TX. 76101

JACK B. BAUGHN
GO INC.
BOX 1286
FORT WORTH, TX. 76101

W.R. GLOVER
HILLCREST CARPETS
P.O. BOX 2905
FORT WORTH, TX. 76101

JERRY L. BROWNLEE
JUSTIN IND.
2821 W. 7TH. AVE. BOX 425
FORT WORTH, TX. 76101

W.R. COWAN
LITTLE DUDE TRAILER
P.O. BOX 4513
FORT WORTH, TX. 76101

J.N. GREENMAN
MFG. DATA SYSTEMS
2109 S. MAIN ST.
FORT WORTH, TX. 76101

B.G. CORBETT
ROBINTECH
P.O. BOX 2342
FORTWORTH, TX. 76101

WALLACE C. JAY
TEXAS CONSUMER FINANCE
P.O. BOX 1290
FORT WORTH, TX. 76101

ROY T. RIMMER
ACC INDS.
1300 SUMMIT AVE.
FORT WORTH, TX. 76102

J.K. MONTGOMERY
BROOKS INT'L. INC.
P.O. BOX 17026
FT. WORTH, TX. 76102

R.D. WOOFTER
COMMUNITY PUBLIC SERVICE
501 W. 6TH
FORT WORTH, TX. 76102

B.E. RAY
ENERGY RESOURCES
1102 EXECUTIVE PLAZA BLDG.
FORT WORTH, TX. 76102

KENNETH McCLAIN
GEO-SEARCH
529 FT. WORTH NAT'L. BANK
FORT WORTH, TX. 76102

KENNETH M. McCLAIN
GLOBAL GAS
2092 FORT WORTH NAT'L. BLDG
FORT WORTH, TX. 76102

LUTHER A. HENDERSON
PIER 1 IMPORTS
2520 W. FREEWAY
FORT WORTH, TX. 76102

B.J. KELLENBERGER
SHENANDOAH OIL CORP.
COMMERCE BLDG.
FORT WORTH, TX. 76102

L.A. HENDERSON
TRINITY TRADE
2520 W. FREEWAY
FORT WORTH, TX. 76102

ROBERT R. LOWDON
STAFFORD-LOWDON
1114 W. DAGGETT ST.
FORT WORTH, TX. 76107

JOHN A. WILSON
TANDY CORP.
2727 W. 7TH ST.
FORT WORTH, TX. 76107

JOHN S. HOWELL
HOWELL INSTRUMENTS
3479 W. VICKERY BLVD.
FORT WORTH, TX. 76107

M.H. SPRINKS, SR.
SPRINKS INDS.
P.O. BOX 11099
FORT WORTH, TX. 76110

HOLLIS TAYLOR
PAMEX FOODS
3500 NOBLE AVE
FORT WORTH, TX. 76111

T.C. DAVIS
STRATOFLEX
220 ROBERTS CUT-OFF
FORT WORTH, TX. 76114

JAMES E. FREEMAN
SCOTTISH INNS OF TEXAS
8345 W. FREEWAY
FORT WORTH, TX. 76116

R.E. KELLERMAN
TEXAS CRUDE OIL
P.O. BOX 12405
FORT WORTH, TX. 76116

F.A. ATTAYA
SILVER MONARCH MINES
P.O. BOX 16548
FORT WORTH, TX. 76133

IRVING N. LEVINE
LOMA INDS.
P.O. BOX 40300
FORT WORTH, TX. 76140

MARVIN SMALL
GALAXY OIL
918 LAMAR ST.
WICHITA FALLS, TX. 76301

R.J. MORAN
MORAN BROS.
1000 PETROLEUM BLDG.
WICHITA FALLS, TX. 76301

B.D. WOODY
LANCHART INDS.
P.O. BOX 2405
WICHITA FALLS, TX. 76307

BARRY B. DONNELL
TOWN & COUNTRY MOBILE HOMES
P.O. BOX 5005
WICHITA FALLS, TX. 76307

ROBERT B. KAMON
BLACK GIANT OIL
1304 AVENUE L
CISCO, TX. 76437

RICHARD F. HARE
INT'L. ROYALTY & OIL
1304 AVENUE L
CISCO, TX. 76437

BONNER HARDEGREE
ARTCO-BELL CORP.
P.O. BOX 608
TEMPLE, TX. 76501

GILBERT B. BOSSE
GRIGGS EQUIPMENT
804 E. 4TH
BELTON, TX. 76513

SAM V. ROCHELLE
MID-TEXAS COMMUNICATIONS
P.O. BOX 1150
KILLEEN, TX. 76541

PAUL J. MEYER
SUCCESS MOTIVATION INST.
107 LAKE AIR CENTER EAST
WACO, TX. 76710

E.P. McNAMARA
MONARCH TILE MFG.
P.O. BOX 2041
SAN ANGELO, TX. 76901

FRANK M. POOL
POOL CO.
P.O. BOX 1940
SAN ANGELO, TX. 76901

BRUCE L. FLY
TUCKER DRILLING
P.O. BOX 1876, PETROLEUM BLDG.
SAN ANGELO, TX. 76901

W. FENTON GUINEE
ANDERSON CLAYTON & CO.
P.O. BOX 2538
HOUSTON, TX. 77001

ANTHONY J.A. BRYAN
CAMERON IRON WORKS
P.O. BOX 1212
HOUSTON, TX. 77001

HERSCHEL G. MALTZ
CENTURY PAPERS
P.O. BOX 1908
HOUSTON, TX. 77001

CAREY CRUTCHER
CRUTCHER RESOURCES
P.O. BOX 3227
HOUSTON, TX. 77001

JACKSON C. HINDS
ENTEX, INC.
P.O. BOX 2628
HOUSTON, TX. 77001

WAYNE CRISMAN
FALCON SEABOARD
P.O. BOX 3348
HOUSTON, TX. 77001

D.L. GOLDY
INTERNATIONAL SYSTEMS
P.O. BOX 2589
HOUSTON, TX. 77001

MILTON E. ELIOT
MOSHER STEEL CO.
P.O. BOX 1579
HOUSTON, TX. 77001

J.M. COURTNEY
PEARSALL CHEMICAL
P.O. BOX 437
HOUSTON, TX. 77001

ISRAEL PROLER
PROLER INT'L.
P.O. BOX 286
HOUSTON, TX. 77001

JOHN C. NELSON
UNITED ENERGY RESOURCES
700 MILAM ST., BOX 1478
HOUSTON, TX. 77001

STANFORD ALEXANDER
WEINGARTEN REALTY
P.O. BOX 1698
HOUSTON, TX. 77001

A.J. LAYDEN
ALLRIGHT AUTO PARTS
1625 ESPENSON BLDG.
HOUSTON, TX. 77002

PAUL R. COLE
AUSTRAL OIL CO.
800 BELL HUMBLE BLDG.
HOUSTON, TX. 77002

C. FRED CHAMBERS
C & K PETROLEUM
#2 HOUSTON CENTER, STE. 2828
HOUSTON, TX. 77002

ROBERT CIZIK
COOPER INDS.
2 HOUSTON CENTER, #2700
HOUSTON, TX. 77002

C.H. PASEUR
CRS DESIGN ASSOCS.
1100 MILAM ST.
HOUSTON, TX. 77002

HARRY B. GORDON
GORDON JEWELRY
820 FANNIN ST.
HOUSTON, TX. 77002

ROBERT H. ALLEN
GULF RESOURCES & CHEMICAL
2125 TENNESSEE BLDG.
HOUSTON, TX. 77002

J.K. DOZIER
HOUSTON TERMINAL WAREHOUSE
701 N? JACINTO ST.
HOUSTON, TX. 77002

PAUL N. HOWELL
HOWELL CORP.
800 HOISTON NATURAL GAS BLDG.
HOUSTON, TX. 77002

IRVING WOLF
INEXCO OIL
1100 MILAM, STE. 1900
HOUSTON, TX. 77002

GEORGE P. MITCHELL
MITCHELL ENERGY & DEVLPT.
ONE SHELL PLAZA
HOUSTON, TX. 77002

R.M. STEWART
PETROLEUM RESERVES
2700 HUMBLE BLDG.
HOUSTON, TX. 77002

CHARLES H. CARMOUCHE
SERNCO, INC.
1200 TRAVIS, STE. 830
HOUSTON, TX. 77002

J.R. PARTEN
SEVEN J STOCK FARM INC.
1603 BANK OF S.W. BLDG.
HOUSTON, TX. 77002

W.S. CHADWICK
SOUTHDOWN, INC.
950 TENNECO BLDG.
HOUSTON, TX. 77002

MELVIN E. KURTH, JR.
SOUTHLAND PAPER MILLS
1111 FANNIN
HOUSTON, TX. 77002

C.J. STEWART, II
STEWART & STEVENSON SVCS.
1719 PRESTON AVE.
HOUSTON, TX. 77002

GENE BIDDLE
STRATFORD OF TEXAS
950 OENNZOIL PLAZA, S. TOWER
HOUSTON, TX. 77002

JOHN F. WOODHOUSE
SYSCO CORP.
1300 MAIN ST.
HOUSTON, TX. 77002

JOHN W. THOMSON
THOMSON INDS. LTD.
1100 MILAM BLDG. STE. 3080
HOUSTON, TX. 77002

STORMY F. SMITH
TRANSOCEAN OIL CO.
1111 FANNIN ST.
HOUSTON, TX. 77002

EVERETT HANLON
FAIRLANE INDS.
419 DOWLING
HOUSTON, TX. 77003

HARRY E. BLAIR JR.
COMPUTER INSTALLATIONS
5514 CAROLINE ST.
HOUSTON, TX. 77004

V.H. VAN HORN
NATIONAL CONVESCIENCE
3200 TRAVIS ST.
HOUSTON, TX. 77006

NATHAN M. AVERY
GALVESTON-HOUSTON CO.
1818 MEMORIAL
HOUSTON, TX. 77007

JAMES A. RAMIN
GLENCO SCIENTIFIC
2802 WHITE OAK DR.
HOUSTON, TX. 77007

A.K. SMITH
BIG 3 INDS.
3602 W. 11TH
HOUSTON, TX. 77008

ZOLTAN ENGEL
CAMCOR PKG.
1225 SEAMIST DR.
HOUSTON, TX. 77008

BERNARD WEINGARTEN
J. WEINGARTEN INC.
600 LOCKWOOD DR.
HOUSTON, TX. 77011

B.B. HOLLINGSWORTH
SERVICE CORP INT'L.
1929 ALLEN PKWY
HOUSTON, TX. 77019

W.L. WAYNE
FLUIDIC INDS.
P.O. BOX 15617
HOUSTON, TX. 77019

JULIUS FEINSTEIN
UNIVERSAL METALS
5906 ARMOUR DR.
HOUSTON, TX. 77020

J.L. PATTERSON, JR.
DATA INDS. CORP OF TX.
P.O. BOX 14130
HOUSTON, TX. 77021

A.J. MONROE
DIXILYN CORP.
P.O. BOX 14067
HOUSTON, TX. 77021

BERNARD SAMPSON
TRIUMPH INDS.
P.O. BOX 14368
HOUSTON, TX. 77021

ALVIN N. LUBETKIN
OSHMAN'S SPORTING GOODS, INC.
2302 MAXWELL LN.
HOUSTON, TX. 77023

G.N. SWANSTROM
ATEC INC.
P.O. BOX 19426
HOUSTON, TX. 77024

C.G. GLASSCOCK
BELL WESTERN
9039 KATY FWY., BLDG. 400
HOUSTON, TX. 77024

W.A. GRIFFIN
DANIEL INDS.
P.O. BOX 19097
HOUSTON, TX. 77024

DAVID L. BROWN
DIGICON, INC.
6 LEISURE LN.
HOUSTON, TX. 77024

E.W. KELLEY
FAIRMONT FOODS
333 W. LOOP NORTH
HOUSTON, TX. 77024

BENJAMIN RONN
INSYTE CORP.
P.O. BOX 19522
HOUSTON, TX. 77024

SCOTT MOYERS
INTERMEDCO
9219 KATY NO. 149
HOUSTON, TX. 77024

H.N. RAIZES
MACGREGOR LEISURE
7311 ALMEDA, BOX 20328
HOUSTON, TX. 77025

JAMES E. SADLER
AUTOTRONIC SYSTEMS
4550 POST OAK PL. DR.
HOUSTON, TX. 77027

MATTHEW HOWARD
CORONADO OIL & MINERALS
P.O. BOX 27567
HOUSTON, TX. 77027

DON E. McMAHON
DIAMOND M DRILLING
P.O. BOX 22738
HOUSTON, TX. 77027

ROBERT L. TOPPER
HOLLY RESOURCES
4615 S.W. FREEWAY
HOUSTON, TX. 77027

EDWARD O. GAYLORD
ROBERTSON DIST. SYSTEMS
2000 W. LOOP S.
HOUSTON, TX. 77027

MICHAEL S. SPOLANE
STERLING COMP. SYSTEMS
4211 S.W. FRY.
HOUSTON, TX. 77027

R. LARRY SNIDER
STERLING ELECTRONICS
4211 S.W. FREEWAY
HOUSTON, TX. 77027

MACO STEWART
STEWART INFO SYSTEMS
2200 W. LOOP S.
HOUSTON, TX. 77027

LE ROY MELCHER, SR.
U TOTE M, INC.
P.O. BOX 22794
HOUSTON, TX. 77027

JAMES H. TICHEMOR
UNITED SALT CORP.
2000 W. LOOP S.
HOUSTON, TX. 77027

R.E. SMITH
WEATHERFORD INT'L. INC.
4605 POST OAK PL., STE 230
HOUSTON, TX. 77027

HAROLD FRIEDMAN
FRIEDMAN INDS.
4001 HOMESTEAD RD.
HOUSTON, TX. 77028

K.S. ADAMS, JR.
ADA RESOURCES
6910 FANNIN ST.
HOUSTON, TX. 77030

H.J. PHILLIPS
BROWNING-FERRIS INDS.
FANNIN BANK BLDG.
HOUSTON, TX. 77030

H.L. SHAW
HI-PORT INDS.
8502 GLENVISTA, BX. 34215
HOUSTON, TX. 77034

WILLIAM E. POWELL
POWELL ELECTRICAL
8550 MOSLEY DR.
HOUSTON, TX. 77034

WILLIAM B. STANBERRY
HYCEL INC.
P.O. BOX 36329
HOUSTON, TX. 77036

RICHARD L. MINNS
PRESIDENT-1ST LADY SPA
P.O. BOX 36706
HOUSTON, TX. 77036

P.W. PIGUE
PRODUCTION OPERATORS
P.O. BOX 36528
HOUSTON, TX. 77036

YANDELL ROGERS JR.
L.L. RIDGEWAY
P.O. BOX 36150
HOUSTON, TX. 77036

GALE REESE
SEISCOM DELTA
P.O. BOX 36789
HOUSTON, TX. 77036

GALEN T. BROWN
KEYSTONE INTL. INC.
P.O. BOX 40010
HOUSTON, TX. 77040

E.E. MARTIN
AMERICAN MEDICAL
8400 W. PARK DR.
HOUSTON, TX. 77042

GEORGE T. RICHARDSON
OFFSHORE
3411 RICHMOND AVE.
HOUSTON, TX. 77046

FRANK V. ROGERS
A.P.S.
3000 PAWNEE ST.
HOUSTON, TX. 77054

GILBERT H. TAUSCH
CAMCO
7010 ARDMORE ST.
HOUSTON, TX. 77054

ROY B. DAVIS JR.
GRAY TOOL
7135 ARDMORE ST.
HOUSTON, TX. 77054

W.C. LEASURE
MIRA-PAK
7000 ARDMORE AVE.
HOUSTON, TX. 77054

O. CHARLES HONIG
ALASKA INTERSTATE
POST OAK TOWER BLVD.
HOUSTON, TX. 77056

J.V. NEUHAUS
DIVERSIFIED DESIGN
1700 POST OAK TOWER
HOUSTON, TX. 77056

JAMES R. WHATLEY
KANEB SERVICES
5433 WESTHEIMER RD.
HOUSTON, TX. 77056

GEORGE A. PETERKIN JR.
KIRBY EXPLORATION
1717 ST. JAMES PL.
HOUSTON, TX. 77056

HENRY F. LE MIEUX
RAYMOND INTL. INC.
2801 S. POST OAK RD.
HOUSTON, TX. 77056

C.R. PALMER
ROWAN CO.
5051 WESTHEIMER ST.
HOUSTON, TX. 77056

BRIAN JONES JR.
BUFFALO BUSINESS
5825 SCHMACHER
HOUSTON, TX. 77057

R.A. WESTERHOUSE
HOUSTON COMPLEX
6116 SKYLINE STE. 106
HOUSTON, TX. 77057

RICHARD A. BEELER
JETERO CORP.
6234 RICHMOND AVE.
HOUSTON, TX. 77057

WENDELL W. GAMEL
TECH-SYM.
6430 RICHMOND
HOUSTON, TX. 77057

E.E. COOK
INVENT
7721 SAN FELIPE NO. 100
HOUSTON, TX. 77063

LELAND C. PICKENS
WESTCHESTER
8989 WESTHEIMER RD.
HOUSTON, TX. 77063

JAMES H. ELDER JR.
ANDERSON, GREENWOOD
5425 S. RICE AVE.
HOUSTON, TX. 77081

A.L. FRIEDLANDER
RICE FOOD MARKETS
5333 GULTON DR.
HOUSTON, TX. 77081

ALLEN G. RENZ
NATL. PETROLEUM CORP.
10333 N.W. FREEWAY
HOUSTON, TX. 77092

ALLEN G. RENZ
PERMEATOR
10333 NORTHWEST FAIRWAY
HOUSTON, TX. 77092

L.D. CRUMBY JR.
RESEARCH FUELS
9800 NORTHWEST FREEWAY
HOUSTON, TEXAS 77092

SHERWIN NEWAR
SAGE INTL.
4645 BEECHNUT ST.
HOUSTON, TX. 77096

WILLIAM S. MACKEY JR.
MEDENCO
3800 BUFFALO SPEEDWAY
HOUSTON, TX. 77098

LEONARD L. MANSON
WASHINGTON OIL
3310 RICHMOND AVE.
HOUSTON, TX. 77098

E.F. FLORIAN
MARK PROD.
10507 KINGSHURST
HOUSTON, TX. 77099

ROBERT J. SHERE
TRANS-TEXAS AIRWAYS
BOX 60188
HOUSTON, TX. 77205

CHARLES P. SIESS JR.
MARATHON MFG.
P.O. BOX 61589
HOUSTON, TX. 77208

H.M. WILLIAMS
IMPERIAL SUGAR CO.
SUGAR LAND, TX. 77478

J.R. HUGHEY
OCEANOGRAPHY INTERNATIONAL
512 W. LOOP
COLLEGE STATION, TX. 77840

G.S. SODERSTROM
ARGONAUT ENERGY
P.O. BOX 12099
AMARILLO, TX. 78101

G.R. RUTHERFORD
T-BAR-M
P.O. BOX 469
NEW BRAUNSFELS, TX. 78130

G.V. SHAW
SOUTH STATES OIL & GAS
MILAM BLDG.
SAN ANTONIO, TX. 78205

JOHN C. HOLMGREEN JR.
ALAMO IRON WORKS
P.O. BOX 231
SAN ANTONIO, TX. 78206

WALTER N. CORRIGAN
SOMMERS DRUG
3130 E. HOUSTON ST.
SAN ANTONIO, TX. 78206

THOMAS N. SMITH JR.
LULING OIL & GAS
8622 CROWNHILL BLDG.
SAN ANTONIO, TX. 78209

DONALD W. BECKER
FOX-STANLEY PHOTO
1734 BROADWAY
SAN ANTONIO, TEXAS 78215

E.L. BIRSONG
PEARL BREWING
312 PEARL PARKWAY
SAN \ANTONIO, TX. 78215

SAMUEL E. BARSHOP
LA QUINTA MOTOR INN.
P.O. BOX 32064
SAN ANTONIO, TX. 78216

WILLIAM K. CLARK
UVALDE ROCK ASPHALT
CENTURY BUILDING
SAN ANTONIO, TX. 78216

JAMES C. PHELPS
TESORO PETROLEUM
8700 TESORO DR.
SAN ANTONIO, TX. 78217

TOM E. TURNER
SIGMOR
P.O. BOX 20267
SAN ANTONIO, TX. 78220

E.R. EVETTS
WINN'S STORES INC.
P.O. BOX 20007
SAN ANTONIO, TX. 78220

KEITH M. ORME
CONROY
3355 CHERRY RIDGE STE. 201
SAN ANTONIO, TEXAS 78230

WILLIAM H. KING
SOUTHERN MINERALS CORP.
2023 OAK SHIRE
SAN ANTONIO, TX. 78232

C.W. CHURCH JR.
CHURCH'S FRIED CHICKEN
P.O. BOX 13320
SAN ANTONIO, TX. 78284

H.E. O'KELLEY
DATAPOINT
8400 DATAPOINT DR.
SAN ANTONIO, TX. 78284

GEORGE H. WENGLEIN
CAFETERIAS
CENTURY BLDG. STE. 200E
SAN ANTONIO, TX. 78286

ROBERT G. MARBUT
HARTE-HANKS NEWSPAPERS
P.O. BOX 269
SAN ANTONIO, TX. 78291

WALLACE C. SPARKMAN
TEJAS GAS
P.O. BOX 2806
CORPUS CHRISTI, TX. 78403

JACK MODESETT JR.
TERRAMAR
200 WILSON TOWER, BX. 896
CORPUS CHRISTI, TX. 78403

F.H. VAHLSING JR.
TEXAS PLASTICS
ELSA, TEXAS 78543

R.L. TAYLOE
TRUE TASTE
P.O. BOX 35
ELSA, TX. 78543

LORNE S. HAMME
TEXSUN
P.O. BOX 327
WESLACO, TX. 78596

GROGAN LORD
TEXAS TELECOM
P.O. BOX 78
GEORGETOWN, TX. 78626

DONALD R. JOSEPH
TOMANET
P.O. BOX 125
ROUND ROCK, TX. 78664

R.W. HUGHES
COMMUNICATIONS PROPERTIES
910 CITY NATL. BANK BLDG.
AUSTIN, TX. 78701

FRANK W. MC BEE JR.
TRACOR
6500 TRACOR LN.
AUSTIN, TX. 78721

JERRY L. BROWNLEE
KINGSTRIP
3445 EXECUTIVE CENTER DR.
AUSTIN, TEXAS 78731

RONALD CARROLL
TCC
3429 EXECUTIVE CENTER DR.
AUSTIN, TX. 78731

EDWARD DICKINSON II
OLIX IND.
P.O. BOX 9147
AUSTIN, TX. 78758

BERNARD A. PESKIN
ACCELERATORS
P.O. BOX 17068
AUSTIN, TX. 78760

DR. EUGENE HADDAD
COLUMBIA SCIENTIFIC
P.O. BOX 9908
AUSTIN, TX. 78766

F.J. MORRIS
LEM
P.O. BOX 1546
AUSTIN, TX. 78767

CHARLES R. PURSIFULL
JOHN ROBERTS
P.O. BOX 2905
AUSTIN, TX. 78767

LEONARD SCHOENBERG
M-G. INC.
P.O. BOX 697
WEIMAR, TX. 78962

JOHN G. CARROTHERS
FRIONA IND.
U.S. HIGHWAY 60
FRIONA, TX. 79035

JOE C. EASLEY
PITMAN-EASLEY
P.O. BOX 1776
HEREFORD, TX. 79045

Z.A. MC CASLAND
SHUR-GRO IND.
P.O. BOX 1150
HEREFORD, TX. 79045

S. GENE HALL
MINCO OIL & GAS
P.O. BOX 2317
PAMPA, TX. 79065

T. BOONE PICKENS JR.
MESA PETROLEUM
P.O. BOX 2009
AMARILLO, TX. 79105

K.B. WATSON
PIONEER
P.O. BOX 511
AMARILLO, TX. 79105

SCOTT M. SPANGLER
PROCHEMCO
P.O. BOX 9197
AMARILLO, TX. 79105

JOHN P. TURNER
STANDARD GILSONITE
P.O. BOX 2009
AMARILLO, TX. 79105

GEORGE E. FEASTER
WESTERN BEEF
P.O. BOX 2638
AMARILLO, TX. 79105

LLOYD E. GEOFFROY
TECKLA
BANK OF SOUTHWEST BLDG.
AMARILLO, TX. 79109

RALPH W. DOUGLAS
ERA
1638 MAIN ST.
LUBBOCK, TX. 79401

CHARLES S. CARTER
SHELDON PETROLEUM
LUBBOCK NATL. BANK BLDG.
LUBBOCK, TX. 79401

CLIFFORD W. ANDREWS
FURR'S CAFETERIAS
P.O. BOX 6747
LUBBOCK, TX. 79413

RICHARD F. BACON
MERCHANTS
P.O. BOX 3257
ABILENE, TX. 79604

B.J. PEVEHOUSE
ADOBE OIL & GAS
1100 WESTERN-LIFE BLDG.
MIDLAND, TX. 79701

R.S. McGRATH
BENGAL OIL & GAS
MIDLAND SAVINGS BLDG.
MIDLAND, TX. 79701

T.C. BROWN
TOM BROWN
315 MIDLAND TOWER BLDG.
MIDLAND, TX. 79701

GEORGE T. CONLY
COQUINA OIL
P.O. BOX 2960
MIDLAND, TX. 79701

NASH J. DOWDLE
DOWDLE OIL
300 W. WALL ST.
MIDLAND, TX. 79701

ROY E. CAMPBELL
ELCOR CHEM.
WILCO BLDG.
MIDLAND, TX. 79701

R.O. MAJOR
MFG OIL
1126 VAUGHN BLDG.
MIDLAND, TX. 79701

S.T. MILLER
MILLER OIL
3612 WEST WALL ST.
MIDLAND, TX. 79701

W.F. JUDD
TEXAS AMERICAN OIL
300 W. WALL ST.
MIDLAND, TX. 79701

D.H. STOLTZ
TIPPERARY
500 WEST ILLINOIS ST.
MIDLAND, TX. 79701

FRANK J. ALLEN
WESTERN OIL SHALE
300 W. WALL ST.
MIDLAND, TX. 79701

DR. LEO J. WINDECKER
WINDECKER IND.
P.O. BOX 6288
MIDLAND, TX. 79701

JACK Q. FRIZZELL
AUSTRALIAN OIL
300 WEST WALL
MIDLAND, TX. 79704

CHARLES D. MC KEE
ROBERT E. MC KEE
1918 TEXAS AVE.
EL PASO, TX. 79901

GLEN JORDAN
PANNATIONAL GROUP
ONE STATE NATL. PLAZA
EL PASO, TX. 79901

FRED HERVEY
CIRCLE K.
P.O. BOX 888
EL PASO, TX. 79908

G.J. RUBIN
HELEN OF TROY
6827 MARKET ST.
EL PASO, TX. 79915

JOSEPH H. LAMA
TONY LAMA
1137 TONY LAMA ST.
EL PASO, TX. 79915

GARY MANN
MANN MFG.
6975 COMMERCE ST.
EL PASO, TX. 79915

AL WILSON
AARONSON BROS.
1138 BARANCA DR.
EL PASO, TX. 79935

JOHN E. TURNER
JETCO
1133 BARRANCA DR.
EL PASO, TX. 79935

M.R. PRESTRIDGE JR.
BORDER STEEL ROLLING MILLS
P.O. BOX 71
EL PASO, TX. 79941

HUGH F. STEEN
EL PASO CO.
P.O. BOX 1492
EL PASO, TX. 79978

WILLIAM C. LEONE
FARAH MFG.
8889 GATEWAY BLVD. WEST
EL PASO, TEXAS 79985

RICHARD D. ARNOLD
BILLY THE KID
100 S. COTTON ST.
EL PASO, TX. 79988

LEO ROTH
PRECISION PLASTICS
5570 HARLAN ST.
ARVADA, COLO. 80002

KENNETH P. GREEN
GREEN BROS. IND.
10401 W. 120TH. AVE.
BROOMFIELD, COLO. 80020

LESTER LERICH
WEJ-IT
ATLAS IND. PARK
BROOMFIELD, COLO. 80020

J. LAWSON COOK
COLORADO MILLING
P.O. BOX 629
COMMERCE CITY, COLO. 80022

A.S. ROSS
MILE HIGH KENNEL CLUB
6200 DAHILA ST.
COMMERCE CITY, COLO. 80022

J.A. YOBLIN
EXPLOSIVE FABRICATORS
1301 COURTESY RD.
LOUISVILLE, COLORADO 80027

VICTOR A. CASEBOLT
STORAGE TECH. CORP.
2270 S. 88TH ST.
LOUISVILLE, COLO. 80027

R.A. BARTON
CODECA
6429 S. MAGNOLIA
ENGLEWOOD, COLO. 80110

W.C. JULANDER
ENERGY MINERALS
5 DENVER TECH.
ENGLEWOOD, COLO. 80110

G.R. JONES
JONES INTERCABLE
880 CONTINENTAL BANK BLDG.
ENGLEWOOD, COLO. 80110

A.J. STEPHENS
MECHANEX
3773 S. JASON ST.
ENGLEWOOD, COLO. 80110

RIKE D. WOOTTEN
MENTOR
P.O. BOX 1533
ENGLEWOOD, COLO. 80110

JOHN R. BILLINIS
MICRON
7524 E. PROGRESS PL.
ENGLEWOOD, COLO. 80110

JAMES M. HANKINS
MOBILE HOME
40 W. DENVER TECH.
ENGLEWOOD, COLO. 80110

D.M. PRATT
NATL. CITY LINES
5 DENVER TECH. CENTER
ENGELWOOD, COLO. 80110

ORAN E. WATSON
PAYLESS CASHWAYS
7935 E. PRENTICE BLDG.   40W.
ENGLEWOOD,COLO. 80110

JOHN S. GOULD
UNIQUE MOBILITY
3700 S. JASON
ENGLEWOOD, COLO. 80110

RICHARD H. SIMON
CENTENNIAL TURF CLUB
LITTLETON, COLO. 80120

RODERRICK D. McCULLOCH
MID-CONTINENT MINING
6202 S. BROADWAY
LITTLETON, COLO. 80120

T.J. GARRITY
AZTEX MINING
6202 S. BROADWAY
LITTLETON, COLO. 80121

R.W. ADAMS
ALLIED NUCLEAR
ONE PARK CENTRA, STE. 387
DENVER, COLO. 80202

G.W. EWING JR.
ARAPAHO PETROLEUM
1110 SECURITY LIFE BLDG.
DENVER, COLO. 80202

GORDON SMALE
ATLANTIC OIL
1825 LAWRENCE ST.
DENVER, COLO. 80202

R.C. QUALLS
BOBCAT OIL CO.
400 DENVER CLUB BLDG.
DENVER, COLO. 80202

RAYMOND JACOBY
CENTRURY OIL& GAS
621 17TH. ST. STE. 1145
DENVER, COLO. 80202

P.V. HOOVLER
CHAPARRAL RESOURCES
444 SEVENTEENTH ST.
DENVER, COLO. 80202

GENE CLARK JR.
CLARCAN PETROLEUM
1960 COLORADO STATE BANK BLDG.
DENVER, COLO. 80202

GEO. P. CAULKINS JR.
DENVER REAL ESTATE
828   17TH. ST.
DENVER, COLO. 80202

J.F. O'DEA
DENVER UNION
CENTRAL BANK WEST
DENVER, COLO. 80202

R.F. DIETRICH
DIETRICH EXPLORATION
444 17TH ST.
DENVER, COLO. 80202

MARVIN NEUMANN
DOMESTIC ENERGY
601 DENVER CLUB BLDG.
DENVER, COLO. 80202

HOLMES P. MC LISH
FLYING DIAMOND OIL
1700 BROADWAY
DENVER, COLO. 80202

C.G. DORN
FOREST OIL
950   17TH ST.
DENVER, COLO. 80202

THOR GJELSTEEN
FRONTIER RESOURCES
515 MAJESTIC BLDG.
DENVER, COLO. 80202

F.F. HAMILTON
HAMILTON BROS. PETROLEUM
1600 BROADWAY
DENVER, COLO. 80202

J.P. COLLINS
HELMET PETROLEUM
475 17TH. ST. METRO BLDG.
DENVER, COLO. 80202

JOHN A. LOVE
IDEAL BASIC IND.
821   17TH. ST.
DENVER, COLO. 80202

DR. W. RICHARD GOODWIN
JOHNS-MANVILLE
P.O. BOX 5108
DENVER, COLO. 80217

R.A. KADANE
K.R.M. PETROLEUM
817 17TH. ST.
DENVER, COLO. 80202

JIM SNYDER
MARLIN OIL
870 DENVER CLUB BLDG.
DENVER, COLO. 80202

G.A. FOUST
MINERALS ENGINEERING
650   17TH. ST. NO. 503
DENVER, COLO. 80202

WESLEY N. FARMER
OCEANIC EXPLORATION
PRUDENTIAL PLAZA TOWER
DENVER, COLO. 80202

RICHARD H. OLSON
OUTDOOR SPORTS IND.
518   17TH. ST.
DENVER, COLO. 80202

DAVID E. PARK JR.
OXFORD EXPLORATION
1030 DENVER CLUB BLDG.
DENVER, COLO. 80202

JEROME A. LEWIS
PETRO-LEWIS
1600 BROADWAY STE. 1400
DENVER, COLO. 80202

TRUMAN E. ANDERSON
PETRO-SEARCH
825 PETROLEUM CLUB BLDG.
DENVER, COLO. 80202

J.A. POLUMBUS
POLUMBUS CORP.
3 PARK CENTRAL STE. 200
DENVER, COLO. 80202

DEAN R. GIDNEY
POTASH CO. OF AMERICA
821 17TH. ST.
DENVER, COLO. 80202

GALE B. AYDELOTT
RIO GRANDE IND.
P.O. BOX 5482
DENVER, COLO. 80202

E.A. BREITENBACH
SCIENTIFIC SOFTWARE
633 17TH. ST.
DENVER, COLO. 80202

ROBERT T. BIRDSONG
WEBB RESOURCES
FIRST OF DENVER PLAZA STE. 2200
DENVER, COLO. 80202

H.E. ZOLLER
ZOLLER & DANNEBERG
633 17TH. ST. STE. 2100
DENVER, COLO. 80202

H.C. PORTER
ANTARES OIL
1660 LINCOLN ST.
DENVER,COLORADO 80203

G.A. KIMMERY
BASIC EARTH SCIENCE
2300 UNITED BANK CENTER
DENVER, COLO. 80203

J.C. WOOD
BALY CORP.
1845 SHERMAN ST. STE. 401
DENVER, COLO. 80203

R.E. BENNETT
BENNETT PETROLEUM
1776 LINCOLN ST.
DENVER, COLO. 80203

R.A. BAILE
CHALLENGE OIL & GAS
1660 LINCOLN ST.
DENVER, COLO. 80203

GORDON S. ROSENBLUM
INTER-AMERICAN PETROLEUM
609 E. SPEER BLVD.
DENVER, COLO. 80203

S.J. ROSENFELD
JUNIPER PETROLEUM
LINCOLN CENTER BLDG.
DENVER, COLO. 80202

J.D. CRANOR
MANNING GAS & OIL
1660 LINCOLN ST. STE. 2322
DENVER, COLO. 80203

ORVILLE M. SHOCKLEY
ROCKY MOUNTAIN NATL GAS
1600 SHERMAN ST.
DENVER, COLO. 80202

C. SILVER
SUNDANCE OIL
1776 LINCOLN ST.
DENVER, COLO. 80203

C.S. DICTLER
WESTERN CRUDE OIL
1100 DENVER CENTER BLDG.
DENVER, COLO. 80203

EDMUND L. EPSTEIN
GOLD BELT MINING
1321 BANNOCK ST.
DENVER, COLO. 80204

S.L.R. McNICHOLS
SILVER BELL IND.
222 MILWAUKEE ST.
DENVER, COLO. 80206

RICHARD A. FORSLING
CABLECOM-GEN.
4705 KINGSTON
DENVER, COLO. 80207

ELBERT L. BARRETT
ELBA SYSTEMS
5909 E. 38TH. AVE.
DENVER, COLO. 80207

A.L. FELDMAN
FRONTIER AIRLINES
8250 SMITH RD.
DENVER, COLORADO 80207

L.E. CLARK
PETRO-SILVER
333 QUEBEC ST. PENTHOUSE F
DENVER, COLO. 80207

MONROE M. RIFKIN
AMERICAN TV.
360 S. MONROE
DENVER, COLO. 80209

J.C. MALONE
TELE-COMMUNICATIONS
P.O. BOX 10727
DENVER, COLO. 80210

E.K. DROULLARD
KEBA OIL & GAS
2460 W. 26TH. AVE. STE. 30C
DENVER, COLO. 80211

ROBERT M. COLLINS
COBE LABS.
1201 OAK ST.
LAKEWOOD, COLO. 80215

W.D. CREW
DAKOTA GRAPHICS
9655 W. COLFAX AVE.
LAKEWOOD, COLO. 80215

ROBERT G. RISK
LEADVILLE
1677 WADSWORTH BLVD.
DENVER, COLO. 80215

R.A. HILDEBRAND
POLARIS RESOURCES
7536 W. 17TH. AVE.
LAKEWOOD, COLO. 80215

WILLIAM C. FOXLEY
FLAVORLAND IND.
P.O. BOX 16345
DENVER, COLO. 80216

JAMES C. SHEARON
STEAK INC.
5100 RACE CT.
DENVER, COLO. 80216

THOMAS W. GAMEL
TIMPTE
5990 N. WASHINGTON ST.
DENVER, COLO. 80216

D.L. VALDEZ
JET-X
2250 WEST 2ND. AVE.
DENVER, COLO. 80217

RICHARD B. TUCKER
PAK-WELL
3500 ROCKMONT DR.
DENVER, COLO. 80217

PAUL D. MEADOWS
RESERVE OIL & GAS
P.O. BOX 5568
DENVER, COLO. 80217

ROBERT M. STANLEY
STANLEY AVIATION
P.O. BOX 20308
DENVER, COLO. 80220

T.A. MANHART
HATHAWAY INSTRUMENTS
5250 E. EVANS AVE.
DENVER, COLO. 80222

R.V. BAILEY
POWER RESOURCES
1660 S. ALBION STE. B27
DENVER, COLO. 80222

D.E. MAY
ROCKY MOUNTAIN VENTURES
4155 E. JEWELL AVE.
DENVER, COLO. 80222

LEE HARRISON III
COMPUTER IMAGE
2475 W. 2ND. AVE. STE. 4
DENVER, COLO. 80223

D. LORNELL
MARKON MFG.
2001 S. PLATT RIVER DR.
DENVER, COLO. 80223

RODNEY G. LOCHMILLER
NAVAJO FREIGHT LINES
1205 S. PLATE RIVER DR.
DENVER, COLO. 80223

LEE C. SCOTT
AERO IND.
12075 E. 45TH. ST. STE. 135
DENVER, COLO. 80239

J.J. GOLDSTEIN
SCOTTS LIQUID GOLD
4880 HAVANA ST.
DENVER, COLO. 80239

R.K. ANDERSON
VALLEYLAB
5441 WESTERN AVE.
BOULDER, COLO. 80301

T.A. WAIBEL JR.
SONTRIX
4593 N. BROADWAY
BOULDER, COLO. 80302

H.J. JONES
BIONIC SCIENCES
P.O. BOX 2189
BOULDER, COLO. 80306

WILLIAM K. COORS
ADOLPH COORS
GOLDEN, COLO. 80401

D.N. STEVENS
EARTH SCIENCES
4565 HIGHWAY 93
GOLDEN, COLO. 80401

T.H. THOMSON
STAODYNAMICS
601 S. BOWEN
LONMONT, COLO. 80501

S.D. ADDOMS
MONFORT OF COLORADO
P.O. BOX G
GREELEY, COLO. 80631

WILLIAM C. RICHARDSON
AMI IND.
P.O. BOX 370
COLORADO SPRINGS, COLO. 80901

JOHN B. BUNKER
HOLLY SUGAR
P.O. BOX 1052
COLORADO SPRINGS, COLO. 80901

J.B. HAIGH
GEO SURVEYS
415 MINING EXCHANGE BLDG.
COLORADO SPRINGS, COLO. 80903

WILLIAM T. WELLS
GOLDEN CYCLE
102 N. CASCADE, 6TH. FL.
COLORADO SPRINGS, COL. 80903

ROBERT J. SLATER
C F & I STEEL
P.O. BOX 316
PUEBLO, COLORADO 81002

D.H. PEAKER
U.S. BERYLLIUM
306 BON SURANT BLDG.
PUEBLO, COLO. 81003

W.H. BURT
IDARADO MINING
P.O. BOX D
QURAY, COLO. 81427

ALLAN SIMPSON
BEAVER MESA URANIUM
1111 S. 7TH. BOX 567
GRAND JUNCTION, COLO. 81501

RICHARD E. REIMER
DIXSON, INC.
P.O. BOX 1449
GRAND JUNCTION, COLO. 81501

THOMAS B. NEFF
DOUBLE X RANCH
GRAND JUNCTION, COLO. 81501

R.C. CUTTER
GEO IND. INC.
P.O. BOX 2065
GRAND JUNCTION, COLO. 81501

W.H. PEASE
WLLARD PEASE OIL & GAS
P.O. BOX 548
GRAND JUNCTION, COLO. 81501

D.R.C. BROWN
ASPEN SKIING
P.O. BOX 1248
ASPEN, COLO. 81611

R.L. PETERSON
VAIL ASSOC.
ONE WALL ST.
VEIL, COLO. 81657

J.T. HAYS
DISCOVERY OIL
P.O. BOX 1407
CHEYENNE, WY. 82001

D.A. FULLERTON
CRESSON CONSOLIDATED
P.O. BOX 818
LUSK, WY. 82225

JOHN S. HERRIN
CURTIS
P.O. BOX 524
THERMOPOLIS, WY. 82443

NICHOLAS KONDUR
LRC
TECHNICAL RESEARCH PARK
RIVERTON, WY. 82501

JOHN LAURITZ LARSEN
RUBY MINING
625 E. MADISON
RIVERTON, WY. 82501

ROY PECK
WESTERN STANDARD
P.O. BOX 1760
RIVERTON, WY. 82501

J.L. LARSEN
U.S. ENERGY
625 E. MADISON
RIVERTON, WY. 82501

J.A. SMITH
NUCLEAR EXPLORATION
550 MAIN ST. DRAWER EE
LANDER, WY. 82520

MORRIS DICKHART
VIPONT CHEMICAL
310 MAIN ST.
LANDER, WY. 82520

C. FERGUSON
AMERICAN NUCLEAR
P.O. BOX 2713
CASPER, WY. 82601

W.J. HAWKS
BURTON-HAWKS
FIRST NAT'L. BANK BLDG.
CASPER, WY. 82601

CLINTON E. ROSS
COYOTE OIL & GAS
P.O. BOX 2895
CASPER, WY. 82601

R.B. LAUDON
DOUBLE EAGLE PETROLEUM
102 RIVERCROSS RD. BOX 766
CASPER, WY. 82601

R.W. KOENEKAMP
EASTERN PETROLEUM
P.O. BOX 3071
CASPER, WY. 82601

J.P. ELLBOGEN
ECHO OIL
P.O. BOX 3036
CASPER, WY. 82601

E.M. CATRON
EMC ENERGIES
1113 W. 25TH. ST.
CASPER, WY. 82601

D.G. CARPENTER
RAINBOW RESOURCES
305 GOODSTEIN BLVD.
CASPER, WY. 82601

ROBERT W. MIRACLE
WYOMING NAT'L.
234 E. FIRST ST.
CASPER, WY. 82601

WILLIAM J. HOLLANDER
EAGLE EXPLORATION
GOODSTEIN BLDG. BOX 520
CASPER, WY. 82602

WILLIAM J. WILSON
GARRETT FREIGHTLINES
P.O. BOX 4048
POCATELLO, ID. 83201

GARY KNUDSEN
CONTROL DEVELOPMENTS
P.O. BOX 796
NAMPA, ID. 83651

P.T. JOHNSON
TRUS JOIST
9777 W. SHINDEN BLVD.
BOISE, ID. 83702

G.J. HAWKINS
RED STEER
939 BOEING ST. BOX 5509
BOISE, ID. 83705

DAVE W. MORROW
ALBERTSON'S
P.O. BOX 20
BOISE, ID. 83707

WILLIAM H. MC MURREN
MORRISON-KNUDSEN
P.O. BOX 7808
BOISE, ID. 83707

P.W. LACZAY
HELENA SILVER MINES
P.O. BOX 488
COEUR D'ALENE, ID. 83814

C.H. HUNTER
MERGER MINES
P.O. BOX 716
COEUR D'ALENE, ID. 83814

HOWARD CARTER
NIAGARA MINING
P.O. BOX 790
COEUR D'ALENE, ID. 83814

P.W. LACZAY
SUMMIT SILVER
P.O. BOX 488
COEUR D'ALENE, ID. 83814

WENDELL R. BRAINARD
NANCY LEE MINES
P.O. BOX 149
KELLOGG, ID. 83837

WRAY D. FARMIN
PEND OREILLE MINES
P.O. BOX 29
KELLOGG, ID. 83837

C.E. NELSON
SUNSHINE MINING
P.O. BOX 1080
KELLOGG, ID. 83837

ARTHUR A. CHELDE
YREKA UNITED
P.O. BOX 147
KELLOGG, ID. 83837

RAYMOND H. GILES
ABOT MINING
BOX 1010
WALLACE, ID. 83873

WRAY FEATHERSTONE
ALICE CONSOLIDATED MINES
P.O. BOX 469
WALLACE, ID. 83873

W.M. YEAMAN
BIG CREEK APEX
THE SCOTT BLDG.
WALLACE, ID. 83873

W.H. MORROW
CANYON SILVER MINES
P.O. BOX 862
WALLACE, ID. 83873

GORDON M. MINER
CHESTER MINING
P.O. BOX 320
WALLACE, ID. 83873

J.L. RICE
COEUR D'ALEN MINES
504 BANK ST.
WALLACE, ID. 83873

ALDEN HULL
CONSOLIDATED SILVER
P.O. BOX 320
WALLACE, ID. 83873

WILLIAM M. CALHOUN
DAY MINES
DAY BLDG. P.O. BOX 1010
WALLACE, ID. 83873

WILLIAM H. LOVE
HECLA MINING
P.O. BOX 320
WALLACE, ID. 83873

F.E. SCOTT
IDAHO SILVER
P.O. BOX 1088
WALLACE, ID. 83873

H.J. HULL
NABOB SILVER-LEAD
P.O. BOX 709
WALLACE, ID. 83873

H.F. MAGNUSON
SILVER DOLLAR MINING
P.O. BOX 469, SCOTT BLDG.
WALLACE, ID. 83873

W.M. YEAMAN
SUNSHINE CONSOLIDATED
P.O. BOX 890, SCOTT BLDG.
WALLACE, ID. 83873

GEORGE M. GRISMER
WESTERN SILVER-LEAD
P.O. BOX 469
WALLACE, ID. 83873

HARMON G. WILLIAMS
BROWNING
RT. 1
MORGAN, UTAH 84050

C.C. WALL
ALTEX OIL
205 N. VERNAL AVE.
VERNAL, UTAH 84078

CRAIG CALDWELL
HIKO BELL MINING
BANK OF VERNAL BLDG.
VERNAL, UTAH 84078

SAM SOUVALL
ALTA IND.
105 N. FOURTH WEST
SALT LAKE CITY, UTAH 84101

M.P. CALER
CONTINENTS GOLD
62 W. 4TH. SOUTH
SALT LAKE CITY, UTAH 84101

F.H. EVANS
EQUITY OIL
AMERICAN OIL BLDG.
SALT LAKE CITY, UTAH 84101

SCOTT L. SMITH
GOLD STANDARD
1019 LEARNS BLDG.
SALT LAKE CITY, UTAH 84101

S.L. ROWLAND
HEALTHGARDE
330 W. FIFTH SOUTH
SALT LAKE CITY, UTAH 84101

GORDON D. STOTT
PARK CITY CONSOLIDATED MINES
68 SOUTH MAIN ST.
SALT LAKE CITY, UTAH 84101

HARRY FRIEDLAND
PROCESS SYSTEMS
356 W. 7TH. SOUTH
SALT LAKE CITY, UTAH 84101

R.K. NEILSON
SKYLINE OIL
ATLAS BLDG.
SALT LAKE CITY, UTAH 84101

K.K.S. FONG
TRAINS ATLAS
10 W. BROADWAY STE. 510
SALT LAKE CITY, UTAH 84101

MILES P. ROMNEY
UNITED PARK CITY MINES
309 KEARNS BLDG.
SALT LAKE CITY, UTAH 84101

RAY ROSS
CLASSIC MINING
731 EAST SOUTH TEMPLE
SALT LAKE CITY, UTAH 84102

JOHN W. BOUD
FASHION FABRICS
P.O. BOX 250
SALT LAKE CITY, UTAH 84102

RICHARD R. STEINER
STEINER AMERICAN
505 E. SOUTH TEMPLE ST.
SALT LAKE CITY, UTAH 84102

G. PHILIP MARGETTS
DYNAPAC
1610 S. IND. RD.
SALT LAKE CITY, UTAH 84104

G.W. JACKSON
HYDRO FLAME
1874 PIONEER RD.
SALT LAKE CITY, UTAH 84104

L.K. HOLBROOK
MED. DEVELOPMENT
2445 S. JETWAY AVE.
SALT LAKE CITY, UTAH 84104

LAMAR H. HOLLEY
AMACAN RESOURCES
1399 S. 700 EAST
SALT LAKE CITY, UTAH 84105

GEORGE H. BADGER
BINGHAM SILVER LEAD
1931 S. 11TH. ST. EAST
SALT LAKE CITY, UTAH 84105

BELNAP PRESIDENT
BASIC METALS
P.O. BOX 576
SALT LAKE CITY, UTAH 84110

EDWARD H. SNYDER
COMBINED METALS
P.O. BOX 150
SALT LAKE CITY, UTAH 84110

W.D. NEBEKET JR.
CROFF OIL
P.O. BOX 2045
SALT LAKE CITY, UTAH 84110

N.W. STALHEIM
FED. RESOURCES
P.O. BOX 806
SALT LAKE CITY, UTAH 84110

H.S. ELLSWORTH
INT"L. LABORATORIES
P.O. BOX 633
SALT LAKE CITY, UTAH 84110

HAROLD D. STOKER
PACIFIC AIR
P.O. BOX 1712
SALT LAKE CITY, UTAH 84110

JOHN HARTMAN
SKAGGS CO.
P.O. BOX 658
SALT LAKE CITY, UTAH 84110

ROWLAND M. CANNON
U & I INC.
P.O. BOX 2010
SALT LAKE CITY, UTAH 84110

H.L. FRANKS
VISTA INTL.
P.O. BOX 1315
SALT LAKE CITY, UTAH 84110

O. DE VERE WOOTTON
BIG PINEY OIL
455 E. 4TH. ST.
SALT LAKE CITY, UTAH 84111

M.C. GODBE III
EAST UTAH MINING
721 FIRST SECURITY
SALT LAKE CITY, UTAH 84111

CLARENCE IRVING JUSTHEIM
JUSTHEIM PETROLEUM
709 WALKER BANK BLDG.
SALT LAKE CITY, UTAH 84111

K.L. STOKER
SILVER KING MINES
1204 DESERET PLAZA,15 E 1ST. SO.
SALT LAKE CITY, UTAH 84111

F.W. CHRISTENSEN
STANSBURY MINING
926 KENNECOTT BLDG.
SALT LAKE CITY, UTAH 84111

G.H. HAMILTON
TINTIC MOUNTAIN
926 KENECOTT BLDG.
SALT LAKE CITY, UTAH 84111

A.G. HATSIS
TOLEDO MINING
322 NEWHOUSE BLDG.
SALT LAKE CITY, UTAH 84111

RAEBURN VAN COALSON
AMERICAN NATL.
P.O. BOX 15817
SALT LAKE CITY, UTAH 84115

F.L. CHRISTENSEN
CHRISTENSEN
1937 S. 300 WEST ST.
SALT LAKE CITY, UTAH 84115

MURRAY WILLIAMS
G & L. EQUIPMENT
1522 S. STATE ST.
SALT LAKE CITY, UTAH 84115

DONALD A MACKEY
GRAND CENTRAL
P.O. BOX 15507
SALT LAKE CITY, UTAH 84115

W. HAGUE ELLIS
INTERWEST
1935 S. MAIN ST. STE. 211
SALT LAKE CITY, UTAH 84115

G.M. LIDDLE
TRANSPORTATION SAFETY
P.O. BOX 387, 1937 S. 300 W.ST.
SALT LAKE CITY, UTAH 84115

FERRIS COLLETT
COLLETT'S INC.
2001 N. EIGHT WEST
SALT LAKE CITY, UTAH 84116

CLARK L. WILSON
N. ILLY MINING
1849 W. NORTH TEMPLE
SALT LAKE CITY, UTAH 84116

RICHARD BOSWELL
VEDCO WAH WAH MINES
2291 E. 4500 SOUTH
SALT LAKE CITY, UTAH 84117

WARREN CLIFFORD
BEEHIVE MED.
870 W. 2600 SOUTH
SALT LAKE CITY, UTAH 84119

E.J. KNUDSON JR.
DYNAMIC AMERICAN
2300 S. 3600 WEST
SALT LAKE CITY, UTAH 84119

H.D. MOYLE JR.
RESEARCH IND.
1847 W. 2300 SOUTH
SALT LAKE CITY, UTAH 84119

LYLE O. KEYS
TELEMATION
2195 S. 3600 WEST
SALT LAKE CITY, UTAH 84119

EDWARD J. GILSON
EMDEKO INTL.
1260 EAST VINE ST.
SALT LAKE CITY, UTAH 84121

A.E. BENNING
THE AMALGAMATED SUGAR
801 FIRST SECURITY BANK
OGDEN, UTAH 84402

DAVID L. DURBANO
IND. SALES
P.O. BOX 1533
ODGEN, UTAH 84402

J.L. ROBERTSON
NEW PRODUCTS CORP.
3505 GRANT
OGDEN, UTAH 84403

CHARLES E. WARD
AMCOR
379 -17TH. ST.
OGDEN, UTAH 84404

DONALD T. WHALEN
HYDROCARBON
90 WEST FIRST NORTH ST.
PRICE, UTAH 84501

R.E. BILLINGS
BILLINGS ENERGY
P.O. BOX 555
PROVO, UTAH 84601

JAMES B. BURR
ROCKY MT. HELICOPTERS
P.O. BOX 1337
PROVO, UTAH 84601

C.L. BATES
VALTEK
100 EAST, BOX 209
PROVO, UTAH 84601

HAROLD A. SAVAGE JR.
SAVAGE IND.
BOX 352
PHOENIX, AZ. 85001

BRUCE MERRILL
AMECO
2960 GRAND AVE.
PHOENIX, AZ. 85002

KARL ELLER
COMBINED COMM. CORP.
P.O. BOX 25518
PHOENIX, AZ. 85002

R.D. FLORI
FLORI
P.O. BOX 25159
PHOENIX, AZ. 85002

F.M. GEDDES
ARIZONA-COLORADO LAND
5001 E. WASHINGTON ST.
PHOENIX, AZ. 85004

ROGER S. HAGEL
A.J. BAYLESS
P.O. BOX 1152
PHOENIX, AZ. 85004

C.H. HALLETT
ALLISON STEEL
1841 W. BUCHANAN
PHOENIX, AZ. 85005

B.L. JOHNSON
GEN. CASSETTE
1324 N. 22ND. AVE.
PHOENIX, AZ. 85009

PAUL SHATUSKY
OMNITEC
2405 S. 20TH. ST.
PHOENIX, AZ. 85009

C. ROBERT MANDEVILLE
 N R G INC.
3443 N. CENTRAL AVE.
PHOENIX, AZ. 85012

W.A. FRANKE
SOUTHWEST FOREST IND.
3443 N. CENTRAL AVE.
PHOENIX, AZ. 85012

ROBERT A. SHEPLER
CLICA IND.
301 WEST INDIAN SCHOOL RD.
PHOENIX, AZ. 85013

HERMAN CHANEN
NATL. HOUSING
301 W. OSBORN RD. STE. 3700
PHOENIX, AZ. 85013

JAMES H. CEDERQUIST
HALLCRAFT HOMES
4747 N. 22ND. ST.
PHOENIX, AZ. 85016

LEONARD SEIDNER
POLYMER OPTICS
2139 E. INDIAN RD.
PHOENIX, AZ. 85016

LEONARD FRANKEL
ASSOC. GRAPHICS
3030 N. 29TH. DR.
PHOENIX, AZ. 85017

G.M. RAYBURN
NEW MEXICO & AZ. LAND CO.
4350 E. CAMELBACK RD. STE. 140B
PHOENIX, AZ. 85018

JAMES N. MELLOR
PATAGONIA
4350 E. CAMELBACK RD. STE. 140E
PHOENIX, AZ. 85018

MELVIN B. RASKIN
INST. OF BROADCAST ART
P.O. BOX 9217
PHOENIX, AZ. 85020

W.R. CLUER
TURF PARADISE
19TH. AVE. & BELL RD.
PHOENIX, AZ. 85022

D.E. MANNESS
HURRICANE CAR WASH SYS.
3418 W. HEARN RD.
PHOENIX, AZ. 85023

JOHN C. DALTON JR.
AVIATION HOLDING
2730 SKY HARBOR BLVD.
PHOENIX, AZ. 85034

GEORGE W. CHANE
NYTRONICS
2405 SOUTH 20TH. ST.
PHOENIX, AZ. 85034

R.W. APPLEGATE
PHOTOTRON
2 N. 30TH. ST.
PHOENIX, AZ. 85034

E.S. WELLS JR.
BOWER IND.
P.O. BOX 21024
PHOENIX, AZ. 85036

A. MILTON WHITLING
KAIBAB IND.
P.O. BOX 20506
PHOENIX, AZ. 85036

JOE F. WALTON
NUCLEAR DYNAMICS
P.O. BOX 20766
PHOENIX, AZ. 85036

H.R. BONE
NEWBERY ENERGY
3826 S. 28TH. ST.
PHOENIX, AZ. 85041

J.G. DUNCAN
UNIVERSAL MAJOR IND.
P.O. BOX 15234
PHOENIX, AZ. 85060

W.L. GREWCOCK
UNION ROCK & MAT. CORP.
2800 S. CENTRAL AVE.
PHOENIX, AZ. 85066

FRANZ G. TALLEY
TALLEY IND.
3500 N. GREENFIELD RD.
MESA, AZ. 85201

RICHARD H. RUDOLPH
DICKSON ELECTRONICS
8700 E. THOMAS RD.
SCOTTSDALE, AZ. 85251

G.F. STOEBERL
INTL. PETROLEUM
7336 SHOEMAN LANE
SCOTTSDALE, AZ. 85251

JOHN P. LEKAS
VIDEO CONTROL
7020 THIRD AVE. STE. 4
SCOTTSDALE, AZ. 85251

G.J. SPRESSER
MARY MOPPET'S DAY CARE
7120 E. OAK ST.
SCOTTSDALE, AZ. 85257

JACK W. FOWLER
W.A. KRUEGER
7301 E. HELM DR.
SCOTTSDALE, AZ. 85260

DALTON L. KNAUSS
GEN. SEMICONDUCTOR IND.
2001 WEST 10TH. PL.
TEMPE, AZ. 85281

M.L. LENTZ
HYDROCULTURE
P.O. BOX 1655
GLENDALE, AZ. 85301

W.H. CLARK
SPACE PLASTICS
5306 W. MISSOURI
GLENDALE, AZ. 85301

DON V. HAMILTON
TEC
9800 N. ORACLE RD.
TUCSON, AZ. 85704

R.E. SHELTON
OLD TUCSON
201 S. KINNEY RD.
OLD TUCSON, AZ. 85705

HAROLD LAZ
FIRST RECREATION
801 N. STONE AVE.
TUCSON, AZ. 85713

ALLAN B. BOWMAN
BANNER MINING
P.O. BOX 4220
TUCSON, ARIZONA 85717

SIDNEY NELSON
HORIZON LAND
P.O. BOX 27324
TUCSON, AZ. 85726

J.J. MELFI
RESERVE OIL
908 PARK AVE. S.W.
ALBUGUERQUE, N.M. 87102

E. SCHNIFANI
SPRINGER
P.O. DRAWER S.
ALBUQUERQUE, N.M. 87103

E.F. CRUFT
NORD RESOURCES
2300 CANDELARIA, N.E.
ALBUQUERQUE, N.M. 87106

M.L. ANDERSON
RANCHERS EXPLOR.
1776 MONTANO RD. N.W.
ALBUQUERQUE, N.M. 87107

G.OL LOTSPEICH
HYDRO NUCLEAR
FIRST NTL. BANK BLDG.E.
ALBUQUERQUE, N.M. 87108

J.S. REINHART
FALLS LAND
3624 MENAUL BLVD., N.E.
ALBUQUERQUE, N.M. 87110

R.L. WALKER
STARLING
P.O. BOX 30127
ALBUQUERQUE, N.M. 871110

JERALD T. BALDRIDGE
GEN. RECREATION
P.O. BOX 87125
ALBUQUERQUE, N.M. 87125

H.J. MITCHELL
ATOM
P.O. BOX 1109
FARMINGTON, N.M. 87401

J.H. DENDAHL
EBERLINE
P.O. BOX 2108 AIRPORT RD.
SANTA FE, N.M. 87501

JOHN P. TURNER
MUTUAL OIL OF AMERICA
DRAWER 1446
SANTA FE, N.M. 87501

J.W. EAVES
SANTA FE DOWNS
227 E. PALACE AVE.
SANTA FE, N.M. 87501

R.F. MADERA
MONUMENT ENERGY
P.O. BOX 78
WINSTON, N.M. 87943

ART JOHNSON
FORTUNA
P.O. BOX 1
SUNLAND PK., N.M. 88063

J. RAYMOND HARRIS
GLOVER
1000 N. GARDEN ST.
ROSWELL, N.M. 88201

R.V. WYMAN
INTL. EXPLORATION
P.O. BOX 473
BOULDER CITY, NV. 89005

F.D. GIBSON JR.
PACIFIC ENGINEERING
P.O. BOX 797
HENERSON, NV. 89015

ARTHUR J. TARLEY
CENTURION CORP.
FIRST NATL. BANK BLDG.# 816
LAS VEGAS, NV. 89101

RAYMOND H. SIEGESMUND
DUKE & CO.
401 S. THIRD ST.
LAS VEGAS, NV. 89101

STEPHEN A. WYNN
GOLDEN NUGGET
129 E. FREMONT ST.
LAS VEGAS, NV. 89101

GEORGE E.D. DISHEIM
RECRION
200 FREMONT ST.
LAS VEGAS, NV. 89101

JOSEPH H. KELLEY
SHOWBOAT
2800 FREMONT ST.
LAS VEGAS, NV. 89104

JACK D. SOLOMON
ADVANCED PATENT
P.O. BOX 4276
LAS VEGAS, NV. 89106

LEO R. FREY
LE ROY
900 BONANZA RD.
LAS VEGAS, NV. 89106

FLOYD SMITH
INVESCO INTL.
99 CONVENTION CENTER
LAS VEGAS, NV. 89109

PAUL R. CHANIN
REGENCY
3651 MARYLAND PARKWAY
LAS VEGAS, NV. 89109

G.C. RIDLAND
SIERRA SILVER MINING
3111 BEL AIR DR. STE. 26-E
LAS BEGAS, NV. 89109

RICHARD K. METS JR.
SUN FRUIT
P.O. BOX 11186 AIRPORT RD.
LAS VEGAS, NV. 89111

C. STEEN
GRAND DEPOSIT
P.O. BOX 366
STEAMBOAT,NV. 89436

A.J. BANFORD
SILVER PINE HOMES
907 TAHOE BLVD. STE. 11
LAKE TAHOE, NEV. 89450

LLOYD T. DYER
HARRAH'S
206 N. VIRGINIA ST.
RENO, NV. 89501

ROLLAN D. MELTON
SPEIDEL NEWSPAPERS
411 W. SECOND ST.
RENO, NV. 89503

EARL W. SMITH
SISKON
P.O. BOX 889
RENO, NV. 89504

ROBERT W. SCHILLINGER
ALTIUS
735 E. GAGE AVE.
LOS ANGELES, CALIF. 90001

KENNETH R. SIMPSON JR.
PACIFIC MOULDED
905 E. 59TH. ST.
LOS ANGELES, CALIF. 90001

JOHN E. McELLIGOTT
LEACH
3915 AVALON BLVD.
LOS ANGELES, CALIF. 90003

KEITH ROWAN
CARTE BLANCHE
3460 WILSHIRE BLVD.
LOS ANGELES, CALIF. 90005

A.L. CANUT
SAGE OIL
3243 WILSHIRE BLVD.
LOS ANGELES, CALIF. 90005

MEYER LUSKIN
SCOPE IND.
4250 WILSHIRE BLVD.
LOS ANGELES, CALIF. 90005

ROBERT E. LAVERTY
THRIEFIMART
1837 S. VERMONT AVE.
LOS ANGELES, CALIF. 90006

MICHAEL SREDNICK
PRO-TEL
1933 S. BROADWAY
LOS ANGELES, CALIF. 90007

SEYMOUR C. FARBRICK
VOGUE SHOE
3660 S. HILL ST.
LOS ANGELES, CALIF. 90007

JAMES K. SWEENEY
COMPUTER MACHINERY
P.O. BOX 92300
LOS ANGELES, CALIF. 90009

SEYMOUR KAHN
IPM TECH. INC.
6851 W. IMPERIAL HIGHWAY
LOS ANGELES, CALIF. 90009

RYAL R. POPPA
PERTEC CORP.
P.O. BOX 92300
LOS ANGELES, CALIF. 90009

WAYNE M. HOFFMAN
TIGER INTL
L.A. INTL. AIRPORT
LOS ANGELES, CALIF. 90009

FRED MAXEY
SAWYER ADECOR INTL.
3780 WILSHIRE BLVD. STE. 1105
LOS ANGELES, CALIF. 90010

J.R. VAUGHAN
KNUDSEN
231 E. 23RD. ST.
LOS ANGELES, CALIF. 90011

ELLIETTE BRYAN
MISS ELLIETTE
1919 SOUTH LOS ANGELES ST.
LOS ANGELES, CALIF. 90011

GERALD L. KATELL
PARKING STRUCTURES
250 E. FIRST ST.
LOS ANGELES, CALIF. 90012

DAVID BLUM
BARRY'S JEWELERS
543 S. BROADWAY
LOS ANGELES, CALIF. 90013

JACK E. LITT
ARPEJA-CALIFORNIA
860 S. LOS ANGELES ST.
LOS ANGELES, CALIF. 90014

F.G. HATHAWAY
LAACO
431 W. 7TH. ST.
LOS ANGELES, CALIF. 90014

DAVID J. THURIN
BENO'S
1515 SANTEE ST.
LOS ANGELES, CALIF. 90015

PETER DE WETTER
BEKING
1335 S. FIGUEROA ST.
LOS ANGELES, CALIF. 90015

HARRY ROSS
CAMPUS CASUALS
1200 S. HOPE ST.
LOS ANGELES, CALIF. 90015

ROBERT COLMAN
ALEX COLMAN
910 S. LOS ANGELES ST.
LOS ANGELES, CALIF. 90015

S. HAROLD WEISBROD
HARLYN PRODUCTS
1515 S. MAIN ST.
LOS ANGELES, CALIF. 90015

JACK MARION
MARION FABRICS
1140 SANTEE ST.
LOS ANGELES, CALIF. 90015

M.H. SALTER
MISS PAT
1515 SANTEE ST.
LOS ANGELES, CALIF. 90015

JEROME CORNGOLD
TOBIAS KOTZIN
1300 SANTEE ST.
LOS ANGELES, CALIF. 90015

ERNIE LEVY
DIKETAN
1920 W. OLYMPIC BLVD.
LOS ANGELES, CALIF. 90016

ALPHONSE A. JACOBELLIS
GREER HYDRALULICS
5930 WEST JEFFERSON BLVD.
LOS ANGELES, CALIF. 90016

S.L. POLLACK
NATL. HYGIENICS
3344 S. LA CIENEGA BLVD.
LOS ANGELES, CALIF. 90016

CARL GOLDMAN
OLYMPIC PLASTICS
5800 W. JEFFERSON BLVD.
LOS ANGELES, CALIF. 90016

L.H. STRAUS
THRIFTY
5051 RODEO RD.
LOS ANGELES, CALIF. 90016

LELAND K. WHITTIER
BELRIDGE OIL
1300 W. FOURTH ST.
LOS ANGELES, CALIF. 90017

MICHAEL A. MORPHY
CALIFORNIA PORTLAND CEMENT
800 WILSHIRE BLVD.
LOS ANGELES, CALIF. 90017

JOHN W. CLUTE
CLUTE INTL.
1725 W. SIXTH ST.
LOS ANGELES, CALIF. 90017

C. WESLEY POULSON
COLDWELL, BANKER
533 FREMONT AVE.
LOS ANGELES, CALIF.90017

ROBERT F. BAUER
GLOBAL MARINE
811 W. SEVENTH ST.
LOS ANGELES, CALIF. 90017

ARTHUR GUYER
HARVEST FARMS
1256 W. 7TH. ST. STE. 226
LOS ANGELES, CALIF. 90017

MERLE H. BANTA
LEISURE GROUP
UNION BANK SQUARE
LOS ANGELES, CALIF. 90017

B.C. McCABE
MAGMA ENERGY
631 S. WITMER ST.
LOS ANGELES, CALIF. 90017

B.C. McCABE
MAGMA POWER CO.
631 S. WITMER ST.
LOS ANGELES, CALIF. 90017

J.R. BOZMAN
MERCHANTS PETROLEUM
1636 W. EIGHT ST.
LOS ANGELES, CALIF. 90017

R. McCOLLUM
NATL. OIL CO.
NATL. OIL BLDG.
LOS ANGELES, CALIF. 90017

JOSEPH T. HOOTMAN
REMOTE COMPUTING
ONE WILSHIRE BLDG. STE. 1400
LOS ANGELES, CALIF. 90017

R.P. STRUB
SANTA ANITA CONSOLIDATED
ONE WILSHIRE BLDG. STE. 2525
LOS ANGELES, CALIF. 90017

J.R. ELLIOTT
STATE EXPLORATION
800 WILSHIRE BLVD.
LOS ANGELES, CALIF. 90017

W.L. BOYER
WESTATES PETROLEUM
811 W. 7TH. ST.
LOS ANGELES, CALIF. 90017

JACK R. LARSON
WESTMOR CORP.
445 SOUTH FIGUEROA ST.
LOS ANGELES, CALIF. 90017

WILLIAM A. KERR
KERR GLASS MANUFACTURING
501 S. SHATTO PL.
LOS ANGELES, CALIF. 90020

S.A. RESNECK
AMERICAN PROTECTION
1501 S. ALAMEDA ST.
LOS ANGELES, CALIF. 90021

ROGER W. COLEMAN
S.E. RYKOFF
761 TERMINAL ST.
LOS ANGELES, CALIF. 90021

MORTON STEINBERG
STAR-LITE
915 SOUTH MATEO ST.
LOS ANGELES, CALIF. 90021

CURTIS H. PALMER
ARDEN-MAYFAIR
2500 S. GARFIELD AVE.
LOS ANGELES, CALIF. 90022

D.A. KOEPPEL
BLUE CHIP STAMPS
5801 SOUTH EASTERN AVE.
LOS ANGELES, CALIF. 90022

J. ROBERT FLUOR
FLUOR CORP.
2500 SOUTH ATLANTIC BLVD.
LOS ANGELES, CALIF. 90022

CHARLES F. FARRELL JR.
LUMINALL PAINTS
2750 SOUTH GARFIELD AVE.
LOS ANGELES, CALIF. 90022

L.J. SCHEID
TEXTONE
6533 BANDINI BLVD.
LOS ANGELES, CALIF. 90022

BERT J. SHERWOOD
CHEMPLATE
4355 E. SHEILA ST.
LOS ANGELES, CALIF. 90023

MORTON M. WEISS
INTER-POLYMER IND.
3141-51 E. WASHINGTON BLVD.
LOS ANGELES, CALIF. 90023

DR. MORRIS S. FRANKEL
ARGO PETROLEUM
10880 WILSHIRE BLVD.
LOS ANGELES, CALIF. 90024

HENRY C. HEIL JR.
CAREX INTL.
924 WESTWOOD BLVD.
LOS ANGELES, CALIF. 90024

R.R. SUSNAR
DIVERSIFIED EARTH
10880 WILSHIRE BLVD.
LOS ANGELES, CALIF. 90024

GERALD D. MURPHY
EARLY CALIF. IND.
10960 WILSHIRE BLVD.
LOS ANGELES, CALIF. 90024

RICHARD G. NEWMAN
GENGE
10960 WILSHIRE BLVD.
LOS ANGELES, CALIF. 90024

DONALD J. OSWALD
IMODCO
10960 WILSHIRE BLVD.
LOS ANGELES, CALIF. 90024

ELI BROAD
KAUFMAN & BROAD
10901 NATINAL BLVD.
LOS ANGELES, CALIF. 90024

C.V. WOOD JR.
MC CULLOCH OIL
10880 WILSHIRE BLVD.
LOS ANGELES,CALIF. 90024

HAROLD SONNERS
NORMAN WIATT CO.
10450 WILSHIRE BLVD.
LOS ANGELES, CALIF. 90024

THEODORE OFF JR.
OJAI OIL
1387 WESTWOOD BLVD.
LOS ANGELES, CALIF. 90024

WILLIAM K. HODSON
PLANNING RESEARCH
1100 GLENDON AVE.
LOS ANGELES, CALIF. 90024

ROBERT J. FOX
RUSCO IND.
1100 GLENDON STE. 1616
LOS ANGELES, CALIF. 90024

H.H. LEACH
TEJON RANCH
10850 WILSHIRE BLVD.
LOS ANGELES, CALIF. 90024

WILLIAM MALAT
WESTERN ORBITS
P.O. BOX 24545
LOS ANGELES, CALIF.90024

G.M. JENNINGS
EVEREST & JENNINGS
1803 PONTIUS AVE.
LOS ANGELES, CALIF. 90025

BERNARD SHAPIRO
FAMILIAN
12353 WILSHIRE BLVD.
LOS ANGELES, CALIF. 90025

JAMES MATARESE JR.
MACRODYNE IND.
1845 S. BUNDY DR.
LOS ANGELES, CALIF. 90025

A.M. HARRISON
MICRON
1519 PONTIUS AVE.
LOS ANGELES, CALIF. 90025

BILL LE VINE
POSTAL INSTANT
10835 SANTA MONICA BLVD.
LOS ANGELES, CALIF. 90025

CHARLES H. BARRIS
CHUCK BARRIS PROD.
1313 N. VINE ST.
HOLLYWOOD, CALIF. 90028

S.A. GREER
CALSTAR PETROLEUM
802 EQUITABLE BLDG.
HOLLYWOOD, CALIF. 90028

C. LAUFER
LAUFER CO.
7060 HOLLYWOOD BLVD.
HOLLYWOOD, CALIF. 90028

C.O. WALLICHS
WALLICHS MUSIC
1515 N. VINE ST.
HOLLYWOOD, CALIF. 90028

FREDERICK N. MELLINGER
FREDERICK'S OF HOLLYWOOD
6608 HOLLYWOOD BLVD.
LOS ANGELES, CALIF. 90028

BARRY P. EPSTEIN
MEDIA CREATIONS
6528 SUNSET BLVD.
LOS ANGELES, CALIF. 90028

P.V. UEBERROTH
TCI TRAVEL
6290 SUNSET BLVD.
LOS ANGELES, CALIF. 90028

LEON J. CANDON
KENNINGTON LTD.
3209 HUMBOLDT ST.
LOS ANGELES, CALIF. 90031

PETER P. WARDLE
BIRTCHER CORP.
4371 VALLEY BLVD.
LOS ANGELES, CALIF. 90032

DENNIS C. STANFILL
TWENITH CENTURY-FOX FILM
10201 W. PICO BLVD.
LOS ANGELES, CALIF. 90035

WILLIAM J. MORRIS JR.
ACTIVE MANAGEMENT
5670 WILSHIRE BLVD. STE.1690
LOS ANGELES, CALIF. 90036

LEONARD A. AARON
AARON BROS.
960 N. LA BREA AVE.
LOS ANGELES, CALIF. 90038

H.V. STANCIL
STANCIL-HOFFMAN
921 N. HIGHLAND AVE.
HOLLYWOOD, CALIF. 90038

ARTHUR N. RYAN
TECHNICOLOR
6311 ROMAINE ST.
HOLLYWOOD, CALIF. 90038

JACQUES URBACH
UROPTICS INTL.
6208 SANTA MONICA BLVD.
LOS ANGELES, CALIF. 90038

AL R. MARKEY
CENTURY MED. INC.
5443 E. WASHINGTON BLVD.
CITY OF COMMERCE, CALIF. 90040

BERNARD MARCUS
HANDY DAN HOME
6915 E. SLAUSON AVE.
CITY OF COMMERCE, CALIF. 90040

FRED P. BURNS
APOLLO LASER
6365 ARIZONA CIRCLE
LOS ANGELES, CALIF. 90045

WARD F. MOORE
FILTROL
5959 W. CENTURY BLVD.
LOS ANGELES, CALIF. 90045

T.A. BRUINSMA
HARVEST IND.
9841 AIRPORT BLVD.
LOS ANGELES, CALIF. 90045

BERNARD BRISKIN
HOGAN FAXIMILE
8700 BELLANCA AVE.
LOS ANGELES, CALIF. 90045

ROBERT NETHERCUTT
MERLE NORMAN COSMETICS
9130 BELLANCA AVE.
LOS ANGELES, CALIF. 90045

LLOYD E. COTSEN
NEUTROGENA
5755 W. 96TH. ST.
LOS ANGELES, CALIF. 90045

WILLIAM R. MATTESON
PORTAFONE
7351 SUNSET BLVD.
LOS ANGELES, CALIF. 90045

JOSEPH R. MEALEY SR.
TEACHING TECH.
6520 ARIZONA AVE.
LOS ANGELES, CALIF. 90045

BERNARD BRISKIN
TELAUTOGRAPH
8700 BELLANCA AVE.
LOS ANGELES, CALIF. 90045

HARRY M. BAKER
WTC
5959 W. CENTURY BLVD.
LOS ANGELES, CALIF. 90045

CHARLES MARTIN
FORWARD FILMS
1041 FORMOSA AVE.
LOS ANGELES, CALIF. 90046

JARRELL D. ORMAND
ORMAND IND.
12001 SAN VICENTE BLVD.
LOS ANGELES, CALIF. 90047

CHARLES S. OFFER
BUDGET IND.
6434 WILSHIRE BLVD.
LOS ANGELES, CALIF. 90048

WILLIAM R. FORMAN
CINERAMA
141 S. ROBERTSON BLVD.
LOS ANGELES, CALIF. 90048

JOSEPH SOLOMON
FANFARE
7666 BEVERLY BLVD.
LOS ANGELES, CALIF. 90048

HAROLD A. LANDERS
LANDERS-ROBERTS
8899 BEVERLY BLVD.
LOS ANGELES, CALIF. 90048

L.L. SLOAN
PRICE/STERN/SLOAN PUB.
410 NORTH LA CIENEGA BLVD.
LOS ANGELES, CALIF. 90048

STANLEY ROWEN
ZENITH AMERICAN LAND
6300 WILSHIRE BLVD.
LOS ANGELES, CALIF. 90048

RAYMOND M. O'KEEFE
A.J. IND.
11454 SAM VICENTE BLVD.
LOS ANGELES, CALIF. 90049

RICHARD K. EAMER
NATL. MEDICAL
11661 SAN VICENTE, STE. 303
LOS ANGELES, CALIF. 90049

BYRON P. WEINTZ
CONROCK
3200 SAN FERNANDO RD.
LOS ANGELES, CALIF. 90051

PAUL RAVESIES
SINCLAIR VENEZUELAN OIL
P.O. BOX 2679,
LOS ANGELES, CALIF. 90051

H.W. WRIGHT JR.
SWECO
P.O. BOX 4151
LOS ANGELES, CALIF. 90051

RICHARD C. SIMPSON
DUCOMMUN
P.O. BOX 2117
LOS ANGELES, CALIF. 90054

A.F. KANE
FAMILY RECORD PLAN
2015 WEST OLYMPIC BLVD.
LOS ANGELES, CALIF. 90054

J.W. JORGENSEN
EARLE M. JORGENSEN
10650 SOUTH ALAMEDA ST.
LOS ANGELES, CALIF. 90054

HAL W. BROWN JR.
PIA MERCHANDISING
P.O. BOX 54917
LOS ANGELES, CALIF. 90054

THOMAS M. ASHER PH.D.
IMMUNO-SCIENCE
1803 WILSHIRE BLVD.
LOS ANGELES, CALIF. 90057

IRVING I. GRONSKY
GOLD-PAK MEAT
3163 E. VERNON AVE.
LOS ANGELES, CALIF. 90058

EARL R. POTTER
IND. WIRE PROD.
2417 E. 23RD. ST.
LOS ANGELES, CALIF. 90058

H. AISLEY
JENSEN IND.
1946 E. 46TH. ST.
LOS ANGELES, CALIF. 90058

H.J. MEANY
NORRIS IND.
5215 S. BOYLE AVE.
LOS ANGELES, CALIF. 90058

ARTHUR FRANKEL
PIC'N'SAVE CORP.
4701 S. SANTA FE AVE.
LOS ANGELES, CALIF. 90058

P.M. HACHIGIAN
COMPUCORP
12401 W. OLYMPIC BLVD.
LOS ANGELES, CALIF. 90064

PAUL S. REISBORD
C & R CLOTHIERS
11916 WEST PICO BLVD.
LOS ANGELES, CALIF. 90064

R.C. HIBBARD
PHOTO-SCAN
2223 CARMELINA AVE.
LOS ANGELES, CALIF. 90064

R.N. FRANK
LAWRY'S FOOD
568 SAN FERNANDO RD.
LOS ANGELES, CALIF. 90065

PAUL SCHOONOVER
NONOLITH PORTLAND MIDWEST
3326 SAN FERNANDO RD.
LOS ANGELES, CALIF. 90065

NORMAN H. HABERMANN
COLLINS FOODS INTL.
12731 WEST JEFFERSON BLVD.
LOS ANGELES, CALIF. 90066

T. L. MC KAY
LONG-LOK
4101 REDWOOD AVE.
LOS ANGELES, CALIF. 90066

BERNARD TABAKIN
NATL. TELEFILM
12636 BEATRICE ST.
LOS ANGELES, CALIF. 90066

MILTON E. MOHR
QUOTRON SYSTEMS
5454 BEETHOVEN ST.
LOS ANGELES, CALIF. 90066

LOGAN J. HINES
UMF SYSTEMS
5521 GROSVENOR BLVD.
LOS ANGELES, CALIF. 90066

BEN C. WANG
WANGCO
5404 JANDY PL.
LOS ANGELES, CALIF. 90066

CORWIN E. DENNEY
AUTOMATION IND.
1901 BUILDING AVE. 2000
LOS ANGELES, CALIF. 90067

THEODORE E. WILLIAMS
BELL IND.
1880 CENTURY PARK EAST STE.400
LOS ANGELES, CALIF. 90067

E.P. MARTINI JR.
BERGEN-BRUNSWIG
1900 AVE. OF THE STARS
LOS ANGELES, CALIF. 90067

WILLIAM H. MC ELNEA JR.
CAESARS WORLD
1801 CENTURY PARK EAST
LOS ANGELES, CALIF. 90067

JOHN J. CONNOLLY
CORDON INTL.
10100 SANTA MONICA NO. 740
LOS ANGELES, CALIF. 90067

JOHN H. DOUGLAS
DEVON GROUP
1880 CENTURY PARK EAST
LOS ANGELES, CALIF. 90067

RICHARD L. BLOCH
FILMWAYS
1800 CENTURY PARK EAST
LOS ANGELES, CALIF. 90067

C.W. HATTEN
GREAT BASINS PETROLEUM
1011 GATEWAY WEST
LOS ANGELES, CALIF. 90067

HARRY GROMAN
HARGROM SERCIE
1900 AVE OF THE STARS
LOS ANGELES, CALIF. 90067

ANGUS A. SCOTT
H M O INTL.
1880 CENTURY PARK EAST STE. 1500
LOS ANGELES, CALIF. 90067

IRVING N. ALPERN
HUNTINGTON HEALTH
10100 SANTA MONICA BLVD.
LOS ANGELES, CALIF. 90067

ALFRED STROGOFF
INTL. FOODSERVICE
1888 CENTURY PARK E. NO. 920
LOS ANGELES, CALIF. 90067

L.B. KORN
KORN-FERRY INTL.
1900 AVE. OF THE STARS
LOS ANGELES, CALIF 90067

BAXTER HALLAIAN
NOLEX CORP.
1800 CENTURY PARK EAST STE. 1118
CENTURY CITY, CALIF. 90067

H.H. KAYE
PACIFIC COAST MED.
421 S. BEVERLY DR.
BEVERLY HILLS, CALIF. 90067

W.R. PAGEN
PAULEY PETROLEUM
10000 SANTA MONICA BLVD.
LOS ANGELES, CALIF. 90067

W.B. ELCOCK JR.
PIEDMONT MANAGEMENT CO.
10100 SANTA MONICA BLVD.
LOS ANGELES, CALIF. 90067

CHARLES F. SMITH
PINEHURST
1800 AVE. OF THE STARS
LOS ANGELES, CALIF. 90067

DONALD BERGMAN
PROSHER
1901 AVE. OF THE STARS
LOS ANGELES, CALIF. 90067

RALPH O. BRISCOE
REPUBLIC
1900 AVE. OF THE STARS
LOS ANGELES, CALIF. 90067

DAN W. BURNS
SARGENT IND.
1901 AVE. OF THE STARS, STE.1251
LOS ANGELES, CALIF. 90067

GRAEME W. HENDERSON
SOURCE CAPITAL
18888 CENTURY PARK EAST
LOS ANGELES, CALIF. 90067

L.A. AULT III
TELECREDIT
1901 AVE. OF THE STARS
LOS ANGELES, CALIF. 90067

MORTON M. WINSTON
TOSCO
10100 SANTA MONICA BLVD.
LOS ANGELES, CALIF. 90067

CHARLES R. COLE JR.
TRATEC
2040 AVE. OF THE STARS
LOS ANGELES, CALIF. 90067

LEONARD ROSS
WYNDON
1900 AVE. OF THE STARS
LOS ANGELES, CALIF. 90067

SEYMOUR HELLER
AMERICAN VARIETY
9220 SUNSET BLVD.
LOS ANGELES, CALIF. 90069

ERIC LIDOW
INTL. RECTIFIER
9220 SUNSET BLVD.
LOS ANGELES, CALIF. 90069

KENNETH LIEBER
CYPRUS MINES
855 S. FLOWER ST.
LOS ANGELES, CALIF. 90071

S.H. BRESSNER
SOUTHERN CROSS IND.
P.O. BOX 505
CONYERS, CALIF. 90207

ROYCE DIENER
AMERICAN MED. INTL.
414 NO. CAMDEN DR.
BEVERLY HILLS, CALIF. 90210

A.A. HOPKINS, JR.
THE DAL PETROLEUM
9437 SANTA MONICA BLVD.
BEVERLY HILLS, CALIF. 90210

DONALD L. LA CAVA
ECI IND.
9171 WILSHIRE BLVD.
BEVERLY HILLS, CALIF. 90210

DONALD E. LIEDERMAN
FEDERATED COMMUNICATIONS
1025 RIDGEDALE DR.
BEVERLY HILLS, CALIF. 90210

HARRY LEWIS
HAMBURGER HAMLETS
322 N. FOOTHILL RD.
BEVERLY HILLS, CALIF. 90210

EARL M. CRANSTON
OIL RESOURCES
1025 RIDGEDALE DR.
BEVERLY HILLS, CALIF. 90210

HAROLD A. HAYTIN
TELECOR
P.O. BOX 5000
BEVERLY HILLS, CALIF. 90210

J.D. WRATHER JR.
WRATHER CORP.
270 N. CANON DR.
BEVERLY HILLS, CALIF. 90210

SAMUEL Z ARKOFF
AMERICAN INTL. PICTURES
9033 WILSHIRE BLVD.
BEVERLY HILLS, CALIF. 90211

JOSEPH BULASKY
ASSOC. HOSTS
8447 WILSHIRE BLVD.
BEVERLY HILLS, CALIF. 90211

RUDOLPH L. SCHAEFER
MET. DEVELOPMENT
8447 WILSHIRE BLVD.
BEVERLY HILLS, CALIF. 90211

EARL SCHEIB
EARL SCHEIB
8737 WILSHIRE BLVD.
BEVERLY HILLS, CALIF. 90211

NATHAM SHAPELL
SHAPELL IND.
8383 WILSHIRE BLVD.
BEVERLY HILLS, CALIF. 90211

GORDON NEAVES
COMSTOCK GOLD, SILVER,COPPER
239 SOUTH BEVERLY DR.
BEVERLY HILLS, CALIF. 90212

DAVID B. CHARNAY
FOUR STAR INTL.
400 SOUTH BEVERLY DR.
BEVERLY HILLS, CALIF. 90212

FRANK ABRAMOFF
FRANKLIN MARKETING
9350 WILSHIRE BLVD.
BEVERLY HILLS, CALIF. 90212

WALTER KORNBLUM
GALAXIE NTL. CORP.
9601 WILSHIRE BLVD.
BEVERLY HILLS, CALIF. 90212

FRANK KING
KING INTL. CORP.
124 LASKY DR.
BEVERLY HILLS, CALIF. 90212

LEOPOLD S. WYLER
TRE
9460 WILSHIRE BLVD.
BEVERLY HILLS, CALIF. 90212

RICHARD A. GRIEBEL
TASSAWAY
P.O. BOX N
BEVERLY HILLS, CALIF. 90213

PETER M. BEHRENDT
CRAIG
921 W. ARTESIA BLVD.
COMPTON, CALIF. 90220

ROBERT B. PHINIZY
GENISCO TECH.
18435 SUSANA RD.
COMPTON, CALIF. 90221

PAUL CHUDNOW
LLOYD'S ELECTRONICS
18601 S. SUSANA RD.
COMPTON, CALIF. 90221

HOWARD M. KLEIN
STANDUM
2943 E. LAS HERMANAS ST.
COMPTON, CALIF. 90221

GUSTAV DALLA VALLE
UNDER SEA IND.
3105 EAST HARCOURT
COMPTON, CALIF. 90221

W.E. BURGET
ACCURATE AIR ENGINEERING
2712 N. ALAMEDA ST.
COMPTON, CALIF. 90222

LEON HAMLIN
GEN. HEALTH SERVICES
3838 HUGHES AVE.
CULVER CITY, CALIF. 90230

WALTER K. CLIFFORD
IMAGE SYSTEMS
11244 PLAYA CT.
CULVER CITY, CALIF. 90230

A.L. FENAUGHTY
INFOMATION INTL.
5933 SLAVSON AVE.
CULVER CITY, CALIF. 90230

V.F. EVERY
MECHMETAL-TRONICS
11431 JOANNE PL.
CULVER CITY, CALIF. 90230

FRANCIS A. DEDONA
SCIONICS
3623 EASTHAM DR.
CULVER CITY, CALIF. 90230

GRAHAM TYSON
DATAPRODUCTION
6219 DE SOTO AVE.
WOODLAND HILLS, CALIF. 90231

FRANKLIN S. BRILES
BRILES MANUFACTURING
1415 EAST GRAND AVE.
EL SEGUNDO, CALIF. 90245

DANIEL R. MASON
COMPUTAX SERVICES
601 NASH ST.
EL SEGUNDO, CALIF. 90245

WILLIAM R. HOOVER
COMPUTER SCIENCES
650 N. SEPULVEDA BLVD.
EL SEGUNDO, CALIF. 90245

RICHARD S. FARR
FARR CO.
2301 ROSECRANS AVE.
EL SEGUNDO, CALIF. 90245

ALLAN B. FOY
TRANSCON LINES
101 CONTINENTAL BLVD.
EL SEGUNDO, CALIF. 90245

STANLEY WAINER
WYLE LAB.
128 MARYLAND ST.
EL SEGUNDO, CALIF. 90245

DAVID KIERMAN
CHALCO IND.
15126 SOUTH BROADWAY
GARDENA, CALIF. 90247

DAVID D. STERNS
ELIXIR IND.
17909 SOUTH BROADWAY
GARDENA, CALIF. 90247

ROBERT J. TAYLOR
PACIFIC AMERICAN IND.
661 W. REDONDO BEACH BLVD.
GARDENA, CALIF. 90247

ARNOLD SCHOTT
PACIFIC ELECTRICORD
747 W. REDONDO BEACH BLVD.
GARDENA, CALIF. 90247

HANS BUEHLER
REX PRECISION
14831 MAPLE AVE.
GARDENA, CALIFORNIA 90247

S.N. LEWIS
ROADCRAFT MFG.
139 W. WALNUT AVE.
GARDENA, CALIF. 90247

KENNETH DONNER
BARCO OF CALIF.
P.O. BOX 350
GARDENA, CALIF. 90248

SAMUEL MYERHOFF
BRENTWOOD IND.
204 W. ROSECRANS
GARDENA, CALIF. 90248

SHELDON BAER
SURVEYOR IND.
15730 SOUTH FIGUEROA ST.
GARDENA, CALIF. 90248

W.B. LOSK
TRICO IND.
15707 S. MAIN ST.
GARDENA, CALIF. 90248

ROBERT E. ANTONACCI
GRAPHIC ARTS
2140 W. 139TH. ST.
GARDENA, CALIF. 90249

LEE HARTSTONE
THE INTEGRITY ENTERTAINMENT
14100 S. KINGSLEY DR.
GARDENA, CALIF. 90249

HYMAN N. COHEN
COMP-SERV CO.
12605 SO. VAN NESS
HAWTHORNE, CALIF. 90250

ROBERT SILVERSTEIN
ELDON IND.
2701 W. EL SEGUNDO BLVD.
HAWTHORNE, CALIF. 90250

ERNEST W. HAHN
ERNEST W. HAHN INC.
2311 W. EL SEGUNDO BLVD.
HAWTHORNE, CALIF. 90250

ARTHUR S. SPEAR
MATTEL
5150 ROSECRANS AVE.
HAWTHORNE, CALIF. 90250

E.R. DICKSTEIN
OMNI-RX HEALTH
11616 HAWTHORNE BLVD.
HAWTHORNE, CALIF. 90250

WALTER C. WOLF
THERMODYNE INTL.
12600 YUKON AVE.
HAWTHORNE, CALIF. 90250

ROBERT S. HOOD
WEMS
4650 W. ROSECRANS
HAWTHORNE, CALIF. 90252

D.W. COX
WESTERN MAGNUM
711 15TH. ST.
HERMOSA BEACH, CALIF. 90254

M.J. LUGASH
MAXON IND.
P.O. BOX 2528
HUNTINGTON PARK, CALIF. 90255

ROBERT J. GARON
LANDSVERK
P.O. BOX 755
LAWNDALE, CALIF. 90260

JAMES E. MENOR
CAYMAN CORP.
608 SILVER SPUR RD.
PALOS VERDES PEN., CALIF. 90274

RONALD P. BALDWIN
GEOTHERMAL RESOURCES
1613 VIA MONTEMAR
PALOS VERDES ESTATES, CALIF.90274

W.F. MONAHAN
OCEANARIUM
MARINELAND OF THE PACIFIC
PALOS VERDES EXTATES, CALIF.90274

HARVEY R. KIBEL
OPEN ROAD IND.
2601 MANHATTAN BEACH BLVD.
REDONDO, CALIF. 90278

GERARD LICCIARDI
ANADITE
10647 GARFIELD AVE.
SOUTH GATE, CALIF. 90280

ROBERT P. LICHT
ANTHONY IND.
P.O. BOX 1131
SOUTHGATE, CALIF. 90280

ROBERT P. LICHT
SIMPLEX IND.
5871 FIRESTONE BLVD.
SOUTH GATE, CALIF. 90280

ROYLE GLASER LASKY
REVELL
4223 GLENCOE AVE.
VENICE, CALIF. 90291

R.L. CALL
SAV-ON-DRUGS
4818 LINCOLN BLVD.
MARINA DEL RAY, CALIF. 90291

D.S. SHANKS
COMPUTER MICROGRAPHICS
5345 W. 120TH. ST.
INGLEWOOD, CALIF. 90301

JOSEPH K. TAUSSIG
JET AIR FREIGHT
900 W. FLORENCE AVE.
INGLEWOOD, CALIF. 90301

JAMES D. HUNTER
VAPORTECH
11010 S. LA CIENCGA BLVD.
INGLEWOOD, CALIF. 90304

M.J. SHAPIRO
WINCORP.
HOLLYWOOD PARK
INGLEWOOD, CALIF. 90306

RUSSELL C. DU BOISE
VARADYNE
P.O. BOX 3710
SANTA MONICA, CALIF. 90403

JOHN J. PHILLIPS
G & H TECHNOLOGY
1649 17TH. ST.
SANTA MONICA, CALIF. 90404

S. DONALD SIMS
HADRON
2520 COLORADO AVE.
SANTA MONICA, CALIF. 90404

LASZLO Z. KERESZTURY
KERONIX
1752 CLOVERFIELD BLVD.
SANTA MONICA, CALIF. 90404

A.W.R. MACKENZIE
MOTHERHOOD MATERNITY
1330 COLORADO AVE.
SANTA MONICA, CALIF. 90404

SYDNEY ROTH
ROTH IND.
3300 OLYMPIC BLVD.
SANTA MONICA, CALIF. 90404

GEORGE E. MUELLER
SYSTEMS DEVELOPMENT
2500 COLORADO AVE.
SANTA MONICA, CALIF. 90404

A.G. SCHEID
WINKLER SCHEID VINEYARDS
1666 NINTH ST.
SANTA MONICA, CALIF. 90404

JOZEF NABEL
C-V AMERICAN
2830 PICO BLVD.
SANTA MONICA, CALIF. 90405

CHARLES M. HOLLIS
GUIDANCE TECH.
2500 BROADWAY AVE.
SANTA MONICA, CALIF. 90406

HOWARD E. VARNER
HOST INTL.
34TH. & PICO BLVD.
SANTA MONICA, CALIF. 90406

EDWARD C. ELLIS
PACIFIC COAST PROPERTIES
P.O. BOX 2116
SANTA MONICA, CALIF. 90406

ROY F. FARMER
FARMER BROS.
20333 S. NORMANDIE AVE.
TORRANCE, CALIF. 90501

JOHN N. GALARDI
DER WIENERSCHNITZEL INTL.
1047 W. CARSON ST.
TORRANCE, CALIF. 90502

RONALD M. SIMON
PERMA-BILT IND.
19106 S. NORMANIE AVE.
TORRANCE, CALIF. 90502

HAROLD ALDEN
BRENTWOOD ORIGINALS
20030 SOUTH NORMANDIE
TORRANCE, CALIF. 90503

J.R. WOODHULL
LOGICON
21535 HAWTHORNE BLVD.
TORRANCE, CALIF. 90503

WILLIAM SHAPHREN
PHONE-MATE
335 MAPLE AVE.
TORRANCE, CALIF. 90503

R.J. BENECCHI
AERONCA
P.O. BOX 2969
TORRANCE, CALIF. 90505

ROBERT L. McKAY
TACO BELL
2424 MORETON ST.
TORRANCE, CALIF. 90505

M.A. MINER
TRIDAIR IND.
3000 W. LOMITA BLVD.
TORRANCE, CALIF. 90505

PERRY A. LUTH JR.
HI-SHEAR IND.
SKYPARK DR.
TORRANCE, CALIF. 90509

JOHN DE GREGORY
STANDARD BRANDS PAINT
4300 W. 190TH. ST.
TORRANCE, CALIF. 90509

RAYMOND E. HIGH
COMPUTER COMM. INC.
2610 COLUMBIA ST.
TORRANCE, CALIF. 90530

A. WALTER ROGNLIEN
WESTERN ICEE
11712 E. WASHINGTON BLVD.
WHITTER, CALIF. 90606

ERNEST E. CHIPMAN
PRODUCTOL CHEM.
P.O. BOX 12
WHITTIER, CALIF. 90608

VERNE H. WINCHELL
DENNY'S
14256 E. FIRESTONE BLVD.
LA MIRADA, CALIF. 90638

HOWARD SHERMAN
SILVERCREST IND.
P.O. BOX 486
NORWALK, CALIF. 90650

R.J. PASAROW
CHB FOODS
7351 CRIDER AVE.
PICO RIVERA, CALIF. 90660

J.I. HATHAWAY
PYRAMID OIL
10707 S. NORWALK BLVD.
SANTA FE SPRINGS, CALIF. 90670

J.J. O'BRIEN
SEABOARD OIL & GAS CO.
P.O. BOX 3608
SANTA FE SPRINGS, CALIF. 90670

JACK L. DAVIES
SUPER-TEMP
11008 SOUTH NORWALK BLVD.
SANTA FE SPRINGS, CALIF. 90670

ROBERT L. UPSHAW
DENTALLOY
P.O. BOX 245
STANTON, CALIF. 90680

A.J. CENTOFANTE
ASTROPHYSICS RESEARCH
1526 WES 240TH. ST.
HARBOR CITY, CALIF. 90710

W.I. THOMAS
PATHCOM
24049 SOUTH FRAMPTON AVE.
HARBOR CITY, CALIF. 90710

WILLIAM R. TINCHER
PUREX
5101 CLARK AVE.
LAKEWOOD, CALIF. 90713

F. VESSELS JR.
LOS ALMITOS RACE COURSE
4961 KATELLA AVE.
LOS ALMITOS, CALIF. 90720

J.P. HYNES
STANDARD COMPUTER
29000 S. WESTERN STE. 210
SAN PEDRO, CALIF. 90732

JOSEPH A. KUEWEMAN
CHEM AERO
231 E. LOMITA BLVD.
WILMINGTON, CALIF. 90744

ROBERT VULCAN
C.M. IND.
231 E. LOMITA BLVD.
WILMINGTON, CALIF. 90744

JOHN V. JONES
TEK-AID
911 WEST B ST.
WILMINGTON,CALIF. 90744

JOHN H. WRIGHT
UNITED COMPUTING
22550 S. AVALON
CARSON, CALIF. 90745

H.B. RODSTEIN
RODAC
1005 E. ARTESIA BLVD.
CARSON, CALIF. 90746

E.R. BALDWIN
FEDERAL STEEL
P.O. BOX 969
LONG BEACH, CALIF. 90801

JOHN C. WALLACE
PETROLANE
1600 E. HILL ST.
LONG BEACH, CALIF. 90801

EDWARD L. LAWLOR
OCEAN SCIENCE
1601 WATER ST.
LONG BEACH, CALIF. 90802

L.L. KAVANAU
SYSTEMS ASSOC.
444 W. OCEAN BLVD.
LONG BEACH , CALIF. 90802

R.K. SUMMY
OIL SECURITIES
5530 THE TOLEDO
LONG BEACH, CALIF. 90803

DAVID G. DAVIDSON
EDG
2400 E. ARTESIA BLVD.
LONG BEACH, CALIF. 90805

D.C. TALLICHET JR.
SPECIALTY RESTAURANTS
2977 REDONDO AVE.
LONG BEACH, CALIF. 90806

RICHARD A. DICK
CAL-STATE AIR LINES
P.O. BOX 8064
LONG BEACH, CALIF. 90808

DAN POCAPALIA
KIT MFG. CO.
1700 SANTA FE AVE.
LONG BEACH, CALIF. 90813

F.J. HOWELL
RAYMAR BOOK
1551 S. PRIMROSE AVE.
MONROVIA, CALIF. 91016

H.F. COLVIN
UNITEK
950 ROYAL OAKS DR.
MONROVIA, CALIF. 91016

CONRAD VON BIBRA
EXETER OIL
1810 FAIR OAKS
SOUTH PASADENA, CALIF. 91030

J.M. GROSSMAN
AREX IND.
201 S. LAKE AVE.
PASADENA, CALIF. 91101

ROBERT W. VAN TUYLE
BEVERLY ENTERPRISES
251 S. LAKE AVE.
PASADENA, CALIF. 91101

MERRILL L. NASH
BROWN
251 S. LAKE AVE.
PASADENA, CALIF. 91101

ROBERT CORNET
CORNET STORES
411 S. ARROYO PARKWAY
PASADENA, CALIF. 91101

R.W. JURGENSEN
JURGENSEN"S
601 SOUTH LAKE AVE.
PASADENA, CALIF. 91101

W.R. NOACK
ARGUS RESOURCES
P.O. BOX 2888
PASADENA, CALIF. 91105

EDWARD J. KORBEL
JACOBS ENGINEERING
837 S. FAIR OAKS AVE.
PASADENA, CALIF. 91105

DR. TERRENCE J. GOODING
KRATOS
403 SO. RAYMOND AVE.
PASADENA, CALIF. 91105

H.K. ABAJIAN
RESDEL IND.
990 S. FAIR OAKS AVE.
PASADENA, CALIF. 91105

J.R. JOHNSON
ROYAL IND.
980 SOUTH ARROYO PARKWAY
PASADENA, CALIF. 91105

L.M. PURCELL
DRESSEN-BARNES
250 N. VINEDO AVE.
PASADENA, CALIF. 91107

MASON PHELPS
V S I CORP.
600 NORTH ROSEMEAD BLVD.
PASADENA, CALIF. 91107

CHARLES D. MILLER
AVERY INTL.
415 HUNTINGTON DR.
SAN MARINO, CALIF. 91108

JOHN K. DUCAN
CRESTMONT OIL & GAS
2622 MISSION ST.
SAN MARINO, CALIF. 91108

EDWARD MEYERS
F.C. NASH
250 E. COLORADO BLVD.
PASADENA, CALIF. 91109

WILLIAM E. LEONHARD
RALPH M. PARSONS AVE.
100 W. WALNUT ST.
PASADENA, CALIF. 91124

GEORGE A. WALKER
SPORTS ARENAS
P.O. DOX 3745
GLENDALE, CALIF. 91201

HAROLD COHEN
TRAID
900 GRAND CENTRAL AVE.
GLENDALE, CALIF. 91201

J.M. BROBERG
JB'S BIG BOY FAMILY
420 N. BRAND BLVD.
GLENDALE, CALIF. 91203

H.G. POWELL
WEBB'S STORES
139 N. BRAND BLVD.
GLENDALE, CALIF. 91203

A.J. ROUSE
TRAILER LIFE PUB. CO.
23945 CRAFTSMAN RD. BOX 500
CALABRASAS, CALIF. 91302

ANTHONY J. JOLLES
NUCLEONIC PRODUCTS
6660 VARIEL AVE.
CANOGA PARK, CALIF. 91303

FRANCIS V. WAGNER
ATAR COMPUTER
P.O. BOX 1452
CANOGA PARK, CALIF. 91304

C.R. SALMON
AEROCEANIC
20315 NORDHOFF
CHATSWORTH, CALIF. 91311

GORDON K. FRESHMAN
BANNER GELATIN
20730 DEARBORN ST.
CHATSWORTH, CALIF. 91311

M.J. SALVIN
BISHOP GRAPHIS
20450 PLUMMER ST.
CHATSWORTH, CALIF. 91311

RICHARD O. BAILY
LEXITRON CORP.
9600 DE SOTO AVE.
CHATSWORTH, CALIF. 91311

NAT LERMAN
NATEL ENGINEERING
8944 MASON AVE.
CHATSWORTH, CALIF. 91311

MIHAI D. PATRICHI
NETWORKS ELECTRONIC
9750 DE SOTO AVE.
CHATSWORTH, CALIF. 91311

JAMES A. REEVES
SPACELABS
20550 PRAIRIE ST.
CHATSWORTH, CALIF. 91311

DONALD SPAR
SPORTSCOACH
9061 CANOGA AVE.
CHATSWORTH, CALIF. 91311

J.S. TUSHINSKY
SUPERSCOPE
20525 NORDHOFF ST.
CHATSWORTH, CALIF. 91311

JOSEPH P. MEYERS
VIKING IND.
21001 NORDHOFF ST.
CHATSWORTH, CALIF. 91311

THOMAS A. O'DONNELL
AMERICAN SAFETY EQUIPMENT
10655 VENTURA BLVD.
ENCINO, CALIF. 91316

BURTON S. SPERBER
ENVIOROMENTAL IND.
16055 VENTURA BLVD.
ENCINO, CALIF. 91316

DR. SHELDON DEUTSCH
MEDICAL TESTING SYSTEMS
16781 OAK VIEW DR.
ENCINO, CALIF. 91316

CHARLES BEDZOW
PACIFIC INTL.
16200 VENTURA BLVD.
ENCINO, CALIF. 91316

H. STUMP
SEMTECH
652 MITCHELL RD.
NEWBURY PARK, CALIF. 91320

WILBERT LLOYD
DIODES
P.O. BOX 2050
NORTHRIDGE, CALIF. 91324

DOUGLAS P. CRONIN
PROPULSION DATA
12670 PIERCE ST.
PACOIMA, CALIF. 91331

PIETRO VITALE
OH BOY-IND.
1516 FIRST ST.
SAN FERNANDO, CALIF. 91340

D.E. RUBENDALL
SAN FERNANDO ELECTRIC
1501 FIRST ST.
SAN FERNANDO, CALIF. 91341

JOHN P. ENDICOTT
THE SIERRACIN CORP.
12780 SAN FERNANDO RD.
SYLMAR, CALIF. 91342

GERALD WEINSTEIN
DATA INSTRUMENTS
16611 ROSCOE PL.
SEPULVEDA, CALIF. 91343

EDGAR I. RAKUSIN
ALPHA GYREX
12161 WOODLEY AVE.
GRANADA HILLS, CALIF. 91344

G.M. JOYCE
FLAMEMASTER
11120 SHERMAN WAY
SUN VALLEY, CALIF. 91352

D.I. SOFRO
HOUSE OF FABRICS
11250 S. HERMAN WAY
SUN VALLEY, CALIF. 91352

J.J. GUARRERA
SACOM
11855 WICKS ST.
SUN VALLEY, CALIF. 91352

R.P. STEVENS
UNIVERSAL BY PRODUCTS
9200 GLENOAKS BLVD.
SUN VALLEY, CALIF. 91352

J.J. DICKASON
THE NEWHALL LAND & FARMING
27050 HENRY MAYOR RD.
VALENCIA, CALIF. 91355

DONALD N. BARBOUR
CONSOLIDATED RESOURCES
5537 ETTWANDA AVE.
TARZANA, CALIF. 91356

ALFRED WHITTELL JR.
RAYPAK
31111 AGOURA RD.
WESTLAKE VILLAGE, CALIF. 91360

LLOYD BALL
AMERICAN NUCLEONICS
6036 VARIEL AVE.
WOODLAND HILLS, CALIF. 91364

WILLIAM C.W. MOW
MACRODATA
P.O. BOX 1900
WOODLAND HILLS, CALIF. 91364

MICHAEL ROTHBART
TERMINAL DATA
21221 OXNARD ST.
WOODLAND HILLS, CALIF. 91364

RONALD M. COLITTI
ACCURATE ELECTRONICS
14545 FRIAR ST.
VAN NUYS, CALIF. 91401

LEWIS R. MALER
BRAEWOOD DEVELOPMANT
15236 BURBANK BLVD.
VAN NUYS, CALIF. 91401

WILLIAM SCOTT
FLAGG IND.
7101 SEPULVEDA
VAN NUYS, CALIF. 91401

JAMES MATHEWSON
HUNGRY TIGER
14265 OXNARD
VAN NUYS, CALIF. 91401

F.C. BUMB
INTERDYNE
14761 CALIFA
VAN NUYS, CALIF. 91401

JOHN E. MEEHAN
REDKEN LAB.
14721 CALIFA ST.
VAN NUYS, CALIF. 91401

D.B. WEISS
GOLDEN STATE HEALTH CENTERS
13347 VENTURA BLVD.
SHERMAN OAKS, CALIF. 91403

LEWIS GREENWOOD
PAY-FONE SYSTEMS
15432 VENTURA BLVD.
SHERMAN OAKS, CALIF. 91403

DAN MC BRIDE
TRANSTECHNOLOGY
UNION BANK PLAZA-15233 VENTURA
SHERMAN OAKS, CALIF. 91403

LOUIS L. BORICK
SUPERIOR IND.
14721 KESWICK ST.
VAN NUYS, CALIF. 91405

GARLAND S. WHITE
DATAMETRICS
7632 GLORIA AVE.
VAN NUYS, CALIF. 91406

DONALD J. FARMER
EXTEK MICROSYSTEMS
6955 HAYVANHURST AVE.
VAN NUYS, CALIF. 91406

MARCIA ISRAEL
JUDY'S
7710 HASKELL AVE.
VAN NUYS, CALIF. 91406

J.J. ERTESKEK
OLGA
7900 HASKELL AVE.
VAN NUYS, CALIF. 91406

W.J. KARPLUS
TORR LAB.
6837 HAYVENHURST DR.
VAN NUYS, CALIF. 91406

ANDREW P. PROUDIAN
XONICS
6837 HAYVENHURST AVE.
VAN NUYS, CALIF. 91406

M.J. SHERMAN
ED. & RECREATIONAL SERV.
5719 SEPULEVEDA BLVD.
VAN NUYS, CALIF. 91407

TRUDE C. TAYLOR
ELECTRONIC MEMORIES
15760 VENTURA BLVD.
ENCINO, CALIF. 91436

P.V. UEBERROTH
FIRST TRAVEL
16055 VENTURA BLVD.
ENCINO, CALIF. 91436

LOUIS S. DREWETT
PENN-PACIFIC
15720 VENTURA BLVD.
ENCINO, CALIF. 91436

WILLIAM W. DREWRY JR.
DREWRY PHOTOCLOR
211 S. LAKE ST.
BURBANK, CALIF. 91502

A.L. KOTLER
GLEASON NATL.
1 W. ALAMEDA AVE.
BURBANK, CALIF. 91502

RALPH J. SCHMIDT
MENASCO MANUFACTURING
805 S. SAN FERNANDO BLVD.
BURBANK, CALIF. 91502

HOWARD W. HILL
ZERO MANUFACTURING
777 FRONT ST.
BURBANK, CALIF. 91502

JOHN W. MYERS
PACIFIC AIRMOTIVE
2940 N. HOLLYWOOD WAY
BURBANK, CALIF. 91503

WILLIAM J. MARCY
RAVEN ELECTRONICS
P.O. BOX 111
BURBANK, CALIF. 91503

H.A. KRAFT
AMERICAN VANGUARD
2909 THORNTON AVE.
BURBANK, CALIF. 91504

A.R. STEARNS
AXIAL
3020 EMPIRE AVE.
BURBANK, CALIF. 91504

GEORGE GREGORY
PRODUCTS RESEARCH
BOX 3008
BURBANK, CALIF. 91504

D.E. BUTLER
SSP IND.
2990 NORTH SAN FERNANDO BLVD.
BURBANK, CALIF. 91504

A.L. KOTLER
TECHNIBILT
P.O. BOX 6819
BURBANK, CALIF. 91505

MELVIN ATLIN
RIDGEWOOD IND.
1104-8 CHESTNUT ST.
BURBANK, CALIF. 91506

JAY KANTER
FIRST ARTIST PRODUCTION
4000 WARNER BLVD.
BURBANK, CALIF. 91522

J.P. SEIDER
RADIANT IND.
7121 CASE AVE.
NORTH HOLLYWOOD, CALIF. 91601

NORMAN KAHN
GRAPHIDYNE
11969 VENTURA BLVD.
NORTH HOLLYWOOD, CALIF. 91604

JOSEPH A. GARCIA
INTL. CONSTRUCTION
4024 RADFORD AVE.
STUDIO CITY, CALIF. 91604

DON FREEBERG
NATL. ACCOMMODATIONS
4070 LAUREL CYN. BLDG.
STUDIO CITY, CALIF. 91604

C.D. OLSON
OLSON FARMS
BOX 70
NORTH HOLLYWOOD, CALIF. 91604

DONALD E. WARNER
AUDIOTRONICS
7428 BELLAIRE AVE.
NO. HOLLYWOOD, CALIF. 91605

J.A. BERG
BLUE HAVEN POOLS
11933 VOSE ST.
N. HOLLYWOOD, CALIF. 91605

WALTER MC BEE
INTL. IND.
6837 LANKERSHIM BLVD.
N. HOLLYWOOD, CALIF. 91605

S. GERALD STONE
MAGNETIC TAPE
8125 LANKERSHIM BLVD.
N. HOLLYWOOD, CALIF. 91605

IRA HIRSCH
PACIFIC VITAMIN
12747 SATICOY ST.
N. HOLLYWOOD, CALIF. 91605

C.L. FOX
SCANFAX SYSTEMS
8110 WEBB AVE.
N. HOLLYWOOD, CALIF. 91605

JACK SCHWADRON
AMERICAN CYTOLOGY
6440 COLDWATER CANYON AVE.
N. HOLLYWOOD, CALIF. 91606

RALPH PEARLMAN
APPLIED LEARNING
12139 RIVERSIDE DR.
N. HOLLYWOOD, CALIF. 91607

VICTOR ALECK
BIOCHEMICAL PROCEDURES
12012 CHANDLER BLVD.
N. HOLLYWOOD, CALIF. 91607

WILLIAM G. VAN BECKUM
IDEAL BRUSHES
6925 TUJUNGA AVE.
N. HOLLYWOOD, CALIF. 91609

SIDNEY J. SHEINBERG
MCA
100 UNIVERSAL CITY PLAZA
UNIVERSAL CITY, CALIF. 91609

RICHARD D. WOOD
OPTICAL RADIATION
6352 N. IRWINDALE AVE.
AZUSA, CALIF. 91702

THOMAS C. BEISEKER
DATA-DESIGN LAB.
P.O. BOX 711
CUCAMONGA, CALIF. 91730

HUGH P. MOORE
GENTEC
9900 BALDWIN PL.
EL MONTE, CALIF. 91731

FOSTER MARKOFF
CROWN CITY PLATING
4350 TEMPLE CITY BLVD.
EL MONTE, CALIF. 91731

NORMAN BLAU
BLAIR OF CALIF.
2439 LOMA AVE.
SOUTH EL MONTE, CALIF. 91733

DR. HENRY L. LEE JR.
LEE PHARMACEUTICALS
1444 SANTA ANITA AVE. BOX 3836
SOUTH EL MONTE, CALIF. 91733

GEORGE KAY
VACCO
P.O. BOX 3096
EL MONTE, CALIF. 91733

HENRY MARCHESCHI
AMERICAN TELECOMMUNICATIONS
4276 BALDWIN AVE.
EL MONTE, CALIFORNIA 91734

WENDELL B. SELL
HOFFMAN ELECTRONICS
HOFFMAN ELECTRONIC PARK
EL MONTE, CALIF. 91734

YEHOCHAI SCHNEIDER
A & E PLASTIK PAK
14505 PROCTOR AVE. BOX 1268
CITY OF IND., CALIF. 91744

NORMAN D. WARD
ROBERTS CONSOLIDATED
600 N. BALDWIN PARK BLVD.
CITY OF IND., CALIF. 91744

W.R. MOORE JR.
GOLDEN OIL
639 SOUTH SEVENTH AVE.
CITY OF IND., CALIF. 91745

W.R. MOORE, JR.
GOLDEN STATE FOOD
639 S. SEVENTH AVE.
CITY OF IND., CALIF. 91745

R.B. GLASSCO
MANSION IND.
14711 E. CLARK
IND., CALIF. 91745

DONALD D. WINN
ARCHON
P.O. BOX 2156
CITY OF IND., CALIF. 91746

ROBERT N. OVERNELL
QUEMETCO
720 S. 7TH. AVE.
CITY OF IND., CALIF. 91747

HAROLD LIPCHIK
WATER TREATMENT
17400 E. CHESTNUT ST.
CITY OF IND., CALIF. 91747

A.L. SIMON
ADVANCED CHEM. TECH.
1100 S. AZUSA AVE.
CITY OF IND., CALIF. 91748

J.R. COONS
COMMODORE ED. SYSTEMS
390 REID ST.
SANTA CLARA, CALIF. 91749

L.R. TOLLENAERE
AMERON
400 SOUTH ATLANTIC BLVD.
MONTEREY PARK, CALIF. 91754

ROBERT S. COPE
AUTO-GRAPHICS
751 MONTEREY PASS RD.
MONTEREY PARK, CALIF. 91754

HARRY BAGRAMIAN
CHANDEL ENTERPRISES
2123 S. ATLANTIC BLVD.
MONTEREY PARK, CALIF. 91754

C.C. VANDERSTAR
INTL. ALUMINUM
767 MONTEREY PASS RD.
MONTEREY PARK, CALIF. 91754

HERBERT HEZLEP III
ACME GENERAL
300 E. ARROW HIGHWAY
SAN DIMAS, CALIF. 91773

JACK GOLDFARB
HERMETIC SEAL CORP.
4232 TEMPLE CITY BLVD.
ROSEMEAD, CALIF. 91775

J.G. CLARY
ADDMASTER
416 JUNIPERO SERRA DR.
SAN GABRIEL, CALIF. 91776

DONALD G. ASH
CLARY CORP.
320 W. CLARY AVE.
SAN GABRIEL, CALIF. 91776

A.K. MELIN
WHAM-O MFG.
835 EAST EL MONTE ST.
SAN GABRIEL, CALIF. 91778

C.C. PASCAL
LUDWIG ENGINEERING
P.O. BOX 626
UPLAND, CALIF. 91786

F.M. McCOWN
SOUTHWESTERN RESEARCH
P.O. BOX 1093
WALNUT, CALIF. 91789

JAMES E MC BRIDE
DAVIDSON OPTRONICS
2223 EAST RAMONA AVE.
WEST COVINA, CALIFORNIA 91790

SAMUEL MINTZ, M.D.
HOSPITAL SERVICES
845 N. LARK ELLEN AVE.
WEST COVINA, CALIF. 91790

W.J. MORAN
MORAN PROPERTIES
P.O. BOX 870
ALHAMBRA, CALIF. 91802

BENJAMIN E. SMITH
LANCER PACIFIC
P.O. BOX 819
CARLSBAD, CALIF. 92008

DONALD O. OLSON
CONTROLLED WATER EMISSION
585 VERNON WAY
EL CAJON, CALIF. 92020

ROGER L. MANFRED
TRAVELODGE INTL.
MAIN AT GUYAMACA
EL CAJON, CALIF. 92020

R.E. EHLY
DATA-LINK
P.O. BOX 1145
EL CAJON, CALIF. 92022

JOE E. LITTLE
TRAILERANCHO
615 E. LEXINGTON
EL CAJON, CALIF. 92022

BUDDY L. DUFT
MATERIAL SYSTEMS
P.O. BOX 2277
ESCONDIDO, CALIF. 92025

WILLIAM DRELL
CALBIOCHEM
10933 N. TORREY PINES RD.
LA JOLLA, CALIF. 92037

E.F. HEIZER JR.
FOTOMAT
7590 FAY ST.
LA JOLLA, CALIF. 92037

GARY L. MC MULLEN
INFONATIONAL
2706 CAMINITO PRADO
LA JOLLA, CALIF. 92037

C.R. SCOTT
INTERMARK
P.O. BOX 2266
LA JOLLA, CALIF. 92037

P.M. RESNICK
JAVELIN
P.O. BOX 2750
LA JOLLA, CALIF. 92037

J.R. BEYSTER
SCIENCE APPLICATIONS
1205 PROSPECT ST.
LA JOLLA, CALIF. 92037

HENRY A. BONEY
SPEEDEE MART
7839 UNIVERSITY AVE.
LA MESA, CALIF. 92041

ALBERT ANDREIKO
CONSYNE
1740 LA COSTA MEADOWS DR.
SAN MARCOS, CALIF. 92069

R.P. KEEHN
VANIER GRAPHICS
8787 OLIVE LANE
SANTEE, CALIF. 92071

KENNETH M. STAYER
COURTESY PRODUCTS
1411 W. PALM
SAN DIEGO, CALIF. 92101

ALFRED P. LENCH II
NATL. COMMUNITY
110 W. A STREET STE. 1210
SAN DIEGO, CALIF. 92101

STANLEY FOSTER
RATNER
730 13TH. ST.
SAN DIEGO, CALIF. 92101

I. RONALD HOROWITZ
VAGABOND MOTOR
1810 STATE ST.
SAN DIEGO, CALIF. 92101

J.V. DRUM
WICKES
110 WEST A ST.
SAN DIEGO, CALIF. 92101

FRED P. OSBORNE
ROYAL INNS
4855 N. HARBOUR DR.
SAN DIEGO, CALIF. 92106

DAVID M. DEMOTTE
SEA WORLD
MISSION BAY
SAN DIEGO, CALIF. 92109

C. TERRY BROWN
ATLAS HOTELS
500 HOTEL CIRCLE
SAN DIEGO, CALIF. 92110

BRUCE R. FARLEY
BRUCE FARLEY
1521 HOTEL CIRCLE WEST
SAN DIEGO, CALIFORNIA 92110

JOHN S. BARRY
WD-40 CO.
1061 CUDAHY PLACE
SAN DIEGO, CALIF. 92110

F.C. GROSS
ESD
4909 RUFFNER RD.
SAN DIEGO, CALIF. 92111

SCOTT G. MILLER
ROYAL PROPERTIES
7000 FASHION HILLS BLVD.
SAN DIEGO, CALIF. 92111

STANLEY A. YALOF
TETRAHEDRON ASSOC.
7605 CONVOY CT.
SAN DIEGO, CALIF. 92111

CHARLES B. MC FADDEN
CALIFORNIA GEN.
P.O. BOX 649
SAN DIEGO, CALIF. 92112

PAUL I. STEVENS
CAMPBELL IND.
FOOT OF 8TH. ST.
SAN DIEGO, CALIF. 92112

W.S. IVANS
COHU
BOX 623
SAN DIEGO, CALIF. 92112

EVERETT H. BROWNELL
DELTA DESIGN
P.O. BOX 421
SAN DIEGO, CALIF. 92112

M.B. LADDON
LANGLEY
310 EUCLID AVE.
SAN DIEGO, CALIF. 92112

WILLIAM R. SHIMP
PSA
P.O. BOX 185
SAN DIEGO, CALIF. 92112

HUGH W. NESS
SPECTRAL DYNAMICS
P.O. 671
SAN DIEGO, CALIF. 92112

ROBERT J. DICKER
WALKER-SCOTT
P.O. BOX 1511
SAN DIEGO, CALIF. 92112

T.G. LAMBORN
HELIX LAND
P.O. BOX 15453
SAN DIEGO, CALIF. 92115

S.N. SATO
IVAC
11353 SORRENTO VALLEY RD.
SAN DIEGO, CALIF. 92121

EDWARD ETESS
MONITOR LABS
4202 SORRENTO VALLEY BLVD.
SAN DIEGO, CALIF. 92121

WALTER J. ZABLE
CUBIC
9223 BALBOA AVE.
SAN DIEGO, CALIF. 92123

P.E. HUMPHREY
HUMPHREY INC.
9212 BALBOA AVE.
SAN DIEGO, CALIF. 92123

JOHN M. THORNTON
WAVETEK
9045 BALBOA AVE.
SAN DIEGO, CALIF. 92123

HANS W. SCHOEPFLIN
THE FED MART
P.O. BOX 80848
SAN DIEGO, CALIF. 92138

J.T. TRILLY
FOUNTAIN OF YOUTH SPA
304 TERRACE CIRCLE
BRAWLEX, CALIF. 92227

PAUL KLEIN
42 PRODUCTS LTD.
P.O. BOX 579
TEMECULA, CALIF. 92390

C.H. ATCHISON
R.L. BURNS
334 WEST THIRD ST.
SAN BERNARDINO, CALIF. 92401

J.P. HENCK
SANTA'S VILLAGE
P.O. BOX 544
SAN BERNARDINO, CALIF. 92403

BETTY GEVIRTZ
MW INTL.
141 N. ARROWHEAD
SAN BERNARDINO, CALIF. 92408

WILLIAM W. WEIDE
FLEETWOOD ENTERPRISES
P.O. BOX 7638
RIVERSIDE, CALIF. 92503

MARLAN E. BOURNS
BOURNS INC.
1200 COLUMBIA AVE.
RIVERSIDE, CALIF. 92507

EDWIN R. GAMSON
GERTRON
1701 SOUTH STATE COLLEGE BLVD.
ANAHEIM, CALIF. 92608

C. RICHARD NELSON
VTN
2301 CAMPUS DR.
IRVINGE, CALIF. 92614

ELLIS F. GARDNER
STACO
1139 BAKER ST.
COSTA MESA, CALIF. 92626

RONALD R. FOELL
STANDARD PACIFIC
1565 W. MAC ARTHUR BLVD.
COSTA MESA, CALIF. 92626

W.R. TIGHE
WILLARD BOAT WORKS
1300 LOGAN AVE.
COSTA MESA, CALIF. 92626

D.F. BROSMAN
MSI DATA
340 FISCHER AVE.
COSTA MESA, CALIF. 92627

W.E. BELLWOOD
WYNN INTL. INC.
2600 E. NUTWOOD AVE.
FULLERTON, CALIF. 92631

HOUSTON C. KIER
VIM
130 W. SANTA FE AVE.
FULLERTON, CALIF. 92632

A.A. MORRIS
MOREHOUSE IND.
1600 W. COMMONWEALTH BLVD.
FULLERTON, CALIF. 92633

LORAN D. COVINGTON
COVINGTON BROS.
P.O. BOX 3128
FULLERTON, CALIF. 92634

DAVID A. SWEDLOW
SWEDLOS INC.
12605 BEACH BLVD.
GARDEN GROVE, CALIF. 92641

AL ROSSO
ROSSO'S CARPET
16672 BEACH BLVD.
HUNTINGTON BEACH, CALIF. 92647

MORRIS E. HARRISON
LION COUNTY SAFARI
8800 MOULTON PARKWAY
LAGUNA HILLS, CALIF. 92653

ROSS W. CORTESE
ROSSMOOR
24321 PASEO DE VALENCIA
LUGUNA HILLS, CALIF. 92653

ROBERT W. CLIFFORD
AIR CALIFORNIA
3636 BIRCH ST.
NEWPORT BEACH, CALIF. 92660

J.W. KLUG
AMERICAN PACESETTER
4540 CAMPUS DR.
NEWPORT BEACH, CALIF. 92660

B.E. DE MERS
COLONY FOODS
1801 DOVE ST.
NEWPORT BEACH, CALIF. 92660

B. LEE KARNS
COMPREHENSIVE CARE
230 NPT CENTER NO. 222
NEWPORT BEACH, CALIF. 92660

JOHN F. BISHOP
DANA ELECTRONICS
500 NEWPORT CENTER DR.
NEWPORT BEACH, CALIF. 92660

NORMAN E. PESSIN
HEALTH IND.
610 NEWPORT CENTER DR.
NEWPORT BEACH, CALIF. 92660

JOHN J. CORLEY
NATL. SYSTEMS
4361 BIRCH ST.
NEWPORT BEACH, CALIF. 92660

A.J. GLASKY
NEWPORT PHARMACEUTICALS
1590 MONROVIA BLVD.
NEWPORT BEACH, CALIF. 92660

R.S. FRIEDBEG
OXOCO
610 NEWPORT CENTER DR. STE. 630
NEWPORT BEACH, CALIF. 92660

G.E. HEWITT
RADIATRONICS
439 VIA LIDO SOUD
NEWPORT BEACH, CALIF. 92660

RANDALL E. PRESLEY
THE PRESLEY CO.
4600 CAMPUS DR.
NEWPORT BEACH, CALIF. 92660

ROLAND R. SPEERS
AMCORD
P.O. BOX 2550
NEWPORT BEACH, CALIF. 92663

JERRY FISHER
SIR SPEEDY
892 WEST 16TH. ST.
NEWPORT BEACH, CALIF. 92663

ALVIN B. PHILLIPS
WESTERN DIGITAL
19242 RED HILL AVE. BOX 2180
NEWPORT BEACH, CALIF. 92663

G.S. HERBERT JR.
ALLERGAN PHARMACEUTICALS
2525 DUPONT DR.
IRVINE, CALIF. 92664

D.J. BENTLEY
BENTLEY LABS.
17502 ARMSTRONG AVE.
IRVINE, CALIF. 92664

R.C. LANGFORD
BERTEA
18001 VON KARMAN AVE.
IRVINE, CALIF. 92664

F.E. VACHON
COLEMAN SYSTEMS
18842 TELLER AVE.
IRVINE, CALIF. 92664

DAVID H. METHVIN
COMPUTER AUTOMATION
18651 VON KARMAN AVE.
IRVINE, CALIF. 92664

MILAN PANIC
ICN PHARMACEUTICAL
2727 CAMPUS DR.
IRVINE, CALIF. 92664

G.E. MOXON
MOXON
2222 MICHELSON DR.
NEWPORT BEACH, CALIF. 92664

DON GALLANT
SYMBOLIC DISPLAYS
1762 MC CAW AVE.
IRVINE, CALIF. 92664

E.H. CLARK JR.
BAKER INTL.
500 CITY PARKWAY WEST
ORANGE, CALIF. 92668

E.L. SHANNON JR.
SANTA FE INTL.
P.O. BOX 1401
ORANGE, CALIF. 92668

W.B. REINHOLD
VARCO INTL.
800 NORTH ECKOFF ST.
ORANGE, CALIF. 92668

WILLIAM J. STOCK
STANG HYDRONICS
P.O. BOX 3217
SAN CLEMENTE, CALIF. 92672

A. ROBERT MAGES
MODULAR DIMENSIONS
6421 IND. WAY
WESTMINSTER, CALIF. 92683

PATRICK F. CADIGAN
ELECTRONIC ENG.
P.O. BOX 58
SANTA ANA, CALIF. 92702

B.E. BRYANS
DATA TECH.
2700 SOUTH FAIRVIEW AVE.
SANTA ANA, CALIF. 92704

PHILIP FREY JR.
MICROSEMICONDUCTOR
2830 S. FAIRVIEW ST.
SANTA ANA, CALIF. 92704

ISADORE DIAMOND
NEWPORT CONTROLS
2727 S. SUSAN ST.
SANTA ANA, CALIF. 92704

M.C. SUKUT
SUKUT CONST.
3401 W. ASTOR
SANTA ANA, CALIF. 92704

ROBERT E. BERRY
IRT
1641 MC GAW
SANTA ANA, CALIF. 92705

D.W. FULLER
MICRODATA
17481 RED HILL AVE.
IRVINE, CALIF. 92705

B.B. WEEKES
NEWPORT LABS.
630 E. YOUNG ST.
SANTA ANA, CALIF. 92705

EDWARD B. ISELL
PLUS PRODUCTS
2681 KELVIN AVE.
IRVINE, CALIF. 92705

DAVID C. DAHLBERG
RB IND.
2323 S.E. MAIN ST.
IRVINE, CALIF. 92705

S.V. EDENS
TELEFILE COMPUTER
17131 DAIMLER ST.
IRVINE, CALIF. 92705

E.W. BAUMGARDNER
STANDARD LOGIC
2215 S. STANDARD
SANTA ANA, CALIF. 92707

H.W. ANDERSON
HALLAMORE
18060 EUCLID ST.
FOUNTAIN VALLEY, CALIF. 92708

MARTIN P. CLEARY
DATATRON
P.O. BOX 11427
SANTA ANA, CALIF. 92711

JERRY GOLDEN
GOLDEN WEST MOBILE HOMES
1929 E. ST. ANDREWS PL.
SANTA ANA, CALIF. 92711

R.D. JOHNSON
SAN-BAR
P.O. BOX 11787
SANTA ANA, CALIF. 92711

G.S. HERBERT JR.
IMAJ INTL.
P.O. BOX 19534
IRVINE, CALIF. 92713

ALLAN L. BRIDGFORD
BRIDGFORD FOODS
1308 N. PATT ST.
ANAHEIM, CALIF. 92801

GEORGE M. CANOVA
CALIF. COMPUTER
2411 W. LA PALMA AVE.
ANAHEIM, CALIF. 92801

PHILIP F. SHEPHERD
CIRCLE SEAL CORP.
1111 N. BROOKHURST ST.
ANAHEIM, CALIF. 92801

WILLIAM N. KENNICOTT
THE MC CARTHY CO.
2535 WEST LA PALMA AVE.
ANAHEIM, CALIF. 92801

W.E. FERRELL
UNITAX
639 N. EUCLID AVE.
ANAHEIM, CALIF. 92801

BERNARD W. HOLMBRAKER
XYTEX
2411 W. LA PALMA
ANAHEIM, CALIF. 92801

WAYNE ODEKIRK
AMREC IND.
2415 S. MANCHESTER
ANAHEIM, CALIF. 92802

THOMAS E. FRANK
EXECUTIVE IND.
P.O. BOX 4508
ANAHEIM, CALIF. 92803

PETER CHURM
FLUOROCARBON
P.O. BOX 3339
ANAHEIM, CALIF. 92803

LAWRENCE GOSHORN
GEN. AUTOMATION
1055 S. EAST ST.
ANAHEIM, CALIF. 92805

E.J. NORMAN
OLSON LABS.
421 E. CERRITOS AVE.
ANAHEIM, CALIF. 92805

WALLACE E. RIANDA
DATUM
1363 S. STATE COLLEGE BLVD.
ANAHEIM, CALIF. 92806

W. ROBERT TUCKER
PLANT IND.
1235 S. STATE COLLEGE BLVD.
ANAHEIM, CALIF. 92806

LAWRENCE PHILLIPS JR.
UNICORN IND.
1511 KRAEMER BLVD.
ANAHEIM, CALIF. 92806

E.J. CARR
NORRIS OIL
P.O. BOX I I
VENTURA, CALIF. 93001

F.R. HUNTSINGER
VETCO
P.O. BOX 1688
VENTURA, CALIF. 93001

DANIEL L. GILLUM
INFORMATION MAGNETICS
5743 THRONWOOD DR.
GOLETA, CALIF. 93017

C. STEHLE
VACA OIL CO.
274 E. FIR AVE.
OXNARD, CALIF. 93030

VOLNEY H. CRAIG
LIMONEIR
P.O. BOX 230
SANTA PAULA, CALIF. 93060

GERARD Q. DECKER III
SLOAN TECH.
414 E. COTA ST.
SANTA BARBARA, CALIF. 93101

VICTOR TERRY
SOVEREIGN
30 W. SOLA ST.
SANTA BARBARA, CALIF. 93101

D.A. WINER
INFRARED IND.
P.O. BOX 989
SANTA BARBARA, CALIF. 93102

W.F. BAUER
INFORMATICS
P.O. BOX 1452
CANOGA FALLS, CALIF. 93104

H.R. FRANK
APPLIED MAGNETICS
75 ROBIN HILL RD.
GOLETA, CALIF. 93105

SAM D. BATTISTONE
SAMBO'S RESTAURANTS
3760 STATE ST.
SANTA BARBARA, CALIF. 93105

C.L. CABANISS
GRIFFIN STEEL
P.O. BOX 1998
BAKERFIELD, CALIF. 93303

WAYNE REEDER
REEDER
1830 BRUNDAGE LN.
BAKERFIELD, CALIF. 93304

DR. DAN HOAK
COMM. INTL.
P.O. BOX 119
SELMA, CALIF. 93663

JAMES R. COSON
BUCKNER IND.
P.O. BOX 232
FRESNO, CALIF. 93708

WILLIAM W. BOGGS
BERVEN CARPETS
2600 VENTURA AVE.
FRESNO, CALIF. 93717

G.B. BREWER
PRODUCERS COTTON
P.O. BOX 1832
FRESNO, CALIF. 93717

C.C. LAVAL III
UNDERGROUND SURVEYS
P.O. BOX 6119
FRESNO, CALIF. 93727

ROBERT V. ANTLE
BUD ANTLE
639 S. SANBORN RD.
SALINAS, CALIF. 93901

JAMES L. RANKIN
SPIEGL FOODS
P.O. BOX 1491
SALINAS, CALIF. 93901

GEORGE H. DIDINGER JR.
VACU-BLAST
501 BRAGATO RD.
BELMONT, CALIF. 94002

J.F. LEISY
WADSWORTH PUBLISHING
10 DAVIS DR.
BELMONT, CALIF. 94002

GEORGE N. KEYSTON JR.
ANZA PACIFIC
433 AIRPORT BLVD.
BURLINGAME, CALIF. 94010

R.V. JARRELL
EBS DATA
1209 DONNELLY AVE.
BURLINGAME, CALIF. 94010

R.P. MC GRATH
METRIC RESOURCES
822 AIRPORT BLVD.
BURLINGAME, CALIF. 94010

J. FRANK LEACH
ARCATA NTL.
2750 SANDHILL RD.
MENLO PARK, CALIF. 94025

J.M. CARTER
CARCO ELECTRONICS
195 CONSTITUTION DR.
MENLO PARK, CALIF. 94025

BERNE A. SCHEPMAN
ENVIROTECH
3000 SAND HILL RD.
MENLO PARK, CALIF. 94025

J.L. SHEPARD
GRANGER ASSOC.
1360 WILLOW RD.
MENLO PARK, CALIF. 94025

HERBERT HINDIN
L.B. NELSON
64 WILLOW PL.
MENLO PARK, CALIF. 94025

PAUL M. COOK
RAYCHEM
300 CONSTITUTION DR.
MENLO PARK, CALIF. 94025

JAMES R. WEERSING
ROYCO INSTRUMENTS
141 JEFFERSON DR.
MENLO PARK, CALIF. 94025

WILLIAM F. SCANDLING
SAGA
1 SAGA LN.
MENLO PARK, CALIF. 94025

M.G. SMITH
DIAGNOSTIC DATA
518 LOGUE AVE.
MOUNTAIN VIEW, CALIF. 94040

WILFRED J. CORRIGAN
FAIRCHILD CAMERA
464 ELLIS ST.
MOUNTAIN VIEW, CALIF. 94040

D.T. MACK
MICROFORM DATA
830 MAUDE AVE.
MOUNTAIN VIEW, CALIF. 94040

CHARLES ASKANSAS
THE QUANTOR
520 LOGUE AVE.
MOUNTAIN VIEW, CALIF.94040

HERBERT M. DWIGHT JR.
SPECTRA-PHYSICS
1250 W. MIDDLEFIELD RD.
MOUNTAIN VIEW, CALIF. 94040

W.D. BELL
ELECTRONIC ARRAYS
550 MIDDLEFIELD RD.
MOUNTAIN VIEW, CALIF. 94043

GEORGE K. BISSELL
DUKOR MODULAR SYSTEMS
2525 E. CAMINO REAL
REDWOOD, CITY, CALIF. 94061

H.R. GOFF
JAMES DOLE
1400 INDUSTRIAL WAY
REDWOOD CITY, CALIF. 94063

P.M. FRIEDENBACH
FARINON ELECTRIC
1691 BAYPORT AVE.
SAN CARLOS, CALIF. 94070

W.J. SANDERS III
ADVANCED MICRO DEVICES
901 THOMPSON PL.
SUNNYVALE, CALIF. 94086

J.J. WOO
AMCOMP
686 WEST MAUDE AVE.
SUNNYVALE, CALIF. 94086

ORION L. HOCH
ADVANCE MEMORY
1276 HAMMERWOOD
SUNNYVALE, CALIF. 94086

RANDOLPH J. KROENERT
BARNES-HIND
895 KIFER RD.
SUNNYVALE, CALIF. 94086

DR. DAVID B. LEESON
CALIF. MICROWAVE
455 W. MAUDE AVE.
SUNNYVALE, CALIF. 94086

J.J. WOO
DATA DISC
686 W. MAUDE AVE.
SUNNYVALE, CALIF. 94086

DR. WILLIAM J. PERRY
ESL
495 JAVA DR.
SUNNYVALE, CALIF. 94086

R.E. FINNIGAN
FINNIGAN
845 W. MAUDE AVE.
SUNNYVALE, CALIF. 94086

BERTIL D. NORDIN
GRT
1286 N. LAWRENCE STATION RD.
SUNNYVALE, CALIF. 94086

HENRY L. SCHOGER
HLS IND.
610 NORTH MARY AVE.
SUNNYVALE, CALIF. 94086

R.H. FRIED
INTL VIDEO
990 ALMANOR AVE.
SUNNYVALE, CALIF. 94086

ROBERT E. WHITESIDE
MICRO MASK
676 N. VAQUEROS AVE.
SUNNYVALE, CALIF. 94086

CHARLES C. HARWOOD
SIGNETICS
811 E. ARQUES AVE.
SUNNYVALE, CALIF. 94086

CHARLES T. GROSWITH
VELO-BIND
650 ALMANOR AVE.
SUNNYVALE, CALIF. 94086

ALAN J. GRANT
WAVECOM IND.
470 PERSIAN DR.
SUNNYVALE, CALIF. 94086

E.L. JORDAN
WESTERN MICROWAVE
1260 BIRCHWOOD DR.
SUNNYVALE, CALIF. 94086

I.T. ALLISON
WCS-INTL.
840 EL CAMINO REAL
SUNNYVALE, CALIF. 94087

SYDNEY J. ROSENBERG
AMERICAN BUILDING
335 FELL ST.
SAN FRANCISCO, CALIF. 94102

JAMES M. METZGAR
ORPHEUM BLDG. CO.
1182 MARKET ST.
SAN FRANCISCO, CALIF. 94102

J. P. GEORGE
CALLON PETROLEUM
703 MARKET ST. STE. 1600
SAN FRANCISCO, CALIF. 94103

NETTLE R. MOSSONI
CSE
989 MARKET ST.
SAN FRANCISCO, CALIF. 94103

DAN A MC MILLAN JR.
THERMAL POWER
785 MARKET ST.
SAN FRANCISCO, CALIF. 94103

HAROLD SCHWARTZ
TOPPS & TROWSERS
5 THIRD ST.
SAN FRANCISCO, CALIF. 94103

HERBERT L. BROWN
ASTRODATA
2570 BANK OF AMERICA CENTER
SAN FRANCISCO, CALIF. 94104

J.D. HANN
BOOTHE COMPUTER
555 CALIFORNIA ST.
SAN FRANCISCO, CALIF. 94104

V.E. BARTOLETTI
COMPUTER USAGE
300 MONTGOMERY ST. STE. 500
SAN FRANCISCO, CALIF. 94104

JAMES B. SCHRYVER
COMSTOCK TUNNEL
105 MONTGOMERY ST.
SAN FRANCISCO, CALIF. 94104

HARRY R. GOFF
JAMES DOLE
235 MONTGOMERY ST.
SAN FRANCISCO, CALIF. 94104

ROBERT J. FEIBUSCH
EDS NUCLEAR
220 MONTGOMERY ST.
SAN FRANCISCO, CALIF. 94104

R.J. SEIDL
SIMPSON LEE PAPER
1600 CROCKER PLAZA
SAN FRANCISCO, CALIF. 94104

J.M. HALLIDAY
SONOMA INTL.
235 MONTGOMERY ST.
SAN FRANCISCO,CALIF. 94104

R.L. WIEL
CYPRESS ABBEY
9 1ST. , RM. 707
SAN FRANCISCO, CALIF. 94105

WILLIAM K. WARNOCK
KORACORP
611 MISSION ST.
SAN FRANCISCO, CALIF. 94105

PETER HAAS
LEVI STRAUSS
98 BATTERY ST.
SAN FRANCISCO, CALIF. 94106

E.A. BENESCH
FRITZI OF CALIF. MFG.
167-199 FIRST ST.
SAN FRANCISCO, CALIF. 94107

GEORGE MARTINEZ
TIA MARIA
2101 THIRD ST.
SAN FRANCISCO, CALIF. 94107

NORMAN SCOTT
AMERICAN PRESIDENT LINES
601 CALIFORNIA ST.
SAN FRANCISCO,CALIF. 94108

RAYMOND F. O'BRIEN
CONSOLIDATED FREIGHTWAYS
INTL. BLDG. 601 CALIF. ST.
SAN FRANCISCO, CALIF. 94108

PAUL C. HENSHAW
HOMESTAKE MINING
650 CALIFORNIA ST.
SAN FRANCISCO, CALIF. 94108

E.F. DERTINGER
LYNCH COMM. SYSTEMS
601 CALIFORNIA ST.
SAN FRANCISCO, CALIF. 94108

DORMAN L. COMMONS
NATL. CO.
INTL. BLDG. ST. MARY'S SQ.
SAN FRANCISCO, CALIF. 94108

JOHN P. MC CLELLAND
ALMADEN VINEYARDS
1 MARITIME PLAZA
SAN FRANCISCO, CALIF. 94111

ALAN RICHARDS
CALIF. WINDSOR
100 CALIFORNIA ST.
SAN FRANCISCO, CALIF. 94111

JAMES W. CONTE
COMM. PSYCHIATRIC
517 WASHINGTON ST.
SAN FRANCISCO, CALIF. 94111

THOMAS F. HERMAN
DELTA CALIF. IND.
600 MONTGOMERY ST.
SAN FRANCISCO, CALIF. 94111

ROBERT C. MC CRACKEN
DI GIORGIO
1 MARITIME PLAZA
SAN FRANCISCO, CALIF. 94111

C.L. GANZ
DYMO IND.
ONE EMBARCADERO
SAN FRANCISCO, CALIF. 94111

F.H. MURPHY
HOLDEN-DAY
500 SANSOME ST.
SAN FRANCISCO, CALIF. 94111

PETER S. REDFIELD
ITEL
ONE EMBARCADERO
SAN FRANCISCO, CALIF. 94111

JAMES H. LEONARD
LAWRENCE SYSTEMS
37 DRUMM ST.
SAN FRANCISCO, CALIF. 94111

JOHN ALIOTO
PACIFIC FAR EAST LINE
ONE EMBARCADERO CENTER
SAN FRANCISCO, CALIF. 94111

JAMES W. SHANNON
PVO INTL.
WORLD TRADE CENTER
SAN FRANCISCO, CALIF. 94111

LOUIS W. WALKER JR.
SAN FRANCISCO REAL ESTATE
633 BATTERY ST.
SAN FRANCISCO, CALIF. 94111

RICHARD J. BRADLEY
VICTORIA STATION
150 CHESTNUT ST.
SAN FRANCISCO, CALIF. 94111

A.P. SCHUMAN
LILLI ANN
2701 SIXTEENTH ST.
SAN FRANCISCO, CALIF. 94116

PETER WIDDRINGTON
GENERAL BREWING
2601 NEWHALL ST.
SAN FRANCISCO, CALIF. 94119

RICHARD B. MADDEN
POTLATCH
P.O. BOX 3591
SAN FRANCISCO, CALIF. 94119

W. DOUGLASS SMITH
AMERICAN MOBILE POWER
450 PACIFIC AVE.
SAN FRANCISCO. CALIF. 94133

ROBERT B. HOOVER
PACIFIC LUMBER
1111 COLUMBUS AVE.
SAN FRANCISCO, CALIF. 94133

CHAUNCEY E. SCHMIDT
BANCAL TRI-STATE
400 CALIF. ST.
SANFFRANCISCO, CALIF. 94145

PAUL RYAN
BEHAVIORAL RESEARCH
LADERA PROFESSIONAL CENTER
PALO ALTO, CALIF. 94302

JAMES L. HOBART
COHERENT RADIATION
3201 PORTER DR.
PALO ALTO, CALIF. 94303

JEROME DREXLER
DREXLER TECH. INC.
3960 FALRAN WAY
PALO ALTO, CALIF. 94303

DAVID P. ROUSH
ROCOR INTL.
2800 WEST BAYSHORE RD.
PALO ALTO, CALIF. 94303

A. ZAFFARONI
ALZA
950 PAGE MILL RD.
PALO ALTO, CALIF. 94304

DANIEL LAZARE
COECON
975 CALIFORNIA AVE.
PALO ALTO, CALIF. 94304

H.W. LE CLAIRE
TAB PRODUCTS
2690 HANOVER
PALO ALTO, CALIF. 94304

H. RICHARD JOHNSON
WATKINS-JOHNSON
3333 HILLVIEW AVE.
PALO ALTO, CALIF. 94304

CARL DJERASSI
ZOECON
975 CALIF. AVE.
PALO ALTO, CALIF. 94304

R.H. WATSON
LOUISIANA-PACIFIC
550 CALIF. AVE.
PALO ALTO, CALIF. 94306

ROBERT S. GUNDERSON
CALIF. JOCKEY CLUB
P.O. BOX 5050
SAN MATEO, CALIF. 94402

CHARLES C. DAVIS JR.
CALNY FOOD
1650 BOREL PL.
SAN MATEO, CALIF. 94402

WILLIAM E. MARTIN JR.
COPICO
4 WEST 4TH. AVE. NO. 204
SAN MATEO, CALIF. 94402

JAMES G. FULLER
MC KEON CONSTRUCTION
400 S. EL CAMINO REAL NO.300
SAN MATEO, CALIFORNIA 94402

JOHN R. NIVEN
PARAGON
155 BOVET RD.
SAN MATEO, CALIF. 94402

A.H. STROMBERG
URS
155 BOVET RD.
SAN MATEO, CALIF. 94402

W.G. McGAUGHEY
DISTRIBUCO
2655 CAMPUS DR.
SAN MATEO, CALIF. 94403

W.R. BOYD
HOLIDAY RESOURCES
640 SANDALWOOD ISLE
ALAMEDA, CALIF. 94501

W.R. BALDWIN
BURLINGAME-WESTERN
ROUTE 1, P.O. BOX D-250
BYRON, CALIF. 94514

GEORGE H. BURNS JR.
SYSTRON-DONNER
ONE SYSTRON DR.
CONCORD, CALIF. 94520

JOHN KILMARTIN
MERVYN'S
25001 INDUSTRIAL BLVD.
HAYWARD, CALIF. 94545

F.L. CARLEY
GUARDIAN PACKAGING
6590 CENTRAL AVE.
NEWARD, CALIF. 94560

JOHN M. LILLIE
LESLIE SALT CO.
7200 CENTRAL AVE.
NEWARD, CALIF. 94560

J.W. GOFMAN
CARDIODYNAMICS
6841 DUBLIN BLVD.
DUBLIN, CALIF. 94566

HARVIE M. MERRILL
HEXCEL
11711 DUBLIN BLVD.
DUBLIN, CALIF. 94566

JAMES L. STELL
LUCKY STORES
6300 CLARK AVE.
DUBLIN, CALIF. 94566

WILLIAM E. MC GLASHAN
BERKELEY BIO-ENGINEERING
600 MC CORMICK ST.
SAN LEANDRO, CALIF. 94577

WALLACE BIRNBAUM
PHYSICS INTL.
2700 MERCED ST.
SAN LEANDRO, CALIF. 94577

JACK B. ROSE
GRODING OF CALIF.
2225 GRANT AVE.
SAN LORENZO, CALIF. 94580

G.W. DESKIN
MB ASSOC.
BOLLINGER CANYON RD.
SAN RAMON, CALIF. 94583

JOSEPH M LONG
LONGS DRUG
141 NORTH CIVIC DR.
WALNUT CREEK, CALIF. 94596

WILLIAM W. SHANNON
NEW IDRIA
1990 N. CALIFORNIA BLVD.
WALNUT CREEK, CALIF. 94596

B.E. SIMON
SIMON STORES
1500 BOTELHO
WALNUT CREEK, CALIF. 94596

JOHN BORETA
BUTTES GAS & OIL
1970 BROADWAY
OAKLAND, CALIF. 94604

RICHARD M. KIRK
E-H RESEARCH
515 11TH. ST.
OAKLAND, CALIF. 94607

MAURICE J. DAY
SEAPORT
1155 SEVENTH ST.
OAKLAND, CALIF. 94607

ROBERT LAUTER
MURPHY PACIFIC MARINE SALVAGE
4300 EASTSHORE HWY.
EMERYVIYLE, CALIF. 94608

J. GARY SHANSBY
SHAKLEE
1900 POWELL
EMERYVILLE, CALIF. 94608

R.S. LAUTER
TECHO
1900 POWELL ST.
EMERYVILLE, CALIF. 94608

KENNETH P. GILL
VACU-DRY
5801 CHRISTIE ST.
EMERYVILLE, CALIF. 94608

WILLIAM R. BREUNER
JOHN BREUNER
2201 BROADWAY
OAKLAND, CALIF. 94612

HOWARD K. HOWARD
SATURN AIRWAYS
P.O. BOX 2426 INTL. AIRPORT
OAKLAND, CALIF. 94614

RICHARD C. LOVORN
SFO HELICOPTER
P.O. BOX 2525
OAKLAND INTL. AIRPORT,CALIF.94614

H.P. HUFF
TRANS INTL AIRLINES
OAKLAND INTL AIRPORT
PAKLAND, CALIF. 94614

EDWARD J. DALEY
WORLD AIRWAYS
OAKLAND INTL. AIRPORT
OAKLAND, CALIF. 94614

R.B. SHETTERLY
THE GLOROX
7901 OAKPORT ST.
OAKLAND, CALIF. 94621

MELVEIN LEMBERGER
COMPUTER DYNAMICS
100 HEGENBERGER RD.
OAKLAND, CALIF. 94621

MERLE M. KRANTZMAN
GRAND AUTO
7200 EDGEWATER DR.
OAKLAND, CALIF. 94621

DONALD J. EATON
PAY LESS DRUG STORES
8000 EDGEWATER DR.
OAKLAND, CALIF. 94621

JAMES B. BOULDEN
ON-LINE DECISIONS
2150 SHATTUCK AVE.
BERKELEY, CALIF. 94704

DAVID DUNBAIR
COMPUTER ELECTION
1001 EASTSHORE HIGHWAY
BERKELEY, CALIF. 94710

LOWELL H. CARLSON
CYCLOTRON
950 GILMAN ST.
BERKELEY, CALIF. 94710

HARVEY L. MORTON
TINSLEY LABS.
2448 -6TH. ST.
BERKELEY, CALIF. 94710

CHARLES L. FRY
FRYS'S FOOD
3558 SAN PABLO DAM RD.
EL SOBRANTE, CALIF. 94803

DAVID SCHWARTZ
BIO-RAD LABS.
32ND. & GRIFFIN AVE.
RICHMOND, CALIF. 94804

MALCOM R. MALCOMSON
MARK SYSTEMS
510 N. PASTORIA AVE.
SUNNYVALE, CALIF. 94806

C.A. RYPINSKI
RYDAX
76 BELVEDERE ST.
SAN RAFAEL, CALIF. 94901

SIMON SIEGEL
LUCKY LANES
13255 SAN PABLO AVE.
SAN PABLO, CALIF. 94908

SHERMAN NAYMARK
NUCLEAR SERVICES
1700 DELL AVE.
CAMPBELL, CALIF. 95008

L.L. BOYSEL
FOUR-PHASE
19333 VALLCO PARKWAY
CUPERTINO, CALIF. 95014

FREDERICK R. ADLER
INTERSIL
10900 NORTH TANTAU AVE.
CUPERINO, CALIF. 95014

BRUCE BLAKKAN
LITRONIX
19000 HOMESTEAD RD.
CUPERTINO, CALIF. 95014

DAVID A. BOSSEN
MEASUREX
ONE RESULTS WAY
CUPERINO, CALIF. 95014

THOMAS J. O'ROURKE
TYMSHARE
10340 BUBB RD.
CUPERTINO, CALIF. 95014

ROBERT C. WILSON
MEMOREX
1180 SHULMAN AVE.
SANTA CLARA, CALIF. 95050

WILLIAM H. ORR
ORROX CORP.
3303 SCOTT BLVD.
SANTA CLARA, CALIF. 95050

W.D. WEAGANT
SIGMAFORM
2401 WALSH AVE.
SANTA CLARA, CALIF. 95050

MICHAEL A. McNEILLY
APPLIED MATERIALS
3050 BOWERS AVE.
SANTA CLARA, CALIF. 95051

GORDON E. MOORE
INTEL CORP.
3065 BOWERS AVE.
SANTA CLARA, CALIF. 95051

C.E. SPORCK
NATL. SEMICONDUCTOR
2900 SEMICONDUCTOR DR.
SANTA CLARA, CALIF. 95051

RAYMOND E. WAKEMAN
PRECISION INSTRUMENT
2323 OWEN ST.
SANTA CLARA, CALIF. 95051

RICHARD E. LEE
SILICONIX
2201 LAURELWOOD RD.
SANTA CLARA, CALIF. 95054

JACK W. MC KITTRICK
PLANTRONICS
345 ENCINAL ST. BOX 635
SANTA CRUZ, CALIF. 95061

HUGH E. MACKENZIE
MONTCALM VINTERS
5950 E. WOODBRIDGE RD.
ACAMPO, CALIFORNIA 95220

RALPH R. CHAPIN
INTERCOLE AUTOMATION
420 N. SCRAMENTO ST.
LODI, CALIF. 95240

JOSEPH J. FRANZIA
FRANZIA BROS.
P.O. BOX 697
RIPON, CALIF. 95366

DR. G.M. BEITZ
HY-LOND
P.O. BOX 1100
SONOMA, CALIF. 95476

J.W. ANDERSEN
SONOMA VINEYARDS
P.O. BOX 368
WINDSOR, CALIF. 95492

A.A. EMERSON
SIERRA PACIFIC IND.
P.O. DRAWER Y
ARCATA, CALIF. 95521

R.F. ILLSLEY
OPTICAL COATING LAB.
P.O. BOX 1599
SANTA ROSA, CALIF. 95602

EDWARD S. TOWNE
THOMSON-DIGGS
1801 SECOND ST.
SACRAMENTO, CALIF. 95804

D.J. LAVELLE
UNIVERSAL CHEM.
P.O. BOX 15318
SACRAMENTO, CALIF. 59813

ROBERT FEUCHTER
AMERICAN RECREATION CENTERS
P.O. BOX 41069
SACRAMENTO, CALIF. 59841

TERRY R. BRANDT
ORCHARD MACHINERY
2700 COLUSA HIGHWAY
YUBA CITY, CALIF. 95991

K.L. BUTTERS SR.
HAWAII BIOGENICS
P.O. BOX BB
HAWI, HAWAII 96719

JAMES P. WOHL
HAWAII LAND
P.O. BOX 362
HILO, HAWAII 96720

JOHN W. A. BUYERS
C. BREWER & CO.
P.O. BOX 3470
HONOLULU, HAWAII 96801

HERBERT C. CORNULLE
DILLINGHAM
P.O. BOX 3468
HONOLULU, HAWAII 96801

JAMES F. GARY
GASCO
P.O. BOX 3379
HONOLULU, HAWAII 96801

J.C. STOPFORD
HUTCHINSON SUGAR
P.O. BOX 3470
HONOLULU, HAWAII 96801

THOMAS J. O'BRIEN
PUNA SUGAR
P.O. BOX 3230
HONOLULU, HAWAII 96801

WILLIAM B. CASE
WAILUKU SUGAR
P.O. BOX 3470
HONOLULU, HAWAII 96801

KARL H. BERG
KEKAHA SUGAR CO.
KEKAHA, KAUAI, HAWAII 96801

NICHOLAS WALLNER
THE HAWAII CORP.
720 KAPIOLANT BLVD.
HONOLULU, HI. 96803

B.W. ROBERTS
CROWN CORP.
P.O. BOX 2117
HONOLULU, HI. 96805

L.S. PRICHER
ALEXANDER & DALDWIN
822 BISHOP ST.
HONOLULU, HI. 96813

CARLO PANFIGLIO
AMELCO CORP.
645 HALEKAUKILA ST.
HONOLULU, HI. 96813

WILLIARD M. P. WONG
PACIFIC LEISURE
919 BETHEL ST.
HONOLULU, HI. 96813

SHELDON E. LEE
GREAT WEST LAND MINING
1650 KANNCE ST. STE. 314
HONOLULU, HI. 96814

K.L. STOKER
PACIFIC SILVER
1441 KAPIOLANI BLVD.
HONOLULU, HAWAI 96814

ROBERT W. BEHNKE
THE SYSTEMS CORP.
1441 KAPIOLANI BLVD.
HONOLULU, HAWAII 96814

RANDOLPH CROSSLEY
AMERICAN PACIFIC
2270 KALAKUAU AVE.
HONOLULU, HI. 96815

WALTER D. CHILD JR.
INTER-ISLAND RESORTS
307 LEWERS ST.
HONOLULU, HI. 96815

SPENCER F. WEAVER JR.
SPENCECLIFF
1826 KALAKAUA AVE.
HONOLULU, HI. 96815

HARRY WEINBERG
HRT LTD.
373 N. NIMITZ HIGHWAY
HONOLULU, HI. 96817

KENNETH CHAR
ALOHA AIRLINES
P.O. BOX 9038
HONOLULU, HI. 96820

JOHN H. MAGOON JR.
HAWAIIAN AIRLINES
P.O. BOX 9008
HONOLULU, HAWAII 96820

C.C. CAMERON
MAUI LAND & PINEAPPLE
P.O. BOX 187
KAHULUI, MAUI, HI. 96732

GLEN R. GORDON
ALOHA IND.
4330 S.W. 142ND.
BEAVERTON, OR. 97005

ALLEN C. EDWARDS JR.
EDWARDS IND.
P.O. BOX 549,10350 S.W.5TH ST.
BEAVERTON, OR. 97005

A.L. RESER
RESER'S FINE FOODS
P.O. BOX 8
BEAVERTON, OR. 97005

GEORGE DEWEY
MULTNOMAH KENNEL CLUB
P.O. BOX 18
FAIRVIEW, OR. 97024

J. LYELL GINTER
GINTER CORP.
610 N.W. OVERLOOK
CRESHAM, OR. 97030

EARL WANTLAND
TEKTRONIX
BOX 500
BEAVERTON, OR. 97077

WILLIAM M. LEE
EXACT ELECTRONICS
P.O. BOX 160
HILLSBORO, OR. 97123

R.H. KLINGER
CASCADE STEEL ROLLING MILLS
P.O. BOX 687
MC MINNVILLE, OR. 97128

GEORGE E. KECK
COLUMBIA CORP.
2300 S.W. FIRST AVE.
PORTLAND, OR. 97201

WALKER M. TREECE
GRANTREE CORP.
2500 S.W. FIRST AVE.
PORTLAND, OR. 97201

T.W. MAC LEAN JR.
INFORMATION SCIENCES
100 S.W. MARKET ST. STE.100
PORTLAND, OR. 97201

C.R. DUFFLE
WILLIAMETTE IND.
1300 S.W. FIFTH AVE.
PORTLAND, OR. 97201

CYRIL K. GREEN
FRED MEYER
3800 S.E. 22ND.
PORTLAND, OR. 97202

WALTER N. MUIRHEAD
ROSS ISLAND SAND & GRAVEL
4129 S.E. McLOUGHLIN BLVD.
PORTLAND, OR. 97202

E.LAWRENCE PERRIN
CHICO'S PIZZA
922 CORBETT BLDG.
PORTLAND, OR. 97204

J.S. HEIGEL
DANT & RUSSELL
1221 S.W. YAMHILL ST.
PORTLAND, OR. 97205

K.E. ROTH
FOMAT FOODS
P.O. BOX 8569
PORTLAND, OR. 97205

ORVILLE M. WILSON
PACIFIC NORTHWEST
2411 S.E. 42ND. AVE.
PORTLAND, OR. 97206

E.H. COOLEY
PRECISION CASTPARTS
4600 S.E. HARNEY DR.
PORTLAND, OR. 97206

GUY POPE
POPE & TALBOT
1700 S.W. 4TH. AVE.
PORTLAND,OR. 97207

B.I. GALITSKI
DISCOUNT FABRICS
P.O. BOX 2769
PORTLAND, OR. 97208

MONFORD A. ORLOFF
EVANS PROD. CO.
1121 S.W. SALMON, BOX 3295
PORTLAND, OR. 97208

WILLIAM J. FRONK
HYSTER CO.
P.O. BOX 2902
PORTLAND, OR. 97208

ROBERT ROTH
JANTZEN
P.O. BOX 3001
PORTLAND, OR. 97208

STANLEY N. BACHMAN
KIRKMAN LABS.
P.O. BOX 3929
PORTLAND, OR. 97208

ROBERT SPROUSE II
SPROUSE-REITZ
P.O. BOX 8996
PORTLAND, OR. 97208

M.A. JUBITZ
FLEET LEASING
P.O. BOX 11264
PORTLAND, OR. 97211

HENRY J. CASEY
METTROPOLITAN MINES
6339 N.E. SANDY BLVD.
PORTLAND, OR. 97213

W.T. TRIPLETT JR.
BAZA'R. INC.
1845 S.E. 3RD. AVE.
PORTLAND, OR. 97214

DONALD L. TISDEL
ORBANCO
P.O. BOX 14490
PORTLAND, OR. 97214

KENNETH T. SHIPLEY
OREGON PORTLAND CEMENT
111 S. E. MADISON ST.
PORTLAND, OR. 97214

ROBERT T. KORDISCH
CONSUMERS BLDG. MARTS
7609 S.E. STARK
PORTLAND, OR. 97215

ELLSWORTH D. PURDY
UNISERVCE
415 N. KILLINGSWORTH ST.
PORTLAND, OR. 97217

B.B. BOLDT
AMERICAN CARE CENTERS
11699 N.E. GLISAN
PORTLAND, OR. 97220

JOSEPH J. BARCLAY
CASCADE
P.O. BOX 20187
PORTLAND, OR. 97220

MERLE R. SHARP
GREGG'S FOOD PRODUCTS
9000 N.E. MARX DR.
PORTLAND, OR. 97220

C. KENNETH MILLER
MILLERS INTL.
11155 N.E. HALSEY ST.
PORTLAND, OR. 97220

EDWARD S. SMITH
OMARK IND.
2100 S.E. MILPORT RD.
PORTLAND, OR. 97222

ROLF G. FRANZ
HEINICKE INTRUMENTS
P.O. BOX 23008
PORTLAND, OR. 97223

JOHN E. GOMINA
LAMB -WESTON
6600 S.W. HAMPTON ST.
PORTLAND, OR. 97223

TONY J. BOSBOOM
FABRIC WHOLESALERS
2035 N.E. 181
PORTLAND, OR. 97230

EDDIE B. WAGNER
WAGNER MINING EQUIPMENT
4424 N.E. 158TH. ST.
PORTLAND, OR. 97230

H. GOLDBERG
GENERAL SALES
1105 N.E. BROADWAY
PORTLAND, OR. 97232

E. GLEN GRODER
ALBANY FROZEN FOODS
745 WEST 30TH. ST.
ALBANY, OR. 97321

E.M..BYER
OREGON FREEZE DRY FOODS
770 WEST 29TH. AVE.
ALBANY, OR. 97321

H.F. PETERS
ORGEGON METALLURGICAL
P.O. BOX 580
ALBANY, OR. 97321

R.G. LEE
REM METALS
P.O. BOX 829
ALBANY, OR. 97321

W.L. MIKKELSON
SMOKE-CRAFT
P.O. BOX 36, 850 W. 30TH ST.
ALBANY, OR. 97321

JESSE E. HARMOND
PROGRESSIVE GOLF
925 WITHAM DR.
CORVALLIS, OR. 97330

LORAN L. STEWART
BOHEMIA
2280 OAKMONT WAY
EUGENE, OR. 97401

WILBUR HOUMES
INTL. KING'S TABLE
2350 OAKMONT WAY
EUGENE, OR. 97401

JOHN R.H. HOLMES
BEAR CREEK
P.O. BOX 712
MEDFORD, OR. 97501

E.E. MOORE
CAROLINA PACIFIC PLYWOOD
P.O. BOX 370
MEDFORD, OR. 97501

RUSSELL J. HOGUE
MEDFORD
P.O. BOX 550
MEDFORD, OR. 97501

R.D. PETERSON
PALMER G. LEWIS
525 C. ST. N.W.
AUBURN, WA. 98002

C.M. PIGOTT
PACCAR
BUSINESS CENTER BLDG.
BELLEVUE, WA. 98004

ROBERT H. LINDBERG
AUDISCAN
P.O. BOX 1456
BELLEVUE, WA. 98009

B.W. JOHNSON
CHEM-NUCLEAR SYSTEMS
P.O. BOX 1866
BELLEVUE, WA. 98009

DONALD R. STENQUIST
HEATH TECNA
19819 84TH. AVE.
KENT, WASHINGTON 98031

D.J. HEERENSPERGER
PAY'N PAK STORES
1209 S. CENTRAL AVE.
KENT, WA. 98031

LESLIE A. LARSEN
TALLY
8301 180TH ST.
KENT, WA. 98031

KENNETH W. MERRITT
OLYMPUS SERVICE
P.O. BOX 2489
LYNWOOD, WA. 98036

JOHN W. ZEVENBERGEN
JOHN FLUKE MFG.
P.O. BOX 43210
MOUNTLAKE TERRACE, WA. 98043

M. RAY DRILLING
INTERFACE MECHANISMS
5503 232 ST. SOUTHWEST
MOUNTLAKE TERRACE, WA. 98043

W.H. SIMPSON
PHYSIO - CONTROL
11811 WILLOWS RD.
REDMOND, WA. 98052

G.S. SUTHERLAND
ROCKET RESEARCH
YORK CENTER
REDMOND, WA. 98052

R.L. GOWER
PERSPECTIVE SYSTEMS
P.O. BOX 2376
RENTON, WA. 98055

M.R. OVERBYE
LEWIS REFRIGERATION
WOODINVILLE, WA. 98072

M.E. MAES
GARNER-MARLOW-MAES
SEATTLE TOWER, PENTHOUSE
SEATTLE, WA. 98101

J.N. NORDSTROM
NORDSTROM
1501 FIFTH AVE.
SEATTLE, WA. 98101

MONTE L. BEAN
PAY'N SAVE
1511 6TH. AVE.
SEATTLE, WA. 98101

H.J. MUSIEL
WESTOURS
100 W. HARRISON
SEATTLE, WA. 98101

J.A. MAC DONALD
PACIFIC WESTERN IND.
3725 SEATTLE-FIRST NATL.BLDG.
SEATTLE, WA. 98104

JAMES H. WIBORG
UNIVAR
1600 NORTON BLDG.
SEATTLE, WA. 98104

HERBERT A. SCHIESSL
FENTRON HIGHWAY
2601 N.W. MARKET ST.
SEATTLE, WA. 98107

LOUIS LAVINTHAL
ABC. RECORD & TAPE
729 SOUTH FIDALGO ST.
SEATTLE, WA. 98108

WILLIAM M. WEISFIELD
WEISFIELDS
800 S. MICHIGAN ST.
SEATTLE, WA. 98108

BRUCE H. BLAKEY
WESTERN MARINE
905 DEXTER AVE. N.
SEATTLE, WASHINGTON 98109

HOLT W. WEBSTER
AIRBORNE FREIGHT
190 QUEEN ANNE AVE. BOX 662
SEATTLE, WA. 98111

J.P. FORD
EPCON
1275 MERCER ST.
SEATTLE, WA. 98111

SAMUEL SCHULMAN
FIRST NORTHWEST IND.
221 WEST HARRISON
SEATTLE, WA. 98119

SAMUEL SCHULMAN
SEATTLE SUPER SONICS
221 W. HARRISON ST.
SEATTLE, WA. 98119

SAM RUBENSTEIN
WHITNEY-FIDALGO SEAFOOD
2360 W. COMMODORE WAY
SEATTLE, WA. 98119

G.A. DE BON
LOOMIS CORP.
55 BATTERY ST.
SEATTLE, WA. 98121

BERT H. HAMBLETON
ASSOC. GROCERS
P.O. BOX 3763
SEATTLE, WA. 98124

DOUGLAS S. GAMBLE
PACIFIC GAMBLE ROBINSON
P.O. BOX 3687
SEATTLE, WA. 98124

EDWIN H. BAIER
TRAILER EQUIPMENT
14561 AURORA AVE. N.
SEATTLE, WA. 98133

WILLIAM F. NIEMI JR.
EDDIE BAUER
1737 AIRPORT WAY S.
SEATTLE, WA. 98134

EDWIN S. COOMBS JR.
RAINIER CO.
3100 AIRPORT WAY, S.
SEATTLE, WA. 98134

WILLIAM H. MOULTRIE
WITS
P.O. BOX 3805
SEATTLE, WA. 98134

O.F. BENECKE
ALASKA AIRLINES
SEATTLE-TACOMA
SEATTLE, WA. 98158

ROBERT M. MC LENNAGHAN
LINDAL CEDAR HOMES
10411 EMPIRE WAY, S.
SEATTLE, WA. 98178

WARREN P. JENSEN
CRUISE-A-HOME
1028 NORTON AVE.
EVERETT, WASHINGTON 98201

JOHN L. THOMAS
UNIFLITE
9TH & HARRIS
BELLINGHAM, WA. 98225

HENRY JANSEN
LYNDEN TRANSPORTATION
8631 DEPOT RD.
LYNDEN, WA. 98264

T.L. LYNOTT
REINELL IND.
14219 HIGHWAY 99
MARYSVILLE, WA. 98270

RONALD R. JENSEN
PAN-ALASKA FISHERIES
P.O. BOX 647
MONROE, WA. 98272

DANIEL R. BATY
HILLHAVEN
1015 CENTER ST.
TACOMA, WA. 98411

LEO M. KRENZLER
AMERICAN MARINE IND.
2556 E. 11TH. ST.
TACOMA, WA. 98421

R.A. SCHMIDT
OLYMPIA BREWING
P.O. BOX 947
OLYMPIA, WA. 98501

L.C. MERTA
MODULINE INTL.
P.O. BOX 209
CHEHALIS, WA. 98532

G.R. OSBORNE SR.
NORTHWEST HOMES OF CHEHALTS
P.O. BOX 896
CHEHALIS, WA. 98532

GORDON N. ALLISON
WAYNE'S PHOTO
141 NAT. AVE.
CHEHALIS, WA. 98532

A.C. RENN
CERTIFIED MFG.
SANDERSON FIELD
SHELTON, WA. 98584

B.O. HALLBERG
TOLLYCRAFT
2200 CLINTON AVE.
KELSO, WA. 98626

R.P. WOLLENBERG
LONGVIEW FIBRE CO.
LONGVIEW, WA. 98632

ARTHUR ABLE
WELSH
PANEL WAY
LONGVIEW, WA. 98632

E.W. STUCHELL
BILES-COLEMAN
OMAK, WA. 98841

WM. M. YEAMAN
CLAYTON SILVER MINES
P.O. BOX 34
YAKIMA, WA. 98901

K.W. FACKLER
COLDEX INC.
803 WASHINGTON MUTUAL BLDG.
SPOKANE, WA. 99201

E.J. ARMSTRONG
IBEX MINERALS
601 W. MAIN ST.
SPOKANE, WA. 99201

ESKIL ANDERSON
LITTLE SQUAW GOLD MINING
PEYTON BLDG. RM. 737
SPOKANE, WA. 99201

TIBOR KLOBUSICKY
MIDNITE MINES
601 GREAT WESTERN BLDG.
SPOKANE, WA. 99201

WAFFORD CONRAD
AMERICAN SILVER MINING
E2503 - 17TH. AVE.
SPOKANE, WA. 99203

F.J. FRANKOVICH
ATLAS MINING
34 E. HIGH DR.
SPOKANE, WA. 99203

EARL A. TENLEY
SILVER SCOTT MINES
WASHINGTON TRUST BANK BLDG.
SPOKANE,WA. 99204

GEORGE F. GARLICK
HOLOSONICS
2950 GEORGE WASHINGTON WAY
RICHLAND, WA. 99352

JAMES J. FLOOD
WIEN AIR ALASKA
INTL. AIRPORT
ANCHORAGE, ALASKA 99502

NEIL BERGT
ALASKA INTL. IND.
P.O. BOX 60029
FAIRBANKS, ALASKA 99701

INDEX